Canadian Retailing

Canadian Retailing

Third Edition

J. Barry Mason
Morris L. Mayer
Hazel F. Ezell

Michel Laroche
Concordia University

Gordon H. G. McDougall
Wilfrid Laurier University

Represented in Canada by:
McGraw-Hill Ryerson Limited

IRWIN
Toronto · Chicago · New York · Auckland · Bogoatá · Caracas ·
Lisbon · London · Madrid · Mexico City · Milan · New Delhi ·
San Juan · Singapore · Sydney · Tokyo

McGraw-Hill
A Division of The McGraw-Hill Companies

CANADIAN RETAILING

This book is printed on acid-free paper.

1 2 3 4 5 6 7 8 9 0 QD QD 9 1 0 9 8 7

ISBN 0-256-19521-8
Library of Congress Catalog number 96-60969

Publisher: *Roderick T. Banister*
Project supervisor: *Lynne Basler*
Marketing manager: *Gary Bennett*
Production supervisor: *Dina L. Genovese*
Designer: *Larry J. Cope*
Prepress buyer: *Jon Christopher*
Compositor: *Carlisle Communications, Ltd.*
Typeface: *10/12 New Baskerville*
Printer: *Quebecor Book Printing Group, Dubuque*

http://www.mhcollege.com

This book is dedicated to Anne Laroche, and to Betty, Michael, and Sandy McDougall

Preface

Since the second edition was published, Canadian retailing has experienced many significant events, from the lingering effects of the recession, to the continuing impact of the North-American Free Trade Agreement (NAFTA), to the ongoing invasion by huge American retailers such as Wal-Mart, and to the development of the information highway. These events have had a substantial impact on Canadian retailers. Inefficient retailers were forced out of business, and many others were prompted to rethink their basic strategic approach, including the opening of big box outlets, a better focus on good customer service and the development of Web sites on the Internet.

The rest of this decade and the beginning of the new millennium will bring even more challenges and opportunities, particularly for the astute entrepreneur who understands retailing in the Canadian environment within a globalized economy. What kinds of new retailing concepts will be introduced, particularly to lower distribution costs? How far will the concept of controlled environment be extended, and will the future bring more megamalls like the West Edmonton Mall or the Mall of America? How far will the information highway go, what new technologies will be introduced, and how will this affect the management of retail institutions, or create new ones? Will the big box phenomena continue its strong growth, or will it decline? How will consumer environmental concerns affect retailing in Canada?

Answers to these and other questions will determine which retailing institutions will survive in a highly competitive and globalized economy. This text emphasizes a managerial, practical approach to retailing, focusing directly on the strategic issues faced by the owner, the manager, or the employee of a retail institution for the rest of the 1990s and the new millennium. It assumes no prior knowledge of retailing, and it covers the conceptual and analytical foundations necessary to understand all aspects of retail management in the current Canadian environment. This is done in a pragmatic, practical point of view, and in simple straightforward language, with many real-life examples.

Each chapter starts with an introduction which sets the stage for the following material. Throughout the chapter, numerous examples and *Retail Highlights* reflecting recent events have been added to provide an in-depth look at important issues and applications. It ends with detailed chapter highlights, a list of the key terms, discussion questions, application exercises, and suggested cases. The complete package is intended to maximize learning while doing. Enhanced pedagogical features have been added to improve student access to important details: page references for end-of-chapter key terms and suggested cases, and end-of-text glossary, as well as new figures and tables.

The book follows a logical sequence towards strategy development for the retail firm.

In *Part 1, The World of Canadian Retailing,* five chapters provide a broad perspective on the institutions, the economy and the markets in the Canadian environment. Chapter 1 introduces the reader to retailing in Canada, its history, role, evolution, structure and trends. Chapter 2 covers the critical environmental factors affecting retail strategy development (legal, economic, social, and technological). Understanding the retail customer is critical to the success of the retail strategy, including individual factors (Chapter 3) and social influences (Chapter 4). Knowledge of markets is essential to succeeding in Canadian retailing, and the retail research methods used to obtain this knowledge are covered in Chapter 5.

In *Part 2, Developing the Retail Strategy,* the conceptual, financial and organizational aspects of the retail strategy are logically developed. Chapter 6 deals with the development of strategic planning, as a method of defining the objectives of the firm, and deciding how to compete. To compete successfully retailers need to understand how to start and finance a retail business (Chapter 7). Franchising as a means of owning and operating a retail firm is examined in detail (Chapter 8). Chapter 9 discusses the critical issues in the recruitment, selection, training and motivation of retail employees, as well as organizing the retail firm.

In *Part 3, Designing the Retailing Mix,* the decisions on the key variables of the retailing mix are discussed. The important issues in the retail location decisions are covered in Chapter 10. Store design, layout and merchandise presentation decisions are covered in Chapter 11. Merchandise and expense planning decisions are the object of Chapter 12. Buying, handling and inventory management decisions are explained in Chapter 13. Determining retail prices is the topic of Chapter 14. In order to successfully promote their products or services, retailers need to: help their employees develop the keys to successful selling (Chapter 15); design effective programs in retail advertising, sales promotion and publicity (Chapter 16); and instill in their employees a customer-focused culture (Chapter 17).

In *Part 4, Evaluating the Retail Strategy,* the tools used to determine how well the retail strategy is doing are explained. Internal evaluation is critical to the retail manager, including the elements involved in developing control systems (Chapter 18), and evaluation of performance through an accounting system (Chapter 19).

In *Part 5, New Dimensions of Retailing,* Chapter 20 is devoted to the developing fields of services retailing and nonstore retailing.

Finally, an appendix on careers in retailing is provided to help students make informed decisions about the many facets of working in retailing.

Another strong feature of the text is the set of cases that follow Chapter 20. These are among the best case materials available in Canada, and they cover all aspects of the text. The cases are keyed to each chapter, and some cases can be used to cover several topics. Some cases were contributed by Canadian academics, and the others by the authors of the text. The mix of cases provides the instructors with some that are very comprehensive, others that are of more restricted scope, and the remainder can be used to focus on very specific issues. Thus, a wide range of teaching material is provided to maximize learning. Available for the instructor is an Instructor's Manual including detailed course outlines, suggested answers to discussion questions, answers to cases, solutions to chapter problems, and transparency masters. With this edition are a testbank of approximately 1,600 true/false and multiple choice questions and the computerized version of the testbank, CompuTest. CompuTest is available on a 3½-inch diskette in Windows and Macintosh platforms. CompuTest enables the instructor to create up to 99 versions of the same test, and add or edit questions.

In the preparation of this edition, many people have provided encouragement, suggestions and material, and we are most grateful for their assistance. Professor David Gilkes, Saskatchewan Institute of Applied Science and Technology; Art Pierce, Ryerson Polytechnic University; Deborah Reyner, Conestoga College; Donna Stapleton, Memorial University of Newfoundland reviewed the second edition of *Canadian Retailing*. Development of the third edition owes much to the thoughtful and thorough reviews of James Boyes, Durham College; Alvina Cassiani, Humber College; Harry Dulat, Red River Community College; Lowell Geddes, New Brunswick Community College; Paul Larson, University of Alberta. Many thanks also to the case contributors who provided material for the book.

The production of this manuscript involved other individuals to whom we are most grateful. Many thanks to Elsie Grogan, who proved once again to be a cheerful, professional individual who met both reasonable and other deadlines, and to Isabelle Miodek and Anne H. Laroche who helped find and develop new material. Our thanks also to Rod Banister, our current and past editor, a great person to work with and dedicated to excellence in publishing. As well, the financial support of Irwin is very gratefully acknowledged.

Finally, we hope this third edition of *Canadian Retailing* will provide you with a useful and rewarding learning experience for many years to come.

Michel Laroche and Gordon H. G. McDougall

Contents in Brief

Contents

Cases

Canadian Retailing

PART

The World of Canadian Retailing

The five chapters in *Part 1, The World of Canadian Retailing* provide a broad perspective on the types of retailers, the economy and the markets in the Canadian environment. Chapter 1 introduces the student to retailing in Canada, its history, role, evolution, structure and trends. Chapter 2 covers the critical environmental factors affecting retail strategy development (legal, economic, social, and technological). Understanding the retail customer is critical to the success of the retail strategy, including individual factors (Chapter 3) and social influences (Chapter 4). Knowledge of markets is essential to succeeding in Canadian retailing, and the retail research methods used to obtain this knowledge are covered in Chapter 5.

1. **Canadian Retailing Today: Structure and Trends**

2. **Analyzing the Canadian Retailing Environment**

3. **Understanding the Retail Customer**

4. **Social Influences on the Retail Customer**

5. **Retailing Research**

Canadian Retailing Today
Structure and Trends

Learning Objectives

After reading this chapter, you should be able to:

1. Relate retailing to the marketing discipline.

2. Explain and describe the descriptive classifications of retail structure.

3. Explain and describe the strategic classifications of retail structure.

4. Review the explanations of retail structural change.

5. Understand the major trends in retailing.

McDonald's first Canadian restaurant

Courtesy McDonald's Restaurant of Canada Ltd.

McDonald's introduces a new retail format.

Courtesy McDonald's Restaurant of Canada Ltd.

Canadian retailers operate in a dynamic, competitive environment. The deep recession of the early 1990s led to bankruptcy for thousands of Canadian retailers, from small independents to large, well-known chains like Woodwards. Major department stores are under siege from U.S. category killers like Wal-Mart, Price Club/Costco, and Home Depot. Some specialty chains in the apparel, footwear, and jewelery store categories are experiencing little growth or declining sales, while other categories, particularly household electronics and appliance retailers, are booming.

New types of retailers are constantly evolving, from "big box" stores to "stores-within-stores," as retailers seek to deliver value and convenience to consumers whose needs are constantly changing depending on economic, family, and personal circumstances. The goal is to survive and prosper in these ever-changing times.

And some retailers do survive and prosper. Whether times are good or bad, there is a group of retailers, led by McDonald's, who continually outperform their competitors. McDonald's outpaces its rivals in the highly competitive fast-food business with strategies and tactics that include adding new outlets, locating in unique, nontraditional sites (e.g., hospitals, train stations, and the SkyDome), adding new product lines like salads, pizza, and Tex-Mex dishes; and advertising to capture the attention of consumers. While other competitors occasionally flounder, McDonald's monitors the environment for opportunities that lead to sales of over $1.6 billion each year.[1] ■

To set the stage, we offer the following overview of retailing in Canada:

- Retailing employs more Canadians than any other industry. More than 1,400,000 people work in retailing, which is approximately 11 percent of Canada's workforce.

- Total retail sales in Canada are more than $21 billion annually; on average, each Canadian spends more than $7,500 on retail goods and services in stores from Prince George (population 70,000, with annual retail sales of more than $628 million) to Sydney (population 113,000, with annual retail sales of more than $665 million).

- More than 200,000 stores dot the Canadian landscape. Although independent retailers account for the majority of total retail sales (because of their sheer numbers), much of the buying power is in the hands of a few large chains that are well known to most Canadians (Table 1–1).

- Canadians spend more than 50 percent of their retail dollars in shopping centres. From regional malls like the Woodgrove Centre in Nanaimo, British Columbia, with 110 stores, to community malls like the Lancaster Mall in Saint John, New Brunswick, with 46 stores, to downtown malls like the Weyburn Square in Weyburn, Saskatchewan, with 28 stores, more than 1,200 shopping centres are the shopping destinations for the majority of Canadians.

- Canadians respond to new retailing concepts. When Price Club, the no-frills giant club warehouse outlet, entered the Canadian market, it generated more than $1 billion in sales in its first full year of operations, and each of its stores has sales of nearly $100 million each year.

- Canadian retailers face many challenges and opportunities including the economic environment, new forms of competition, and shifting demographics (Retail Highlight 1–1).

Retailing in Canada is a competitive, dynamic business. As the above examples show, retailers must continually adjust to an environment where consumers,

Table 1-1   Major Canadian Retail Chains

Department Stores	Revenue ($000)	Characteristics
Hudson's Bay Company	$5,900,000	Comprises two chains, The Bay (100 stores) and Zellers (292 stores). Employs 57,000 people.
Sears Canada	3,900,000	Has 100 retail stores and 1,432 catalog units across Canada. Employs approx. 38,000 people.
Wal-Mart Canada	2,600,000	World's largest retailer, with 122 stores in Canada.
Price Club/Costco Canada	2,400,000	Warehouse club chain, with 45 locations in Canada.
Eaton's	2,000,000 (Est.)	Probably Canada's best-known department store chain, a private company.
K mart Canada	1,300,000	U.S.-owned 127-store chain, which has experienced competitive pressures.
Clothing Stores		
Dylex	1,300,000	Restructured retailer, which operates a number of chains including Fairweather, Tip Top, Thrifty's, Club Monaco, and BiWay. Has over 600 stores. Has experienced considerable difficulties in recent years.
Reitman's	350,000	Operates more than 700 stores under various banners including Reitmans, Smart Set, Penningtons, Wearhouse, Dalmys, Antels, and Cactus.
Suzy Shier	570,000	Operates over 260 Suzy Shier and La Senza stores.
Mark's Work Wearhouse	198,000	Calgary-based chain of more than 135 corporate and franchise stores.
Château Stores	148,000	Operates 154 stores under the Le Château name and 56 in-store boutiques in Sears stores across Canada.
Specialty Stores		
Canadian Tire	3,800,000	A Canadian landmark, with over 420 stores.
Shoppers Drug Mart	3,300,000	Part of the Imasco Group, including more than 680 franchised Shoppers Drug Mart and Pharmaprix stores and 135 Big V Pharmacies.
Leon's Furniture	283,000	Operates 50 company-owned and franchise stores.

Source: *The Financial Post 500,* 1996, and various annual reports.

Retail Highlight 1–1

The Retailing Challenges to Year 2000

- *Economic environment.* The recession of the early 1990s reduced the profitability of most retailers. The challenge is to manage a retail business in a slow growth environment where consumers have become more value conscious.
- *Demographic environment.* The Canadian population is aging, non-traditional household groups are emerging, and ethnic markets are increasing. The challenge is to respond to the diverse needs of these new market segments.
- *Competitive environment.* New forms of competition including foreign retailers entering the Canadian market, "big box" stores emerging as a new retail format, and off-price retailers are changing the competitive landscape. The challenge is to identify the competition and revise retail strategy to reflect this new retailing era.

- *Customer satisfaction.* Many consumers have expressed dissatisfaction with the merchandise, value, and service offered by retailers. The challenge is to address these consumer concerns by focussing on customer satisfaction through the merchandise mix and services offered, including retail staff training.
- *Store location.* Shopping centres have lost their glamour for a number of Canadians. The challenge is to rejuvenate these centres by rethinking the store mix, store cluster, and physical design.
- *Positioning.* A number of Canadian retailers do not have a clear image in the consumer's mind. The challenge is to design and implement a positioning strategy that presents the consumer with a complete picture of what the retailer offers.

---

segments, and competitors are constantly changing. Success in retailing is not easy but it's always exciting.

Retailing consists of all activities involved in the sale of goods and services to the ultimate consumer. A retail sale occurs whenever an individual purchases groceries at a Sobey's supermarket, a compact disc at Sam the Record Man, a coffee at Tim Horton Donuts, a haircut at Magicuts, or a membership at a fitness centre. Not all retail sales are made in stores. Some are made by door-to-door salespeople employed by firms such as Avon, by mail-order firms such as Eddie Bauer, by telemarketers such as the Canadian Home Shopping Network, by the use of automatic vending machines, or by farmers selling produce at the roadside.

Marketing is the process by which individuals and groups obtain what they need and want through creating and exchanging products and value with others. Retailing is the final part of that process, satisfying individual and organizational objectives through exchanges.

Structure is the arrangement of parts, elements, or constituents considered as a whole rather than a single part. Thus, the **retail structure** comprises all the outlets (organizations, establishments) through which goods or services move to the ultimate consumer. The structure is complex and can be classified in various ways to help understand its components.

Retailing is thus a part of marketing from a process point of view and is a complex structure from an institutional perspective. Finally, retailing is primarily carried out by organizations that link manufacturers to consumers in the distribution channel. **Channels of distribution** are systems through which products or services are marketed. Figure 1–1 presents a diagram of the place of retailing in the classic marketing channels of distribution.

Figure 1–1   Typical Channels of Distribution

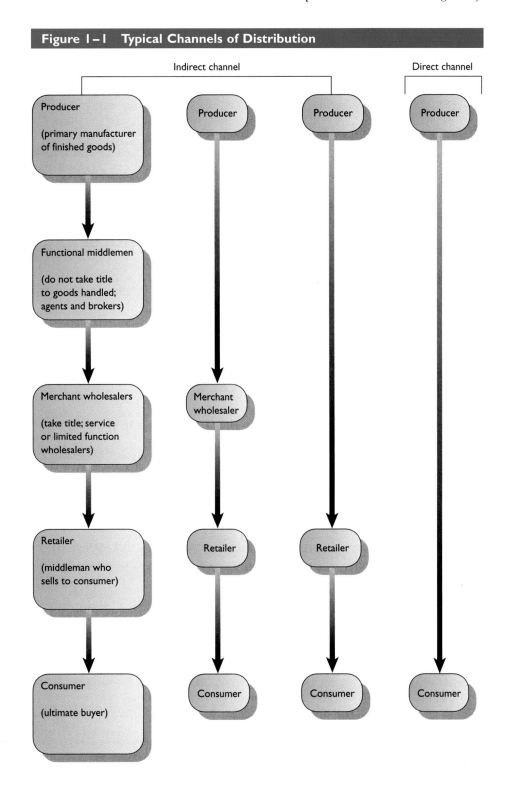

A direct channel—from producer to consumer—provides
"fresh" and "natural."

Photo by Betty McDougall

Alternative Ways to Classify the Retail Structure

The complexity and dynamics of retailing can best be understood by analyzing
its structure. Analyzing retail structure and understanding competition is
critical to developing and implementing retail strategies. By analyzing the
structure, better ways of serving consumer needs through new types of retailing
organization may be revealed. These new approaches can serve as a competitive
advantage that may be difficult for competitors to copy in the short run.

The retailing structure can be classified in various ways, and for two broad
purposes—for describing and understanding (descriptive classifications) and
for strategy assistance (strategic classifications).

Descriptive classifications

The four main descriptive ways of classifying retail structures are (1) type of
ownership, (2) variety and assortment, (3) kind of business, (4) and location.

Type of ownership

The most common classification is based on ownership, and the two major types
are independent and chains. The *independent* with a single store constitutes
around 61 percent of total retail sales.[2] Single-unit organizations tend to be
small businesses operated by family members.

The small independent store can compete with chains because: (1) the store's
cost of doing business is usually low due to low rents, location in a lower traffic
neighbourhood or rural area, and ownership by the proprietor; (2) the store is
often located closer to customers than are larger chain stores; (3) a personal

Retail Highlight 1–2

Canadian Department Stores: The Originals

Two of Canada's department store chains, the Bay and Eaton's, have considerable importance from an historical perspective. The Hudson's Bay Company is Canada's oldest enterprise. The original charter, granting them trading rights in Hudson's Bay, was given on May 2, 1670. During its first century of operation the company established forts and the Bay and traded with the First Nations. The merger of the company with a rival trading firm in 1821 led to the Hudson's Bay Company. The company played an important role in Canada's development from its early inception to today. It is now a conglomerate with sales exceeding $5 billion annually.

Timothy Eaton, generally acknowledged in Canada as the "father of the department store," opened his first

store in 1860 in St. Mary's, Ontario. Nine years later he opened a store on Yonge Street in Toronto, and in early 1870 he added a slogan to his handbills and advertisements that was to revolutionize Canadian retailing: "GOODS SATISFACTORY OR MONEY REFUNDED." By 1929, three chains, one being Eaton's, accounted for 80 percent of all department store sales. Today Eaton's is one of the largest department store chains in Canada, with over 100 retail outlets and sales exceeding $2 billion each year.

Sources: *Hudson's Bay Company*, Annual Report, 1995; William Stephenson, *The Store That Timothy Built*, McClelland and Stewart, Toronto, 1969; and *Department Stores in Canada: 1923-1976*, Ottawa: Statistics Canada, 1979.

---

relationship between customers and the manager is more likely to occur, allowing the smaller store to develop a unique personality, and (4) the manager can be very flexible in meeting the needs of customers. Still, the failure rate among small, independent retail stores remains high. Such failures can be attributed to inexperience, incompetence, or other management shortcomings.

A **chain** is a retail organization consisting of two or more centrally owned units that handle similar lines of merchandise. In food retailing and the general merchandising field, chain stores control a substantial proportion of the market. The six largest department and discount store chains—The Bay, Zellers, Sears Canada, Wal-Mart, K mart, and Eaton's—have total sales exceeding $14 billion annually. Two of these chains—The Bay and Eaton's—have operated in Canada for close to 100 years or more and have historical importance (Retail Highlight 1–2).

The large supermarket chains, including Safeway, Loblaws, Provigo, Atlantic & Pacific, Sobeys, and the Oshawa Group, have achieved dominance in food retailing through vertical integration and buying power.

A number of specialty retail chains have become major forces in Canadian retailing—Reitmans and Dylex in the clothing field, Home Depot and Beaver Lumber in the home improvement area, SportChek in sporting goods, Lewiscraft in leisure products, Future Shop in home entertainment and consumer electronics, and Canadian Tire in the automotive and hardware business. The size of these chains provides them with many opportunities including buying power, advertising economies, and in-store specialists. Overall, these chains can use their size to create efficiencies in distribution, management, and purchasing.

Retail stores can be owned by manufacturers, such as Bata Shoes; by governments, such as provincially-owned liquor stores, or by consumers. **Consumer cooperatives** are retail stores owned by consumers and operated by a

Canada's oldest enterprise continues to adapt to the changing environment.

Courtesy Hudson's Bay Company Ltd.

hired manager. Co-ops have prospered in some rural areas of Canada where the benefits of group buying are more important than in larger communities. However, some co-ops have been successful in larger communities, such as Co-op Atlantic with its reduced prices to members and its slogan "It Pays to Belong."

Variety and assortment

Variety is the number of lines of merchandise carried; **assortment** is the choice offered within a line. *Variety* can be thought of as the width or breadth of a store's merchandise selection, and *assortment* can be thought of as the depth of a store's selection, including sizes, colours, and types of material. Figure 1–2 illustrates the concept of width and depth for sports shoes carried in a specialty store, a department store (Eaton's), and a discount department store (Zellers).

In this example, the number of items reflects the models offered by each manufacturer. The specialty store carries more types of shoes (width) and more depth (brands and items) within each type than either Eaton's or Zellers. The width of Eaton's and Zellers sports shoe lines are the same but, Zellers offers more depth, including a store brand (Venture). The specialty store, with its wide and deep line, provides a wider choice, which is appealing to customers but requires more inventory. The strategy is to attract more customers and hopefully generate more sales because of the variety and assortment.

Kind of business

Outlets may also be classified by kind of business or merchandise group. Such a classification is helpful to management in analyzing retail sales by merchandise groups such as drug stores, shoe stores, men's clothing stores, women's clothing stores, and the like.

Figure 1-2   Types and Brands of Sports Shoes Offered

Types of Sports Shoes	Specialty Store	Eaton's	Zellers
Running	Reebok Nike Brooks Adidas Asics Saucony New Balance Avia (47 items)	Reebok Nike Brooks (18 items)	Nike Brooks Venture (22 items)
Basketball	Nike Reebok Adidas Converse Asics (26 items)	Nike Reebok (4 items)	Nike Adidas Converse Venture (19 items)
Cross-training	Nike Reebok Avia (30 items)	Nike Reebok (12 items)	Nike Venture (14 items)
Tennis	Adidas Nike Reebok (14 items)		
Volleyball	Asics Kangaroo (3 items)		
Soccer	Reebok Nike Mitre Adidas (32 items)		
Golf	Nike Reebok (4 items)		

Location

An analysis by location is helpful in establishing long-term trends in regional levels of retail sales. The three major types of locations are the central business district, shopping centres, and stand-alone locations. As mentioned earlier, shopping centres account for over 50 percent of all retail sales in Canada but many retailers do very well by locating in the downtown area or in a stand-alone location. The characteristics of these locations and trends within these locations are discussed in Chapter 10. Trading area, another concept dealing with location, is also discussed in Chapter 10.

A specialty store carries a deep range of jogging shoes to target serious runners as well as casual joggers.

Photo by James Hertel

Strategic Classifications

The following strategic classifications help to understand retailing and they also assist retailers in achieving differential advantages in the market. The classifications include strategic dimensions that may provide helpful ideas for achieving a competitive advantage.

The margin-turnover classification

The margin-turnover framework for retail structure may be applied to all types of outlets. The framework is useful for understanding basic strategic choices along financial dimensions.

Margin is defined as the difference between the cost and the selling price or as the percentage markup at which the inventory in a store is sold. **Turnover** is the number of times the average inventory is sold, usually expressed in annual terms.

Figure 1–3 diagrams four quadrants, defined by margin and turnover, into which any retail outlet can be placed. Typically, the low-margin, high-turnover retailer focusses on price, offers few services, and carries a large variety of merchandise. Three leading retailers—Wal-Mart, Zeller's, and Sears—have adopted this strategy. The high-margin, high-turnover retailers focus on convenience by having numerous locations and extensive open hours, charge prices above the market, and provide a large variety of merchandise, considering the store size. Mac's Milk, 7-11, and a host of convenience stores pursue this strategy. The high-margin, low-turnover stores focus on service, charge prices

Figure 1–3 The Margin-Turnover Classification

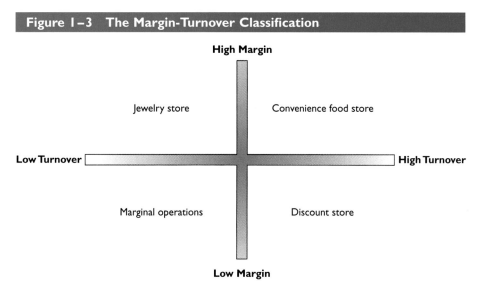

Strategic Dimensions	Low Margin—High Turnover	High Margin—Low Turnover	High Margin—High Turnover
Merchandise	Presold or self-sold	Sold in store	Presold or self-sold
Services	Few	Many	Many
Locations	Stand-alone	Cluster	Numerous
Organization	Simple	Complex	Simple
Variety	Large	Small	Large
Assortment	Small	Large	Small
Prices	Very competitive	Less competitive	Less competitive
Promotion	Price focus	Merchandise focus	Minimal

above the market, and offer a limited variety of merchandise, often on an exclusive basis. Holt Renfrew, the exclusive women's wear chain, typifies this category. The low-margin, low-turnover retailers have a poor strategy that requires adjustment to regain profitability.

Retail price and service strategy classification

A second classification utilizes two major value dimensions—price and service. In Figure 1–4, quadrants 1 and 4 are not viable in the long run and are in fact "traps." Quadrants 2 and 3 are promising strategic options.

In Quadrant 1, even though customers would be pleased with high service/low prices, the strategy would be unwise for the retail firm because it is unlikely to generate sufficient profits. Customers would not be interested in Quadrant 4's poor value of low service at high prices. Retailers must monitor this strategy carefully as they reduce service in an attempt to be more price competitive. A popular strategy recently has been that illustrated by Quadrant 3 and represented by such firms as Price Club/Costco. Zellers, K mart, and Wal-Mart also fit into that quadrant.

Quadrant 2, high price/high service, illustrates the business practices of firms such as Liptons and Lands' End in catalog retailing.

Holt Renfrew offers exclusive, classic merchandise which allows it higher margins.

Courtesy Holt Renfrew

Retail Structural Change

Figure 1–5 illustrates selected changes in the retail institutional structure that have occurred during the past 100 years. The **life cycle** describes the stages a retail institution goes through from its beginning to its decline and possible disappearance from the retailing scene. In general, the life cycle has four stages: (1) introduction, where the new form begins (e.g., the West Edmonton Mall that combined retail and amusement concepts in 1979), (2) growth, where new competitors enter the market (e.g., the current situation with wholesale clubs), (3) maturity, where intense competition is often the major characteristic (e.g., warehouse retailers with their advertising and price wars), and (4) decline, where the store type slowly fades from the landscape (e.g., variety stores). In Figure 1–5 we indicate the period of fastest growth for each type of institution, the stage in the life cycle of each store type, our own explanation for the development of each type, and an example of each. The table provides a framework for the discussion that follows.

No single theory can explain the evolution of all types of retail outlets. At best, the existing theories discussed are descriptive and perhaps somewhat explanatory. Certainly they are not predictive of institutional change.

Figure 1-4   The Retail Price/Service Strategy Classification

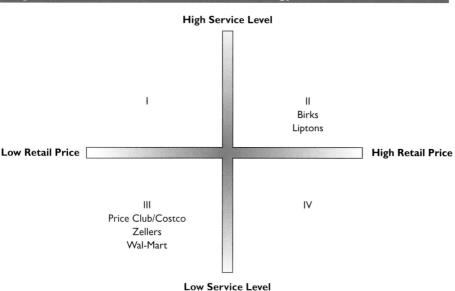

Theories of Retail Institutional Change

In response to changing consumer needs, increased competition and other environmental factors, new types of retailers enter the market to capture new opportunities, and existing retailers modify their merchandise and service mix to match the changing market requirements. A number of theories have been proposed to help explain and understand these changes in retail structure.

The wheel of retailing

The **wheel of retailing** hypothesis is the best-known explanation for changes in the structure (Figure 1-6). This theory states that new types of retailers enter a market as low-margin, low-priced, low-status merchants. Gradually, they add to their operating costs by providing new services and improving their facilities in the trading-up phase. Over time, they become high-cost merchants and are vulnerable to new types of competition that enter the marketplace as low-cost, no-frills competitors. Recently, the warehouse club has entered the low-priced, low-status area. Price Club/Costco has proven to be a formidable competitor in Canada, resulting in a strong reaction from many existing competitors including Canadian Tire and Loblaws.

The theory has been criticized because not all institutions begin as low-margin outlets with few services.[3] Upscale fashion stores did not follow the model and have never fit the wheel of retailing.

The retail accordion

An alternative explanation for change is the concept of the **retail accordion** (see Figure 1-7). Proponents of the theory argue that changes in the merchandising mix, not prices and margins, are a better explanation for changes in retail

Figure 1–5 Selected Changes in Retail Institutional Structure

Institutional Type	Period of Fastest Growth	Period from Inception to Maturity (years)	Stage of Life Cycle	Examples of Explanatory Hypotheses*	Representative Firms†
General store	1800-40	100	Declining/obsolete	Ra	A local institution
Single-line store	1820-40	100	Mature	Ab	Sam the Record Man
Department store	1860-1940	80	Mature	Dp	Eaton's
Variety store	1870-1930	50	Declining/obsolete	Ab	Kresge
Mail-order house	1951-50	50	Mature	Ab	Gifts Unlimited
Corporate chain	1920-30	50	Mature	Ab	The Bay
Discount store	1955-75	20	Mature	Ad,Dp	K mart
Conventional supermarket	1935-65	35	Mature/declining	Dp	Loblaws
Shopping centre	1950-65	40	Mature	Ab	Oakridge
Cooperative	1930-50	40	Mature	Ab	Home Hardware
Gasoline station	1965-75	45	Mature	Dp	Esso
Convenience store	1960-75	20	Mature	Ra	Mac's Milk
Fast-food outlet	1965-80	15	Mature	Dp	McDonald's
Home improvement centre	1975-85	15	Late growth	Ra	Beaver Lumber
Super specialists	1975-85	10	Growth	Ra	One Stop Battery
Warehouse retailing	1970-80	10	Maturity	Wr	Leon's
Regional shopping malls (megamall)	1979-90	12	Maturity	Ab	West Edmonton Mall
Computer store	1980-87	7	Mature	Ra	Computerland
Electronics superstores	1982-	6	Growth	Ra	Future Shop
Off-price retailer/factory outlet	1980-	?	Growth	Dp	Apparel Clearance Centre
Electronic home shopping	1989-	?	Introduction	Ab	Canadian Home Shopping Network
Wholesale clubs	1990	?	Introduction/Growth	Wr	Price Club/Costco

* Ra = Retail accordion; Ab = Adaptive behaviour; Dp = Dialectic Process; Wr = Wheel of retailing.
†These firms are representative of institutional types and are not necessarily in the stage of life cycle specified for the institutional group as a whole.

institutional structure than the wheel of retailing. The accordion theory is based on the premise that retail institutions evolve over time from broad-based outlets with wide assortments to outlets offering specialized, narrow lines. Over time the outlets again begin to offer a wide assortment, thus establishing a general-specific-general pattern. Retailers contract their lines to focus on more specific target markets, higher margin lines, and higher turnover merchandise. Then, the retailers expand their lines to attract more customers to increase overall sales. Then, the explanation is that the retailer makes the decision to focus again. This evolution suggests the term *accordion*, which reflects a contraction and expansion of merchandise lines.

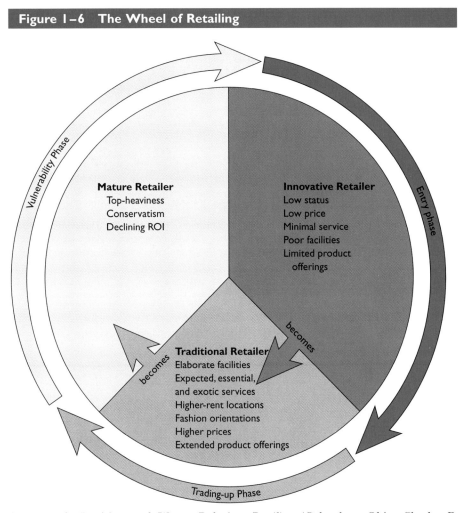

Figure 1-6   The Wheel of Retailing

Mature Retailer
Top-heaviness
Conservatism
Declining ROI

Innovative Retailer
Low status
Low price
Minimal service
Poor facilities
Limited product
  offerings

Traditional Retailer
Elaborate facilities
Expected, essential,
and exotic services
Higher-rent locations
Fashion orientations
Higher prices
Extended product offerings

Vulnerability Phase
Entry phase
Trading-up Phase
becomes
becomes

Source: Dale Lewision and Wayne Delozier, *Retailing* (Columbus, Ohio: Charles E. Merrill, 1982), p 37.

For example, modern retailing in Canada began with the general store, a one-stop outlet with wide assortments of merchandise. Then came the urbanized department stores, more specialized than the general store. As urbanization continued, single-line and specialty stores (e.g., bookstores, drugstores) emerged. Over time, the single-line and specialty stores added complementary lines. For example, grocery stores over time added faster-moving merchandise to the traditional lines. Some stores added small appliances, convenience-food items, and paper products. Many supermarkets now offer nonfood items such as drugs and cosmetics, and discount stores offer a variety of soft goods. More recently, a new form of specialty store has emerged. These retailers, referred to as category killers or category specialists, such as Toys "Я" Us and Sportchek, offer consumers deep selections of a limited number of merchandise categories.

Two further theories have been proposed to explain changes in retailing. One theory, the **dialectic process**, is based on the adage, "If you can't beat

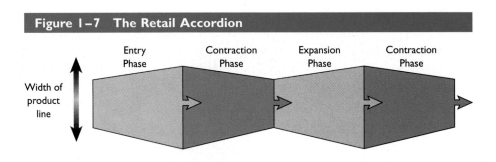

Figure 1–7 The Retail Accordion

them, join them."[4] As a new store, for example the discount store, gains a share at the expense of existing stores, for example department stores, a new form emerges that is a blend of both stores, for example the discount department store such as Wal-Mart and Zellers. The second theory, the **adaptive behaviour** explanation, suggests that the retailing institutions that can most effectively adapt to economic, competitive, social, technological, and legal environmental changes are the ones most likely to survive.[5] The variety store is often cited as an institution that failed to adapt to the changing environment and is seldom seen today. On the other hand, video stores grew rapidly with the advent of videocassette recorders.[6]

Trends in Canadian Retailing

The final section of this chapter discusses the major trends that are likely to affect retail strategies in the future. Retailing strategies probably change more quickly than any other component of the business structure. The reason is that retailing is closer to the consumer than any other part of the corporate world. As a consequence, retailing strategies are constantly changing in response to shifts in the external environment and as new forms of competition are developed to meet consumer needs.

The major trends that retailers are facing are (1) the globalization of markets, (2) shift to a marketing orientation, and (3) merchandising trends.

The globalization of markets

There has been a continuous trend to reduce trade barriers around the world to encourage more international trade. As well, a number of economic communities have been formed to eliminate all trade barriers and create a common market between a group of nations. As one example, the European Community, a group of the major Western European nations, has created a "common market" with a population exceeding 320 million people.

In North America, Canada and the United States signed the Free Trade Agreement (FTA) in 1989, which over a 10-year period will eliminate most trade barriers and liberalize trade practices. In 1994, the North American Free Trade Agreement (NAFTA) established a free trade zone between Canada, the United States, and Mexico, which will eliminate most trade barriers between the three countries over the next 15 years. The agreement creates a market of

Photo by Betty McDougall

360 million people who produce and consume over $8 trillion worth of goods and services.

To date, the major impact for Canadian retailers has been the influx of U.S. retailers into Canada. The list is extensive and includes Wal-Mart, Home Depot, Business Depot, Price Club/Costco, Sports Authority, Michaels, Petstuff, and The Gap. Between 1990 and 1995 total retail sales in Canada increased by $16 billion and one analyst estimated that new U.S. retailers entering Canada captured all of the increase.[7] Canadian retailers had to improve their competitive strategies to defend their markets in Canada in the face of this strong competition from U.S. retailers opening stores in Canada. For example, some retailers sourced outside of Canada to maintain and advertise lower prices (e.g., Bata), while Eaton's introduced a "Made in Canada" theme in its advertising.

Another strategy was to form joint ventures or partnerships with U.S. retailers, where each side helps the other penetrate its market. A third strategy was for Canadian department stores to lease departments to U.S. retailers, especially in smaller markets.

The strategy pursued by Zellers when Wal-Mart entered the Canadian market in 1994 illustrates one approach to a major competitive challenge. In response to Wal-Mart's entry, Zellers renovated 62 stores, reconfigured stores to provide for broader, more competitive merchandise assortments, and revised their pricing to maintain its dominant price position against all competitors, including Wal-Mart. The result led to increased sales and market share but a decline in profits.[8] Even with the competitive responses of retailers like Zellers, Wal-Mart has had a substantial impact since its arrival in Canada (Retail Highlight 1–3).

ghlight 1–3

he Impact on Competitive Retailers

In a study or Wal-Mart's impact on the Canadian retail environment, Stephen Arnold, a marketing professor at Queen's University School of Business, found that in the first year that Wal-Mart was in Kingston it had a large impact. In surveys before (1994) and one year after (1995) Wal-Mart arrived (it took over the Woolco store), Dr. Arnold found the following:

First Choice to Shop in Kingston	1994	1995
• Zellers	40%	39%
• Woolco/Wal-Mart	7%	22%
• Sears	19%	10%
• The Bay	16%	13%
• S&R Dept. Store	9%	8%
• K mart	9%	8%

Which Store Has the Lowest Prices	1994	1995
• Zellers	55%	37%
• Woolco/Wal-Mart	8%	44%
• Sears	N/A	N/A
• S&R Dept. Store	N/A	N/A
• K mart	9%	7%

His report noted that the dramatic increase in Wal-Mart having the lowest prices did not bode well for any of its competitors. The report also mentioned that this was accomplished by Wal-Mart in a single year, a remarkable achievement for any retailer.

Source: Paul Brent, "How Hard Did Wal-Mart Hit?" *Financial Post*, February 24, 1996, p. 3.

Shift from a merchandising to a marketing orientation

Evidence indicates that retail management's focus will continue to shift from merchandising to marketing. **Merchandising** means that the primary focus of the firm is to have the right merchandise, at the right place, at the right time, in the right quantities, and at the right price. *Marketing* means that all of the retailer's activities support an integrated marketing strategy with a strong consumer focus. This shift does not lessen the importance of the merchandising function within retailing. Rather, it means that merchandising is no longer more important than other functions.

Today, finding the right goods and creatively displaying them no longer ensures that a retailing firm will grow and prosper. Management can no longer simply "mind the store"; it must run the business with a constant eye on the consumer. Historically, retailers have felt that profitability and market share would follow if they presented consumers with the right goods at the right price. Financial systems and business operations under such a philosophy were merely necessary housekeeping chores.

Today, firms ranging from Zellers to Loblaws are creating new types of retail organizations to meet the new competitive pressures and the changing and varying consumer needs. For example, Loblaws has several core stores like Loblaws, Zehrs, or Valu-Mart, discount stores like No Frills or Econo-mart, convenience stores like Quick Mart, superfood stores like City Farms or Extra Foods, as well as combination stores like Centres, Super Loblaws, and the Superstores. Successful retailers today are reorienting their organizations toward:

1. Thinking about the following questions: What business are we in? How are we positioned competitively? Have we tried to be all things to all people?

How can we distinguish ourselves from our competitors in the minds of our target customer? Who is our target customer? Why does it matter?

2. A broader business perspective that examines the impact of each functional specialty on others and strives for excellent, effective business decisions at all levels.

3. Increased financial sophistication and skill in asset management to ensure optimum financial results.

4. Skill in working through people to achieve effective implementation, encourage creativity, and retain valued employees with changed life-style expectations.[9]

Merchandising Trends

Significant changes in merchandising are also occurring. These include an improved merchandising mix and productivity improvements.

Improved merchandise mix

Many department stores are reducing the number of marginal lines carried. Department stores are vulnerable in consumable items, health and beauty aids, and various houseware categories because they compete with every discounter, drugstore, and mass merchandising outlet in the city. In specific merchandise categories, fashion areas are where department stores perform best—fashion apparel, accessories, jewelery, and cosmetics. Department stores are dropping lines subject to heavy discounting and low margins. Major appliances, in particular, offer little return relative to their space and inventory costs. Retailers are realizing that consumers have no special inclination to shop for these products at department stores, no matter how favourable a store's image.

As one example, Canadian Tire has decided to focus on three merchandise categories: auto parts and accessories, sports (hockey, bicycling, fishing, and basketball equipment), and home products (hardware and housewares). Canadian Tire's goal is to achieve market dominance in these three categories and it hopes that customers will see three "specialty stores" under one roof.[10]

Productivity improvements

Through the use of technology, improved distribution systems, and better inventory management, Canadian retailers are becoming more efficient. As one example, Shoppers Drug Mart/Pharmaprix launched a three-year program to improve operating efficiency. Part of the program involves centralized supplier negotiations to better leverage buying power and the introduction of point-of-sale technology to generate on-line inventory data to improve merchandising and inventory control.[11]

These trends reflect the competitive and dynamic nature of Canadian retailing. In response, retailers must constantly anticipate the implications of the trends.

Chapter Highlights

- Marketing is the process by which individuals and groups obtain what they need and want through creating and exchanging products and value with others. Retailing is the final part of the process, satisfying individual and organizational objectives through exchanges.

- The dynamics of retailing can best be understood by analyzing its structure, which also helps illustrate the strategies by which retailers compete in the marketplace.

- Descriptive classifications of retailing structure include ownership, variety and assortment, kind of business, and location.

- Strategic classifications include margin-turnover and price and service.

- The retail structure is dynamic. Retail types appear to follow a pattern of evolution, but no single theory explains the evolution of all types of retail outlets. The existing theories are, at best, descriptive and perhaps somewhat explanatory.

- The wheel of retailing theory is based on the premise that retailers evolve through three phases: entry, trading-up, and vulnerability. A second explanation for change is the retail accordion where retail institutions evolve from broad-based outlets with wide assortment patterns to specialized narrow lines and then return to the wide-assortment pattern.

- Two further theories are the dialectic process ("If you can't beat them, join them") and adaptive behaviour (those that most effectively adapt to the changing environment will survive).

- Retailers are facing three major trends: (1) the globalization of markets, (2) shift to a marketing orientation, and (3) merchandising trends.

Key Terms

adaptive behaviour 20	marketing 8
assortment 12	merchandising 22
chain 11	retail accordion 17
channel of distribution 8	retail structure 8
consumer cooperative 11	retailing 8
dialectic process 19	turnover 14
life cycle 16	variety 12
margin 14	wheel of retailing 17

Discussion Questions

1. Explain the following concepts: retailing, marketing, retail structure, and channels of distribution.

2. Why is it important to classify the retail institutional structure?

3. Discuss the margin-turnover classification model (Figure 1–3). Given an example of a retail outlet that may exist in each of the four quadrants of the margin-turnover model.

5. What are some bases for the classification of retail outlets other than margin-turnover and ownership of the establishment?

6. How might the owner of an existing store benefit from a study of retail structure in a given market area?

7. What does it mean to say that retail management is shifting its emphasis from a merchandising to a marketing orientation?

8. Summarize the major trends that are projected for the year 2000 in the competitive structure of retailing.

Application Exercises

1. Select a full city block or a shopping centre in your city. Classify each store according to its margin-turnover classification scheme.

2. Place five different stores in your community in each quadrant of the margin-turnover figure (Figure 1–3). Explain the reasons for their placement.

3. Using the classification schemes in the text, choose the major stores in the retail structure in your community and make a complete classification chart of the structure. Then draw some strategy conclusions.

Suggested Cases

1. Videofile
2. Retailing Newswatch
3. Canadian Life-Styles

Notes

1. Leonard Kubas, "Navigating the New Retail Landscape," *Marketing*, August 7, 1995, pp. 11, 12.

2. *Retail Chain and Department Stores* (Ottawa: Statistics Canada, Catalog 63–210), Annual.

3. Rom J. Markin and Clovin P. Duncan, "The Transformation of Retailing Institutions: Beyond the Wheel of Retailing and Life Cycle Theories," *Journal of Macromarketing*, Spring 1981, pp. 58–66; Stephen Brown, "The Wheel of Retailing," *International Journal of Retailing* 3, 1, 1988, pp. 16–37; and Stephen Brown, "Variations on a Marketing Enigma: The Wheel of Retailing Theory," *Journal of Marketing Management* 7, 1991, pp. 131–55.

4. Thomas J. Maronick and Bruce J. Walker, "The Dialectic Evolution of Retailing," *Proceedings: Southern Marketing Association,* (Atlanta: Georgia State University, 1975), pp. 147–51.

5. A.C.R. Dressmann, "Patterns of Evolution in Retailing," *Journal of Retailing* 44 (Spring 1968), pp. 64–81.

6. For more information on the evolution of retail institutions, see Adam Finn and John Rigby, "West Edmonton Mall: Consumer Combined-Purpose Trips and the Birth of the Mega-Multi-Mall?" *Canadian Journal of Administrative Sciences,* June 1992, pp. 134–45.

7. Rod McQueen, "Retailers 'Without Mercy,' " *Financial Post,* February 24, 1996, pp. 12–13.

8. Hudson's Bay Company, *Annual Report,* 1994.

9. Debra J. Cornwall, "Say Goodbye to the Merchant Mystique," *Business Horizons,* September/October 1984, p. 82. © 1984 by the Foundation for the School of Business at Indiana University. Reprinted by permission.

10. Canadian Tire, *Annual Report,* 1994.

11. Imasco, *Annual Report,* 1994.

Analyzing the Canadian Retail Environment

Chapter Objectives

After reading this chapter you should be able to:

1. Describe the major federal regulations affecting retailers.

2. List the key economic indicators that reflect the state of the economy.

3. Evaluate the demographic environment.

4. Discuss how changes in competition affect retailing.

5. Describe trends in technology and its impact on retailing.

Photo by Betty McDougall

The past decade has brought many changes to the Canadian retail environment. Ten years ago, few stores were open on Sunday. Now, three provinces—Alberta, British Columbia, and Ontario—have wide open, seven-day shopping, whereas in some other provinces Sunday shopping is a controversial political and legal issue. And the Competition Act, passed by the federal government in 1986, has a series of measures that directly affect retailers.

In the past decade, the Canadian economic environment has experienced inflation, high unemployment rates, a recession, as well as years of strong economic growth. Many Canadians experienced difficult times in the deep recession of the early 1990s when the unemployment rate was 11 percent and incomes declined, and a large number of personal and retail bankruptcies occurred. In the mid 1990s, the economy grew, the unemployment rate declined, but average consumer incomes showed little or no growth.

The past decade has seen only moderate increases in the total population (less than 1 percent per year). However, some age groups, such as the baby boomers, grew at a far more rapid rate than the overall population.

And in the next 10 years the "seniors," those people age 65 and over, will grow more rapidly than any other age group.

In the past decade over 1.6 million women entered the labour force. The overall participation rate in the labour force for married women increased by 4 percent, and today 63 percent of female heads of household with children are in the labour force; 56 percent with children under three years of age. Dual-income households are now the norm, not the exception.

In the past decade technology has had a tremendous impact on retailing. In particular, point-of-purchase scanners allow firms to evaluate tactical decisions on a daily basis and to optimize the merchandising mix. As well, electronic data interchange provides the basis for quick response delivery systems, which can improve customer service and reduce inventory and distribution expenses.

Today, retailers are faced with many forms of competition that did not exist 10 years ago. Stores within stores, superstores, mixed-use stores, warehouse retailers, and the world's largest shopping mall have created a new competitive environment.

In the past decade, Canadian retailers have experienced intensive competition from foreign firms entering the market. Beginning with the giant warehouse clubs, Price Club and Costco (since merged), and followed by others such as The Gap and Home Depot, these firms brought new capabilities and services to Canada. But the major new entrant was Wal-Mart, the world's largest discount retailer who is defining the retail experience in Canada. Wal-Mart has, and will continue to have, a substantial impact on Canadian retailing. ■

Progressive retailers know that the next decade will bring more changes. These retailers constantly monitor the environment so they can anticipate and react to these changes. New strategies are developed to capture opportunities and avoid threats in the retail environment.

The retail strategies to be discussed in Chapter 6 cannot be developed in a vacuum. The strategies emerge after an analysis of both the internal and external environments facing the firm. Careful analysis of shifts in the economy, in competitive behaviour, in population demographics, in the legal environment, and in technology are important in order to base planning efforts on realistic assumptions about the future. Consumer responses to economic and social trends are complex, and they reveal themselves in changing patterns of consumption.

The ability to anticipate and respond to such changes is the key to strategic success in retailing. Forward-thinking managers have established approaches to monitor trends and determine their impact. This chapter discusses the major environmental forces affecting retailers, beginning with the legal environment.

The Legal Environment

Retailing decisions are affected by the legal environment, which is made up of legislation (federal, provincial, and municipal), government agencies, and various action groups. These laws, agencies, and groups regulate and influence

---

Table 2–1   Major Federal Legislation Affecting Retailers

1. Trade Practices

- **Competition Act:** encourages competition in the marketplace and benefits consumers by reducing upward pressure on prices, rewarding innovation and initiative, increasing choice and quality of goods offered, and preventing abuses of market power by ensuring that firms compete with each other on a fair basis.
- **Bankruptcy Act,** intellectual property laws (e.g., **Copyright Act, Trade-marks Act, Patents Act** and **Industrial Design Act, the National Trade Mark and True Labelling Act** and the **Canada Business Corporations Act;**) make rules for the marketplace that impact on consumers.
- **Tax Rebate Discounting Act:** protects consumers who use tax discounting services.
- Other legislation involving trade practices include **Broadcasting Act, Canadian Human Rights Act, Income Tax Act, Official Languages Act, Small Loans Act, Employment Equity Act,** and **Multiculturalism Act.**

2. Health and Safety

- **Food and Drugs Act** (partly administered by Health and Welfare Canada): protects consumers from hazards to health, and from fraud or misleading representations associated with the sale of foods.
- **Hazardous Products Act:** protects the health and safety of consumers by prohibiting or regulating the sale, advertisement, and importation of products considered to be dangerous to the public.

3. Product Standards and Grades

- **Consumer Packaging and Labelling Act:** specifies what product information must be made available to consumers on prepackaged products, and how it must be displayed.
- **Weights and Measures Act:** sets national standards for fair measure in trade for most measured commodities.
- **Textile Labelling Act:** requires that information on fibre content and dealer identity be provided on the labels of consumer textile articles.
- **Precious Metals Marking Act:** protects consumers from false claims for articles containing adulterated or substandard precious metals.

Source: "The Marketplace in Transition: Changing Roles for Consumers, Business and Governments?" *Consumer and Corporate Affairs Canada,* 1992.

retailers' strategies and tactics. This section introduces you to the federal, provincial, and local regulations, agencies, and groups that can impact strategy and implementation.

Legislation regulating retailers

More regulations affecting retailing have been introduced in the past two decades than in the previous 100 years. Devising effective ways to regulate the marketplace while sustaining an environment of healthy competition, innovation, and economic growth is a major challenge confronting retailers, the government, and consumers. A description of the major federal legislation affecting retailers is provided in Table 2–1.

In 1986, the federal government enacted the Competition Act—the major legislative act regulating marketing and retailing practices in Canada. The Act is designed to protect companies, consumers, and the interests of society. It does this by prohibiting mergers that reduce competition to the detriment of the

Table 2–2   The Competition Act—Major Sections Affecting Retailers

Mergers:	Section 33 prohibits mergers by which competition is, or is likely to be, lessened to the detriment of, or against the interest of the public.
Pricing:	Sections 34 and 35 prohibit a supplier from charging different prices to competitors purchasing like quantities of goods (price discrimination), and prohibit price cutting that lessens competition (predatory pricing).
Pricing and Advertising:	Section 52 prohibits prices that misrepresent the regular selling price (misleading price advertising). Section 53 prohibits advertising activities that misrepresent warranties, guarantees, and testimonials. Provisions for double ticketing (if two prices are shown on a product, the lower price is the price to consumers) and pyramid selling are included in Sections 54 and 56. Pricing and advertising are also covered under Section 37, which prohibits "bait and switch" selling (the nonavailability of advertised bargains) and prohibits selling above the advertised price.
Pricing:	Section 38 prohibits suppliers from requiring subsequent resellers to offer products at a stipulated price (**resale price maintenance**).
Distribution:	Section 48 prohibits consignment selling if the purpose is to control prices or discriminate between dealers. Exclusive dealing, when retailers agree to handle the products of only one supplier, is prohibited where the result is that competition is, or is likely to be, substantially lessened. Tied selling, where a supplier will sell a line of merchandise only if the retailer also agrees to purchase other merchandise from the supplier, is also prohibited if competition is lessened.

public. For example, in 1995 Canada's two largest book retailers, Smith Books and Coles, were merged, creating a chain with 430 stores and annual sales of over $340 million. The merger was approved by the Competition Bureau (created by the Act) with a number of conditions including the elimination of covenants in leases with shopping malls that prevented other book retailers from opening in these malls and a monitoring (by the Competition Bureau) of their trade activities for the next three years.[1] As well, the Act forbids unfair trade practices, such as **predatory pricing, price discrimination,** and **exclusive dealing,** and prohibits misleading price advertising. The important sections of the Competition Act that directly affect retailers are shown in Table 2–2, and examples of the types of activities that retailers have been prosecuted for are shown in Retail Highlight 2–1.

At the provincial level, each province has business practices acts that are similar to or extend the federal legislation. For example, all provinces regulate the activities of door-to-door retailers and allow for "cooling-off" periods, ranging from 2 to 10 days, where consumers can cancel contracts with this type of seller. Also, most provinces have consumer protection acts, which regulate retailers' activities, including the hours and days a retailer can open. In 1984, the Supreme Court repealed the Lord's Day Act and the provinces were then faced with the Sunday shopping issue. The controversy led to wide open, seven-day shopping in Alberta, British Columbia, and Ontario, and to some provinces letting each municipality decide the issue. Now, in Canada, regulations governing Sunday shopping vary widely across provinces, cities, and even types of stores.

Retailers operating in Quebec need to comply with language requirements for their signs and displays. For example, all outdoor signs must be in French, but within the store, English signs and messages are allowed. Quebec retailers

Retail Highlight 2–1

Examples of Prosecution of Retailers under Section 36 of Competition Act

- A Winnipeg sporting goods retailer stated in newspaper advertisements that a discount of "30-40 percent" off the ordinary selling price was available for golf clubs. Investigation revealed the statements were untrue and the retailer was fined $2,000.
- A national paint and wallpaper retailer was fined $225,000 because, for certain stains, paints, and wallpaper, most of the sales were at the discount sale price, not the ordinary sale price.
- A furniture retailer compared its sale price to a regular price in advertising matters. It was found that the regular price was substantially exaggerated and the retailer was fined $115,000.
- A national womenswear retailer was offering its clothing at discount prices, with price tags indicating the original amount, the special price, and the amount of the discount. It was found that the clothing was never sold at the original price as the clothing was already tagged "special" before even entering the store. The retailer pleaded guilty and was fined $300,000.
- A national book retailer stated in newspaper ads and on in-store price tags a regular and a special price for each featured book. Investigation revealed that the quoted regular prices were inflated and the retailer was fined $25,000.
- An Ontario supermarket chain displayed two (or more) prices on various grocery products. It was established that the products were being sold at the higher of the two prices indicated and the chain was fined $2,000.
- A department store chain distributed more than a million "scratch-and-win" cards, which gave the impression that consumers had one chance in four of winning a 25 percent discount on merchandise. It was established that over 90 percent of the cards offered only a 10 percent discount and the chain was fined $100,000.
- A department store chain compared its sale price to its regular price in advertising tires. It was established that the chain had systematically misled the public in misrepresenting the regular price and it was fined $135,000.

Sources: "Misleading Advertising Bulletin," *Consumer and Corporate Affairs Canada* (various issues), and "Keeping an Eye on Advertising Tricks," *The Record*, July 4, 1995, p. B7.

are also governed by regulations concerning advertising to children and roadside advertising.

Government agency activities

Consumer affairs departments at the federal and provincial levels make sure that retailers comply with legislation. They also act as a "watchdog" for consumers and can act on consumer complaints. In this capacity, these departments ensure that individual consumers receive fair treatment by retailers. At the provincial level, the consumer affairs departments will often provide information to consumers as to their rights when buying merchandise. These guides include such things as facts on refunds and exchanges and tips on buying a car.

Action group activities

Various consumer groups also affect the activities of retailers. On a formal basis, groups like the Consumers Association of Canada (CAC) lobby governments, manufacturers, and retailers for changes that safeguard and protect consumer

hopping
da; for
y shop-
ence to
ers.

Photo by James Hertel

interests. The Better Business Bureau, which operates branches in 17 Canadian cities, provides a strong voice for consumers who have complaints against specific retailers.

Consumers will band together on an informal basis when they have a common interest or goal. Because retailers are in constant touch with consumers, they often bear the brunt of consumer protests. Retailers have been petitioned and boycotted by these citizen groups who have protested Sunday shopping, the selling of war toys, the selling of fur coats, nonunion products, and retail bank charges. As a result of a consumer lobby group, the Ontario government passed legislation banning the sale of cigarettes in drugstores and pharmacies in 1995. Two months before the Ontario legislation took effect, Wal-Mart announced that it was voluntarily removing cigarettes from all its stores across Canada.[2]

Consumer concern over environmental issues is reflected in retailer actions. Although recent studies show a decline in the percentage of Canadians expressing a willingness to pay more for environmentally safe products, a segment of Canadians is committed to improving the environment.[3] Retailers such as Loblaws, Becker Convenience Stores, and The Body Shop have been actively marketing environmentally safe products to these individuals.

Industry codes

Various industry codes also affect Canadian retailers. This is particularly true in the area of advertising, where broadcast codes and industry guidelines lead to considerable control of advertising. For example, the Canadian Advertising Foundation has developed the Canadian Code of Advertising Standards, which deals with how products or services, including cosmetics and nonprescription medicines, should be advertised. The Foundation also provides guidelines for the use of comparative advertising. Additional broadcast codes administered by other associations provide guidelines for advertising to children and sex-role stereotyping.[4]

Conclusion

Various government regulations affect both growth strategies and marketing plans. More than ever, managers must be sensitive to the liabilities they can face from various actions or lack of action. The retailer who is interested in serving the public by providing complete and accurate information and merchandise at fair prices is not likely to encounter difficulties. Legislative remedies are designed to ensure fairness in competitive behaviour and to protect consumers from unscrupulous sellers.

Management needs to develop a positive response to these pressures. Simply put, government regulations are designed to provide consumers with useful and honest information that makes it easier for them to function as rational shoppers.

The Economic Environment

Retailers need to monitor the economic environment to anticipate the conditions that are likely to occur in the future. This is done by paying close attention to the key economic indicators that reflect the state of the economy. These indicators include the gross domestic product, personal saving rates, unemployment rates, the consumer price index, the prime interest rate, new housing starts, and the foreign exchange rate (Table 2–3).

In the early 1990s Canada's economy was in a recession with high unemployment and reduced consumer expenditures. During that time, retail sales and profits declined and retail bankruptcies increased dramatically. A number of well-known retail chains went out of business during these times (see Retail Highlight 2–2). This period was particularly difficult for Canadian retailers because they faced the introduction of the goods and services tax in 1991, the loss of revenue due to cross-border shopping because of a relatively favourable exchange rate, and the increase in federal, provincial, and municipal taxes on

Table 2–3   Key Economic Indicators— Highs and Lows in the Past Decade

Gross Domestic Product—$794 billion in 1996

a. the highest increase was 9.8% in 1984
b. the lowest increase was .8% in 1991

Personal Savings Rate—7.0% in 1996

a. the highest savings rate was 17.8% in 1982
b. the lowest savings rate was 6.9% in 1995

Unemployment Rate—9.2% in 1996

a. the highest unemployment rate was 11.3% in 1992
b. the lowest unemployment rate was 7.5% in 1989

Consumer Price Index—134.1 in 1996

a. the highest increase was 6.7% in 1991
b. the lowest increase was −.2% in 1994

Prime Interest Rate—6.0% in 1996

a. the highest prime rate was 14.0% in 1990
b. the lowest prime rate was 6.0% in 1996

New Housing Starts—120,000 in 1996

a. the highest increase was 29.2% in 1983
b. the lowest increase was −29.3% in 1982

Foreign Exchange Rate (in US$)—$.73 in 1996

a. the highest rate was $.87 in 1991
b. the lowest rate was $.73 in 1995

Source: *Canadian Outlook,* The Conference Board of Canada (various issues). Indicators for 1996 are estimates.

consumers. In particular, the increased taxes considerably reduced the spending power of Canadian consumers. Real spending by consumers, after inflation, declined by 4 percent in the two recession years.[5] Although the Canadian economy began a recovery in 1993, consumers continued to face financial pressures. Household debt (mortgage debt plus consumer credit) rose from 79 percent of after-tax income in 1989 to 92 percent in 1995, the result of higher taxes, fewer jobs, and few pay increases. The result is lower retail spending, as Canadians pay down their debt, more emphasis on products and services that are durable and practical, and more bargain hunting. In summary, total retail sales in Canada grew by 2 percent in 1992, 5 percent in 1993, 7 percent in 1994, and 2 percent in 1995.[6]

Many retailers suffered dramatic declines in sales during the early 1990s. Sears Canada sales declined $500 million in 1991 and have not increased since that time. However, some retailers were able to implement strategies that led to continued growth in both sales and profits during the turbulent times. For example, Zellers, with its Club Z and "where the lowest price is the law" strategy increased its share of the market and its sales. Loblaws, with its extensive "no name" and Club Pack merchandise lines, also increased its sales during the early 1990s. Clearly, certain retailers are better positioned than others to respond to changing economic conditions. Through monitoring the economic environ-

Retail Highlight 2–2

Retail Casualties of the Recession

Many retailers were unable to survive the ravages of the recession and its after-effects and went out of business or closed many of their stores. Among the casualties were:

Retailer	Stores Closed	Number of Employees	Announced
Beaver Canoe	20	180	April 1992
Bargain Harold's	160	4,000	February 1992
Groupe Selection	100	650	December 1991
Town & Country[1]	162	1,300	November 1991
Mac's/Mike's Mart[2]	150	750	June 1992
Marks & Spencer[3]	25	300	May 1992
Grafton-Fraser[4]	114	N/A	December 1991
Maher[5]	290	1,275	May 1992
Elks[6]	79	700	January 1991
Ayres[7]	60	750	December 1991
A&A Records and Tapes[8]	140	N/A	March 1993
Woodwards	26	N/A	December 1991
Woolworth	240	3,000	October 1993
Steel[1]	86	N/A	October 1993
K mart	25	N/A	January 1994
Dylex[9]	200	1,800	January 1995

[1] Part of the Dylex chain.
[2] Part of the Silcorp chain.
[3] Forty-two stores remain open in chain.
[4] Grafton-Fraser is part of the Grafton Group. Stores closed included Madison, Bimini, Jack Fraser (some remained open), and George Richard's Kingsize Clothes.
[5] The footwear chain that was part of the Grafton Group.
[6] The menswear chain that was part of the Grafton Group.
[7] Operated J. Michael's, Kristy Allan, and Berries chains.
[8] A&A went bankrupt twice, the first time in 1991.
[9] Dylex closed 200, or 27 percent, of its 738 stores operating under the Tip Top Tailors, Fairweather, BiWay, and Thrifty's store names.

Sources: Mark Evans, "Grim Outlook for Retailing," *Financial Post*, December 12, 1991, p. 5; Barrie McKenna, "Rag Trade Facing Disaster," *Globe & Mail*, May 12, 1992, p. B6; Mark Evans, "Silcorp Shakeup Shuts 150 Stores," *Financial Post*, June 18, 1992, p. 1; Mark Evans and Neville Nankivell, "Big Cuts at M&S Canada," *Financial Post*, May 13, 1991, p. 3; Matthew Ingram, "Shopping for Retail Survivors," *Financial Times*, April 2, 1994, pp. 1, 6–7; and Paul Brent, "Dylex to Shut 200 Stores as It Bids to Restructure," *Financial Post*, January 12, 1995, pp. 1, 2.

ment, retailers can take a proactive position and adjust both strategies and tactics to maximize opportunities and minimize threats.

Economic conditions vary considerably across Canada. For example, the Maritimes, particularly Newfoundland, has experienced greater unemployment than most other areas of Canada. As a result, the income rating index for Newfoundland in 1996 was 25 percent below the national average and the market rating index was 20 percent below the national average (Table 2–4). On the other hand, Ontario often has a favourable economic climate and was 18 percent above the national average on the income rating index but was 3 percent below on the market rating index.[7]

Table 2–4   The Canadian Markets, 1996

	Population (000)	% Population Change (1986–96)	Market Rating Index[a]	Income Rating Index[b]
Newfoundland	581	2.2	80	75
Prince Edward Island	134	5.5	81	84
Nova Scotia	935	7.1	93	87
New Brunswick	758	6.8	84	84
Quebec	7,395	13.2	97	92
Ontario	11,274	23.9	97	108
Manitoba	1,129	6.2	86	87
Saskatchewan	1,001	(.8)	84	85
Alberta	2,782	17.6	114	102
British Columbia*	3,888	31.4	118	109
Canada	29,877	18.0	100	100

*Includes Yukon and North West Territories
[a]Market Rating Index = Retail Sales/Population
[b]Income Rating Index = Per Capita Income/Population

Source: *Market Research Handbook, 1995,* Statistics Canada, Catalog 63-224 and Canadian Markets 1995, *Financial Post,* 1995. Based on estimates.

The Demographic Environment

Changing demographics are important because of their impact on retail strategy and responses to competition. Recent changes in the population's age distribution, in the rate of household formation, geographic shifts in the population, relative income gains among selected market segments, and increasing ethnic markets all can affect retail strategy.

The changing age distribution

The 35-to-49 age group now constitutes the largest segment of the population and is dominated by baby boomers (persons born between 1946 and 1966) who are in the middle of their careers, raising children, and paying into investment plans (Table 2–5). The baby boomers are aging and will continue to have major implications for retailers as they move through life. They are responsible for the "Echo Boom" and will eventually join the "Countdown Generation" (Retail Highlight 2–3).

As one example of the impact of the baby boomers, in terms of outdoor recreation activities, the highest forecasted growth rates between 1996 and 2001 will be in natural environment activities (e.g., hiking, pleasure walking) followed by general recreation (e.g., picnicking, sightseeing). These growth rates are fueled by the large number of baby boomers reaching middle age. Lower growth rates are predicted for recreational sports, water-based sports, and winter sports (e.g., tennis, water skiing, and skating) because of the smaller numbers of Canadians in the age groups who participate in these activities.[8] For retailers specializing in leisure products, this will have significant implications for their merchandising mix.

Table 2–5 Population Age Distribution (1976-2006)							
	Thousands				Percent Change		
Age Group	1976	1986	1996	2006	1976–1986	1986–1996	1996–2006
Children (0-9)	3,620	3,630	3,980	3,480	0	(10)	(13)
Youth (10-19)	4,260	3,730	4,030	4,240	(19)	(8)	(5)
Young adults (20-34)	5,750	6,930	6,840	6,620	21	(1)	(3)
Early middle age (35-49)	3,850	4,980	7,170	7,800	29	44	8
Late middle age (50-64)	3,150	3,590	4,200	6,050	14	17	44
Retirees (65 and over)	2,000	2,730	3,650	4,300	37	34	18
	22,990	25,590	29,870	32,490	11	17	9

Source: *Marketing Research Handbook 1995*, Statistics Canada, Catalogue 63-224.

The changing age mix of the population will result in different growth rates for various age groups for the next two decades. Overall, the three age segments under 34—children, youths, and young adults—will decline, while the three older groups—early middle age, late middle age, and retirees—will increase. These shifts will have significant impacts on the purchase of many products and services.

In the longer term, the 50-plus age group market will represent about one-third of all Canadians and about 40 percent of all households. An important fact is that this population segment will account for about three-quarters of all of Canada's population growth in the next 20 years. Proactive retailers should be developing strategies now to capitalize on the future potential of the 50-plus market. Research has shown that these Canadians, who control most of the personal wealth in Canada, are active shoppers with an intense interest in specials. They want to believe they are saving money whenever they spend and they have a strong value orientation that is based on "getting your money's worth," a reflection of the economic hardship many experienced in their youth.[9]

Rate of household formation

The rate of household formation has been increasing slightly faster than the growth in population. Between 1986 and 1996 the population grew by 17 percent while households grew by 18 percent, and between 1996 and 2006 it is estimated that the population will grow by 9 percent while households will grow by 11 percent. Among the reasons for this is an increase in nonfamily households. The number of one-person households has increased while the number of households with more than four people has declined. Now, about one-quarter of all Canadian households are people who live alone and about 44 percent of all households are nonfamily or single-parent households. This group includes singles, widows, empty nesters, childless and unmarried couples, and younger couples planning to have children later. These small households are prime prospects for townhouses, condominiums, kitchen mini-appliances, and packaged goods in single servings. SSWDs (single, separated, widowed, and divorced) spend more money on travel and entertainment, but they save less and tend to buy more services.

Retail Highlight 2–3

The Echo Boom and the Countdown Generation

In 1987, the birth rate in Canada dropped to an all-time low. But that is changing as the baby boomers (those Canadians born between 1946 and 1966) who are now in their early 30s to late 40s are now making the decision to have children (more than one-third of the babies born in 1990 were born to women 30 and over). Called the "Echo Boom," the birth rate in Canada has been increasing since 1987 and now over 400,000 live births are recorded each year. Opportunities are now available for retailers who target this group. Many couples with new babies change residences, buy cars, and change brands to ones best suited for their babies. They need products such as car seats, playpens, baby foods, and diapers.

The Countdown Generation is at the other end of the age spectrum. The 12 percent of Canadians who expect to retire in the next few years control almost half the personal wealth in Canada. This group, representing about 3 million Canadians, is mature, secure, and relatively rich. The Countdown Generation is used to saving because of economic hardship in their youth. They have paid off their mortgages and now have considerable wealth, mainly in the value of their home. This group will provide many opportunities to retailers who can satisfy their needs for experiences (e.g., travel, entertainment), quality products, and personal growth (e.g., recreational activities).

Sources include: Jo Marney, "The Psychology of Age," *Marketing*, August 21, 1995, p. 12; Hugh Filman, "Baby Books Benefit from Echo Boom," *Marketing*, March 30, 1992, p. 30; Stephen Strauss, "Baby Boomlet Continues, Statistics Canada Reports," *Globe & Mail*, March 3, 1992, pp. A1, A6; and Marina Strauss, "Retirees Have Big Bucks to Spend," *Globe & Mail*, March 17, 1992, p. B7.

Population shifts

Canadians are a mobile people with about 1 in 10 moving each year. In the past decade, the populations of the Western provinces and Ontario grew more than the national average while Quebec and the Maritime provinces grew less than the national average. For the remainder of the 1990s, it is predicted that Ontario, British Columbia, and Alberta will have the fastest growing populations. These population shifts offer opportunities for retailers locating in the faster-growing areas.

Canadians are also moving from rural to urban areas. These concentrated urban areas, called Census Metropolitan Areas (CMAs) by Statistics Canada, now hold the majority of the population. About 61 percent of Canadians live in the 25 CMAs and the three largest markets—Toronto, Montreal, and Vancouver—account for about 32 percent of Canada's population. These large markets provide opportunities for retailers to cater to very specific segments and stores carrying narrow and deep product lines (e.g., a mystery-book store) are found in these locations.

Skewed income distribution

Income distribution in Canada is very skewed. While the average household income in 1994 was $53,500, 47 percent of the households earned less than $35,000, 27 percent between $35,000 and $60,000, and 25 percent earned more than $60,000.[10] The bottom 47 percent accounted for only 20 percent of the total income earned by all Canadians while the top 25 percent accounted for 51 percent of the total income earned.[11]

Table 2–6   Regional Population, Personal Income, and Retail Sales

	Population		Personal Income per Capita		Retail Sales per Capita	
	1996 (000)	Percent Change 1986–96	1996	Percent Change 1986–96	1996	Percent Change 1986–96
British Columbia	3,889	33	$21,000	59	$8,800	69
Prairies	4,912	12	18,200	48	7,500	36
Ontario	11,274	25	20,800	50	7,200	24
Quebec	7,395	13	17,700	48	7,300	43
Maritimes	2,408	4	16,000	60	6,500	35
Canada	29,877	18	$19,200	51	$7,500	38

Source: Canadian Markets, *Financial Post,* various issues.

Retailers need to consider the size and spending power of these income groups when making strategic decisions. For example, BiWay is a chain of stores retailing lower-price men's and women's casual wear to price- and value-conscious shoppers. On the other hand, Harry Rosen menswear stores target the upper-income professional man, and one location in the heart of downtown Toronto features three levels of shopping, including an entire floor of designer boutiques.

Regional differences

While retailers need to monitor each environmental factor to determine the effect on the firm, additional insights can be gained when two or more factors are examined together. For example, population and personal income per capita together have an important impact on retail sales. This is illustrated in Table 2–6 for the five major regions of Canada. Over the past 10 years, the population of British Columbia grew by 33 percent, more than the national average of 18 percent, and income per capita grew by 59 percent, again more than the national average of 51 percent. As a result, retail sales grew by 67 percent, a far greater increase than the national average of 38 percent. In the past 10 years, only Quebec and British Columbia outpaced the national average on retail sales, while the remaining regions were below the average, reflecting the impact of both population and income changes. To thoroughly understand the impact of the many environmental factors, retailers combine them to get a more complete picture of changes that are occurring.

Increasing ethnic markets

A major demographic factor for the 1990s is continuing immigration, the major bulk of net population increase. These immigrants are primarily from Asia (Hong Kong, Philippines, India, Vietnam, and China), Europe (Poland, Britain, and Portugal), Lebanon, and the United States.[12] The five largest ethnic groups in Canada are Germans, Italians, Ukrainians, Native people, and Chinese. About one-third of the Canadian population is non-British and non-French. Canada is largely a multicultural society, with varied tastes and needs, and presents many opportunities for retailers.

In addition, many of these ethnic groups are concentrated in metropolitan areas. It has been estimated that 37 percent of visible (non-Caucasian and non-aboriginal) minorities live in Toronto, 15 percent in Vancouver, and 13 percent in Montreal. About 50 percent of Canada's visible minority population live in Ontario, 19 percent in British Columbia, and 14 percent in Quebec.[13] This concentration is again favourable to retailers. For example, the major Canadian banks are targeting the Asian Canadians, particularly Chinese-speaking ones in Toronto, Vancouver, and other Canadian cities, using Chinese-speaking employees and other services to make these consumers feel as comfortable as possible.[14]

The Competitive Environment

Understanding competition

Competition among retailers is a fact of life. The most familiar type is intratype competition. **Intratype competition** is competition between two retailers of the same type, such as two drugstores. Intratype competition is the model most frequently described in basic economics texts. Examples include The Bay and Eaton's (traditional department stores), Zellers and Wal-Mart (discount department stores), McDonald's and Harvey's (fast-food retailers), and Reitman's and Braemar (women's specialty stores).

A second competitive model is **intertype competition,** which is competition between different types of retail outlets selling the same merchandise. Intertype competition is a common type of retail competition today. For example, Loblaws competes with Sears in many of the nonfood lines sold by Loblaws. The acceptance of scrambled merchandising has allowed similar merchandise to be sold by many different types of retailers. Many convenience products, such as chewing gum, candy, magazines, and soft drinks, are sold in a wide variety of stores ranging from convenience stores to supermarkets to department stores to drugstores. For example, convenience store chains like Becker's and Mac's have suffered losses and closed stores, due in part to the heightened competition from drugstores who expanded their product line to include snacks, soft drinks, and easy-to-prepare foods. As one response, Mac's has entered into agreements with Subway and Pizza Hut to allow them to open branded food service outlets within Mac's stores.[15]

Corporate systems competition occurs when a single-management ownership links resources, manufacturing capability, and distribution networks. Bata Shoes is an example of corporate systems competition. They manufacture most of their merchandise, handle their own storage and distribution functions, and perform all management activities necessary for the sale of goods and services at the retail level.

Total systems networks can be formed either backward or forward. In **forward integration,** a manufacturer establishes its own wholesale and retail network. Examples are Goodyear and Sherwin Williams. **Backward integration** occurs when a retailer or wholesaler performs some manufacturing functions. Most of the large supermarket chains in Canada have, through various holding companies, engaged in backward integration. For example, Loblaws, part of the Weston empire, has access to numerous products manufactured by Weston-owned companies.

The above types of competition do not exist in isolation. Retail firms in all types of channel structures face competition from retailers in any or all of the other systems. Also, our comments must be regarded only as broad generalizations about the nature of competition and the various types of channel systems because numerous exceptions exist.

The new face of competition

The competitive structure of retailing is changing radically. The changes are causing a rethinking of the concepts of retail competition and are also causing changes in consumer shopping habits. **Secondary market expansion** (expansion into small markets) is an increasingly attractive move. Thus, firms such as Stedman's, Metropolitan, and Saan typically face less competition, are able to pay lower wages, and face fewer zoning and other restrictions in these communities of 50,000 or fewer persons. They provide more viable markets than many of the large metropolitan markets, which are already served by almost every major retailer. Recently, two of Canada's largest retailers began pursuing this strategy. Wal-Mart plans to introduce its stores in many of Canada's smaller communities and Sears is opening specialty stores in rural communities across Canada, tailoring each store to local needs.[16]

Supermarket retailing

The supermarket concept, long familiar in the food field, has been adopted by many other types of retailers. The key elements of **supermarket retailing** are (1) self-service and self-selection, (2) large-scale but low-cost physical facilities, (3) a strong price emphasis, (4) simplification and centralization of customer services, and (5) a wide variety and broad assortment of merchandise. This concept has been successful in many lines of trade including sporting goods—Sporting Life and Sportcheck; home improvement—Home Depot; furniture and housewares—Ikea; and business office supplies—Business Depot.

A recent and successful use of this concept are the giant no-frills warehouse stores such as Price Club/Costco. They have entered the Canadian market and generate annual sales per store of $200 to $300 million. Consumers pay $25 a year to join and shop in large warehouse outlets that carry a limited product selection of groceries, office supplies, appliances, and other merchandise at discount prices. These stores cater to bulk buyers more interested in discounts than in convenience and selection. Canadian retailers have responded by opening their own discount operations including Loblaw's with Fortino's supermarkets, the Real Canadian Superstores, and Canadian Tire with its All Out Retail outlets.

The international dimension

Canadian retailers now face new competition on an international basis. It comes in two forms, cross-border shopping and foreign retailers, primarily from the United States, entering the Canadian market. At its height in 1992, Canadian cross-border shoppers spent about $10 billion in the United States, business lost by Canadian retailers. More recently, the substantial decline in the value of the

Canadian dollar against the U.S. dollar has seen a reversal in cross-border shopping; fewer Canadians are shopping in the United States and more Americans are shopping in Canada. Also contributing to this reversal is the entry of Wal-Mart into Canada. Wal-Mart's entry forced Canadian retailers to cut prices and offer better service to compete.[17]

Although the list of foreign retailers entering the Canadian market grows each year, the entry of Wal-Mart had the most dramatic impact on the Canadian retail scene. In January 1994, Wal-Mart, the world's largest discount retailer, purchased 122 Woolco stores for $300 million (U.S.) and began converting them to Wal-Mart stores. Since that time, the major Canadian department store chains, including the Bay, Eaton's, Zellers, Sears Canada, K mart Canada, and other large merchandisers, like Canadian Tire, have changed their strategies to meet the Wal-Mart challenge. These changes include efforts to streamline operations, reduce costs, or focus on satisfying defined customer segments. As well, they have improved merchandise quality, lowered prices, offered better customer service, and instituted loyalty programs.[18] Eaton's is remodelling most of its department stores across Canada at a cost of over $300 million to combat competition and attract customers.[19] Many other international retailers, such as Price Club/Costco, HMV, The Gap, Tiffany, Lenscrafter, Pier 1 Imports, IKEA, The Body Shop, Toys "Я" Us, Home Depot, and Business Depot, have success-fully entered the Canadian market. Predictions are that by the year 2000, 25 percent of retail firms in Canada will be headquartered in the U.S.[20] Among the reasons for the success of foreign retailers in Canada is their experience in highly competitive markets, their high operating efficiency, their clearly defined target markets, and their focus on hiring, training, and motivating salespeople to provide quality customer service. Many of the weaker Canadian retailers have been driven out of business by the intense competition of foreign retailers, particularly the "big box stores" (large stores such as Wal-Mart, Home Depot, and Business Depot), with their emphasis on price and selection.[21]

The Technology Environment

Changes in technology are affecting virtually every dimension of the retailing outlet. Detailed information that can aid retailers in making decisions ranging from merchandise elimination to credit authorization is now available on a timely basis through point-of-sale (POS) technology and electronic data inter-change (EDI). This information forms the basis of the management informa-tion system, the structure necessary to gather, analyze, and distribute informa-tion needed by management. Other technology changes include new methods of merchandising presentation ranging from video kiosks to home video shopping through such channels as the Canadian Home Shopping Network.

Point-of-sale technology

A **point-of-sale (POS)** cash register (or terminal) is the key input device for many retailing systems. POS terminals record a variety of information at the time a transaction occurs. The terminals are usually connected to the retailer's computer information system, which provides on-line information on which

Canadian Tire's "new format" stores provide selection, service, and value.

Courtesy Canadian Tire

merchandise, styles, and colours of various manufacturers are selling most rapidly and allows buying staff and managers to effectively manage the store's merchandise. POS information provides the basis for the sales reports, which are key to inventory control, sales forecasting, and scheduling sales staff.

POS information, combined with customer information from credit and debit cards, can be of assistance in identifying target groups for promotional activities and reward programs. For example, by knowing the buying patterns of various target groups, retail managers can design promotions that can be directed, through personal letters, to these groups. More retailers are using direct targeting to encourage their customers to continue shopping with them.

Electronic data interchange

Electronic data interchange (EDI) is the computer-to-computer transmission of data and business documents between retailers and suppliers. EDI allows retailers to instantly transmit purchase orders to their suppliers, reducing inventory costs for both parties. Other benefits include reduced administrative

---

Retail Highlight 2–4

Bedford Furniture Industries and EDI

Bedford Furniture Industries, located in Toronto, manufactures bedding and upholstery for more than 1,000 customers, including Sears, Eaton's, and The Bay. It is connected to all its large customers through EDI and has implemented a rapid delivery system with one of them. Here's how the system works:

When a consumer selects a Bedford product, the retailer's sales department keys in the order, complete with label information. The order is transmitted to Bedford's electronic mailbox that evening. Bedford's computer picks up orders at half-hour intervals between 2 A.M. and 10 P.M. They're processed by the translator software, summarized by shipment, and entered into the host mini, where they await the start of the production day at 6 A.M.

Finished goods are bar-coded at the shipping dock. Consumer labels are applied and bar codes scanned during loading, when serial numbers are also recorded, to produce an advance shipping notification or electronic bill of lading. When the retailer receives the shipment, it can check it against the advance shipping notification prior to reloading the goods for delivery to consumers.

Bedford's EDI system also generates electronic invoices for some customers; allows others to make receipt-driven payment, eliminating the need for an invoice; and permits the electronic transfer of funds by the retailers into Bedford's bank account.

As a result of becoming EDI-capable, Bedford now devotes fewer resources to order processing and other administrative functions, makes fewer errors, does a greater volume of business using the same number of employees, and has happier customers.

Source: Sandy Fife, "E-Commerce," *Challenges*, Summer 1995, pp. 8–11.

---

costs such as filing, storing, and retrieving documents and productivity gains because data are entered only once. For example, Bedford Furniture Industries makes Bedford, King Koil, and private-label bedding and upholstery for more than 1,000 Canadian retailers, including Sears, Eaton's, and The Bay. Bedford and one of its major retail customers have implemented a rapid delivery system that allows products to be shipped within 24 hours of the order date and allows the retailer to do away with inventory (see Retail Highlight 2–4).

EDI has allowed retailers to develop quick response (QR) delivery systems, a form of inventory management system that lowers inventory investment, improves customer service, and reduces distribution costs. Both the retailer and its vendors share the inventory, sales, and marketing data (in most cases, the vendors have access to the retailer's POS terminal data so they can track sales of their products) and they use the EDI system to transmit orders. QR will be discussed further in Chapter 13 (Buying, Handling, and Inventory Management).

Universal vendor marking

Universal vendor marking (UVM) is an identification system for marking merchandise at the vendor level. The need to mark the items when they are received at the store level can be eliminated largely by the use of such a standardized format. Stores like Price Club/Costco, Aikenhead's, and Canadian Tire are using vendor marking. The major advantage is the ability of the retailer to "handle" incoming merchandise through the use of computers and electronic data input, leading to major increases in productivity.

Other technology advances

Other new technology advances will include wireless telephones, microwave communications, communication satellites, and fibre optics, all of which are bringing in an era of low-cost, convenient, universal communications. These devices are already transforming many forms of retailing as a result of the electronic information links that allow retailers to break out of building walls and shopping malls. Increasingly, the new technology will go directly into households and present images, comparative data, and product descriptions. Electronic bulletin boards will provide the latest information to in-store customers. Similarly, technology will allow shoppers to try on outfits electronically (see how they look on screen) before deciding on the one to purchase.

Artificial intelligence will also provide devices that can listen, understand, and respond to customer queries. Smart cards (credit cards with a memory chip) will allow retailers to tailor product lines to precise consumer demand since life and family histories of each customer can be recorded on the card.

Emerging technologies

Other changes are occurring in the way technology is used in retailing. These changes involve customer communications, electronic shopping, and similar activities.

Videodisc mail order catalogues

Sears has led the way in experimenting with video catalogues. The retailer has placed some of its catalogues on laser discs for in-home and at-store viewing. Product demonstrations, fashion shows, and footage from Sears TV commercials were part of their experiment. Harry Rosen, the men's clothing chain, has used a CD-ROM format for a men's clothing catalogue. The disc combines text, sound, and motion to show designer fashions to encourage more men to come to Harry Rosen's for their clothes.[22] The discs contain motion sequences plus colour pictures. Videodisc use is limited in retailing today.

Video technology

Home television shopping began in Canada in the late 1980s. The Canadian Home Shopping Network (CHSN) combined traditional merchandising with modern technology to offer consumers a wide variety of products via cable television. While television shopping has grown rapidly in the United States, consumer acceptance has been slower in Canada. The CHSN has an average weekly reach of 1.6 million viewers in Eastern Canada and generates approximately $50 million in annual sales.[23]

Cable marketing is also being used by real estate firms to interest potential home buyers in various properties and by automobile traders to sell used cars. Two or more channels in many Canadian communities are devoted to cable marketing shows.

Interactive in-store video sales aids

Increasingly, retailers are turning to the use of in-store video to provide prerecorded answers to questions frequently asked by customers. The devices help increase productivity because they reduce the need for salespersons to provide basic information. For example, the Atari electronic retail information centre exists in a variety of retail outlets. The device self-activates when customers come near the machine, and it allows customers to have hands-on experience with an Atari computer. The device responds to the customers' button-pushed questions and provides answers by tailoring the video presentation directly to their needs. HMV uses in-store videos and "listening posts" to allow consumers to see and hear musicians and music before they buy it.

Retailers are also experimenting with interactive, electronic in-store couponing. In one form, a kiosk in a supermarket dispenses coupons in 15 to 20 grocery categories, which are valid only the same day at the same store. In another form, a kiosk displays nine retailer categories and after the consumer has selected a category, it displays the names of up to six retailers. The consumer can then select coupons for products from that retailer. One test recorded sales increases of 37 percent for video products.[24]

The Internet

The Internet's World Wide Web (WWW) allows retailers to make an interactive connection with existing or new customers. The "Web" is a vast collection of pages of information and graphics that are assembled into locations or "sites." The pages of these sites are interconnected by links, which users see as buttons to click onto with their mouse. Each particular site has an address, like an 800 number, on the Internet.

Retailers have used the WWW to provide information on their products and services, to offer consumers an opportunity to buy, and to collect opinions from their customers. Many consumers are now using the Internet to purchase everything from computers to compact discs, to buy stocks and bonds or arrange a mortgage, and to comparison shop for upcoming purchases.[25]

Chapter Highlights

- **The major federal regulations affecting retailers include acts dealing with trade practices (Competition Act, Bankruptcy Act), health and safety (Food and Drug Act, Hazardous Products Act), and product standards and grades (Consumer Packaging and Labelling Act, Textile Labelling Act). In particular, the Competition Act is important as it regulates unfair trade practices such as misleading price advertising.**

- The economic environment can be understood, in part, by paying close attention to key economic indicators, such as interest rates, unemployment rates, and the consumer price index.

- The primary demographic factors of importance to retailers include the changing age distributions, the rate of household formations, changing family relationships, population shifts, skewed income distribution, regional differences, and increasing ethnic markets.

- The primary types of competition include intratype competition, intertype competition, and corporate systems competition. The competitive structure of retailing as a whole is undergoing change including secondary market expansion, supermarket retailing, and the international dimension.

- Changes in technology that have impacted on retailing include the use of point-of-sale technology and electronic data interchange to improve merchandising and reduce costs and new emerging technologies that offer new ways of shopping.

Key Terms

backward integration 42
corporate systems competition 42
exclusive dealing 32
forward integration 42
intertype competition 42
intratype competition 42

point-of-sale (POS) 44
predatory pricing 32
price discrimination 32
resale price maintenance 32
secondary market expansion 43
supermarket retailing 43

Discussion Questions

1. What are some retail activities covered by the Competition Act?

2. List four key economic indicators that retailers should monitor. What type of retailer is most likely to be affected by changes in each indicator?

3. Why is competition so intense in retailing today? Does this competitive intensity have an impact on retailers' needs to monitor and forecast environmental changes? Explain your answer.

4. Summarize the changes that are occurring in the demographic profile of consumers and households in our society, and the likely impact on retail operations.

5. Summarize the information presented in the text relative to changes in the competitive environment. Explain how these changes are impacting retailing.

6. Why is the Canadian market so attractive to many foreign-based retailers?

7. What are the major benefits of electronic data interchange (EDI) to retailers? to suppliers?

8. What are some of the technological advances occurring today that are impacting nonstore shopping?

Application Exercises

1. Visit the managers of two or three of the retail stores in your city. Find out their major problems, if any, with government regulations. Which aspects of the business seem to be most affected? Does the manager think the regulations serve a useful purpose?

2. Develop a sample of fast-food outlets, sit-down restaurants, coffee shops, and supermarkets, and determine which of the outlets are offering breakfast menus. Compare and contrast the offerings and seek to identify the demographic characteristics of the primary customer base.

3. Review the Statistics Canada catalogue and identify the publications that would be of primary interest to department store managers who want to understand the most significant trends that will influence their business in the next five years.

Suggested Cases

3. Canadian Life-Styles
4. Canadian Population, Household, and Retail Sales Trends

Notes

1. John Heinzl and Val Ross, "Smith Books-Coles Deal Okayed," *Globe & Mail*, March 22, 1995, pp. B1, B4.

2. Paul Brent, "Wal-Mart Canada Pulls Cigarettes from Shelves," *Financial Post*, November 5, 1994, p. 3.

3. Gordon H. G. McDougall, "The Green Movement in Canada: Implications for Marketing Strategy," *Journal of International Consumer Marketing*, 5, no. 3, 1993, pp. 69–87; Peter Boisseau, "Consumers Wary of Green Products," *The Record*, October 17, 1994, p. B5.

4. More information on industry guidelines can be obtained from The Canadian Advertising Foundation, Advertising Advisory Board and Advertising Standards Council, the Canadian Association of Broadcasters, and the Canadian Radio-Television and Telecommunications Commission. The Canadian Code of Advertising Standards outlines the major industry codes.

5. Bruce Little, "Bigger Tax Bites Stifle Consumers," *Globe & Mail*, July 6, 1992, pp. B1, B2.

6. Paul Brent, "Retail Sales a Disaster," *Financial Post*, February 22, 1996, p. 1; Bruce Little and Susan Bourette, "It's Pay-Back Time," *Globe & Mail*, July 29, 1995, pp. B1-2.

7. "Canadian Markets 1995," *Financial Post*, 1995.

8. David K. Foot, "The Age of Outdoor Recreation in Canada," *Journal of Applied Recreation Research*, 15, 1990, pp. 159–78.

9. Leonard Kubas, "Grey Power," *Retail Directions*, November/December, 1988, pp. 10, 11, 30. For more information on retailing to the 50-plus age group, see John Straiton, "Here Are the Goods on the Over-50 Crowd," *Marketing*, December 12,

1988, p. C10, Clayton Sinclair, "The Growing Wave of Seniors' Publications," *Financial Times of Canada,* February 29, 1988, p. 14; Alanna Mitchell, "Seniors' Housing Boom," *Financial Post,* October 31, 1988, pp. 17, 20; Stan Sutter, "Chasing the Over-50 Market," *Marketing,* April 4, 1988, pp. 25, 28; and Marina Strauss, "Retirees Have Big Bucks to Spend," *Globe & Mail,* March 17, 1992, p. B7.

10. Alan Freeman, "Family Income Falls for Fourth Year," *Globe & Mail,* December 24, 1994, p. B5.

11. Bruce Little, "Guess Where Incomes Land When They Rise," *Globe & Mail,* December 18, 1995, p. A8.

12. John Robert Colombo, *The 1995 Canadian Global Almanac,* Macmillan Canada, 1995.

13. Ibid.

14. John Schreiner, "Hongkong Bank Grabs Asian Business," *Financial Post,* March 9, 1995, p. 8.

15. *Silcorp Limited,* Annual Report 1994.

16. Susan Bourette, "Sears Expanding in Rural Markets," *Globe & Mail,* November 10, 1995, p. B3.

17. Barrie McKenna, "Attention U.S. Shoppers . . . ," *Globe & Mail,* July 4, 1995, pp. B1, B3.

18. Mark Stevenson, "The Store to End All Stores," *Canadian Business,* May 1994, pp. 20–29.

19. John Heinzl, "Eaton Plans $300 Million Face Lift," *Globe & Mail,* November 8, 1995, pp. B1, B2.

20. Anne Bokma, "Raking in the Dough," *Financial Post Magazine,* January, 1992, pp. 32–35.

21. Gordon McDonald, "Bankruptcies Climb 15% in First Half," *Globe & Mail,* August 10, 1995, p. B5.

22. "Menswear Ads Tailored to Tradition and High-Tech," *Financial Post,* April 4, 1995, p. 13.

23. Louise Leger, "The Hard Sell," *Broadcast Week,* August 5, 1995, pp. 8-9; James Pollack, "Shopping Network Gets $10 Million Makeover," *Marketing,* February 5, 1996, p. 3.

24. Ken Riddell, "Reaching Consumers In-Store," *Marketing,* July 13, 1992, p. 10.

25. Dean Hopkins, "Building an Internet Presence," *Marketing,* May 29, 1995, p. 18; John Long, "On Line and Onside," *Marketing,* May 15, 1995, p. 16.

Understanding the Retail Customer

Chapter Objectives

After reading this chapter you should be able to:

1. Describe the retail consumer as a problem solver.

2. Explain the motives for shopping other than buying.

3. Discuss where consumers buy, how they buy, what they buy, and when they buy.

4. Explain the role of image in affecting consumer buying decisions.

5. Emphasize the importance of responding to dissatisfied consumers.

Zellers, a retailer that understands its customers.

Courtesy Hudson's Bay Company Ltd.

The key challenges facing mass retailers today are the intense competition, similar low-margin pricing policies, similar product lines, saturation of retail outlets, and lack of market growth. In addition to these changes, when Wal-Mart entered Canada through its purchase of the Woolco chain, the managers at Zellers knew they faced a formidable competitor.

To meet these challenges, Zellers counts on a thorough understanding of the consumer. Research has shown that consumers want good value (price, quality, service), convenience, and thank you's for shopping in a particular store (service). Further, many customers see mass retailers as similar and, as a result, customer loyalty equals the best sales price.

The prime target market of Zellers is women between the ages of 25 and 55, with a family, who shop frequently for basic clothing and staples, with little discretionary income.

In 1990, Zellers decided that they needed to differentiate the store from competition with a program that could not easily be copied. This led to the creation of the Club Z membership program. Every time a "member" makes a purchase at Zellers, the salesperson enters the membership number into the computer and the member is credited with points based on the amount purchased. This program rewards customer loyalty, is easy to use, is value added, and provides a long-term commitment to Zellers. The television commercial, the in-store supports, and circulars all contribute to this objective.

In addition to the promotion, Zellers' pricing policy is very competitive, with the slogan: "Zellers . . . where the lowest price is the law." With the entry of Wal-Mart, Zellers has provided a broader, more competitive merchandise assortment and repriced thousands of products to maintain its dominant price position. It also launched a huge 15,000 m^2 store called Zellers Plus, with wider aisles, a complete home entertainment centre, a complete paint department, a pharmacy, a hair salon, a portrait studio, and a restaurant; all of these amenities are designed to appeal to broader needs of consumers, at the lowest prices.

It is not surprising that Club Z is one of the most successful customer loyalty programs in North America, with more than 6 million members, and that Zellers is holding its share of the discount chain market. Zellers's marketing program is based on a thorough understanding of its customers.[1] ∎

Development of retail strategies begins with an understanding of the consumer. An old saying is that "nothing happens until a sale is made." Sales occur only when the retailer understands and responds to how consumers buy, what they buy, where they buy, and when they buy. Retailers must also understand the consumer as a problem solver and seek to develop merchandise offerings to address unmet needs, as Zellers has done. An additional critical dimension is knowing how consumers form images of retail outlets and how to develop merchandising and marketing strategies compatible with the desired image.

Types of Consumer Decisions

You might like to keep in mind the following points about consumers when studying this chapter:

- *Consumers are problem solvers.* The role of the retailer is to help them solve their buying problems.

- Consumers try to *lower their risk* when buying merchandise by seeking information. They also seek information for reasons other than risk reduction.

- Store choice and merchandise choice depend on variables such as location, image, hours, and price, which are under the influence of the retailer.

- Many other factors, such as store atmosphere and courtesy of sales clerks, affect the in-store behaviour of consumers.

Motives for Shopping

Consumers shop for reasons other than buying, as shown in Figure 3–1. These reasons can be grouped into personal and social motives. *Personal motives* include role playing, diversion, sensory stimulation, physical activity, and

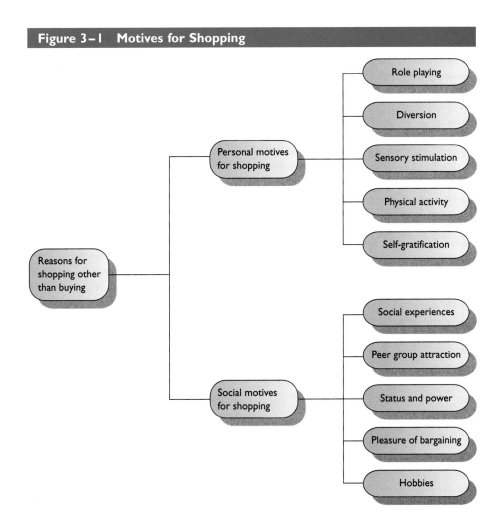

Figure 3–1   Motives for Shopping

self-gratification. *Social motives* include the desire for social experiences, peer group attraction, status and power, the pleasure of bargaining, and hobbies. Careful planning by a retailer can influence shoppers to make purchases even when the primary purpose of the trip is for social or personal reasons.

Personal motives

Personal motives result from internal consumer needs, which are different from the needs that are fulfilled in purchasing a good or service.

Role playing   Consumers often engage in activities that they perceive as associated with their role in life. Familiar roles include those of housewife, student, husband, or father. For example, a husband may perceive that in his role he should purchase only high-quality gifts from prestigious outlets for his wife; or that he should be able to fix things in the house when they break or need adjustment (and proper advice from a well-trained retail clerk may prove invaluable for someone who is not too handy).

Diversion   Shopping often provides the opportunity to get a break from the daily routine. Simply walking through a shopping centre can allow a person to keep up with the latest trends in fashion, styling, or innovation. Similarly, malls often schedule antique or auto shows in an effort to attract consumers. Regional shopping malls are popular browsing sites because of their comfortable surroundings and appealing atmosphere.

Research has shown that many consumers derive enjoyment from the simple activity of shopping for some types of goods. This is the *hedonic value of shopping,* in contrast with the *utilitarian* value.[2] Stores that carry deep product assortments and unique brands are especially attractive to browsers because of the novelty and stimulation inherent in such outlets. Heavy browsers are more involved with the merchandise, more knowledgeable, and more likely to be opinion leaders than are other consumers.[3]

Sensory stimulation   Shoppers often respond favourably to background music, scents, and other types of sensory stimulation as part of the shopping process. Research has shown that customers feel more at ease, spend more time, and shop more often in a store that plays soft background music, compared to no music or loud music.[4]

Physical activity   Many people, particularly older people, welcome the opportunity to walk for exercise in a safe, temperature-controlled environment. Thus, some malls have organized walking and health clubs in response to such needs. The malls are opened for walking before the shops are opened for business. Large cities such as Toronto or Montreal have extensive underground malls, often connected to each other in the downtown areas. These large malls have often replaced, particularly in the winter months, the "main street" as the favourite strolling areas for the whole family or friends.

Self-gratification   Shopping can alleviate loneliness or other emotional stress. It has been shown that shopping is often used to compensate for negative moods and complement positive ones, with the act of shopping displacing cigarettes or chocolate bars. In addition, people in a good mood are more likely to buy if they are involved in the shopping experience and when the experience itself is a good one.[5] Another study showed that young Canadians, in trying to

Today, malls are designed to satisfy personal and social motives.

Photo by Betty McDougall

find their identity, tend to shop and buy objects with a high symbolic value, such as clothes or music tapes. This quest for self-gratification by young Canadians could lead to more shopping and buying activities.[6]

Social motives

Social motives for shopping are also illustrated in Figure 3–1. These motives include the desire for group interaction of one sort or another.

Social experiences   For many people shopping has become a social activity. They take advantage of such opportunities to meet friends or to develop new acquaintances. Some malls feature morning promotions especially designed to serve older persons. Others arrange cooking demonstrations and similar activities.

Peer group attraction   Individuals may shop so as to be with a peer or reference group. Patronage of elite restaurants reflects such behaviour. Similarly, one will often find teenagers at a compact disk shop that offers music styles that appeal to their tastes. Also, some outlets have advisory boards composed of influential people in a city. Local opinion leaders are also often used in advertising and promotion programs.

Status and power   Some consumers seek the opportunity to be served and catered to as part of the shopping experience. Such an activity may be one of their primary ways to get attention and respect.

The pleasure of bargaining   Some persons enjoy the opportunity to negotiate over price. They get ego satisfaction as a result of bargaining.

Hobbies   Interest in a hobby may bring people together, as it is a common desire to meet people like oneself. Thus, retailers can provide a focal point for persons with similar interests or backgrounds. Retail computer outlets sponsor hobbyist clubs for this reason.

Shopper profiles

Consumer attitudes toward shopping, as distinct from motives for shopping, also affect shopping behaviour. Understanding consumer attitudes, therefore, is also important in strategy development. For illustrative purposes, consumers can be categorized as follows, based on their attitudes toward shopping:

- The buy-for-one consumer.
- The stability-seeking consumer.
- The get-my-money's-worth consumer.
- The time-buying consumer.

The **buy-for-one-consumer** represents the rapidly increasing number of single-person households, comprising divorced people and both young and elderly single people. These people seek food items packaged in single servings. They use utensils especially made for preparing meals for one person. They have more time for leisure and consequently spend more on entertainment and travel.

Many of these people are upwardly mobile professionals with high earning power but high expectations from the marketplace. They are good customers who expect quality products and quality salespeople to wait on them.

The **stability-seeking consumer** normally represents the blue-collar, middle-class household. Such people provide a good market for many products and services, including durables such as recreation equipment and equipment for various do-it-yourself activities, home satellite dishes, and high-definition TVs and VCRs.

Stability-seeking consumers are somewhat overwhelmed by the rapid changes occurring around them. They seek a return to yesterday (by watching old movies on TV), a return to nature (by buying indoor plants), and life simplification (with hobbies and do-it-yourself activities that give them a sense of control over their destiny). This group of consumers readily responds to friendliness, personal attention, the work ethic, and the traditional values and morality structure.

The **get-my-money's-worth consumer** is something of a consumer activist and a supporter of various social activist causes. People in this category look for good values—though not always at the lowest price. They seek energy-efficient homes and appliances, and look for durability and retailers who are socially responsible and environmentally sensitive. They substitute consumer labour for consumer costs. This group uses self-service gasoline stations and is willing to use unbranded products. This group and the stability-seeking segment have fuelled the growth of retailers such as Crate & Barrel, a retail chain that sells cooking items, kitchen accessories, and home furnishings, and Lechter's, a retail chain specializing in household organization and storage items. Both chains have capitalized on the "back to basics" movement.

The **time-buying consumer** reflects the rapidly growing number of households with two or more incomes. The female often maintains the household in addition to a full-time job outside the home. Such households are prone to use telephone shopping services and catalogues, to use the Internet to obtain information on products, to purchase well-known national brands, and to be receptive to such appliances as microwave ovens. They are also prime markets for cellular telephones, fax machines, laptop computers, personal shopper services, lawn care, and home delivery of groceries.

A Model of the Consumer Decision Process

The decisions facing shoppers seeking to make a buying decision differ widely and depend on their past experiences with the merchandise to be bought. Many decisions, such as buying a loaf of bread, are routine because consumers have made similar purchases many times before.[7] Such activities are known as *low-involvement decisions* and require little thought by the shopper and no comparison shopping. Other decisions, such as buying an automobile, may be difficult for some consumers because of their lack of experience or the risk involved in making a wrong decision. Consumers exhibit *high involvement* in such situations as they actively compare merchandise and retail outlets before making a buying decision.

When making these more difficult purchases, the consumer normally goes through six decision stages, shown in Figure 3–2. The stages are: (1) problem recognition, (2) search for alternatives, (3) evaluation of alternatives, (4) risk reduction, (5) the purchasing decision, and (6) postpurchase behaviour. Retailers can influence consumer choices and actions at each stage of the decision process. Such efforts by retailers are key components of their segmentation and positioning strategies.

Figure 3–2   A Model of the Consumer Decision Process

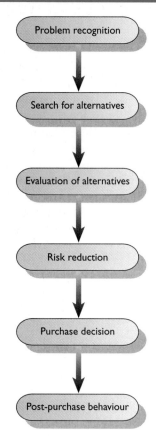

Problem recognition

The decision process begins when the consumer realizes that a difference exists between an existing and preferred state of affairs.[8] Sometimes consumers may simply discover that they need to purchase gasoline for their automobile. Other things that may trigger problem recognition are: a lack of satisfaction with an existing product or service; a raise; a spouse beginning to work (more money is now available); the need to purchase a gift for someone; or a change in fashions. Retailers can also trigger problem recognition through advertising, in-store displays, or the creative use of sight, sound, or smell.

Search for alternatives

The consumer seeks and evaluates information after problem recognition occurs. The search may be physical or mental. Mental search means drawing on past experience for information.[9] The consumer may need up-to-date information about products, prices, stores, or terms of sale. Physical or mental search may be required to obtain the needed information. The search may occur for the merchandise or for the preferred store at which the purchase will be made. Consumers evaluate the store on the basis of factors important to them and choose the outlet that most closely matches these factors.[10]

Table 3–1 Problem-Solving Behaviour		
Level Required	**Typical Products**	**Retailer Response**

Extensive	Personal computers
	Cellular phones
		Provide information on the following:
		  Uses of product or service
		  Reasons why consumer needs
		    product
		  Important characteristics

Limited	Small appliances Clothes Breakfast cereal	Facilitate brand-to-brand comparisons Target features important to consumer
Routinized response	Health and grooming aids Food items Automobile gas	Convenience of location

Problem-solving behaviour

Depending on the consumer's background and experience, he or she may exhibit extensive, limited, or routinized response behaviour (Table 3–1). Each type of problem solving requires a different response by the retailer.

Extensive problem solving   Consumers engage in extensive problem solving when faced with a first-time purchase in an unfamiliar product category, perhaps during the introductory or early growth stages of the life cycle of the product or service class. Examples include cellular phones and personal computers. Retailers should provide consumers with information on uses of the product or service, reasons why they need it, and characteristics of the product or outlet important to consider in the purchase.

Limited problem solving   The consumer who is familiar with the class of product or service engages in limited problem solving; the decision becomes a choice between brands or outlets. An example for many of us would be small appliances. Shoppers evaluate brands by comparing prices, warranties, after-sale service programs, knowledge and friendliness of salespeople, or similar features. At this stage, facilitating brand-to-brand comparisons is often a key element of the retail marketing plan. Retailing research, as discussed in Chapter 5, can help retailers discover which features consumers find important. Marketing programs can then reflect that information.

Routinized response behaviour   Many consumers reach a stage of routinized response behaviour after they become familiar with a product class, the brands within the class, or an outlet. Such buyers tend not to engage in any kind of information search before a purchase. They exhibit **low-involvement behaviour.** Low-involvement products are of limited interest to the consumer, carry little risk of a wrong choice, and are not socially visible. Low involvement typifies the purchase of a loaf of bread or a tank of gasoline at the most convenient outlet. Neither the brand nor the outlet is important to the customer.

Information sources

The retailer can make information available to consumers in a variety of forms to help them in their search. Consumers are normally exposed to (1) marketer-dominated sources, (2) consumer-dominated sources, and (3) neutral sources of information, as shown in Figure 3–3.

Figure 3–3   Sources of Consumer Information

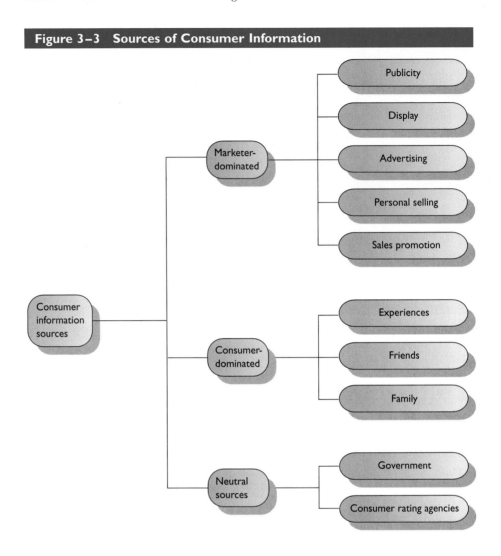

Marketer-dominated sources   **Marketer-dominated information sources** include advertising, personal selling, displays, sales promotion, and publicity. The retailer exercises control over their content. Typically, the retailer provides information on price, product features, and terms of sale.

Consumer-dominated sources   **Consumer-dominated information sources** include friends, relatives, acquaintances, or others. Consumer-dominated information is normally perceived as trustworthy. Satisfied consumers become especially important since they tend to talk to others about their shopping experiences. Additional consumer-dominated sources of information are persons who are known and respected by their peers. Consumers are likely to respect information from such individuals. Retailers may therefore be able to utilize such groups as sports leaders, college class presidents, and other socially active persons to convey product and store information. Word of mouth information from such persons is likely to be received favourably. Dissatisfied customers can also have a negative impact on an outlet. They often talk to many people about their bad experiences. Satisfied consumers typically are less vocal.

Table 3–2 Factors Influencing the Choice of Merchandise and the Choice of Retail Outlet

Factors Affecting Merchandise Choice		Factors Affecting Store Choice	
Product	Service	Store	Employee
Features	Features	Characteristics	Characteristics
Fashion	Credit terms	Hours	Knowledge
Brands	Installation	Layout	Friendliness
Quality	Accessories	Cleanliness	Helpfulness
Styles	Delivery	Displays	Courteousness
Colours	Layaway	Decor	
Assortments		Image	

Dissatisfied consumers in positions of influence can have a damaging impact on an outlet because of the large number of people to whom they talk and because of their role as influentials.[11]

Neutral sources of information **Neutral sources of information** are also likely to be perceived as accurate and trustworthy. The Consumers' Association of Canada and federal and provincial consumer protection agencies are examples of neutral information sources. Government agencies, for example, provide information on gasoline consumption for autos and energy efficiency ratings for appliances.

Typically, most information is provided by commercial sources even though consumers may rely more on personal sources. Marketer-dominated sources may serve to create initial awareness while personal and neutral sources are then used to help evaluate specific outlets or brands of merchandise.

Evaluation of alternatives

After background information is acquired, the consumer evaluates the outlet and product attribute alternatives. Examples of these attributes are shown in Table 3–2. Attribute importance varies among consumers. Knowledge of the importance of attributes is critical to management in helping consumers make choices compatible with their personal preferences. Product trial and demonstration, for example, is one way of reducing risk.

Risk reduction

A desire to reduce the risk of a poor decision influences the evaluation of alternatives. Six types of risks affecting outlet and merchandise choice decisions as they evaluate merchandise in terms of want satisfaction have been identified:

- **Performance risk**—the chance that the merchandise purchased may not work properly.
- **Financial risk**—the monetary loss from a wrong decision.
- **Physical risk**—the likelihood that the decision will be injurious to one's health or likely to cause physical injury.
- **Psychological risk**—the probability that the merchandise purchased or outlet shopped will not be compatible with the consumer's self-image.

Personalized service and individual customer attention are
ways of reducing customer
risks.

Courtesy Hudson's Bay Company Ltd.

- **Social risk**—the likelihood that the merchandise or outlet will not meet with peer approval.
- **Time-loss risk**—the likelihood that the consumer will not be able to get the merchandise adjusted, replaced, or repaired without loss of time and effort.[12]

The task of the retailer is to minimize each of the risks for the consumer. For example, performance risk and financial risk can be addressed by guarantees or exchange privileges. Performance risk can also be addressed by offering instruction in training programs. Psychological and social risks can be minimized by focussing on the brands carried, national advertising programs that support the merchandise, and the individuals serving as advisors to the outlet. Time-loss risk can be addressed by stressing the chainwide applicability of warranties for repair, availability of on-site repair or replacement, and similar services.

The purchasing decision

After evaluating some of the alternatives available, a substantial percentage of shoppers make their final decision while in the store. For example, research has shown that 80 percent of grocery shoppers make their final buying decision while in the store, and that 60 percent of grocery purchases are unplanned or impulse decisions.[13]

Choosing the outlet and the merchandise does not end the purchasing process. The consumer has to decide on the method of payment, accessories for the merchandise (such as a camera lens for a camera or a belt for a pair of trousers), whether to purchase an extended warranty, and delivery of bulky merchandise. Retailers frequently offer a variety of options designed to meet a diverse array of consumer preferences.

Postpurchase behaviour

Retailers need to reassure consumers after the purchase that they made the right decision. When making a major purchase, consumers are often afraid that they may have spent their money foolishly. This feeling is called **cognitive dissonance,**[14] and retailers must find ways of reducing this level of dissonance. A follow-up letter from the retailer or a phone call often can help reassure and satisfy the customer. As well, a policy of "satisfaction guaranteed or your money back" provides customers with the assurance that stores, such as Eaton's, stand behind their merchandise. The level of consumer satisfaction also influences whether the store and its merchandise will be recommended to a friend. Satisfied customers help to generate stronger customer loyalty, repeat business, reduced vulnerability to price wars, the ability to command a higher relative price for merchandise without affecting market share, lower marketing costs, and growth in market share.[15] Retailers need to be sensitive to the uncertainties in the minds of the consumers, then work to alleviate their concerns.

In conclusion, understanding the decision-making process of consumers is essential for retailers because of the implications for strategy development. How retailers can influence consumers is detailed in the next part.

Understanding the Where, How, What, and When of Shopping

Retailers may have the most influence on the behaviour of consumers during the information search and evaluation stage of the decision process. An understanding of the *where, how, what,* and *when* of consumer shopping behaviour can help retailers respond to consumer needs for information during their search and evaluation efforts.

The retailer needs to have the right merchandise at the right place, at the right time, and at the right price and quality to match consumer decisions on where to buy, what to buy, how to buy, and when to buy, as shown in Figure 3–4.

- *Where* means the choice of a downtown location, a free-standing location, a shopping centre and the specific outlet.
- *How* includes decisions on whether to engage in store or nonstore shopping.
- *What* includes consumer decisions on merchandise price and quality, whether to purchase store brands or national brands, and criteria used in evaluating merchandise.
- *When* includes decisions on such matters as time of day and day of week to shop.

Where do consumers shop?

Consumers have a large variety of places at which to shop, some of which are discussed next (see a more complete discussion of this topic in Chapter 10).

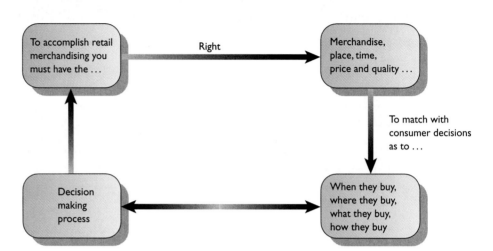

Figure 3–4   Retailers Must Match Their Merchandising to the Consumer Decision Process

Shopping centres   Consumers may choose shopping centres because of convenience, a controlled climate, and the merchandise assortment available. Others go to shopping centres because they can meet friends there, as shopping centres provide a festive atmosphere and a convenient way to keep up with the latest trends in fashion. By 1987, for the first time Canadians spent more money in the 3,270 shopping centres than in all other retail outlets combined.[16]

Some people prefer shopping at "strip" shopping centres as opposed to the enclosed malls. Strip centres require less walking and generally involve less hassle in shopping. Additionally, access is typically easier than to major enclosed malls, but the merchandise selection is limited in comparison.

Downtown   Some people prefer to shop downtown because of convenient public transportation and the availability of nonshopping facilities, such as financial institutions. Others work downtown and find it convenient to shop there. Finally, some consumers, often those with lower incomes and no transportation, live near the downtown area and shop in the outlets closest to their homes.

In most large Canadian cities, the downtown area has seen the opening of *urban centres* such as the Eaton's centres in Calgary, Edmonton, Winnipeg, Toronto, and Montreal; Midtown Plaza in Saskatoon; Pacific Centre in Vancouver; Confederation Court Mall in Charlottetown; Barrington Place in Halifax; Atlantic Place in St. John's; Brunswick Square in Saint John (NB); or the underground centres like Les Promenades de la Cathédrale in Montreal, built underneath a church!

Outshopping   Some consumers go out of town to shop (**outshopping**) because (1) the selection may be better, (2) they may want to get out of town for a visit, including, perhaps, a good meal, (3) they may work out of town and do their shopping after work, and (4) store hours, store personnel, and services such as repair may be better in the other community.

Some people like to shop in markets.

Photo by Betty McDougall

Outshopping (also called **cross-border shopping** when applied to the United States) activities are particularly important in Canada for a number of unique reasons:[17] (1) the concentration of a large percentage of the Canadian population along the American border, and near some large U.S. cities (about 80 percent of Canadians live within 200 km of the U.S. border); (2) the large distances between Canadian cities, particularly on an east-west axis; (3) economic variables such as price and currency differentials, as well as promotional enticements; (4) the lessening of border controls under the Free Trade Agreement; (5) the severe climatic conditions in Canada, particularly during the winter months; and (6) the tendency to travel south for vacations ("Canadian snow birds"). In one study of Maritime consumers, it was estimated that about 88 percent were outshoppers.[18]

After the advent of the goods-and-services tax (GST), cross-border shopping all across Canada had a strong influence on the Canadian retail scene; however, a large tax cut on cigarettes, followed by a dramatic drop in the Canadian dollar, and the entry of Wal-Mart lessened the blow to Canadian retailers. Retail Highlight 3–1 derives useful lessons from these recent experiences.

Nonstore shopping Catalogue, telephone, and electronic shopping are the primary types of **nonstore shopping,** although in-home, personal selling of merchandise by firms such as Avon or Tupperware is also common (see Chapter 20). Nonstore shopping is popular because it allows consumers to make purchase decisions at their leisure without leaving home. Nonstore shoppers tend to have higher incomes and higher education. Higher incomes allow them to make more discretionary purchases, and education often widens the opportunity for selling merchandise to these individuals. Because they have more education, nonstore shoppers often see less risk than other consumers in buying

Retail Highlight 3–1

Cross-Border Shopping: Can Canadian Retailers Learn from Their Experiences?

Although outshopping has been around for a long time in Canada, the cross-border shopping phenomenon until about 1993 can be traced to two key events:

- The signing of the Free Trade Agreement with the United States: The FTA took effect on January 1, 1989, and it gave the impression that the border was now 'open,' i.e., the tariffs were being eliminated.
- The introduction of the goods and services tax (GST): the GST took effect on January 1, 1991, and it created a public wave of anger.

To the misperception about tariffs and the anger toward the GST, one must add the belief by many Canadians that prices in the United States were much lower than those in Canada. This belief is not true in every case (it may be true for about 6 or 8 out of 10 items). On the other hand, there are negatives: the costs of driving to the United States, long lines at the border, the obligation to pay the GST and some provincial sales taxes, and problems with warranties.

All of these factors taken together represented a strong motivation to shop in the United States, and the U.S. retailers have been very obliging (e.g., advertising in Canadian media, staying open on Sundays, posting bilingual signs, and taking Canadian dollars at par). In fact, many retailers in U.S. bordertowns would not be viable without Canadian shoppers. For example, a study in Plattsburgh found that 41 percent of retailers depend in major part on the patronage of Quebecers, and would not otherwise be located there.

This became a major problem for Canadian retailers, since about 60 million one-day trips were taken in 1991, costing retailers an estimated $10 billion, and about 250,000 jobs being lost or in danger of being lost. Surveys have shown that 62 percent of cross-border shoppers did it because of the lower prices and to beat the GST. Only 3 percent did it because of the variety of goods available, 2 percent because it is recreational activity (e.g., a shopping vacation, particularly on Sundays when working people have some time for shopping), and 1 percent because of the quality of service or the convenience. Other research also shows that cross-border

shoppers do not feel guilty about the negative consequences on the local economy of their shopping in the United States.

Thus, the main response by retailers had to be to *lower their prices,* and cut costs. Part of the problem for retailers are inefficient distribution systems and higher margins. Another pressure to reduce prices has been the entry of Wal-Mart in Canada. Recently, Canadian retailers have reduced their prices (some advertise that they will pay the GST) and improved their service. Changes in the distribution system may take longer and the lower Canadian dollar will give them some breathing time.

Also, the federal government has accelerated the tariff exemptions on many items, particularly electronic products, thus allowing retailers to reduce their prices further. At the same time, governments have erected new nontariff barriers, such as surcharges on cross-border mail-order shopping, or the collection at the border of GST. Many provincial governments have eliminated the prohibition of Sunday shopping. These actions and the lower Canadian dollar have led to a dramatic decrease in cross-border shopping, still around 40 million. And retailers have seen an increase of U.S. visitors shopping in Canada.

The main lesson of the story is that retailers and governments must listen to consumers and find innovative ways to satisfy their needs. U.S. retailers have benefited from their understanding of consumers and have taken advantage of situational factors such as the FTA, the GST, the 1991–92 recession, and a then higher Canadian dollar. Retailers have reacted in positive ways, and they were helped by a lower Canadian dollar, but what if the exchange rate is again unfavourable to Canadian retailers?

Sources: "Cross-border shopping trend reversed by weak C$," *The Financial Post,* February 21, 1995, p. 16; G.L. Fullerton and T. Navaux, "A Profile of the Cross-Border Shopper: Some Preliminary Findings," *Marketing,* vol. 15, ASAC, 1994, pp. 75–84; E.R. Bruning, L. Lockshin, and G. Lantz, "A Conjoint Analysis of Factors Affecting Intentions of Canadian Consumers to Shop in U.S. Retail Centres," *Marketing,* vol. 14, ASAC, 1993, pp. 12–21; A. Toulin, "Lower Prices Only Way to Stem Border Shopping," *The Financial Post,* February 10, 1992, p. 9; "$10-billion Loss Cited in Border Shopping," *Globe & Mail,* June 24, 1992, p. B8; M. Evans, "Shopping Study Faults Mark-ups," *The Financial Post,* May 15, 1992, p. 9; L. Héroux et al., "Do U.S. Bordertown Retailers Adapt Their Marketing Strategies to Accommodate Canadian Shoppers?" unpublished document, S.U.N.Y. Plattsburgh.

in a nonstore setting.[19] Direct merchants can stress several important factors in nonstore purchases by consumers. Making purchases from their homes is a great convenience to consumers. Good product guarantees are important in assuring consumers that risks in nonstore purchases are not unreasonable. The ease of credit-card buying offered by major merchants such as Eaton's also is a major factor in determining purchase decisions.

Choosing a store

Consumers make decisions about outlets at which to shop after deciding whether to shop downtown or at a shopping centre if in-store purchases are to be made. The *image* of a retail outlet is important in such a decision.[20] The major attraction characteristics include the type and quality of merchandise and services offered, physical facilities, employees, and other shoppers. For example, consumers may be seeking a particular brand or quality of merchandise, specific services such as credit or delivery, an attractive outlet, courteous employees, and an outlet where consumers with similar **life styles** are likely to shop. All of these characteristics other than the characteristics of other shoppers are under the direct influence of retailers. Research has shown that quality customer service has a greater effect on sales than any other variables under the control of the retailer.[21]

Research is often necessary to help management develop an understanding of the importance of these characteristics to shoppers. The information may help retailers do a better job of meeting consumer needs. Most of Canada's foremost retailers, such as Eaton's and The Bay, are spending hundreds of millions of dollars remodelling all their stores across Canada in order to improve their image and withstand the competition of the discount stores. The idea is to project a strong image of quality, fashion, and sophistication.[22]

There are a number of useful methods for measuring store image from using open-ended questions, semantic differential scales (using bipolar adjectives such as "helpful/unhelpful"),[23] or a multiattribute model (more details on retail research are provided in Chapter 5).

The **multiattribute model** of consumer choice is one that is frequently used to help retailers understand the importance of various outlet features to consumers.[24] The model can be applied as follows:

$$As = \sum_{i=1}^{n} B_i\, W_i$$

where:

As = Attitude toward the store

B_i = Belief by a consumer that a store possesses a particular attribute i

W_i = The importance of the attribute to consumers

n = Number of attributes important to consumers in their choice of a store

Example Assume that the four attributes shown in Table 3–3 are important in the consumer's choice of a store at which to shop. The *belief* about each attribute in store choice is rated on a scale of 1 to 5, with a score of 5 indicating that the store rates high on that attribute, and 1 indicating that it rates low.

		Beliefs (B_i)		
Attributes	Importance (W_i)	Store 1	Store 2	Store 3
Low prices	4	1	3	5
Wide merchandise assortment	5	5	3	3
Courteous personnel	2	4	3	2
After-sale service	4	4	3	1
Attitude toward the store		53	45	43

Table 3–3   The Multiattribute Model of Store Choice

Consumers rate the *importance* of each attribute on a scale of 1 to 5, with 5 reflecting a very important one to consumers, and 1 a very unimportant one.

As shown in Table 3–3, the importance and belief scores are multiplied for each attribute and summed to develop a measure of the consumer's attitude toward each of the three stores being evaluated. Scores could range from 4 to 100 (5×5×4) with 4 being the least favourable score and 100 the most favourable.

Store attributes clearly vary in importance to consumers. Store 1 (for example, a sporting goods store) may offer the widest selection of merchandise and the most qualified salespersons. Store 3 (for example, a discount store), on the other hand, may offer little, if any, advice and stock only the fastest-moving items. However, its prices are likely to be lower than those at other outlets. Store 2 (for example, a junior department store) rates average on all the attributes.

Based on the customer's stated importances in Table 3–3, it is likely that he or she will shop in the first type of store, since the attitude is the highest among the three (i.e., 53 versus 45 and 43). Other types of consumers may express different importances, which may lead to different attitudes toward the three stores.

Understanding store image

The above model is one way to determine a consumer's image of a retail outlet. **Image** is the way consumers "feel" about an outlet. The image is what people believe to be true about an outlet and how well those beliefs coincide with what they think it should be like. The image may be accurate, or it may be quite different from reality. Knowing how consumers feel about an outlet is important in developing strategies for attracting them.

Why think about store image?

The retailer should be concerned about store image because the flow of customer traffic depends on it. Management may have what they think is the right merchandise, at the right price, in the right style, and in the desired size, colour, and quality. But it is what the customer thinks of the price, the quality, and the service that is important.

Also important is the impression that customers have of the employees. If they like the employees, they are more apt to have favourable impressions of what the outlet offers.

How are images formed?

Specific features of an outlet provide the elements that make up its image. By examining each of the elements management can determine the importance of these elements to consumers. For example, a study of Canadian grocery shopping habits found an absence of store loyalty. The main factors for choosing a store for grocery shopping were the presence of fresh products, a clean, well-lit store, well stocked, low prices, friendly service, and name brand products—in that order.[25] Supermarkets should implement a strategy that creates and delivers a positive image based on these elements.

Price policy   *An outlet's price line influences the way people think of its other aspects.* Therefore, prices must be consistent with the other elements of the retailing mix. To illustrate, a supermarket learned that when it installed carpeting, it created a higher price image. Customers felt that prices had gone up even though they had not. Yet, it isn't always necessary for an outlet to give the impression that it is a "bargain centre." A low-price policy may create an unfavourable image. Some customers feel that low quality goes with low prices and will not shop at these outlets. Yet, other customers like bargain stores. The importance of price varies with a number of factors such as the type of product, family income, and competitive offerings.

Customers usually make up their mind about an outlet's prices from the store's advertising displays, merchandising practices (such as stocking national brands), and location. They also rely on their impression of the outlet's pricing policies rather than on actual knowledge.[26]

Two questions that can be helpful in image-building efforts are:

- What price do the customers expect to pay?
- Do the customers consider price as important as quality, convenience, dependability, and selection?

Merchandise variety   Image improves when customers find a product that they like but don't find in other outlets. On the other hand, failure to carry certain items may give a retailer's whole product line a bad name. Similarly, when customers find one product that displeases them, they are apt to become more critical of the rest of the offering. The key is in knowing the preferences of the customers.

Employees   Salespeople and other employees who are seen by customers affect the outlet's image. Customers may react negatively if the educational level of an outlet's personnel is different from theirs. Whether an outlet appeals primarily to professional or working class people, salespeople should dress and speak in such a way that the customers feel comfortable talking to them. Telephone personnel should be knowledgeable, friendly, and efficient, as should back-office personnel.

Employee perceptions of customer service are fundamental to the delivery of quality service and, furthermore, are consistent predictors of sales. If every employee does not perceive that quality service is important, then the employees are unlikely to deliver a quality service response in relating to the customer.[27]

Outlet appearance   What people see as they pass by an outlet is another important element in its image. Even people who never enter an outlet form an impression from its outside appearance. That impression may be the reason

The outlet appearance creates an image of the products and services offered by La Cache.

Photo by Anne Laroche

they don't break their stride when they go by the outlet. Consumers form images of nonstore retailers based on their reliability in filling orders, the knowledge of employees, the ease of resolving complaints, and similar attributes.

Inside the outlet, the layout and the decor reinforce customers' impressions about the products and salespeople. For example, classic design fixtures usually appeal to older and more conservative groups. The new redesigned department stores (Eaton's and The Bay) with polished, richly decorated emporiums are meant to create excitement and project an image of quality.[28] Plain, inexpensive-appearing fixtures help to build a good image with young families whose incomes are limited. Low ceilings may make the store more personal, and indirect lighting usually makes the customer think of higher quality. Some colour schemes are considered masculine, feminine, or neutral, which may be important in displaying certain types of merchandise.

Type of clientele   The image that some people have of an outlet is influenced by the type of people who shop there. Some people, for example, think of a shop as one where professional people usually shop. They think of other outlets as ones where blue-collar workers usually shop.

Advertising   Advertising tells people whether the outlet is modern or old-fashioned, low-price or high-price, small or large. It also communicates other things of both a physical and psychological nature.

For example, when printed ads are full of heavy black print, customers get an image of low prices. Conversely, white space often connotes quality. A food store could improve its image by including a personal interest feature in its weekly ad of special prices. The outlet could feature a recipe, perhaps with the picture of the chef who originated it.

Catalogues are also very useful in forming a store image. Major department stores like Eaton's and The Bay produce beautiful catalogues, in particular during the Christmas season.

Changing the outlet's image

An image is a complex affair, and managers should not try to change an outlet's image without careful thought and planning. However, if a retailer is dissatisfied with the store image customers seem to have, three questions should be asked:

- What kind of image will best serve the existing market?
- What kind of image does the store have now?
- What changes can be made to improve the image?

A store cannot be all things to all people. In fact, one of the competitive strengths in retailing is that each outlet can be different. Many outlets are successful because they specialize and their owner-managers build an image around that particular specialty, and the recent spending by the leading department stores builds on this theme.[29]

Keeping the image sharp

Like the human face, an outlet's image does not stay bright by itself. Maintaining an outlet's image—regardless of the type of outlet—can be handled in the same way as other management problems. Managers should review the image periodically just as they periodically review financial statements. They can then find potential trouble spots and correct them before they get out of hand, as in the case of most Simpson's stores.

Listen to customers   Management can ask customers what they like about an outlet and why they prefer it to others. Their answers give an idea of the strong points in the marketing mix and its image. They can also indicate what products and services should be advertised and promoted.

All customers speak in sales. What they buy, or don't buy, speaks louder than words. Keeping track of sales by item can help to determine what customers like or don't like.

Customer complaints can help deal with reluctant customers—those who shop for one or two items that they can't get elsewhere. In most cases, their reluctance is caused by the image they have of the store. Management can change that image only by learning its cause and making adjustments.

Management should also look at competitors. They can do some comparison shopping with the goal of trying to find out the strong points competitors use to create attractive images.

IKEA creates a store image through advertising.

Courtesy IKEA

Listen to noncustomers   Management often finds that there are more people in their neighbourhood who don't patronize them than who do. Why? Often only one or two aspects of an operation irritate and keep some people from having a good image of it. Because of a grouchy cashier, for example, such potential customers think poorly of the whole store.

How do consumers shop?

The way in which consumers select products and services and the distance they will travel to shop also affect merchandising decisions.

The costs of shopping   Many consumers try to minimize the costs of shopping when making a shopping trip. The costs of shopping are money, time, and energy. **Money costs** are the cost of goods purchased and the cost of travel. **Time costs** include the time spent getting to and from the store(s), time spent in getting to and from the car, and time spent paying for merchandise. **Energy costs** include carrying packages, fighting traffic, parking, waiting in line, and various psychological costs as shown in Table 3–4.

Management can be responsive to these problems by having the proper store hours and by offering shoppers credit, delivery, and similar services.

Consumers are willing to travel farther for specialty goods than for either shopping goods or convenience goods because they believe the satisfaction they obtain from getting exactly what they want more than offsets the cost of the extra effort.

- **Convenience goods** are frequently purchased items for which consumers do not engage in comparison shopping before making a purchase decision. Among convenience goods are staple goods (e.g., bread and fruits), impulse goods (e.g., a chocolate bar), and emergency goods (e.g., batteries).

Table 3–4 Costs in Shopping and Buying	

• **Cost of merchandise**
 • **Other monetary outlays**
   1. Parking fees
   2. Automobile gasoline and wear and tear
   3. Installation
   4. Credit
   5. Repairs
   6. Wrapping
   7. Babysitting fees
   8. Warranties
	• **Non-monetary costs**
	   1. Time away from other activities
	   2. Waiting in line
	   3. Comparison of merchandise between stores
	   4. Comparison of alternative merchandise offerings
	   5. Travel time
	 • **Emotional costs**
	   1. Frustration from out-of-stock items
	   2. Dealing with surly or indifferent sales assistance
	   3. Bargaining over price and terms of sale
	   4. Concern over a wrong decision
	   5. Effects of crowding

- **Shopping goods** are products for which consumers make comparisons between various brands in a product class before making a purchase.

- **A specialty good** is a product that consumers know they want and for which they are willing to make a special effort to acquire.

It is not possible to generalize as to what types of merchandise can be described as convenience, shopping, or specialty goods. Consumers view merchandise differently. What is a shopping good to one consumer may be a convenience good to another one. However, typical examples of convenience, shopping, and specialty goods can be identified. Household salt is a convenience good for most shoppers. They will make the purchase at the nearest available outlet. Household durables or appliances are shopping goods for many persons. A lawnmower is an example of such a product. Consumers often do not have strong brand preferences for such an item. As a result they will compare price, warranties, and various features before making a purchase. Designer label merchandise such as Benetton is a specialty good for many shoppers. Similarly, a Rolex watch may be regarded by many shoppers as a specialty good. They will travel considerable distances to purchase the item they want and will not compare alternative merchandise offerings.

Overall, less time is spent today in shopping than in the past. The reasons include: (1) advertising, which makes information more easily available, (2) the higher cost of gasoline, and (3) the increased number of women who now work outside the home and have less time for shopping, and (4) increasing nonstore alternatives for purchases.[30] Many shoppers do not visit more than two stores even when buying items such as TV sets.

How far are consumers willing to travel?   Most shoppers at grocery stores live within a kilometre of the store. Shoppers usually will travel 10 minutes or so to shop for higher-priced merchandise. Typically, 75 percent of the persons travelling to a large shopping centre live within 15 minutes of the centre. However, shoppers will travel much further to purchase specialty goods, particularly to the new **big-box** or **warehouse-style stores** such as Wal-Mart, Zellers Plus, Price Club/Costo, Home Depot, or Future Shop.

What do consumers buy?

Price and brand are two major attributes that affect consumer purchases   Price is important because it is often a measure of worth and quality. Brand is often relied on as a measure of quality.[31] Other factors that are important in merchandise choice include open code (freshness) dating, nutritional labelling, unit pricing, shelf displays, shelf location, and coupons.

Price   Consumers ordinarily do not know the exact price of a merchandise item. But they usually know within well-defined ranges.[32] The higher-income consumer usually is less price conscious than the lower-income consumer seeking the same merchandise. The more of a shopper's income that is spent on an item, the greater price awareness there is likely to be. Also, price is not as important to the nondiscount shopper as to the discount shopper.

Brands   Some consumers purchase only well-known brands of manufacturers such as Del Monte. These **national brands** are the brands of a manufacturer such as Procter & Gamble, which are sold through a wide variety of retail outlets. Purchasing these brands helps consumers avoid unsatisfactory purchases. But many consumers are now buying *nonbranded* items, as they can save up to 30 to 40 percent when compared to national brands. These nonbranded products, called **generics,** are unbranded merchandise offerings carrying only the designation of the product type on the package. Consumers rely on the reputation of the store as an assurance of quality in buying the items. Many stores, such as Sears, Eaton's, Canadian Tire, and Loblaws, sell their own brands. Known as **private brands,** they are brands of merchandise that retailers develop and promote under their own label.

Private brands have been especially important to department stores and specialty stores in recent years. During much of the previous decade these outlets had relied heavily on designer labels such as Calvin Klein to develop upscale, somewhat exclusive images. However, as the sales volume of the designer labels levelled off due to the rather exclusive pattern of distribution through department and specialty stores, suppliers began selling the merchandise through mass market outlets. The merchandise thus lost its exclusivity and in many instances was heavily price discounted. Department and specialty stores as a defensive strategy began developing their own private labels to maintain desired margins on the merchandise and to protect the integrity of their image.[33]

Open code dating   **Open code dating** means the consumer can tell the date after which a product should not be used, and food shoppers often use this information. The strongest users tend to be young consumers with higher incomes and higher levels of education, who live in the suburbs.

Nutritional labelling   **Nutritional labelling** is important for people with some allergies, or people on a specific diet. The usage pattern for nutritional labelling is similar to that for open code dating.

Unit pricing[34]   **Unit pricing** states price in such terms as price per kilogram or litre. Shoppers use this information as a guide to the best buys. Here again, the younger, higher-income consumers are more likely to use the data. Brand switching often occurs when prices are stated on a per-unit basis.

Shelf displays and location   Retailers tend to give the most shelf space to merchandise with the highest profit margins. Profits tend to drop, however, if managers shift store displays and layout too often. Point-of-sale materials, even simple signs, can increase item sales by as much as 100 percent. End-of-aisle and special displays can have even larger effects on consumer buying behaviour. Today with computerized cash registers, managers know exactly how often a product sells. As a result they often will stock only the two or three best-selling brands in each product category. The subject of shelf space allocation is discussed in greater detail in Chapter 11 on layout and merchandise presentation.

Shelf location becomes especially critical for **low-involvement** *products since consumers are likely to purchase the first item that catches their attention.* Examples include cleaning supplies or paper products. Conversely, consumers are likely to make brand comparisons in a **high-involvement** product class such as salad dressings in which shoppers may compare products on such bases as content or number of calories. Shelf location may be a less critical factor for high-involvement products since consumers will be making a more concerted effort to compare alternative offerings. Merchandise located on the lowest shelves may present difficulties for elderly or infirm consumers, and merchandise on the higher shelves may be difficult for some individuals to reach. The ideal shelf location depends on the consumer. For example, merchandise directed primarily at children should be on a lower shelf where they can easily see it.[35]

Coupons and other sales promotions   **Coupons** can be used to draw new customers to a store and to increase purchases by regular consumers. They can also be used to offset the negative features of a store by drawing customers to a poor location. Coupons can be issued by manufacturers (*manufacturer coupons*) or by retailers (*store coupons*). Retailers may provide coupons in a variety of ways, the most popular ones being in their weekly advertisements (*retailer-initiated coupons*), on the shelves (*in-store-shelf coupons*), in booklets, or at the cash register (electronically printed coupons). In 1994, of all the coupons distributed, 3.3 billion were regular (i.e., manufacturers') coupons and 12 billion were retailers' coupons. Of the 15.3 billion coupons distributed, 260 million were redeemed and the average face value was $0.68.[36]

The coupon users tend to have slightly higher incomes than the average household and normally have children. They are especially good customers for retailers. In Canada, coupons have achieved a high level of acceptance, and more than three-quarters of all retail customers reported using coupons for food, household items, transportation, and dining. More than half reported clipping coupons at least once a week, and over 60 percent of coupon users felt that they were really worth it.[37]

Trading stamps, rebate offers, and similar strategies also can be used to attract new consumers and to retain the loyalty of current customers.

When do consumers buy?

Sunday and 24-hour openings are attractive to many shoppers. Sunday is often the only time some families can shop together, and working wives are more likely to shop in the evenings and on Sunday.

Many retailers do not like Sunday openings or long hours because they feel that costs are going up without helping profits. However, consumer preference for these hours and competitive pressures (locally or from cross-border U.S. retailers) are making these openings increasingly common (as provincial governments are forced to allow it).

Retailers may also experience great seasonal variations. Some retailers make one-third or more of their annual sales in November and December. Spring

Retail Highlight 3-2

The Economics of Customer Dis/Satisfaction

According to author William A. Band, each time a company loses a customer, it forfeits the investment it made in the first place. For example, if it cost the retailer a conservative $20 to acquire each customer, and the retailer lost on a national basis over 100,000 customers because of poor service, the lost business would be over $2 million annually.

Since it is at least five times more costly to acquire a new customer than to retain a current one, the retailer must develop a relationship with customers to keep them patronizing its stores. This is called *relationship marketing*.

On the negative side, research shows that 96 percent of unhappy customers never complain, and of these

91 percent never return; but each one them may tell 9 other people about their bad experience, and 1 in 8 may tell at least 20 other people.

On the positive side, if the complaint is resolved satisfactorily, 7 out of 10 will return, and as high as 9 if the complaint is resolved on the spot. That customer will then tell 5 other people how well the complaint was handled.

Sources: Adapted from William A. Band, *Creating Value for Your Customers*, Wiley, New York, 1991; R.M. Morgan and S.D. Hunt, "The Commitment-Trust Theory of Relationship Marketing," *Journal of Marketing*, vol. 58 (July 1994), pp. 20–38; Michel Huet, "Keeping the Customer Happy," *Marketing* (June 20, 1994), p. 16; Clay Carr, *Front-Line Customer Service: 15 Keys to Customer Satisfaction*, Wiley, New York, 1990.

dresses sell well just before Easter. Picnic supplies sell best in the summer, and ski equipment during the fall and early winter.

Responding to Consumer Dissatisfaction

Consumer complaints are a signal that all is not well in the business. Retailers must make a concerted effort to understand customers' satisfaction and dissatisfaction with their services.[38] Retailers should actively seek feedback from customers—what they like and don't like; how they can be better served; their satisfaction with store policies; and so forth. Unfortunately, too few stores do this, and as Retail Highlight 3–2 illustrates, the consequences are dramatic.

It is too simple to say the customer is always right. Some consumers do not pay their bills. They shoplift, switch price tags, and so forth. Nor is the customer always wrong. Retailers sometimes use bad credit information, make errors in customers' accounts, and sell inferior merchandise.

The level of satisfaction varies with the product category. A nationwide survey of Canadian consumers found that a majority were satisfied with large household appliances. Of those dissatisfied, at least half took some form of action to resolve the problem.[39] For clothing and footwear, they complained about quality, workmanship, and assortment; for groceries, they complained about prices and freshness.[40]

How do consumers view retailers?

Overall, retailers are rated poorly in communicating with consumers, in being interested in customers, in providing good value for money, and in honesty concerning what they say about merchandise. Chains tend to rate highest in the quality of the job they perform; appliances and automobile repair service rank at the bottom of the list.[41] Also, retailers are often held responsible for the products they distribute and the problems consumers encounter with these products.

What consumers consider a serious product violation depends on the product category and whether it is a quantity, a labelling, or a quality violation.[42] A study provides some indication about the seriousness Canadian consumers attach to each type of violation. The most serious **quantity violations** are for entertainment articles, and the least serious for fresh fruits and vegetables. The most serious **labelling violations** are for precious metal articles (e.g., gold jewellery), and the least serious for pet supplies. The most serious **quality violations** are for precious metals, home improvement products, and automotive products; and the least for eggs, fresh fruit and vegetables, and other foods and beverages. Finally, quality violations are perceived to be much more serious than quantity violations, which in turn are more serious than labelling violations.

What's being done about problems?

Retailer responses   As noted earlier, freshness dates now appear on many products, nutritional labelling is also being practised, and unit pricing is another aid to the consumer. Some stores provide in-store consumer consultants, consumer advisory panels, consumer affairs forums, buyer guides, employee training on consumer rights, and signs, sales notices, and applications in languages other than English when appropriate.

Voluntary action groups   Voluntary action groups are organizations sponsored by an industry that are designed to respond to consumer complaints about products or services sold by retailers. The groups also provide needed information to consumers to help them make important buying decisions. However, some studies find a level of scepticism about these voluntary business efforts.[43]

Consumers also need to react responsibly to help avoid unnecessary problems in their capacity as consumers. Consumers are likely to have fewer problems with merchandise when they understand how to operate the items they purchase, if they use proper care in handling the equipment, if they bring defective merchandise to the attention of retailers, if they are aware of their rights as consumers, and if they make comparisons before their purchases. Finally, as seen in Chapter 2, Better Business Bureaus serve a useful purpose in handling consumer problems at the local level.

A philosophy of action for management

Retailers need to be alert to changing attitudes and demands of consumers and to practice better customer relations. The demand of consumers normally is not unrealistic. Customers simply want more, better, and honest information. Retailers may need to do research from time to time to learn how customers feel about a store and its products. They should take a positive approach in dealing with customers. Most retailers do not want to make money by selling merchandise that may hurt customers or simply drive them away. Customers simply want such things as better values, labelling, honesty in advertising, and full information on credit terms.

Chapter Highlights

- Consumers shop for reasons other than buying, which can be grouped into personal and social motives. Personal motives include role playing, diversion, sensory stimulation, physical activity, and self-gratification. Social motives include the desire for social experiences, peer group attraction, status and power, the pleasure of bargaining, and hobbies. Careful planning by a retailer can influence shoppers to make purchases even when the primary purpose of the trip is social or personal.

- Consumer attitudes toward shopping, as distinct from motives for shopping, also affect shopping behaviour. For strategy purposes, consumers can be categorized based on their shopping behaviour. Typical categories include the buy-for-one shopper, stability-seeking shopper, get-my-money's-worth shopper, and the time-buying shopper.

- Consumers go through a series of stages in making a purchase decision. The stages, for other than routine purchases, include problem recognition, information search, evaluation of alternatives, risk reduction, the actual purchase decision, and postpurchase behaviour. Retailers can influence consumer choices and actions at each stage of the decision process.

- Retailers can have the most influence on the behaviour of consumers during the information search and evaluation stage. An understanding of the how, when, where, and what of consumer shopping and buying behaviour can help retailers be responsive to their needs for information.

- Consumers use consumer-dominated, marketer-dominated, and neutral sources of information in making store and product choices. Marketer-dominated sources include advertising, personal selling, displays, sales promotion, and publicity. Consumer-dominated sources include friends, relatives, acquaintances, or others. Neutral sources include federal and provincial government consumer protection agencies.

- Consumers seek to minimize risks during the purchase evaluation stage. The risks they are seeking to avoid include performance risk, financial risk, physical risk, psychological risk, social risk, and time-loss risk.

- Consumers may seek to go to shopping centres, downtown stores, out of town (outshopping), or out of the country (cross-border shopping), or simply shop from their own home (nonstore shopping).

- Store image is an important consideration in store selection. It is formed based on information such as price, merchandise variety, employee behaviour and appearance, store appearance, type of clientele, and advertising. Efforts must be made to improve, change, or maintain the store's image.

- Many consumers try to minimize the costs of shopping when making purchase decisions. These costs include money, time, and energy. Actual purchases by consumers are influenced by many factors, including price and brand, shopping aids such as open code dating and unit pricing, shelf displays and shelf locations, coupons, trading stamps, and rebates.

- Retailers also need to be sensitive to consumer concerns that often take the form of consumerism. Efforts at solving consumer dissatisfaction often start with the retailer from whom a purchase was made. In recent years, a variety of retailers have responded by including in-store consumer consultants, consumer advisory panels, consumer-affairs forums, buyer guides, and employee training on consumer rights.

Key Terms

big-box store 75
buy-for-one consumer 58
cognitive dissonance 65
consumer-dominated information
    sources 62
convenience goods 74
coupon 77
cross-border shopping 67
extensive problem-solving
    behaviour 61
energy costs 74
financial risk 63
generics 76
get-my-money's- worth
    consumer 59
high involvement 61
image 70
labelling violation 79
life styles 69
limited problem-solving
    behaviour 61
low involvement 61
marketer-dominated information
    sources 62

money costs 74
multiattribute model 69
national brands 76
neutral sources of information 63
nonstore shopping 67
nutritional labelling 76
open-code dating 76
outshopping 66
performance risk 63
physical risk 63
private brands 76
psychological risk 63
quality violation 79
quantity violation 79
routinized response behaviour 61
shopping goods 75
social risk 64
specialty goods 75
stability-seeking consumer 59
time-buying consumer 59
time costs 74
time loss risk 64
unit pricing 76
warehouse-style store 75

Discussion Questions

1. Briefly describe each of the stages (steps) of the consumer decision process discussed in the text.

2. What are some of the reasons consumers might prefer to shop downtown? Why do some people prefer to shop in shopping centres?

3. What is the importance of image to the retailer? How does it affect the shopping behaviour of consumers? Think of the two largest department stores in your community. How would you describe their images?

4. How does open code dating and unit pricing information aid consumers in making purchase decisions? Develop a profile of those consumers who are the most likely to use these types of shopping information.

5. What are some of the things retailers can do to reduce each of the six types of risks discussed in the chapter?

6. **Provide an example of each of the personal and social motives discussed in the chapter as reasons for shopping but not buying.**

7. **What are some of the things that retailers can do to help consumers minimize the costs of shopping?**

8. **What are some retailers doing to help consumers buy more effectively?**

Application Exercises

1. Visit a national supermarket in your community, a discount or warehouse grocer food outlet, and a 24-hour type of food store. Prepare a paper that points out the similarities and differences between the three types of stores. Write a brief statement that summarizes your thoughts about the image of each type of outlet. Describe the characteristics of the people whom you think are most likely to shop at each of the three outlets.

2. Briefly interview 10 to 15 of your fellow students. Find out the latest experience about which they were dissatisfied with a retail outlet. What action did they take, if any? What was the response of management to the situation if it was called to their attention? Will the situation cause the dissatisfied person not to shop at the outlet again? Write a short paper summarizing their experiences.

3. Interview a local retail manager of your choice and try to identify the methods used by that manager to track and understand the store's customers. Write a report presenting your results according to the framework of this chapter.

Suggested Cases

4. Canadian Population, Household, and Retail Sales Trends

5. Buying an Oriental Rug

6. A Buying Experience

7. York Furniture Company

Notes

1. J. Heinzl, "Zellers Steps up Discount War," *Globe & Mail*, November 9, 1995, p. B1; C. Green, "The 'Law' of Retail," *Marketing*, October 28, 1991, pp. 1, 3; J. Heinzl, "Club Z Leaving Its Mark," *Globe & Mail*, December 6, 1991, p. B1.

2. B.J. Babin, W.R. Darden, and M. Griffin, "Work and/or Fun: Measuring Hedonic and Utilitarian Shopping Value," *Journal of Consumer Research*, vol. 20 (March 1994), pp. 644–56.

3. T.K. Clarke and F.G. Crane, "Are Leisure Shoppers Really Different?" in *Marketing*, vol. 10 (ed. Alain d'Astous), ASAC, 1989, pp. 58–65; G.R. Jarboe and C.D. McDaniel, "A Profile of Browsers in Regional Shopping Malls," *Journal of The Academy of Marketing Science* 15 (Spring 1987), pp. 45–52; C.W. Park, E.S. Iyer, and D.C. Smith, "The Effects of Situational Factors on In-Store Shopping Behaviour," *Journal of Consumer Research* 15 (March 1989), pp. 422–33.

4. E.S. Iyer, "Unplanned Purchasing: Knowledge of Shopping Environment and Time Pressure," *Journal of Retailing* 65 (Spring 1989), pp. 40–57.

5. W.R. Swinyard, "The Effects of Mood, Involvement, and Quality of Store Experience on Shopping Intentions," *Journal of Consumer Research*, vol. 20 (September 1993), pp. 271–80; C. Berneman and R. Heeler, "Shoppers' Mood and Purchases," *Marketing*, vol. 7 (ed. Thomas E. Muller), ASAC, 1986, pp. 152–61.

6. M. Strauss, "Young Pleasure Seekers Born to Shop, Study Says," *Globe & Mail*, January 27, 1989, p. B6.

7. M. Laroche, J.A. Rosenblatt, J.E. Brisoux, and R. Shimotakahara, "Brand Categorization Strategies in RRB Situations: Some Empirical Results," in *Advances in Consumer Research*, vol. 10, ed. R.M. Bagozzi and A.M. Tybout (Ann Arbor: Association for Consumer Research, 1983), pp. 549–54.

8. R.E. Nisbett and D.E. Kanouse, "Obesity, Food Deprivation, and Supermarket Shopping Behaviour," *Journal of Personality and Social Psychology*, August 1969, p. 290.

9. P. Thirkell and H. Vredenburg, "Individual and Situational Determinants of Prepurchase Information Search: A National Study of Canadian Automobile Buyers," in *Marketing*, vol. 3 (ed. M. Laroche), ASAC, 1982, pp. 305–13.

10. R.N. Maddox, T. Moore, G. McPherson, C. Kruitwagen, and G. Clark, "Business Person's Criteria for Restaurant Selection for Lunch," in *Marketing*, vol. 7 (ed. T.E. Muller), ASAC, 1986, pp. 201–11.

11. J.A. Quelch, S.B. Ash, and M.J. Grant, "Consumer Satisfaction with Appliances and Personal Care Equipment," in *Marketing*, vol. 1 (ed. V.J. Jones), ASAC, 1981, pp. 289–97; W.O. Bearden and R.L. Oliver, "The Role of Public and Private Complaining in Satisfaction with Problem Resolution," *Journal of Consumer Affairs* 19 (Winter 1985), pp. 222–40.

12. M. Dunn, P.E. Murphy, and G. Skelly, "The Influence of Perceived Risk on Brand Preferences in Supermarket Products," *Journal of Retailing* 62 (Summer 1986), pp. 204–16.

13. J. Marney, "Moment of Decision Is in the Store," *Marketing*, September 27, 1987, pp. 13–4; J. Oldland, "Brand Loyalty Reasons Are Changing," *Marketing*, November 23, 1987, p. 9.

14. L. Festinger, *A Theory of Cognitive Dissonance*, Stanford: Stanford University Press, 1957.

15. L.L. Berry, D.R. Bennett, and C.W. Brown, *Service Quality*, Homewood, IL: Dow Jones-Irwin, 1989, p. 29; G. McDougall and T. Levesque, "The Measurement of Service Quality: Some Methodological Issues," in *Marketing, Operations and Human Resources Insight into Services*, ed. P. Eiglier and E. Langeard, Aix, France: I.A.E., 1992, pp. 411–31; G. LeBlanc, "The Determinants of Service Quality in Travel Agencies: An Analysis of Customer Perceptions," in *Marketing*, vol. 11 (ed. J. Liefeld), ASAC, 1990, pp. 188–96.

16. "The Mall Overtakes Main Street," *Canadian Business*, December 1988, p. 10; M. Salter, "Shoppers' Heaven," *Report on Business Magazine*, June 1989, pp. 62–69.

17. G.L. Fullerton and T. Navaux, "A Profile of the Cross-Border Shopper: Some Preliminary Findings," *Marketing*, vol. 15 (ed. B. Smith), ASAC, 1994, pp. 75–84; E.R. Bruning, L. Lockshin, and G. Lantz, "A Conjoint Analysis of Factors Affecting Intentions of Canadian Consumers to Shop in U.S. Retail Centres," *Marketing*, vol. 14 (ed. A. Carson), ASAC, 1993, pp. 12–21; N.G. Papadopoulos, L. Heslop, and G. Philips, "A Longitudinal Perspective on Consumer Outshopping," *Marketing*, vol. 9 (ed. T. Barker), ASAC, 1988, pp. 58–67; N.G. Papadopoulos, "Consumer Outshopping Research in Canada," *Marketing*, vol. 4 (ed. J.D. Forbes), ASAC, 1983, pp. 288–98.

18. M. Smith and G. Fullerton, "Outshopping in Maritime Canada: Some Preliminary Research Results," *Marketing*, vol. 7 (ed. T.E. Muller), ASAC, 1986, pp. 173–80.

19. G. Moschis, J. Goldstucker, and T.J. Stanley, "At-Home Shopping: Will Consumers Let Their Computers Do the Walking?" *Business Horizons*, March-April 1985, pp. 22–9.

20. N.J. Church, M. Laroche, and J.A. Rosenblatt, "Consumer Brand Categorization for Durables with Limited Problem Solving: An Empirical Test and Proposed Extension of the Brisoux-Laroche Model," *Journal of Economic Psychology*, vol. 6, 1985, pp. 231–53; M.A. Elbeik, "Image Determinants of an Ideal Hospital," *Marketing*, vol. 7 (ed. T.E. Muller), ASAC, 1986, pp. 91–100.

21. W. Weitzel, A. Schwarzkopf, and E.B. Peach, "The Influence of Employee Perceptions of Customer Service on Retail Store Sales," *Journal of Retailing* 65 (Spring 1989), pp. 27–39.

22. J. Heinzl, "Eaton Plans $300 Million Face Lift," *Globe & Mail*, November 8, 1995, pp. B1–2; "Department Stores Spend Millions on Improvements," *The Kitchener Record*, November 13, 1995, p. D3.

23. G.H.G. McDougall and J.N. Fry, "Combining Two Methods of Image Measurement," *Journal of Retailing*, Winter 1974–75, pp. 53–61.

24. M. Fishbein, "The Relationships Between Beliefs, Attitudes and Behaviour," in *Cognitive Consistency*, ed. S. Feldman (New York: Academic Press, 1966), pp. 199–223.

25. "An Absence of Store Loyalty among Women," *Marketing*, August 31, 1987, p. 4.

26. T.E. Muller, "Information Load at the Point of Purchase: Extending the Research," in *Marketing*, vol. 3 (ed. M. Laroche), ASAC, 1982, pp. 193–202.

27. Weitzel et al., "The Influence of Employee Perceptions."

28. J. Heinzl, "Eaton plans $300 million face lift."

29. "Department Stores Spend Millions on Improvements," *The Kitchener Record*, November 13, 1995, p. D3.

30. J. Marshall, T. Deutscher, and B. Portis, "Convenience Food Purchasing: A Proposed Model," *Marketing*, vol. 3 (ed. M. Laroche), ASAC, 1982, pp. 144–54.

31. M. Laroche, J.A. Rosenblatt, L. Wahler, and F. Bliemel, "Economic Considerations for Dispensing Pharmacists: the Impact of Price-Quality Evaluations on Brand Categorization," *Journal of Pharmaceutical Marketing and Management* 1, no. 1, 1986, pp. 41–60.

32. T.E. Muller, "In Search of Dr. Weber's K: Market Response to Supermarket Information," in *Marketing*, vol. 2 (ed. R.G. Wyckham), ASAC, 1981, pp. 246–55; T.E. Muller and K.K. Leung, "Price Awareness in the Supermarket," *Marketing*, vol. 4 (ed. J.D. Forbes), ASAC, 1983, pp. 238–46.

33. F. Schwadel, "Complaints Rise about Clothing Quality," *The Wall Street Journal*, June 27, 1988, p. 17.

34. C.L. Herbert and R.D. Johnson, "Does Unit Pricing Matter? An Inferential Beliefs Analysis," *Marketing*, vol. 14 (ed. A. Carson), ASAC, 1993, pp. 106–12.

35. A. Swasy, "More Businesses Put Out Welcome Mat for Children," *The Wall Street Journal*, May 31, 1989, p. B1.

36. K. Riddell, "Reaching Consumers In-Store," *Marketing*, July 13/20, 1992, p. 10; K. Riddell, "Couponers Show Record Year," *Marketing*, February 10, 1992, p. 2.

37. J. Marney, "Marketing: A Push and Pull Situation," *Marketing*, October 3, 1988, pp. 14–16.

38. J. Langer, "Upscale Department Stores often Provide Low-End Service," *Marketing News*, March 13, 1987, p. 17.

39. J.A. Quelch, S.B. Ash, and M.J. Grant, "Consumer Satisfaction with Appliances and Personal Care Equipment," *Marketing*, vol. 1 (ed. V.J. Jones), ASAC, 1980, pp. 289–97.

40. J.D. Claxton and J.R.B. Ritchie, "Consumer Prepurchase Shopping Problems: A Focus on the Retailing Component," *Journal of Retailing*, Fall 1979, pp. 23–43.

41. P. Filiatrault, "The Automobile Repair Consumption Problem: The Point of View of Producers," *Marketing*, vol. 6 (ed. J.C. Chebat), ASAC, 1985, pp. 118–25.

42. J.C. Bourgeois and M. Laroche, "The Measurement of the Seriousness of Product Violations," *Journal of Public Policy & Marketing*, vol. 6, 1987, pp. 1–15.

43. F.A. Salem and A.K. Sarkar, "Consumer Protection: A Look at Consumer Awareness, Attitudes and Preferences in the Canadian Prairies," in *Development in Canadian Marketing* (ed. R.D. Tamilia), ASAC, 1979, pp. 116–23.

Social Influences on the Retail Consumer

Chapter Objectives

After reading this chapter you should be able to:

1. Understand the decision-making process within a family.

2. Understand the role of reference groups and opinion leaders.

3. Explain the influence of social class on retail strategy.

4. Explain the influence of culture and subculture on retail strategy in Canada.

5. Understand the concept of lifestyle.

6. Describe the role of lifestyle merchandising in the retail strategy mix.

The Five & Diner uses its sign to attract a social group: the early boomers.

Photo by Betty McDougall

*T*he social influences on retail strategies are often subtle, but very real. Consider the following:

• Although the target of preference of retailers has traditionally been the baby boomers, another important and different group has been gaining in importance, i.e., the "baby busters," also called "Generation X," which is the group currently between 18 and 29 years old. The key characteristics of the Xers are: (1) they are *demanding* that products live up to their claims and their expectations; (2) they are *suspicious* of product claims, and will scrutinize the product, the company that makes it, and the retailer that sells it; (3) they are *knowledgeable and savvy*, requiring clean stores to examine products and trained salespeople to answer questions; (4) they are *value conscious,* always looking for the best deal; and (5) they are looking for *honesty and simplicity* in products, store layout, and advertising, being turned off by hype, preferring soft-sell messages telling the simple truth in an interesting way (e.g., humour or a touch of irony). The current teenagers, the children of the baby boomers, are called "Generation Y," love to shop, and as such should be of interest to many retailers. They are 2.8 million strong, have $6 billion a year to spend, and are the first generation to grow up within a multimedia, computer-literate environment at home and at school.[1]

- On the other side of the age spectrum are the *mature adults,* aged 50 and over (from 50 to 64 they are called *bridgers*), and retailers must understand their buying habits. In 1996, they number 7.6 million, or 28 percent of the population. They are strong readers of newspapers, magazines, and books. As consumers, they are very discriminating, aware of the value of bargains, and very willing to travel to get lower prices. They save a greater proportion of their income, own rather than rent, and are interested in wellness, health, lifestyle, financial planning, travel, and leisure, especially after they have retired. In advertising, sex and impulse marketing are ineffective, since these consumers are more driven by logic and rational appeals.[2]

- Recent patterns of immigration to Canada, particularly from Hong Kong, have boosted the Asian population to over 600,000 (projected to grow to over 800,000 by 2000), settling mostly in Toronto or Vancouver, which have strong established Chinese communities. Most of the new immigrants are young, they are starting families, and they need houses, major appliances, and cars, which they tend to buy with cash. They are highly educated and have high incomes (the average annual household income for those living in Toronto is $52,800). They are status conscious and prefer prestige brands, like Courvoisier cognac (used as an aperitif). Retailers need to understand what kinds of products they need and how to appeal to them, in terms of store displays, signs, advertising media and copy, as well as service quality. For example, in the past five years, Leon's Furniture has used advertising in Chinese, adapted or created specifically for that market, using television (CFMT) and Chinese newspapers. Leon's has also been advertising in Italian and Portuguese for the past 10 years.[3] ■

As these three examples illustrate, demographics alone are not enough to understand and serve markets. The previous chapter focussed on understanding the decision-making process of individual consumers. However, consumers are also influenced by others, including family members, friends and colleagues, other members of their social class, and their cultural or subcultural group (Figure 4–1). This chapter will focus on these influences. Finally, the concept of lifestyle, as a customer's pattern of living, has emerged as a major influence on retail merchandising, and is covered in the last part of the chapter.

Family Buying Behaviour

Buying decisions may be influenced by one or several members of a family. Shopping behaviour may involve the husband, the wife, and some of the children. This pattern of influence evolves also over time, both in terms of family life cycle and in terms of changing roles within the family.

Family life cycle

The concept of **family life cycle** reflects the combined effect of several demographic factors: marital status (legal or common law), age of the adult(s), employment status, and number and age of the children. Although 1 in 10

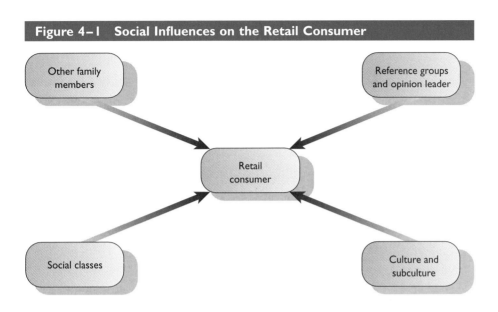

Figure 4–1   Social Influences on the Retail Consumer

Canadian couples is living in a common-law relationship, and 42 percent include children, Statistics Canada counts these common-law couples as families, and in the following discussion, we will use the same convention.[4]

The various stages of a family life cycle are represented in Table 4–1 for the traditional view, and in Figure 4–2 for a modified version that takes into account some more recent family patterns in terms of divorces.

Table 4–1 also provides an indication of financial needs and behavioural patterns at each stage of the family life cycle. As a family passes through some of these stages, their financial resources and needs vary in fairly predictable ways. For instance, the arrival of children for young couples will change their financial situation due to the expenses incurred in terms of housing, appliances, toys, and other child-related costs.

Retail strategies can be based, in part, on the size and location of families in a given stage of a family life cycle. For example, more than 2 million childless couples live in Canada, and many of them are choosing to be childless. These are often two-income households with a large disposable income, and needs that are very different from other couples of the same age. For retailers, these customers represent an attractive market for fine furniture, appliances, and travel and luxury products.[5] Similarly, other stages or subgroups within a stage (for example, higher-income groups) may be targeted by retailers.[6]

Decision making within the family

For many products, such as cars or homes, several family members play a role in the purchase decision. There are four basic types of decisions within a family, as indicated in Table 4–2:[7]

Wife-dominant   A decision is said to be **wife-dominant** when the decision to purchase a product is made most of the time by the wife. In the example of Table 4–2, this is the case for the wife's and children's clothing.

Table 4–1 The Traditional Family Life-Cycle Stages and the Financial Situation and Buying Behaviour at Each Stage

| | Bachelor, Young, Single, Not Living at Home | Young Married Couples | | | Older Married Couples | | | Solitary Survivor | |
| | | Newly Married, No Children | Full Nest I, Youngest Child under Six | Full Nest II, Youngest Child Six or Over | Full Nest III, with Dependent Children | No Children Living at Home | | In Labour Force | Retired |
						Empty Nest I, Head Working	Empty Nest II, Head Retired		
Financial situation	Few financial burdens.	Better off financially than they will be in near future.	Home purchasing at peak. Liquid assets low. Dissatisfied with financial position and amount of money saved.	Financial position better. Some wives work.	Financial position still better. More wives work. Some children get jobs.	Home ownership at peak. Most satisfied with financial position and money saved.	Drastic cut in income. Keep home.	Income still good but likely to sell home.	Drastic cut in income.

Behaviour with Respect to Marketing Dimensions

	Bachelor, Young, Single, Not Living at Home	Newly Married, No Children	Full Nest I, Youngest Child under Six	Full Nest II, Youngest Child Six or Over	Full Nest III, with Dependent Children	Empty Nest I, Head Working	Empty Nest II, Head Retired	In Labour Force	Retired
General	Fashion opinion leaders. Recreation oriented.	Highest purchase rate and highest average purchase of durables.	Interested in new products. Like advertised products.	Less influenced by advertising. Buy larger-sized packages, multiple-unit deals.	Hard to influence with advertising. High average purchase of durables.	Interested in travel, recreation, self-education. Make gifts and contributions. Not interested in new products.		Special need for attention, affection, and security.	
Specific (products)	Basic kitchen equipment, basic furniture, cars, equipment for the mating game, vacations.	Cars, refrigerators, stoves, sensible and durable furniture, vacations.	Washers, dryers, TV, baby food, chest rubs and cough medicine, vitamins, dolls, wagons, sleds, skates.	Many foods, cleaning materials, bicycles, music lessons, pianos.	New, more tasteful furniture, auto, travel, nonnecessary appliances, boats, dental services, magazines.	Vacations, luxuries, home improvements.	Medical appliances, medical care, products that aid health, sleep, and digestion.		Some medical and product needs as other retired group.

Source: Adapted from W. D. Wells and G. Gubar, "The Life-Cycle Concept in Marketing Research," *Journal of Marketing Research* 3 (Published by the American Marketing Association, November 1966), p. 362.

Figure 4–2   Family Life-Cycle Stages

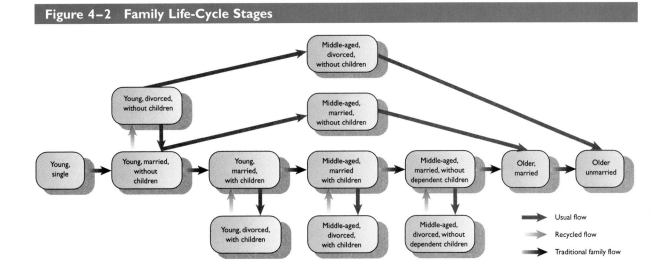

Husband-dominant   A decision is said to be **husband-dominant** when the decision is made most of the time by the husband. In the same example, this is the case for life insurance.

Autonomous   A decision is said to be **autonomous** when the decision is made over time independently by the husband or the wife. Thus, on one occasion, it may be the husband, and in another, it may be the wife. In the example, this is the case for savings, alcohol, and the husband's clothing. Contrary to the previous two types of decisions, the retailer should target both spouses in advertising or in-store selling.

Syncratic   A decision is said to be **syncratic** when the decision is made jointly by both spouses. In the example, this is the case for vacations, housing, and living room furniture. As in the previous type of decision, the retailer must make sure that the needs of both spouses are met. For example, in selling living room furniture, the salesperson must interact with both spouses, instead of only one or the other.

Role of children in decision making

There are about 5.5 million children 12 years and younger in Canada, and these numbers are expected to rise due to a small reversal of the birthrate. After reaching a low in 1987, the birthrate has risen to approximately 400,000 births annually. This "echo boom" has led to the launching of new magazines and a renewed interest in marketing baby and children's products, such as car seats, playpens, and baby foods. However, this pattern may be affected by the decision of many couples to remain childless for a variety of reasons. Retailers must keep abreast of such changes.[8]

Thus, decision making within the family may be affected by the presence of children. A study on vacation decisions by Canadians found that husbands tended to be more dominant when children were present than in childless couples. However, the influence of children on decision making was found to be mainly through "alliances" with one of the spouses.[9] Another study found

Table 4–2 Examples of the Four Basic Types of Decision within a Family and Associated Products	
Wife-Dominant	**Husband-Dominant**
Cleaning products	Life insurance
Kitchenware	Other insurance
Child's clothing	
Wife's clothing	
Food	
Other furnishings	
Autonomous	**Syncratic**
Husband's clothing	School
Alcoholic beverages	Vacation
Garden tools	Housing
Housing upkeep	Outside entertainment
Appliances	Living room furniture
Savings objectives	Children's toys
Forms of savings	Television set
Car	
Non-prescription drugs	
Cosmetics	

Source: Adapted from H.L. Davis and B.P. Rigaux, "Perceptions of Marital Roles in Decision Processes," *Journal of Consumer Research,* June 1974, pp. 51–62.

that four out of ten times, the children will determine the choice of a restaurant for a family.[10]

In addition to influencing the family decision process, children are also consumers. In one study, the average weekly income of 10-year-olds was found to be $11.[11] These SKOTIES (Spoiled Kids of the Eighties) represent a major market for many retailers of cereal, candy, chewing gum, soft drinks, clothing, toys, and video games (e.g., the Nintendo craze).

Role of teenagers in family decision making

With about 3 million teenagers (i.e., aged 13 to 19) in Canada, this is another important market for retailers, with an estimated market size of $6 billion. Retail Highlight 4–1 further profiles this segment. Among retailers who have been very successful targeting the teenage market are Benetton, HMV Stores, Roots Natural Footwear, and Château Stores of Canada.[12]

The changing roles of men and women

The last 30 years have seen major changes in the respective roles of men and women within the family, and these have important implications for retailers.

First, more women are now working than at any time in the past; about two-thirds of the 10 million women of working age are now in the labour force, and 2 out of 5 working women consider themselves career women, i.e., they are mostly interested in developing their career.[13] By contrast to this group, the other working women enter the work force primarily for generating additional income for the family. Different job orientations within the family have been found to lead to different behaviours, as illustrated in Table 4–3. For dual

Retail Highlight 4–1

Understanding the Teen Market

Many Canadian teenagers are compulsive, enthusiastic consumers, searching for self-gratification and pleasure, willing to live their life to the fullest. They are struggling to find their own identity and use consumption for their symbolic value. They 'wear' these products as 'badges' of the image they want to project to their peers. About 55 percent of teenagers have a part-time job, and their average income is about $6,000 per year or $115 per week. They spend about 60 percent of that income weekly, and save the rest for larger purchases. In a six-month period, 45 percent of teenagers had bought clothes, jackets, and footwear, 17 percent a new stereo, a TV set, or a VCR, 13 percent had bought large gifts, and 11 percent had spent a substantial amount on sport equipment. In terms of shopping habits, in a typical two-week period, 51 percent shop in a grocery store, 64 percent in a drugstore, 43 percent in a music store, 75 percent in a convenience store, 86 percent visit a shopping mall, and 80 percent a clothing store. Finally, 82 percent of teenagers influence the buying decisions of their families, and their influence is strong.

In addition, research revealed that teenagers:

- Share similar goals, motivations, and values.
- Are prepared to work hard to succeed in life.
- Struggle between being conformists and innovators.

- Enjoy friendship and music (from the 1960s and 1970s) the most.
- Feel that growing up these days is difficult, worry about time, money, school, life after school, unemployment, and the environment.
- Choose clothes to express their selves and their relationships with peers.
- Want to conserve, preserve, and under-consume, and dislike waste.

The picture that emerges is that teens, when compared to their parents, are more conservative, less optimistic about the future, and price-sensitive when they are spending their hard-earned money (the average income is $6,000). However, they are brand- and status-conscious and knowledgeable about current social issues (e.g., environment, AIDS, drunk driving).

As an example, HMV Stores, selling recorded music, understand that the store environment is essential to attracting teens ("the medium is the message"), and that in order to provide the right kind of service to demanding teens, it uses teenage employees.

Sources: Jo Marney, "Brand Loyalty: A Marketer's Teen Dream," *Marketing,* December 9, 1991, p. 14; Jo Marney, "Teen Loyalty Targeted with a Variety of Promotions," *Marketing,* December 16, 1991, p. 18; *TG Magazine,* reproduced in *Marketing,* November 19, 1990, supplement, p. 2.

---

career and dual income families, the job orientation is the same for both spouses. In the traditional family, the wife does not work outside the home.

Some implications of these changes for retailers are that shopping is viewed as a chore by working women, and that the emphasis should be on convenience, in terms of location and opening hours (evening and Sunday shopping). Another implication is that the additional income puts the family in higher income and social groups, allowing the purchase of time-saving products and services such as microwave ovens, freezers, convenience foods, and vacation packages. Also, these families spend their time differently, and must be reached with different kinds of media (e.g., prime time television, week-end newspapers, and billboards). Finally, a recent study shows that women *still* have the major role for planning for grocery shopping, meal planning, and meal preparation, and that the men who actually carry out these plans may decide on where to shop, what brand to buy, and how much to spend.[14]

Men have reacted in different ways to this new reality. Four distinct types have been identified:[15]

Table 4–3   Some Behavioural Differences for Families with Different Job Orientations

	Dual Career	Dual Income	Traditional
Grocery Shopping			
Who does it?	Whoever enjoys it	Wife usually	Wife
How often?	Once a week or once a month	Once a week or once a month	Once a week
When?	No specific day	Same day	Same day
Store loyalty	No	Yes	Yes
Household Chores			
Cooking	Both spouses	Wife usually	Wife
Cleaning and laundry	Both spouses	Wife usually	Wife
Housekeeper	Yes	No	No
Attitude toward chores	Routine during week to free weekends	Ongoing, but haphazard	Ongoing, but organized
Household Conveniences			
Dishwasher and microwave oven	Yes	No	No
Freezer	For bulk purchase, extra cooking	For bulk purchases	For garden harvest
Attitude toward conveniences	Appreciate time saved	To save money	To save money
Family Finances			
Accounts	His, hers, ours	Some pooling	One account
Who keeps track?	Household—wife	Wife	Wife
Major expenses	Conferences, each spouse contributes	Priorities—family needs	Priorities—spousal territory
Budget	Informal, periodic reviews	More formal	More formal
Attitude toward money	Can have what we want, "cushions"	Work to get what we want	Have what we need; some wants
Credit	Convenience, consolidation of bills	Convenience and instalment buying	Considered dangerous
Payment	Pay off each month	Pay interest	Pay interest
Household Durables			
Who decides?	Both spouses	Both spouses	Wife
Who buys?	Both spouses	Wife, sometimes with husband	Wife
Criteria	Timesaving, style, price not a factor, very little shopping around, quality stores	Price major factor, comparison shopping, mid-quality stores	Price major factor, comparison shopping, mid-bargain stores
Lifestyle			
	Integration of career and family life by both spouses. Affluence allows for conveniences that make both family and individual leisure-time pursuits possible.	Both spouses focus on the family, although the wife usually tends to household and child concerns. Both spouses work to provide needs of family.	The wife's domain is the home; the husband's domain is work. Range of individual and family activities is influenced by sex roles and the earning power of the husband's job.

Source: Adapted from James W. Hanson and Rosemary Polegato, "Identifying Dual Career, Dual Income and Traditional Family Segments," in *Marketing*, vol. 4, ed. James D. Forbes (Montreal: Administrative Sciences Association of Canada, 1983), pp. 137–39.

Progressives (13 percent)   They are young, educated, with above-average incomes, and tolerant of their wives' employment. About two-thirds do the main food shopping.

All talk, no action (33 percent)   Their attitudes, but not their behaviour, are similar to the progressives. About 20 percent do the main food shopping.

Ambivalents (15 percent)   Because of economic pressures, they reluctantly accept their wives' employment. About 60 percent do the main food shopping.

Traditionalists (39 percent)   Older, less educated, they believe that their wives' place is at home.

Some of the implications of these changes for retailers are in terms of targeting both spouses for store loyalty, merchandise selection, pricing, and promotion. In particular, the increase in food shopping by men may affect store layout and placement of impulse products.[16]

Reference Groups and Opinion Leaders

A **reference group** is any group for which a consumer is a "psychological participant," that is, a group with which he or she will identify and accept its norms or judgment. Examples of reference groups are family, relatives, friends, colleagues, professional or religious associations, celebrities, and salespersons.

Retailers can use their knowledge of reference group influences in various ways. For example, they may use recognized members of a group (such as a local celebrity) in their advertisement or in their direct selling, or they may indicate to the customer that members of a certain reference group routinely patronize their store. They may also post letters from or photographs of such persons.

When retailers can identify persons whose product-specific competence is recognized by others (called **opinion leaders**), they can attempt to influence them in a number of ways. These individuals may be consulted when new products are introduced and they may receive free samples or trial use of a product. The objective is to win over the opinion leader, who through positive word-of-mouth will generate traffic and sales.

Finally, a good salesperson may act as a reference person for several customers, if they have come to trust and depend on such a salesperson. Some customers may be unsure about their choice, either because they do not have the expertise, or do not trust their own judgment. When they find a salesperson that is credible and sincere, and has made the "right" choice for them in the past, they will continue to depend on that person for what may be a very long time.

Influence of Social Classes

Social classes are divisions of society that are relatively homogeneous and permanent, and in which individuals or families often share similar values, lifestyles, interests, and types of behaviour. This applies also to shopping behaviour and, as such, is of great importance to retailers because many studies have found that social classes affect the consumption of products and services, the selection of a retail outlet, and the use of credit cards.[17]

In practice, social class membership is measured using major components such as how prestigious the occupation of the family head is, the area of residence of the family, and the type of dwelling (e.g., detached house or apartment), the source of family income (e.g., salary, investment, or welfare), and/or the level of education.

Social classes in Canada

A recent study provides the distribution of the Canadian population among four major social classes:[18]

Upper classes (11 percent)   These include self-employed and employed professionals, and high-level management. They tend to shop at the better retail outlets, and buy high-quality goods and clothing, jewelry, luxury cars, appliances, and furniture. They represent the best market for luxury goods and status symbol products.

Middle class (28 percent)   These include semi-professionals, technicians, middle managers, supervisors, foremen, and skilled clerical-sales-service. With the working class, they represent the mass market for most goods and services. They tend to shop at department stores, and buy good quality goods, clothing, and furniture. They tend to be price sensitive while selecting quality items.

Working class (41 percent)   These include the skilled tradesmen, the farmers, the semi-skilled manual and clerical-sales-service. They tend to shop at discount stores and promotional department stores, and spend less than the middle class on clothing, travel, and services, and more on sporting goods and equipment. They tend to prefer national brands.

Lower classes (20 percent)   These include the unskilled clerical-sales-service, and manual and farm labourers. They tend to spend most of their income on the basic necessities of life, little on luxury products. They purchase second-hand cars and used furniture, and less expensive goods and clothes.

Many implications for retailers are based on social class structure including merchandise mix, store image, design and layout, pricing, and advertising.

Influence of Culture and Subculture

Culture

As individuals grow up within a cultural group, they learn a set of values, attitudes, traditions, symbols, and characteristic behaviours. In a sense, **culture** affects and shapes many aspects of consumption behaviour, including shopping behaviour. This section deals with the cultural and ethnic groups comprising the Canadian "salad bowl" and their importance to retailers.

In looking at Canadian cultural groups, retailers should recognize that the differences among them stem from a variety of sources, including:

- The system of inherited values, attitudes, symbols, ideas, traditions, and artifacts that are shared by the members of the group. These differences will affect the merchandising mix, the pricing policy, and the promotional strategies of the retailer, depending on the group(s) targeted.

- The dominant religion of the group, which may be confounded with culture, and which may affect some values and attitudes, for example, toward Sunday shopping.
- The dominant language spoken by the group, which may also be confounded with culture, and which may require different promotional or selling strategies—for example, advertising in French or Italian, or using salespeople with certain language skills.

Cultural groups in Canada

A brief overview of the most significant cultural groups in Canada and their characteristics of interest to retailers is as follows:

English Canadians   They represent the largest group in Canada with about 12 million people. They are present in all major markets in Canada, although they are not a homogeneous group, with regional differences, and differences among those of Scottish descent, Irish descent, and recent immigrants from England.[19] However, as a group they exhibit consumption and shopping behaviour that is different from that of other groups. Compared to the French Canadians, they consume more frozen vegetables, less beer and wine, and more hard liquor, shop at more stores, and purchase furniture more at department or furniture stores than at discount stores.[20]

French Canadians   They represent the second largest market in Canada, with about 7.5 million people, and they account for over $54 billion in retail sales. French Canadians reside mostly in Quebec, Ontario, and New Brunswick. In many respects, their consumption and shopping behaviour may be vastly different from that of the English Canadians, not only in terms of degree, as illustrated in the previous paragraph, but also in terms of approach. For example, in advertising, they respond better to an emotional approach, and react more to the *source* (the spokesperson) of the advertisement, while English Canadians react more to the (rational) *content* of the message.[21] Many retailers, including Burger King, have developed specific campaigns to meet the needs of French Canadians. Retail Highlight 4–2 provides additional characteristics of this major group.

German Canadians   They number about 1 million, and are mostly concentrated west of Ontario, comprising 14 percent of the population of Kitchener, 13 percent of Regina, and 12 percent of Saskatoon. They are maintaining their ethnicity through celebrations and rituals, but only 10 percent speak German at home. The four major values of this group are a strong sense of family, work ethic, drive for education, and sense of justice.

Italian Canadians   The vast majority of the 700,000 Italian Canadians are concentrated in the metropolitan areas of Quebec and Ontario. They represent 9 percent of the population of Toronto, 8 percent in St. Catharines-Niagara, 7 percent of Thunder Bay and Windsor, and 5 percent in Montreal.

They have maintained a strong culture by developing a community with their own stores, cinemas, newspapers, radio stations, and TV programs, and

Burger King targets the French Canadian market with a humorous campaign.

Courtesy Burger King Canada/Marketel

about 37 percent speak Italian at home. Their primary relations are with people of their own background, and as their level of affluence increases, they become more status conscious, want to own their homes, buy new cars, and send their children to university.

A study in Montreal shows very distinct consumption and shopping patterns. For example, 72 percent shop in a large supermarket once or twice a week and 39 percent in a department store.[22]

Asian-Canadians   They number about 600,000 and more immigrants are expected from Hong Kong as the colony approaches 1997. Projections are that they will number at least 800,000 by 2000. As mentioned earlier, they have unique behavioral patterns and needs, high levels of education, high incomes, and, thus, present interesting opportunities for many retailers. For example, 70 percent of the Chinese in Toronto are exposed to Chinese TV, 78 percent in Chinese newspapers, and retailers advertising in Chinese may get more business from this group. Only 10 percent of the Chinese in Toronto consider themselves truly bilingual.[23]

Ukrainian-Canadians   About 400,000 strong, they are mostly concentrated west of Ontario, including 7 percent of the population of Winnipeg, and 6 percent in Saskatoon and Edmonton. Although Ukrainian is the mother tongue of 46 percent of them, only 10 percent speak it at home. They are known for their distinct types of food, crafts, clothing styles, techniques for building and decorating homes, and leisure activities.

Other significant groups   Other significant groups are the Native people (370,000), the Dutch (350,000), the South Asians (260,000), the Jewish

Retail Highlight 4-2

How Are French-Canadians Different Compared to English-Canadians?

French-Canadians in general

- Are more willing to pay premium prices for convenience and premium brands.
- Buy few "no-name" products but make greater use of cents-off coupons.
- Patronize food warehouses less, and convenience stores and health food outlets more.
- Are less likely to consume tea, diet colas, jam, tuna, cookies, and eggs, but more likely to consume pre-sweetened cereals, regular colas, instant coffee, and butter.
- Give more importance to personal grooming and fashion, and more often visit specialized clothing boutiques.
- Are less likely to use medicated throat lozenges, cold remedies, and nasal sprays.
- Have a higher propensity to drink wine and beer, and to smoke cigarettes, but a lower one for hard liquor.
- Are less likely to play golf, jog, garden, go to the movies, and entertain at home.
- Buy more lottery tickets, subscribe to book clubs, and make fewer long-distance phone calls.
- Have more life insurance but fewer credit cards.

The mature Quebecers (55-plus)

- Go to the supermarket more often and seldom to food warehouses.
- Consume less canned foods, cranberry-based items, frozen vegetables, ginger ale, boxed chocolates, and bran cereals.
- Drink more milk, fresh orange juice, prune nectar, bottled water, cognac, gins, French wines, and vermouth.
- Are less active, travel less, but are more likely to go dancing.
- Are less likely to use automatic banking machines and credit cards, and to own cats, dogs, or cars.

Source: François Vary, "Sizing up 55-plus," *Marketing*, October 5, 1995, pp. 13–14; François Vary, "Quebec Consumer Has Unique Buying Habits," *Marketing*, March 23, 1992, p. 28.

(245,000), the Polish (220,000), the Portuguese (200,000), the Blacks (175,000), the Scandinavians (170,000), and the Greeks (140,000).

They are being studied to learn more about their consumption and shopping behaviour. What is learned could help retailers to attract more customers belonging to targeted ethnic groups.

Conclusion on ethnic groups in Canada   What can be gathered from this brief discussion is that Canadian retailers must thoroughly understand the ethnic origins of their customers, and adjust their strategies accordingly, particularly in the areas of merchandise mix, advertising and sales promotion, store location and design, in-store selling, and pricing.

Lifestyle Merchandising

Lifestyle and psychographics

Lifestyle is a customer's pattern of living as reflected in the way merchandise is purchased and used. **Psychographics** are the ways of defining and measuring the lifestyles of consumers. They can be measured with a series of questions called the lifestyle (or AIO) inventory, which includes questions on various *a*ttitudes (e.g., I find shopping enjoyable), *i*nterests (e.g., I often go to the movies), and *o*pinions (e.g., all retailers are honest businesspeople). The respondent is asked to agree or disagree with these types of statements.

Lifestyle concepts influence almost every dimension of merchandise presentation in retailing. Why has lifestyle merchandising become so important? We live in an age in which large differences exist in the behaviour of people with similar demographic profiles. This diversity makes it hard to offer merchandise to consumers based only on an analysis of their age, income, and education. Instead, retailers need to know (1) how people spend their time, (2) how they spend their money, and (3) what they value, so that they can serve the customers better. Market segmentation based on lifestyle characteristics (as measured by the AIO inventory) gives retailers a more realistic picture of the customers they want to serve.

Lifestyle retailing has grown in importance since the early 1970s. Previously, retailing had been characterized by a sameness in operations. Large retailers such as Sears, Eaton's, and The Bay had few significant differences in strategy. Managers could be shifted from one store to another across the country and would find few differences between the stores.[24]

The marketing concept

The marketing concept was developed in the early 1960s by packaged goods firms such as Procter & Gamble as a response to the lack of attention to the needs of consumers in merchandising decisions. The marketing concept involves focussing on consumers' needs and integrating all activities of the store to satisfy the needs identified.

Retailers in the 1960s, even though insisting that "the customer is always right," often implemented the marketing concept only in the context of day-to-day operations, not in the context of the broader strategic dimensions of the store (Chapter 6 will discuss this point further). Refund policies, hours of operation, and customer service were developed with a consumer focus. Product lines, store location, style of merchandise, and other strategic issues still retained the sameness of earlier years.

The positioning concept

The concept of **market positioning** emerged during the early 1970s as the forerunner of contemporary lifestyle merchandising and as part of an effort to implement the marketing concept. Management began to tailor merchandising strategies to specific consumer segments. The segments to be served were defined, however, largely in terms of demographics such as age, income, and education.

Outlets such as Colour Your World, a decoration store, experienced success by market positioning, based on demographics, and by offering narrow but deep lines of merchandise to carefully defined consumer segments.

Lifestyle merchandising

Retailers quickly realized that defining consumers in terms of demographics alone was not sufficient for fast growth. The concept of lifestyle merchandising thus evolved. The new focus was on understanding and responding to the living patterns of customers rather than making merchandising decisions primarily on

Eddie Bauer uses lifestyle merchandising to serve its target.

Photo by Betty McDougall

the basis of consumer demographics, and in doing so integrating all the social dimensions discussed in the first part of the chapter.

A portfolio of lifestyle-oriented outlets then emerged as the next evolutionary stage for some retailers. Management recognized that a portfolio of outlets is likely to be more profitable than focussing on only one or two target groups. Even such a traditional mass merchant as K mart has opened a variety of lifestyle-oriented retailing specialty outlets, such as Builders Square, targeted to the do-it-yourself market, also served by Home Depot and Northern Reflections, the latter launched in Canada as a faux-country chain stocked with casual clothes. At the Toronto-based Sporting Life, the entire store format, including the salespeople and the merchandise, appeals to the individual who loves the outdoors and many kinds of sports.

Why worry about lifestyle merchandising?

As just illustrated, lifestyle analysis offers retailers (1) an opportunity to develop marketing strategies based on a lifelike portrait of the consumers they are seeking to serve, (2) the ability to partially protect the outlet from direct price competition by developing unique merchandise offerings that attract shoppers for reasons other than price, and (3) the opportunity to better understand the shopping behaviour and merchandise preferences of customers.

Management is simply better able to describe and understand the behaviour of consumers when thinking in terms of lifestyle. Routinely thinking in terms of the activities, interests, needs, and values of customers can help retailers plan merchandise offerings, price lines, store layout, and promotion programs that are tightly targeted. However, lifestyle analysis only adds to the demographic, geographic, and socioeconomic information retailers need in serving markets effectively. Lifestyle analysis is not a substitute for this information. Rather, all the information sources taken together give retailers a richer view of their customers and help them recognize and serve consumer needs.

What shapes lifestyles?

We are all a product of the society in which we live. We learn very early concepts such as honesty and the value of money. And these stay with us throughout our lives. These cultural influences, plus individual economic circumstances, produce consumer lifestyles—traits, activities, interests, and opinions reflected in shopping behaviour. Individuals can be grouped into distinct market segments based on the similarities of their lifestyles.

Where do lifestyles come from?

The lifestyles of consumers are rooted in their values. Values are beliefs or expectations about behaviour shared by a number of individuals and learned from society. Some of these values do not change much over time, whereas others can change quite rapidly. The major forces shaping consumer values include family, culture, religious institutions, schools, and early lifetime experiences.

A study of cultural and economic lifestyle influences offers some of the most important and interesting ways of understanding consumers. This information helps in serving them more effectively. The following examples of such analyses will help you understand the impact of lifestyles on consumer buying behaviour.

Values and lifestyles (VALS)   Stanford Research International (SRI) has developed a trademarked program entitled VALS (values and lifestyles) that can help retailers understand the effect of consumer preferences and expectations on market planning decisions.[25] Their program is summarized in Figure 4–3. VALS was modified with the introduction of VALS 2, which places less emphasis on values and more emphasis on the psychological underpinnings of behaviour.

The VALS program allows retailers to predict consumer responses to merchandise or to outlets based on the VALS categories established. For example, people who use yogurt regularly have been found to be societally conscious, as have the experiencers and achievers. Similarly, the experiencers are more likely to buy imported cheese than domestic cheese. Achievers, experiencers, and societally conscious individuals shop more frequently at supermarkets and convenience stores than other groups do, and they also buy more on each trip to the store.

Furthermore, VALS information can help retailers develop promotional campaigns targeted at specific groups. Societally conscious consumers read magazines often but do not watch much television. When they do, it is often a cable channel. They listen to radio on an average basis but focus on news, soft rock, and classical music.

VALS's limitation was that it did not account for how well consumers' motivations matched with their ability to buy the goods and services they wanted. For this reason, SRI developed VALS 2, which explains not just what consumers buy, but why and how they make purchase decisions. The system introduces and defines the notions of psychological and material resources and describes the critical role they play in the translation of psychological motivation into purchasing behaviour.[26]

The VALS 2 system divides consumers into eight groups, determined by their psychological makeup or self-orientation, and their financial resources.

Figure 4–3   VALS and VALS 2

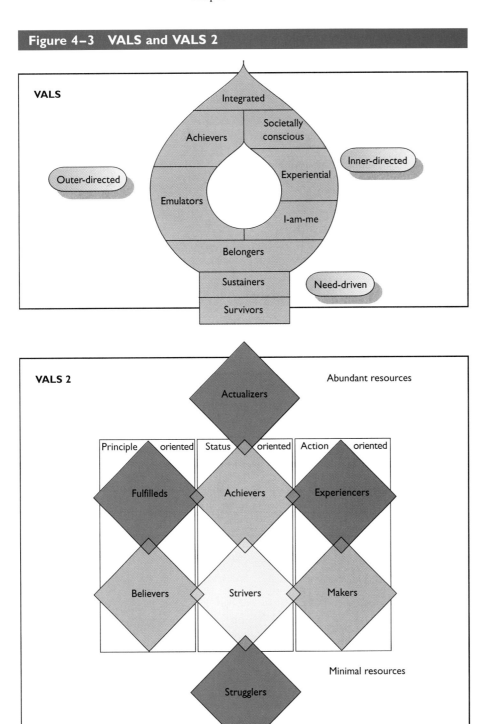

Source: Reprinted with permission from Marsha Farnsworth Riche, "Psychographics for the 1990s," *American Demographics*, July 1989, p. 26. For subscription information call (800) 828-1133.

Self-orientation refers to the patterns of attitudes and activities that help people reinforce, sustain, or modify their social self-image.

For VALS 2 purposes, resources include education, income, self-confidence, health, eagerness to buy, intelligence, and energy level. Resources generally increase from adolescence through middle age and decrease with extreme age, depression, financial reverses, and physical or psychological impairment.

VALS finds three patterns to be highly effective predictors of consumer behaviour: principle, status, and action orientations. **Principle-oriented consumers** are guided in their choices by their beliefs or principles, rather than by feelings, events, or desire for approval. **Status-oriented consumers** are heavily influenced by the actions, approval, and opinions of others. **Action-oriented consumers** are guided by a desire for social or physical activity, variety, and risk taking.

Each of the groups has distinctive attitudes, lifestyles, and life goals. Consumers within each group buy products and services and seek experiences characteristic of themselves.

With those factors as a foundation, a thumbnail sketch of the eight VALS 2 segments follows:[27]

- **Actualizers** are successful, sophisticated, active, take-charge people with high self-esteem and abundant resources. Their possessions and recreation reflect a cultivated taste for the finer things in life.

- **Fulfilleds** are mature, satisfied, comfortable, reflective people who value order, knowledge, and responsibility. Most are well educated, and in, or recently retired from, professional occupations. Although their income allows them many choices, they are conservative, practical consumers, concerned about functionality, value, and durability in the products they buy.

- **Believers** are conservative, conventional people with concrete beliefs and strong attachments to traditional institutions: family, church, community, and the nation. They follow established routines, organized in large part around their homes, families, and social or religious organizations. As consumers, they are conservative and predictable, favouring national products and established brands.

- **Achievers** are successful career-oriented people who like to, and generally do, feel in control of their lives. They value structure, predictability, and stability over risk, intimacy, and self-discovery. They are deeply committed to their work and their families. As consumers, they favour established products that demonstrate their success to their peers.

- **Strivers** seek motivation, self-definition, and approval from the world around them. They are striving to find a secure place in life. Unsure of themselves, and low on economic, social, and psychological resources, they are deeply concerned about the opinions and approval of others. They emulate those who own more impressive possessions, but what they wish to obtain is generally beyond their reach.

- **Experiencers** are young, vital, enthusiastic, impulsive, and rebellious. They seek variety and excitement, savouring the new, the offbeat, and the risky. Still in the process of formulating life values and patterns of behaviour, they quickly become enthusiastic about new possibilities but are equally quick to

Targeting actualizers and fulfilleds with an image and product mix.

Photo by Anne Laroche

cool. They are avid consumers and spend much of their income on clothing, fast food, music, movies, and videos.

- **Makers** are practical people who have constructive skills and value self-sufficiency. They live within a traditional context of family, practical work, and physical recreation, and have little interest in what lies outside that context. They experience the world by working on it (for example, building a house or canning vegetables), and have sufficient skill, income, and energy to carry out their projects successfully. They are unimpressed by material possessions other than those with a practical or functional purpose.

- **Strugglers'** lives are constricted. Chronically poor, ill-educated, low-skilled, without strong social bonds, aging, and concerned about their health, they are often despairing and passive. Their chief concerns are for security and safety. They are cautious consumers, and although they represent a very modest market for most products and services, they are loyal to favourite brands.

According to SRI, the VALS 2 segments are balanced in size so that each truly represents a viable target for retailers. In addition, some of the segments with similar characteristics interconnect with one another, so they can be combined in various ways to suit particular retailing purposes.

What else do we know about changing cultural patterns?

There are a number of cultural and lifestyle trends that have important implications for retailers.

The divorce rate remains high. In the 1991 census, there were 1 million single-parent families in Canada, or 14 percent of all families (82 percent were female lone parents). Although the divorce rate has dropped recently, it remains at around 80,000 a year.[28] As a result, the value patterns of today's children are shifting. More children are being raised without fathers in the home. So, many children now learn some of their values from individuals other than family members.

Parents are spending less time with very young children. For example, today more than 30 percent of preschool children are in day care centres, a segment that will continue to grow rapidly.

People move more often than in the past. Thus, less influence comes from grandparents and aunts and uncles as part of the extended family. Many of today's young people lack "roots" and a sense of traditional family values.

Religion is not important in many people's lives. As a consequence, the moral standards of previous years are changing. People are more prone to pursue pleasure and less likely to practice self-denial, although this might be changing as a consequence of the 1991–92 recession.

Schools are becoming more important in shaping values. More young people are staying in high school, and approximately half now go to college. Young people are being exposed to a larger number of different values than in the past and are more willing to experiment and try alternative lifestyles.

Individuals in each generation have different experiences. More than 80 percent of consumers today were not alive during the depression of the 1930s. Many have little awareness of World War II. Today's middle-age people (the baby-boom generation) grew up in an era of low-cost credit, plentiful jobs, job security, and loyalty to one's country and parents. Yet, these same people also lived through high inflation and an energy "crisis." On the other hand, the teenagers (i.e., their children) have been experiencing low inflation, a severe recession, and poor employment prospects.

Small family sizes and more single-person households. The small family size of the 1990s (at about 3.1 persons) is continuing and their lifestyle patterns continue to create new merchandising opportunities. Many of these households have high discretionary income and spend more on restaurants, educational products, and travel services than larger families. Their homes are typically smaller than in the past and the furnishings also are smaller.

Single-person households reflect lifestyles that are not impacted by family norms and the preferences of other family members. Activities are on a per person basis as opposed to a household basis. Products and services for such households are being personalized rather than standardized. Such retail services as health care, personal finance, and insurance are now offered on a per person rather than a per household basis.

The increasing emphasis on the family is being accompanied by an increase in adult-oriented lifestyles. More and more adult-oriented programming is available to households through cable television and the networks. The popularity of adult soap operas reflects this trend in society. In addition, the penetration of VCR and of video stores is making it easier to watch movies at home.

The yuppies (young, urban professionals) are getting older. The number of persons aged 35 to 44 will increase rapidly, while persons aged 25 to 34 will actually shrink in numbers by about 20 percent by 2000.[29] Such households typically have two incomes, are well educated, and have the money to spend to support their lifestyle preferences. The yuppies are placing more emphasis on their households than they did when they were in their 20s. They are purchasing more expensive home furnishings, and quality art, and are major consumers of services. Banks, stock-brokerage houses, and other financial institutions are rejoicing at the opportunity to serve these markets. These consumers are conspicuous in their consumption and are willing to spend heavily to support their lifestyles. The values of the aging yuppie are characterized by the term "couch potatoes" and by what is popularly described as "cocooning." They are increasingly inclined to buy things that provide control, comfort, and security against what they perceive as a harsh outside world. Domino's Pizza, capitalizing on this lifestyle, became a national force in the pizza business by providing home delivery. The La-Z-Boy Showcase Shops have profited from this trend, which has also fuelled retail markets for VCR ownership and videotape rentals.

Families earning more than $50,000 a year are growing at a rapid rate although they only comprise 20 percent of the population. An important number of these affluent families represent retirees who have earned good pensions during the last 50 years (called the Countdown Generation).[30] Affluent buyers seek products and services that reflect their self-image and are interested in aesthetics as much as performance. From retailers, they seek the highest-quality merchandise that reflects prestige and fashion. They expect high-quality service and expect consultation. Affluent dual-income households provide strong markets for luxury products such as satellite dishes, boats, and premium cars.[31] Retailers such as Holt Renfrew are positioned to serve these markets.

No longer are the roles of the male and the female in the household as clearly defined as in the past. More and more women are buyers of financial services and other male-oriented products. Men are increasingly becoming purchasers of household products, and young adults of both sexes are learning how to manage households and to cope with problems of school and education. Many retail promotions are universal in content and not targeted specifically to either males or females.

One of the most dramatic changes has been the effects of technology on consumer lifestyles. The development of videocassette players led to the emergence of video outlets that specialize in the rental of movies and VCR equipment. Busy consumers are responding to the opportunity to view films at their convenience in the privacy of their homes rather than go to movie houses. Microwave ovens have led to changes in the types of foods eaten, and in-home interactive shopping offered through cable services is beginning to redefine how and when consumers shop.

Not all consumers are sharing in the affluence of some demographic segments. Such consumers, as part of their lifestyles, are very responsive to coupons and other promotions. They use generic products, buy at flea markets and garage sales, are willing to accept less service in return for lower prices, and are active in seeking goods that last longer and require less maintenance. Such consumers are responsible for the growth of warehouse outlets for various types of merchandise.

There is a major shift in attitudes and values. In the last few years, there have been some subtle and important shifts in attitudes and values among consumers that will profoundly affect the economy in the future:[32]

Table 4–4 Key Differences between the Values of the 1980s and Those of the 1990s	
1980s	**1990s**
New	Old
Future	Past
Prestige	Comfort
Trend	Tradition
State-of-the-art	Enduring
Fast track	Sure-footed
Wealth	Contentment
Make-believe	Real
Image	Character
Leading-edge	Heritage
Avant-garde	Classic
Fitness	Wellness
Nutrition	Health
Good for you	Feels good
High-tech	High-touch
Me	You

Source: "Torlée Targets Marketing in the 1990s," *Marketing*, December 9, 1991, p. 6.

- The return to conservative ideals, in terms of life, work, love, and family.
- The rejection of the legacy of conspicuous consumption.
- The demand for real intrinsic value, including product quality and durability.
- The growth of altruism.
- The search for balance and moderation, in particular the search for simplicity and convenience.

These shifts are summarized in Table 4–4.

The more money people have to spend, the less time they have to spend it. The most affluent households typically have two wage earners, which means that they have little time for shopping. As a result, they are willing to pay for time-saving goods including lawn care services and cleaning services. They also have been responsible for the rapid growth in specialty shops, in supermarkets and in downtown department stores. Such consumers also seek high-quality recreation because of the limited amount of time available to them. They are prone to go to fashionable ski resorts, take sun-and-surf winter vacations (Canadian snowbirds), and go to theme restaurants and expensive golf and tennis resorts.

Segmenting Markets by Lifestyle

The information used in forming lifestyle market segments is developed from consumer research. Marketing researchers question consumers about the merchandise they purchased, their media habits, as well as their activities, interests, and opinions.[33] One research study yielded five fashion segments, which can

Retail Highlight 4–3

An Illustration of Psychographic Segmentation: The Female Clothing Market

Opinion leaders. These women shopped most frequently, but placed the least weight on brand, salesperson's evaluation, and store loyalty. They frequently used mail brochures and overseas fashion magazines. This group was willing to pay the most for given items of clothing, and spent the largest percentage of income on clothing purchases. They were younger, more likely to be single, better educated, and more mobile.

Discontents. These women bought the least amount of ready-made clothing, being most inclined to do their own sewing. They saw price as very important, had the lowest reasonable price perceptions for an average garment, and were not store loyal. This group was in the lowest family income bracket and spent the least on clothes.

Conservatives. This group spent the lowest percentage of income on clothing. They shopped the least frequently, but were prepared to pay well when they did shop. Fabric and instructions for care were seen as particularly important when buying clothes, and they particularly emphasized the importance of quality and garment care.

Followers. These women did not pay much attention to fashion trends, and checked to see what is fashionable only when buying new clothes. They saw brand as important, and were most likely to be store loyal. They were in the average family income bracket and had the lowest level of education.

Socializers. This group saw the type of fabric, price, and the store where purchased as unimportant when buying clothes, but instructions for care as particularly important. They bought virtually all of their clothes ready-made, spent more on clothing than all others, and were in the highest income group. They were older, most inclined to shop at prestige fashion stores, and enjoyed reading local fashion magazines.

Source: Peter Thirkell, "Opinion Leadership and Attitudes toward Fashion of Female Consumers: A Segmentation Study," in *Developments in Canadian Marketing: Proceedings of the Administrative Sciences Association of Canada*, ed. Robert Tamilia (1979), p. 67.

---

provide a key to understanding how **lifestyle segmentation** can be used in a retail setting.[34] The five segments are profiled in Retail Highlight 4–3, as an illustration of the use of lifestyle analysis in merchandise planning.

Idea-oriented presentations

Merchandise is often brought together from all areas of the store for its lifestyle appeal. Lifestyle merchandising breaks down departmental barriers. This approach allows salespeople to sell primarily to customers with similar lifestyles. Management seeks to group merchandise the way customers want to buy it, not the way the store thinks it is easiest to sell. Simply putting dresses into departments labelled better, moderate, and budget can help. Consumers match their lifestyles with the departments. Many complementary items are placed together to encourage multiple purchases. For example, all items of sporting equipment may be grouped in one department, women's accessories may be grouped in another, or furniture and accessories may be grouped in a single-room setting. Such efforts break down departmental rigidities, encourage multiple sales, and increase space productivity.

Increasingly, merchants are using idea-oriented presentations to convey an idea by clustering complementary items to motivate multiple purchases, but without the extensive involvement of sales clerks. A typical example is the bath

Leisure-time active sportswear fits into the current
physical-fitness lifestyles.

Photo by James Hertel

shop, where the entire merchandise presentation is idea oriented. Customers
find all items related to the bath brought together from different merchandise
categories throughout the store.

Lifestyle merchandise classifications

One of the trends in merchandising for males is selling to "the better young
man," defined as "a fashion-aware young man in a college or university, who
doesn't have the budget yet for more expensive clothes."

Some stores have opened separate shops with an updated, traditional flair,
giving fashion direction with designer jeans by such names as Sasson.

Super specialty retailing

The super specialists include such firms as Toys "Я" Us. Their exceptional
profitability and rapid growth have made them formidable competitors for
department/general merchandise stores and small independent retail operations.

The stores offer a limited assortment of contemporary merchandise aimed
at specific segments—typically, adults aged 18 to 35 with an interest in fashion.

Management is centralized, and the organizations are able to respond to
market trends almost instantly. Personal service, breadth, and depth in merchandise, and the ability to keep pace with fashion trends give these outlets a
strong image relative to department stores and independent outlets.

The role of ambience

The essence of visual lifestyle retailing is reflected in the concept of **ambience**
(or atmospherics). Ambience is a term loosely defined but critical to lifestyle

Courtesy Hard Rock Cafe

merchandising. Adolph Novak, a leading store designer, defines ambience as "the general quality of design which expresses the character of a store, resulting in an institutional personality immediately recognized by the consumer public."

Ambience is a lifestyle reflection of two elements: (1) the interior decor, which includes everything within the store, such as walls, ceilings, floor, lighting fixtures, customer services, signing, and merchandise; and (2) exterior design. The interior and exterior designs should be in harmony. Exterior design often draws customers to the outlet by identifying the type or quality of the firm.

Considerable research has been done on ambience in the context of hedonic consumption as part of the overall lifestyle experience. **Hedonic consumption** has been defined as those facets of consumer behaviour that relate to the multisensory and emotional aspects of the shopping experience and product consumption.[35] In other words, consumers may be attracted by sights, sounds, smells, colour, and displays as part of the retailing experience.

An excellent example of a store as theatre is the Hard Rock Cafe in Montreal. The Cafe is a place that people do not easily forget.

Serving customers with unique lifestyles

Continuing market fragmentation has made lifestyle sensitivity even more critical to retail success. Cultural differences require unique types of information for shoppers, as do pressures of time faced by professionals, exemplified by the need for longer store hours and personal shopping services. More knowledgeable salespeople are often required.

Information   Large retailers in such metropolitan markets as Montreal, Toronto, and Vancouver offer multilingual services to attract and serve foreign tourists. Many of these stores maintain lists of employees with foreign language abilities. Store directions and information pamphlets are sometimes printed in foreign languages. The service is offered free to make shopping easy for tourists.

Shopping services   Shopping services are becoming increasingly popular with working women (and men). Customers make an initial visit to an outlet and provide retailers with essential measurements and other information needed to help make merchandise selection decisions for the customers. They can then call ahead and have several outfits assembled for their approval when they arrive at the store. Such services require creative talent by salespeople but can lead to significant "plus" sales for the outlet.[36]

Store hours   Longer shopping hours are especially common in suburban areas where stores may be open late each night of the week and even on Sunday (where it is allowed by law). Increasing numbers of two-income households are likely to demand that retail outlets remain open in the evening and on Sundays to serve the needs of individuals who are unable to shop during "normal" store hours.

Effects on retail salespeople   Retail salespeople have to identify both with the items being sold and the lifestyle of the customer buying the items. Even store branches need to be tailored to the lifestyles of the customers living in that particular area. For example, the salesperson selling tennis equipment should ideally be an avid tennis player.

Better promotion efforts   Lifestyle merchandising is changing the media mix used by retailers. Lifestyle programming by various stations that offer sports, "middle-of-the road" music, or all-news programs represent attempts to reach specific target audiences. Tightly defined media audiences are being sought by retailers today.

Visual merchandising   Attractively displayed merchandise in harmony with a consumer's lifestyle increases that consumer's desire to buy. Lifestyle merchandising based upon this psychology is a highly refined art. Promotional displays are likely to be strong, dramatic, and striking, and support the theme of the other promotion efforts.

Creating the artistic environment so essential in lifestyle merchandising requires a unique blending of lighting, background, and props. All visual merchandising themes should start with what the customer wants and should communicate important merchandise information. These points are discussed in further detail in Chapter 11.

Understanding emerging global lifestyles

Global telecommunications, frequent cross-border travel, and a global economy are creating an international youth culture whereby fashion, music, and food are becoming part of a universal, international lifestyle that is essentially the same in Vancouver, Madrid, and Osaka. "It is consumer-driven: drinking cappuccino and Perrier; furnishing the apartment with IKEA; eating sushi; dressing in the united colours of Benetton; listening to U.S.-British rock while driving the Hyundai over to McDonald's."[37] Groups of consumers in Toronto and Milan often have greater similarities than consumers do in Calgary and Halifax.

Television media deliver the same images around the world. McDonald's competes for the same expensive real estate whether in Montreal's Crescent street, the Ginza in Japan, or the Champs-Elysées in Paris. Sushi bars have flooded Canadian cities, Tex-Mex cuisine is served in Israel, and numerous oriental restaurants operate in Canada.

Fashion, especially, is becoming international in this era of global travel and telecommunications. Italian youths today tend to dress in blue denim, and Canadians are switching to Italian suits. Fashion-conscious youth favour clothes from such international fashion retailers as Laura Ashley, Benetton, and Esprit, all outfitters of the global lifestyle. Benetton's "All the Colours of the World" oozes international flavour unmatched in history. Esprit, based in California, is also one of the world's leading sportswear merchants. Habitat, a British home furnishings merchant, operates its stores worldwide, as does IKEA, the Swedish unassembled furniture merchant, whose catalogues are published in 12 languages.

Global pricing is the result of global merchandising and global electronics. Prices are controlled electronically so that outlets around the world for any particular chain are largely immune to currency fluctuations. A Chanel suit sells for essentially the same price on Rodeo Drive, in Hong Kong, and in Paris.

The Wall Street Journal, the British-based *Economist,* and the *Financial Times* are transmitted around the world by satellite transmission. The *Economist* is read by people in more than 170 countries. Less than 25 percent of its readers live in Great Britain. Vast cultural exports from the United States essentially have conquered the world. The first all-American Disneyland outside the United States opened in Japan. EuroDisneyland opened in Paris in 1992.

English has emerged as a universal language as the cultures of English-speaking countries increasingly dominate world trends. More than 1 billion English speakers live in the world today. English is the language of the international youth culture, who are equally comfortable singing the lyrics of Bryan Adams, U2, or Janet Jackson. Global lifestyles are slowly helping to overcome cultural nationalisms. No longer can progressive merchants think in terms of North American lifestyles only as nationalist borders become unimportant for other than political reasons.

Chapter Highlights

- **Retailers must understand how decisions are made within a family, the respective roles of men, women, and children, and the changing needs during different stages of its life cycle.**

- **Retailers may often use reference groups and opinion leaders such as local celebrities to improve the image of their store and the credibility of their salespersons.**

- Social class distinctions have often been used instinctively by retailers in defining their targets and their marketing strategies.

- Most Canadian retailers should be sensitive to the Canadian "salad bowl," and understand the subtleties of attitudes and behaviour of the various subgroups.

- Retailers can more readily meet the needs of customers if they understand how people spend their time and money and what they value. The essence of this type of information is lifestyle analysis.

- Lifestyles are based on the values of people. The forces affecting consumer values are the influence of the family, religious institutions, schools, and early life-time experiences.

- Retail management philosophies in meeting the needs of consumers have evolved gradually over time. Until the 1950s retailers were supply oriented. By the 1960s the marketing concept was introduced as a philosophy of management that required a total consumer orientation in all activities of the firm.

- Positioning, an extension of the marketing concept, emerged in the early 1970s. Management began to target their offerings to narrow groups of consumers defined in terms of demographics. By the mid-1970s, lifestyle merchandising emerged with an emphasis on the activities, interests, and opinions of consumers.

- The latest development in marketing strategy is a lifestyle portfolio of stores owned by a single organization but with each store targeted toward the needs of a different group of consumers.

- The Stanford Research International VALS program offers retailers the opportunity to structure lifestyle-focussed marketing programs. The SRI analysis combines the notions of psychological and material resources and shows the cultural role they play in the translation of psychological motivations into purchasing behaviour.

- Society today is characterized by parents who spend less time with young children than in previous generations, high divorce rates, and the relative unimportance of religion. The increasing importance of schools in shaping the values of youth, the decreasing family sizes, the increasing number of single-person households, and the redefinition of the role of the male and female are affecting shopping behaviour. Similarly, health awareness, poverty of time, and lifestyle changes brought about by dramatic changes in technology are redefining shopping behaviour.

- Sensitivity to lifestyle differences affects the retailing strategist in various ways, including making him or her aware of the importance of lifestyle merchandise classifications, the psychological effects of design and layout on purchasing behaviour, and ambience on targeted consumer markets.

- Retailers are offering personal shopper services in response to the expectations of certain lifestyle segments, seeking to match retail salespeople with the merchandise they are selling, and harmonizing visual merchandising displays with customer lifestyle segments.

- Understanding global lifestyles is becoming more important to the marketing strategy decisions of many retailers.

Key Terms

achievers 104
action-oriented consumers 104
actualizers 104
ambience 110
autonomous decision 91
believers 104
boomers 87
bridgers 88
culture 96
experiencers 104
family life cycle 88
fulfilleds 104
Generation X 87
Generation Y 87
hedonic consumption 111
husband-dominant decision 91

lifestyle 99
lifestyle segmentation 109
makers 105
market positioning 100
opinion leader 95
principle-oriented consumers 104
psychographics 99
reference group 95
social classes 95
status-oriented consumers 104
strivers 104
strugglers 105
syncratic decision 91
VALS 102
wife-dominant decision 89

Discussion Questions

1. What are the major changes occurring within the modern Canadian family, and what impact would these changes have on retailers?

2. Why is it important for the backgrounds of salespeople to match the lifestyles of the customers they will be serving? How does this relate to the notion of reference group?

3. In what ways does social class affect the kind of strategic decisions retailers must make? Give some specific examples.

4. Select three cultural groups in your community, and describe in detail how local retailers should adjust their strategies to better serve these groups.

5. Summarize changes occurring today in society that are shaping Canadian values and discuss the resulting effects on consumer behaviour.

6. What is meant by the term "super specialty retailing"? What are some of the operating characteristics of super specialists?

7. What are the things that some retailers are doing now to better serve customers with unique lifestyles?

8. Trace the differences in management philosophy between homogeneous retailing, retailing based on the marketing concept, and lifestyle retailing.

Application Exercises

1. Examine the range of retail outlets in your community for a specific group of items (e.g., fashion clothes, jewelry, gifts). Either by personal visits or by studying their advertising, regroup the stores who tend to appeal to a similar clientele. Then define this clientele in terms of age groups, gender, and/or social class. In each case, explain your reasoning.

2. Visit a mall or the CBD and identify as many stores as you can that represent lifestyle merchandising in action. Relate the strategy to the positioning that you believe management is attempting. Discuss whether you feel management of the stores you identify need to be more alert to changes in lifestyles.

Suggested Cases

5. Buying an Oriental Rug
6. A Buying Experience
7. York Furniture Company

Notes

1. E. Blais, "Generation X: Targeting a Tough Crowd That Is Not Easily Impressed," *Marketing,* June 6, 1994, pp. 13–15; J. Marney, "The psychology of age," *Marketing,* August 21/28, 1995, p. 14; E. Carey, "It's Generation Y: Teens Born to Shop," *The Toronto Star,* November 15, 1995, p. A1.

2. J. Marney, "The Psychology of Age"; C. Guly, "Selling to Seniors," *Today's Seniors,* October 1995, pp. 3–6.

3. "The Marketing Report on the Chinese Market," *Marketing,* September 18, 1995, pp. 17–24; J. Lynn, "Approaching Diversity," *Marketing,* July 3/10, 1995, p. 11.

4. A. Mitchell, "Common-Law Households on the Rise," *Globe & Mail,* June 8, 1992, pp. A1–2.

5. F. Taylor, "More Choosing to Be Childless," *Globe & Mail,* July 8, 1995, p. A3.

6. J. Gadd, "From Monster Home to White Elephant," *Globe & Mail,* November 10, 1995, p. A8; J. Marney, "Woopies, Muppies . . . The List Grows," *Marketing,* February 2, 1987, pp. 10–12.

7. H. L. Davis and B.P. Rigaux, "Perception of Marital Roles in Decision Processes," *Journal of Consumer Research,* June 1974, pp. 51–62.

8. F. Taylor, "More Choosing to Be Childless," p. A3; H. Filman, "Baby Books Benefit from Echo Boom," *Marketing,* March 30, 1992, p. 30; "Canada's Birth Rate Rises for Third Year," *Kitchener-Waterloo Record,* March 31, 1992, pp. A1–2.

9. P. Filiatrault and J.R.B. Ritchie, "Joint Purchasing Decisions: A Comparison of Influence Structure in Family and Couple Decision-Making Units," *Journal of Consumer Research,* September 1980, pp. 131–40.

10. J. Marney, "Advertising to Children Isn't Kid Stuff," *Marketing,* October 31, 1985, p. 19.

11. J. Marney, "Woopies."

12. J. Marney, "Youth Culture Is Key to a Huge Market," *Marketing,* August 5, 1991, p. 16; J. Marney, "Teen Loyalty Targeted with a Variety of Promotions," *Marketing,* December 16, 1991, p. 18; J. Marney, "Teen Market Offers Growing Opportunities," *Marketing,* November 18, 1991, p. 18.

13. J. Gadd, "Women Gain More of Employment Pie," *Globe & Mail,* August, 9, 1995, p. A1; J. Marney, "Complex Female Market," *Marketing,* October 7, 1991, p. 14.

14. J.J. Marshall, L. Duxbury, and L. Heslop, "Grocery Shopping and Food Preparation in Dual Income Families: Implications for Marketing," *Marketing,* vol. 15 (ed. B. Smith), ASAC, 1994, p. 41; C. Kim, "Working Wives' Time-Saving Tendencies:

Ownership, Convenience Food Consumption, and Meal Purchases," *Journal of Economic Psychology* 10, 1989, pp. 391–409; W.K. Bryant, "Durables and Wives' Employment Yet Again," *Journal of Consumer Research* 15, June 1988, pp. 37–47; M.H. Strober and C.B. Weinberg, "Working Wives and Major Family Expenditures," *Journal of Consumer Research*, December 1977, pp. 141–47; "Strategies Used by Working and Non-Working Wives to Reduce Time Pressures," *Journal of Consumer Research*, March 1980, pp. 338–48.

15. J. Marney, "Measuring the Macho Market," *Marketing*, October 14, 1991, p. 22; J. Marney, "A New Masculine Force Is Emerging in the Marketplace," *Marketing*, April 29, 1985, p. 12.

16. J. Meyers-Levy and D. Maheswaran, "Exploring Differences in Males' and Females' Processing Strategies," *Journal of Consumer Research* 18, June 1991, pp. 63–70; R.N. Maddox, "The Importance of Males in Supermarket Traffic and Sales," *Marketing*, vol. 3 (ed. M. Laroche), ASAC, 1982, pp. 137–43.

17. P. Martineau, "Social Class and Spending Behaviour," *Journal of Marketing*, October, 1958, pp. 121–30; L.H. Mathews and J.W. Slokum, Jr., "Social Class and Commercial Bank Credit Card Usage," *Journal of Marketing*, January 1969, p. 73; S.M. Clarke, F.G. Crane, and T.K. Clarke, "Social Class and Adolescent Buying Behaviour," *Marketing*, vol. 7 (ed., T.E. Muller), ASAC, 1986, pp. 309–16.

18. G.S. Kindra, M. Laroche, and T.E. Muller, *Consumer Behaviour: The Canadian Perspective*, Toronto: Nelson Canada, 1994, Chapter 12.

19. C. Lawrence, S.J. Shapiro, and S. Lalji, "Ethnic Markets—A Canadian Perspective," *Journal of the Academy of Marketing Science*, Summer 1986, pp. 7–16.

20. C.M. Schaninger, J. Bourgeois, and W.C. Buss, "French-English Canadian Subcultural Differences," *Journal of Marketing*, Spring 1985, pp. 82–92; A. Joy, C. Kim, and M. Laroche, "Ethnicity as a Factor Influencing Use of Financial Services," *International Journal of Bank Marketing*, Vol. 9, 1991, pp. 10–16.

21. R.D. Tamilia, "A Cross-Cultural Study of Source Effects in a Canadian Advertising Situation," *Marketing 1978* (ed., J.M. Boisvert and R. Savitt), ASAC, 1978, pp. 250–56.

22. J. Lynn, "Approaching Diversity"; "Montreal Ethnics Focus of New Study," *Marketing*, March 5, 1984, pp. 12–13.

23. "Focus on the Chinese in Canada," *The Financial Post*, November 18, 1994, pp. C1–C24; J. McElgunn, "Wave of New Ethnic Media Is Announced," *Marketing*, September 4, 1994, p. 3; J. Pollock, "Opening Doors of Opportunity," *Marketing*, September 18, 1995, pp. 17–24.

24. J.N. Sheth, "Marketing Megatrends," *The Journal of Consumer Marketing*, Summer 1983, Volume 1, no. 1, pp. 5–13.

25. J.L. Lastovicka, J.P. Murry, Jr., and E.A. Joachimsthaler, "Evaluating the Measurement Validity of Life Style Typologies with Qualitative Measures and Multiplicative Factoring," *Journal of Marketing Research* 27, February 1990, pp. 11–23.

26. M.F. Riche, "Psychographics for the 1990s," *American Demographics*, July 1989, pp. 25–31.

27. Reproduced with permission from "New VALS 2 Values and Lifestyles Segmentation," *Stores*, 1989, p. 37. Copyright © The National Retail Federation. All rights reserved.

28. A. Mitchell, "Affair with Divorce Shows Signs of Cooling," *Globe & Mail*, March 23, 1992, pp. A1–2.

29. J. McElgunn, "Foot Puts Boot to Current 'Life-Cycle' Trends," *Marketing*, June 15, 1992, p. 7.

30. M. Strauss, "Retirees Will Have Big Bucks to Spend," *Globe & Mail*, March 17, 1992, p. B7.

31. "Affluentials: The Class Mass Market," *Marketing Communications,* December 1983, pp. 17–21.

32. "Torlée Targets Marketing in the 1990s," *Marketing,* December 9, 1991, p. 6.

33. R. Haley, "Benefit Segments: Backwards and Forwards," *Journal of Advertising Research,* February/March 1984, pp. 5–22.

34. P. Thirkell, "Opinion Leadership and Attitudes towards Fashion of Female Consumers: A Segmentation Study," *Developments in Canadian Marketing* (ed. R.D. Tamilia), ASAC, 1979, pp. 66–67.

35. E. Hirschman and M.B. Holbrook, "Hedonic Consumption: Emerging Concepts, Methods and Propositions," *Journal of Marketing,* Summer 1982, pp. 92–101.

36. R. Maynard, "Satisfaction Guaranteed," *Report on Business Magazine,* January 1988, p. 58.

37. J. Nesbitt and P. Aburdene, *Megatrends 2000* (New York: William Morrow and Company, 1990), p. 18.

Retailing Research

After reading this chapter, you should be able to:

1. Discuss the issues involved in gathering, analyzing, and presenting data for retail decision making.

2. Highlight the types of internal and external secondary data useful to retail managers.

3. Identify sources of secondary data for retail managers.

4. Describe the primary data collection process.

5. Highlight the components of a merchandising information system.

6. Discuss the role of environmental scanning in developing and implementing retailing strategy.

7. Explain the evaluation and control mechanisms helpful in assessing retail performance.

Scanning equipment offers major benefits to retailers, including research.

Courtesy Tokyo Electric Canada Ltd.

A major component of the success of retailers is to make correct decisions based on the best information available. Research properly conducted provides valuable information to retailers. Consider the following examples:[1]

- Research can help the retailer find answers to questions such as: How is store loyalty created? How does the use of smell (e.g., freshly baked goods) or music affect the customer's impression of the store? How many shoppers make their final decisions while in the store (the answer is over 80 percent)?

- Research can assist in determining merchandise selection and pricing: for example, customer brand loyalty continues to decline, and 60 percent of grocery shoppers think that generics are just as good as manufacturers' brands, and they would pass up their preferred brand in favour of a cheaper one. In addition, 1 in 10 shoppers regularly patronizes discount "club" stores such as **Price Club/Costco**, and 38 percent of these shoppers have household incomes of **$50,000** and over.

- **Research can also help check the complex system of hotel services. For example, consultants with formal training in the hospitality industry posed as guests and tested every feature of the service from wake-up calls to cleanliness. The resulting 200-page report provided a comparison of the hotel against its competitors, and included examples of $250 rooms where no one changed the sheets!**

- **Finally, planned research helps retailers generate sales on a continuing basis: for example, the many uses of identification codes help retailers (1) keep track of their sales (by scanning the UPC codes on products) on a daily basis, (2) through loyalty programs, such as Air Miles, find out who is buying what, (3) get paid immediately thanks to debit cards, and (4) thanks to people meters, find out what television programs are being watched, including the commercials.**

These examples illustrate the many uses of research by the modern retail firm. It is clear that research plays a role in understanding customer behaviour, and in evaluating the quality of service. ■

A strategic plan can be no better than the information on which it is based. In today's highly competitive environment, the need for better information becomes essential to the success of retail strategy. Retail managers need information on consumer market trends, competitive actions, and customer perceptions of each element of the firm's and competitors' retail strategies.

Information Needs of Retailers

Retail managers need information to add to their intuition and experience as they make decisions within the firm's external and internal environments. The **external environment** consists of the political, social, technological, and economic forces surrounding the organization. The **internal environment** consists of forces at work within the organization. *Internal information* is information generated within the retail business. *External information* is information about outside factors that may affect the business on a regular basis. The key external factors on which information may be needed include technological trends, legislative trends, work force availability, and the actions of potential competitors. Examples of internal information include financial resources, company strengths and weaknesses, and merchandise quality.

Information needs vary widely within an organization because of the various responsibilities of managers. The level of detail needed in data analysis, the frequency of data use, the need for updating, and the source and uses of data differ depending on the purpose of the activity. A chief executive officer needs one type of data when making high-risk, strategic decisions, whereas lower-level management requires different kinds of data to make detailed, practical, policy-based decisions. Some examples are as follows:

- *Monitoring sales by merchandise type:* Data are needed frequently and are available from internal sales records. The data can be used to decide which types of merchandise to reorder.

- *Monitoring the sales levels of retail salespeople:* Such data are evaluated often on a monthly basis to determine whether salespeople are meeting their quotas.

- *Evaluating the actual percentage of markdowns and expenses:* This is compared to the objectives established at the beginning of the year.

- *Obtaining information on demographic and lifestyle trends, forecasts of interest rates and inflation, and likely technological changes* that will affect the firm. Such data can be used in planning new store locations, in repositioning the firm, and in planning expansion into new markets.

Strategic issues in gathering and analyzing data

Management gathers and analyzes data to help avoid surprises, to develop benchmarks for objective evaluation, and to identify opportunities that might not otherwise be available. Any time a firm begins research, management must decide (1) what data are needed, (2) what priorities should be established, and (3) what indicators should be monitored. Similarly, management must decide how data will be analyzed, and how the resulting information will be presented. The overall process for gathering data and transforming it into useful information occurs in the context of a retail decision support system.

The Retail Decision Support System

A **retail decision support system** is the structure of people, equipment, and procedures to gather, analyze, and distribute the data that management needs for decision making. Depending on the size of the retail firm, such a system may vary from very informal to very formal and structured. The important point is that the firm must have an ongoing procedure to provide simple statistics, to allow for statistical analyses to be undertaken, to develop new products and services, and to measure advertising effectiveness.[2] In addition, the availability of inexpensive microcomputers, and the development of accompanying software can provide retailers, whatever their size, with tools that were once only available to large firms.[3] Retail Highlight 5–1 describes in detail how a small chain developed a system to improve the effectiveness of its retailing mix.

The components of a retail decision support system, shown in Figure 5–1, include (1) data sources, (2) a merchandise information system, (3) a management information system, and (4) model building.

The **data sources** include internal data, secondary data, and primary data. **Internal data** help management systematically determine what's going on in the firm. Examples include records of customer complaints, reports on out-of-stock items, analysis of customer charge accounts, information from warranty cards, and observations of customer traffic flow in a store. **Secondary data** are existing data that have been previously collected for their own purposes, but may help answer some management problems. Secondary data are gathered by groups or organizations and made available to the retail firm. Examples include census

Improving Effectiveness with an "Accountable" System

Perfect Portions, a chain of 11 Southwestern Ontario stores, is enjoying dramatically increased sales on a much leaner marketing budget thanks to an "accountable" system developed by consultant Tri-Media Marketing & Publicity. The idea behind the system is to analyze promotion, product, and purchase data to fine tune the firm's marketing mix.

First, Tri-Media asked 1,500 customers, using in-store questionnaires, where they saw their most recent Perfect Portions ad. Tri-Media director Albert Iannantuono discovered that flyers and newspaper ads were the most effective media, so all other media, including radio, were dropped, generating important savings in promotional spending. The effectiveness of the flyer program led to the launch of a newsletter to promote sales items and offer new product information and recipes. This newsletter generated chainwide sales increases. The in-store survey also revealed that the average shopper patronized a Perfect Portions store every two weeks, so all specials were harmonized to last two weeks.

Tri-Media also introduced a coupon coding system to evaluate the effectiveness of the various media. Based on the coupon tally, more customers redeem flyer coupons than newspaper ones, suggesting a 60-40 mix of coupons to be produced in favour of flyers.

Next, the stores' electronic cash registers were replaced by point-of-sale computer systems linking registers with PCs, and forwarding individual store information to the head office in Welland for analysis and interpretation. By using a Lotus spreadsheet covering 2,000 products and sales variables, owner André Champagne knows the traffic count by the hour, the number of featured items sold, and what other products were also sold at the same time. "From the data, we try to figure out why a customer bought something." For example, after a flyer offered a 1.4 kg box of chicken fingers for $0.99 with every box purchased at the regular price of $17.99, sales went up 1,300 percent. Comparisons with other promotions indicated that customers respond more to "buy one, get one at a special price" offers than straight discounts. In addition, the system revealed that, excluding chicken fingers, sales-per-customer almost doubled during the special.

Source: J. Low, "Results-Based Promotions Help Retailer Beat Cross-Border Blues," *Profit*, September 1991, pp. 47–48.

data from Statistics Canada, data from syndicated services such as A.C. Nielsen, and trade association data. **Primary data** collection occurs when the firm must collect data because neither internal nor external sources can supply the data the firm needs. Examples include analysis of the firm's image, the effectiveness of promotion, and competitors' merchandise assortments.

Merchandise information systems are computer-based systems that provide retail managers with better and faster information on their merchandising activities. The system can provide a series of reports that allow retailers to find quick answers to issues such as establishing seasonal plans, measuring performance against plans, order management, vendor analysis, price revisions, and sales promotion evaluation.

Management information systems have a broader focus than merchandising issues. They are designed to provide information on operating and macro environments and to aid in evaluation and control. Operating environments include competitors, customers, suppliers, creditors, and shareholders. The macro environments include the economic and resource environments, technological environment, social environment, and legal environment. Evaluation

Figure 5–1   The Components of a Retail Decision Support System

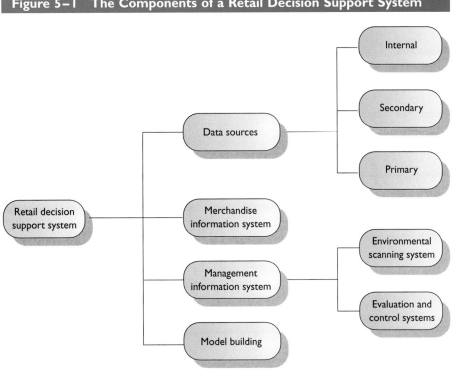

and control involves the application of various measures such as financial ratios in monitoring organizational performance.

Model building includes the application of statistical principles in the analysis of data important to management. The models use primary, secondary, and internal data as inputs. Examples of model building include developing sales forecasting models, site evaluation models, and performance effectiveness models. Computers are usually used to help generate these models.

Data sources[4]

Internal data

Internal data are probably the least expensive type of data. Some data generation, such as sales by merchandise line, can be provided on a daily basis, whereas other data may be collected only periodically.

As shown in Figure 5–2, internal data can be developed from (1) customer feedback, (2) salespeople, (3) an analysis of customer charge accounts, (4) consumer panels, and (5) financial records.

Customer feedback   Customer feedback can include information obtained based on product returns, warranty cards, coupon redemptions, or customer service records. Customer correspondence, such as complaint letters, can also provide useful information on product quality and service problems.

Customer records are essential as part of database marketing, as shown in Retail Highlight 5–2. **Database marketing** is the use of customer-specific

Figure 5–2   Examples of Internal Information Sources

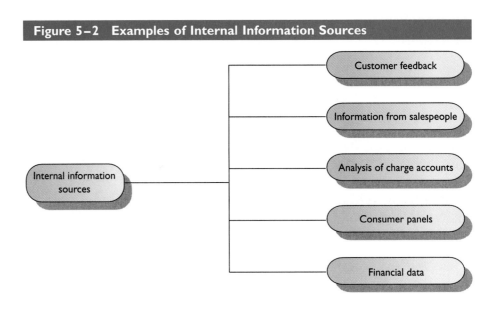

information to allow retailing programs to be narrowly targeted to specific groups of customers.[5] As an example, Sears keeps track of the purchases made by each of its customers who use its store credit card, other credit cards, its mail-order business, and its brokerage and insurance units. These files are merged to give Sears a powerful marketing tool that helps identify needs, increase revenues, and win customer loyalty.[6]

Information from salespeople   Salespeople have the closest continuing contact with customers. They are in the best position to recognize shifts and trends in consumer demand. Salespeople can be especially important in providing information on missed sales opportunities because of merchandise that was out of stock or that the firm does not carry.

Many retailers require salespeople to complete "want slips" each time a customer requests merchandise the retailer does not stock. Managers also have regular meetings, some even daily, with salespeople to generate suggestions, criticisms, and feedback, which are not easily communicated by a written system.

Analysis of charge accounts   Retailers who maintain their own credit systems have a highly valuable source of information. These records can form the basis of consumer surveys to determine why some accounts are relatively inactive and others very active. Lists of customers can also be used to test special mailings or merchandise and to track consumer purchases over time. Plotting the addresses of credit card holders is also an inexpensive way of estimating a store's trading area.

Consumer panels   Retailers sometimes assemble panels of consumers to elicit information for making better merchandising decisions. The following are two common types of consumer panels:

1. *The continuous-purchase record panel*   Such panels consist of groups of consumers who record their purchases of particular types or brands of products on a continuing basis. The panels provide valuable information on any changes that may be taking place in consumer purchasing of products and brands.

Retail Highlight 5–2

Database Retailing: Strengthening Relationship Marketing

Years ago, retailers were on a first-name basis with most of their customers. They understood their tastes, needs, and preferences, and strived to meet them. Retailing over the years has become more impersonal and transaction focussed. The consequence is that management today often knows little about their customers and has difficulty building and maintaining customer loyalty.

The new electronic technologies are allowing retailers to once again customize merchandising strategies at the store level. The core of database retailing is the name and address of each customer, purchase frequency, and the amount, recency, and type of merchandise purchased. Computer technology then allows retailers to develop detailed customer buying profiles and to predict selling opportunities by customer segment. Buying behaviour profiles should be combined with information such as the customer's age, income, distance from the store, and other measures of purchase potential. Retailers can then use the integrated databases to develop promotion plans consistent with the customers' lifestyles and consumption patterns as reflected in prior purchases. For example, purchasers of fishing equipment are also probably candidates for camping or other outdoor equipment.

Toys "Я" Us started buyer clubs—some for kids, others for parents and grandparents—anchored in their databases. The key is the extent to which the customer can be recognized as an individual, not simply as a member of an income bracket or geographic market. Targeted groups of customers can be identified as recipients for customer newsletters, educational programs, frequent buyer award programs, and customer clubs, to strengthen customer relationships.

Source: Based on "Targeting the Right Customers," *Enterprise*, Winter 1991-1992, pp. 30–34.

---

2. *The consumer advisory panel* A selected group of consumers can be used by the retailer to give its opinion on a variety of matters, ranging from possible new products that the store should consider carrying to store services and policies and advertising copy. With respect to merchandise assortment planning, the consumer advisory panel can be a good source of ideas for decisions regarding product additions or deletions.

Financial data   Financial data can reveal a wealth of useful information. Such information can include sales trends over time by merchandise lines, profitability by merchandise lines and departments, frequency of maintained markup by merchandise line, and information on merchandise turnover. Other valuable information can be obtained on vendors, such as which vendor is offering the best financial terms, the relative popularity of selected brand names by vendor, the frequency of unfilled orders, or orders that have been incorrectly filled.

Secondary data

Information published by various sources helps management determine what is going on outside the firm. As shown in Figure 5–3, information is available from (1) syndicated services; (2) government reports; (3) guides, indexes, and directories; (4) trade associations; and (5) computerized searches.

Syndicated services   **Syndicated services** specialize in collecting and selling information to clients, either financial or market information.

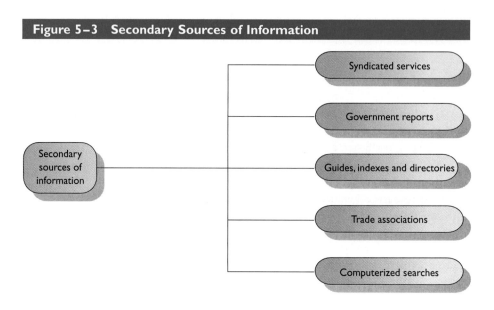

Figure 5–3   Secondary Sources of Information

Financial data   The major suppliers of financial data are provided in Table 5–1. For example, Dun & Bradstreet provides average operating ratios of various companies. *The Financial Post* annually publishes its Survey of Markets, and the *Globe & Mail Report on Business* publishes the Top 1000 Companies in Canada.

Market data   Such information may be in the form of store audits, warehouse withdrawal services, or consumer purchase panels. One of the most widely known firms providing such information is the A.C. Nielsen Company. Nielsen-type data on product movement is tracked by retailers to determine which merchandise is most popular with various consumer market segments.

An important source of syndicated information is related to electronic scanning of product purchases at the checkout. The use of scanners has been greater in the supermarket than in other sectors of retailing. Today, more than 90 percent of dry groceries are marked with the universal product code (UPC), as well as more than 85 percent of the merchandise stocked by deep-discount stores.[7] Products equipped with the familiar bar code, when passed over a laser beam scanner, allow management to capture detailed information far more quickly than was possible before the bar-coding system was developed. The data captured includes brands and sizes of products purchased, prices paid, and frequency of purchase. Such information on product movement can help management quickly drop slow-moving items and increase shelf space allocated to more popular items.

Some firms have developed systems that allow product purchases to be identified with specific households. Retailers are then able to determine differences in product sales by household characteristics. Product promotions can then be targeted to households that have been shown to be the best markets for the items. Systems like these offer several benefits:

- Automatic purchase recording is more accurate than conventional research techniques of keeping a diary or interviewing consumers.

- Response rates are high since respondents' work is simplified. This makes the data more representative of the population.

Table 5–1 Typical Secondary Sources of External Information

Statistics Canada (available in printed and electronic formats)

1. Census of Canada: conducted every five years, it contains detailed information on population by census tract, enumeration area, and census subdivision.
2. Reports on Commerce, Construction, Finances, and Prices: cover the retail trade.
3. Reports on Employment, Unemployment, and Labour Income.
4. Income Tax data, including the *Taxfiler* data, can be obtained by Forward Sortation Area (FSA, first three digits of postal codes).
5. *Market Research Handbook:* published yearly.

Other Government Sources

1. Consumer and Corporate Affairs: conducts studies on consumer problems and regulations; publishes the *Misleading Advertising Bulletin.*
2. Public Archives of Canada: provides information on machine readable format.
3. Federal Royal Commission Reports.
4. Health and Welfare Canada: provides information on families with children (including their age) and Canadians 65 and over.
5. Provincial Governments: references are listed in the ProFile Index.

Syndicated Commercial Information

1. Financial data: *Financial Post,* Moody's, Dun & Bradstreet, and Standard & Poor's.
2. Market data: Store audit panels (Nielsen's Retail Index Services), consumer panels (Market Facts of Canada, International Surveys, Dialogue Canada), various market reports (Maclean Hunter Research Bureau), market data (Financial Post Survey of Markets), psychographics (Polk/Compusearch).

Other Published Sources

1. Trade and Professional Associations: *Supermarketing, Progressive Grocer, Journal of Retailing,* etc.
2. Indexes and Directories: *Canadian Periodical Indexes, Business Periodical Index, Canadian Trade Index, Fraser's Canadian Trade Directory, Canadian Directory of Shopping Centres,* etc.
3. *Handbook of Canadian Consumer Markets.*

Sources: Adapted from D. Huck, "Some Data on Data Sources," *Marketing* (October 11, 1993), pp. 11–12; R.Y. Darmon, M. Laroche, and K.L. McGown, *Marketing Research in Canada,* Toronto: Gage (1989), Chapter 5.

- Perhaps the greatest advantage is that a kind of information is provided that has hitherto been unavailable—what people didn't buy. Researchers know what alternatives were open to the consumer in the scanner stores. What is bought can be related both to previous history and to those alternatives.

Scanner-store panels are taking over as the usual form of manually tracking product sales auditing. It is possible to track very small markets and to change item specifications retrospectively. Among the major developments of this technology are the following:

1. Data are automatically transmitted by telephone line to the computers analyzing the figures, then on to the retailer, and in turn for use by the sales clerks.[8] This makes data available according to the clients' needs: weekly, daily, or even hourly. They are truly continuous data. The collection of in-store information about promotions, stockouts, facings, and so forth also becomes a normal part of a store's own requirements.

2. Instead of predetermined regions, users are able to specify their own area requirements in relation to sales regions, climatic regions, or income characteristics. They also are able to pick out groupings of towns or districts for tests.

Other new services also promise retailers greater insight into the hearts and minds of consumers. During the past decade, new research tools, such as the categories developed by Compusearch, Goldfarb, VALS (Stanford), or Thompson, Lightstone, have been introduced to track changes in consumer attitudes and lifestyles.

These methods track shifts in consumer lifestyles and are providing information about consumer behaviour that has made it easier to implement market segmentation strategies based on lifestyles, as described in Chapter 4. The emphasis on these services is on the "nonrational, emotional aspects of decision making, as well as the kind of information that can be obtained from such techniques as trade-off modelling and conjoint analysis. The services have emerged as retailers began to realize that there is more to understanding the consumer than just demographics and turned to lifestyle and psychographic information to 'explain some of the things that previously weren't explainable' by demographic analysis."[9]

Government reports   Provincial and federal governments maintain detailed information on many aspects of the economy that can be useful to management. Among the censuses conducted by Statistics Canada are the Census of Canada, as well as surveys covering many areas, including retail trade. Examples of these publications of interest to retailers are *Family Expenditures in Canada, Retail Trade, Operating Results* (various categories), and *Direct Selling in Canada.* Results of these and other studies are available in virtually every library. The *Marketing Research Handbook* also contains such information in capsule form, including average sales per square metre for various categories of retailers.

Provincial agencies typically publish similar information at the provincial level.

Guides, indexes, and directories   Other valuable sources of external information include guides, indexes, and directories. Examples of such information are also shown in Table 5–1. Guides such as the *Canadian Periodical Index* provide complete references by subject matter to articles in a wide array of journals. Specialized indexes such as the *Financial Post Index* or the *New York Times Index* provide information for those specialized sources only and are available as computerized databases. Finally, the *Canadian Trade Index* is an index for information on specific companies and industries.

Directories are often helpful in identifying diverse sources of information. For example, the *Fraser's Canadian Trade Directory* is organized by industrial sectors. Other directories, such as the *Canadian Directory of Shopping Centres,* provide detailed information on shopping centres of various sizes and regions of Canada.

Trade associations   Most retailers belong to trade groups that collect and publish data for association members. For example, the Grocery Products Manufacturers of Canada published a research report entitled *Grocery Attitudes of Canadians,* based on research conducted by Dialogue Canada.[10] Such information can be useful for comparing the retailer's performance to industry averages. Associations may also publish annual industry forecasts that can be used as a guide to firms making their own forecasts. As well, the Retail Council of Canada is an association that actively promotes the interests of retailers to governments, the public, and manufacturers.

Computerized searches   The amount of new information generated each year is multiplying so quickly that keeping up-to-date in a specialized field can be difficult. New journals are started each year, specialized reports appear, and information of interest is published in literally thousands of often obscure publications. Organizations specializing in abstracting, storing, and retrieving such information by subject area are thus often the starting point in information development by management. These computerized databases often contain thousands of items by subject, which are available for quick retrieval. Organizations may subscribe to the specialized services for an annual fee or may pay a research firm a fee to retrieve information on a project-by-project basis. The required information is often available through library online searches, Internet searches, or CD-ROM searches (e.g., Canadian Business and Current Affairs, ABI/Inform, and Statistics Canada's CANSIM).[11]

Strengths and weaknesses of secondary data

Secondary data can be gathered quickly and inexpensively, although using them can present problems. Some data—for example, a survey on attitudes toward the environment—may become out-of-date, as such attitudes may rapidly evolve in response to external events (e.g., an oil spill or illegal dumping of chemicals).

Another problem is a lack of standardized reporting units. One organization may define the West as British Columbia, the Yukon, and the Northwest Territories; another may say the region also includes Alberta. Both organizations use the West as the unit for reporting, but the information is not comparable. Similarly, various organizations may use different breaking points in reporting information by age or income.

Another issue is the accuracy and objectivity used in collecting the data. Management should go to the source of external data whenever possible. This reduces the possibilities for errors made in publishing the information. Management also needs to know the magnitude of sampling errors and possible nonsampling errors. Were the persons gathering the data qualified to do so? What was the motive for gathering the data? A chamber of commerce, for example, might present only positive information about a community. Similarly, advocacy groups such as the Canadian Pharmaceutical Association tend to publish only information favourable to their causes.

However, despite these problems, secondary data are a very valuable research tool for retailers.[12]

Primary data collection

When management cannot find what it needs to know from any existing source, it must generate first-hand information. For example, among the research projects Sears conducts at the corporate level are studies of credit, public relations, and home installations. Similarly, Eaton's corporate research department conducts economic research to track economic trends and help evaluate sales trends, and consumer research to determine consumer attitudes and buying habits. Large retailers such as Sears and Eaton's conduct new-product research with the same vigour that manufacturers do. Advertising is also subject to the same intensive scrutiny.[13]

In this section the focus is on primary data-gathering activities. Primary data collection can take many forms: observation, exploratory research, surveys, or experimentation.

Observation

Observation can be an accurate method of collecting certain information. Competitors, for example, will not volunteer information on their prices, in-store displays, and other promotional efforts. Observing competitors is the only way to collect such information. Also, observation may be the least expensive way to collect certain types of data.

Methods of observation can be classified into 1 of 5 categories: (1) natural or contrived situation, (2) open or disguised observation, (3) structured or unstructured observation, (4) direct or indirect observation, and (5) human or mechanical observation.

Natural versus contrived situation   Natural observation occurs when management records the normal shopping behaviour of consumers without intervening in the shopping process. A *natural situation* for data collecting occurs when researchers observe the characteristics of individuals who enter or leave a retail outlet in a specified time period.

A *contrived situation* occurs when management observes the reaction of salespersons in an artificially created stressful situation. Thus, management might send an individual disguised as a shopper to pose a particularly difficult problem for a sales clerk to see how the person will react.

Open versus disguised observation   An example of *open observation* is a supervisor observing the sales presentation of a retail salesperson to a prospective customer. *Disguised observation* occurs when researchers act as salespeople and mingle with the shoppers to observe how they handle merchandise, move up and down aisles, and generally react to various in-store displays.

Structured or unstructured observation   *Structured observation* occurs when an individual is given a checklist or questionnaire to use in observing behaviour or a situation. For example, management might have a checklist for evaluating the cleanliness of company-owned gasoline service stations. Similarly, management might have a checklist to determine whether employees are adhering to dress codes. *Unstructured observation* occurs when an individual is told to observe a particular situation and record whatever is of interest.

Direct versus indirect observation   Using mechanical counters to identify the volume of traffic moving past a location is one of the most frequent uses of *indirect observation* by management. Using cameras to record shopping patterns within a store for later analysis by management is a similar example. *Direct observation* would involve the use of humans to record the same information.

An example of structured, direct observation   Shopping the competition is a time-honoured dimension of the retailers' marketing intelligence system. Merchants tend to look at six elements when shopping competitor stores: (1) shifts and emphasis in merchandise classifications, (2) stock content, (3) display and presentation, (4) pricing, (5) traffic patterns, and (6) service. Most competing stores today carry basically the same merchandise. Management thus needs to check the competition and find out what everybody else is doing that might be different. Retailers can be quite aggressive in their competitor shopping programs. As one individual observed, "Hit or Miss will do anything, as long as it's legal, to get a leg up on the competition... We'll buy merchandise at a competitor if we can't recognize the source. We'll do whatever it takes to find out who a resource is and what a direction is. We're there to find out."[14]

Exploratory research

Management may not be able to carefully specify the problem about which it is concerned. In such situations, exploratory research is needed to help define the problem. **Exploratory research** *is characterized by flexibility in design and the absence of a formal research structure.* Management, in seeking to more carefully define a problem, may obtain some qualitative information from three major sources:[15]

1. Evaluate data either internal or external to the firm. Internally, there may be reports and sales analyses that may assist the manager in more clearly defining the problem. Externally, some secondary sources may contain information bearing on the situation faced by the manager: for example, trade publications may explain that consumers are becoming more environmentally conscious and that they may avoid buying certain types of products.

2. Talk to knowledgeable people about the issue. These may include some suppliers, other retailers, and even customers. The retailer may even ask 8 to 12 suppliers, customers or noncustomers, to meet around a table to talk informally about the issue, with the assistance of a trained interviewer. This is called a **focus group,** and it is often used because it is a quick and inexpensive way to obtain qualitative information.[16]

3. Observe the behaviour of consumers who may be making purchase decisions. If necessary, this may be followed by an in-depth interview, using a trained interviewer, to ascertain some of the reasons for the behaviour.

Once the problem has been defined, a formal research design may be necessary to collect the data on which to base a decision. Such efforts may involve survey research or experimental designs for determining the presence of cause-and-effect relationships.

Survey research

Survey research often includes the collection of information on the opinions or perceptions of persons in a market segment of interest to management. The process can be quite complex. For example, developing a questionnaire, normally the first step in survey research, is an art one can best learn by experience. Many different decisions have to be made. Survey research is probably the most frequently used method of data collection by management. The major steps in survey research must answer the following questions:[17]

- *Objectives:* What are the objectives of the survey?
- *Questionnaire:* What information should be collected to meet these objectives?
- *Sample:* From whom will the information be obtained?
- *Survey method and organization:* How will the information actually be collected?
- *Analysis and reporting:* How should the data be prepared for analysis, analyzed, and the findings be reported?

Questionnaire development

The **questionnaire** used for the survey must respond as closely as possible to the information needed by the retail manager. In developing a questionnaire, a number of decisions must be made:

Question format   Questions can be either *open-ended,* in which the respondents are simply asked to give their opinions without a formal response structure, or *close-ended,* in which response choices are prespecified.

Open-ended questions   An example of an **open-ended question** is:
What is it that you like most about shopping at Loblaws?

Closed-ended questions   Closed-ended questions may use one of five popular formats:

Dichotomous, which pose yes or no answers, for example:
Do you shop at Eaton's at least once a month?
YES _____   NO _____

Multiple choice, which allow a respondent to choose from among several predetermined answers, for example:
Which of the following stores do you shop at most often for your shoes?
Bata _____   Kinney's _____
Ingledew's _____   Other _____

Likert scale, which allows respondents to express their level of agreement or disagreement with various statements, for example:
Canadian Tire offers the best selection of bicycles in this city.

Strongly Disagree	Disagree	Neither Agree nor disagree	Agree	Strongly Agree
_____	_____	_____	_____	_____

Semantic differential scale, which allows respondents to select the point representing the direction and intensity of their feelings between two bipolar words, for example:
How would you describe Harvey's Restaurants?

Clean ___ ___ ___ ___ ___ ___ ___ Dirty
Friendly ___ ___ ___ ___ ___ ___ ___ Unfriendly

Importance scale, which allows the respondents to indicate the level of importance they attach to an attribute, for example:

When I go grocery shopping, free parking is:

Extremely Important	Very Important	Somewhat Important	Not Very Important	Not at All Important
1	2	3	4	5

Number of questions   The number of questions to be included in a questionnaire is often a function of the type of data collection that will be used: few if by telephone, more if by mail, and even more if by personal interview. In addition, in a questionnaire dealing with a "fun" subject (like cars), more questions may be added.

Content of the questions   Only questions for which one may expect relatively accurate answers should be asked. An example of questions that will elicit inaccurate answers is: How many times did you go to a restaurant last year? (it would be extremely difficult to estimate in most cases). In addition, sensitive issues should be avoided or worded differently: these involve age, income, personal issues, etc. For example, instead of asking: What is your age? _____, it is better to ask:

In which age category do you fall?
15-24 _____   25-34 _____   35-44 _____   45-54 _____   55-64 _____

Order of the questions   The order of the questions should be logical, avoid biasing the answers, and make the questionnaire easier to answer. The first questions should be simple, just to make the respondent feel at ease. Questions should be placed so that the answer to one does not influence the answer to a subsequent one. Open-ended questions are usually placed toward the end, as well as classification questions (such as age, income, education).

Sample selection

Sampling is also often a major part of both survey and experimental research. The **sample** chosen can be either nonprobability or probability.

Nonprobability samples   *Nonprobability samples* are chosen in such a way that each unit does not have a known chance of selection, and thus they cannot be evaluated using standard statistical techniques. Nonprobability samples do not allow management to make the assumption that the sample is representative of the overall population.

The most common nonprobability sample is a **convenience sample.** When using convenience samples, researchers simply talk to the most readily available individuals. Convenience samples are often used in the preliminary testing of a questionnaire to make sure that respondents understand and can answer all the questions.

Probability samples   **Probability samples** are those in which each sampling unit has a known chance of selection, and it has been selected using a random procedure. Probability samples allow researchers to select samples in such a way that the results of the findings are representative of the group in which management is interested.

A simple **random sample,** a special type of probability sampling, is selected so that each sampling unit has an equal chance of selection. For example, a researcher who was going to choose a sample from the telephone directory

Table 5–2 Strengths and Weaknesses of the Most Frequent Means of Respondent Contact				
Issues	**Mail**	**Telephone**	**Personal**	**Computer**
Cost per subject	Low	Low	High	Low
Amount of time required	Large	Small	Medium	Small
Response rate	Low	High	High	Low
Ability to collect complex data	Good	Poor	Good	Good
Control over responses	Poor	Good	Good	Good

would first have to number each telephone listing in the directory and then select the sample from the list of household numbers using a standard table of random numbers (found in any statistics book).

A **systematic sample** is often chosen when researchers want a probability sample because it is simpler to generate (i.e., you do not need to refer to a table of random numbers). In systematic sampling, researchers choose a random beginning—for example, the 4th listed number in the telephone directory—and then choose every nth number thereafter. Thus, if management decided on a 10 percent sample, the first telephone number chosen would be the 4th, the second one the 14th, the third the 24th, and so forth.

Using an **area sampling** is often a useful way for retailers to obtain a representative sample of the trading area for the store (which may not be possible or feasible with the telephone directory, for example). First, the retailer defines the trading area on a map; next, some blocks are randomly selected (for example, census tracts or enumeration areas); third, some streets are randomly selected; and finally, houses or apartments are either systematically or randomly selected. Questionnaires are then distributed or administered door-to-door to the selected addresses.

Data collection

The next step is a decision on how the data are to be collected. The four primary methods of contact with respondents are (1) personal interviews, (2) telephone interviews, (3) mailed questionnaires, and (4) computer interviews. Personal interviews can be conducted either at the respondents' homes or in central locations, such as shopping malls. Each of the four methods of contact has unique strengths and weaknesses, as shown in Table 5–2. Management weighs these strengths and weaknesses in choosing the method most suited to its needs.

Personal interviews   Personal interviews are expensive and time-consuming but allow interviewers to get more information than do the other methods. Personal interviews often are the only way to collect data if researchers need to demonstrate merchandise or to use visual aids.

Telephone interviews   Telephone interviewing is the quickest of the four methods. However, the amount of time the respondents are willing to spend on the telephone often is limited, the questioning process must be kept simple, and the use of visual aids is not possible.

Mailed questionnaires   Mailing questionnaires, the slowest of the four methods, is the least expensive. A major drawback, however, is the lack of control over who responds to the questionnaire. Researchers may want responses from adult males over 18 years of age. A mailed survey gives researchers no assurance that such an individual actually responds to the questionnaire. Response rates are also low, often less than 20 percent.

Computer interviews   Computer technology also has made possible in-store survey research by means of electronic push-button questionnaires or touch-screen computer (also called interactive kiosks)[18] for a fraction of the cost and time of personal interviews in malls or households. This technology allows management to measure consumer perceptions of retail service performance, store image, and advertising effectiveness. The equipment is positioned in a prominent location in an outlet. Signs invite customers to express their viewpoints on the issues of interest to management. The machine can tabulate customer responses by count, computer averages, and cross tabulations. The result can be a fairly sophisticated analysis of the data.

Field work

Careful control over the persons involved in data collection (**field work**) is necessary. Researchers must guard against cheating and ensure that sampling instructions are followed and that callbacks, if necessary, are made according to a predetermined plan. Essentially, management wants to be sure that the most representative set of data possible is collected.

Even in the best of circumstances, some potential respondents will refuse to cooperate and others will not be at home. Plans must be made for substituting for such persons. Careful training of interviewers is necessary to minimize the biases that can enter the data collection process because of the interviewer's attitudes, preconceived notions about the research findings, or the degree of care with which they conduct the interviews.

Experimental methods

Some issues on which management wants information may not be resolved easily by survey research. Experimental research may be the only way to answer such questions as: What is the effect of a reduction in price on sales levels? Which of several advertising themes is most preferred by customers? Which of several package designs is the most effective in stimulating sales?

Experimental designs allow management to infer cause-and-effect relationships in variables of interest. Thus, management seeks to rule out explanations for changes in a variable such as sales (a dependent variable) other than those caused by changes in such variables as price or advertising (independent variables). For example, field experiment can answer the question: How does a small retailer measure the profitability of a couponing promotion?[19]

Ruling out alternative explanations for change in a dependent variable such as sales is important to management. Unless other explanations can be eliminated, management might mistakenly assume that a 10 percent reduction in the price of a carton of soft drinks would increase sales from 20 to 25 units per week. Part of the five-unit change, however, might be caused by unusually hot weather during the week of the research. Such a possibility must be evaluated if management wants to determine whether the increase in sales is due either in whole or in part to the reduction in price. Establishing cause-and-

Canada Trust uses interactive kiosks to learn what customers think of its services.

Courtesy Canada Trust

effect relationships is quite difficult because of the possibility of intervening variables.

Retailers can use a before/after experimental design with a control group to measure the reaction of demand to price changes in a product. In the research design shown in Table 5–3, the retailer selects two stores that are

Table 5–3 A Research Design	Before/After with Control	
Measurement	**Test Group (Store 1)**	**Control Group (Store 2)**
Measurement of sales before price change (sales)	Yes (10)	Yes (10)
Price reduction of 10 percent	Yes	No
Measurement of sales after price reduction of 10 percent (sales)	Yes (20)	Yes (15)

matched in terms of customer profiles, management, policies, store size, and other features so that they are as similar as possible. Unit sales in both stores are then determined for the product of interest. Since the stores are matched, the level of sales should be the same—10 units in each outlet. The price level for the product in Store 1 is reduced by 10 percent and left unchanged in Store 2. At the end of the specified period of time, sales are measured in both stores. As noted, sales increased from 10 units to 20 units for the store in which the price was reduced. However, sales also increased from 10 units to 15 units in the store for which the price was not reduced. This five-unit increase was due to various forces beyond the control of management and probably would also have occurred in Store 1 even without the reduction in price. The net effect of the price reduction was five units: 20 − 15 = 5.

In another example, an unobtrusive field experiment in four supermarkets found that price-elasticity differed sharply between stock-up (i.e., frequently consumed) and non-stock-up (i.e., perishable or infrequently consumed) items. The first group of items showed much higher price elasticity than the second one.[20]

Test markets

Regional or national retail chains test products or store concepts on a limited basis (**test market**) to help decide on whether to make changes in the merchandise mix, decor, store layout, or similar variables. Management may test colour schemes, price points, or menu variations before introducing the changes in all outlets, as for example, McDonald's Restaurants testing their pizza in Montreal, prior to national rollout (in Canada and then in the United States). Major test cities are, among others, Peterborough, Sherbrooke, and Edmonton.

Test marketing assumes that the results obtained from the test cities can be projected to the national market, which may be questionable if the test cities collectively are not representative of Canada. For example, would success of the McDonald's pizza in Montreal guarantee success in Toronto, Winnipeg, Calgary, Vancouver, or Halifax?

However, retailers may learn more about customers' reactions to the new concept (leading to improvements), and they can pre-test alternative strategies such as pricing or promotion (using several cities, with one set of alternatives per city).

Nevertheless, test marketing is difficult, risky, and expensive in Canada because of its diversity of lifestyles and geographic cultures.

Model building

Sophisticated retailers are moving beyond ad hoc research investigations and are building models that allow them to simulate various dimensions of their businesses and answer the "what if" questions that are becoming necessary in today's environment. Many retailers use sophisticated models to forecast sales, test the price elasticity of selected merchandise, and plan the size and timing of promotions.

Such systems may have built-in models that allow management to conduct "what if" analyses to determine whether an idea makes sense before it is implemented throughout the organization. Inventory control specialists who think that a new item is similar to one from the previous year might access the model for the previous year's item and then use it to develop forecasts for the new one.

Information Systems

Recall from Figure 5–1 that additional components of the retail decision support system are the merchandise information system and the management information system. Such systems tend to be technology driven. Today, virtually all retail decisions, including on-the-floor activities, merchandise replenishment, inventory control, and other essential dimensions of implementing competitive strategy, are computer driven. Personal computers have proliferated throughout retailing and have helped to streamline decision making.

The new retail technology, however, has a language all its own that anyone interested in retailing today must understand.[21]

Understanding the terminology

Retailers used mechanical cash registers for many years to ring up sales and make change. The original purpose of the cash register was to reduce employee theft by having cash under the control of one employee.

The first machines were really adding machines set on top of a cash drawer. A clerk pushed buttons and cranked an arm to enter information into the register. Later versions displayed the price of each item in large numbers for both the clerk and customer to read. Finally, mechanical registers printed a record of each sale and calculated the amount of change due.

Electronic cash register The **electronic cash register** (ECR) was introduced in the 1960s. The ECR uses electric light beams to enter information at high speed. More and more ECRs are being used as part of a computer support system to provide management with up-to-date reports. The equipment has the ability to store data and transfer it from one location to another.

The new electronic technology has brought about changes in the way merchandise is marked, the way money and credit are handled, and the way the merchant works with financial institutions and vendors. ECRs produce increased savings through better inventory management, reduction of under-rings at the cash register, and higher labour productivity.

POS in-store technologies A **point-of-sale (POS) cash register** is the input device for many retailing systems. A POS device scans and records a variety of information when a transaction occurs. The information is stored and can be called up whenever it is needed. The system can reveal which merchandise, styles, and colours are selling best.

Scanning and wanding   **Scanning** and **wanding** are the most widely used methods of data entry at the POS terminal. More than 90 percent of the retailers in a survey were scanning at the point of sale. In addition, more than 50 percent were scanning goods with hand-held scanners on the shelf or rack, and 25 percent were scanning goods as part of backroom inventory.[22] Scanning began in supermarkets, where bar codes are read by a fixed slot scanner. Wanding has been used primarily in general merchandise retailing. Many items in general merchandise retailing, such as apparel, cannot easily be passed over a fixed slot scanner.

Hand-held scanning and slot scanning (fixed scanning) are now roughly comparable in cost. The result is a mixture of fixed and hand-held scanning in retail outlets. Fixed scanners are typically used in the front of the store. Hand-held scanners are more likely to be used in individual departments. A combination of fixed and hand-held scanners is typically used in the back areas for such functions as receiving and marking.

One factor fuelling the drive for automation is the emergence of industry standard systems that allow retailers to create their own software. Such software can be developed by the vendor, the retailer, or an independent third party, who then offers it on a standard industry platform.

The universal product code.   The **universal product code** (UPC) is the marking standard in both food and general merchandise retailing. Most people are familiar with the small black-and-white bars on supermarket and general merchandise items. The bars are codes that contain information about the product and the manufacturer. The bar codes are passed over an electronic scanner, and the information is transferred into computer memory for later retrieval.[23] Computers may then automatically update the store's inventory, look up the price of the item in question, print a receipt for the customer, or perform other functions. UPC scanner and marking systems offer the following benefits:

1. Improved accuracy.
2. Improved customer satisfaction. Speed, accuracy, quietness, and the detailed receipt are consumer pluses.
3. Time and labour savings. Some stores report productivity gains of up to 45 percent when item-price marking is eliminated.
4. Improved inventory and financial control.

Scanning's greatest long-term benefit is its ability to generate totally new marketing information:

1. Accurate readings, item by item, of actual item movement at the point of sale.
2. Daily store-by-store readings of consumer buying behaviour.
3. Fast, accurate feedback on test-market experiments.
4. Measurement of the effects of marketing and promotional activity.

Most retailers thrive on the right assortment of merchandise, minimal inventory, and rapid turnover. The POS systems and scanner technology allow frequent and up-to-date information on product sales rates, stock outages, sales patterns, and similar information that can be grouped for buyers by department.

Universal Vendor Marking   **Universal vendor marking** (UVM) is a standard vendor-created merchandise identification system. The need to mark items at the store level can be eliminated largely by the use of such a standardized format. Indeed, much of the ticketing for Sears, Toys "Я" Us, Wal-Mart, and Provigo is now done at the vendor level.

Electronic data interchange   Retailers are increasingly using **electronic data interchange** (EDI) to communicate with vendors. (EDI is a computer-to-computer exchange of data.) Approximately 46 percent of retailers are using programs that electronically remit payments and invoice data directly to vendors.[24]

Wal-Mart and Price Club/Costco, among others, are using computerized direct store delivery systems requiring vendors to send invoice information electronically as part of a **quick response (QR) partnership. QR partnerships** require sharing of information between vendors and retailers to allow timely replenishment of inventory without the necessity of a large backroom inventory at the store level.

The systems use the **uniform communication standard** (UCS) codes developed by the Universal Code Council to allow direct exchange of information between the vendor and store computers. The generic standard in North America is ANSI X.12, and EDI FACT is the international standard.

Other common uses of EDI, in addition to processing payment, include order entry and materials management systems that keep track of shipments. Savings from EDI are of two kinds: the direct mechanical benefits and the indirect strategic benefits. The mechanical benefits include error reduction, the elimination of key entry, and reduced response time. The indirect benefits occur as a result of enhanced business systems capabilities.

The merchandise information system

No single merchandise information system can apply to all types of retailing. However, the concepts underlying such systems are the same for all retailing sectors. They include establishing design objectives and developing the necessary system modules.

Establishing merchandising objectives

Agreeing on merchandising objectives is a first step in taking advantage of the retail technology and information base available to merchandise planners. A typical objective is to facilitate planning and decision making at all levels to increase gross margins, reduce markdowns, and optimize inventory turnover. System design objectives logically flow from merchandising objectives.

Establishing system design objectives

Establishing system design objectives requires decisions about input, processing, and output design requirements.

Examples of *input requirements* include (1) the need to capture information for both units and dollars so that the financial and the unit control systems are in balance; (2) the need to capture information at an economically feasible level of detail; (3) system capability for both batch and on-line data entry functions; and (4) the ability to add classifications, departments, and merchandise divisions as needed.

Processing requirements include retention and maintenance of data files and security procedures so that information and data entry functions are provided only to authorized individuals.

Output requirements call for a system that limits the information provided on a regular basis, but that can provide additional information as needed.

Components

Agreeing on the components of the system is the final step. The components include a planning system, a processing system, and an information reporting system, as shown in Figure 5–4.

Planning system module   An online planning system allows merchandise planners to maintain an optimal inventory for meeting customer demands, keep purchases in line with the financial resources available, and provide the information needed at each selling location to meet merchandising objectives. The merchandise system works interactively, allowing executives to develop a seasonal merchandising plan for each merchandise classification. Modules of the system are designed to enable management to prepare seasonal plans in both units and dollars, monitor performance against the plan, and establish exception reporting and inquiry (results outside control limits).

Processing system module   A processing system includes all activities associated with the ordering, receiving, handling, and distribution of merchandise from the time the decision to buy is made until the items are available for sale in the store. The system requires five separate modules: order management, receiving and checking, marking, distribution, and systems control and monitoring, as shown in Figure 5–4.

Information reporting system module   An information reporting system allows merchandise planners to establish a record of sales and merchandise on hand and on order at multiple selling and nonselling locations. The information is available by store, merchandise, division, department, and class, as well as by vendor, style, colour, size, price, and perhaps other merchandise assortment characteristics. This information often is organized into such reporting modules as style status and summary reporting, vendor analysis, price revisions, merchandise replacement, and sales promotion evaluation.

The management information system

A management information system provides two additional sources of information that aid in decision making: information on operating and macro environments and assessments of performance at the department and store levels.

Environmental scanning

In addition to the data requirements just discussed, management also needs ways to identify long-term strategic problems and opportunities.

Critical environments to monitor for decision-making purposes are the operating environment and the macro environment. The **operating environ-**

Figure 5–4   Components of a Merchandise Information System

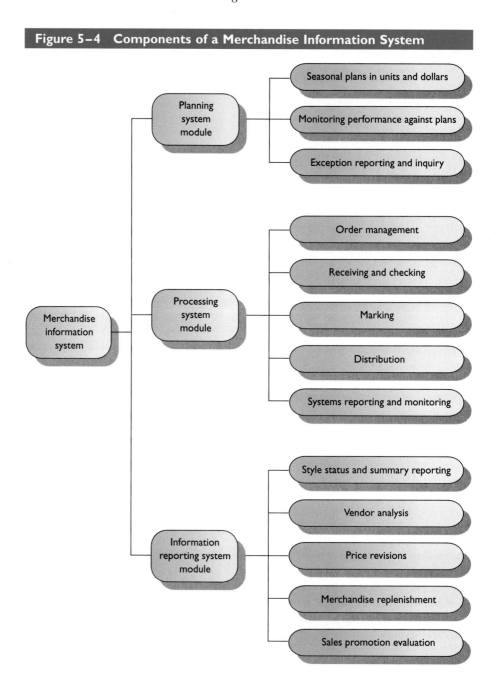

ment consists of all organizations or groups that either directly affect or are affected by the retailer's competitive strategy. Examples include customers, competitors, suppliers, and shareholders. The **macro environment** includes the larger forces beyond the control of the firm, such as technology or social trends, that can affect its future. The key to success is to recognize the implications of the identified factors for retail strategy.

The operating environment audit   This is an important task for management to perform. Key issues are highlighted in Table 5–4.

Table 5–4   Key Issues in an Operating Environment Audit

Customers

1. Can you describe the customer base for the retail sector of interest in such terms as age, income, stage in life cycle, lifestyle, or similar dimensions?
2. What is the projected growth in the primary customer base over the next five years?
3. Do customers see the merchandise sold primarily as impulse, convenience, shopping, or specialty goods?
4. What are the key customer shopping strategies for the merchandise?
5. What is the purchase frequency?
6. Are brands important to the customers?
7. Are customers in this retail sector prone to shop by mail, by phone, or in person?
8. Are the customers likely to make purchases more on a rational, or utilitarian basis, or more on the basis of ego satisfaction?
9. How do customers view the offerings of the various competitors? Which firm seems to be most differentiated from the competition?
10. Do buying decisions vary by market segment?
11. What attributes appear to determine patronage (e.g., price, merchandise, quality, or location)?

Competitors

1. Which are the primary competitors, and what are their market shares?
2. What are the financial and other resources of the primary competitors?
3. Does entry appear readily possible for another competitor?
4. What are the marketing and positioning strategies of the various competitors?
5. Are the competitors part of a vertical marketing system? If so, what type of system?
6. Are any of the competitors especially innovative or aggressive?
7. Do any of the competitors appear to have unique cost advantages? If so, why?
8. Which competitors are leaders, and which are followers?

Suppliers

1. What is the power of key suppliers?
2. Are key suppliers likely to practice forward integration in the near future?
3. How important is the retailer to the supplier?
4. Are alternative sources of supply readily available?
5. How difficult would it be to switch suppliers?

Shareholders

1. Are shareholders satisfied with the dividend structure if the firm is publicly traded?
2. Is there any evidence of shareholder dissatisfaction about the social responsibility and environmental sensitivity policies of the firm?
3. Is the level of community involvement at the local level sufficiently strong?

Important *customer issues* include size of and trends in the market, key customer shopping strategies, the nature of customer buying decisions, and factors affecting patronage.

Key *competitor issues* include trends in the market shares of primary competitors; the strength of the competition; positioning strategies of the competition; unique cost advantages, if any, of competitors; and which competitors are leaders and which are followers.

The behaviour of *suppliers* must be carefully evaluated. Suppliers can become powerful competitors if they engage in a process of forward integration,

Table 5–5   The Ingredients for a Macro Environmental Audit

Economic/Resource Environment

1. What are the current and forecasted rates of inflation?
2. What is the forecasted real growth in the economy for the next few years?
3. What are the likely influences of foreign competition?
4. Are raw materials essential to the products of the firm likely to be in short supply or to be available only at increasing prices?
5. Are growth rates for the offerings of the firm (if the firm is geographically dispersed) likely to vary widely by regions of the country over the next few years?
6. What are the trends in unemployment?
7. What are the trends in energy, construction, and rental costs?
8. What are the likely effects of import quota and tariff changes?
9. What are the likely effects of a lower/higher dollar on importing/exporting goods?

Technological Environment

1. Is new technology on the horizon that will require the firm to expend large sums of money to remain competitive?
2. Are electronic funds transfer, two-way interactive television, and similar advances likely to pose a challenge?
3. Are near-term product substitutes likely to be developed?

Social Environment

1. What are the current and likely future pressures from consumerism as they relate to the firm under analysis?
2. What are the current trends in consumer lifestyles, and how are these likely to affect the firm?
3. What are the population trends among the age groups that are primary markets for the firm?

Legal Environment

1. Are pending actions by the regulatory agencies likely to affect the firm in the near future?
2. Is the firm likely to be vulnerable to affirmative action measures, equal credit opportunity regulations, or privacy regulations?
3. Are the firm's pricing, promotion, and product safety actions in compliance with existing regulations?

for example, and establish retail outlets. They can also be of critical importance if only a few suppliers exist, giving them strong bargaining power with the retailer. Similarly, suppliers have substantial power if the retailer would encounter large switching costs in changing suppliers.

Shareholders can be important in determining both short-term and long-term marketing plans. Managers of publicly held companies must always keep the market value of the company stock in mind when developing corporate strategies. Concerns over social responsibility, environmental sensitivity, and similar issues can influence retail strategy, as we saw in Chapter 2.

The macro-level audit   A macro-level assessment must include evaluation of economic and resource factors, technological factors, and social and legal environments, as discussed in Chapter 2. Key issues are highlighted in Table 5–5.

Changes in the macro environments are important because they are often accompanied by changes in customer preferences, which, in turn, may require major changes in the strategic priorities of the firm.

Scanning the *economic and resource environment* consists of an assessment of trends in inflation, the nature of the business cycle, import quotas and tariffs, and similar issues. For example, accelerating unemployment with an attendant drop in consumer purchasing power characterizes a recession. Consumers in such situations are less likely to spend resources on leisure activities but to accelerate do-it-yourself projects.

The *social and cultural environments* reflect the beliefs and values that guide the thoughts and actions of individuals and organizations. These beliefs and values change over time and can alter consumer preferences and marketing practices. Consumerism was a driving force in the 1970s, as was social activism. During the mid- to late-1980s, concern over AIDS dramatically changed the patterns of sexual behaviour for many people and the resulting marketing programs for some retailers. Environmental sensitivity is a driving force in the 1990s that is guiding the consumption patterns of many consumers.

The *legal and political environments* affect every dimension of the retail firm from merchandising to promotion to location. Regulations may prohibit or discourage certain practices, permit previously prohibited practices, or provide new and unique opportunities. The changes reflect society's changing expectations, which can significantly alter supplier or customer relationships.

Technological changes can significantly affect the relationship between customer and retailer. New and improved technologies can lead to dramatic shifts in customer preferences. Technology can also affect every dimension of the marketing mix.

Assessing performance

Assessing performance needs to occur throughout the organization as part of a retail decision support system. The measures may occur on a daily, weekly, monthly, quarterly, or annual basis, depending on the dimensions of performance being evaluated. Profitability analysis, for example, may be conducted quarterly, or even monthly, to measure the performance of various merchandise lines or departments. In contrast, the appropriateness of competitive strategy may be evaluated every three to five years.

A variety of control devices can be used to track performance and may be implemented at either the departmental level or the store level. Store level measures include customer feedback, market share analysis, and operating ratio analysis. Departmental level measures include analysis of sales variance and sales-to-expense ratios.

Store-level controls   Continuing *customer feedback* is necessary for sound management decisions. Customer surveys can be undertaken, for example, to establish the organization's actual image, compared with the one desired by management; customer perception of the friendliness and competence of the sales staff; and the level of customer satisfaction with after-sale service, the merchandise mix, and similar dimensions.

Management often focusses on sales growth as a measure of performance. Such an analysis is not sufficient unless it tells management how the firm is performing relative to its competition. If a firm's *market share* is increasing relative to its competitors', the organization probably is on firm ground. Still, care and attention are necessary in evaluating such information.

Early warning indicators of problems are important. Monitoring selected *financial ratios* can help determine whether problems are developing. The reason the ratios are important is that an organization is essentially a pool of cash, and the objective of the firm is to effectively manage cash flows. Comparisons of ratios to similar stores as reflected in published trade data can alert management to problems. We advise managers to become familiar with industry-specific information for their line of retailing. For more on financial ratio analysis, see Chapter 19.

Department-level control measures   **Sales variance analysis** enables management to compare actual sales to sales goals. A variance analysis can then be conducted to determine why the firm is outside target limits.

A periodic evaluation of the **sales-to-expense ratio** can also help management determine whether the firm is either overspending or underspending in its efforts to reach sales targets. Disaggregated ratios can include the ratio of sales force costs to sales, advertising to sales, sales promotion (such as displays and in-store sampling) to sales, and sales administration to sales. Such expense ratios should be charted, and upper and lower limits established. When a ratio exceeds either limit, management needs to determine why the deviation is occurring.

Ethics and the Use of Information

Ethics should always be the foremost issue when management is collecting and utilizing research-based information. Some of the ethical issues involve the question of confidentiality of the respondents, the use of surveys as a disguised means of selling, misrepresentation of results, and truthfulness in advertising.[25]

In addition to the moral aspects of questionable behaviour, adverse publicity will almost always affect the profits of the firm.

Chapter Highlights

- **The transition from a merchandising to a marketing orientation increases the need for quality information ranging from data on consumer market trends and competitive actions to market share measurement and measurement of consumer perceptions.**

- **The components of a retail decision support system include data sources, a merchandise information system, a management information system, and model building.**

- **The data sources of a retail decision support system include internal data, secondary data, and primary data.**

- **Internal information is probably the least expensive source of data and can be developed from customer feedback, by feedback from salespeople, by** analysis of charge accounts, by the use of consumer panels, and by analysis of internal financial data.

- Frequently used secondary sources of information include information available from syndicated services, government reports, guides, indexes and directories, trade associations, and computerized bibliographic searches. One of the most promising sources of syndicated information is emerging as a result of the rapid advances in electronic scanning of product purchases at the checkout.

- Primary data collection can take many forms, including observation, exploratory research, survey research, and experimental research.

- Observational approaches to data collection can be natural or contrived, open or disguised, structured or unstructured, direct or indirect, and human or mechanical.

- Survey research is the collection of information on the opinions or perceptions of market segments of interest to management. The process includes questionnaire development, sample selection, data collection, and field work.

- Experimental methods allow management to make inferences about cause-and-effect relationships in data. Such efforts can be especially important in pricing decisions, in shelf space allocation decisions, and in merchandise-mix decisions.

- The cash register and the computer are two of the major electromechanical inventions that have occurred in the history of retailing. This technology is affecting almost every aspect of retailing, including merchandise management, buying, pricing, promotion, location, operations, and personnel.

- The point-of-sale (POS) terminal allows all sales data to be captured at the point of sale. The data can then be recalled for processing and analysis to give management timely, detailed information to aid in decision making.

- Scanning and wanding, electronic data interchange, and standardized communication technologies are among the newer technologies affecting retailing.

- A retail decision support system is useful in helping the retailer to plan and implement marketing strategy and to assess the success of the strategy implementation decisions.

- The new retail technology has allowed the development of merchandising information systems to assist in all dimensions of the merchandising process. Such systems typically include a planning system module, a processing system module, and an information reporting system module.

- Environmental scanning allows management to identify long-term strategic problems and opportunities. Retailers are usually interested in assessing trends in the operating and macro environments. Operating environment issues include customers, competitors, suppliers, and shareholders. Macro environment issues include the economic and resource environments, social environment, legal environment, and technological environment.

- Assessing performance is also an important dimension of the management information system. Performance is assessed through both store-level controls and departmental-level control measures. Examples of store-level controls include customer feedback, market share analysis, and operating ratios. Departmental-level control measures include sales variance analysis and analysis of sales-to-expense ratios.

Key Terms

area sampling 136
convenience sample 135
data sources 123
database marketing 125
electronic cash register 140
electronic data interchange 142
environmental scanning 143
experimental design 137
exploratory research 139
external environment 122
field work 137
focus group 133
internal data 123
internal environment 122
Likert scale 134
macro-environment audit 146
merchandise information
 systems 124
observation 132
open-ended question 134
operating-environment audit 144
panel 126
point-of-sale (POS) cash register 140

primary data 124
probability sample 135
questionnaire 134
quick response partnership 142
random sample 135
retail decision support system 123
sales variance analysis 148
sales-to-expense ratio 148
sample 135
scanning 141
secondary data 123
semantic differential scale 134
survey research 133
syndicated services 127
systematic sampling 136
test market 139
uniform communication
 standard 142
universal product code (UPC) 141
universal vendor marking
 (UVM) 142
wanding 141

Discussion Questions

1. What is the difference between primary and secondary data?
2. What are the various stages and decision areas involved in developing an effective merchandise information system?
3. What are some internal sources of information available to retailers?
4. What secondary sources are available to retailers?
5. How does exploratory research differ from survey and experimental research?
6. Define these terms: probability sample, nonprobability sample, convenience sample, and random sample.
7. Discuss the advantages and disadvantages of telephone interviews, personal interviews, mailed questionnaires, and computer interviews as methods of contact with respondents.
8. Explain the differences among the five most popular types of closed-ended questions. Under what conditions should each one be used?

Application Exercises

1. Visit the library and list all the indexes or directories. Note the kinds of information contained in each. Project this exercise into the future and predict how you might use each index or directory in a specific kind of work with a retailing company.

2. Work with your university or college bookstore (or some other retailer with whom you or your instructor have a good relationship) and identify an "image problem" the outlet experiences. Define the problem; devise a questionnaire to seek answers (assuming it is a problem for which a survey may be helpful) or an observation sheet for in-store research; collect and analyze your data; write up your findings; and present conclusions to the retailer.

3. Interview a retailer in each of the major "kinds" of businesses, such as grocery and department stores. Determine the "image" that person perceives of retailing as a career opportunity. Summarize the perceptions; generalize your findings; present conclusions and recommendations.

Suggested Cases

8. Diego's
9. The Undercover Agency
19. The Gourmet Palace

Notes

1. J. Marney, "Moment of Decision Is in the Store," *Marketing*, September 28, 1987, pp. 13–14; M. Strauss, "Brand Loyalty Losing Impact with Shoppers," *Globe & Mail*, April 14, 1992, p. B8; M. Evans, "The Tricky Art of Changing Formats," *The Financial Post*, January 13, 1992, p. 3; R. Maynard, "Satisfaction Guaranteed," *Report on Business Magazine*, January 1988, pp. 58–64; "Supermarket Big Brother Is Watching," *The Kitchener Record*, February 11, 1995, p. C4; D. McKay-Stokes, "Too Close for Comfort," *Marketing*, September 15, 1995, pp. 11–13.

2. T. O'Brien, "Decision Support Systems," *Marketing Research* (December 1990), pp. 51–55.

3. "Many Software Programs Available, but Customized Often Yields Best Results," *Marketing News* (February 18, 1991), pp. 11, 22.

4. For more details see R.Y. Darmon, M. Laroche, and K.L. McGown, *Marketing Research in Canada*, Toronto: Gage, 1989, Chapter 5.

5. "A Potent New Tool for Selling: Database Marketing," *Business Week* (September 5, 1994), pp. 56–62.

6. M. Mayer, "Scanning the Future," *Forbes* (October 15, 1990), pp. 114–117.

7. G. Rowan, "Deciphering the Bar Code," *Globe & Mail* (August 3, 1993), p. A7.

8. S. Fortin, op. cit.; L.N. Gold, "Support the Sales Staff with Scanning Data," *Marketing News*, April 10, 1989, pp. 2, 5.

9. J.J. Louviere and R.D. Johnson, "Reliability and Validity of the Brand-Anchored Conjoint Approach to Measuring Retailer Images," *Journal of Retailing* 66, 4, Winter 1990, pp. 359–382.

10. Grocery Products Manufacturers of Canada, *Grocery Attitudes of Canadians*, 1988, Don Mills, Ontario.

11. E. Campbell, "CD-ROMs Bring Census Data In-House," *Marketing News* (January 6, 1992), pp. 12, 16.

12. T. Powell, "Despite Myths, Secondary Research Is a Valuable Tool," *Marketing News* (September 1, 1991), pp. 28, 33.

13. "Using Computers to Divine who Might Buy a Gas Grill," *Wall Street Journal* (August 16, 1994), pp. B1, B6.

14. J. Abend, "Busman's Holiday," *Stores,* July 1982, p. 37.

15. Darmon, Laroche, and McGown, *Marketing Research in Canada,* pp. 95–98, 101.

16. S. Kelman, "Consumers on the Couch," *Report on Business Magazine,* February 1991, pp. 50–53.

17. Ibid., pp. 150–58.

18. A. Kryhul, "You Ought to Be in Kiosks," *Marketing,* June 6, 1994, pp. 11–12.

19. R.G. Chapman, "Assessing the Profitability of Retailer Couponing with a Low-Cost Field Experiment," *Journal of Retailing* 62:1, Spring 1986, pp. 19–40.

20. D.S. Litvack, R.J. Calantone, and P.R. Warshaw, "An Examination of Short-Term Retail Grocery Price Effects," *Journal of Retailing* 61:3, Fall 1985, pp. 9–25.

21. "Partners in Survival," *Marketing* (August 1/8, 1994), p. 17; "How to Get Wired," *Business Week* (October 17, 1994), pp. 242–244; "All You Need to Go Online," *PC World* (June 1995), pp. 141–152.

22. Ernst & Young Survey of Retail Information Technology Expenses and Trends, as reported in *Chain Store Age Executive,* September 1991, p. 42.

23. G. Rowan, "Deciphering the Bar Code."

24. Ernst & Young Survey.

25. Darmon, Laroche, and McGown, *Marketing Research in Canada,* pp. 461–469.

PART

Developing the Retail Strategy

In *Part 2, Developing the Retail Strategy,* the conceptual, financial and organizational aspects of the retail strategy are systematically developed. Chapter 6 deals with strategic planning, as a method of defining the objectives of the firm, and deciding how to compete. To compete successfully, retailers need to understand how to start and finance a retail business (Chapter 7). Franchising as a means of owning and operating a retail firm is examined in detail (Chapter 8). Chapter 9 discusses the critical issues in the recruitment, selection, training, and motivation of retail employees, as well as organizing the retail firm.

6.   **Strategic Retail Management**

7.   **Starting and Financing a Retail Business**

8.   **Franchising**

9.   **Developing the Human Resources Plan**

Strategic Retail Management

Chapter Objectives

After reading this chapter, you should be able to:

1. List the steps involved in strategic retail planning.

2. Understand the concept of an organization's mission statement.

3. Evaluate the issues involved in a situation analysis.

4. Identify the major strategic alternatives available to retailers.

5. Discuss the factors involved in deciding on markets in which to compete.

6. Review the components of retail positioning strategy.

7. Understand the implementation of the strategy.

8. Discuss the issues involved in evaluating and controlling retail operations.

HMV's strategy has led to increased sales and profits.

Courtesy HMV Canada

The battle for leadership in the $1.5 billion music retail industry has led to brutal competition since HMV entered the arena. In 1991, A&A Records and Tapes filed for bankruptcy (it was reborn and went bankrupt a second time in 1996), Discus Music World went bankrupt, and many independent music retailers went out of business. HMV, part of a massive British conglomerate, opened its first Canadian store in 1987, but the intense competition really began with the launching of its flagship Toronto store in 1991. By the end of 1991, HMV's 51 stores sold more than $100 million in CDs, cassettes, and videos, closing in fast on the market leader, Sam the Record Man, which sold about $135 million in its 140 stores. For 1995, HMV's 80 stores sold more than $225 million in CDs, cassettes, videos, and computer software, surpassing Sam the Record Man (now in third place) and Music World with its 110-store chain.

These "big three" face new and formidable competition. Future Shop, the computer and appliance chain, added CDs to its product mix in 1994 and sells the top hits at discount prices. More recently, Tower, the giant U.S. chain, opened its first Canadian superstore in Toronto, and Virgin Records from the United Kingdom plans to open 15 to 20 stores in the near future. The mail-order segment, dominated by Columbia House and BMG Direct, has captured about 25 percent of all record music sales in Canada with the popular "buy one CD, get nine free" type campaigns.

The Canadian music retailing industry has experienced dramatic changes in the past few years—the shift from records to CDs and cassettes, the dramatic increase in video and computer software sales, the changing demographics—yet many retailers sell their product with little innovative marketing or customer service.

HMV continues to shake up the industry by pursuing an aggressive strategy that includes the following elements:

- Location—many stores are located in upscale shopping centres across Canada on very favourable terms (shopping centre developers are keen to have HMV with many retailers falling into bankruptcy).

- Atmosphere—from the displays, to banks of video screens, to "listening posts" where customers can play the latest hits, to in-store concerts, HMV provides a new experience for shoppers.

- Customer service—from the helpful, knowledgeable staff who are re-warded, in part, based on the store's performance.

- Selection—a wide and targeted selection provided by the staff, many of whom "run" a part of the store and decide what titles to carry in their particular section.

- Prices—on average higher than other chains like Sam's because HMV decided that customers would be willing to pay something extra in terms of helpful staff and a broad selection.

- Product mix—HMV added a computer software department because its young staff are convinced that serving the Internet and personal computer market is going to be "as big as the music business."

The strategy has led to greater sales and profit increases for HMV than for any other music retailer in the industry. Since he opened HMV in Canada, the president, Paul Alof (who left in 1995) had a goal: to make HMV the number one music retailer in Canada. The goal was accomplished but the continuing challenge for the new president is to remain on top.

The success of any strategy depends on how the retailer implements its plan and meets the needs of customers. In a highly competitive market a well-designed and well-executed strategic plan is essential for survival and growth.[1] ■

Strategic planning includes defining the overall mission or purpose of the company, deciding on objectives that management wants to achieve, and developing a plan to achieve these objectives. HMV evaluated the retail music industry in Canada and identified strategies that would allow the firm to prosper and grow. The strategies will be implemented through pricing, promotion, and physical facility plans in order to accomplish the overall mission of the firm.

Figure 6–1 illustrates the steps involved in strategic planning. The plan begins with a statement of the mission or purpose of the organization. Objectives management wants to achieve are then established. An analysis of internal strengths and weaknesses and external threats and opportunities is

Figure 6–1   Strategic Planning

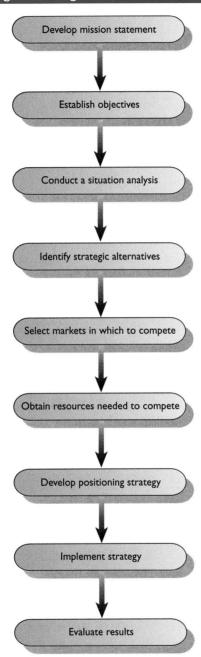

then undertaken to help management decide on the best way to carry out the organization's mission and to achieve its objectives. Next, management identifies the major strategic alternatives it could pursue. Markets in which to compete must be selected, and resources needed to compete must be obtained. A positioning strategy outlines how the organization will serve the needs of chosen markets. An important aspect of the positioning strategy is determining how the retailer will develop and exploit its competitive advantage. The strategy must then be implemented. Finally, results must be measured and evaluated to ensure that the strategy is working.

Defining the Mission or Purpose of the Organization

Management begins the planning process by identifying the organization's mission or purpose. The **mission statement** describes what the firm plans to accomplish in the markets in which it will compete for customers it wants to serve. A mission statement normally includes the following elements:

1. What products and services will be offered, what customers will be served, and what geographic areas will be covered.

2. How the physical assets, financial assets, and human resources will be used to create customer satisfaction.

3. How the firm intends to compete in its chosen markets.

The mission statement provides a clear sense of direction for the organization and distinguishes the firm from all others. Retail Highlight 6–1 provides

One of Mark's Work Wearhouse's goals is to provide quality products at competitive prices.

Courtesy Mark's Work Wearhouse

Retail Highlight 6–1

Canadian Retailers' Mission and Goal Statements

Many retailers today are focussing on customer satisfaction as their primary goal. Listed below are mission statements from a number of Canadian retailers. Which retailers seem to have adopted a mission of customer satisfaction?

Mark's Work Wearhouse provides quality name brand, private, and captive label products competitively priced and supported by active sales promotion. Our stores are easily accessible, one stop retail outlets offering a complete range of workwear, casual wear, and related apparel including custom uniforms.

The company's mission is to grow consistently as a mature and stable enterprise known for:

Being the most customer-sensitive and responsive specialty retail organization in the markets in which it operates.

Having a people-oriented work environment where people are allowed the greatest possible freedom to carry out their responsibilities, own what they do, have fun, learn, and earn fair financial rewards.

Providing a superior financial return to investors as a result of being customer driven and people oriented.

Empire (the diversified Canadian food and pharmaceutical retailer and distributor) has three components to its mission statement:

Goal: Empire is committed to building shareholder value through long-term profitability and growth by becoming a market leader in its core operating businesses and by investing in opportunities to augment this growth in value.

How: Empire will achieve this goal by treating employees in ways that create extraordinary customer service and shareholder value.

Value: Empire will be a good corporate citizen, upholding the highest standards of integrity and ethical conduct.

Sears Canada is a full-time, full-service department store and catalogue retailer dedicated to providing its customers with quality merchandise and exceptional service, coast to coast. Our vision is to be Canada's most successful retailer ... providing total satisfaction for our customers, opportunities for our associates to grow and contribute, and superior returns for our shareholders.

Canadian Tire's vision, which guides the daily activities and long-term strategy of the enterprise, is to be the best at what customers value most. To achieve the vision, the company's efforts will be dedicated to the mission—to be the first choice for Canadians in automotive, sports, leisure, and home products by providing total customer value through focussed assortments, competitive operations, and customer-driven service.

Le Château is a vertically integrated retailer of the latest fashion apparel at moderate prices. We adapt mainly European designs of clothing, accessories, and footwear for North American men and women. Our clientele is predominantly 15 to 30 years of age, although we continue to attract more consumers of all ages. Our ability to provide unique clothing and respond quickly to upcoming fashion trends is greatly enhanced by our vertical approach to retailing. In addition to extensive product development, approximately 70 percent of the Company's goods are manufactured in our Canadian production facilities.

The Bay's mission is to be Canada's best fashion department store by offering broad, dominant assortments, quality and value, fashion and trend leadership, a high level of customer service, and an unremitting guarantee of performance. *Zellers*' goal is to lower the cost of living for ordinary Canadians by dedicating ourselves to providing our customers with exceptional value—everyday.

Sources: Mark's Work Warehouse; Empire Company Ltd.; Sears Canada Inc.; Canadian Tire; Le Château; and Hudson's Bay Company *Annual Reports*.

examples of Canadian retailers' mission and goal statements, presented in their annual reports. Most of these retailers have more detailed mission statements that are provided to their employees.

Mission statements often reflect an organization's values or corporate culture. **Corporate culture** establishes the values of greatest importance to the organization. These are values on which emphasis is constantly placed. Often these values reflect the personal goals of top management. A firm's values are often stated in the company motto, as shown in the following examples:

> McDonald's: (QSCV) Quality, Service, Convenience, and Value. This slogan is emphasized to all employees as they are brought into the organization.

> Eaton's: Satisfaction guaranteed or your money refunded. This motto has been a policy of Eaton's since its beginning over 120 years ago.

Setting Objectives

Management's task, after agreeing on the mission statement, is to establish objectives. **Objectives** are statements of results to be achieved. Objectives may include profitability, sales volume, market share, or expansion results.

Management normally sets both long-term and short-term objectives. One- or two-year time frames for achieving specific targets are short term. Long-term objectives are less specific than short-term targets and reflect the strategic dimensions of the firm. Retailing is too dynamic to establish specific targets much beyond five years.

Good objectives are measurable, are specific as to time, and indicate the priorities for the organization. To illustrate, Mark's Work Wearhouse's specific goals related to profits, debt-to-equity ratio, current ratio, and other measures on an annual basis.[2] Examples of well-stated and poorly stated objectives appear in Table 6–1.

Table 6–1 Examples of Well-Stated and Poorly Stated Objectives	
Examples of Well-Stated Objectives	**Examples of Poorly Stated Objectives**
Our objective is to increase market share from 15 percent to 18 percent in 1997 by increasing promotional expenditures 15 percent.	Our objective in 1997 is to increase promotional expenditures.
Our objective for 1997 is to earn after-tax profits of $5 million.	Our objective is to maximize profits.
Our objective is to open three new units by 1997 in each of the following provinces where the chain presently has no units: Nova Scotia, New Brunswick, and Prince Edward Island.	Our objective is to expand by adding units to the chain.

Conducting a Situation Analysis

Once objectives are set, management must decide on a plan for achieving them within the context of the firm's mission. This plan is based on an analysis of the strengths and weaknesses of the organization and the threats and opportunities in the environment. This assessment of internal strengths and weaknesses and external threats and opportunities is referred to as a **situation analysis,** popularly known as SWOT analysis (strengths, weaknesses, opportunities, and threats).

Internal factors are those variables largely under the control of store management. Such factors include financial resources, physical assets (for example, buildings, display fixtures), management skills, sales force composition, merchandise lines carried, the reputation of the firm, and employee attitudes toward the company. The questions the retailer wants to answer are shown in Table 6–2.

External factors are those over which store management has very little or no control. The external environments on which management focusses were discussed in Chapter 2. These include the legal environment, the economic and social environments, the competitive environment, and the technological environment. Management examines trends in these environments and determines whether the trends pose threats or opportunities, or whether they have no relevance for the organization.

For example, Mark's Work Wearhouse views its performance management system, which includes setting objectives for all company employees, as a strength of the firm. The "On Concept" stores, which are large (10,000 to 15,000 square feet or 930 to 1,400 m^2) and have a dominant position in their retail location, are also a strength. Current weaknesses include poor performance of stores in the Quebec and Vancouver markets. On the external side, Mark's Work Wearhouse recognizes threats from "Big Box" retailers (large freestanding stores, like warehouse stores, that offer merchandise with limited service and an emphasis on price) and electronic shopping. Opportunities include the custom uniform, corporate wear, and winter workwear segments. Mark's has taken steps to address its threats and capitalize on its opportunities.[3]

Table 6–2 SWOT Appraisal	
Internal Appraisal	**External Appraisal**
Strengths:	*Opportunities:*
What is the firm's present position?	In what areas could success be achieved?
What is the firm good at?	What favourable environmental trends exist?
What major resources/expertise exist?	How are markets developing?
Weaknesses:	*Threats:*
What is the firm's present position?	Where is performance likely to suffer?
What are the major problems faced?	What unfortunate environmental trends exist?
What is the firm poor at doing?	How are competitors behaving and developing?
What major resources/expertise deficiencies exist?	

Source: Nigel Piercy, "Analyzing Corporate Mission: Improving Retail Strategy," *Retail and Distribution Management,* March/April 1983, p. 35.

The result of the situation analysis forms the foundation for identifying the major strategic alternatives. Management may stay the course and make only minor adjustments in strategy. In other instances major changes may be made in markets served and in strategies for serving the new markets. In the recession period in the early 1990s, many Canadian retailers made major changes to their strategies to reflect the harsh economic times. For example, the Oshawa Group, which operates Food City and supplies IGA stores, has reduced operating expenses by restructuring its stores, warehouses, and offices. As well, it is expanding its Price Choppers stores—standard size supermarkets that offer limited selections of groceries, fresh meat, and produce at lower prices. The Oshawa Group hoped to win back consumers who cut back spending, shopped more often in the United States, and sought bargains in discount warehouse-style stores.[4]

Identifying Strategic Alternatives

In broad terms, a retailer may consider pursuing one or more of four major strategic options; market penetration, market development, retail format development, and diversification (Figure 6–2). As well, retailers often refine their strategies through a range of productivity improvements.

Market penetration

Retailers following a strategy of **market penetration,** which targets existing market segments with existing formats, seek a differential advantage over competition by a strong market presence that borders on saturation. Market penetration is often used by retailers because it builds on the firm's existing strengths, which include knowledge of current customers and their preferences and the firm's familiarity with the merchandising lines. Such a strategy is

---

Figure 6–2   Major Retail Strategic Options

Retail format		Market segment	
		Existing	**New**
Existing		**Market Penetration** • Increase number of customers • Increase quantity purchased by customers • Increase purchase frequency	**Market Development** • Reach new segments with existing formats • Expand markets
New		**Retail Format Development** • Offer new retail formats to existing customers	**Diversification** • Develop new retail formats targeted at new segments

designed to increase (1) the number of customers, (2) the quantity purchased by customers, and (3) purchase frequency.

Increasing the number of customers

Strategies designed to increase the number of customers is one way of increasing sales and profitability. Adding stores and modifying in-store offerings can lead to more customers. Sears Canada has added new national brands, devoted more space to apparel, and added more private labels to attract more customers to its stores.[5] For years, Sobey's has added new stores in Atlantic Canada to increase its dominant position in this market. Sobey's also continues to remodel existing stores—making them brighter and larger—to attract more customers. As well, a penetration strategy could include the use of the retailing mix variables to ensure:

1. The lowest price lines and the lowest prices within the market area.
2. Extensive width and depth of consumer goods such as health and beauty aids and housewares.
3. Aggregate convenience including location, parking, hours, and ease of purchase; features such as supermarket-like front ends, total merchandise display, wide aisles, easy-to-see-and-locate merchandise groups, shopping carts, and usually a single display floor.

Increasing the quantity purchased

Improving the store layout and merchandise presentation can help to create an atmosphere that is conducive to more spending. Loblaws invests substantial sums to renovate existing stores to provide a comfortable shopping environment, and has expanded produce, seafood, deli, and bakery departments to get more customers into the stores and to increase the quantity purchased.[6] Another approach is to encourage salespeople to cross-sell. Cross-selling involves salespeople from one department attempting to sell complementary merchandise from other departments to their customers. For example, a salesperson who has just sold a pair of dress pants to a customer would take the customer to the shirt and tie area to sell the customer a shirt and tie that complements the pants.

Increasing purchase frequency

Toy supermarkets such as Toys " Я " Us, the U.S. chain with 56 stores in Canada, have been quite successful in implementing strategies designed to increase purchase frequency. The firm offers a complete selection of items that sell year-round. Customers know that when they buy a toy at Christmas they will find a good selection after Christmas to accommodate returns. Toys in the low- to medium-price ranges, often with strong licensed characters and video games, provide sales day in and day out. High-impulse items like peg-boards, die-cast toys, and hobby kits lead to high customer traffic. The firm capitalizes not only on birthdays and Christmas but also on other holidays and special occasions like Valentine's Day, Easter, Halloween, and back-to-school.

Market development

A strategy of **market development** focusses either on attracting new market segments or completely changing the customer base. Market development

Loblaw introduces in-store
pharmacies to attract new
segments.

Courtesy Loblaw Company Ltd.

normally involves bolder strategy shifts, more capital, and greater risk than a
market penetration strategy. Examples of market development efforts include
reaching new segments and market expansion.

Reaching new segments

Fast-food restaurants provide a good example of the strategy of attracting new
segments in existing markets. McDonald's, through the years, has added
chicken, breakfast items, salads, pizza, and Tex-Mex dishes to their menu. This
helps attract consumers who are looking for something nonfried, less filling,
with lower calories, and more nutritious than many traditional fast-food offerings. Harvey's has broadened its product line to include sandwiches to attract
new segments. Tim Horton's has added muffins, soup, and sandwiches to its
doughnuts and coffee to attract new segments. McDonald's also seeks to reach
new segments by opening restaurants in unique, non-traditional sites including
hospitals, subway and train stations, and tourist areas. In the Toronto SkyDome,
McDonald's has four outlets, including one seating 600 people. Toys "Я" Us is
reaching a new segment with its Baby Boutique, an expanded merchandise line
of high-end nursery items for expectant parents.[7]

Market expansion

An effective strategy for many retailers is to expand on a geographic basis. The
basic premise is that if the store concept works in one locale, it should work in
another. Franchise retailers have successfully used geographic expansion for
many years. Probably one of the most interesting and well-documented franchise expansions was McDonald's Canada's expansion to Moscow. With over
1,000 outlets in Canada, in 1995, Tim Horton's has aggressively pursued market
expansion. The takeover of Tim Horton's by Wendy's will allow more rapid
expansion for Wendy's and Tim Horton's as they plan to open a number of

McDonald's introduces a new retail format; a limited menu outlet in a high traffic location.

Courtesy McDonald's Restaurants of Canada Ltd.

combo units (combining both Wendy's and Tim Horton's in one location) in both Canada and the United States.[8]

Retail format development

A retail format development is introducing a new retail format to customers. For example, Sears Canada has opened a number of freestanding furniture stores, called Whole Home, in Ontario, and plans to have up to 40 locations across Canada within a few years. At 3,252 square metres (35,009 square feet) the Whole Home Furniture Store has tripled the selling space for furniture, rugs, and decor items over what is offered by the typical Sears store. Sears Canada identified an opportunity for this kind of furniture store, which offers a wide range of value-priced and higher-end fashionable merchandise.[9] Other examples are fast-food retailers like McDonald's and Subway who offer limited menus in smaller locations inside major stores (e.g., Wal-Mart) or gasoline stations.

Diversification

Diversification is a move to an entirely new retail format directed toward a market segment that the retailer currently does not serve. CIBC's strategy of selling automobile insurance through telemarketing is an example of diversification.

The major Canadian bank's strategy of taking over investment firms and offering these services through the Internet is another example of diversification.

Productivity improvement

The strategy of **productivity improvement** focusses on improved earnings through cost reductions, increased turnover through an improved merchandise mix, and increased prices and margins. Productivity improvement often occurs in firms in the mature or declining phases of their life cycles. During these stages, strategies requiring major infusions of cash are not acceptable to management. Rather, the emphasis is on squeezing as much profit as possible from the operation. The strategy is more a refinement of existing strategies than a dramatic new way of doing business. Dalmy's women's clothing chain, after suffering losses in four of five years, improved productivity through reducing overheads, closing unprofitable stores, reducing head office expenses, tightening control over inventories, and conserving working capital.[10]

Cost reductions

Some retailers concentrate on cost reductions as a competitive weapon in increasing productivity. A key to such a strategy often is to increase self-service to hold down labour costs. Reducing store hours, making better use of part-time help, and cutting back on customer services are other actions that can be taken to reduce costs.

Provigo, a large Canadian wholesale and retail organization (retail operations include Provigo, Maxi, and Héritage), focusses on a sophisticated information technology system to achieve significant cost reductions in its distribution system. Information obtained from the company's point-of-sale scanners in their supermarkets allows the firm to measure the contribution of individual products to profitability. Provigo uses information technology to achieve productivity improvements through reducing costs and improving the merchandise mix. As well, the company processes virtually all its orders with suppliers through electronic data interchange, resulting in significant cost savings.[11]

Improved merchandise mix

Most stores attempt to improve productivity by increasing their turnover through a better merchandise mix. The key is to ensure that the new merchandise satisfies the needs of the target market while maintaining the store's desired position. Mark's Work Wearhouse encourages in-store product managers and product category coordinators to introduce new items into the product assortment on a test basis. By using local knowledge of customer needs, this ongoing testing allows Mark's to respond quickly to changing market demands. Video chains, like Jumbo Video, have broadened their merchandising mix to include games and laser disk rentals.

Price and margin increases

Price and margin increases can be a key element in productivity-based strategies. Higher-than-normal prices may be possible on low-visibility items or infrequently purchased products. Charging for services such as delivery or installation may also be feasible. Many furniture retailers charge a fee for delivery of merchandise. Adding high-margin items to the merchandise mix, as is done by superstores, is a further dimension of such a strategy. Banks vary service charges to retail customers based on account balances.

Based on the strategic alternatives the retailer identifies as providing the best opportunity for growth and profits, the retailer decides on the target markets where it plans to compete.

Deciding on Markets in Which to Compete

Market segments are the groupings of consumers based on homogeneous responses to merchandise offerings. Segment descriptors provide the ways in which market segments can be described.

Typical descriptors based on demographics (age, income, occupation, etc.) are the most frequently used ways of segmenting markets. Psychographics (the activities, interests, and opinions of consumers) are often used to supplement demographic data.

Target markets are the segments that management decides to serve. Market positioning is how management plans to compete in target markets that appeal to the firm. Let us briefly use the Harvey's hamburger chain to show the relationships between segmentation, targeting, and positioning in strategy development before we discuss each concept in more detail.

Business	Hamburger chain
Market segment descriptors	Age
	Income level
	Occupation
Target market selected	Adults aged 18 to 30
	Education: completed secondary degree
	Personal income: $22,000 and over
	White-collar professional
Positioning strategy in target market	Superior-quality product at a premium price in attractive surroundings

You can probably better understand segmentation, targeting, and positioning if you think about how McDonald's, Wendy's, Burger King, and A&W chains compete against Harvey's by choosing different market targets and positioning strategies.

Segmenting markets

Requirements of segmentation. The market segments selected by management must be:

1. Measurable—Is the segment measurable and identifiable?

2. Accessible—Will focussing marketing efforts on a particular market segment have a positive impact on eliciting desired responses?

3. Economically viable—Is the segmentation variable shared by enough potential customers to justify the expense and effort of focussing marketing efforts on that segment?

4. Stable—Are the consumer characteristics stable indicators of market potential?

In strategy development, consumers can be viewed in one of three ways, depending on the product or service offered:

1. Similarity—All consumers are viewed as basically similar. Although differences such as age, income, needs, and preference exist among them, these differences are not thought to be important influences on the purchase of the firm's specific product class. A standard product will essentially satisfy most consumers. For example, in retailing, convenience stores provide a merchandise mix, wide variety, and little depth, all of which focus on the customer's primary reason for shopping at the store—convenience—and ignore the differences.

2. Differences/similarities—Consumer differences and similarities are important sources of influence on market demand. These differences and similarities facilitate the grouping of consumers in aggregates and appeal to these aggregates on common bases. For example, most womenswear retailers target specific segments based on various descriptors including age and lifestyle. The Dalmy's chain, which has five store banners to target different segments, has defined its target for the Dalmy's division as younger fashion-conscious women in the mid-price market.[12]

3. Uniqueness—All consumers are somewhat different. The differences among them make a standardized offering unacceptable. Market offerings must be tailored specifically to the needs of a very narrowly defined group of consumers. For example, high-end menswear retailers, like Harry Rosen, provide a made-to-measure service for men wanting custom-made suits.

Target market selection

No single best way exists for selecting target markets in which to compete. Often, management begins by looking at the entire market in terms of both the size and consumer segments to which it might appeal. From these segments, it identifies a smaller number of segments that hold the most promise for the firm—these are the possible targets. Next, management zeros in on these possible targets and applies a set of screening criteria to help select the final targets. A number of variables are normally evaluated for each target to determine the ones most compatible with the organization's resources and skills. Typical criteria are shown in Table 6–3. They include the growth potential of

Table 6–3   Market Attractiveness Analysis

Critical Market Factors	Weight	Young Professionals	Teens	Seniors	Middle Age
Future growth potential	20	9	8	6	4
Present size	15	8	5	7	7
Investment required	10	8	5	6	7
Strength of competition	10	7	7	9	9
Ability to meet the needs of the market	20	8	9	6	8
Profit potential	25	6	5	5	4
Score	100	760	660	620	605

Note: Each target is rated from 1 (very unattractive) to 10 (very attractive).

each likely target market, the investment needed to compete, and the strength of the competition. The possible market targets are evaluated by deciding (1) on a weight for each factor and (2) how each possible target rates on each factor. Multiplying the weights by the ratings yields a score that is summed for each target. The total score for each target allows management to objectively evaluate each target. This lets management select targets for further development of marketing strategies. Table 6–3 provides an example of a retailer who has evaluated four targets, with young professionals scored as most attractive and middle-age as least attractive.

Once retailers have chosen target markets in which to compete, a plan must be developed for attracting targeted consumers. The basis for such planning is a thorough understanding of those consumers—their behaviour, values, motives, and expectations. Especially important is an understanding of the decision process customers go through in making merchandise and store choice decisions. Because of the importance of this topic, a separate chapter in the text is devoted to a discussion of buyer behaviour. Chapter 3 focussed on the consumer as a problem solver and highlights a number of different issues related to the behaviour of consumers. Chapter 4 provided an in-depth look at consumers by focussing on social characteristics and living patterns of customers. Knowledge of consumer behaviour helps retailers better understand consumers' merchandise and store preferences and their shopping behaviour.

Obtaining Resources Needed to Compete

As part of the planning process, retailers must evaluate the alternatives for owning a business as well as avenues for entering a retail business. For example, a retail firm can be operated as a sole proprietorship, a partnership, or a corporation. To enter retailing, a person can start his or her own business, can buy an existing business, or can become part of a franchise operation. Such issues are the topics of Chapters 7 and 8. Chapter 7 focusses on different forms of ownership, issues in buying a retail business, determining capital needed for a new business, and sources of needed funds. Because franchising is one of the fastest growing segments in retailing today, a separate chapter, Chapter 8, is devoted to a discussion of franchising as a retail business concept.

Store location, a crucial element of retail planning, is the topic of Chapter 10. For example, Home Depot and Price Club/Costco need sites that have a large amount of space and are located near major highways. Because of this, these retailers are willing to pay over $1 million per acre in markets like Vancouver and Calgary to obtain prime sites.[13]

Human resources are just as vital to the success of a retail operation as are financial resources and physical facilities. As will be shown in Chapter 9, the human resources plan must be consistent with the overall strategy of the retail organization. Human resources management also involves a variety of issues such as recruiting, selecting, training, compensating, and motivating personnel as well as organizing, and it is essential that these activities be managed effectively and efficiently.

Figure 6–3   Hypothetical Positioning Map for Women's Apparel Retailers

Developing a Positioning Strategy

After target markets are selected and the necessary resources are obtained, a positioning strategy is developed. **Positioning** is the design and implementation of a retail mix to create an image of the retailer in the customer's mind relative to its competitors.[14] A positioning map is often used to portray the customer's image and preference for retailers. A hypothetical positioning map for women's apparel retailers is provided in Figure 6–3. The two dimensions, fashion and assortment, are two criteria that consumers might use in forming images of the stores. In this example, Sarah's Classics and Fudge's Apparel are close to each other because consumers see them as similar in terms of fashion and assortment. In contrast, Biba Boutique and Suzy Shier are far apart, suggesting that consumers have quite different images of them. Retailers use these maps to determine how consumers perceive them and their competition. Based on these consumer perceptions, a particular retailer can reinforce its position or consider repositioning if its current position is unsatisfactory.

One example of positioning is Zellers, the discount department store chain. Zellers is positioned to appeal to the budget-minded customer with the assurance of the lowest price. Zellers focusses directly on this position with its slogan: "Where the lowest price is the law." A profile of Zellers is provided in Retail Highlight 6–2.

The importance of developing and maintaining a positioning strategy must be stressed, especially in an era when competition in retailing is fierce. When Zellers' positioning was threatened by the entry of Wal-Mart into Canada, it reconfigured its stores to provide for broader, more competitive merchandise

Retail Highlight 6–2

Zellers' Profile

Zellers is the leading national chain of discount department stores. It targets the budget-minded customer with the assurance of the lowest price. Excellent values are offered in both national and private-brand merchandise and these are communicated aggressively with frequent advertising in both print and electronic media. Zellers is further distinguished by Club Z, its customer rewards program. Zellers is successful in its competitive retail segment by operating with a very low expense rate.

Zellers stores are characterized by self-service and central checkout. Zellers markets its own credit card and accepts those of the major banks. Merchandising and sales promotions are centrally directed. Zellers operates 292 stores across Canada mainly in shopping malls. The average store is 72,000 square feet (6,700 m^2) with new stores in excess of 100,000 square feet (9,300 m^2).

Source: Hudson's Bay Company, *Annual Report*, 1994.

Zellers reconfigures its stores to maintain dominance in the discount market.

Courtesy Hudson's Bay Company Ltd.

assortments and repriced its merchandise to maintain its dominant position against all competition.

The positioning strategy involves the use of retailing mix variables. The **retailing mix** consists of all variables that can be used as part of a positioning strategy for competing in chosen markets. As shown in Figure 6–4, the retailing mix variables include product, price, presentation, promotion, personal selling, and customer service. Issues related to the retailing mix variables are included in Chapters 10 to 17 of the text.

Figure 6–4   Variables of the Retailing Mix and Types of Decisions

Variable	Types of Decisions
Product	Merchandise lines (width, depth, assortment)
	Brand lines (national, store, generic)
	Supplier selection
	Inventory levels
Price	Pricing policy (above, at, below the market)
	Price levels
	Price adjustments
Presentation	Store design
	Store layout
	Merchandise presentation
Promotion	Advertising budget, copy, and media
	Sales promotions
	Publicity and public relations
Personal selling	Sales force size, training, and compensation
	Motivation of staff
Customer service	Support services
	Credit policies
	Returns policies

Strategy Implementation

A sound strategy is no guarantee of success if it cannot be well executed. To implement a firm's desired positioning effectively, every aspect of the store must be focussed on the target market. Merchandising must be single-minded; displays must appeal to the target market; advertising must talk to it; personnel must have empathy for it; and customer service must be designed with the target customer in mind.

The Gap, a popular and profitable specialty clothing chain, will be used to illustrate how the marketing mix variables play a critical role in positioning efforts within target markets. The Gap has over 1,200 stores in the U.S. and Canadian markets, targeting consumers with a simple, yet powerful positioning strategy—good style, good quality, and good value. The blend of some of the retailing mix variables in support of this position strategy is:

Product	The Gap designs its own clothes with the focus on simplicity. New collections hit the stores about every eight weeks and unpopular designs are marked down and quickly sold off.
Price	Strict quality control procedures and using manufacturers in 40 countries ensures high quality, low costs, and a very good price for customers.
Presentation	Merchandise is displayed to emphasize the deep assortment of colours and is laid out on tables and shelves where it can be easily touched.
Promotion	Advertising for The Gap has been striking, including the "Individuals of Style" campaign, a series of black-and-white photos of personalities from Miles Davis to k.d. Lang. The message communicates an individual sense of style.
Personal selling	Sales staff receive no commission but constant contests are run to motivate the staff to provide quality service.
Customer service	The Gap accepts all credit cards.[15]

Evaluating and Controlling Operations

Once a strategy is implemented, managers need feedback on the performance of the new strategy. Some types of information are needed on a routine, ongoing basis to help management determine whether objectives have been met. Chapter 19 focusses on several types of control systems that help management assess the success of operations.

The effectiveness of the long-term competitive strategy of the firm, however, must also be evaluated periodically. Such an evaluation covers all elements of the plan, as shown in Table 6–4. This type of evaluation guarantees that the firm's plan does not degenerate into fragmented, ad hoc efforts that are not in harmony with the overall competitive strategy of the business. Management can also use the process to decide what changes, if any, should be made in the future to ensure that the combination of retailing mix variables supports the firm's strategy.

Table 6-4   Evaluating Competitive Strategy

Merchandising Plan

1. What is the growth pattern of existing merchandise lines?
2. Is the merchandise line portfolio balanced? Should merchandise lines be added or deleted?
3. Should product line breadth or depth be modified?
4. What is the strength of the individual brands carried?
5. Are the merchandise lines properly positioned against the competition and in support of the marketing plan?
6. Does the firm have an adequate open-to-buy plan?
7. Are adequate inventory controls in place?

Pricing Plan

1. What are the profit margins on the merchandise lines carried? Are they increasing or decreasing? How do they compare to those of competition?
2. Are the pricing policies, including price lines (at, equal to, or above the competition), appropriate for each target market?
3. Does pricing have a primary or secondary role in the marketing plan?
4. Is a realistic system for planned markdowns in place?

Advertising and Sales Promotion Plan

1. Are the objectives for advertising and sales promotion clearly stated? Do they support the marketing plan?
2. Is the media mix supportive of the marketing plan?
3. Are budgets adequate to accomplish the objectives? How are budgets established?
4. Are the creative strategies compatible with the marketing plan?
5. Does the firm have weekly, monthly, and seasonal plans for such activities in place?

Distribution and Sales Support Plan

1. Are customer service levels such as on warranties and repairs satisfactory? What weaknesses exist?
2. Are mail and telephone sales programs compatible with the overall marketing plan?
3. Are the after-sales delivery programs, if any, compatible with the marketing plan?
4. Are the credit programs offered cost effective? Should credit options be added or deleted?
5. Is the breadth and intensity of market coverage satisfactory for a firm with branches or multiple outlets?

Financial Plan

1. Is a profit analysis possible, including a break-even analysis and analysis of ROI and leverage?
2. What are the profit margins by merchandise line? Are they increasing or decreasing? How do they compare to those of the competition? Compare with trade statistics where possible.
3. Does the firm have a sound accounting and information system?
4. What are the trends in such indicators as return on assets, earnings per share, and net profits?

Physical Facilities Plan

1. Is adequate emphasis placed on space productivity?
2. Is flexible fixturing used whenever possible?
3. Does signing provide adequate information to shoppers?
4. Do the atmospherics support the other elements of the marketing plan?
5. Is merchandise arranged for easy cross-selling whenever possible?
6. Is lighting appropriate for each area?

The Retail Information System

1. Does the merchandise information system provide the information needed for key operating decisions?
2. Is a sound, competitive shopping system in place?
3. Is someone in the firm responsible for evaluating environmental trends that can affect the continuing success of the firm?
4. Are the financial and merchandising ratios of the firm regularly compared to comparable trade statistics?

Human Resources Plan

1. Does the firm have the talent to execute its marketing strategies?
2. Is the firm adequately staffed?
3. Are the firm's selection and recruiting efforts and training programs adequate?
4. Are the firm's pay scales adequate? Are opportunities for promotion available? Are performance appraisals and feedback occurring?
5. If several outlets exist, are personnel decisions centralized or decentralized?
6. Are disciplinary procedures in place?
7. Do union/management relations receive adequate attention?

Chapter Highlights

- The steps involved in strategic planning are: (1) develop a mission statement, (2) establish objectives, (3) conduct a situation analysis, (4) identify strategic alternatives, (5) select markets in which to compete, (6) obtain resources needed to compete, (7) develop a positioning strategy, (8) implement the strategy, and (9) evaluate the results.

- The beginning point in developing a strategic plan is identification of the organization's mission or purpose. The mission statement tells what the firm intends to do and how it plans to do it. The mission statement often reflects the firm's values or corporate culture.

- The retailer's plan for achieving objectives within the context of the mission statement is based on an analysis of the strengths and weaknesses of the organization and threats and opportunities in the environments. Such an analysis is called a situation analysis.

- The situation analysis helps store management identify the strategic alternatives available including market penetration, market development, retail format development, and diversification.

- The factors involved in deciding on markets in which to compete include segmentation and screening criteria (such as future growth potential and strength of competition). The markets that management decides to serve are referred to as target markets.

- In obtaining the resources needed to compete, the retailer has various options for owning and operating the business.

- The retailer must develop a positioning strategy. The positioning strategy is a plan of action that outlines how the organization will compete in chosen markets and how it will differentiate itself from other organizations competing for the same customers. The positioning strategy is developed through a combination of the retailing mix variables. These variables include product, price, presentation, promotion, personal selling, and customer service.

- A sound strategy is no guarantee of success if it cannot be implemented successfully. The retailing mix variables must be blended appropriately in implementing a store's positioning strategy.

- Once a strategy is implemented, managers need feedback on how the organization is performing based on its strategy. Some types of information are needed on a routine, ongoing basis to help management determine whether objectives are being met. However, the effectiveness of the long-term competitive strategy of the firm must also be periodically evaluated.

Key Terms

corporate culture 162	positioning 172
market development 165	productivity improvement 168
market penetration 164	retailing mix 173
market segments 169	situation analysis 163
mission statement 160	strategic planning 158
objectives 162	target markets 169

Discussion Questions

1. Indicate the steps involved in developing a strategic plan.

2. What is meant by an organization's mission statement? What does this statement normally include?

3. What is the difference between long-term and short-term objectives?

4. What is a situation analysis? Which factors are evaluated in such an analysis? What is the ultimate value and use of a situation analysis?

5. Explain the relationships between target markets, positioning strategy, and the retailing mix.

6. Discuss each of the following strategy alternatives: market penetration, market development, retail format development, and diversification.

Application Exercises

1. Mission statements of a number of Canadian retailers are included in the text. Visit your library and find mission statements of other retail operations from their annual reports. Be prepared to discuss if they provide a clear sense of direction for the organization.

2. Select at least three fast-food operations in your community. Indicate each firm's target market and positioning strategy and discuss how the elements of the retailing mix are combined in implementing the positioning strategy.

3. Select at least four women's clothing stores in your community. Suggest how each store might be segmenting the market. Recommend how their segmentation approach could be improved.

Suggested Cases

8. Diego's

9. The Undercover Agency

10. Clean Windows Inc.

11. Donna Holtom

12. Omer DeSerres

13. Wing and a Prayer

14. West Coast Furniture

Notes

1. Sources include: Christian Alland, "Loony Tunes," *Canadian Business,* August 1995, pp. 73–74; James Pollock, "Luckhurst Rising Fast on HMV's Charts," *Marketing,* February 5, 1996, p. 7; "A Musical Success," *The Record,* July 25, 1995, p. B7; and Mathew Ingram, "The Battle for the Music-Sales Market," *Financial Times,* November 4, 1991, pp. 1, 12.

2. Mark's Work Wearhouse, *Annual Report,* 1995.

3. *Ibid.*

4. Marina Strauss, "Oshawa Group Pins Hope on Price Chopper," *Globe & Mail,* June 6, 1992, p. B7.

5. Sears Canada, *Annual Report,* 1994.

6. Loblaw Companies Limited, *Annual Report,* 1994.

7. "Toys-Я-Us Gears up for New Market," *Financial Post,* July 7, 1995, p. 12.

8. Scott Anderson, "Wendy's Puts US$ 42.5M Bite on Tim Horton's," *Financial Post,* August 9, 1995, pp. 1,2.

9. Miles Socha, "Triple the Pleasure," *The Record,* August 26, 1995, p. B4.

10. Dalmys, *Annual Report,* 1994.

11. Univa, *Annual Report,* 1994.

12. Dalmys, *Annual Report,* 1995.

13. Susanne Craig, "Box Retail Expansion Pushing up Land Prices," *Financial Post,* August 26, 1995, pp. 1–2.

14. David A. Aaker and J. Gary Shansby, "Positioning Your Product," *Business Horizons,* May-June, 1982, pp. 56–62; George Lucas and Larry Gresham, "How to Position for Retailing Success," *Business,* April-June, 1989, pp. 3-12; and Martin R. Lautman, "The ABCs of Positioning," *Marketing Research,* Winter 1993, pp. 12–18.

15. Russell Mitchell, "The Gap," *Business Week,* March 9, 1992, pp. 58–64 and Mario Shao and Laura Zinn, "Everybody's Falling into the Gap," *Business Week,* September 23, 1991, p. 36.

Starting and Financing a Retail Business

Chapter Objectives

After reading this chapter you should be able to:

1. Describe the risks and advantages of ownership.

2. Explain the differences between a sole proprietorship, partnership, and a corporation.

3. Define issues in buying a retail business.

4. Discuss the importance of planning in starting a business.

5. Estimate the operating capital needed for a new business and the sources of the funds.

Garlic's Restaurant: from an idea to reality

Photo by Betty McDougall

In the spring of 1990, Kathy Burns was laid off after six years as operations manager in the food services unit of a large institution. At that time, she saw three options: find another job in a big organization, enrol in an MBA program, or open her own restaurant. Fourteen years earlier she had enjoyed operating a Mexican restaurant for about a year. She decided to take an MBA but she didn't abandon her restaurant dream.

While in the MBA program, she thought a lot about the restaurant idea and decided that if she opened a restaurant it would specialize in garlic dishes—garlic is a passionate food, it is multi-ethnic, and it has a folklore of being healthy. She talked to a lot of people about her idea—some thought it was crazy but most said, "Why not?" Her family—two children, aged 5 and 10, and a husband—said, "If you want to do it, go for it." Kathy did and today runs Garlic's Restaurant in London, Ontario. It is successful but how she got from the idea to a profitable business will be explored throughout this chapter. It is a story full of challenges and initiative and is a fascinating example of starting a retail business.[1]

Many people have the dream of owning their own business in spite of the long hours, the financial risks, and the fiercely competitive nature of retailing. They can get started in many ways. Examples include: starting a business and operating as an independent organization; banding together with other retailers or wholesalers to have more power in buying goods but still operating as an independent business; buying an existing business; becoming a franchiser; or becoming a franchisee. (Franchising is discussed in the next chapter.)

A successful retail venture depends not only on successful marketing strategies, but also on the legal form of the organization, access to the types of capital needed, and a business plan.

Over one million people are employed in retailing in Canada. Two-thirds of retail firms have less than four employees, and 90 percent are single-unit establishments. Clearly, most retail businesses are small by any standard. Persons who want one day to manage a family business or open a business may decide to start their retail career by working in a small firm. Higher quality and more specialized training are normally available in a chain organization.

The Advantages of Ownership

Retailing offers more opportunities for ownership than virtually any other type of business. Read the newspaper on almost any day and you can probably find several retail businesses for sale. Also, many suppliers and bankers will loan the funds to help people open their own firms; they will, however, probably want to see a cash flow plan, as discussed later in this chapter, and will need to understand the organization's planned business strategy.

Most retailing is local in nature so independent retailers can often compete successfully with large national firms. Store trading areas are small and the outlets are viewed as part of the local neighbourhood. At the local level, small retailers can do things that a national firm cannot do. Most national firms do not vary their operations from town to town. Consequently, local merchants can offer unique merchandise lines, more specialized services, and more personal attention than are normally available from chain-store merchants.

As one example, Robert Zaurrini operates Olifruits Ltée, a fruit and vegetable store he founded in Laval, Quebec, 16 years ago at the age of 24. Since then, Zaurrini has expanded the operation from strictly a fruit, vegetable, and cheese store to one that includes deli and grocery sections, gift baskets (an Olifruits specialty), and prepared vegetarian meals. In spite of increased competition in the neighbourhood, he maintains annual sales of more than $4 million by offering good prices, quality, service, and aggressiveness.[2]

The Risks of Ownership

Going-out-of-business signs are a part of every community, although few people voluntarily go out of business. But aspiring entrepreneurs should not be discouraged from starting their own business if they are willing to take a risk, because the rewards can be large.

Early failure is likely

The first five years are the toughest for the business owner. Of the businesses that fail, more than 50 percent fail in the first five years.[3] For example, one study showed that between 1978 and 1986, over 58,000 retail firms ceased operation in Canada. On the other hand, over 90,000 retail firms started up during the same time.[4] In general, about 150,000 business are started each year in Canada, 50 percent to 60 percent survive the first year, and about 30 percent survive more than three years.[5]

What are the causes of failure?

The most common reasons for failure are incompetence, unbalanced experience, lack of experience in the line, and a lack of managerial experience. Among the specific reasons for failure are a lack of research before starting the business, no break-even analysis conducted, no business plan completed, and poor inventory management skills. Failure because of neglect, fraud, or disaster is unusual.[6] The early 1990s saw an increase in business and retail failures due to the harsh economic climate. In 1991, there were 13,500 business bankruptcies in Canada, most of them in the retail sector. A total of 28,000 jobs were lost in retailing during that year.[7] More recently, Canada has experienced an increase in business failures in the retail sector due to the impact of the big-box stores, like Wal-Mart, which has forced some smaller retailers into bankruptcy.[8]

Systematic differences exist between businesses that survive for three years and those that fail. The surviving businesses are more likely to use business plans, to get started with higher levels of capital, and to use professional advisors. Similarly, the owners are more likely to have college degrees and to run the business full-time as opposed to hiring a professional manager.

Starting a New Business

People interested in opening a new business can form a sole proprietorship, a partnership, or a corporation. The advantages and disadvantages of each form of business are shown in Table 7–1. Management may also decide to purchase an existing business instead of starting a new one. The forms of business are the same whether starting a new business or buying an existing firm.

The sole proprietorship

The **sole proprietorship** is the most common form of ownership today. Everything belongs to the owner.

Being the sole owner of a business has several advantages. Such a business is the easiest to start, as less paper work is necessary and fewer restrictions exist other than for inspection or licensing. As well, the owner is the boss, the owner keeps all the profits, and the owner decides on the goods to be sold, store hours, and so forth. The owner can go out of business very quickly, often simply by locking the door and hanging a sign in the window which says "Closed." In addition, because both the federal and provincial governments view small

Table 7–1	The Advantages and Disadvantages of Each Form of Ownership		
	Sole Proprietorship	**Partnership**	**Corporation**
Advantages	• Easy to organize • Easy to dissolve • Owner keeps all profits • Preferential government treatment	• Easy to organize • Greater capital availability • Combined management experience	• Limited financial liability • Easier to raise capital • Specialized management skills • Easier to transfer ownership
Disadvantages	• Unlimited financial liability • Difficult to raise capital • Limited life of firm • The business is based on the heartbeat of one individual • Limited by owner's skills	• Unlimited liability • Dividend authority • Hard to dissolve	• Complex government regulations • Expensive to organize • Various tax disadvantages • Lack of personal involvement

businesses as important to Canada's economy, certain financial aid and consulting programs may be available to small retailers.

Disadvantages also exist. For example:

1. The full risk of loss is borne by the owner who can be forced to pay business debts out of personal assets.
2. The firm has limited borrowing power.
3. Qualified people may be hesitant about working for the firm.
4. Such a business can probably offer fewer fringe benefits to employees than could larger employers.
5. No one is legally able to make business decisions except the owner.

The partnership

A **partnership** exists when two or more people jointly own a retail business. Partnerships can take various forms. For example, in a *general partnership* the partners share all of the responsibilities and benefits of the partnership, including profits and management authority. *Limited partners* are persons whose input is limited to one area of the business. For example, a lawyer may be a limited partner. The liability of limited partners is restricted to their investment.

Silent partners likewise have limited liability. They are not active in the business but are willing to allow their names to be used as one of the partners. Often, these partners are well known in the community and the use of their names is an asset to the firm. *Secret partners* do not allow their names to be used. They do not always have limited liabilities.

The disadvantages of partnerships, shown in Table 7–1, make them less popular than other forms of organization, and the problems can be complicated when a firm has several partners. Partnerships often cease to exist when one of the partners becomes incapable of continuing in the business. Likewise, the unlimited liability for the debts of the business can be a drawback, as can the fact that the actions of any one partner are binding on the others.

Consequently, the articles for a partnership are very important. They need to carefully spell out the roles of the partners, the ways for a partner to get out of the business, and what happens when one of the partners dies or becomes disabled.

A corporation

A **corporation** is a separate legal entity apart from the owners. Thus, liability is limited to the amount that each individual stockholder has invested in the firm. Since management is separate from ownership, it may be easier for a corporation to attract strong managerial talent. It may also be easier to raise capital, either by issuing stock or through loans. Since corporations are often large and have greater earning power than single proprietorships, they have easier access to borrowing money at favourable rates.

Again, some disadvantages exist. For example, earnings are taxed more heavily. Corporate earnings are taxed as well as dividends to stockholders.

Corporations may be either private or public. **Private corporations** are those owned by a few people (a maximum of 50 shareholders is allowed), often a family, and persons outside the corporation cannot buy the stock on the open market. The stock value does not have a known market value and does not vary widely in price. In Canada, many small businesses are private corporations with a single owner or a few people. In these instances, the costs of incorporation are relatively low, government regulations are relatively simple, and the individuals have considerable personal involvement. **Public corporations** are those in which the stock of the firm can be purchased on the open market. Normally, only larger retailers are public corporations.

Incorporating is relatively easy to do and can be done under the Federal Canada Business Corporations Act or under a Provincial Corporations Act. A corporation can be established by a single individual. The individual or group is issued a corporate charter, which is a contract between the province or federal government and the person or group. The corporate charter allows the business to operate. The advice or counsel of a lawyer should be sought on the details for such an arrangement.

Two of the more important factors in deciding on the form of ownership are the liability of the owners and tax considerations. In general, only corporations provide for limited liability with respect to debts incurred by the business. With respect to taxes, knowledge of the Canadian tax system and the tax laws relating to personal income and corporate income should be obtained before making the decision. The advice of an accountant should be sought on tax matters.

Kathy Burns decided to form a private corporation to launch her venture. She estimated that start-up costs would be $200,000. In spite of the fact that she had a detailed business plan, experience, education, and enthusiasm, these were not assets that the various lenders she approached could touch and feel. The only loan she obtained was a $15,000 New Ventures Loan, guaranteed by the federal government. Fortunately some friends said they would provide equity and they agreed to hold non-voting stock in a private corporation. A comprehensive shareholders' agreement was signed, well after the friends put up the money. In fact, they gave her the money before there was a business licence, a liquor licence, a location, or even a company!

Buying a Retail Business

A person may decide to buy an existing business instead of starting a new one. Buying a retail business is a complex process. The potential buyer needs the help of professionals such as accountants, bankers, brokers, and lawyers on specific issues.

Deciding on the type of retailing

The type of retailing depends on the personal characteristics of the potential buyer, including his or her personality, interests, experiences, and skills. The amount of financing available may also determine the type of business that can be purchased. The growth potential is also important. Information on the future prospects of the business can be developed by talking with executives in trade associations, with bankers, suppliers, and others knowledgable about the business.

Identifying potential stores

Newspaper classified ads are a source of possible leads. Prospective buyers can also place "business wanted" ads in the newspaper. Persons specializing in buying and selling retail firms often can provide valuable assistance. The potential buyer needs to remember, however, that the broker represents the seller and gets a commission based on the sales price.

Other potential sources of leads are suppliers, distributors, trade publications, and trade associations. Occasionally accountants or other management consultants may also be able to identify a business that is for sale.

Evaluating the business opportunity

The potential buyer needs to determine the reasons why a business is for sale. Old age, poor health, and pending bankruptcy are reasons that can be easily spotted. Other less obvious reasons include excessive competition, problems with creditors, excess accounts receivable, or a pending lease loss.

Assessing earnings potential

The potential buyer should look at past profits, sales, and expenses. Operating ratios should be compared with industry data provided by such sources as the Retail Council of Canada and Dun & Bradstreet Canada before making an offer for a business.[9] In particular, key performance measures such as those shown in Table 7–2 should be examined and, if possible, compared with similar businesses. An independent accountant who specializes in retailing may need to analyze the profit and loss performance of the business over the past three to five years. The buyer should be wary of a seller who will not provide background information including financial statements, income tax returns, purchases, and bank deposits.

When Kathy Burns was initially considering opening a restaurant she could have examined an industry profile of the restaurant sector prepared by Dun & Bradstreet Canada. As shown in Table 7–3, for the 1992 to 1994 period, the restaurant industry had low profit margins (return on sales after tax was around 2 percent) and poor returns

Table 7–2   Selected Key Performance Measures

Profitability

Net profit after tax to net sales—measures amount of net profit produced by each dollar of sales.
Net profit after tax to total assets—measures return on all invested funds.
Net profit after tax to net worth/invested—measures return on net equity invested.

Productivity

Space:
Sales per sq. metre of selling areas—measures sales generated through a store.
Gross margin per sq. metre of selling area—measures gross margin dollars generated by use of space.
Transactions per sq. metre of selling area—measures traffic per sq. metre.
Inventory:
Gross margin percent—indicator of gross profit level.
Gross margin return on inventory—measures the relationship between investment in inventory and gross margin generated by that margin.
Inventory turnover—used to determine how effectively managers utilize their investment in inventory.
Personnel:
Sales per selling employee—measures staff levels relative to volumes.
Gross margin per employee—measures gross profit generated per employee.
Accounts Receivable:
Days outstanding in receivables—measures quality of credit management.
Total Assets:
Net sales to total assets—used to evaluate how effectively managers use their assets.

Financial Management

Leverage:
Total assets to net worth—the relationship between how much a firm owes to how much the firm owns.
Total liabilities to net worth—the relationship between how much a firm owns to how much the firm owes.
Liquidity:
Current ratio (times)—indicator of liquidity.
Quick ratio (times)—indicator of liquidity.

(return on assets was under 5 percent). Liquidity, the ability to cover costs with incoming cash, was also poor (the quick ratio of .28:1 for 1994 meant there were $.28 of short-term assets to cover every $1.00 of current liabilities). To quote an industry expert from Dun & Bradstreet Canada, "You're really living hand-to-mouth and you've really got to have the magic all together to be successful with a restaurant."[10]

A detailed analysis will sometimes indicate a business is not profitable. The potential owner must then make an assessment about whether it is possible to earn a profit from the business. Perhaps the person has better management skills, is willing to invest more time and energy, or has identified industry trends that make the business attractive in the near future.

Evaluating the assets

The assets of the business should also be carefully considered. Independent appraisers should determine the dollar value of the inventory and its age, style,

Table 7–3   Canadian Restaurants—Profile and Mortality*

Industry Profile

	1994	1993	1992
1. Quick ratio	0.28:1	0.27:1	0.29:1
2. Current ratio	0.77:1	0.65:1	0.65:1
3. Total liabilities to net worth	83.59%	83.10%	77.84%
4. Return on sales, after tax	2.11%	1.43%	1.36%
5. Return on assets, after tax	4.77%	2.56%	2.69%
6. Return on net worth, after tax	8.38%	11.50%	15.64%

	Current	3 Months Ago	6 Months Ago	9 Months Ago
7. Stability score	5.0	5.2	5.1	5.2
8. Paydex score	62	61	62	62
9. Average number of employees:	20			

10. Failure rate for 1995, as of Oct. 30: 1.51%

Footnotes:

1. Indicates liquidity: cash and accounts receivable vs. current liabilities. A ratio of 1:1 is considered good. Current levels are weak.
2. Also a measure of liquidity: cash, accounts receivable, and inventory vs. short-term liabilities. 2:1 is considered good. Current levels are weak.
3. Measures how much debt is leveraged against the worth of the business. Debt levels are light.
4. Measures profitability. The trend is good, but the figure is low.
5. Shows how efficiently a business leverages its assets to make profits. Returns are poor.
6. Return on equity has been dismal and weakening.
7. Measures the profitability of a business closing in the next six months, measured out of 10, with 10 the safest and 1 the riskiest. In percentage terms, the risk of closing within six months has increased to 3.66 percent from 2.58 percent.
8. Measures how quickly they pay their bills, by number of days. Payments are slow.

Source: Dun & Bradstreet Canada survey of 1,151 restaurants.

Annual Mortality Rate of Restaurants

Using a historical database of 16,513 restaurants that failed in their first 12 years, figures show percentage of companies that went under in each year of operation. Failures jump in the eighth and ninth years.

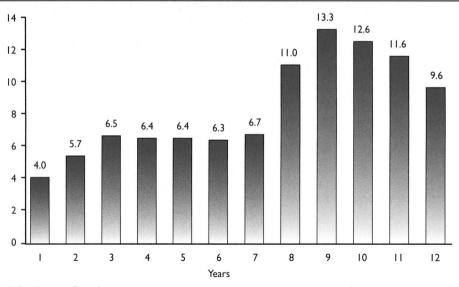

Source: Dun & Bradstreet Canada.
*As reported in Janet McFarland, "Eateries Live Hand-to-Mouth," *Globe & Mail,* November 13, 1995.

condition, and quality. Is the inventory compatible with the trading area of the store? How much inventory would have to be liquidated at a loss? What is the market value of the furniture and fixtures? Will they have to be replaced? Are the fixtures compatible with the business?

Accounts receivables should also be studied to determine their age, the credit standing of some of the larger customers, and the success of the firm in collecting past due accounts. Are too many of the credit customers slow in paying their bills? Would customers be lost if stricter credit requirements were established? Similarly, what is the condition of accounts payable? Are any lawsuits pending against the retailer?

The potential buyer should also determine if the lease is transferable. Also, what are the terms of the lease and how much time is left on the lease? Will mailing lists and customer lists be included as part of the sale? Is the business name included as part of the sale?

Finally, the potential buyer should check to determine whether the business has a good reputation and a satisfied clientele. Do the potential customers have a unique attachment to the present owner such that they might not continue to shop at the outlet if it is sold? Finally, any sales agreement should include a provision that keeps the seller from opening a similar business within the same market for a specified period of time.

The Importance of Planning

In beginning the new business, proper planning is the most important ingredient in success. As stated earlier, over half of all retail firms fail in their first five years. Effective planning will do more than anything else to help avoid becoming a part of this alarming failure rate. Success and planning go together. The owner/manager should:

1. Plan together with partners/associates.
2. Make performance expectations clear to everyone.
3. Provide for feedback on progress to keep plans on track.
4. Make plans goal oriented (i.e., what is to be accomplished) rather than activity oriented (i.e., the tasks involved).
5. Remember that hard work is vital to success, but this should be accompanied by efficient work.

Five "friends" who can help make it go

The retailer can improve the chances for success by securing the services of these professionals: lawyer, accountant, banker, insurance specialist, and professional consultants. In planning the business, some basic questions also need to be considered:

- Why am I entering retailing?
- What business am I entering?

- What goods or services will I sell?
- What is my market and who is my consumer?
- Who is my competition?
- Can I compete successfully with my competition?
- What is my sales strategy?
- What marketing methods will I use?
- How much money is required?
- Where will the money come from?
- What technical and management skills do I need?
- Can I make just as much money working for someone else?

Answering the above questions honestly and objectively will help assure the new businessperson is well on the way to building a successful business plan.

A quality business plan can be important in many ways:

1. A business plan provides the retailer a path to follow. It sets out goals and steps that allow the retailer to be in better control of steering the firm in the desired direction.

2. A business plan allows one's banker, accountant, lawyer, and insurance agent to know clearly what the business is trying to do. A plan will give them insight into the situation so that they can be of greater assistance to the business.

3. A business plan can help the owner communicate better with the staff, suppliers, and others about operations and objectives of the business.

4. A business plan can help the owner develop better management skills and abilities. It can help management consider competitive conditions, promotional opportunities, and what situations are most advantageous to the new business. In short, a business plan will help the owner to make sound business judgments.

There are no set requirements as to the contents of the plan. The contents depend on the type and size of the business being started. The most important consideration is the quality of the plan, not its length. The plan should include all aspects of the proposed business. Any possible problem areas in starting the venture should be listed with possible methods of dealing with them. Bankers would rather know the problems before the business is started than down the road where possible solutions may be limited. In fact, the major Canadian banks, including the Royal Bank and the Bank of Montreal, provide information on how to start a new business and how to prepare a business plan. The banks now provide software to help the individual prepare the plan. Suggested contents for a business plan are provided in Table 7–4. Each plan will be different and subject to variations of this list, but these suggestions will at least help to get started.[11]

Kathy Burns spent a considerable amount of time preparing her business plan. As shown in Retail Highlight 7–1, the executive summary provides the key elements of her plan.

Table 7–4   Contents for a Business Plan

1. Summary of the mission of the retail firm—a few paragraphs on what the owner is doing, and the plans for the future.
2. The retail industry in the community as a whole, the company, and its products or services. A paragraph on each.
3. Market research and analysis.
   (a) Consumers.
   (b) Market size and trends.
   (c) Competition.
   (d) Estimated market share and sales.
4. Marketing plan.
   (a) Overall marketing strategy.
   (b) Merchandise and services.
   (c) Pricing.
   (d) Sales tactics.
   (e) Advertising and promotion.
5. Management team.
   (a) Organization.
   (b) Key management personnel—who are they and what will they do?
   (c) Ownership and compensation.
   (d) Board of directors.
   (e) Any supporting services.
6. The financial plan (you may need accounting help).
   (a) Profit and loss forecasts.
   (b) Pro forma cash flow analysis.
   (c) Pro forma balance sheets.
7. Proposed company offering.
   (a) Desired financing.
   (b) Capitalization.
   (c) Use of funds.
8. Overall schedule of activities for the next three years.

Operating Capital Needed

After the business plan is developed, sources of capital must be obtained. The nature of retailing affects the types of capital needed. The main thing to do is avoid an early shortage of funds. Therefore, retailers need to begin by estimating the capital needed to open a business. Many have a tendency to underestimate the needed opening capital.

As noted, Kathy Burns estimated that $200,000 was required to open the business. Her cost estimates for equipment were $100,000, which were fairly accurate, but she had forgotten to add GST and PST, which added $15,000 to her equipment costs. The consequence was that she had to find an extra $15,000, which was difficult to do.

Retailers need to plan for two categories of costs: (1) *opening costs,* which are one-time costs, such as the cost of fixturing and decorating; and (2) *operating expenses,* which are the estimated ongoing expenses of running the business for a designated time period. Examples of these costs are shown in Table 7–5.

Garlic's Restaurant Business Plan

Executive summary

In November 1993, the first Garlic's Restaurant will open in London, Ontario. It will be located at 481 Richmond Street, just two doors north of the Grand Theatre. Garlic's will be an 80-seat bistro, which will specialize in foods cooked with lots of garlic. To accommodate the 'non-garlic lovers in the crowd' there will be a few items on the menu not seasoned with garlic. The menu will be very international and the portions will be "small plates." The menu will be inexpensive; items will range from $4.95 to $6.95.

Garlic's primary market is expected to be theatre patrons and downtown business professionals. Its secondary market will be tourists and university students.

Garlic's will cost approximately $200,000 to start up. Included in the start-up costs are: leasehold improvements, equipment, fixtures, and furnishings, training, prepaid lease, and professional service fees.

Pro forma statements for the first three years of operation have been developed. The first year's projections consider three scenarios in which sales volume, food costs, and lease expense are sensitive variables. Sales are estimated to grow 20 percent in the second year and 10 percent in the third year. In the most likely scenario, Garlic's will yield an attractive return on investment of 20 percent in year one, 33 percent in year two, and 43 percent in year three.

Customers of the 1990s are increasingly value greedy, health conscious, globally informed, and demanding of high levels of service. Garlic's Restaurant will offer its customers superb value, healthful eating, the pleasures of international cooking, and customer service *nonpareil*.

Source: Kathy Burns, "The Sweet Smell of Success," *Business Quarterly*, Summer 1995, pp. 82–88, here at p. 83.

Developing a cash flow forecast

Cash flow projections are helpful in planning for the opening and preparing for unforeseen difficulties, and they are a necessity when approaching a bank about loans.

A cash flow forecast is designed to predict when cash will be received by the firm and when payments need to be made. Cash inflow and outflow vary by type of retailer, especially for those that are seasonal and who stock merchandise based on varying seasonal sales levels.

Management can use a cash budget, as shown in Table 7–6, to help estimate cash flow. Negative cash flow (when outlays exceed income) should be funded with the initial capital developed for the new venture. Retailers can base the projections on experience, an estimate published in trade magazines, and information from their banker. A retailer should ideally know approximately what the operating costs and the cash inflow will be before opening the business. A person should have enough money to cover all expenses for about six months. Management should be conservative if it is uncertain about how much money is needed. They should borrow too much rather than too little, in order to avoid having to come back later for additional funds.

In reflecting on her business, Kathy Burns felt that a well-thought-out business plan was worth its weight in gold. She used her plan to estimate her costs and profits and she entered the financial part of the plan into a spreadsheet on a computer. She updated it daily during the early start-up days when a river of cash was flowing out. Later she

Table 7–5 Opening Costs and Operating Expenses for a Typical Retail Business	
Opening Costs	**Operating Expenses**
Inventory	Rent (including one month's deposit)
Fixtures and equipment	Taxes, licenses, and permits
Leasehold improvements (wiring, plumbing, lighting, air conditioning)	Advertising and promotion
	Legal and accounting fees
Security system	Wages (including owner's)
Exterior sign	Utilities
	Supplies
	Depreciation
	Insurance
	Maintenance and repair
	Auto expenses
	Miscellaneous

recognized that she did too much advertising and had she lowered advertising expenditures earlier, she would have saved some badly needed cash.

As an example, in Table 7–6, anticipated sales for a restaurant in the first three months of operation are $53,000, $58,000, and $66,000 per month. Average monthly sales based on a sales forecast of $750,000 are $62,500 ($750,000 divided by 12). Management expects a $200 loss at the end of the first month, to break even at the end of the second month, and to show a profit at the end of December.

Sources of funds

Having prepared a business plan, including a cash flow projection, the prospective retailer typically has three potential sources of funds for the business; equity, suppliers, and financial institutions, including government agencies. Equity is the amount the prospective owner can invest plus the amount that can be raised from others who are willing to invest in the business. The investors typically share in any profits generated by the business.

Suppliers will often provide merchandise based on terms of sale such as net 30 (invoice must be paid within 30 days to maintain a good credit rating). Negotiating skills are important for the prospective owners in dealing with suppliers when starting their business as the owners have no track record.

Depending on the business plan, prospective owners can obtain loans from banks to assist in financing inventory and accounts receivable as well as some fixed assets. The Business Development Bank of Canada is a source of government funds, as is the Small Business Office of the Ministry of Industry, Trade and Technology, which has developed a loan guarantee plan. At the provincial level, a number of provinces have established small business development departments, which may also provide assistance.

Once the business is up and running, future sources of financing can be obtained either from internal or external sources. The major way to generate capital inside the firm is from profitable operations. The external sources of capital have been discussed above, except that once the business is profitable, a further option is to issue stock or perhaps bonds if the business is a corporation.

Table 7–6 Projected Cash Flow Budget for a Restaurant for Three Months Ending December 19—			
	October	November	December
Anticipated cash receipts:			
Payment for credit sales	$53,000	$58,000	$66,000
Cash sales	2,000	4,000	4,500
Total receipts	55,000	62,000	70,500
Anticipated payments:			
Cost of food and beverages	27,500	31,000	32,250
Payroll	15,500	18,200	18,200
Promotion	5,200	5,800	7,600
Loans to be repaid	1,500	1,500	1,500
Rent	4,500	4,500	4,500
Utilities	600	600	700
Outside accounting and legal fees	400	400	400
Total	55,200	62,000	65,150
Expected surplus at end of month	(200)	—	5,350
Desired cash operating balance	2,000	2,000	—
Short-term loan needed	2,200	2,000	—
Cash available	—	—	5,350

The first year

Because many retail firms fail in their first year of operation, it is critical that the owner do everything in his or her power to increase the probability of success. The experience of Kathy Burns provides an excellent example of the elements that contributed to her success in the first year.

- *Location. In any business start-up there is at least one critical factor that will, to a large extent, determine the early success of the venture. In the case of Garlic's Restaurant, as with many retail ventures, it was location. Kathy Burns spent months searching for the right location for her concept.*

- *Drive. The determination to see it through, no matter what happens. When things go wrong, you can't remain down for too long; you have to keep going. As an example, a month after Garlic's opened, the local newspaper ran a highly critical review of the restaurant attacking both the taste of the food and the service. Kathy Burns was devastated, called the staff together, and they went through the review. Based on this incident, they vowed that never again would they present any reviewer with a reason to be so critical.*

- *Energy. During the start-up, 80 to 90 hours a week were typical because the owner is the one individual that shapes the venture.*

- *Support network. Nothing goes smoothly—bureaucrats are frustrating, suppliers do not keep promises, staff lack enthusiasm, customers complain, and the owner must bear the brunt of the problems. At these times, family, friends, and investors listen and provide support.*

- *Business plan. As noted earlier, a well-thought-out business plan is worth its weight in gold because it provides the road map for the venture and the benchmarks to measure performance.*

Garlic's Restaurant survived its first year. In fact, the business plan estimated three levels of sales—pessimistic, most likely, and optimistic—$397,000, $440,000, and $533,000—for the first year. Actual first-year sales were $1,000,000 and the forecast is for a 10 percent increase in the second year. Kathy Burns is now considering future options including adding a function room for private parties and opening a second restaurant. Like many entrepreneurs, she has an eagerness for change.

Chapter Highlights

- The main risk of ownership of a retail business is the possibility of failure, but the main benefit is the independence of being your own boss. The important traits for success as a retail owner/manager include self-confidence, willingness to take risks, persistence and determination, initiative, a high level of drive and energy, and the ability to live with uncertainty. The most common reasons for failure in retailing are management incompetence, unbalanced experience, and the lack of experience in the line of trade. Failure because of neglect, fraud, or disaster is unusual.

- Retailers have the choice of forming a new business as a sole proprietorship, a partnership, or a corporation. Also, they can operate as an independent firm or become part of a marketing system. The major differences between a sole proprietorship, a partnership, and a corporation are in terms of organization (sole proprietorship is easiest to organize), ability to raise capital (partnerships and corporations have greater access to capital), and financial liability (corporations have limited financial liability).

- Many persons enter retailing by buying an existing business. Such persons have to decide on the type of business they want to buy based on their interests, skills, and experience, as well as the financing they can arrange. Available opportunities for buying a business can be discovered by working with business brokers and realtors, by studying newspaper ads, and by contacts with trade sources. In making the decision on whether to buy a business the potential buyer should determine the reasons the business is for sale, whether a profit is being earned, the operating ratios of the business as compared to industry averages, and the worth of the business assets.

- Proper planning is the most important ingredient for success in starting a business. The plan includes setting clear performance objectives, measuring progress towards achieving the objectives, and addressing basic questions in preparing the plan.

- Capital is needed for two categories of cost in starting a business: (1) opening costs, which are one-time costs, and (2) operating expenses, which are the estimated ongoing expenses of running the business. Sources of cash include owners' equity, the credit available from suppliers, loans from financial institutions and government, and the sale of stock.

Key Terms

corporation 185
partnership 184
private corporation 185

public corporation 185
sole proprietorship 183

Discussion Questions

1. **Why are the risks of business ownership so high today?**

2. **What are the major causes of retail business failure?**

3. **Evaluate the three forms of business ownership (sole proprietorship, partnership, and corporation) in terms of the strengths and weaknesses of each.**

4. **How does a retailer determine the amount of capital needed?**

5. **Describe the various sources of capital that are available to a retailer opening a new retail operation.**

6. **What are the key financial ratios an individual needs to examine in deciding whether or not to buy a retail business? What do each of these ratios measure?**

7. **What factors determine the value of a retail business?**

Application Exercises

1. Visit four independent retail firms in your community that have opened in the last five years. Identify the factors that prompted the owner/manager to go into the business, the background of the owner before entering the business, the biggest mistakes the owner has made thus far, and the advice the owner/manager would offer to individuals contemplating opening a new retail business. Write a brief essay that summarizes your findings.

2. Review the material in the chapter on the characteristics essential for success. Interview three people employed in retailing—an owner/manager, a manager, and a clerk—and ask them to what extent they agree with each of the characteristics. Write a brief report that summarizes your findings.

3. Visit a local bank and ask for any material it has on starting and financing your own business. Write a brief report that summarizes the material.

Suggested Cases

8. Diego's

9. The Undercover Agency

10. Clean Windows Inc.

11. Donna Holtom

13. Wing and a Prayer

15. The Maaco Franchise

Notes

1. Kathy Burns, "The Sweet Smell of Success," *Business Quarterly*, Summer, 1995, pp. 82–88. All references throughout the chapter to Kathy Burns and Garlic's Restaurant are based on this article.

2. Contained in *Royal Bank Business Report*, Fall 1995.

3. *Royal Bank Business Report*, Fall 1995, and David A. Whyte, "Interest Rates as a Factor in Small Business Failures," *Journal of Small Business-Canada*, vol. 2, Winter 1984/85, pp. 44–46.

4. Russell M. Knight, "Business Growth and Job Creation in Canada 1978–1986," *Journal of Small Business and Entrepreneurship*, vol. 6, Fall 1988, pp. 29–39.

5. Don Layne, "Beating the Odds," *Business Quarterly*, Summer 1995, pp. 89–94.

6. See *The Canadian Business Failure Rate*, Dun & Bradstreet various years. For further reading on small business failures in Canada see: A. Bakr Ibrahim, "Is Franchising the Answer to Small Business Failure Rate? An Empirical Study," *Journal of Small Business and Entrepreneurship*, 3, Fall 1985, pp. 48–54, and A. Bakr Ibrahim and W. Ellis, "An Empirical Investigation of Causes of Failures in Small Business and Strategies to Reduce It," *Journal of Small Business and Entrepreneurship* 4, Spring 1987, pp. 18–24.

7. Alan Toulin, "Ottawa Attacked Over Record Bankruptcies," *Financial Post*, February 5, 1992, p. 3; and *Canadian Economic Observer*, Statistics Canada, Catalog 11-010, May 1992.

8. Gordon McDonald, "Bankruptcies Climb 15% in First Half," *Globe & Mail*, August 10, 1995, p. B5.

9. See, for example, *Canadian Business Financial Ratios*, Dun & Bradstreet, Canada.

10. Janet McFarland, "Eateries Live Hand-to-Mouth," *Globe & Mail*, November 14, 1995, p. B6.

11. For further insights on preparing a retail plan, see John C. Williams and John A. Torella, *Strategic Retail Marketing*, (Toronto: Retail Council of Canada, 1984). For more information on key performance measures, see *Key Performance Measures For Retail Businesses*, Government of Canada, Regional Industrial Expansion, Ottawa. For more information on preparing a business plan, see Raymond W.Y. Kao, *Small Business Management*, 3rd Edition, Dryden Canada, 1992; Douglas Gray and Dianna Gray, *Complete Canadian Small Business Guide*, 2nd Edition, McGraw-Hill Ryerson, 1994; and Lee A. Eckart, J.D. Ryan, Robert J. Ray, and Ronald A. Knowles, *Canadian Small Business: An Entrepreneur's Plan*, Dryden Canada, 1994.

Franchising

Chapter Objectives

After reading this chapter, you should be able to:

1. Discuss the importance of franchising in the Canadian economy.

2. Evaluate the advantages and disadvantages of becoming a franchisee.

3. Describe the basic types of franchise arrangements.

4. List the types of costs involved in becoming a franchisee.

5. Evaluate franchise opportunities.

6. Explain the items contained in a typical franchise contract.

7. Discuss the trends and outlook for franchising.

M & M Meat Shops, a successful Canadian franchise

*I*n early 1980, Mac Voisin, a home builder in Kitchener, Ontario, was talking with his brother-in-law, Mark Nowak, about why people don't always get a perfect steak in the supermarket like they do in a restaurant. One idea led to another, and the concept for selling food service products to people who wanted something quick but good was born. Voisin said, "Microwave ovens were in most homes. Women were going back to work in droves. We had sensed a desire by people to spend less time in the kitchen—they wanted to have high-quality meals in a short period of time."

Voisin was convinced they had a winning idea: to provide frozen quality meat and specialty food items to the public at reasonable prices. They opened their first M&M Meat Shop in Kitchener in late 1980.

Unfortunately, the consumers were not as excited about the concept as the two partners were. The first few months were terrible but they got a break when a writer for the local paper wrote a feature story on the M&M concept. People started coming to the store, the partners devised stunts to attract business, sales increased , and the losses turned into profits. In 1983, they opened their first franchise store in Cambridge, Ontario, and never looked back. Since that time, M&M Meat Shops has expanded to 153 franchise stores across Canada, has annual sales of over $142 million, and plans to double in size in the next four years.

Mac Voisin's franchise strategy, which has led to M&M Meat Shops becoming Canada's largest specialty frozen food retail chain, includes the following components:

- *Mission*—to create a friendly food shopping experience that makes the customers say, "I'll be back."

- *Concept*—reasonably priced, high-quality meats and specialty food items. The product line includes a wide variety of flash-frozen, wholesome products including steaks, burgers, pork, chicken, and seafood. Party foods, desserts, cheeses, and vegetables are also available. All items are ready for the oven, **BBQ**, or microwave. All items are flash-frozen to ensure retention of flavour and nutrition.

- *Marketing and Advertising*—continuously increase consumer awareness of stores as well as promote the dedication to store image, cleanliness, and service.

- *Selection of Franchisees*—preference is given to team players who appreciate the benefits of working within a proven system of operation. Franchisees should have good interpersonal and communication skills, be familiar with and involved in the community where the store is located, ensure success by working in and managing the store, and have the financial capacity to invest in the store as well as the financial ability to survive the first year with only a small salary.

- *Commitment to Franchisees*—M&M Meat Shops is committed to developing the strongest franchisor-franchisee relationship in the industry. To be part of the team is to be in business for yourself but not by yourself.

Mac Voisin, the president (his brother-in-law left the business in 1985), has received numerous awards for his efforts, but he is particularly proud of the "Award of Excellence in Franchise Relations" he received from the Canadian Franchise Association. He says, "The strength of the franchise system is the franchisees." He believes that communication, motivation, and trust are the prime factors that bolster the company's success and bind the franchisees together. Monthly newsletters keep franchisees informed of company happenings, and franchisees get together 10 times a year. Mac's Fax, a direct fax line to Voisin's home, allows franchisees to share ideas and concerns.

Voisin also stars in a bimonthly 30-minute video, with personnel and customers, which is used at staff meetings. The video is called "What's Cooking," and features sales tips, operational ideas, new product launches, and contests.

The company also returns a part of its profits back into the community. It is the largest supporter for the Canadian Foundation for Ileitis and Colitis. Every year it holds a nationwide burger day with the proceeds donated to the charity, and over the last six years it has raised more than $1.3 million for the foundation.

All in all, it adds up to a successful franchise system that has never seen a franchisee fail and continues to outperform the competition.[1] ∎

A **franchise contract** is a legal document that enables a firm (the **franchiser**) to expand by allowing an independent businessperson (the **franchisee**) to use the franchiser's operating methods, financing systems, trademarks, and products in return for the payment of a fee. Franchisers may sell products, sell or lease equipment, or even sell or rent the site and premises.

Franchising is one of the fastest-growing segments of retailing in Canada and accounts for about 40 percent of all retail sales. Experts predict continued growth in new franchises and sales.[2]

Franchises exist in virtually every line of trade today including lawn care, maid services, baby-sitters, dentists, tutors, funeral homes, dating services, skin care centres, legal offices, and many others. About 1,300 franchising companies are operating in Canada today, with over 50,000 outlets across the country. Surprisingly, even though many of the best-known franchises are the foreign giants—McDonald's, Pizza Hut, Kentucky Fried Chicken—nearly 75 percent of all franchises in Canada were started in Canada. From Shoppers Drug Mart to Canadian Tire, from Provi-Soir to Harvey's, from Becker's to Uniglobe Travel, numerous franchises are owned and operated by Canadians.

Franchising has become a powerful force partly because economic factors have made growth through company-owned units difficult for many businesses. Therefore, by emphasizing independent ownership, franchising provides an effective method of overcoming such problems as shortage of capital, high interest rates, and finding and hiring competent employees.

Advantages of Becoming a Franchisee

A number of advantages exist for franchisees as part of a franchising program. The advantages include training programs that teach the retailer how to operate the business. Also, such programs allow individuals to enter a business with no previous experience. Less cash may be required to enter the business since the franchiser is often willing to provide credit to a prospective franchisee.

The purchasing power of the franchiser can result in lower costs and higher gross profits for the franchisee. The franchisee also benefits from the national advertising and promotion by the franchiser, which exceeds the advertising of conventional independent businesses. Additionally, up-to-date merchandise assistance, displays, and other materials are prepared by the franchiser and distributed to franchisees.

An equally important advantage is the program of research and development that is designed to improve the product or service. Firms such as Wendy's and McDonald's have regular, ongoing programs of research designed to identify new menu additions to help increase the sales base. Franchisees may also have access to a variety of fringe benefits such as dental plans at lower rates than are available to independent retailers.

The franchiser can also provide advice for handling special problems. Help is available in site selection, record-keeping, taxes, and other issues. As a result, around 90 percent of all franchises succeed in Canada whereas around 80 percent of all new small businesses fail. However, these statistics are somewhat misleading, as the top 20 franchise operations account for over 80 percent of the business. More than 50 percent of Canadian franchisers have been in business for less than five years and most of these for less than two years. While the well-established franchises have excellent track records, some of the newer companies may not be as successful. Oversaturation is also a problem in the franchise area. Two of the hot franchises of the 1980s—fast food restaurants and quick printing shops—declined during the early 90s and some went bankrupt due to the recession and oversaturation.[3]

Disadvantages of Becoming a Franchisee

Some disadvantages to franchising do exist. A major problem is the high cost of the franchise. Many franchisees feel they have to pay too much for supplies, fees, and other arrangements. In some cases, franchisees have found that they could purchase their supplies for less and have more favourable credit and payment terms if they dealt directly with a supplier rather than the franchiser.[4]

Also, the franchisee gives up flexibility in return for the right to a franchise. Operations are handled centrally at the corporate office and standard policies apply to all outlets. Individuals who want to run a business their own way would probably find a franchise unsuitable because of the inflexible nature of franchise operations. For example, in evaluating prospective franchisees, M&M Meat Shops prefer "team players" rather than "entrepreneurs" who want everything their own way.[5] The rigidity that results from centralized operations can also be detrimental to franchisees who face unusual local market conditions.

Decisions on how profits are to be shared between the franchiser and the franchisee typically favour the franchiser because of its financial strength. However, the major complaint typically is the nature of the contract itself. Often franchisees do not understand the document. They also have problems in terminating a franchise as the conditions of termination typically favour the franchiser.

Another problem is that the overall franchise may get into trouble, creating problems for both the franchiser and franchisee. Burger King, faced with intense competition in the fast-food business, tried a strategy of discounting and coupon promotions to hold market share during the 1991-92 recession, but it led to reduced profits for the franchisees. As well, the franchise had internal problems including rapid management turnover and erratic advertising. The result was that Burger King was reduced from 202 to 172 stores in Canada within two years. Franchise agreements were cancelled, franchisees sued Burger King, and one franchisee withdrew 15 restaurants from the chain.[6]

A study of Canadian franchisees found that they were moderately satisfied with their franchise agreement and ongoing relationship with the franchisers. Franchisees with larger systems were more satisfied than those with smaller systems.[7]

The franchiser's perspective

From the franchiser's perspective, the primary advantage in franchising is the opportunity to enjoy rapid expansion without decreasing the ownership or working capital of the company. Even a large firm like Beaver Lumber, owned by The Molson Companies, decided that it could gain greater market share without stretching its financial resources by franchising stores. It began franchising in 1977, and of over 130 Beaver Lumber outlets today, over 70 percent are franchised.

However, one of the serious problems facing franchisers is finding management with the ambition and incentive to make a franchise a success. Still, the franchise system is often better than hiring employee/managers, since the franchisee has a financial investment in the outlet and can benefit directly from its profits.

Types of Franchises

Franchises are of two basic types. The first is **product and trade-name franchising,** used, for example, by automobile dealers and gasoline outlets. The second is **business format franchising,** in which firms that have developed a unique method of performing a service or of doing business decide to expand by selling the rights to use the concept.

Product and trade-name franchising

Product and trade-name franchising began as an independent sales relationship between a supplier and a dealer where the dealer acquired some of the identity of the supplier. Franchised dealers concentrate on one company's product line and to some extent identify their business with that company. Typical of this segment of franchising are automobile and truck dealers (Ford, Chrysler, General Motors), gasoline service stations (Petro Canada, Sunoco), and soft drink bottlers (Pepsi Cola). This type of franchise dominates the field, accounting for over one-half of all franchise sales in Canada. For strategic reasons, Coca-Cola began buying back their franchises in Canada in 1986, and now only 2 percent of sales are accounted for by franchisees.[8] Pepsi Cola Canada is also buying back their franchises.

Business format franchising

Business format franchising is characterized by an ongoing business relationship between the franchiser and franchisee that includes not only the product, service, and trademark, but the entire business format. Such franchises include a marketing strategy and plan, operating manuals and standards, quality control, and continuing two-way communications. Restaurants (Cultures), nonfood retailing (Colour Your World, Cyclepath), personal and business services (Uniglobe), rental services (Rent-A-Wreck, Jumbo Video), lawn care services (Nutri-Lawn), and a long list of other service businesses fall into the category of business format franchising. Business format franchising, particularly in the fast-food business, has been responsible for much of the growth of franchising in Canada and will probably continue to offer excellent opportunities. The top 10 Canadian business format franchises in the fast-food industry are presented in Table 8–1.

Table 8–1	Top Ten Business Format Franchises (Fast-Food)		
Company	**1994 Revenue ($ millions)**	**Units**	**Business/Operations**
McDonald's Canada	$1,622	824	McDonald's Restaurants
Cara Operations	995	1,544	Franchiser/operator of Harvey's, Swiss Chalet, Church's Chicken
Scott's Hospitality	698	915	Franchiser of Kentucky Fried Chicken; operator of Manchu Wok, Sizzler, and Sbarro
KFC Canada	630	850	Franchisee of Kentucky Fried Chicken in Canada
TDL Group	600	961	Franchiser/operator of Tim Horton Donuts
Pizza Hut Canada	382	462	Franchiser of Pizza Hut in Canada
A&W Food Services Canada	317	469	Franchiser/operator of A&W Restaurants, Shoppsy's, and Frisco Jacks
Subway Franchise	311	871	Franchiser of Subway Sandwiches and Salads
Dairy Queen Canada	248	557	Franchiser/operator of Dairy Queen and Orange Julius
Burger King Canada	240	203	Franchiser/operator of Burger King in Canada

Source: "Top 100 Listings," *Foodservice and Hospitality*, July 1995.

McDonald's, Canada's and the world's leading franchise, with another creative ad

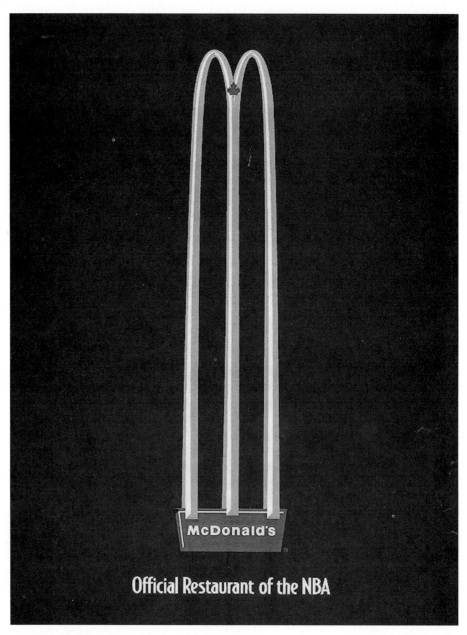

Courtesy McDonald's Restaurants of Canada Ltd.

Forms of Franchise Arrangements

Product and trade-name franchises and business format franchises can assume a variety of forms. The franchiser may sell individual franchises to persons who will develop each one. Alternatively, franchisers may sell **master franchises,** or **area-development franchises.**

Master franchisees buy the rights to an extensive geographic area but do not build and operate franchises. Rather, they divide the area into segments and sell the rights within the territory to individual franchisees. Franchisers often are attracted to the master franchise concept because it is easier for corporate management to work with one large franchisee than many small ones. Persons granted such franchises have substantial financial strength, which increases their likelihood of success. Southland Corporation, which franchises 7-Eleven convenience stores, uses the master franchise format.

A second alternative is the area-development franchise. The franchisees purchase a large territory and open a large number of shops themselves. As an example, Ramtron Pre-entry Alarm Systems of Winnipeg sells area-development franchises on a provincial basis.

The Costs of Franchising

Typically, a franchisee agrees to sell a product or service under contract and to follow the franchiser's formula. The franchiser is normally paid an initial fee for the right to operate at a particular location and a franchise fee based on monthly sales. The various costs involved in becoming a franchisee can include the following: the initial cost, the franchise fee, opening costs, working capital, premises expenses, site evaluation fees, royalties and service fees, and promotion charges. Each cost is briefly described below.

- *Initial costs.* Franchisees typically must pay an initial sum for the right to operate under the terms and conditions of the franchise. The amount may be only a down payment with the remainder financed by the franchiser or from other financing sources.
- *Franchise fee.* The right to use the trademark, license, service mark, or other operating procedures of the franchise.
- *Opening costs.* Payments for equipment, inventory, and fixtures.
- *Working capital.* The operating expenses needed until the business breaks even.
- *Premises costs.* The costs of building, remodeling, and decorating.
- *Site evaluation fee.* The charge by the franchiser to determine the market potential at alternative sites.
- *Royalties.* A continuing service charge or payment based on monthly gross sales. In return for the charge, the franchiser provides such services as product research, management advice, accounting services, inventory records, and similar activities.
- *Promotion costs.* A percentage of gross sales, normally 1 or 2 percent, to support local advertising and promotion.

Typical franchise fees are structured as follows:

- Soapberry Shop - Franchisees pay a $20,000 franchise fee and require between $130,000 and $180,000 in start-up costs. They do not pay a royalty on sales but they do purchase all their supplies from the franchiser.
- Tim Horton's - The franchise fee is $50,000 and start-up costs range between $200,000 and $245,000. Franchisees pay 4.5 percent of gross sales as royalties.

- McDonald's - Franchisees invest, on average, $700,000 to open a new outlet. The money pays for the equipment within the store and entitles the franchisees to a 20-year operating license. Additionally, the franchisee pays fees generally totalling about 12.5 percent of annual gross sales in return for services that include training for management and crews, operating assistance, marketing, financial advice, and menu research.

- College Pro Painters - There is no franchise fee and the start-up costs are estimated at $2,000 to $3,000. The royalty fee ranges between 14 percent and 17 percent of gross sales. All College Pro franchisees start out as university or college students.

- Yogen Fruz - Franchisees pay a franchise fee of $25,000 and the start-up costs range between $55,000 and $130,000. They are required to pay 6 percent of gross sales for royalty fees and 2 percent for advertising.

Identifying Franchise Opportunities

Franchise opportunities are easy to identify. Choosing the right one is difficult. Intense competition exists among franchisers in attracting interested franchisees and advertisements for franchise opportunities are common in many newspapers. Both the *Financial Post* and the *Globe & Mail* have an advertising section devoted to franchise opportunities ranging from travel agencies to submarine sandwich shops to total body care retail concepts. Various publications also provide information on available franchises. The *Franchise Annual* and the *Buyer's Guide to Franchise and Business Opportunities* contain listings of Canadian franchise opportunities.[9] *The Rating Guide to Franchises* rates a number of franchises including some Canadian operations.[10] Each franchise is rated on six criteria: industry experience, franchising experience, financial strength, training and services, fees and royalties, and satisfied franchisees. Each criterion receives a rating between one and four stars. Business fairs are also held at which franchisers try to attract franchisees.

Evaluating the Franchise and the Franchise Company

Provincial legislation

Alberta is the only province in Canada that has regulations governing franchising companies. Ontario is considering legislation that is similar to Alberta's. The Alberta Franchise Act is designed to protect potential franchisees by requiring the franchiser to provide complete disclosure of all the facts relating to the franchise being offered. A prospectus must be filed with The Alberta Securities Commission outlining the franchiser's financial capabilities, the history of the franchise company, its principals, and franchisees who have left the system. Potential franchisees in Alberta are entitled to a copy of the prospectus.[11] Because most Canadian franchisees are not protected by specific legislation, individuals considering buying a franchise should proceed with caution and a lawyer should be consulted before any franchise purchase is made.

Evaluating the company

The franchising company should have a good credit rating, a strong financial position, and a favourable reputation in the business community. The firm also should have been in business for a sufficient period of time to demonstrate expertise and the ability of its products or services to prosper in a competitive environment. The local and national offices of the Better Business Bureau should be contacted to determine if there have been complaints about the franchise company and, if so, how they were resolved. Also, the Canadian Franchise Association and the appropriate provincial Ministry of Consumer Affairs should be contacted about the reputation of the company and its product.[12] Various books and other information sources are also available to help guide the potential franchisee through the evaluation process.[13]

Evaluating the product or service

Interested buyers should make sure the product or service has been tested in the marketplace before signing a franchise agreement. An independent investigation to determine the likelihood of the franchise's success in a local market is also in order. Equally important is an evaluation of the product warranties as part of the franchise agreement. The prospective buyer should understand the terms and conditions of the warranty, who is issuing the warranty, and the reputation of the company for keeping its promises. The buyer should also determine the legitimacy of claimed trademarks, service marks, trade names, and copyrights.

Understanding the franchise contract

The franchise contract varies by franchiser. The contract is a legal document that specifies the rights and responsibilities of the franchiser. The advice of a lawyer should be sought before signing the document. The critical areas to be considered in deciding whether to sign a franchise agreement include the nature of the company, the product, the territory, the contract, and assistance available.

All franchise contracts contain a variety of provisions to which the franchisee must agree. For example, the franchisee typically must agree to abide by the operating hours established by the franchisee. The franchisee often must also agree to use a standardized accounting system, follow companywide personnel policies, carry a minimum level of insurance, use supplies approved by the franchiser, and follow the pricing policies established by the franchiser.

The franchiser often retains the right to require the franchisee to periodically remodel his or her establishment(s) and to allow the franchiser to conduct unscheduled inspections. Territorial restrictions are typically stated in the contract agreement and provisions for expanding into additional territories are carefully stated.

Some contracts impose sales quotas that are designed to ensure that the franchisee vigorously pursues sales opportunities in the territory. Most contracts also prohibit a franchisee from operating competing businesses and prohibit an individual whose franchise has been terminated from opening a similar type of business for a specified period of time.

Most franchise contracts cover a minimum period of 15 years. They typically contain provisions for termination and renewal of the contract, the franchisee's right to sell or transfer the business, and a provision for arbitration of disputes between the franchiser and franchisee.

Termination

Franchise contracts typically contain a provision for cancellation by either party upon 30 to 60 days' notice. Normally, franchises can only be terminated when the franchisee fails to meet the conditions of the franchise contract, including minimum payments required, sales quotas, and the need to keep the premises in good condition.

Renewal

The franchiser can refuse to renew the contract of any franchisee who does not fully comply with the terms of the contract, including maintaining required quality standards. Termination provisions give the franchiser substantial power over franchisees.

Transferring a franchise

The franchisee normally does not have the right to sell or transfer the franchise to a third party without the concurrence of the franchiser. However, sale or transfer to a third party typically is not a problem.

Buy-back provisions

The franchiser often has the option to purchase a franchise unit or the inventory if the franchisee decides to sell. The buy-back provision is an advantage to the franchisee because it can provide a ready sale for the outlet.

Deciding on the price for the sale is often not easy. Some franchisers will offer a price that will only cover the value of the building and the equipment and will not consider payment for goodwill. Goodwill is the price set for the intangible assets of a business including its future earning power and its condition at the time of the sale. Franchisers often maintain that the goodwill of the business is reflected in the trademark or tradename.

Arbitration provisions

Arbitration (the settlement of a dispute by a person or persons chosen to hear both sides and come to a decision) may be used to settle disputes between franchisers and franchisees. Arbitration is faster and less expensive than litigation and, with many franchise agreements today, disputes are settled by arbitration.[14]

Franchisee advisory councils

Some franchisees have established franchisee advisory councils to represent individual owners in dealing with the franchiser. The purpose of joining together is to allow the franchisees to accomplish common goals and to exert greater power over the franchiser in resolving issues that are of concern to the individual franchisees. The franchisees as a group can also support needed legislation, exchange ideas, and generally work to strengthen their position relative to the franchiser.[15]

Photo by Betty McDougall

Trends and Outlook

All trends indicate that franchising will continue to expand, creating great opportunities for existing and new businesses, developing new entrepreneurs, new jobs, new products, and new services. With long-term prospects for franchising bright, growing numbers of smaller companies, operating in local or regional markets, are turning to franchising for new ways to distribute their goods and services. Continuing economic improvement, stable prices, a slower-growing population, and increased competition for market share are turning many companies, both large and small, to franchising. Franchising can enable these firms to cover existing markets or penetrate new markets at minimal cost.

Although the overall trend for franchising is positive, some caution is warranted. Many markets are crowded with franchise outlets and new entrants have difficulty surviving. As well, whereas many of the large franchise markets, such as car dealerships, fast-food outlets and auto-service shops, are profitable, often the newer franchises are operating in markets that are considerably smaller and have limited opportunity. For example, franchises in home inspection, portable shelter, custom closets, and flavoured shaved ice have limited profit potential because the overall market size is relatively small.

Two new trends in franchising that are growing in popularity are "minifranchising" and "twinning." *Minifranchising* is a smaller version of a franchise, often located in a unique setting, such as a McDonald's in Wal-Mart. These Mc-Donald's offer limited menus and rely on the store traffic to generate their business. Silcorp, which operates the Mac's and Mike's Mart chains in Canada, has entered franchise agreements with Subway and Pizza Hut to open limited

Retail Highlight 8–1

Wendy's and Tim Horton's: The Fast-Food Alliance

In late 1995, when Wendy's and Tim Horton's merged, it was the largest example of "twinning" or alliances in the fast-food business in Canada. The benefits to combination restaurants like Tim Horton's-Wendy's are:

- More product offerings to meet different tastes.
- More use of dining areas throughout the day (Tim Horton's for breakfasts and snacks, Wendy's for lunches and dinners).
- More cost savings by pooling supplies, staff administration, and real estate.
- Entry into smaller towns because of the added draw of both restaurants.

Other franchise chains have pursued twinning so consumers can have:

- Frozen yogurt and donuts (Yogen Fruz and Country Style Donuts).
- Fried chicken and burgers (Church's or Swiss Chalet and Harvey's).
- Pizza and chicken (Pizza Delight and Le Coq Roti).
- Cookies and fries (Mrs. Field's Cookies and New York Fries).

Industry experts see these firms as trying to create a new market and draw more people into their stores at a time of day when the stores usually don't attract customers. As well, many consumers prefer to buy food from familiar and trusted brand names.

Sources: Marina Strauss, "Marriage All the Rage in Fast-Food Field," *Globe & Mail*, August 10, 1995, p. B7; and Greg Ip, "Dollars for Doughnuts," *Financial Post*, September 2, 1995, p. 7.

menu versions of these franchises in a number of its locations. The advantage for the franchiser, like McDonald's or Pizza Hut, are the franchise fees and royalties from locations that would not be available with their existing formats. For the franchisee, the advantages are reduced dependence on existing product lines, increased sales from new product lines, and increased traffic because of the well-known franchises like McDonald's. The disadvantage for the franchiser may be some customer disappointment because the minifranchise does not offer the complete product line and for the franchisee, the possibility of a low return on investment because of the location.

Twinning is a concept that puts two different franchise operations under the same roof. The idea is to find a combination where consumers shop for two different types of product at different times of the day or to offer consumers more choice and thereby attract a wider market segment. For example, combining doughnut and ice cream franchises may lead to a more balanced and profitable operation. The $400 million merger of Wendy's and Tim Horton's is probably the most well-known example of twinning, but a number of franchise firms have pursued this option (Retail Highlight 8–1). Harvey's, one of Canada's largest restaurant chains, is adding Church's Chicken franchises into some of its Harvey's restaurants and Swiss Chalet into others. The strategy of twinning has improved sales and profits for Harvey's.[16]

Business and personnel franchise services in particular are expected to continue to rise significantly for the next few years. Companies will need additional business and management consulting services to provide innovative marketing ideas geared to a better-educated and more affluent consumer in highly segmented markets.

In summary, major changes are in progress in the economy as a whole. As we move toward the year 2000, creativity and imagination in the treatment of

Tim Horton's, the leader, with over 1,000 franchises in Canada

Photo by Betty McDougall

goods and services will be richly rewarded. The continuing trend toward a service economy and the desire of individuals to "be their own boss" suggest that franchising will be a growing method of doing business in the future.[17]

Chapter Highlights

- Franchising is a way of doing business that allows an independent business person (the franchisee) to use another firm's (the franchiser) operating methods, financing systems, trademarks, and products in return for payment of a fee.

- Franchising is one of the fastest-growing segments of retailing in Canada and accounts for about 40 percent of retail sales. Experts predict continued growth in new franchises and sales. About 1,300 franchising companies are operating in Canada today with over 50,000 outlets across the country.

- The overriding advantage of a franchising program is the ability to quickly expand a company with limited capital. Another advantage of franchising is the training programs that are available that allow an individual to enter a business with no experience. The franchisee can also benefit from the purchasing power of the franchiser. Equally important are the programs of research and development that many franchisers have established to improve their product or service.

- A major disadvantage of a franchise is the high initial fee. The franchisee also gives up some flexibility in return for the right to purchase a franchise. Complaints may arise over the nature of the franchise contract.

- Franchises are of two basic types: product and trade-name franchises such as automobile dealers and gasoline outlets, and business format franchising in which firms that have developed a unique method of performing a service or of doing business sell the concept to others.

- Franchisers may grant individual franchisees to businesspersons. Alternatively, they may sell master franchises. Some persons purchase area-development franchises, which give them the right to an extensive territory in which they develop a large number of outlets.

- The various costs involved in becoming a franchise can include the initial cost, the franchise fee, opening costs, working capital, premise expenses, site evaluation fees, royalties and service fees, and promotion charges.

- Evaluating franchise opportunities includes determining the credit rating, financial position, and reputation of the franchiser. As well, the product or service offered should be market tested and the franchise concept should be thoroughly understood.

- The typical franchise contract gives the franchisee the right to sell a product or service under an arrangement that requires the individual to follow the franchiser's formula. The franchiser is usually paid an initial fee for the right to operate at a particular location and a franchisee fee based on monthly sales.

- Trends indicate that franchising will continue to expand, creating opportunities for new businesses, jobs, and products and services.

Key Terms

arbitration 208
area-development franchise 204
business format franchising 202
franchise contract 200
franchisee 200

franchiser 200
master franchise 204
product and trade-name
   franchising 202

Discussion Questions

1. What are the differences between product and trade-name franchising, and business format franchising?
2. Discuss why franchising has become a powerful force in retailing.
3. Write a brief essay on the cost elements that are typically included as part of a franchising contract.
4. What are the issues a prospective franchisee should evaluate in deciding whether to purchase a franchise?
5. What are the ingredients of a typical franchise contract?

6. **Highlight the advantages and disadvantages of becoming a franchisee and of franchising as a way of doing business.**

7. **What are the legal restrictions on franchising?**

8. **Discuss the trends and outlook for franchising.**

Application Exercises

1. Review the various sources cited in the chapter (these typically are found in your local library) to establish the initial opening costs for the following types of franchises: A national food franchise such as Tim Horton Donuts, a personnel service franchise such as Weed Man, a retail cosmetics franchise such as Faces, and a car rental business such as Rent-A-Wreck.

2. Talk to the owner/managers of three fast-food franchises in your community and write an essay outlining the primary advantages and disadvantages they see in being a franchisee.

3. Interview the owner of a local automobile agency (an example of a product and tradename franchise) and the owner of a business format franchise. What are the similarities and differences between the two types of franchises? Which type of franchise is likely to generate the greatest loyalty to the franchiser?

Suggested Cases

8. Diego's
10. Clean Windows Inc.
15. The Maaco Franchise
16. Dans un Jardin

Notes

1. Based on material provided by M&M Meat Shops.

2. Paul Brent, "Franchising at New Highs, But Be Wary," *Financial Post,* February 17, 1995, p. 15; and David Thomas, "Franchise Industry Up, Up and Away," *Financial Post,* February 16, 1996, p. 15.

3. Bruce Gates, "Predictability Breeds Profitability," *Financial Post,* March 20, 1992, p. 11; and Andrew E. Server, "Trouble in Franchise Nation," *Fortune,* March 6, 1995, pp. 115–129.

4. "Franchising Today," *Canadian Business,* Supplement to March 1995 Issue, p. B24. For more on franchisee problems, see John Lorinc, "War and Pizza," *Canadian Business,* November 1995, pp. 86–97.

5. John Southerst, "If You're 'Entrepreneurial,' Forget Franchising," *Globe & Mail,* May 8, 1995, p. B5.

6. John Heinzl, "Burger King Makes It His Way, Right Away," *Globe & Mail,* April 17, 1992, p. B1.

7. Bernadette Schell and Sheila McGillis, "Franchise Legislation Disclosure Information: Views from Franchisers and Franchisees on Its Impact on Franchisees' Satisfaction and Commitment Levels," *Journal of Small Business and Entrepreneurship,* October-December, 1993, pp. 83–104.

8. Coca Cola Beverages, Annual Report, 1994.

9. *The 1995 Franchise Annual,* Info Press, Inc., St. Catharines, Ontario, 1995; and *1996 Buyer's Guide to Franchise and Business Opportunities,* Entrepreneur Magazine, 1995.

10. Dennis L. Foster, *The Rating Guide to Franchises,* Facts on File Publications, New York, 1994.

11. John Southerst, "Tougher Franchise Disclosure in the Works," *Globe & Mail,* October 9, 1995, p. B7; and David Thomas, "National Franchising Rules Are in the Works," *Financial Post,* February 16, 1996, p. 16.

12. Douglas Gray and Norman Friend, *The Canadian Franchise Guide,* McGraw-Hill Ryerson, 1994.

13. Michael M. Coltman, *Franchising in Canada: Pros and Cons,* Self Counsel Press, North Vancouver, 1995; Lynn Beresford, "The Right Stuff," *Entrepreneur,* August 1995, pp. 158–164; John Lorinc, *Opportunity Knocks: The Truth About Canada's Franchise Industry,* Prentice-Hall Canada 1995; and Canadian Franchise Association, *Invest Before Investing,* Monograph.

14. John Southerst, "The Warning Signs in Franchise Deals," *Globe & Mail,* August 21, 1995, p. B7.

15. David Thomas, "Franchise Advisory Councils Can Be Good for Business, *Financial Post,* February 17, 1995, p. 20.

16. Cara Operations Limited, Annual Report, 1995.

17. For more on franchising, see Andrew J. Sherman (ed.), *The Franchise Handbook,* American Management Association, New York, 1993; and John Lorinc, *Opportunity Knocks: The Truth About Canada's Franchise Industry,* Prentice-Hall Canada, 1995.

Developing the Human Resources Plan

Chapter Objectives

After reading this chapter you should be able to:

1. Understand the importance and content of personnel policies.

2. Discuss how to determine needed job skills and abilities.

3. Plan and conduct an effective retail personnel recruitment and selection process.

4. Discuss the need to train employees.

5. Outline and describe the various methods for evaluating and compensating retail employees.

6. Discuss the issues involved in employee motivation and job enrichment.

7. Explain how to organize for profits.

Salespeople are critical to a specialty store like Birks.

*A*ccording to a recent Angus Reid poll, 56 percent of Canadians said they had not had a recent shopping experience where the customer service was excellent, and 30 percent said the service was so bad, they swore never to return to that store. About 18 percent blamed rude employees, and 11 percent fingered slow service or a long wait. On the other hand, many Canadians indicate that they like to shop in the United States because of the excellent service they receive. There is more to good customer service than a smiling and polite salesperson. A large part of excellent customer service is a highly trained and competent staff. Consider the following examples:[1]

- When a regular customer complained that her favourite lunch selection, "black bean fried rice," was not on the menu, Christine Renner, manager of Vancouver's Fortes Seafood House, responded in a positive way. If that valued customer would call the day before her next lunch, she would make arrangements. And, when the customer showed up, she was handed a menu where her favourite dish was featured as the first special of the day. This level of service is no accident, but the result of lots of planning and special training by Bud Kanke, the owner of Joe Fortes Seafood House, The Cannery, and The Fish House. In 1995, companywide training cost $200,000, and *all* employees, including bussers, have to go through the program.

- Much of the success of British-owned HMV can be credited to its former president Paul Alofs, who ran what he called "superstores with a soul." According to Alofs, Canadian retailers tend to overlook the importance of their most obvious asset: their employees. This, in turn, explains the generally poor customer service tradition in Canada. "I go to the Young Presidents' organization and the Retail Council of Canada and they say the customer is number one . . . but if you ask them what their incentive programs are like, or how much they spend on training and development, they answer, 'Well, what does that have to do with customer service?' " At HMV, all staff, from clerks to managers, are paid above the industry norm, and HMV spends "more than all of our competitors put together times five" on staff training and development. Store managers earn 10 to 20 percent above competition, and at Christmas they receive higher bonuses than the senior management team and the board of HMV receive for the entire year. Says Alofs: "We put our money where our mouth is. It's not us taking the glory and us taking the money."

- In the field of retail jewelry, you hear a similar story: according to a jewelry manager, "no matter how well you watch your cash flow, manage your inventory, or make your store attractive to customers, you'll lose business if you don't work to develop your salespeople. In a high-service business such as jewelry retailing, contact between the salesperson and the customer makes or breaks the bond between your store and your clientele. However, many jewelers still don't recognize how important that connection is. A retailer who is doing a poor job of developing employees' potential will see a high turnover rate among salespeople, combined with a general lack of motivation and bad customer relations. Employees will be more interested in coffee breaks and quitting time and less interested in taking care of customers." ■

The unique success of well-known retail outlets such as Joe Fortes Seafood House or HMV depends to a substantial degree on the skills, motivation, and dedication of their employees. Employees should not be regarded as throw-away assets. All dimensions of the human resources plan, ranging from selection and placement to pay and performance appraisal, should be structured to allow employees to feel they are a vital part of the organization. Sensitivity to the issues inherent in employee motivation and job enrichment are also important in progressive organizations.

The Retail Human Resources Challenges

The human resources environment has become increasingly volatile in recent years as a result of such issues as testing for illegal drug use, concern over child care, the impact of mergers, acquisitions, restructuring, and the Canada-U.S. Free-Trade Agreement on human resources.

Human resources staffs, as never before, are looking for ways to motivate and empower employees. The challenges are numerous:

- Training a nontraditional work force consisting increasingly of immigrants and older people.
- Competing against other industries that normally pay more for entry-level and mid-level management employees.
- Identifying innovative approaches to finding and keeping good employees.
- Meeting expectations for sales increases, productivity, and customer satisfaction.
- Finding ways to remain competitive as mid-level managers and top-level executives continue to be eliminated in downsizing programs.[2]

All managers need to understand and appreciate the importance of good personnel policies in the recruiting, training, and compensation of employees in addition to organizational issues. Understanding the goals and values of employees can also be of great benefit in avoiding unnecessary conflicts in the enterprise.

The development of a human resources plan in helping to implement competitive strategy is thus becoming increasingly important in retailing. One reason is that the age of growth through expansion seems to be almost over for many firms. More emphasis is being placed on market share management and improving productivity through better use of people, current assets, and facilities.

Both of these avenues for growth put stress on human resources personnel because of the labour-intensive nature of retailing. The payroll/sales ratio runs to as much as 25 percent in the higher-price/better-service stores such as Holt Renfrew. The specialty store is the most labour-intensive type of retailer, with payroll ratios as high as 30 percent.

Success in maintaining a results-oriented focus in the organization depends on defining or enforcing performance standards at each level in the organization. Specific performance measures are needed not only for the entire organization but for each line of business and each functional area. Normally, multiple measures are needed. Some measures are objective; others are necessarily somewhat subjective and include employee morale, customer satisfaction, and employee-management relations.

The focus should always be on achievement, producing results by using the full array of rewards and punishments outlined in this chapter. Intense people orientation, constantly reinforced, is the key to getting everyone in the organization committed to the goals to be achieved. The key element is making champions out of the people who turn in winning performances. Disney (see Retail Highlight 9–1) refers to employees as *cast members,* and McDonald's uses the term *crew member.* Such firms seek out reasons and opportunities to reward good performance.

The remaining portions of this chapter focus on four things: what employees are expected to do for the company, what the company can do for the employee, how the two can work together to accomplish organizational objectives, and how to effectively organize the company.

What the employees are expected to do for the company

1. Prepare a job description and job analysis.
2. Recruit applicants.
3. Select employees.

Retail Highlight 9–1

Good Employees Are a Major Part of the Retail Offering

Everyone who is "employed" by Disney, from dishwasher to monorail operator, begins with three days of training and indoctrination at Disney University.

Disney never hires an employee for a job. The "actors" are "cast" in a "role" to perform in a "show." Sometimes the show is called Walt Disney World, sometimes Disneyland, sometimes The Disney Store, and so forth. Their main purpose is to look after the "guests." Disney has never had customers.

Every "cast member" is provided with a "costume," not a "uniform." That way a guest doesn't have to ask: "Do you work here?" Each cast member is told not to hesitate to get a new costume if the old one gets dirty. Cast members do not work the floor; they are "on stage." The stock rooms and other nonpublic areas are "backstage."

One cast member is always designated to be the "greeter." The greeter position is a very important one. The role is to greet all guests as they enter and as they leave, and to thank them for "visiting our store," not for shopping. The greeter sets the tone for the guests' visit and also acts as a small deterrent to shoplifting because people are less likely to shoplift if they have been recognized by someone when they enter the store.

The words *no* and *I don't know* are not part of the Disney script. Everything is positive. Instead of "I don't know," cast members say, "I'll find out." Instead of, "We don't have any," cast members say, "We are out of," and instead of saying, "That item won't be available until," they say, "That item will be available on." Any response to the guest is phrased in a positive manner.

The Disney Store does not have stuffed animals; it has "plush" animals. A Disney Store cast member always points with an open palm, not the index finger. When you point with the index finger, four fingers are pointing back at you. Besides, when you were younger and your parents pointed at you, you knew you were in trouble.

The Disney show is several things. It's the entire experience that is created by the environment, the merchandise, the attractions, the music, and so forth, but, most importantly, it is the people. The cast members have a certain look that includes style of hair, makeup, name tags, and so on, all of which are a part of the Disney script.

What dimensions of the Disney employee culture appear to set the firm apart from other retailers?

Source: Prepared by Donald Smith, a cast member at The Disney Store, a Division of Walt Disney Enterprises.

What the company can do for the employee

1. Develop an employee pay plan.
2. Plan employee benefits.
3. Make employee performance appraisals.

How the company and employees can work together to accomplish organizational objectives

1. Improve employee relations and develop personnel policies.
2. Work on job enrichment.

How to effectively organize the company

1. Develop organizing principles.
2. Develop organizational structure.

The Job Analysis and Job Description[3]

A manager looking for someone to fill a job should spell out exactly what he or she wants in the job description. Imagine an owner/manager advertising for a "sales clerk." What should the applicant be able to do? Just tally sales receipts accurately? Keep a customer list and occasionally promote products? Run the store while the manager is away? The job of sales clerk means different things to different people. Retailers should determine what skills are needed for the job, what skills an applicant can get by with, and what kind of training should be given to the employee.

Good *job descriptions* and *job specifications* are excellent tools but they will not, by themselves, assure the best possible selection and assignment of employees to jobs, nor will they assure that the employees will be trained and paid properly. If good job descriptions and clear job specifications exist, however, selection, training, and salary decisions will be much easier and better.[4] Job descriptions and job specifications are written from a *job analysis.*

Job analysis

Job analysis is a *method for obtaining important facts about a job.* Specifically, the job analysis obtains answers to four major questions that the job description and job specification require:

1. *What* physical and mental tasks does the worker accomplish?
2. *How* does the person do the job? Here the methods used and the equipment involved are explored.
3. *Why* is the job done? This is a brief explanation of the purpose and responsibilities of the job, which will help relate the job to other jobs.
4. What *qualifications* are needed for this job? Here are listed the knowledge, skills, and personal characteristics required of a worker for the job.

A job analysis thus provides a summary of job (1) duties and responsibilities, (2) relationships to other jobs, (3) knowledge and skills, and (4) working conditions of an unusual nature.

Conducting a job analysis

An easy way to begin a job analysis is to think about the various duties, responsibilities, and qualifications required for the position and jot them down on a note pad. The ingredients of a job analysis outline are shown in Table 9–1. Management should talk with the job supervisor or a person who now holds the job to fill in the details about the job.

When conducting a job analysis, it is important to describe the job and the requirements of the job rather than the employee performing it. (The present employee may be overqualified or underqualified for the job or simply have characteristics irrelevant for the job.)

It is also a good idea to keep in mind the ultimate goals of job analysis: to simplify and improve employee recruitment, training, and development, and to evaluate jobs for determination of salary and wage rates.

Table 9–1   Job Analysis Outline for a Sales Manager
Duties
Assist customers with purchases
Develop expertise of staff
Achieve sales goals
Schedule hours and assign work to subordinates
Complete performance reviews on time
Present merchandise
Manage inventory
Open and close store
Provide floor supervision
Education
University or college graduate
Relationships
Report to store manager daily
Meet daily with subordinates
Knowledge/Skills
Transaction entry
Merchandising and operating procedures
Selling skills and product knowledge
Sales analysis knowledge
Knowledge of company's human resources standards and procedures
Performance review skills
Merchandise program knowledge
Inventory control procedures
Employee training
Supervisory skills
Physical Requirements
Capable of basic manual skills
Able to work on feet all day
On-the-Job Hazards/Working Conditions
No danger if safety rules and regulations are followed.

Source: Sears Canada.

Using the job analysis

After a job analysis has been conducted, it is possible to write a job description and job specification from the analysis. A **job description** is that part of a job analysis that describes the content and responsibilities of the job and how the job ties in with other jobs in the firm. The **job specification** is that part of a job analysis that describes the personal qualifications required of an employee to do the job.

Figure 9–1 demonstrates the relationship of job analysis to job description and job specification.

In addition to their usefulness in explaining duties and responsibilities to the applicants, job descriptions and specifications can help with:

- **Recruiting.** Job descriptions and specifications make it easier to write advertisements or notices announcing the job opening, or explaining the job to an employment agency.

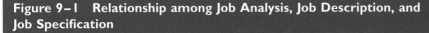

Figure 9–1   Relationship among Job Analysis, Job Description, and Job Specification

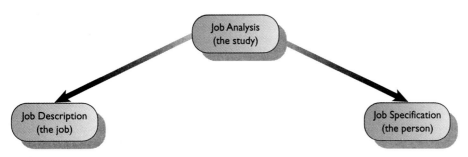

- **Interviewing applicants.** Since a job description provides a written record of the duties and requirements of a particular job, and a specification provides the qualifications needed for the job, they can be very helpful in planning an interview, especially as guidelines for asking the applicant questions about his or her abilities.

- **Training and development of new employees.** Having the duties of each job clearly defined can provide a basis for determining what knowledge and skills should be taught to new employees and helps to plan training so that (1) important skills are learned first and (2) the training is comprehensive.

- **Coordination.** Job descriptions, when they are available, can ensure that people know what is expected of them and that their activities are coordinated.

- **Setting wage rates and salaries of employees.** By providing a perspective of the relative amounts of work required and qualifications needed for different positions, fairer wage rates and salaries may be established. Remember that the minimum wage varies at the federal level, and from province to province (the highest is British Columbia and the lowest is Newfoundland).[5]

- **Employee relations.** The information about the job in the description can assure that fewer misunderstandings will occur about the respective duties and responsibilities of various jobs.

Job description

A job description is a summary of the important facts about a particular job. It states in a concise, clear way the information obtained in a job analysis. A fully adequate job description should be outlined on less than one page. For instance, a job description for a buyer at Sears Canada could be written as in Figure 9–2.

Job specification

A job specification, like a job description, is written from the job analysis and describes those personal requirements that should be expected of anyone who is placed on the job, as well as any unusual or hazardous environmental

Considerable product knowledge is required for many retail positions.

Photo by James Hertel

conditions that the jobholder must be prepared to accept. A job specification thus describes the type of employee required for successful performance of the job. One way to prepare a job specification is shown in Figure 9–3.

Recruiting Applicants

When the owner/manager knows the kind of skills needed in a new employee, he or she is ready to contact sources that can help recruit job applicants. Application forms help screen and select the best candidates.

Selecting the right recruiting methods

The recruiting methods used depend upon what type of employee is sought and how hard the retailer wants to search for the best available candidate.

Each recruiting method has its advantages and disadvantages. Some may be time consuming, such as direct newspaper ads, which require screening of all

Figure 9–2   Job Description for a Buyer

JOB DESCRIPTION

JOB TITLE: Buyer   Date: _____

Statement of the Job

Develops a marketing plan and advocates what is best for the company—item by item, line by line—and brings forth those recommendations to the company via the department/group marketing plan.

Major Duties

1. Makes recommendations on items and/or lines. This includes private label/national brand or combination, selling plan, item price by geographic region, vendor, inventory investment, and assortment and depth by store volume.
2. Purchases goods as agreed to in the marketing plan.
3. Ensures that sales personnel and customers understand the value of the product line.

Relationships

The buyer works with other buyers and store managers in preparing the group marketing plan. The buyer works with vendors to obtain merchandise and store personnel to market merchandise.

Source: Sears Canada.

who apply, or notices on college and university bulletin boards, which may be very slow in bringing in an adequate number of applicants. Others can be fairly costly, such as employment agencies, where competent applicants often expect the retailers to pick up the fee.[6] Some can be used concurrently, but it would be inefficient to use others in such a way.

In each province there is an employment service with several **Canada Human Resources Centres.** All are affiliated with the Federal Department of Human Resources Development Canada, which operates a computerized, nationwide job databank. Local Canada Human Resources Centres are ready to help businesses with their hiring problems. A retailer should be as specific as possible about the skills required for a job, and notify the Canada Human Resources Centre, who will post the notice of a job opening, with its requirements on its bulletin board. All interested applicants are interviewed by a Centre counsellor, and if the assessment is positive, a referral is made to the retailer.

Private employment agencies can also help in recruitment. However, the employee or the employer must pay a fee to the private agency for its services.

Another method of recruiting is a "Help Wanted" sign in the front window. But there are drawbacks to this method: a lot of unqualified applicants may inquire about the job, and a retailer cannot interview an applicant and wait on a customer at the same time.

Newspaper advertisements are another source of applicants. They reach a large group of job seekers, and retailers can screen these people at their convenience. But a retailer should think twice before listing the store's phone number in the ad. He or she may end up on the phone all day instead of dealing with customers.

Job applicants are also readily available from schools, colleges, and universities. The local high school may have a distributive education department,

Figure 9–3　Job Specification for a Sales Manager

JOB SPECIFICATION

JOB TITLE: Sales Manager　　　　　Date: _____

Education: (List only that which is really necessary for the job, e.g., high school, college, trade school, or other special training.)

University or community college graduate

Experience: (The amount of previous and related experience that a new employee should have.)

None specifically.

Knowledge/Skills: (List the specific knowledge and skills that the job may require.)
Must know how to:

- Enter customer transactions.
- Work within the merchandising and operating procedures (the list would include the elements listed in the job analysis in Table 9–1).

Physical and Mental Requirements: (Mention any special physical or mental abilities required for the job, e.g., 20/20 eyesight, availability for irregular work hours, ability to work under time pressure, etc.)

Must have a good personality and be able to lead and motivate people.

Source: Sears Canada.

where the students work in the store part-time while learning about selling and merchandising in school. Many part-time students stay with the store after they finish school. Colleges and universities also provide placement services for students, and are a good source of talent for retailers.

Retailers may also find applicants from a variety of informal sources (e.g., friends, neighbours, customers, suppliers, present employees) or local associations such as the Chamber of Commerce, or service clubs.

A combination of the many sources for job applicants may serve best. The important thing is to find the right applicant with the right skills for the job, whatever the source.

Reviewing recruiting practices

It is useful to review the firm's recruiting practices from time to time to see how they can be improved. The retailer may wish to simply note what brought success, as well as the methods that did not seem to work well. For example, it may turn out that the store's employees have often been able to refer better applicants than the employment agencies. Or it could be that advertising in the local newspaper seems to bring better applicants than posting notices on college or university bulletin boards.

Developing application forms

Some method of screening the applicants and selecting the best one for the position is needed. The application form is a tool that can be used to make the task of interviewing and selection easier. An example is shown in Figure 9–4. The form should have blank spaces for all the facts needed as a basis for judging

Figure 9–4   Sample Employee Application Form

APPLICATION FOR EMPLOYMENT

Name: _____   Date: _____

Last   First   Middle

Present address: _____   Social insurance no.: _____

Telephone number: _____   Driver's license no.: _____

Indicate dates you attended school:

Elementary from _____ to _____

High school from_____ to _____

College from_____ to _____

Other (specify type and dates) _____

Can you be bonded? _____ If yes, in what job? _____

Do you have any physical limitations that preclude you from performing certain kinds of work? _____

If yes, describe each and specify work restrictions: _____

_____

List below all present and past employment, beginning with most recent:

Name and address of company	From Mo/Yr	To Mo/Yr	Name of supervisor	Reason for leaving	Weekly salary	Describe the work you did

May we contact the employers listed above? _____ If no, indicate which ones you do not wish us to contact:

_____

Remarks: _____

_____

the applicant. Retailers will want a fairly complete application so they can get sufficient information. However, the form should be kept as simple as possible.

The retailer must not abuse the information from the application in hiring. The Canadian Human Rights Act prohibits discrimination in employment based on race, national or ethnic origin, religion, age, sex, marital status, family status, disability, and conviction for which a pardon has been granted.[7] This act applies to all departments and agencies of the federal government, all Crown corporations, and businesses under federal jurisdiction. The act is administered by the **Canadian Human Rights Commission** and a tribunal with broad powers to order an end of the discriminatory practice, some financial compensation for the victim, or to develop and implement an affirmative action program (Section 15). This last application of the act has been strengthened by the Constitution Act of 1982, especially the Charter of Rights and Freedoms.

Table 9–2   Major Laws Related to Employment Practices in Canada and the Provinces

Federal Jurisdiction

Canada Labour Code
Canadian Human Rights Act
Employment Equity Act
Equal Wages Guidelines
Fair Wages and Hours of Labour Act
Holidays Act
Wages Liability Act

Alberta

Employment Standards Code
Individual's Rights Protection Act
Family Day Act

British Columbia

Employment Standards Act
Human Rights Act
Skills Development and Fair Wage Act

Manitoba

Employment Standards Act
Human Rights Code
Pay Equity Act
Payment of Wages Act
Remembrance Day Act
Retail Business Holiday Closing Act
Shops Regulation Act
Vacations with Pay Act

New Brunswick

Days of Rest Act
Employment Standards Act
Human Rights Act
Minimum Employment Standards Act
Pay Equity Act

Newfoundland

Human Rights Code
Labour Standards Act
Remembrance Day Act

Nova Scotia

Human Rights Act
Labour Standards Code
Pay Equity Act
Remembrance Day Act
Retail Business Uniform Closing Day Act

Ontario

Human Rights Code
Employment Standards Act
Labour Relations Act
One Day's Rest in Seven Act
Retail Business Establishment Holidays Act
Wages Act

P.E.I.

Employment Standards Act
Human Rights Act
Pay Equity Act
Retail Businesses Holidays Act

Quebec

Charter of Human Rights and Freedoms
Civil Code
Collective Agreement Decrees Act
Hours and Days of Admission to
Commercial Establishments Act
Labour Standards Act
Manpower Vocational Training and
Qualification Act
National Holiday Act

Saskatchewan

Human Rights Code
Labour Standards Act
Lord's Day Act
National Holiday Act

Northwest Territories

Employment Standards Act
Fair Practices Act
Labour Standards Act
Wages Recovery Act

Yukon

Human Rights Act
Employment Standards Act
Lord's Day Act

Source: Adapted from Labour Canada, *Employment Standards Legislation in Canada, 1995–1996 Edition* (Hull: Supply and Services Canada, 1995).

In areas not under federal jurisdiction, which include most retailers, protection is given by provincial human rights laws, which are similar in contents and remedies to the federal law.

The list of laws related to employment practices is provided in Table 9–2, and they are compared in Table 9–3.

Table 9–3   A Comparison of Antidiscrimination Laws in Canada and in the Provinces

Jurisdiction	Federal	British Columbia	Alberta	Saskatchewan	Manitoba	Ontario	Quebec	New Brunswick	Prince Edward Island	Nova Scotia	Newfoundland	Northwest Territories	Yukon
Race	•	•	•	•	•		•	•	•		•	•	•
National or ethnic origin[1]	•					•	•	•	•	•	•		•*
Ancestry		•	•	•	•	•		•				•	•
Nationality[7]				•	•						•		
Based on association[8]										•			•
Place of origin		•	•	•		•	•				•		
Colour	•	•	•	•	•	•	•	•	•	•	•	•	•
Religion	•	•		•	•	•	•	•	•	•	•	•	•
Creed[2]			•	•	•	•	•				•		•
Age	•	•	•	•	•	•	•	•	•	•	•	•	•
(age limits)		(45–65)	(18+)	(18–65)		(18–65)	(19+)			(40+)	(19–65)		
Sex[6]	•	•	•	•	•****	•	•					•	•
Pregnancy or childbirth[6]	•		•	•	•	•							
Marital status[3]	•	•	•	•	•	•	•	•	•	•		•	•
Family status[3]	•					•						•	•
Pardoned offence						•							
Record of criminal conviction		•					•						•
Physical handicap or disability	•	•	•	•	•	•	•	•			•	•	•
Mental handicap or disability	•	•	•	•	•	•	•				•	•	•
Dependence on alcohol or drug[9]	•									•			
Place of residence												•	
Political belief		•			•		•			•			•**
Assignment, attachment or seizure of pay[4]											•		
Source of income					•								
Social condition[4]							•						
Language							•						
Social origin[4]											•		
Sexual orientation[5]						•	•						•
Harassment[5]	•					•***	•				•		•

[1] New Brunswick includes only "national origin."

[2] Creed usually means religious beliefs.

[3] Quebec uses the term *civil status*.

[4] In Quebec's charter, "social condition" may include assignment, attachment or seizure of pay and social origin.

[5] The federal, Ontario, Quebec and Yukon statutes ban harassment on all proscribed grounds. Ontario and Newfoundland also ban sexual solicitation.

[6] Sex includes ground of pregnancy. Pregnancy or childbirth is included within ground of sex. Based on policy for B.C., N.B., P.E.I., Nova Scotia, Newfoundland, Northwest Territories, Supreme Court of Canada has held that sex includes sexual harassment.

[7] Ontario's Code includes only "citizenship."

[8] Association with individuals determined by prohibited grounds of discrimination.

[9] Based on the policy for British Columbia, Saskatchewan, Manitoba and P.E.I.

   *Includes linguistic background.

  **Includes political activity or political association

 ***Does not include sexual orientation.

****Includes gender determined characteristics.

Source: Canadian Human Rights Commission, 1992.

Selecting Employees

After recruiting a number of job candidates, the retailer has to weed out the unqualified ones and then select the best remaining candidates for the job. The main tools will be the questions asked and perhaps pre-employment tests. Answers to some questions may be obtained through a resume, but by far the most informative answers come from a job interview and the job application form.

Many different selection methods are available. These include personal interviews, tests, and recommendations from various people who had contact with the candidates. The personnel office seeks to develop objective criteria in screening applicants to achieve the best match of person and position. One frequent approach to this problem is the development of performance criteria. Such an approach involves identifying the characteristics of those who perform the job in a superior manner. These characteristics are then sought in potential new employees. Ideally, a limited number of characteristics can be isolated. Executives can use the performance criteria in predicting which applicants will perform most satisfactorily. Such predictors may include intelligence scores, tests of manual dexterity, formal education, or past related job experiences.

One potential problem, however, is bias against some applicants because of the measures being used. Federal, provincial, and local governments actively challenge selection tools that can lead to bias in hiring. Companies can use employment tests if they can show that the tests are valid and reliable in predicting job success and that no better way exists to make such evaluations. This process is difficult and requires the use of statistics, including coefficients of correlation and other measures. Tests may also be biased because of cultural or language problems for some applicants.

The burden of proof rests with the employer. The employer must be able to show that the procedure utilized is capable of predicting job performance and does not systematically discriminate against any one group of applicants. Arbitrary job descriptions that specify minimum education levels, age, sex, marital status, or similar requirements are open to challenge. Management cannot use that "gut" feeling any more, because a rejected applicant may sue, charging unlawful discrimination on a variety of grounds.

Preliminary screening of applicants   It is wise to ask applicants to send resumes before scheduling appointments for interviews. This has two advantages:

- Reviewing resumes will enable the retailer to screen out some unacceptable job candidates. Priorities can also be assigned to the resumes so that the most promising candidates are seen first. In this way, the retailer will run less risk of losing the best ones to job openings in other firms while going through the selection procedure.
- When the retailer decides to interview a candidate, some background information on the person will be available from the resume and thus will enable the retailer to ask better questions and conduct a better interview.

The job interview

The objective of the job interview is to find out as much information as possible about the applicant's work background. The major task is to get the applicants to talk about themselves, their skills, and their work habits. The best way to go about this is to ask each applicant specific questions, such as: What did you do on your last job? How did you do it? Why was it done? Questions that have no relationship to the ability of a person to do the job in question cannot be considered in making a hiring decision.

As the interviews go along, evaluate the applicants' replies. Do they know what they are talking about? Are they evasive or unskilled in the job tasks? Can they account for discrepancies?

When conducting an interview, the following guidelines can be helpful:

- *Describe the job in as much detail as is reasonably possible.*
  Give descriptions of typical situations that might arise and ask the applicant how he or she would handle it. "What would you say to a customer with a complaint?" "What colour blouse would you recommend to complement a red plaid skirt?" Interviewers shouldn't expect responses to be as expert as their own, but training could make them so. Do not be discouraged or discouraging. Offer praise such as, "That is a good way to go about it. If we hire you, we can teach you several other ways to handle situations such as that."[8]

  A detailed description lets the applicant know the expectations from the earliest stage. It also lets the applicant make a realistic personal judgment as to his or her ability to fill the job.

- *Discuss the pluses and minuses of the job.*
  No job is without its minuses. If they are known initially, they are less likely to become obstacles later. If the person is expected to work nights, weekends, or holidays, say so. Disclosure can prevent many misunderstandings later.

- *Explain the compensation plan.*
  What is the salary? What fringe benefits are offered? What holidays are allowed? What is the vacation policy?

- *Weigh all factors in reaching a decision.*
  Of all the factors mentioned above, no single one is overriding. Perhaps the most important characteristics to look for are common sense, an ability to communicate with people, and a sense of personal responsibility. Only personal judgment will tell the interviewer whether the applicant has these characteristics.

Making the selection

When the interviews are over, the applicants should be asked to check back later if the interviewers are interested in the applicant. The interviewers should never commit themselves until they have talked with all likely applicants.

Next, the interviewers should *verify the information obtained*. Previous employers are usually the best sources. Sometimes, previous employers will give out information over the telephone that they might hesitate to put on paper for fear of being sued. But it is usually best to request a written reply.

To help ensure a prompt reply, retailers should ask previous employers a few specific questions about the applicant that can be answered with a yes-or-no check, or with a very short answer. For example: How long did the employee work for you? Was his or her work poor, average, or excellent? Why did the employee leave your employment?

Helping a customer find the "right" clothes and ensuring the best fit require excellent training.

Courtesy Hudson's Bay Company Ltd.

After the retailers have verified the information on all the applicants, they are ready to make the selection. The right employee can help the firm make money. The wrong employee will cost the firm much wasted time and materials, and may even drive away customers.

The Need to Train Employees[9]

The next step is to train employees. Sales training programs will be covered in Chapter 15, so this section will discuss the evolving nature of sales training in the context of the human resources plan.

In the past, sales training programs have been related to the hiring sequence and perhaps to retraining. Today, with the evolution of retail systems, the complexity of the environment, and the need to improve the delivery of customer service, old ideas of integrating an employee into the retail operation are no longer useful. In addition, the situation is complicated by different educational or cultural backgrounds of employees.

Today, employees must deal with complicated automated systems, and retailing requires candidates with higher intellectual qualities for a successful training program. These kinds of candidates are difficult to find even during recessions. Once found and selected, they must be given a customized training program covering all aspects of modern retail operations. In the introductory example of Bud Kanke, each of the 30 managers have to fill out a two-page goal planner; all 250 staff members have to go through a rigorous training program run by Executive Development Services which cost $250,000 in 1995. For example, waiters are told that they run a micro-business of six tables, and they have to succeed in that business, with daily performance sheets posted on a board.[10]

Retail Highlight 9-2

Masterminding Success by Training and Good Customer Service

One important strategy for independents to beat large, often impersonal chain stores is by emphasizing *product knowledge,* i.e., knowing just about all there is to know about products, related goods, and services, and how they are used. To provide this knowledge requires commitment, a trained staff, and low turnover. Jonathan Levy, co-owner of the 10 Toronto-area Mastermind stores (which sell educational toys and computer and science wares) knows that salespeople have to know what's appropriate for children of different ages and interests. But sales also depend on his staff giving out reliable, on-the-spot , easy-to-understand information.

Training is a priority. Levy holds regular seminars, bringing in suppliers "to transplant as much product knowledge as possible from the source to the end-user of the knowledge." But just to be sure, he has built in a fail-safe system. When store employees can't answer a customer's question, they can call any of three designated "experts," one for books, one for science, or Levy for other subjects, who work in the combined head office and warehouse. Levy says that the trio respond to three or four calls a day from each store.

Reaching out to customers after the sale keeps the information flowing, and sparks interest in new purchases. Three times a year, Levy publishes a newsletter that goes out to 20,000 customers, containing news, product reviews, and children's activities. "It's a way to reach out and touch our customers, to keep them informed about what we're doing," says Levy. What the newsletter does also is educate consumers (who are easier to sell to) *and* reinforce employee knowledge (ongoing training).

Source: Marlene Cartash, "Catching a Falling Store," *Profit,* December 1990, pp. 27–28.

Retail Highlight 9–2 further illustrates how important training employees is to excellent customer service.

An additional complication in today's environment is the changing demographic and cultural profile of the market, providing a pool of candidates who are culturally different from past employees, and from current customers. Again, the training program must try to bridge these gaps. Otherwise, the retailer may anticipate problems in terms of customer service perceptions.

Developing the Pay Plan[11]

Pay administration may be another term for something management is already doing but has not bothered to name. Or, perhaps the organization has not been paying employees according to any system, but waiting until unrest shows up to make pay adjustments—using payroll dollars to put out fires, so to speak.

A formal pay plan, one that lets employees know where they stand and where they can go as far as salary is concerned, will not solve all employee-relations problems. It will, however, remove one of those areas of doubt and rumour that may keep the work force anxious, unhappy, less loyal, and more mobile.

What is the advantage of a formal pay plan for the firm? In business, it is good people who can make the difference between success and failure. Many people like a mystery, but not when it is how their pay is determined. Employees working under a pay plan they know and understand can see that it is fair and uniform, and that pay is not set by whim. They know what to expect and can plan accordingly. In the long run, such a plan can help to (*1*) recruit, (*2*) keep, and (*3*) motivate employees, and (*4*) build a solid foundation for a successful business.

Types of salary plans

A formal pay plan does not have to be complex nor cost a lot of time and money. Formal does not mean complex. In fact, the more elaborate the plan is, the more difficult it is to put into practice, communicate, and carry out.

The foremost concern in setting up a formal pay administration plan is to get the acceptance, understanding, and support of management and supervisory employees. A well-defined, thoroughly discussed, and properly understood plan is a prerequisite for success.

The steps in setting up a pay plan are: (1) define the jobs as discussed earlier in the chapter, (2) evaluate the jobs, (3) price the jobs,(4) install the plan, (5) communicate the plan to employees, and (6) appraise employee performance under the plan.

Job evaluation and compensation

The question of how much to pay an employee in a particular position is an important but complicated matter. If management offers too little pay for a particular position, the good employee will leave to perform the same work elsewhere and only the less motivated, less able employee will remain for the lower pay. On the other hand, management has very little to gain by paying an employee far more than what is being paid in other organizations for the same work.

Job evaluation   **Job evaluation** is a method of ranking jobs to aid in determining proper compensation. Figure 9–5 can now be used to demonstrate the relationship of these four basic personnel management tools.

Figure 9–5   Relationship of Job Evaluation with Respect to the Other Three Management Tools

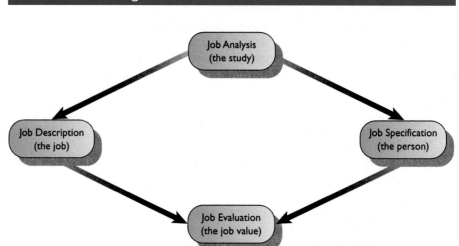

Thus, a job evaluation is obtained by evaluating both the responsibilities from a job description and the items on a job specification. The reason for job evaluation is to establish a fair method of compensating employees for their work.

Compensation   In determining pay rates, it is important to take several principles into consideration:

- Equal pay for equal work. This is a very important principle that has been slowly gaining acceptance by legislators in the federal and provincial levels. The federal government and some provincial governments have some form of pay equity regulations.
- Higher pay for work requiring more knowledge, skill, or physical exertion.
- Reasonable pay, in comparison, to pay for similar work in other organizations.
- Overqualified employees not paid more (or much more) than a qualified employee in the same position.
- After several years, very little or no extra pay for the length of time an employee has remained with the firm.
- Total earnings reflecting, in some way, the employee's contribution to the organization.
- As much as possible, pay scales known to employees.
- Fairness in application of these principles.

One general but fairly effective rule of thumb to follow when determining salaries and wage rates is to pay the most important nonsupervisory job as well as or somewhat better than the job receives elsewhere and to do the same for the least important full-time job. Rates for all other jobs can then be set in a reasonable way, in between. Job descriptions are often helpful in finding similar positions in other businesses with which to compare pay rates.

Management can obtain information on *competitive salaries* from various sources, including:

- Local surveys conducted by nearby business associations and organizations.
- Informal contacts, such as meetings with other owners/managers in social, civic, or community functions. Usually this information is useful only to get a general feel of things, since competitors may not wish to disclose salaries of jobs, and noncompetitive companies may be different from your firm.
- Industry meetings and conventions.
- Job advertisements in local newspapers and trade journals.
- National surveys, if they are available.

It is not always possible to compare salaries with pay rates in other businesses. This is especially true if some of the jobs in a business are not standard or common jobs.

Methods of job evaluation   Another way, then, to establish salaries and pay rates for jobs is to evaluate the worth of the job to the business, so that more important jobs receive more pay. In this way, management is able to take into

Table 9–4   Application of Job Ranking

Job Rank	Job Title	Salary or Wage Rate
1	Manager	$30,000 to $35,000 per year
2	Assistant manager	?
3	Cook 1	$24,000 to $26,000 per year
4	Cook 2	$8.00 to $8.50 per hour
5	Head waiter/waitress	$7.50 to $8.00 per hour
6	Cook's helper	?
7	Waiter/waitress	Minimum wage plus tips averaging $6.50 per hour
8	Dishwasher	?

consideration all but one of the principles of salary administration discussed earlier. This principle concerns providing a reasonable pay level, in comparison to pay for similar work in other organizations.

There are two different ways to evaluate jobs. They are:

- Ranking—comparing a job against a job.
- Classification—comparing the jobs with the aid of a scale.

These two methods are described in detail in the next sections.

The rank method of job evaluation

Job ranking, possibly with the aid of job descriptions, is the simpler and usually more practical way to evaluate jobs. The most valuable and complex job is assigned a "1"; the job that is second in complexity and importance, a "2," and so on until all jobs have been assigned a number. Jobs that are equal in importance may be assigned the same number. If management uses this method, they know that the higher the job's position on the list, the more important the job is to the business, and can assign pay levels accordingly.

In creating new jobs, management can then place them into their proper places in the ranking.

Example: Suppose that a restaurant owner/manager who is looking for an assistant manager, a cook's helper, and a dishwasher has the situation indicated in Table 9–4. In this case, the assistant manager should be paid more than a cook, but less than a manager, somewhere between $25,000 and $30,000 a year. A cook's helper seems to fit in the range of less than $8.00 per hour, but more than $6.50 per hour. The dishwasher, being the least important job, would receive the minimum wage or only a little above it.

The classification method of job evaluation

In the **job classification** method, jobs are evaluated and rated on two scales:

- *The complexity* of the various responsibilities and qualifications that are required on the job and their respective importance to good performance.
- *The length of time* the respective responsibility and qualification are utilized during the average day.

For each responsibility and qualification, two rating numbers are assigned—one for the complexity and importance to the job, and the other for the length of time during which it is used. For instance, if knowledge of computer programming is required on a job, it may receive a 7 for responsibility and qualification, but if that knowledge is required only a few hours out of each week, it may receive a 2 for length of time. These two numbers can then be multiplied and averaged with all other qualifications and responsibilities of that job, to provide a classification number. Large numbers indicate the more difficult and important positions. The method of evaluating jobs based on classification is a complex one and cannot be adequately described in this book.

Planned pay structure   In general, a planned pay structure makes it possible to tie individual rates of pay to job performance and contribution to company goals. Table 9–5 shows the most frequently used retail sales pay plans.

A *straight salary* is most likely to be paid in a small store in which employees have a variety of responsibilities other than selling. This pay plan also avoids the temptation for employees to engage in "pressure" selling. The drawback of the plan is that it does not provide an incentive for extra effort, which may lower employee motivation.

A *salary plus commission* is the most frequently administered plan in retailing, primarily because it emphasizes both selling and customer service. It provides an extra incentive for "plus sales" and also provides a stable income for employees.

The *quota-plus-bonus plan* provides for the payment of a bonus as a varying percentage of sales achieved above a quota established for each category of merchandise. The program allows unique sales incentives to be established by category of merchandise/tasks, does not encourage overly aggressive selling, and does provide a stable income during periods of slow sales. The disadvantages are that the plan can be misunderstood by employees and must be changed to reflect changes in the merchandise mix by season.

The *straight commission* pay plan provides a strong financial incentive for outstanding salespersons and thus is likely to attract strong sales personnel. The disadvantage is that the arrangement can promote overly aggressive "pressure" selling, which can antagonize customers. Employees may also be prone to focus excessive attention on high-cost goods, creating ill will and tension among salespersons.

Drawing account   A drawing account is a cash advance paid to retail salespeople. The account is established as a "draw" for the employee as needed. The amount withdrawn is repaid to the company out of the sales commissions earned during each period. A drawing account may or may not be guaranteed. Under a *nonguaranteed* plan, the advance is a loan. The balance of the debt is carried over to the next period if the salesperson does not earn a sufficient amount in commissions to pay back the advance in a single period.

A *guaranteed* draw account is one in which the loan debt is cancelled if the salesperson's commissions are less than the draw. In effect, a guaranteed draw is much like a salary. For that reason, the nonguaranteed draw is more widely used because it is less of a financial burden on the retailer.

Drawing accounts are designed to offset some of the disadvantages of the straight commission plan. They provide both security and regularity of income. The accounts are subject to abuse, however. Salespeople may view the draw as salary rather than a loan. In addition, employees in arrears may simply quit.

Table 9–5   Strengths and Weaknesses of Selected Forms of Retail Salesperson Compensation Plans

Method of Payment	Formula	Advantages	Disadvantages
Straight salary	Amount of pay established in advance for a defined pay period	Definite and easy for employees to understand Generally best for smaller stores Minimizes temptation to use "pressure" selling Encourages more conscientious and careful work Provides easier managerial control Good for inexperienced/new employees Simplifies payroll Provides a definite income to employees Fair	Inflexible Provides no financial incentive for extra effort Compensation does not fluctuate in proportion to sales volume Lack of incentives could promote laziness Strong supervision often required No opportunity to earn extra income

Example: Calculate the earnings of a salesperson who worked 40 hours during a week at the rate of $6 per hour.
Solution: 40 × $6 = $240

Salary plus commission	Guaranteed minimum salary plus an additional percentage based on amount of sales	Easy for employees to understand Emphasizes selling and customer service Stable income guaranteed when volume is low Provides financial incentive for extra effort Incentives easily controlled by management Good opportunity to earn extra income Less managerial supervision necessary	Small incentives could be ineffective Even ineffective salespeople receive commissions Increases departmental selling costs Poor salespeople could lose customers with "pressure" selling

Example: A salesperson who earns $6 per hour plus 2 percent commission on sales worked 39 hours during the week and had sales of $2,400 for that period.
Solution: (39 × $6) + ($2,400 × 2%) = $234 + $48 = $282

Quota bonus plan	Various percentages of sales are paid for different levels of sales achieved above the quotas set for each category of merchandise	Effective in smaller establishments Good incentives for special sales or tasks Encourages competitive spirit Stable income guaranteed when volume is low Does not overly promote "pressure" selling Very flexible for managerial use Automatic check against excess personnel Ensures prompt service to customers Less managerial supervision necessary	Not as easily understood by employees Sales returns could cause withheld bonuses and thus ill feelings Setting rates for quota bonuses is a delicate task Quota could be difficult to set from past sales Bonuses must be changed often for seasonal goods Unattainable bonuses destroy incentive

Example: A salesperson earns an 8 percent commission on sales made in excess of $2,000. Calculate the weekly earnings for an employee whose sales equaled $4,000, assuming the salesperson earns a weekly base salary of $200.
Solution: ($4,000 − $2,000) × 8% = $160 + $200 = $360

Table 9–5   (continued)

Method of Payment	Formula	Advantages	Disadvantages
Straight commission	Salary is based entirely on a percentage of sales. The percentage is typically higher for the most profitable merchandise.	Provides strong incentives to salespeople Easy for employees to understand Attracts better salespeople Guarantees planned selling cost for store Easy for management to operate Drawing account to ensure a definite income per pay period could be established by management to offset some disadvantages of this method (When necessary, pay is charged against future commissions)	Employees must be well trained and supervised No guaranteed income Factors beyond salesperson's control could substantially diminish earnings Too uncertain for average retail salesperson "Pressure" selling strongly encouraged Customers could be antagonized Focussed generally on high-cost goods Senior salespeople take high-cost goods, leaving juniors with low-cost goods Ill will and tension level among salespeople

Example: Calculate the earnings of a salesperson whose sales for the week were $5,200 at the commission rate of 7 percent.
Solution: $5,200 × 7% = $364

Method of Payment	Formula	Advantages	Disadvantages
Drawing account	Cash advance to a salesperson against future sales	Provides security Guarantees regular income Stabilizes income when sales are highly seasonal Discourages overly aggressive selling	Employee may view the draw as a salary, not a loan Employees in arrears may quit

Example: A retail salesperson draws $1,000 at the beginning of each month, and she earns a commission of 10 percent on sales volume. Her monthly sales during this period are $30,000, then $5,000, and finally $20,000.
Solution

Month	Draw	Sales Volume	Commission Earned	End-of-Month Payment
December	$1,000	$30,000	$3,000	$2,000
January	$1,000	$ 5,000	$ 500	0 (rep owes $500)
February	$1,000	$20,000	$2,000	$500, computed as follows: Commission = $2,000 Less draw − $1,000 Less February debt −$500 Net $500

Drawing accounts are declining in popularity because of the problems involved in administering them. Retailers instead are more prone to supplement a commission with a salary.

Installing the plan

At this point, employers have a general pay plan, but they do not, of course, pay in general. They pay each employee individually. They must now consider how the plan will be administered to provide for individual pay increases.

There are several approaches for administering the pay increase feature of the plan:

- **Merit increases,** granted to recognize performance and contribution.
- **Promotional increases,** given to employees assigned different jobs in higher pay levels.
- **Tenure increases,** given to employees for time worked with the company.
- **General salary increases,** granted to employees to maintain real earnings as required by economic factors and in order to keep pay competitive.

These approaches are the most common, but there are many variations.[12] Most annual increases are made for cost of living, tenure, or employment market reasons. Obviously, employers might use several, all, or combinations of the various increase methods.

Employers should document salary increases for each employee and record the reasons for them.

Updating the plan

To keep the pay administration plan updated, the employer should review it at least annually. Adjustments should be made where necessary, and supervisory personnel should be retained in using the plan. This is not the kind of plan that can be set up and then forgotten.

During the annual review, the owners/managers should ask themselves these important questions: Is the plan working? Are they getting the kind of employees they want or are they just making do? What is the turnover rate? Do employees seem to care about the business? What matters is how the plan helps employers achieve the objectives of the business.

Planning Employee Benefits[13]

Employee compensation includes wages or salary, commissions, incentives, overtime, and benefits. **Benefits** include holidays and paid vacations, employment insurance, Canada/Quebec pension, health care, company pensions, welfare benefits (life insurance, supplementary health, dental plan), disability payments, and services like credit unions, product or service discounts, legal assistance, travel clubs, education subsidies, profit-sharing plans, and food services.

After productivity, employee compensation is the most difficult employee-relations issue for management. Employee benefits can help develop a stable and productive work force, but employers must have effective cost and administrative controls. Legally required benefits (e.g., Canada Pension, employment insurance) can be managed with minimal difficulty by keeping records, submitting forms to the proper authorities, and paying for the required coverage. But when choosing and managing other types of benefits, employers should get professional advice in planning and setting up programs.

As the benefits cost increases as a percentage of total compensation, the direct pay cost percentage decreases. Employers cannot recognize outstanding achievement with direct pay increases because funds for direct pay are diminishing as benefits spending gets bigger. As a result, unfortunately, the compensation differential between the mediocre employee and the outstanding achiever is narrowing. Managers need to recognize the advantages, limitations, and cost impact that employee benefits have on business operations and net profit.

Analyzing benefits costs can be accomplished by grouping them into the following categories:

- Legally required benefits (Canada/Quebec pension plan, workers' compensation, employment insurance).
- Private pensions.
- Group insurance.
- Supplementary insurance.
- Payment for time not worked.
- Employee services such as day care.
- Perquisites such as employee discounts or merchandise.

Many employers now pay for most, if not all, of the employees' life, medical, and disability insurance. The rapid escalation of benefits cost, as compared to direct pay compensation, has caused managers to become more diligent in controlling these costs and in getting better employee relations.

Selecting employee benefits

Benefits should be designed with the help of an individual who is a competent planner and manager. Employers need an approach that allows them to offer employee benefits designed to meet the company's and the employees' needs. For example, employees who are older and no longer have the responsibility of a family will have different requirements from the employees who have families. Also, employees whose spouses are employed by another employer's plan might be considered in such a way as to minimize double coverage.

Employee Performance Appraisal

Many retail employees are under a merit increase pay system, though most of their pay increase may result from other factors. This approach involves periodic review and appraisal of how well employees perform their assigned duties. An effective employee appraisal plan (1) achieves better two-way communications between the manager and the employee, (2) relates pay to work performance and results, (3) provides a standardized approach to evaluating performance, and (4) helps employees see how they can improve by explaining job responsibilities and expectations.

Such a performance review helps not only the employees whose work is being appraised, but also the manager doing the appraisal to gain insight into the organization. An open exchange between employee and manager can show the manager where improvements in equipment, procedures, or other factors might improve employee performance. Managers should try to foster a climate in which employees can discuss progress and problems informally at any time throughout the year.[14]

Again, to get the best results, it is a good idea to use standardized forms of appraisal. A typical form includes job performance factors such as results achieved; quality of performance; volume of work; effectiveness in working with others in the store; effectiveness in dealing with customers, suppliers, etc.; initiative; job knowledge; and dependability.

Employers can design their own forms, using examples in books on personnel administration, if necessary. The forms should be tailored to the jobs and should follow from job analyses as discussed earlier.

Employee Relations and Personnel Policies[15]

There are many ways to manage people. The manager can be strict or rigidly enforce rules. Communications can be one-way from boss to employee. The job might get done, but with fairly high turnover, absenteeism, and low morale.

Or the owner can make an extra effort to be a "nice guy" to everyone on the payroll. This management style may lead to reduced adherence to the rules, and employees may argue when they are asked to do work they do not like. Controlling the daily operation of the business may become more and more difficult. The business may survive, but only with much lower profit than if the owner followed more competent personnel policies. But there is another way, a way where employees can feel a part of the firm, where manager and employees can communicate effectively with each other, where rules are fair and flexible, yet enforced with positive discipline. The job gets done efficiently and profitably, and the business does well.

Large companies have a separate personnel department. Most managers of a small firm view this "personnel function" as just part of the general job of running a business. It is good practice, though, to think of the personnel function as a distinct and separate part of management responsibilities—only then are personnel responsibilities likely to get the priorities they deserve.

The human resources function is generally considered to include all those policies and administrative procedures necessary to satisfy the needs of employees. Not necessarily in priority order, these include:

1. Administrative personnel procedures.
2. Supervisory practices based on human relations and competent delegation.
3. Positive discipline.
4. Grievance prevention and grievance handling.

5. A system of communications.

6. Adherence to all governmental rules and regulations pertaining to the personnel function.

Administrative personnel procedures

Favourable employee relations requires competent handling of the administrative aspects of the personnel function. These include the management of:

1. Work hours.

2. The physical working environment:
   a. Facilities
   b. Equipment

3. Payroll procedures.

4. Benefit procedures, including insurance matters, and vacation and holiday schedules.

Developing job commitment

If an employee's job satisfies his or her needs, the employee responds more favourably to the job. Such employees tend to take their responsibilities seriously, act positively for the firm, and are absent from work only rarely. The key point is that when a job satisfies needs, the employee may bring greater commitment to the job.

There are five factors that generally cause a deep commitment to job performance for most employees. These are:

1. *The work itself.* To what extent does the employee see the work as meaningful and worthwhile?

2. *Achievement.* How much opportunity is there for the employee to accomplish tasks that are seen as a reasonable challenge?

3. *Responsibility.* To what extent does the employee have assignments and the authority necessary to take care of a significant function of the organization? Properly used, the empowerment of service workers may bring high dividends to retailers, as in the introductory example.[16]

4. *Recognition.* To what extent is the employee aware of how highly other people value the contributions made by the employee?

5. *Advancement.* How much opportunity is there for the employee to assume greater responsibilities in the firm?

These five factors tend to satisfy certain critical needs of individuals:

1. The feeling of *being accepted* as part of the firm's work team.

2. *Feeling important*—that the employee's strengths, capabilities, and contributions are known and valued highly.

3. The chance to *continue to grow* and become a more fully functioning person.

If the kinds of needs just described are met by paying attention to the five factors previously listed, management will have taken significant steps toward gaining the full commitment of employees to job performance. To do this, several practical strategies can be used, such as:

- Establishing confidence and trust with employees through open communication and the development of sensitivity to employee needs.
- Allowing employees to participate in decision making that directly affects them.
- Helping employees to set their own work methods and work goals, as much as possible.
- Praising and rewarding good work as clearly and promptly as inadequate performance is mentioned.
- Restructuring jobs to be challenging and interesting by giving increased responsibilities and independence to those who want it, and who can handle it.

Positive discipline

The word *discipline* carries with it many negative meanings. It is often used as a synonym for punishment. Yet discipline is also used to refer to the spirit that exists in a successful ball team where team members are willing to consider the needs of the team as more important than their own.

Positive discipline in a retail firm is an atmosphere of mutual trust and common purpose in which all employees understand the company rules as well as the objectives, and do everything possible to support them.

Any disciplinary program has, as its base, that all the employees have a clear understanding of exactly what is expected of them. This is why a concise set of rules and standards must exist that is fair, clear, realistic, and communicated. Once the standards and rules are known by all employees, discipline can be enforced equitably and fairly.

A good set of rules need not be more than one page, but can prove essential to the success of a business. A few guidelines for establishing a climate of positive discipline are given below:

1. There must be rules and standards, which are communicated clearly and administered fairly, and these must be reasonable. In addition, employees should be consulted when rules are set.

2. Rules should be communicated so they are known and understood by all employees. An employee manual can help with communicating rules. While a rule or a standard is in force, employees are expected to adhere to it. Even though rules exist, people should know that if a personal problem or a unique situation makes the rule exceptionally harsh, the rule may be modified or an exception granted.

3. There should be no favourites and privileges should be granted only when they can also be granted to other employees in similar circumstances. This means that it must be possible to explain to other employees, who request a similar privilege with less justification, why the privilege cannot be extended to them in their particular situation.

4. Employees must be aware that they can and should voice dissatisfaction with any rules or standards they consider unreasonable as well as with working conditions they feel hazardous, discomfiting, or burdensome.

5. Employees should understand the consequences of breaking a rule without permission. Large companies have disciplinary procedures for minor violations that could apply equally well in small companies. They usually call for one or two friendly reminders. If the problem continues, there is a formal, verbal warning, then a written warning, and if the employee persists in violating rules, there is a suspension and/or dismissal. In violations of more serious rules, fewer steps would be used. It is not easy to communicate this procedure since it should not be so firm that it can be expressed in writing. If it is made clear to employees who violate a rule at the first reminder, the procedure soon becomes understood by all.

6. There should be an appeals procedure when an employee feels management has made an unfair decision. At the very least, the employee should be aware that management is willing to reconsider a decision at a later time.

7. There should be recognition for good performance, reliability, and loyalty. Negative comments, when they are necessary, will be accepted as helpful if employees also receive feedback when things go well.

Corrective action   No matter how good the atmosphere of positive discipline in a business, rules are bound to be broken, by some people, from time to time. In those situations, corrective action is sometimes necessary. In some rare cases, the violation may be so severe that serious penalties are necessary. If an employee is caught in the act of stealing or deliberately destroys company property, summary dismissal may be necessary. In all other severe cases, a corrective interview is needed to determine the reasons for the problem and to establish what penalty, if any, is appropriate. Such an interview should include all, or most, of the following steps:

1. Outlining the problem to the employee, including an explanation of the rule or procedure that was broken.

2. Allowing the employee to explain his or her side of the story. This step will often bring out problems that need to be resolved to avoid rule violations in the future.

3. Exploring with the employee what should be done to prevent a recurrence of the problem.

4. Reaching agreement with the employee on the corrective action that should be taken.

Even in the best environment, though, employees will occasionally feel unhappy about something. They may not get paid on time, or may feel that the room is too hot, too cold, or too dark. They may feel that they deserve a merit increase, or that someone has hurt their feelings inadvertently. When this happens, good personnel policies require that employees know how they can express their dissatisfaction and obtain some consideration.

A written grievance procedure, known to employees, can be very helpful in creating a positive atmosphere. It informs employees how they can obtain a hearing on their problems and it assures that the owner/manager becomes aware that the problem exists. When employees know that someone will listen to them, grievances are less serious and hearing a complaint carefully often is half the job of resolving it.

A good grievance procedure begins with the manager making it a point to be actively looking for signs of possible sources of dissatisfaction, and by noticing changes in employee behaviour that signal that a problem may exist. This often makes it possible to handle a situation when it is still easy to resolve.

Job Enrichment

Too many companies today treat employees as throw-away assets. The average annual turnover rate among restaurant workers, for example, is 250 percent, whereas management turnover is about 50 percent. Many employees leave within 30 days of employment, wasting whatever training they have been given.[17] The retail investment is too high to take such an approach. Forward-thinking managers view the employee as a total person. They are concerned with what the employee does during working hours and during time off the job. They try to help employees get more education, sharpen job skills, and participate in worthwhile non-job activities.

Keeping employees satisfied at work is more than a matter of salary. Employees want to feel they belong and that the company cares about them as total human beings. Careful attention to these needs will contribute to higher employee productivity and a lower turnover rate.[18]

Motivation and job enrichment cannot be separated. **Motivation** is normally related to work policies and supervisor attitudes. Motivated employees will devote their best efforts to company goals. As a result, management is recognizing the benefits of flexibility in work schedules, enrichment programs, and building employee motivation. Yesterday's human resources solutions don't work with today's lifestyles. Programs such as flex time, job sharing, on-site day care, and quality circles have emerged in retailing in recent years as management has sought ways to increase productivity and enrich the job by reducing worker stress at home and at work.

Typical programmes

Flex time   **Flex time** is a system by which workers can arrive and depart on a variable schedule. Flex time programs contribute to improved employee morale, a greater sense of employee responsibility, less stress, and reduced turnover. Retailers with flex time programs include Sears and the Bank of Montreal.

Job sharing   **Job sharing** occurs when two workers voluntarily hold joint responsibility for what was formerly one position. In effect, two permanent part-time positions result from what was one full-time position. Job sharing differs from work sharing. **Work sharing** usually occurs in organizations during economic recessions where all employees are required to cut back on their work hours and are paid accordingly. Job sharing is a way to retain valuable employees who no longer want to work full-time. Management has found that the enthusiasm and productivity in such programs is high. This practice is particularly prevalent among large department stores such as Eaton's.[19]

Child and people care programs   Young children pose a special problem for working mothers. About 57 percent of all single mothers with preschool children are now in the work force. There is a growing recognition in Canada about the value of providing good day care services, with the increased assistance of governments.

Some companies, such as the Bank of Montreal, are giving their employees paid time off, called "people care days," to deal with personal matters such as taking a driving test, applying for a mortgage, or doing volunteer work in the community.[20]

Employee assistance programs   Drug abuse and alcohol abuse are two of the most obvious areas in which employers can provide counselling and assistance. Other programs include scholarships for children of employees and encouraging community volunteer work.

Total quality management (TQM)   TQM programs create situations in which employees at all levels have input into decisions that affect the retail organization. Employees gain an increased sense of self-worth by taking part in the process. Management also benefits from the ideas of dedicated workers at all levels in the organization. Managers and workers seek consensus on company operations instead of having orders simply passed down from above. The total quality concept was initially started in the United States, popularized in Japan, and then imported back into North America. The benefits from such programs include higher productivity, less turnover, and less absenteeism.

Improved communications   Mechanisms should be in place for regular communication between managers and hourly employees. Opportunities should be provided for the employees to communicate their concerns to management.

Organizing

Decisions must also be made on how the retail firm will be organized. Most merchants are all-arounders. They do all jobs as the need arises, or assign tasks to employees on a random, non-specialized basis. Employees are extensions of the managers to carry out the tasks they lack time to do themselves. Small merchants don't think of setting up distinct functions and lines for the flow of authority, nor do they select specialists to handle each function. As a store grows, however, specialization becomes necessary. The primary purpose of organizational structure is to "support market-driven values and behaviour and reinforce desired behaviour across the business."[21] For some thoughts on organizing from the man who built the world's largest retail chain, see Retail Highlight 9–3.

Basic organization principles

Before discussing organizational structure, certain management principles need to be considered in organizing the firm.

- The principle of specialization of labour.
- The principle of departmentalization.
- The span-of-control principle.
- The unity-of-command principle.

Retail Highlight 9–3

Mr. Sam's Thoughts on Organizing

Sam Walton, who died in 1992, built the world's largest retail chain, Wal-Mart, with more than 2,000 stores and sales of over $55 billion. Recognized as one of the best and brightest retailers ever, he offered these thoughts on organizing a retail firm:

• Keep your ear to the ground. Managers and buyers should spend most of their time in stores seeing what customers are and are not buying.
• Push responsibility and authority down. As companies, like Wal-Mart, get bigger, the more important it becomes to shift responsibility and authority toward the front lines, toward that department manager who is stocking the shelves and talking to the customer.

• Force ideas to bubble up. Encourage store employees to push their ideas up through the system.
• Stay lean, fight bureaucracy. If you are not serving the customer or supporting the folks who do, Wal-Mart does not need you.

Wal-Mart also has a profit-sharing plan in which all employees can participate. Sam Walton felt this was critical to Wal-Mart's success because the salespeople then feel that they are part of the company and treat customers better than salespeople in other stores do.

Source: "Sam Walton in His Own Words," *Fortune*, June 29, 1992, pp. 98–106.

Specialization

Modern organizations are built on the concept of **specialization.** More and better work is performed at less cost when it is done by specialists than when it is done by employees who shift from one job to another and who continually improvise.

Specialization is of two kinds: *tasks* and *people.* Specialization of tasks narrows a person's activities to simple, repetitive routines. Thus, a relatively untrained employee can quickly become proficient at a narrow specialty.

Specialization of people involves not simplifying the job, but developing a person to perform a certain job better than someone else can. Training and experience improve the quality and quantity of the work.

In the smaller retail store, most of the specialization is of the second type; but in larger stores there is more need for narrow task specialization. For example, certain special records must be kept, and certain phases of merchandise handling must be done by a well-trained person.

Departmentalization

Management will probably find that it can use **departmentalization** and group jobs into classes such as the following (each demanding a certain combination of skills for good performance):

• Merchandising—buying and managing inventory for different groups of merchandise.
• Direct and general selling and adjustments—customer contact.
• Sales promotion—largely concerning advertising and display.
• Accounting and finance—records, correspondence, cash handling, insurance, and sometimes credit.

- Store operation—building, equipment, and safety measures.
- Merchandise handling—receiving, marking, storing, and delivering.
- Personnel—employment, training, employee benefits, and personnel records.

Recognizing the many functions to be performed doesn't mean that a specialist is necessary for each of them. Management can combine some functions. But management should look ahead and have an organization plan that provides for various specialized positions when they are needed.

Span of control

Span of control addresses the question of how many subordinates should report to a supervisor. Generally, a supervisor's span of control should be small because an individual can work effectively with only a limited number of people at one time. Span of control, however, depends on factors such as the competence of the supervisor and subordinates, the similarity of the functions to be performed, and the physical location of people.

Unity of command

The **unity of command** concept involves a series of superior-subordinate relationships. This concept states that no person should be under the direct control of more than one supervisor in performing job tasks. Thus, an employee should receive decision-making power from and report to only one supervisor. An unbroken chain of command should exist from top to bottom. Otherwise, frustration and confusion will occur.

How to organize for profitable operations

The two functions that probably will be organized first are *merchandising* and *operations,* or store management. Such an organization would look like the one illustrated in Figure 9–6.

The *merchandise manager* has other functions in addition to being responsible for buying and selling. This person supervises or prepares merchandise budgets (or both); handles advertising, displays, and other promotions; and is responsible for inventory planning and control.

The *operations manager* is responsible for building upkeep, delivery, stockrooms, service, supplies, equipment purchasing, and similar activities.

As a store continues to grow in size, specialization of labour occurs. The organization structure may begin to look like the one in Figure 9–7.

Figure 9–6 The Simplest Organization

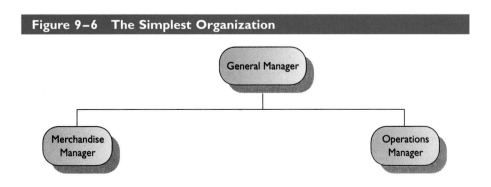

Figure 9–7   Five-Function Organizational Plan

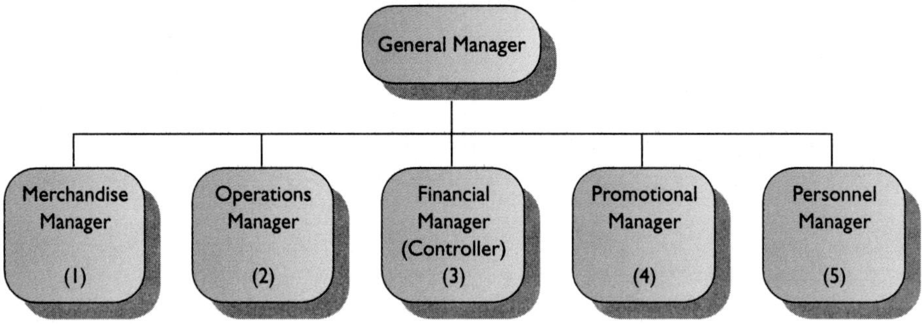

As shown in Figure 9–7, the next managers who should be added are financial, promotion, and personnel managers. The financial manager, or controller, handles the finances of the firm and probably has an accounting background. The organization structure in the figure is typical of most department stores. A food operation, however, performs the same functions, as do all retail firms.

Trends in organizing

Before World War II, the typical organization plan gave the merchandising manager responsibility for *both* buying and selling. But after World War II, shopping centres were developed, and downtown stores "branched" to the shopping centres. The merchandise manager became responsible not only for buying and selling merchandise in the downtown (main) store, but also in the branches. This situation proved to be impossible. One merchandise manager could not be responsible for buying, supervising sales, and general management of both the main store and the branch stores. So a trend developed during this "branching" era to separate the buying and selling functions.

Separation of buying and selling

There are arguments for and against the separation of the buying and selling responsibilities in the organization.

Those *opposing* the separation of the two functions pose the following arguments:

- The buyer must have contact with consumers to be able to understand their needs.
- Those who buy merchandise should also be responsible for selling it.
- It is easier to pinpoint merchandising successes and failures when the two functions are combined.

Those who *favour* the separation of the two functions counter their opposition as follows:

- If the two functions are combined, buying is likely to have more importance than selling.
- Buying and selling require two different types of job skills.

Figure 9–8   Organization for Separation of Buying and Selling

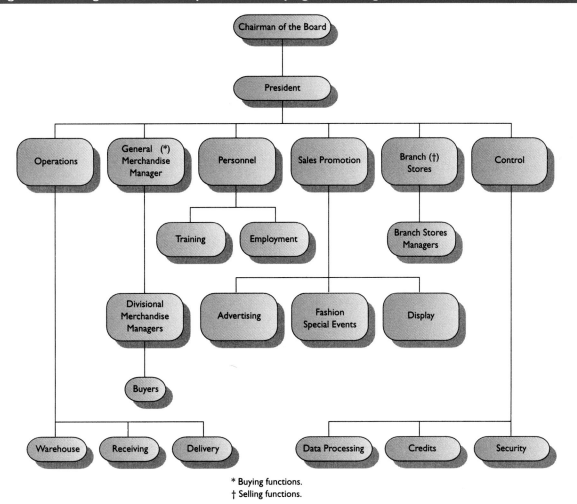

* Buying functions.
† Selling functions.

- With technology, reports, and so forth, it is not necessary for the two functions to be combined.
- Salespeople can be shifted more easily under this arrangement.

The arguments against separating the buying and selling functions do not seem as strong as the counterarguments. The branch store problem seems to demand separation. Thus, the trend is to separate the two. Figure 9–8 shows a department store that is organized for the separation of buying and selling. The general merchandise manager is responsible for buying, and the vice president of branch stores is responsible for selling.

Food stores could have faced the same conflict, but their expansion history actually solved their problems. Rather than branching, these companies expanded as chain-store organizations. No main stores exist in a chain organization. Buying and selling are always separated. Many Canadian retailers, including Loblaws, have buyers who focus on maximizing the rate of return on shelf space investment.[22] Using computer analysis, Loblaws' buyers know the volume and rate of return that competitive products are delivering to a store. A new buyer-seller relationship is evolving where the buyer works very closely with the seller to develop a mutually beneficial relationship. Called **reverse marketing,** it reflects the proactive stance taken by many buyers today.[23]

Centralization versus decentralization[24]

Specialty stores

Specialty stores historically have been highly centralized. For example, The Limited, until around 1990 consisted of roughly a dozen major fashion divisions controlled by the chairman. The organizational philosophy was that synergies between the divisions in distribution, real estate and legal departments, and so forth could be achieved by centralization. The firm has moved since 1990 to aggressively decentralize its business. Each division now has autonomy in merchandising and operations. The only issues controlled centrally are finances and reporting relationships. Toys "Я" Us made the decision to operate its Kids "Я" Us and its international divisions as separate, autonomous units.

Department stores

Department stores are exhibiting a countertrend to the decentralization trend among specialty stores. Traditionally, each department store division in a multidivision holding company was allowed to operate independently and to compete not only with other department stores but also with other divisions of the parent organization.

In essence, department stores have recognized that they do not need a buyer for each classification in every division to be efficient. Rather, operating information systems and electronic merchandising have made it possible for the buyers to make chainwide decisions. For example, the Hudson's Bay Company has moved to greater centralized buying, and at the same time, to provide more flexibility for individual store managers to select a merchandise mix that reflects local market needs. The link between buying and selling is provided by sophisticated computer information systems that allow managers to identify merchandise trends at the local, regional, and national levels.[25]

Chapter Highlights

- **Staffing a store with the right people is a critical part of the strategic plan for a retailer. Staffing needs vary depending on the type of merchandise carried, services the store will offer, the image management wants to project to customers, and the way in which the firm wants to compete.**

- **The initial step in developing a human resources plan for the firm is to develop good job descriptions and job specifications. These are written after a job analysis has been undertaken to obtain important facts about the job. The job description provides the content and responsibilities of the job and** how it ties in with other jobs. The job specification describes the personal qualifications required to do the job.

- Recruiting, attracting the right people, is a critical element of the plan. Recruits may be sought either inside or outside the firm. Specific guidelines exist that management must follow in administering selection tests and in otherwise screening employees.

- Simply hiring the right people is not enough. Training is often necessary for new employees and should be offered as an ongoing part of the personnel program.

- Employees need to know about their rights and responsibilities within the firm, the history of the firm, and specific information about their job responsibilities. Sales personnel may also need training in technical dimensions of the merchandise for which they will be responsible.

- An equitable employee pay plan is a further important component of a personnel plan and can contribute to higher employee productivity and satisfaction. A wage survey within the surrounding area can determine the wages paid for comparable jobs. Retailers should make sure that employees understand how the pay plan was developed, how it will be administered, and how they will be evaluated for pay increases or promotions. Closely related to the pay plan is establishing the level and type of employee benefits to be paid.

- Employee performance appraisal also needs to occur on a regular basis; normally employees are appraised annually. Standardized forms should be developed for this purpose. Ratings by supervisors should be discussed with the employees and suggestions should be given as to how the employees can improve their performance.

- Employee motivation and job enrichment are also important elements of the personnel plan. Management must recognize that employees have needs such as the desire for recognition and achievement, which cannot be satisfied by money alone.

- Basic organizational principles are specialization of labour, departmentalization, span of control, and unity of command.

- The two functions that probably will first be organized in a retail store are merchandising and operations (store management).

Key Terms

benefits 240
Canadian Human Rights
  Commission 227
compensation 235
departmentalization 248
employee compensation 240
flex time 246
general salary increases 240
job analysis 221
job classification 236
job description 222
job evaluation 234
job ranking 236

job sharing 246
job specification 222
merit increases 240
motivation 246
people care programs 246
promotional increases 240
reverse marketing 252
span-of-control 249
specialization 248
tenure increases 240
unity-of-command 249
work sharing 246

Discussion Questions

1. What are the key federal and provincial laws that affect recruiting, selection, and compensation of employees? What are the likely effects as a result of these regulations?

2. Assume you are the manager of a men's clothing outlet located close to a major university campus. What would be the basic elements of a training program for the outlet? How would your program likely differ from the type of training that might be offered for new employees who have been hired by Sears?

3. Briefly describe the steps that must be carried out in developing a formal compensation plan.

4. What is likely to be the most effective method for compensating (1) a retail salesperson, (2) an accountant, and (3) a department buyer?

5. Why should retail management institute an employee performance appraisal plan? What might be some of the performance factors that are evaluated?

6. Why should an employee grievance procedure and a procedure for handling disciplinary matters be established, even in the absence of a union?

7. What are some of the things retail management can do to enhance greater job enrichment and motivation among employees?

8. Discuss the following four principles of organization: specialization of labour, departmentalization, span of control, and unity of command.

Application Exercises

1. Devise a format and interview at least five people who have worked in the retailing industry in some capacity. Determine the individual's honest views on wages, working conditions, superior-subordinate relationships, and so on. Prepare a report for class discussion on what you have discovered.

2. Select several different retail companies (differing in organizational arrangement, number of stores and sales volume, and product line) and make an appointment with the executive responsible for the personnel functions. Describe the employment process of each (include selection, training, and benefits including compensation) and draw comparisons among the group. See if you can explain the differences in apparent effectiveness of the programs. See if you can get them to discuss affirmative action.

3. Arrange through your college or university placement office to have a few minutes with all the recruiters coming to campus to interview people for retailing companies. Structure a questionnaire to administer to each recruiter to find out what he or she is looking for in a student; how the interview on campus enters into the selection process; what kinds of questions are asked of the interviewee; what the recruiter expects the interviewee to know about the company; what variables are considered in evaluating the student; and what the subsequent steps are in the employment process.

Suggested Cases

17.   Who's the Best Candidate?
18.   Diamond Clothiers

Notes

1.   R. Williamson, "Motivation on the Menu," *Globe & Mail,* November 24, 1995, p. B7; A. Bokma, "Raking in the Dough: Canadian Retailers Are Folding, While Foreigners Flourish," *The Financial Post Magazine,* January 1992, pp. 32–35; "Retailers Add Insult to Injury," *Profit,* September 1991, p. 48; R. Outcalt, "Human assets," *Canadian Jeweler,* April 1987, p. 12.

2.   P. Waldie, "Canadian Retailers Warned: Shape up or Face Extinction," *Globe & Mail,* October 18, 1995, p. B11; J. Abend, "Personnel Strategies," *Stores,* September 1990, p. 42.

3.   The material on job analysis, job descriptions, and job specifications is reproduced, with modifications, from *Job Analysis, Job Specifications, and Job Descriptions, a Self-Instructional Booklet,* No. 1020 (Washington, D.C.: U.S. Small Business Administration).

4.   This material is reproduced, with modifications, from Walter E. Green, "Staffing Your Store," *Management Aid* No. 5.007 (Washington, D.C.: U.S. Small Business Administration).

5.   R.M. Hodgetts, K.G. Kroeck, and M.E. Rock, *Managing Human Resources in Canada,* Dryden, Toronto, 1996, pp. 94–96.

6.   R. Henkoff, "Finding, Training and Keeping the Best Service Workers," *Fortune,* October 3, 1994, pp. 110–122.

7.   *Canadian Human Rights Act,* paragraph 2, subsection (a). See also Hodgetts, Kroeck, and Rock, *Managing Human Resources in Canada,* Chapter 3.

8.   Henkoff, "Finding, Training and Keeping the Best Service Workers."

9.   Henkoff, "Finding, Training and Keeping the Best Service Workers;" "Training Programs Must Reflect Today's Environment," *Chain Store Age Executive,* June 1989, pp. 60–61.

10.   R. Williamson, "Motivation on the Menu," *Globe & Mail,* November 24, 1995, p. B7.

11.   This material is condensed from J.F. Scolland, "Setting up a Pay System," *Management Aid,* No. 5.006 (Washington, D.C.: U.S. Small Business Administration).

12.   See, for example, "System Boost Productivity—Immediate Feedback on Job Performance," *Chain Store Age Executive,* June 1992, p. 42.

13.   This material is condensed from J.B. Hannah, "Changing Employee Benefits," *Management Aid,* No. 5.008 (Washington, D.C.: U.S. Small Business Administration); *Managing People, Retailing's Prime Resource,* Retail Council of Canada (1988).

14.   Williamson, "Motivation on the Menu."

15.   For further reading, see L. Berry and P. Parasuraman, *Marketing Services: Competing Through Quality,* New York: The Free Press, 1991, pp. 167–69.

16.   Williamson, "Motivation on the Menu;" D.E. Bowen and E.E. Lawler, III, "The Empowerment of Service Workers: What, Why, How and When?" *Sloan Management Review,* Spring 1992, vol 33, no. 2, pp. 31–39.

17.   Ibid.; B. Bremner, "Among Restaurateurs, It's Dog Eat Dog," *Business Week,* January 9, 1989, p. 86.

18. F.N. Sonnennberg, "A Strategic Approach to Employing Motivation," *Journal of Business Strategy,* May/June 1991, p. 41.

19. S. Nolen, "It's Far Better than Being Laid Off," *Globe & Mail,* August 13, 1993, p. A12; S.L. Dolan and R.S. Schuler, *Personnel and Human Resource Management in Canada,* West Publishing, New York, 1987, p. 145.

20. B. Brennan, "Employers Try to Show They Care," *Kitchener-Waterloo Record,* July 9, 1992, p. E8.

21. G.S. Day, *Market Driven Strategy,* New York: The Free Press, 1990, pp. 360–361.

22. J. Oldland, "Beware of New Breed of Buyers," *Marketing,* June 5, 1989, p. 14.

23. M.T. Leenders and D.L. Blenkhorn, *Reverse Marketing: The New Buyer-Supplier Relationship,* New York: The Free Press, 1988.

24. Based on W.F. Loeb, "Unbundle or Centralize: What Is the Answer?" *Retailing Issues Letter* 4, no. 3, May 1992, pp. 1–4.

25. Hudson's Bay Company, *Annual Report, 1994.*

PART

Designing the Retailing Mix

In *Part 3, Designing the Retailing Mix*, the various decisions on the major variables of the retailing mix are discussed. The key issues in the retail location decisions are covered in Chapter 10. Store design, store layout and merchandise presentation decisions are covered in Chapter 11. Merchandise and expense planning decisions are the focus of Chapter 12. Buying, handling, and inventory management decisions are explained in Chapter 13. Determining retail prices is the topic of Chapter 14. In order to successfully promote their products or services, retailers need to: help their employees develop the keys to successful selling (Chapter 15); design effective programs in retail advertising, sales promotion, and publicity (Chapter 16); and instill in their employees a customer-focussed culture (Chapter 17).

Making the Retail Location Decisions

Chapter Objectives

After reading this chapter you should be able to:

1. Explain the strategic dimensions of the location decision.

2. Explain how to make the market selection.

3. Explain and use the various techniques and procedures for trading area evaluation.

4. Determine the volume of business that can be done in a trading area.

5. Explain and use the principles of site evaluation to assess the value of alternative sites.

Retailers are attracted to malls with open designs.

*H*ow difficult and complex the retail location decisions are can be illustrated by the following cases:[1]

- Sales were falling at **Warden Woods Mall,** a shopping centre located in the industrial section of Scarborough. The Bay, Dylex, and many other tenants had left, and the mall was failing. Then, recently, it underwent a complete face-lift, a $9-million remake to give the mall a totally new image. The old Warden Woods Mall has been replaced by a **Warden Power Centre,** "big box" stores selling everything from radios to rollerblades. The centre has responded to the new consumer demands—low prices, wide selection, better quality. Instead of fighting the superstores, the mall has joined them. Advertising and promotion have been used extensively to promote the new centre, and a successful loyalty card has shown that the centre's trading area is expanding.

- After pre-testing them successfully in 15 locations across Canada, **Sears** has decided to open, starting in 1996, 50 specialty stores across the country, with selling areas between 400 and 600 m^2, and with a variety of products from televisions to sewing machines. Some announced locations are Greenwood, N.S.; Sept-Iles, Quebec; and Campbell River, B.C. With these new specialty stores, Sears wants to better serve markets that are currently serviced by a Sears catalogue outlet.

- **Leonard Kubas,** a noted retail consultant, has observed that the **Toronto Eaton Centre** has become a major tourist attraction, and that contrary to some predictions, and until the 1991-1992 recession hit, surrounding streets did not suffer an absence of pedestrians and an abundance of bankrupt stores. Instead, the chains went into the mall, and the more specialized and innovative stores remained at street level attracting spillover customers from the mall. However, since 1991, a similar situation (although not as dramatic) as in Montreal has happened with many stores closing or hurting financially, due to similar factors.

- **The West Edmonton Mall, dubbed the "eighth wonder of the world," has exerted an enormous power of attraction from Americans and Canadians, all the way to Japanese tourists. However, it also created major problems for downtown Edmonton merchants who saw their business drop dramatically after the mall opened in 1981. With facilities such as an indoor palace, zoo, public aquariums, a 360-room hotel, a 35,000-square-metre indoor amusement park, a 42,000-square-metre indoor water park, and a 1-hectare miniature golf course, it has been a major attraction, although its novelty has declined over time. The West Edmonton Mall has 800 tenants, including eight anchors, such as Canadian Tire, Zellers, Sears, Eaton's, The Bay, and Ashbrooks—a total leasable area of more than 350,000 square metres and a market population of 4.7 million! During the last recession, economic factors have hurt the profitability of the West Edmonton Mall. In 1992, its American sister, called the Mall of America, opened in Minnesota, further eroding its base of American and Japanese tourists. If its planned expansion is carried out, the Mall of America may take the title of largest shopping mall in the *Guinness Book of Records*, again diminishing the power of attraction of the West Edmonton Mall. ■**

Location decisions are essential elements of the competitive strategy of any retail organization. Outlets such as Canadian Tire can succeed in a stand-alone location. Other firms, such as Eaton's, seem to function best as an anchor tenant in a major shopping centre. Small specialty firms, lacking the ability to attract customers on their own, often choose a high-traffic location in a shopping mall.

We cannot overemphasize the importance of a carefully developed location strategy. Such a strategy is the spacial expression of a retailer's goals. Location decisions must be made in the context of the demographics of the target market segments, the patronage behaviour of consumers within the segments, the geographic dimensions of demand, and all other dimensions of the marketing program.

The selection process begins with an assessment of the firm's strategy, followed by (1) choice of region or metropolitan area, (2) trade area analysis, (3) site analysis and evaluation, and (4) selection. Choice of location in essence determines how goods and services are made available to the customer. Even small differences in location can have a major impact on profitability and market share because location affects both the number of customers attracted to the outlet and the resulting level of retail sales.

Competitive Strategy and Location Decisions

Differences in competitive strategy can result in different location objectives even for firms with similar types of merchandise. For example, discount stores, specialty retailers, and chain department stores sell clothing and may even feature the same national brands. Still, each firm may be targeting a different market segment as reflected in their location strategies. Firms such as Home

Depot are likely to be free-standing. Major department stores will serve as anchor tenants in shopping centres. They may also locate in the downtown section of major metropolitan areas.

Competition among firms offering similar merchandise and shopping experiences occurs primarily on the basis of location, promotion, and price. Consumers, in choosing between highly similar outlets, are likely to shop at the most conveniently located outlet offering the best prices. The result is that firms such as gasoline stations are likely to be tightly clustered. Frequently such outlets will be located on all four quadrants of a major high-traffic artery. Supermarkets are another example of a type of retailing with interchangeable merchandise. Grocery outlets also rely on convenience of location, and price competition is likely to occur among such outlets in a narrowly defined area.

Thus, key strategic decisions in retail location relate to (1) type of market coverage, and (2) the type of goods sold.

Type of market coverage

Three primary strategies are possible: (1) regional dominance (primarily for large retail outlets), (2) market saturation, and (3) emphasis on smaller towns and communities. These decisions are important even when a retailer is opening an initial outlet because they indicate the path of greatest growth over the years.

Regional dominance

The retailer may decide to become the dominant retailer in a particular geographic area rather than locate the same number of outlets over a much wider geographic area. Examples of regionally dominant retailers include Sobeys in the Maritimes; Provigo in Quebec; Loblaws in Ontario; Safeway in Manitoba, Alberta, and British Columbia; and Co-op in Saskatchewan.

The advantages of **regional dominance** include:

1. Lower costs of distribution because merchandise can be shipped to all the stores from a central warehouse.
2. Easier personnel supervision.
3. The ability to better understand customer needs.
4. The likelihood of a strong reputation in the area.
5. Better economies in sales promotion since the outlets are concentrated in one region.

Retailers practising regional dominance can offset their high fixed costs by high market share. Typically, the retailers, measured on a city-by-city basis, that have the leading market shares have the highest profits.[2] In addition, high market share increases the number of stores in an area, which in turn improves customer convenience.

Market saturation

This strategy is similar to regional dominance. However, **market saturation** is often limited to a single metropolitan market, such as Toronto, Montreal, Vancouver, Calgary, or Halifax, where the population base is large. The advantages are the same in both instances. Dominance simply occurs on a larger scale than a single metropolitan market.

Smaller communities

Why are smaller communities so popular in location decisions today? One reason is that building codes make it more difficult to build in large cities. Also, costs are higher and competition is tougher.

Secondary markets, communities of less than 50,000, present some advantages to retailers: (1) These communities often welcome new business, such as pulp mills and sawmills in Grande Prairie (Alberta), tourism in Whistler (B.C.), and an auto plant in Bromont (Quebec),[3] (2) the quality of life is often higher, (3) wage rates are lower, (4) unions are less of an issue, (5) the markets are easier to serve, and (6) competition is often less intense.

Some retail chains like Stedmans and Metropolitan operate primarily in small towns (less than 50,000 population), as these companies feel that they can more effectively serve these markets. For example, the Metropolitan chain operates over 450 stores across Canada under various names (e.g., Metropolitan, Greenberg, and Red Apple Clearance Centre), mainly in secondary markets. Others, like Sears Canada, are opening specialty stores in rural communities to better service its current catalogue markets and to increase its market share in several product categories, such as snowblowers, stereos, and dishwashers.[4]

Type of goods sold

Merchandise can be classified as convenience, shopping, or specialty goods based on customer buying habits. Stores can be classified in the same way, as shown in Table 10–1. Understanding how consumers perceive merchandise and stores can help in evaluating the importance of location.

Convenience goods

Convenience goods are often purchased on the basis of impulse at outlets such as Mac's Milk. The volume of traffic passing a site is thus the most important factor in selecting a site at which to sell convenience goods. Some convenience goods outlets such as card shops are often located close to major department stores in shopping malls and depend on the department stores to attract traffic for them.

Shopping goods

Consumers purchasing *shopping goods* prefer to compare the offerings of several stores before making a buying decision. A store such as Chapters is an example of a shopping goods outlet. Thus, consumers will travel farther for purchasing shopping goods than convenience goods but will not make a special effort to reach an outlet if others are more easily accessible.

Specialty goods

Specialty goods are items for which consumers will make a special effort to purchase a particular brand or shop at a given store. Such outlets generate their own traffic. As a result, retailers of such merchandise can choose a somewhat isolated site relative to outlets offering shopping goods or convenience goods.

In summary, if management offers "shopping goods" (items such as men's and women's clothing, major appliances, or expensive jewelry), the best

Table 10–1   Matrix of Consumer Goods and Stores

		Stores		
		Convenience	**Shopping**	**Specialty**
Goods	**Convenience**	Consumers prefer to buy the most readily available brand and product at the most accessible store. 1	Consumers are indifferent to the brand or product they buy, but shop among different stores in order to secure better retail service and/or lower retail prices. 4	Consumers prefer to trade at a specific store, but are indifferent to the brand or product purchased. 7
	Shopping	Consumers select a brand from the assortment carried by the most accessible store. 2	Consumers make comparisons among both retail-controlled factors and factors associated with the product (brand). 5	Consumers prefer to trade at a certain store, but are uncertain as to which product they wish to buy and examine the store's assortment for the best purchase. 8
	Specialty	Consumers purchase their favoured brand from the most accessible store that has the item in stock. 3	Consumers have strong preference with respect to the brand, but shop among a number of stores to secure the best retail service or price for this brand. 6	Consumers have preference for both a particular store and a specific brand. 9

Source: Yoram Wind, *Product Policy: Concepts, Methods, and Strategy* (Reading, Mass.: Addison-Wesley Publishing, 1982), p. 71.

location is near other stores carrying shopping goods. Conversely, locating a shopping goods store in a convenience goods area or centre is not recommended. Take a look at shopping centres in your area. Invariably, you'll find a clothing or shoe store—in trouble—in a shopping centre that carries mainly convenience goods.

Stores that carry shopping goods and those that offer convenience goods often locate in the same regional shopping centre. But it is still important to locate in a section of the centre that is compatible with the retailer's product lines. For example, a pet store should not be located immediately adjacent to a restaurant or a dress shop. Management would want to locate a gift shop near department stores, theatres, restaurants—in short, any place where lines of patrons may form, giving potential customers several minutes to look in the gift shop's display windows.

Stores and merchandise cannot always be classified as neatly as this discussion suggests. Stereo shops, for example, sell blank tapes, and beauty salons sell shampoo, conditioners, brushes, and so forth for the convenience of their customers. Still, for strategic purposes, focussing on the core strategy implied by the type of merchandise and the store is important in targeting customers.

The process of selecting a retail location

As noted above, the location strategy for the firm ultimately reflects both growth and expansion objectives. Developing the location plan after making such decisions requires a careful study of potential markets. Assessment of markets

Figure 10–1   The Four-Step Process of Selecting a Retail Location

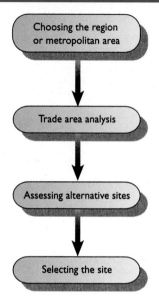

begins with *choices among regions or metropolitan areas* that appear to offer the greatest market potential in meeting the firm's growth objectives.

Choices must then be made within the regions or the cities chosen. Considerable variation within such areas can occur because of the geographic configuration of the area, housing patterns, or land use. Analysis of the different subareas of a city is known as *trade area analysis.* Finally, *site analysis and evaluation* decisions must be made. At this point, management assesses the cost of land and development, traffic flows, ingress (i.e., going in) and egress (i.e., going out or exiting), and similar issues in making specific site choices.

Thus, selection of a retail location typically follows a four-step process, as indicated in Figure 10–1: (1) choosing the region or the metropolitan area; (2) analyzing the trade area; (3) assessing alternative sites; and (4) selecting the site. It must be clear that every step is a refinement of the previous one, and that the process is not necessarily linear. The remainder of the chapter will be devoted to detailing these steps.

Choice of Region or Metropolitan Area

In making the market selection, management evaluates the economic base of targeted regions, the level of competition, size and socioeconomic characteristics of the population, and the overall potential of the area, as shown in Table 10–2.

Population characteristics

For example, a retailer needs to study the number of people, their education, income, ages, and family composition, as well as probable population increases in the area. Census data are a useful source of such information and are

Table 10-2 Factors to Consider in Area Selection

Population Characteristics

Total size
Age and income distributions
Growth trends
Education levels
Occupation distribution and trends

Competitive Characteristics

Saturation level
Number and size of competitors
Geographic coverage
Competitive growth trends

Labour Characteristics

Availability of personnel
    Management
    Clerical
    Skilled
Wage levels
Unions
Training

Economic Characteristics

Number and type of industries
Dominant industry
Growth projections
Financial base

Supply Source Characteristics

Delivery time
Delivery costs
Availability and reliability
Storage facilities

Location Characteristics

Number and type of locations
Costs
Accessibility to customers
Accessibility to transportation
Owning and leasing options
Utility adequacy

Promotion Characteristics

Type of media coverage
Media overlap
Costs

Regulation Characteristics

Taxes
Licensing
Zoning restrictions
Local ordinances

available for all markets in the yearly publication *Canadian Markets*. For example, the detailed listing on Moose Jaw indicates a 1996 population of 34,500, a per capita income of $15,000 (16 percent below national average), and total retail sales of $226 million (on a per capita basis, 9 percent below national average).[5]

Labour availability

Management talent is most readily available in larger areas, but is more expensive, as is clerical help.[6] In smaller communities, local management talent may not be available, and outsiders may not want to move to the area. However, clerical labour is less likely to be a problem.

Distribution problems

These include the timing and frequency of delivery schedules to the store and the reliability of delivery, as well as the distance between the store and the company-owned or the distributor's warehouses.

Media mix issues

These include the availability of newspapers, of radio stations, and of television coverage of the market. Also, good production facilities are needed to help ensure high-quality commercials.

Types of industries in the area

Large manufacturing plants with highly skilled union workers provide better market potential than small plants that use unskilled labour and pay low wages. However, unionized firms are more subject to strikes that can hurt retail sales.

Service organizations such as hospitals and government offices provide a stable or declining economic base, but pay low wage rates. Retailers typically seek a community with a more balanced economic base. They also seek a community with a history of growth and aggressiveness in seeking new industry. They tend to avoid a community with a history of labour problems or which is losing population.

Competition

Who are the likely competitors? Are any national retailers located in the area? How long have they been present? Can the market support another retailer without taking too much business from competition?

Availability of locations

Does the community have several shopping centres with vacancies? Does the downtown area look "alive"? Are plans under way to revitalize downtown? Is land available at reasonable prices for building a stand-alone location? During a recession (like that in 1991-1992), vacancy rates tend to be high, forcing rents down, and providing better choices.[7]

Regulations

Can a business license to operate be obtained, and how much will it cost? Can the firm be open on Sundays? Is the community aggressively seeking new retailers?

Index of retail saturation

One of the more commonly used measures of market attractiveness is the *Index of Retail Saturation (IRS)*. The index is based on the assumption that if a market **A** has a low level of **retail saturation,** the likelihood of success is higher than would otherwise be the case. The calculation of the IRS can be made as follows, and Figure 10–2 provides a concrete example of the use of the formula:

$$\text{Index of Retail Saturation}_1 = \frac{\text{Demand}}{\text{Square metres of retail selling space}}$$

Thus, for market 1:

$$\text{IRS}_1 = \frac{C_1 \times RE_1}{RF_1}$$

where:

$$IRS_1 = \text{Index of retail saturation for market 1}$$

$$C_1 = \text{Number of consumers in market 1}$$

$$RE_1 = \text{Retail expenditures per consumer in market 1}$$

$$RF_1 = \text{Retail facilities in market 1}$$

Figure 10–2   Evaluating the Saturation for Women's Clothing Stores in Fredericton

Teresa Juppe, the owner of a small chain of women's clothing stores, is interested in opening a new store in Fredericton, New Brunswick, and she is concerned about the women's clothing store retail saturation in this market. Through some research, she has been able to gather the following information:

- The 120,000 consumers in Fredericton spend an average of $189.17 per year in women's clothing stores.
- There are numerous women's clothing stores serving Fredericton, with a total of 10,000 square metres of selling area.

This information allows her to calculate an index of retail saturation for women's clothing stores in this market:

$$\text{IRS} = \frac{120{,}000 \times 189.17}{10{,}000} = \frac{22{,}700{,}000}{10{,}000} = \$2{,}270.00$$

The revenue of $2,270.00 per square metre of selling area measured against the revenue per square metre necessary to break even provides her with the measure of saturation in Fredericton. The $2,270.00 figure is also useful in evaluating relative opportunities in different market areas.[8]

Source: *Canadian Markets, 1994* (Toronto: The Financial Post Information Service, 1994), pp. 8, 18.

Census data, which are published every five years, can provide information on the number of potential customers within a trading area. Statistics Canada reports expenditure data by product category for households by income level. The number of competitors within the trading area can be determined by counting them, although selling areas would have to be estimated. Another very useful source is the *Canadian Markets,* published annually.

Trade Area Analysis

Trade area analysis occurs after management agrees on a specific geographic region or a general area of a city as a possible retail location.

Understanding trade areas

Retail sales forecast accuracy depends on the ability to estimate the trade area for an outlet. The **trading area** is the geographic region from which a store primarily attracts its customers, and it is further subdivided into two major parts: the **primary trading area** includes the majority of the store's customers, living within a certain range of the store and having the highest per capita sales; the **secondary trading area** includes almost all of the customers, situated outside the primary area (the rest is called the *fringe trading area*). For example, for the Sahili Centre Mall in Kamloops, the primary area includes 75,000 customers within 5 minutes' driving range, and the secondary area includes 95,000 customers within 25 minutes.[9]

A variety of factors determine trading area size, and they include:

1. The price of the good at one place compared to its price at another place.

2. The number of inhabitants concentrated in various places.

3. The density and distribution of the population.

4. The income and social structures of the population.

5. The proximity of other shopping opportunities.

What does this all mean for students of retailing? It means that the more highly specialized a product or service being offered, the larger the trading area must be before the service can be supported.

Population characteristics

We earlier mentioned the importance of population in market selection. An analysis of population characteristics is even more critical when evaluating a *trading area*. Management needs to understand such features as the population profile of the trading area, population density, and growth trends. The population of a trading area may not change over time, for example, but the characteristics of the people in the area may change dramatically. Some older inner-city areas in recent years have experienced the return of young urban professionals (yuppies). Similarly, minorities can become the dominant force in a trading area and can change its suitability for a particular type of retailing.

Such variables as sex, occupation, education, and age are also important, as are family size and family life cycle. An outlet selling lawn supplies would be interested in the number of single-family homes in the vicinity. On the other hand, retailers seeking suitable sites for a day care centre would be more interested in the number of families with preschool children.

Evaluating a trade area

Retailers differ from manufacturers because they have to be close to their target market since consumers typically shop at the nearest retail outlet that will meet their needs. Techniques for measuring a trade area range from a simple "seat-of-the-pants" approach to complex mathematical models.

Information from existing stores

Retailers with existing stores have an advantage over a person seeking to open an outlet for the first time. The experienced retailers can use information that they have obtained about their existing stores in making decisions about a planned new store. If the new store is similar to the old one, the sales generated will likely be similar. But retailers must, of course, make sure that the stores are alike in all key respects.

Cheque clearance

Cheque clearance data, when available, may also be used to determine a store's trading area. Some stores, such as supermarkets (e.g., Provigo), provide their customers with a privilege card that allows them to pay by cheque. However, this is based on the assumption that the distributions of cash customers and charge customers are basically the same. Plotting the addresses from the customers' cheques makes it possible to determine the characteristics of the trading area for an existing store. More and more customers are using the debit card that allows direct payment to the retailer from the customer's bank account. The information on these customers may be added to the information from cheque clearance and charge accounts to get a fuller picture of the trade area.

Credit records

Credit records can be analyzed to determine the trading area of an existing store. A sample of charge accounts is selected and customer addresses are plotted on a map. Of course, this is only possible if the retailer has developed a credit-granting procedure.

Customer spotting

Customer spotting is a technique used for determining the location of target customers. Target customers must first be defined, say by income group, or profession. Next, a mailing list of these types of customers within a defined region may be purchased from mailing list suppliers (such as direct marketing companies, or research companies such as CompuSearch). Then the home addresses of the target customers are spotted on a map and a circle is drawn to define the primary trading area for the outlet.

Driving time analysis

Driving time analysis can also be used to define a trading area by determining how far customers are willing to travel to reach an outlet. Trading areas typically are measured in terms of time instead of distance because of problems of congestion and physical barriers. A rule of thumb is that customers will travel no more than five minutes to reach a convenience outlet. Three-fourths of the customers of a large regional shopping centre normally will drive 15 minutes to reach the centre. Of course, the West Edmonton Mall is a major exception since it attracts people from the United States and even Japan!

Customer survey

A good way to determine a trading area is to conduct or sponsor a customer survey. The survey can be done by mail, telephone, or personal interview, and each method has its good and bad points, as explained in Chapter 5. The interview can be conducted at the store if it is a personal interview. Alternatively, a sample of respondents can be chosen from customer records and called on the phone or mailed a questionnaire. Retailers may also be able to participate in surveys sponsored by the local chamber of commerce or a similar organization, or buy into an omnibus survey.

The customer survey can provide information on where people shop for items similar to the planned merchandise offering. For example, if a store interviews its own customers, the addresses can be plotted on a map to measure the store's trading area. Also, retailers can do a survey of noncustomers and establish trading areas for competitors.

Drawing circles with a radius of one, two, and five kilometres makes it possible to see how far most customers travel to shop at the outlet. If a retailer is planning the first store, the information for an outlet similar to the planned one can be plotted.

A customer survey can provide other useful information as well. Such information might include: (1) *demographics* (e.g., age, occupation, number of children); (2) *shopping habits* (e.g., type of store preferred, how often consumers

---

Figure 10–3   Reilly's Law

According to Reilly's Law, the "breaking point" in retail trade between two communities a and b is calculated as follows:

$$D_b = \frac{D}{1 + \sqrt{\dfrac{P_a}{P_b}}}$$

where

P_a, P_b = Population sizes of centres a and b (b is the smaller community)
D_b = Break-point distance of trade to centre b
D = Distance between centres a and b

Example: In applying the formula, assume the following information:

P_a = 97,000 population, and **a** is Kelowna
P_b = 41,000 population, and **b** is Penticton
D = 65 kilometres

$$D_b = \frac{65}{1 + \sqrt{\dfrac{97,000}{41,000}}} = \frac{65}{1 + 1.54} = 25.6 \text{ kilometres}$$

The breaking point between Kelowna and Penticton is thus 25.6 kilometres from Penticton (and 39.4 kilometres from Kelowna).

---

shop, or area of town preferred); (3) *purchasing patterns* (e.g., who does the family buying); and (4) *media habits* (e.g., radio, TV, and newspaper habits).

Reilly's law of retail gravitation[10]

Retail **gravity models** are an improvement over other methods of trading area analysis. They are based on both population size and distance or driving time as the key variables in the models.

Reilly's Law is the oldest of the trading area models.[11] The model, as described in Figure 10–3, allows the calculation of a "breaking point" in retail trade between two communities.

These breaking points can be calculated between several cities and, when joined together, form a set of trading area boundaries for a community, as shown in Figure 10–4 for four smaller cities around city *A*.

The formula can be modified in several ways including the substitution of driving time for distance, and square metres of retail floor space for population.

Reilly's law works satisfactorily in rural areas where distance has a major impact on the choice of a community at which to shop. Breaking points do not exist in metropolitan areas, however, because consumers typically have several shopping choices available within the distance that they are willing to travel.

In essence, Reilly's Law states that the size of a trading area increases as population density decreases. For example, people may travel several kilometres to shop at a small rural village. However, the same persons would only be willing to travel a few blocks in a major metropolitan area. Further, the use of Reilly's Law is appropriate only for communities of roughly similar size. Also, trade areas vary by type of good sought, a reality not reflected in Reilly's model. Patronage is also assumed to be linearly related to time or distance from the consumer's household.

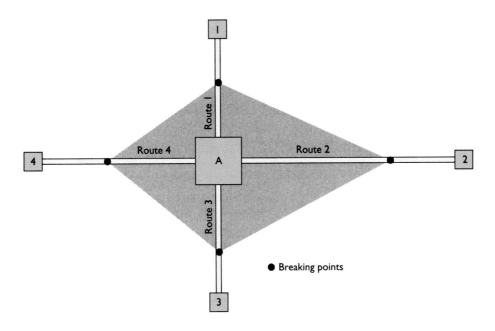

Figure 10–4   The Breaking Points between City *A* and Each of Four Smaller Cities Help Define the Boundaries of the Trading Area for a Store in City *A*.

The Huff model

The model developed by David Huff helps overcome the limitations of Reilly's model. For example, Huff's models are premised on the assumption that the likelihood of consumer patronage increases with the size of a centre. Thus consumers are willing to travel greater distances when additional merchandise is available at a central location. The probability of patronage is also assumed to be linearly related to time or distance from the consumer's household.

The formal expression of the model is as follows:[12]

$$P(C_{ij}) = \frac{\dfrac{S_j}{T_{ij}^{\lambda}}}{\displaystyle\sum_{j=1}^{n} \dfrac{S_j}{T_{ij}^{\lambda}}}$$

where

$P(C_{ij})$ = Probability of a consumer at a given point of origin i travelling to a given shopping centre j

S_j = Square metres of selling space devoted to the sale of a particular class of goods at shopping centre j

T_{ij} = Travel time involved in getting from a customer's travel base i to shopping centre j

λ = A parameter estimated empirically to reflect the effect of travel time on the various kinds of shopping trips

The most frequently used method of estimating λ is a computer program developed by Huff and Blue.[13] After estimating λ, management can determine the trading area of a shopping centre for any product class. The steps involved are as follows:

1. Divide the area surrounding a shopping centre into small statistical units within a constructed grid. Such units are represented by i in the model.
2. Determine the square metres of retail selling space of all shopping centres (the j's) included within the area of analysis.
3. Ascertain the travel time involved in getting from each statistical unit i to each of the specified shopping centres j.
4. Calculate the probability of consumers in each of the statistical units going to each shopping centre for a given product purchase, using the above formula.
5. Map the trading area for the shopping centre by drawing lines connecting all statistical units having the same probabilities.

A concrete example of application of the Huff model is given in Figure 10–5.

Still, the Huff model has its weaknesses. It assumes that consumers with comparable demographic characteristics will exhibit similar retail patronage behaviour. Huff's model includes all potential retail centres in the system although all centres might not be patronized. Recent research has shown that allowing consumers to specify their choice set of shopping centres as opposed to an arbitrarily imposed set in the traditional Huff model substantially improves the performance of the model and can be used for predictive and explanatory purposes.

How much business can be done in the trading area?

Retailers need five sets of data to help estimate the amount of sales available in a trading area: (1) number of people in the trading area; (2) average household income; (3) amount of money spent each year by the households on the type of goods sold by the firm—i.e., groceries, drugs, or apparel; (4) the total market

Before locating a new store, Loblaws does extensive trading area analysis to determine potential sales.

Courtesy Loblaw Company Ltd.

Figure 10-5   A Numerical Application of the Huff Model

Alice Middleton, the owner of a women's clothing store, is interested in opening a new store in one of the three major shopping centres (Thorncliffe, Westmount, and Eaton Plaza) serving the West Park residential area, a high-income community. After doing some research, she has been able to ascertain the following facts:

Square metres of selling space devoted to the sale of women's clothing at each shopping centre:

$S_1 = 1000 \text{ m}^2$, for Thorncliffe Shopping Mall
$S_2 = 1500 \text{ m}^2$, for Westmount Shopping Centre
$S_3 = 2000 \text{ m}^2$, for Eaton Plaza

Travel time involved in getting from a customer's home in West Park to each shopping centre:

$T_{i1} = 2 \text{ km}$, from West Park to Thorncliffe Shopping Mall
$T_{i2} = 3 \text{ km}$, from West Park to Westmount Shopping Centre
$T_{i3} = 4 \text{ km}$, from West Park to Eaton Plaza

$\lambda = 2$

Probability of a consumer from West Park travelling to each shopping centre:

$$P(C_{i1}) = \frac{\dfrac{1000}{2^2}}{\dfrac{1000}{2^2} + \dfrac{1500}{3^2} + \dfrac{2000}{4^2}} = \frac{250}{250 + 167 + 125} = 0.46, \text{ for Thorncliffe.}$$

Similarly, $P(C_{i2}) = 0.31$, for Westmount;
                                 $P(C_{i3}) = 0.23$, for Eaton Plaza.

One can easily verify that $0.46 + 0.31 + 0.23 = 1.00$.

From this information, one can deduce that Alice would have a potential 46 percent of West Park residents if she located in Thorncliffe, compared to 31 percent for Westmount and 23 percent for Eaton Plaza.

If the population of West Park is 100,000 residents, and the average per capita sales of women's clothing is $240, each centre would generate in women's clothing sales:

Thorncliffe:	$100,000 \times \$240 \times 0.46 = \$11,040,000$
Westmount:	$100,000 \times \$240 \times 0.31 = \$ 7,440,000$
Eaton Plaza:	$100,000 \times \$240 \times 0.23 = \$ 5,520,000$

Next, Alice must estimate the share of these total sales that she could realistically expect, given the competition already there for each centre. By multiplying these market shares by the total sales, she will get an estimate of the sales from West Park residents in each location to be compared to the costs of opening a store in each centre. Of course, if each centre draws customers from other areas, the same calculations should be made and aggregated into total expected sales for each location.

---

potential; and (5) the share of the total market potential management can expect to get.

The number of people in a trading area can be obtained from an analysis of Statistics Canada census data in almost any library, as noted above. The data are reported by **census tracts** (small areas with 2,500 to 8,000 people) for all cities with a population of 50,000 or more. There are over 5,000 census tracts in Canada, and these can be used for large shopping centre location decisions. A finer breakdown can be obtained by using **enumeration areas,** which contain 100 to 200 households. There are about 40,000 enumeration areas in Canada, which are very useful for small store location decisions. Finally, distances can be entered into the analysis by using the **universal transverse mercator (UTM) system,** which gives the coordinates of every possible location in Canada, including the centres of the enumeration areas.[14]

Table 10–3   Estimating Annual Sales in a Retail Store's Trading Area

Method:	(1) Number of households in a census tract in retail trading area	×	(2) Median annual income of the households in the census tract	×	(3) Proportion of a household's annual income spent on type of items sold by store	×	(4) Proportion of money spent on item that will be spent in this store	=	(5) Proposed store sales revenue from census tract
Census tracts in trading area:									
354XX	6,500	×	$10,000	×	.20*	×	.10†	=	$1,300,000
354XY	8,500	×	8,000	×	.15	×	.15	=	$1,530,000
Total projected annual sales									$2,830,000

*The proportion of .20 means that 20 percent of the typical household's annual income of $10,000 is spent on merchandise sold by this store.
†The proportion of .10 means that management anticipates that 10 percent of the total merchandise purchased in this census tract will be purchased at this specific store.

The average household income in each census tract is published by Statistics Canada every five years. Information about the amount of money spent each year on various types of merchandise can be found in Statistics Canada publications on family expenditures.[15]

Multiplying average annual household income by the number of families in the trading area yields total sales potential. Multiplying total sales potential by the percentage of the average annual household income spent on each type of good (for example, groceries) yields total sales potential by type of good.

Retailers then decide on the amount of the available sales potential they can get. One way to do this is by plotting competitors in the trading area on a map and trying to establish the sales levels of each. Indicators may be the number of checkouts, number of employees, square metres, and industry trade averages for sales per square metre. Retailers must also decide on the amount of business they need to make a profit. Then, they decide on whether and how much business they can take from the competition. Table 10–3 shows this five-step process.

Site Analysis and Evaluation

Site analysis and evaluation is the third step in the selection of a retail location. The retailer has three basic choices for a site: a shopping centre, the central business district (the "downtown" shopping area), or a solo (or stand-alone) location. Within these major types, there are more categories to choose from.

Understanding the dynamics of the local retail structure

The urban business pattern is constantly changing as new retail outlets are built, inner cities decay and are rebuilt, and central business districts lose their attraction as magnets for major retailers. Understanding the shopping centre structure, the dynamics of central business districts, and the nature of stand-

Table 10-4 Strengths and Weaknesses of Selected Location Alternatives		
Type of Location	**Strengths**	**Weaknesses**
Regional shopping centre	Large number of stores Drawing power of large anchor stores Parking availability Balanced tenant mix	Occupancy costs Some inflexibility (e.g., store hours, merchandise sold)
Community shopping centre	Operating costs Shopping convenience Shared promotions	Poor tenant mix Facility condition High vacancy rate
Neighbourhood shopping centre	Shopping convenience Very low operating costs Distance from customer	Few tenants Susceptible to competition Facility condition
Central business district	Mass transit Urban redevelopment Business/work traffic generates exposure	Parking Limited shopping hours Facility condition Suburban shift Rent costs
Solo location	Lack of close competition Lower rent More space for expansion Greater flexibility	Harder to attract customers Probably have to build instead of rent Higher promotion costs

alone sites available is important at this stage of the analysis. The following sections describe the different types of locations and provide criteria for selecting a particular site. Table 10–4 gives an overview of the strengths and weaknesses of the basic choices.

Shopping centres

Shopping centres are a geographic cluster of retail stores collectively handling an assortment of varied goods that satisfy one or more categories of the merchandise wants of consumers within convenient driving time of the centre. Shopping centres with a mix of stores that meet a very large variety of needs are said to have a **balanced tenancy.** These **planned shopping centres** are the traditional and original shopping centres.

In recent years, other types of shopping centres have emerged by catering to more narrow needs (e.g., only food, clothing, or home decoration). Retail Highlight 10–1 explains the nature of shopping centres in Canada.

What are shopping centre strengths and weaknesses?   The strengths of shopping centres are: (1) balanced tenant mix for the traditional type, depth of assortment in the category for most of the others; (2) common store hours; (3) centrewide promotions; (4) controlled climate; (5) few parking problems; (6) longer store hours; and (7) a pleasant environment for attracting shoppers.

Small stores in shopping centres can take advantage of the traffic-drawing ability of large, mass merchandisers or outlets with national reputations. Often, people will shop in the small shops even though they came to the shopping centre primarily to shop at the large, mass merchandisers.

But shopping centres also have weaknesses. The primary problems centre around what the individual merchant can and cannot do. Specifically, tenants face restrictions on (1) what can be sold and (2) store hours. Also, the policies

Retail Highlight 10–1

Shopping Centres: Are They the New Town Centres?

The recession of the early 1990s has challenged the notion that shopping centres could be compared to the ancient city square, a meeting place for people to socialize and to be seen. Consider the following examples:

- When it opened its doors in 1975, the TransCanada Mall in Calgary was a shiny example of modern consumerism. It seemed ideally located, at a major intersection, dominating an established neighbourhood where no competing malls would likely be built. It obviously was not enough of an attraction for the nearby residents, and the mall was torn down to be replaced by a strip shopping centre of food and convenience stores, all facing the street.

- In downtown Halifax, along Spring Garden Road, there are several "ghost malls." According to Geri Shepard, manager of Bayer's Road Shopping Centre, "Spring Garden Road was a wonderful pedestrian place bounded by parks. It was a residential neighbourhood with seniors, young families, and university students. The developers saw that traffic and translated it into shopping centre traffic. But it would not work ... The empty malls are huge statues for the ego that built them."

What these examples illustrate is that the success of shopping centres is not only a function of traffic or competition, but it must correctly account for the needs of the population, and develop a competitive advantage beyond location. For example, industry analysts have pointed out that:

- Middle-aged couples, many juggling children and two jobs, found that they had less time and inclination to browse through the malls.
- The *mix* of retailers is the second most important factor after location, particularly for customers who do not want to go through several malls to find an item.
- Malls must provide more services, for example, day care for children and medical offices for seniors.
- Some developers have increased the *density* of nearby population by adding office towers, hotels, and car showrooms at mall locations.

The success of a mall as a popular town centre will depend on how well it meets the needs of the population.

Sources: Barbara Wickens, "Misery at the Malls," *Maclean's*, March 23, 1992, pp. 30–31; Andrew Allentuck, "Is the Mall Beginning to Pall?" *Globe & Mail*, May 5, 1992, p. B23.

---

of the centre are often dictated by the large **anchor tenant(s).** Finally, rent will be higher than in a stand-alone location.

What are the choices?[16]   Whether a retailer can get into a shopping centre depends on the market and management. A small shopping centre may need only one children's shoe store, for example, whereas a regional centre may expect enough business for several.

In order to find tenants whose line of goods will meet the needs of the market to be reached, the developer-owner first signs prestige merchants as lead tenants. Then, other types of stores are selected that will complement each other. This bolsters the centre's competitive strength against other centres, as well as supplying the market area's needs. However, many malls in Canada tend to have the same types of tenants, especially the large chains such as Eaton's, or the specialty chains such as Dylex. This may adversely affect new entries with this kind of sameness, and favour new malls with a special flavour.

Strong anchor tenants, like Zellers and Canadian Tire, are critical to the success of a mall.

Photo by Anne Laroche

To finance a centre, the developer needs major leases from companies with strong credit ratings. Lenders favour tenant rosters that include the triple-A ratings of national chains. When most spaces are filled, a developer may choose small outlets to help fill the remaining vacancies.

However, a person who is considering a shopping centre for a first-store venture may have trouble. Financial backing and merchandising experience may be unproven. The problem is to convince the developer that the new store has a reasonable chance of success and will help the tenant mix.

Factors to consider in a shopping centre choice   Suppose that the owner-developer of a shopping centre asks a retailer to be a tenant. In considering the offer, the retailer needs to make sure of what he or she can do in the centre. What rules will affect the operation? In exchange for the rules, what will the centre do for the firm?

Even more important, the trading area, the location of competition, and the location of available space need to be considered. These factors help to determine how much business can be done in the centre.

The centre's location   In examining the centre's location, look for answers to questions such as these:[17]

1. Can the store hold old customers and attract new ones?

2. Would the centre offer the best sales volume potential for the kind of merchandise to be sold?

3. Can management benefit enough from the centre's access to a market? If so, can it offer the appeal that will make the centre's customers come to the store?

A retailer should conduct an analysis of the market the developer expects to reach. In this respect, money for professional help is well spent, especially when the research indicates that the centre is not right for the type of firm planned.

Store space   Determine where the space will be. The location within a centre is important. Does the store need to be in the main flow of customers as they pass between the stores with the greatest "customer pull"? What will be the nature of the adjacent stores? What will be their effect on sales of the planned firm?

The amount of space is also important   Using their experience, retailers should determine the amount of space needed to handle the sales volume expected. The amount of space will also determine the rent to be paid.

Total rent   Most shopping centre leases are negotiated either on a percentage basis or on a fixed fee per square metre. The contents of a lease will be covered later in the chapter.

Rental expenses may begin with a minimum guarantee that is equal to a percentage of gross sales. Although this is typically between five and seven percent of gross sales for non-anchor tenants, it varies by type or size of business and other factors. For anchor tenants, this percentage is usually lower.

Alternatively, fixed annual rents in most Canadian shopping centres tend to average between $100 and $200 per square metre, and may go higher in some instances; for example, in the West Edmonton Mall, the average annual rent can go as high as $350 per square metre.[18]

Table 10–5 Description of the Three Types of Shopping Centres			
	Neighbourhood	**Community**	**Regional**
Number of stores	5-15	16-30	More than 30
Leading tenant	Supermarket or drugstore	Variety or junior department	At least one full-line department store
Typical leasable space	5,000 m²	10,000 m²	20,000 m²
Typical site area	1.6 hectare	4 hectares	12 hectares
Minimum trade population	7,500 to 25,000	25,000 to 75,000	75,000 or more

Other charges are assessed in addition to the minimum guarantee or the monthly rent. A retailer may have to pay dues to the centre's merchant association and for maintenance of common areas.

Rent, then, should be considered in terms of "total rent." If "total rent" is more than the present rent in an existing location, the space in the centre will have to draw enough additional sales to justify the added cost.

Finishing out   Generally, the developer furnishes only the bare space in a new centre. The retailer does the "finishing out" at his or her own expense. For example, a retailer pays for lighting fixtures, counter shelves, painting, and floor coverings. In addition, heating and cooling units may have to be installed.

Some developers help tenants plan store fronts, exterior signs, and interior colour schemes. They provide this service to ensure store fronts that add to the centre's image rather than detracting from it.

Types of shopping centres   Because planned shopping centres are built around a major tenant, centres are classified, in part, according to the leading tenant. The classification includes three types: neighbourhood, community, and regional. The typical characteristics of these are described in Table 10–5.

Neighbourhood shopping centre   Statistics Canada defines a **neighbourhood shopping centre** as one with 5 to 15 stores, and which offers free parking.[19] The supermarket or the drugstore is the leading tenant in a neighbourhood centre. This type is the smallest in size among shopping centres, with few stores, and caters to the convenience needs of a neighbourhood. For example, Westsyde Shopping Centre in Kamloops is anchored by Cooper's Market and Quality Bakery, has 11 stores, a gross leasable retail area of about 5,200 m², a primary population of 7,000, and a secondary population of 25,000.[20]

Community shopping centre   Statistics Canada defines a **community shopping centre** as one with 16 to 30 stores, and which offers free parking.[21] Variety or junior department stores are the leading tenants in the community centre. Such centres include some specialty shops, wider price ranges, greater style assortments, and more impulse-sale items. For example, Country Fair Mall in Summerside (P.E.I.) is anchored by Zellers and Sobey's, has 25 stores, a gross leasable retail area of about 14,530 m², and a population base of 37,700.[22]

Regional shopping centre   Statistics Canada defines a **regional shopping centre** as one with more than 30 stores, and which offers free parking.[23] The department store, with its prestige, is the leader in the regional centre—the largest type of shopping centre. When a retailer finds that a second or third

Regional shopping centres, like the Woodgrove Mall in Nanaimo, B.C., attract shoppers from Ladysmith to Duncan.

Courtesy Cambridge Shopping Centres Ltd.

department store is also locating in such a centre, he or she will know that the site has been selected to draw from the widest possible market area. The smaller tenants were picked to offer a range of goods and services approaching the appeal once found only downtown. The biggest regional shopping centre is the West Edmonton Mall, described at the beginning of the chapter. A more typical regional shopping centre is the Fredericton Mall with three anchors, 79 tenants, a gross leasable area of 20,560 m^2, and a market population of about 100,000.[24] Retail Highlight 10–2 provides some interesting facts about shopping malls in Canada.

When considering a mall, retailers should weigh the benefits against costs. At the outset, it may be difficult to measure savings, such as the elimination of store fronts, against costs. For example, the cost of heating and air-conditioning may be higher in the enclosed mall. In an enclosed mall centre, tenant groupings include drugstores and supermarkets in a separate building at the edge of the parking area. Relatively high-priced women's goods stores tend to cluster together. Service and repair shops are located where customers have direct access from the parking lot for quick in-and-out pickup of goods.

The mega-multi-mall[25]   The West Edmonton Mall has forced a reexamination of malls as a new format of retail institution. Whereas regional malls were designed and managed to satisfy a major purpose, i.e., shopping, the mega-multi-mall is a multifunctional centre where several needs, in addition to shopping, could be satisfied (e.g., entertainment, recreation, eating, drinking, socializing, working, and sightseeing).

Urban arterial developments   **Urban arterial developments** are often found in an older part of the city. The sites were initially developed to provide good locations on busy streets for shoppers. Typical examples include home repair centres, appliance stores, automobile repair shops, and office equipment firms, which serve either a commercial or consumer market. Highway-oriented strip developments occur on the outskirts of major cities and are characterized by such facilities as motels and restaurants.

Power strip centres   **Power strip, or destination, centres** are a hot new development. They are typically anchored by what are known as destination-

Retail Highlight 10–2

Edmonton: The Mall Capital of Canada

Major malls have been built in most regions of Canada, but nowhere to the extent of Edmonton, which on a per capita basis has *three and a half times* the national average of per capita square metres of mall retail area. Here is the ranking for the top 22 census metropolitan areas in Canada:

Metropolitan Area	Number of Malls	Leasable Area (000 m^2)	Area Per Capita (m^2)
Edmonton	9	885	0.99
Quebec City	6	457	0.67
Sherbrooke	1	84	0.58
London	4	234	0.57
Calgary	7	436	0.54
Hamilton	5	332	0.52
Vancouver	12	903	0.51
St. Catharines/Niagara	3	193	0.50
Halifax	3	157	0.46
Ottawa/Hull	5	410	0.41
Chicoutimi	1	66	0.39
Oshawa	1	102	0.38
Toronto	20	1,636	0.38
Sudbury	1	56	0.34
Montreal	15	1,086	0.33
Trois-Rivières	1	47	0.33
Winnipeg	3	213	0.31
Regina	1	57	0.29
Saskatoon	1	65	0.29
Windsor	1	80	0.29
St. John's	1	48	0.27
Kitchener	1	70	0.18
Canada	**113**	**8,100**	**0.28**

Of Canada's 113 malls, 34 can be called "super regional malls," with more than 75,000 m^2 of leasable area. Of the 113 malls, 54 were built in the 1970s, 20 were added in the 1980s, and only one so far in the 1990s.

Sources: *1996 Directory of Shopping Centres;* Statistics Canada, *Annual Demographic Statistics, 1994,* Cat. 91-21, p. 71; B. Little, "Amazing Facts," *Globe & Mail,* January 18, 1992, p. B19.

oriented retailers or superstores, as in the Warden Power Centre example at the beginning of the chapter. The most frequently represented power centre anchor tenants, in descending frequency, are: toy/children's superstores, off-price apparel outlets, soft lines promotional department stores, discount department stores, consumer electronic superstores, deep-discount drugstores, or consumer-oriented home improvement outlets. In essence, a power centre is an oversized strip centre. Typically, it has the drawing power of a regional shopping centre. Everything is visible from the street, and consumers can drive directly to where they want to go. Such centres have smaller acquisition, building, and maintenance costs than regional malls. Additionally, the developers achieve a greater merchandise depth than the typical strip centre. The strongest candidates for power centres are national, regional, and local retailers with a strong presence and name recognition. A strong value image is also important.

Power strip centres include superstores like Michaels to create a strong value attraction for consumers.

Photo by Betty McDougall

Specialty attraction centres   In addition to the traditional shopping centres that dominate the retail scene, there are several types of specialized centres, described next.

Theme or specialty centres[26]   These theme or specialty centres can be quite diverse in thematic format, size, and market orientation, but all share features that distinguish them from other centres: a common architectural theme that unites a wide range of retailers who repeat the theme in their spaces; tenants who offer unusual merchandise; restaurants and entertainment that serve as anchors, rather than supermarkets or department stores; and a strong appeal made to tourists as well as local shoppers.

Fashion-oriented centres   These fashion-oriented centres consist mainly of apparel shops, boutiques, and craft shops carrying selected merchandise of high quality and price. They appeal to high-income shoppers. Growth was strongest for fashion-oriented centres in the mid-1980s but has slowed recently.

Discount centres   A discount centre is usually anchored by one or more discount stores with a strong representation of discount merchants. The centres appeal mainly to lower-income groups, as compared to off-price centres.

Off-price centres   These are centres with a heavy concentration of specialty and department stores selling brand-name goods at 20 to 70 percent off manufacturers' suggested retail prices. Examples include Super Carnival. The quality of goods is higher than in discount stores, so off-price centres draw upon middle- and upper-middle-income shoppers. These centres do not compete directly for the K mart or Zellers clientele in that the former offer high-quality merchandise at reduced prices.

Factory outlets   In contrast to factory outlets of the past, typically found at the factory site, these centres consist of retail outlets owned and operated by manufacturers where goods are sold directly to the public. Factory outlet malls draw a combination of middle- and lower-income customers and often include some off-price stores. (Some researchers combine off-price centres with factory outlet centres.)[27] Vanity Fair, Burlington, and Bally are examples. The factory outlet is the low end of the off-price branded field. *Complete centres devoted to factory outlets have become a permanent fixture in the shopping centre field because they combine two of the key draws that lure shoppers: perceived value and one-stop shopping.* Add to that plenty of parking space, fast-food restaurants, a movie theatre, and a recreation store with blinking electronic games.

Festival or entertainment centres   With a strong representation of restaurants, fast food, specialty retailers, and entertainment facilities, festival or entertainment centres tend to be large. Opportunities for new growth are considered limited. These include Le Faubourg in Montreal, a collection of food stalls, specialty shops, and restaurants in an old warehouse building. Often these enterprises are the result of young entrepreneurial merchants who fill an indoor marketplace with boutiques selling items ranging from towels to hats to strawberry-scented soaps. Ultra-small retailers are a fixture in many such operations. Many of the urban centres built by developers as part of a commercial building offer local neighbourhood customers (including the "office crowd") and tourists a new experience.

Catalogue centres   These are centres anchored by one or more catalogue showroom stores. This category experienced strong growth in the 1970s and virtual disappearance in the 1980s.

Service-oriented centres   These centres depend heavily upon service-oriented retailers, such as opticians, dentists, repair services, health clinics, legal services, and so forth. Their present share is expected to grow in strip centres, the largest industry component and one with much space to fill.

Home improvement centres   These centres are anchored by a large home improvement retailer or feature a concentration of home improvement and hardware specialty retailers. As yet, numbers are not significant, but this concept is expected to grow.

Single-theme centres   Zeroing in on consumer needs in a narrow range such as auto care, home decorating and design, or weddings, this new approach calls for tenanting the centre solely with retailers and services that match the theme.

Niche malls   These malls are targeted to a very specific group of customers, which is why the name *niche* was selected. In Canada, for example, these have been targeted toward the Chinese population in areas of large concentration such as in the metropolitan areas of Montreal, Toronto, and Vancouver. In the United States, niche malls have targeted working women and blacks.[28]

A downtown location

Central business district (downtown) locations also offer several advantages:

1. Rents are lower than in many shopping centres.
2. Public transportation may be more readily available to downtown.
3. The locations are usually close to large office complexes, which employ many people.
4. Entertainment districts offering theatres, restaurants, bars, and similar facilities are often available.

However, disadvantages can exist. They include the following:

1. Downtown stores are often not open in the evening.
2. Crime rates may be higher.
3. Traffic congestion is bad.
4. Downtown areas are sometimes decaying and rundown.

The high concentration of commercial buildings makes the central business district (CBD) one of the important components of urban structure. The CBD attracts people from throughout the metropolitan area, often including visitors. Mass transit also brings people into the CBD in many metropolitan areas. Such areas contain a wide variety of stores and often include the flagship of one of the leading department store chains. Examples include Eaton's in Toronto, and Ogilvy in Montreal. Some have suggested that municipalities try to emulate the appearance of the malls to give their downtown a more inviting and exclusive look, in the same way the malls have borrowed heavily design elements from the downtown (such as parks, fountains, and plazas).[29]

In addition, "old towns" in Montreal and Vancouver are examples of revival of the CBDs. Medical districts around large hospitals also fit this description, as do streets known for their high-class fashion stores or art galleries, such as Sherbrooke Street in Montreal.

A solo location

Statistics Canada defines a **solo location** (also called an on-street or stand-alone location) as a store or outlet located in a residential neighbourhood, commercial section, or major traffic arterial and which is not in a shopping plaza or other type of shopping mall.[30] Superstores such as Wal-Mart, Home Depot, IKEA and Future Shop often choose solo locations. Other organizations, such as Canadian Tire, Sears, and Zellers, have developed their own "big box" stores; for example, in 1995, Sears opened in Kitchener (Ontario) a giant furniture store (3,250 m^2) called the Sears Whole Home Furniture Store, and Zellers opened in Gatineau, Quebec, a 12,000 m^2 giant store called Zellers Plus.[31]

Solo locations on heavily travelled areas have several advantages including:

- The lack of close competition.
- Lower rent.
- More space for parking and expansion.
- Greater flexibility in store hours and other methods of operation.

But, disadvantages also exist. For example:

- Such stores may have difficulty attracting consumers because comparison shopping is not easy.
- Advertising costs are often higher than if the firm was in a shopping centre with other stores that would advertise together.
- The retailer will probably have to build a store rather than rent one.

The most successful stores in on-street locations are those with a strong customer loyalty and a wide assortment of national-brand merchandise from which consumers can choose. After deciding on an acceptable general location,

IKEA can use a solo-location strategy because it has strong customer loyalty and a wide assortment of merchandise in home furnishings.

Courtesy IKEA Canada

a retailer then assesses the economic potential of the trading area to determine whether it can support the planned store.

Making the choice

Ultimately the choice of a location depends on the retailer's strategy for growth. The choice also depends on the market to be served, the characteristics of the customers who will be shopping at the outlet, the image of the firm, the current or projected competitive position of the retailer, and the growth objectives and capabilities of the firm.

Table 10–6 provides a checklist of specific site evaluation criteria.

Accessibility is affected by physical barriers such as rivers, ease of ingress and egress from the site, traffic congestion, and road conditions. As a generalization, the higher the volume of traffic, the higher the level of potential sales. However, the composition of traffic is also important. A high volume of commercial or truck traffic, for example, is not desirable. Similarly, a high volume of pedestrian traffic with little time for browsing is also not desirable.

The amount of parking needed depends on frequency of vehicle turnover, the type of merchandise sold, and peak parking requirements. However, peak parking should be evaluated in a "normal" period as opposed to a heavy shopping period such as Christmas. Otherwise, the retailer will find excess parking spaces sitting vacant most of the year.

Traffic counts can be of critical importance in evaluating the suitability of a site. The general objective of a traffic count is to count the passing traffic—both pedestrian and vehicular—that would constitute potential customers who would probably be attracted into the store.[32] Data from traffic counts should not only show how many people pass by but generally indicate what kinds of people they

Table 10–6 Site Evaluation Checklist	
Zoning	**Land use**
Type	Vacancies
Surrounding zoning patterns	Terrain
Likelihood of getting changes if needed	Parking availability
Utilities	Building patterns
Water, sewer, gas	Amenities
Adequacy	**Growth potential**
Cost	Trends in income
Location of lines	Trends in number and mix of population
Accessibility	Trends—building permits issued
Quality of ingress and egress	Location pattern of competitive businesses
Traffic volume and flow	
Public transportation availability	

are. Analysis of the characteristics of the passing traffic frequently reveals patterns and variations not readily apparent from casual observation.

In order to determine what proportion of the passing traffic represents potential shoppers, some of the pedestrians should be interviewed about the origin of their trip, their destination, and the stores in which they plan to shop. This sort of information can provide a good estimate of the number of potential customers. The season, month, week, day, and hour all have an effect upon a traffic survey. For example, during summer there is generally an increased flow of traffic on the shady side of the street. During a holiday period, such as the month before Christmas or the week before Easter, traffic is denser than normal. The patronage of a store varies by day of the week, too, as store traffic usually increases during the latter part of the week. In some communities, on factory paydays and days when social security checks are received, certain locations experience heavier-than-normal traffic.

Management also has to decide whether they want to locate near the competition. Locating near competitors can encourage comparison shopping. Some areas of a community, for example, have a concentration of automobile dealers or furniture outlets for that reason.

Other factors to consider

Most first-time business owners have no idea how effective a strong merchants' association can be in promoting and maintaining the business in a given area. Management should always find out about the merchants' association. The presence of an effective association can strengthen the business and save management money through group advertising programs, group insurance plans, and collective security measures.

A strong merchants' association can accomplish through group strength what an individual store owner could not even dream of. Some associations have persuaded city planners to add highway exits near their shopping centres. Others have lobbied for (and received) funds from cities to remodel their

Retail Highlight 10-3

For Effective Landlords, a Lease Agreement Is a Partnership

For a landlord, a good tenant is a steady source of revenue, particularly when the lease agreement includes a percentage of sales, and when the economy is faltering. It is, thus, extremely important for the landlord to help current and potential tenants succeed. Some examples help illustrate the benefits of this proactive approach:

• When Confed Realty Services bought for $1 the Eaton Centre mall in downtown Edmonton from Triple Five Corp., the mall was doing very poorly, and tenants were asking for rent concessions. Sandy McNair, a proprietor and manager of the mall, knew that rent concessions would not increase sales, which is what was needed to make the mall profitable. By using the amount of money that would have gone into rent concessions, he was able to invest it in a program that produced impressive results. Some of the elements were: *(1)* a complete interior renovation of the mall to make it more appealing to customers; *(2)* an ongoing program to advise retailers on improving their operations, including window displays and store designs (using consultants paid by Confed); *(3)* the Eaton Centre Retail Management Institute taught by professional consultants (again paid by Confed) giving an eight-week course on customer service, salesmanship, time management, and human resources; *(4)* a customer-loyalty program developed, run, and financed by Confed, which serves as a database for marketing, providing useful information to retailers about who their customers are, and serving as a basis for targeted promotion.

• Trilea Centre, a Toronto-based shopping mall operator, has devised a program to allow aspiring retailers to test-market their ideas while lowering their financial risk. For the last few years, several of its malls have been renting small carts by the week (for as little as $300 a week), or a 10-square-metre shop by the month. By comparison, renting a space in a shopping centre would require an investment of about $200,000, with a five-year lease. In addition, mall managers give basic advice and some, like the Lougheed Mall in Burnaby, run workshops to first-time retailers. The program has been very successful in helping mini-retailers gain valuable experience and go on to lease full-fledged quarters, once they are convinced that the idea is profitable.

Sources: John Southerst, "The Reinvention of Retail," *Canadian Business,* August 1992, pp. 26-31; Jerry Zeidenberg, "Malls Give Entrepreneurs a Chance to Test Market," *Globe & Mail,* December 23, 1991, p. B4.

---

shopping centres, including extension of parking lots, resurfacing of buildings, and installation of better lighting.

Merchants' associations can be particularly effective at organizing store promotions around common themes or events and during holiday seasons. The collective draw from these promotions is usually several times that which a single retailer could have mustered.

Responsiveness of the landlord

Directly related to the appearance of a retail location is the responsiveness of the landlord to the individual merchant's needs. Unfortunately, some landlords of retail business properties actually hinder the operation of their tenants' businesses. They are in fact responsible for the demise of their properties. Retail Highlight 10-3 provides examples of effective landlords.

By restricting the placement and size of signs, by foregoing or ignoring needed maintenance and repairs, by renting adjacent retail spaces to incompatible—or worse, directly competing—businesses, landlords may cripple a retailer's attempts to increase business.

Sometimes landlords lack the funds to maintain their properties. Rather than continuing to invest in their holdings by maintaining a proper appearance for their buildings and supporting their tenants, they try to "squeeze" the property for whatever they can get.

In addition to speaking with current tenants, management should talk to previous tenants of the possible locations. Find out what businesses they were in and why they left. Did they fail or just move? What support or hindrances did the landlord provide? If the opportunity presented itself, would they be retail tenants of this landlord again?

Leases

A lease is a legal contract that conveys property from the landlord to the tenant for a specified period of time in return for an agreed-on fee. Leases can take several forms. Under a **fixed-payment lease,** the landlord charges the tenant a fixed amount each month. In a **variable-payment lease,** the retailer pays a guaranteed minimum rent plus a specified percentage of sales. The minimum rent typically covers the landlord's expenses, such as taxes, insurance, and maintenance. The percentage of sales component of the rent allows the landlord to share in the profits the retailer makes as a result of being in a choice location.

The rent to be paid is determined by several factors. The primary factor is the sales per square metre that can be generated at the site. Retailers with high sales per square metre typically pay a lower percentage rent than retailers with lower sales per square metre. Outlets with high sales per square metre generate higher volumes of customer traffic and as a result are able to negotiate lower percentage rents because they are more desirable tenants.

Other considerations for retail site decisions

A host of other considerations have varying importance in choosing a retail location, depending on the line of business. Although they certainly do not exist in all possibilities, the following questions may help in deciding the retail location:

1. How much retail, office, storage, or workroom space is needed?
2. Is parking space available and adequate?
3. Does the business require special lighting, heating or cooling, or other installations?
4. Will the advertising expenses be much higher if management chooses a relatively remote location?
5. Is the area served by public transportation?
6. Can the area serve as a source of supply of employees?
7. Is there adequate fire and police protection?
8. Will sanitation or utility supply be a problem?
9. Is exterior lighting in the area adequate to attract evening shoppers and make them feel safe?
10. Are customer restroom facilities available?
11. Is the store easily accessible?
12. Does the store have awnings or decks to provide shelter during bad weather?

13.   Will crime insurance be prohibitively expensive?

14.   Will space be needed for pickup or delivery?

15.   Is the trade area heavily dependent on seasonal business?

16.   Is the location convenient to where the employees will live?

17.   Do the target customers live nearby?

18.   Is the population density of the area sufficient?

Selecting the Site

A perfect location rarely exists. Ideally, management will find a location with easy accessibility, high traffic flow, at a reasonable price, and in a desirable shopping environment.

Rating sites

The final choice among alternative sites can be made after management decides on (1) the *importance* of selected factors in choosing a site and, (2) the *attractiveness* of the site based on the factors identified as important. Multiplying importance by attractiveness as shown in Table 10–7 yields a weighted score for each factor. The total score for each site allows management to compare and rank alternative sites more objectively in making a final choice.

Consider the future

Management should look ahead. Try to picture the situation 10 years from now. Try to determine whether the general area can support the firm as the business expands. Also, management must consider whether a site that fills its present needs will allow for future expansion. If management has to move a second time and the distance is too far, the firm is apt to lose a majority of its customers.

Relocate for growth?

Sometimes an owner-manager should consider relocating although the need for it is not apparent—even though the present space may seem adequate, and customers are being served without undue complaints.

Table 10–7   Rating Sheet for Sites

Factor	Importance*	Attractiveness[+] Ranking of Site	Weighted Score
Growth potential	2	2	4
Rental conditions	6	4	24
Investment required	5	5	25
Strength of competition	1	1	1
Ability to serve target	3	6	18
Profit potential	4	3	12
Total Score for Site			*84*

* 1 is most important to the owner-manager.

[+] For the site considered, 1 is most attractive to the owner-manager.

If a facility has become a competitive liability, moving to another building may be the most economical way to become competitive again. For example, if a new high-quality shopping centre in a downtown area is expected to attract a lot of traffic away from the street merchants, the owner of a retail store situated in an old building should seriously consider relocating inside the centre.

The company that prospers is the one whose owner-manager chooses the best possible site and remains there only until the factors indicate that the present location's benefits no longer outweigh the advantages to be gained by moving.

Chapter Highlights

- **Location is a key factor in the retailing mix. Retailers should consider such a decision as carefully as pricing, promotion, and other elements of the marketing mix.**

- **Key strategic decisions in retail location relate to the desired type of market coverage and the type of goods sold. The process of selecting a retail location goes from region or metropolitan area choice, to trade area analysis and site analysis and evaluation.**

- **Key factors in making the market selection include its size, composition of the population, labour market, closeness to the source of merchandise supply, media mix available, economic base of the community, existing and probable future competition, availability of store sites, and local, provincial, and federal regulations.**

- **Trade area analysis is done once the market has been selected. Retailers can employ a variety of techniques in assessing the size of the probable trading area (primary and secondary). These techniques include a study of existing stores, cheque clearance analysis, an analysis of credit records, consumer spotting, driving time analysis, gravity models, and conducting a customer survey to help understand customer shopping behaviour.**

- **After establishing the size of the trading area, management then has to determine the amount of business that can be done in the trading area. The amount of business is a function of the number of people in the trading area, the average household income, the amount of money spent each year by households on the type of goods sold by the firm, the total market potential available, and the share of the total market potential that management expects to attract.**

- **Analyzing and evaluating alternative sites within a trading area is the third step in selecting a retail location. Retailers can decide on a shopping centre, a downtown, or a solo location. The retailer has the choice of locating in a neighbourhood centre, a community centre, a regional centre, a mega-multi-mall, a power strip centre, or some specialty centres (theme or specialty centres, fashion-oriented centres, discount centres, off-price centres, factory** outlet centres, festival or entertainment centres, catalogue centres, service-oriented centres, home improvement centres, single-theme centres and niche malls).

- Analyzing specific sites also involves assessing the adequacy and potential of vehicular or passenger traffic passing a site, the ability of the site to intercept traffic en route from one place to another, the nature of adjacent stores, type of goods sold, and adequacy of parking.

- Finally, there are a number of other factors to consider, including the responsiveness of the landlord and the contents of the lease agreement.

Key Terms

anchor tenants 278
balanced tenancy 277
census tract 275
central business district 285
community shopping centre 281
enumeration area 275
factory outlet centre 284
fixed-payment lease 290
gravity models 272
market saturation 263
niche mall 285
neighbourhood shopping
  centre 281
planned shopping centre 277

power strip centre 282
primary trading area 269
regional shopping centre 281
regional dominance 263
retail saturation 268
secondary trading area 269
solo location 286
trading area 269
traffic count 287
universal transverse mercator
  (UTM) 275
urban arterial developments 282
variable-payment lease 290

Discussion Questions

1. Explain why regional dominance, market saturation, and emphasis on smaller towns and communities are seen today as the best three location strategies.

2. What do you consider to be the important factors in selecting a site for a fast-food outlet? How do these contrast, if at all, with your notion of the key factors for the location of an outlet selling stereo components?

3. In deciding whether to locate in a particular shopping centre, what are the factors (questions) the retailer needs to consider?

4. Distinguish among the following: neighbourhood shopping centres, community shopping centres, and regional shopping centres.

5. What factors have led to the decline of downtown areas as desirable locations for many retail outlets? What can downtown areas do to better compete with the suburban shopping centres?

6. Distinguish among the following techniques used by retailers to determine the size of a trading area: cheque-clearance analysis, gravity models, credit-records analysis, and customer surveys.

7. **What are the various types of information a retailer needs to estimate the amount of likely sales within a trading area? What are some of the sources from which this information may be obtained?**

8. **Why is information about a retail store's target market an essential factor to consider when conducting a pedestrian traffic count?**

Application Exercises

1. Devise a questionnaire to obtain the following information for the shopping centre at which a sample of consumers most frequently shop:
   a) Distance travelled to the shopping centre.
   b) Number of visits per week/month.
   c) Items usually purchased at this shopping centre.
   d) Factors most liked about the shopping centre.
   e) Dominant reason for shopping at the centre.
   f) Opinion about the prices of merchandise.
   g) Opinion about the quality of merchandise.
   h) Opinion about selection of merchandise.
   i) Opinion about salespeople.
   j) Opinion about the convenience of location.
   k) Amount spent here on the average per week/month.

   Expand this questionnaire to obtain similar information about the shopping centre frequented second most. Using the data obtained from your questionnaire, do an analysis to isolate the factors that determine the choice of shopping centres. Which factors are the most important? Which are the least important? Are greater dollar amounts spent at the shopping centre visited most frequently? What meaning does this have for the retailer? What are the similarities and differences in the reasons given for the shopping centre visited most and second most?

2. A topic of interest in many cities is the future of the central business district (CBD). If you are in a city that has gone through a downtown revitalization program, arrange to have interviews with the public servants (and volunteers) who were responsible for getting the project "going." Describe it; indicate the views of success; and indicate future directions. If you are not in such a situation, search the current literature for examples of cities that have done downtown revitalization jobs. Contact the chambers of commerce for information and indicate some of the national efforts along these lines.

3. Prepare a location and site analysis for a good-quality cafeteria (other types of service retailers or tangible goods establishments may be used) for your local community based on the information in the text. Assume that the cafeteria is a regional chain with excellent regional recognition and acceptance but that it is not in your community. Prices are higher than "fast-food" outlets but lower than "service restaurants" of comparable quality food.

Suggested Cases

20. F. B. Smith/McKay Florists Ltd.

21. Housewares Unlimited

Notes

1. Adapted from J. Heinzl, "How a Dying Mall Found New Life," *Globe & Mail,* October 18, 1995, p. B11; S. Bourette, "Sears Expanding in Rural Markets," *Globe & Mail,* November 10, 1995, p. B3; R. Melnbardis, "The Decline and Fall of Montreal," *Financial Times of Canada,* December 23, 1991, pp. 8-10; *Canadian Directory of Shopping Centres, 1996,* Toronto: Maclean Hunter Limited, pp. 158-60; M. Cernetig, "A Wonder Wobbles," *Report on Business,* December 14, 1992, p. B18.

2. G.L. Crittenden, "Retailing's Critical Link: Market Share and Profitability," *Retail Control,* October 1990, p. 10.

3. B. Simon, "Good Times Have Arrived in Some Surprising Places," *The Financial Post,* May 15, 1989, p. 17.

4. S. Bourette, "Sears Expanding in Rural Markets," *Globe & Mail,* November 10, 1995, p. B3.

5. *Canadian Markets, 1996,* Toronto: The Financial Post Information Service, p. 14.

6. A. Bokma, "Hard Labour," *Retail Directions,* November/December 1988, pp. 20-25.

7. S. Craig, "Nouveaux Landlords," *The Financial Post,* August 26, 1995, p. 7.

8. *Canadian Markets, 1994,* Toronto: The Financial Post Information Service, pp. 8, 18.

9. *Canadian Directory of Shopping Centres, 1996,* p. 19.

10. W.J. Reilly, *Methods for the Study of Retail Relationships,* Research Monograph #4, University of Texas Bulletin #2944 (Austin: University of Texas Press, 1929).

11. P.P. Yannopoulos, "Salient Factors in Shopping Centre Choice," in *Marketing,* vol. 12 (ed. Tony Schellinck), ASAC, 1991, pp. 294-302; A. Finn and J. Louviere, "Shopping-Centre Patronage Models," *Journal of Business Research,* vol. 21, 1990, pp. 259-75; H. Matsusaki, "The Estimation of Retail Trading Areas by Using a Probabilistic Gravity Model: An Evaluation from a Cross-Cultural Perspective," in *Marketing,* vol. 1 (ed. Vernon J. Jones), ASAC, 1980, pp. 248-57; G.H. Haines, Jr., L.S. Simon and M. Alexis, "Maximum Likelihood Estimation of Central-City Food Trading Areas," *Journal of Marketing Research,* vol. IX, No. 2 (May 1972), pp. 154-9.

12. D.L. Huff, "A Probabilistic Analysis of Shopping Centre Trade Areas," *Land Economics,* vol. 39. Copyright 1963 by the Board of Regents of the University of Wisconsin System, p. 86.

13. D.L. Huff and L. Blue, *A Programmed Solution for Estimating Retail Sales Potential* (Lawrence, Kansas: Centre for Regional Studies, 1966).

14. R.E. Turner, "Marketing Applications of the 1981 Census Data," in *Marketing,* vol. 6 (ed. J.C. Chebat), ASAC, 1985, pp. 335-42.

15. Statistics Canada, *Family Expenditures in Canada,* Cat. 62-555, Ottawa: Information Canada.

16. J.R. McKeever, "Factors to Consider in a Shopping Centre Location," *Small Marketers Aid, #143* (Washington, DC: Small Business Administration); E. Peterson, "Site Selection," *Stores,* July, 1986; "Firm Anchors Secure Small Centre Financing," *Chain Store Age Executive,* September, 1986.

17. An interesting approach can be found in A. Finn and J. Louviere, "Shopping-Centre Patronage Models," *Journal of Business Research,* vol. 21, 1990, pp. 259-75.

18. *Canadian Directory of Shopping Centres, 1996,* Maclean Hunter, pp. 158-60.

19. Statistics Canada, *Sales per Selling Area of Independent Retailers,* Cat. 61-522, Ottawa: Information Canada (1986), Appendix I.

20. *Canadian Directory of Shopping Centres, 1996,* p. 20.

21. Statistics Canada, *Sales per Selling Area of Independent Retailers.*

22. *Canadian Directory of Shopping Centres, 1996,* p. 584.

23. Statistics Canada, *Sales per Selling Area of Independent Retailers.*

24. "Festival Market Places: Entertaining the Shopper," *Chain Store Age Executive,* October 1985, pp. 51-57; *Canadian Directory of Shopping Centres, 1996,* p. 529.

25. A. Finn and J. Rigby, "West Edmonton Mall: Consumer Combined-Purpose Trips and the Birth of the Mega-Multi-Mall," *Canadian Journal of Administrative Sciences,* vol. 9, June 1992, pp. 134–45.

26. Based on R. O'Neill, "What's New in Shopping Centre Positioning," *Monitor,* May 1990, pp. 68-70.

27. S.A. Forest, "I Can Get It for You Retail," *Business Week,* September 18, 1995, pp. 84-88; H. Schlossberg, "Factory Outlets 'Mills' Growing but Long-Term Success Questioned," *Marketing News,* September 30, 1991, p. 1.

28. K. Shermach, "Niche Malls: Innovation or an Industry in Decline," *Marketing News,* February 26, 1996, pp. 1, 2.

29. S. Lagerfeld, "What Main Street Can Learn from the Mall," *Atlantic Monthly,* November 1995, pp. 110-20.

30. Statistics Canada, *Sales per Selling Area of Independent Retailers.*

31. J. Heinzl, "Zellers Steps up Discount War," *Globe & Mail,* November 9, 1995, p. B1; M. Socha, "Triple the Pleasure: Sears Canada Opens Giant Free-Standing Furniture Store," *The Kitchener Record,* August 26, 1995, p. B4.

32. J.R. Lowry, *Using a Traffic Study to Select a Retail Site* (Washington, DC: Small Business Administration).

Store Design and Layout, and Merchandise Presentation

Chapter Objectives

After reading this chapter, you should be able to:

1. Discuss the main dimensions of exterior and interior store design.

2. Describe typical store layout arrangements.

3. Explain how to allocate space to selling departments and nonselling activities.

4. Explain how to measure selling-space productivity.

5. Evaluate factors to consider in locating selling departments and sales-supporting activities within the store.

6. Describe the essentials of merchandise presentation.

Black's design and layout invite customers in. The focus on the colour reinforces name recognition and creates an image of elegance and quality.

Courtesy Black's

$\mathcal{T}$he importance of store design, layout, and merchandise presentation is illustrated with the following examples:[1]

- *Fairweather:* The Fairweather chain has completely changed its image and moved to a new upscale look. It has spent over $1 million on its new spacious design for its flagship store in the Toronto Eaton Centre. The new design incorporates more mirrors, extra-large fitting rooms, redesigned cash areas, and a broad marble aisle directly down the centre of the store leading to a series of distinct boutiques, recreating the prestige environment of an upscale department store. Good design not only creates customer space; it shows the merchandise to best advantage. Fairweather management knew that the more elegant the store was, the more attractive the merchandise will seem.

- *Nike Town:* When customers walk into Nike Town, located in downtown Portland, Oregon, they see plaster casts of Andre Agassi and Bo Jackson and, suspended from the ceiling, a statue of Michael Jordan going up for a slam dunk. The 2,000 m^2 store (which stocks every one of Nike's products—more than 1,000 new products each year) includes 14 shops featuring products for 25 sports. The store appeals to every one of a customer's senses. Sounds, temperature, and lights are manipulated in each of the 14 shops. Each one, for example, plays a new age sound

track of soothing mantras that hum louder when a customer pulls merchandise off a shelf. In the Aqua Gear shop, the temperature is warmer than in the Town Square outside. Customers hear surf crashing and seagulls squawking. In the All-Conditions Gear room, where biking and hiking goods are displayed, customers hear the sound of wind and feel a breeze from strategically placed fans. The temperature is 15 degrees cooler than in the Town Square outside. In the International running pavilion, the sound of a runner pounds out first on a surface that sounds like pavement, then gravel, then dirt. The basketball shop (The Force) looks like a gym, complete with a wooden floor and girders. Customers hear the sound of a ball dribbling and the squeak of sneakers on a wooden floor. Scattered throughout the store are autographed memorabilia such as Nolan Ryan's baseballs, Michael Jordan's first pair of Nikes, John McEnroe's busted racquets, and Bo Jackson's dirty cleats. ■

As these examples illustrate, innovative retailers take great care in the design and layout of their store and the presentation of their merchandise. This chapter focusses on these decision areas. The end goals are to show how effective layout and presentations can lead not only to increased sales levels but also to greater space productivity.

Store layout and design and merchandise presentation are critical elements of a firm's positioning strategy. At times, firms may need to redesign their stores' interiors and exteriors as part of a new image projection for the organization.

Ideally, design creates a store that invites customers to shop, makes them feel comfortable, helps them find the merchandise, and increases their satisfaction. The major goal of store design and layout and merchandise presentation is to get the shopper into the store to spend as much money as possible on a given shopping trip. In many instances, identical merchandise can be found in directly competing stores. Thus, it is very important for any given store to create a general atmosphere and specific presentations that will trigger buying decisions on its own sales floor rather than that of competitors.

Creating the Physical Environment

In order to more easily discuss the important physical environment of a store, a few terms should be defined.

- **Store planning** includes exterior and interior building design, the allocation of space to departments, and the arrangement and location of departments within the store.

- **Store design** refers to the style or atmosphere of a store that helps project an image to the market. Store design elements include such exterior factors as the store front and window displays and such interior factors as colours, lighting, flooring, and fixtures.

- **Store layout** involves planning the internal arrangement of departments— both selling and sales supporting—and deciding on the amount of space for each department. Figure 11–1 shows the relationships among these three terms.

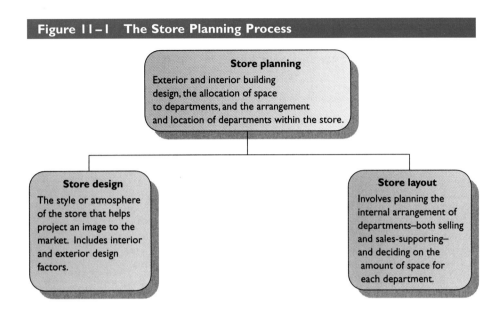

Figure 11–1   The Store Planning Process

Store planning
Exterior and interior building design, the allocation of space to departments, and the arrangement and location of departments within the store.

Store design
The style or atmosphere of the store that helps project an image to the market. Includes interior and exterior design factors.

Store layout
Involves planning the internal arrangement of departments—both selling and sales-supporting—and deciding on the amount of space for each department.

Store Design

Store design is an important image-creating element and should begin with an understanding of the preferences, desires, and expectations of the store's target market. For example, store design for warehouse food stores, whose target segment is price-conscious shoppers, would feature tile floors, harsh lighting, and limited in-store signing. Similarly, a design using bold colours, flashing lights, and eye-popping displays might be very appropriate for a store targeting young people, but inappropriate for a store focussing on older, conservative shoppers.

Demographic characteristics such as income and age are not the only variables of the target market to affect store design. Increasingly, store design is influenced by the lifestyles of target customers. A store that specializes in tennis equipment could reflect the lifestyle of its intended clientele by using murals with large photographs of tennis courts, and of famous tennis players.

Retailers must also constantly monitor changes occurring in the external environment and alter store design to be responsive to such changes. Retailers must use store design as a competitive weapon, appealing to the changing lifestyles of their target shoppers. For example, retail store design is being affected by the changing buying roles of men and women. With women becoming bigger buyers of hardware and automotive products, some hardware and auto-parts stores are changing their store design to shed their "macho" image. When a store changes its target market, repositioning requires changes in store design, as in the Fairweather example in the introduction.

Design and store image

In developing an image for the store, the design should answer five fundamental questions:[2]

- Can the concept and merchandise being sold in your store be explained in one or two sentences?
- Will the customer distinguish your store from the competition?
- Can you explain the concept of your competitors that appeals to customers?
- Will your name, logo, and store design reflect the image that you want to project?
- Will your store design still look good two or five years from now?

Store design is a reflection of two elements: (*1*) the exterior design, and (*2*) the interior design, which includes everything within the store such as walls, floor, ceiling, lighting fixtures, colours, scents, and sounds. The exterior and interior designs should be in harmony with the store's merchandise and customers.

Exterior design

Store designers indicate that many retailers make the mistake of concentrating only on the inside of the store and fail to give adequate attention to the exterior of the building. However, a store's exterior is a most important aspect of image creation.

The building's architecture and entrances, display windows, and signs are some of the image-creating elements related to exterior design.

Architecture and entrances

A store's architecture can create image impressions in a number of ways. The architectural design may reflect the nature of the products sold in the store. A restaurant emphasizing Mexican dishes may use yellow and green colours with adobe-style walls and Mexican decorations (e.g., sombreros or piñatas).

The store's architectural style may also reflect the size of the store. For example, a huge food store may design a building on the model of a "French Market," with a large curved glass ceiling and big columns to give a feeling of space and scale.

A store's entrance should provide for easy entry into the store. However, some designers may also see entrances as a "transition zone"—for example, using corridors leading to courtyards—in order to ease the customer into a busy or large area.

Finally, some designers emphasize the importance of consistency between the exterior and interior design elements, in order to carry through the same theme associated with the design.

Display windows

Window shopping is quite often very important for many types of retailers, and window displays should primarily be used to attract the attention and interest of the customer, leading to entering the store.

Window displays were downplayed during the 1970s and early 1980s because of increased cost cutting and energy consciousness among retailers. Also, during this period emphasis was placed on building stores in malls; thus, attention was focussed more on interior merchandise presentations than on window displays.

Today, however, there is a renewed interest in store window displays, especially among department stores and higher-priced retailers and especially

Classic architecture at Birks. The emphasis is on tradition, elegance, and sophistication.

Photo by Anne Laroche

in cities where walking and window shopping are still in style. This is also true for stores located inside the malls, especially the large malls with many competing stores. Whether in city streets or in "mall streets," window displays may be used to enhance store image, to expose would-be shoppers to new products, or to introduce a new season.

Retailers put much effort in designing window displays for Christmas, since for many of them this is the best selling period. Properly decorated Christmas windows will put the customers into the right mood, bring back childhood memories, break down their inhibitions, and put them into the spirit of giving, as illustrated in Retail Highlight 11–1. For Eaton's, Christmas represents the largest decorating expenditure and is the responsibility of a special committee who works 12 months to plan and order for the upcoming season.[3]

Much art is involved in developing window displays, as illustrated in Retail Highlight 11–1. Principles of good design—balance, proportion, and harmony—are all essential. Errors retailers sometimes make are using too much or too little merchandise, inappropriate props and lighting, or simply not changing a display frequently enough, with the result that it loses its special significance. The ideal is to change the window displays about 15 to 20 times a year.[4]

Management can evaluate the results of window displays by (1) the number of people passing the window in a certain period, (2) the number of passersby who glance at the window, (3) the number that stop, and (4) the number that enter the store after looking at the window display.

Signs

The creative use of an easy-to-read outdoor sign serves the purpose of identifying the store and providing some information about it. The sign can also be an important factor in creating a favourable image for the store. Some retailers

Especially during the Christmas Selling Season, Window Displays
Put Shoppers in the Spirit of Giving

There is much art and imagination in designing windows for the Christmas season. The general idea is well known by most: Santa Claus, the nativity scene, gift-giving, and holiday festivities and activities, such as skating in the pond. The challenge is to find an interesting execution, one that would say to the shopper: "That's an innovative retailer, let's see what's inside." Some examples from the 1994 season in Toronto are:

- At Tiffany's, on Bloor Street, the idea is to have the shopper bang his or her head into the glass trying to get a glimpse at the various tableaux. The story is developed around Santa's preparations for the big event. Santa himself is never seen, but he is there: picking up his laundry (such as his darned red socks), checking his list of who was nice and who's naughty,

having tea and cookies in this cold night. Of course, all around the tableaux, tastefully arranged, are Tiffany's products.
- At The Bay, on Queen Street, the idea is to enchant the shopper by a fantastic rendition of Santa's bedroom in Victorian style, with a twin-unicorn headboard, a carousel horse, a wonderful Victorian bird cage, an armoire, and a sleigh full of porcelain dolls, stuffed bears, and a nutcracker.
- At Grafix, an art supply store, the idea is to make fun of artists, such as Matisse, Van Gogh, and Cezanne, with "self-portraits with Santa Claus hats." The message is, "If these people can paint, you can, too."

Source: Judy Margolis, "Windowonderlands," *Globe & Mail,* December 8, 1994, p. D11.

have developed distinctive signs that are widely recognized by consumers. An example is McDonald's with its golden arches.

Interior design

Within the store, consumers not only respond to the products or services being offered but also to their surroundings. Environmental factors can affect a shopper's desire to shop or not shop at the store and the amount of time spent in the store. The internal environment can also influence the customer's desire or willingness to explore the environment and to communicate with salespeople. Thus, retailers must consider the psychological effects of their outlets on consumer purchasing behaviour. Fast-food restaurants do this by utilizing hard chairs and fast-tempo music to encourage rapid turnover during lunch times.

As has been observed: "A subtle dimension of in-store customer shopping behaviour is the environment of the space itself. Retail space, i.e., the proximate environment that surrounds the retail shopper, is never neutral. The retail store is a bundle of cues, messages, and suggestions that communicate to shoppers. Retail store designers, planners, and merchandisers shape space, but that space in turn affects and shapes customer behaviour. The retail store . . . does create moods, activates intentions, and generally affects customer reactions."[5] This observation was confirmed in a recent study that showed that lighting and music interact with friendliness of employees to affect customers' pleasure and willingness to buy.[6]

Some retailers view the interior of their stores as a stage in a theatre and realize that theatrical elements can be used to influence customer behaviour.

An interesting window display, where the composition, including the use of a few clothes and a beautiful table, all connote high fashion and good taste.

Photo by Anne Laroche

They feel the customer should be entertained and excited. This principle is illustrated in Retail Highlight 11–2.

Many fast-food outlets have undergone interior design changes as a way of attracting customers in an intensely competitive environment. Many feel that a more upscale design attracts a broader range of customers, with less plastic, metal, and bright primary colours. Typically, operators are aiming for subtler lighting and are using pastel colours, marble, mirrors, brass, wood, and greenery to create a warm, earthy environment. Other Canadian store designers use state-of-the-art fixtures as well as borrow some European flavour, particularly in designing fashion stores where the trend is on using sophisticated mannequins and "invisible fixturing," and showing less rather than more in terms of merchandise.[7]

The store's interior design should be based on an understanding of the customer and how design contributes to the strategy for reaching the target market. This is a very important decision, and the selection of a store designer should be done with a great deal of care.[8]

A store's interior design includes everything within the store walls that can be used to create store atmosphere. These elements include floor, wall, and ceiling materials; lighting; fixtures; colours; scents; and sounds. The following sections focus on colour, lighting, sound, and scents as store image-creating variables.

Colours

The use of colours should be done with a great deal of thought, since colours often create an atmosphere for the store. For example, a children's store needs primary bright colours. A bookstore needs soothing and reflective colours. Traditional menswear is best set with country club colours (like forest green),

Retail Highlight 11–2

To Many Avid Readers, a Bookstore Is More than a Big Box Full of Shelves

While the recent trend in the book industry has been to bigger and bigger stores—some big-box stores stock more than a million titles—serious readers always look for a store "with a sense of occasion."

Vancouverites, who have the distinction of being Canada's most avid readers, now have such a store called Bollum's Books, at the corner of Georgia and Granville. It stocks 85,000 titles in over 200 m² of old fir floor space, with travertine marble walls, and cherry-wood shelves. There is classical music playing, overstuffed sofas for comfort, intimate alcoves, a fireplace with a beautiful wood mantlepiece, brass lamps everywhere, and a café with free newspapers on bamboo rods.

At Bollum's Books, authors come regularly for reading and signing sessions. There is a special-orders desk, a large multimedia section, a large Chinese department, and a wide selection of magazines and newspapers (including out-of-town newspapers).

If you feel comfortable in the store, it is open every weekday and Sunday from 8 A.M. to 10 P.M., and until midnight on Friday and Saturday!

Source: John Masters, "Bookstore Bravura," *Financial Post,* May 20, 1995, pp. 26–27.

and young womenswear in a pastel environment. For food services, Retail Highlight 11–3 provides an interesting example.

Research has determined that colour can affect store and merchandise image and customer shopping behaviour. People, regardless of colour preferences, are physically drawn to warm colours such as red and yellow. Thus, warm colours (red and particularly yellow) are good colour choices for drawing customers into a retail store, department, or display area. Warm colours are appropriate for store windows and entrances as well as for buying situations associated with impulse purchases. Think of "red tag sale" or "red dot special," for example. Cool colours (such as blue and green) are appropriate where customer deliberations over the purchase decision are necessary.[9]

Background colours for product presentations are also a major concern for retailers. For example, the colours white, pink, yellow, and blue should not be used in the "toddler" department. Those are the colours of most of the merchandise; thus the garments would merely "fade into the walls." Sometimes, the colour that is used to show off the product should be related to the final use of the product. Fine jewelry, for example, may look dramatic against bold colour backgrounds, but the colour fine jewelry is most often seen against is flesh. On the other hand, costume jewelry is best presented against vivid tones.

Lighting

Lighting can be used to spotlight merchandise, to affect shopping behaviour, and to lower operating costs. Some supermarket retailers have chosen to make the produce area dark and then put light on the merchandise to make it stand out. Others, however, feel that customers are not comfortable in a dark area and thus are moving away from the overall dark, theatrical effect while still focussing light on the product.

Other retailers switched from a fluorescent system to high-intensity discharge (HID) fixtures, which resulted in better visibility and reduced energy costs. With HID fixtures, the light goes up and then is redistributed down at

Retail Highlight 11–3

The Proper Use of Colour and Lighting Can Lead to Dramatic Changes in Customer Perceptions

The 25-year-old IGA store in Toronto was dark and gloomy, with outdated lighting fixtures, and an ugly orange and yellow paint job. Worse, the store was losing customers, and profits were down 15 percent. Then, Cal Stewart, the franchise owner, decided on a complete remodeling.

The lighting system was completely replaced with Promolux fluorescent tubes, which increase effective lighting, bring out the true colour of meat, and reduced the monthly electric bill by $600 to $800.

After considering several colours—green mixed with woods to convey a country, homey feeling, or pastels against beige to create a peaceful, soothing feeling—Cal Stewart decided to use elegant white to let the products provide the colour, to make the store appear clean and bright, and to have the signage stand out in better contrast. The floor can add some colour and patterns to guide the customer through the store.

Since half the customers are seniors and long-time residents of the area, the store is made unique by the placements on the walls of enlarged historic black-and-white photographs of the neighbourhood in the 1920s and 1930s.

The renovation must have been a success, since business is up in most departments by at least 5 percent, and by as much as 12 percent in some departments.

Source: K. Pocock, "Supermarket Makeover," *Canadian Grocer*, September 1994, pp. 37–40.

different angles. Thus, the fixtures direct the light to the ceiling and walls in addition to illuminating the merchandise on display. Improved light distribution is important when the retailer stacks its merchandise high in a warehouse-style setting. Shoppers have an easier time reading package labels. The HID units are also well suited for those retailers who use up to three times more in-store signage than other retailers. Finally, the new lighting system may add to the overall appearance of the store, enhancing the store's colour scheme and making flooring and its patterns more attractive.[10] Retail Highlight 11–3 provides an example of the use of lighting for a supermarket.

Sounds

Music has been found to have an impact on shopping behaviour. Research has found that shoppers spend less time in a store when music is played loudly.[11] A 30 percent increase in supermarket sales was experienced when the store played slow music compared to fast music. Also, in a restaurant, customers spent more time at their tables, consumed more alcoholic beverages, but ate no more food when slow music was played compared to fast music.[12] These improvements in sales were attributed to customers spending more time in the outlet, usually because they moved at a slower pace. Of interest is that a significant number of these customers, after they left, did not recall that music was being played. The implication is that shopping behaviour was altered by the music without their awareness.

Scents

Research has shown that scents can affect consumer behaviour; for example, if a grocery store pumps in the smell of baked goods, sales in that department will increase; scents coming out of stores like Body Shop or Soapberry can draw customers in. Some department stores pump fragrances, carefully choosing them to match their target audience.

Interestingly, scents can affect the perception of products that don't naturally smell—such as shoes. In a study sponsored by Nike, participants examined a pair of Nike gym shoes in two separate rooms. One room was completely odour free; the other was filtered with a pleasing floral scent. The scent had a direct positive effect on the desirability of the sneakers on 84 percent of the participants. The results of the study suggest that stores could boost sales by releasing scents that appeal specifically to targeted audiences. For example, retailers might use a spicy odour if they are targeting men in their thirties; a mixed floral scent would be more appropriate for females in their sixties. Furthermore, retailers should choose scents to suit the area of the store and the time of the day.[13]

Store Layout

Store layout is a very important element of store planning. Layout not only affects customer movement in the store but also influences the way merchandise is displayed. The following elements are part of layout planning:

1. The overall arrangement of the store.
2. Allocation of space to selling departments and sales-supporting activities.
3. Evaluation of space productivity.
4. Location of selling departments and sales-supporting activities within the store.

Arrangement of the store

Typical layout arrangements are the grid, the free-flow or open plan, the boutique concept, and the racetrack plan. Let's look first at the grid layout.

Grid layout

In a **grid layout,** merchandise is displayed in straight, parallel lines, with secondary aisles at right angles to these. An example is shown in Figure 11–2. A supermarket typically uses a grid layout.

The grid arrangement is more for store efficiency than customer convenience, since the layout tends to hinder movement. Customer flow is guided more by the layout of the aisles and fixtures than by the buyer's desire for merchandise. For example, 80 to 90 percent of all customers shopping in a supermarket with a grid layout pass the produce, meat, and dairy counters. Fewer shoppers pass other displays, because the grid forces the customers to the sides and back of the supermarket.

In department stores, a grid layout on the main floor usually forces traffic down the main aisles. Thus, shoppers are less likely to be exposed to items along the walls. Shopping goods (highly demanded merchandise) should be placed along the walls, and convenience goods should be displayed in the main part of the store. Customer traffic then is drawn to otherwise slow-moving areas.

Free-flow layout

In a **free-flow layout,** merchandise and fixtures are grouped into patterns that allow an unstructured flow of customer traffic, as shown in Figure 11–3. The free-flow pattern is designed for customer convenience and exposure to

Figure 11–2   Grid Layout

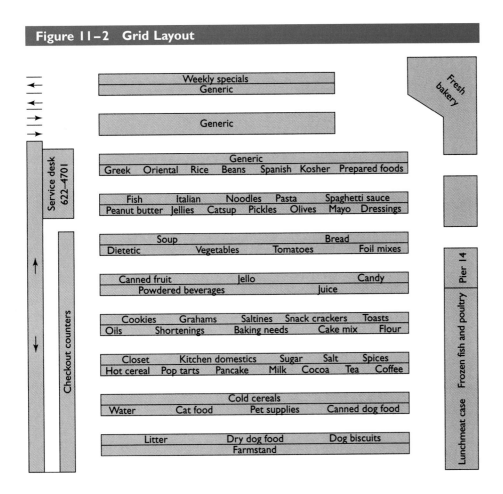

merchandise. Free-flow designs let customers move in any direction and wander freely, thus encouraging browsing and impulse buying. Merchandise divisions are generally made on the basis of low fixtures and signage. The visibility of all departments is possible from any point in the store, which allows for better departmental interselling. The layout, however, is more costly and uses space less efficiently than the grid layout. A free-flow arrangement is often used in specialty stores, boutiques, and apparel stores.

Boutique layout

A variation of the free-flow layout is the **boutique layout** where merchandise classifications are grouped so that each classification has its own "shop" within the store, as shown in Figure 11–4. The boutique concept is an outgrowth of lifestyle merchandising wherein a classification is aimed at a specific lifestyle segment often featuring merchandise from a single designer or company.

Each shop has its own identity, including colour schemes, styles, and atmosphere. Even though greater flexibility is possible with this arrangement, construction costs and security costs are higher. As a result, the concept is used in high-status department stores and other outlets where the sale of higher-priced merchandise allows absorption of the increased costs. However, some discounters are experimenting with the store-within-the-store concept.

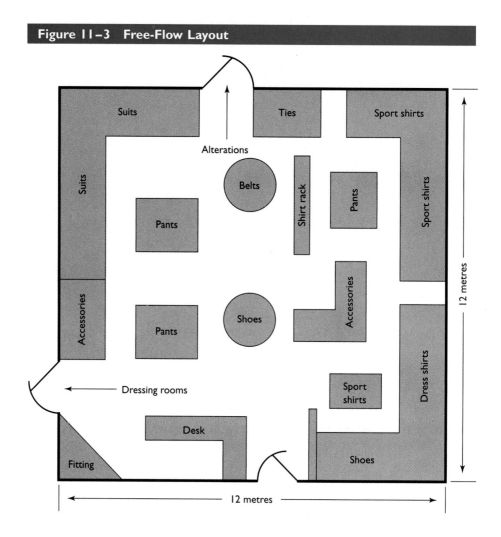

Figure 11–3   Free-Flow Layout

Racetrack (or loop) layout

The **racetrack (or loop) layout** encourages customers to visit several departments (or boutiques) by providing a major aisle that loops through the store (or floor), as shown in Figure 11–5. Customers are constantly stimulated by various arrangements, and are encouraged to complete the loop.

Store size and the allocation of space

Store size

For a variety of reasons, some retailers are reducing store size. Downsizing is becoming increasingly important, for example, as the cost per square metre of retail space soars. However, retailers who are reducing the sizes of their stores are attempting to maximize space productivity so that merchandise presentation and sales will not be negatively affected by the smaller store size. Industry analysts refer to this concept as "maximizing the cube." The concept requires maximum utilization of space, especially of the walls of the store: for example,

Figure 11–4   Boutique Layout

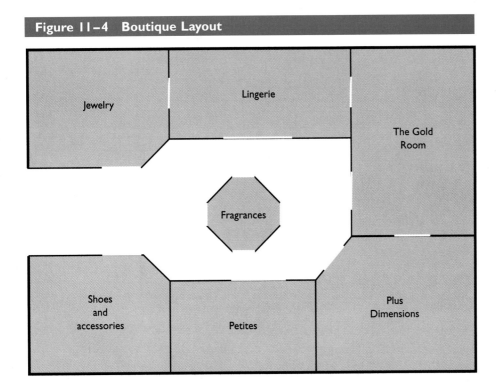

the use of free-standing fixtures and glass display counters; the merchandise displayed on two-tiered hangrods or on shelves that have been built into the walls; a vaulted ceiling to provide the illusion of space; or a rear wall that is mirrored to make a small space appear larger.

Overseas expansion may lead to smaller stores. For example, when Talbots opened its first store in Japan, the store was 200 square metres, about half the size of one of its North American stores. Two factors were at work here. One was the high cost of retail space; the other was a smaller inventory requirement owing to a smaller range of sizes. Whereas in North America the company would have a size run starting at size 4 and go up to 18 or 20, in Japan the stores have a size run of only three or four sizes.[14]

As firms move into smaller markets, smaller outlets may be needed. For example, McDonald's wants to add stores, but major markets already are at or near saturation. Thus, a key to growth is entering smaller markets, and McDonald's sees towns with populations of up to 4,000 as a revenue source it wants to tap. The company has learned, however, that its traditional outlets can't produce enough volume from smaller, rural markets to make profitable franchises. Thus, in these smaller markets, McDonald's is opening units called McDonald's Express, about half the size of standard McDonald's restaurants that seat 50, including counter seating.[15]

One reason that the concept of hypermarkets has been unsuccessful in North America is their size. Wal-Mart, for example, built only four hypermarket stores before stopping its program. K mart stopped at just three such stores. According to industry analysts, customers think these stores are just too big. Not only do customers object to the size, but hypermarkets have to cope with the

boutique layout featuring merchandise from a single designer

Photo by James Hertel

high cost of running such vast operations, including air-conditioning and heating costs and the hiring of 400 to 600 workers rather than continuing with hypermarkets, these retailers are concentrating on supercentres—combination discount department stores and grocery stores—that average around 15,000 m^2.[16]

Allocation of space

Dividing total space between selling and sales-supporting areas is the first step in space allocation. In general, the larger a store, the higher its ratio of sales-supporting space to selling space. As a general rule, retailers—other than specialty or fashion outlets—devote as much space to the sales area as possible. However, the amount of sales space varies by size and type of store. In a very large department store, selling space may account for roughly 65 percent of total space. Jewelry stores need almost no sales-supporting space. A home improvement centre, however, may use more space for warehousing than for selling. A warehouse-type store will put all its inventory on the selling floor, this practice seems to have sparked a trend in the industry, with more and more stores using a larger proportion of space for selling. For example, a regular Canadian Tire store devotes just 40 percent of its space to selling, while the Canadian Tire's warehouse concept has 80 percent of its space accessible to customers.[17]

The amount of space allocated to non-selling areas may be impacted by the advent of electronic data interchange (EDI) and greater UPC vendor marking. With EDI and UPC, merchandise moves more quickly and accurately through the distribution channel, with smaller quantities arriving at the store more frequently. Since large "cushion" stocks will not be required, backroom can be greatly reduced in size, and greater use will be made of store space by merchandising.

Figure 11–5   Racetrack Layout

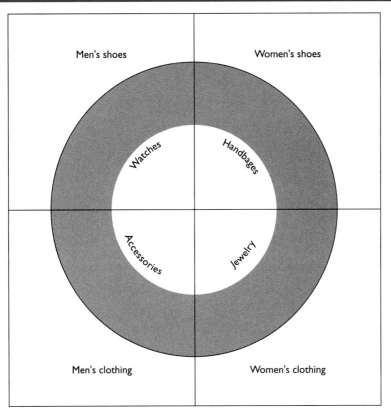

Management can use three basic methods for allocating selling space:

1.   Industry averages by type of merchandise.
2.   Sales productivity of product lines.
3.   The build-up (model stock) method.

Industry averages   Management can use the national average percentage of selling space that a particular merchandise line occupies in a certain type of store. For example, assume that the health and beauty aids department accounts for 4 percent of total selling space as an average in a superstore. Thus, in a superstore with 3,400 square metres of selling space, management would set aside 136 square metres for the health and beauty aids department $(3,400 \times .04 = 136)$.

Sales productivity method   Sales productivity is measured by sales per square metre of selling space. Assume that the planned sales for health and beauty aids is $136,000. If the national average sales per square metre for this department is $1,000, then management would allocate 136 square metres to the department

Table 11–1 Average Sales per Square Metre for Selected Types of Stores	
Type of Store	**Average Sales per m² ($)**
Wine stores	7,632
Appliance, television, radio, and stereo stores	7,117
Pharmacies	6,929
Liquor and beer stores	6,053
Jewelry stores	5,846
Camera and photographic supply stores	5,282
Record and tape stores	4,847
Supermarkets	4,784
Grocery stores	4,739
Gift, novelty, and souvenir stores	4,514
General stores	4,270
Luggage and leather goods stores	4,207
Household furniture stores (without appliances and furnishings)	3,791
Shoe stores	3,615
Sporting goods stores	3,486
Men's clothing stores	3,428
Women's clothing stores	3,331
Pet stores	2,836
Book and stationary stores	2,759
Toy and hobby stores	2,403
Floor covering and drapery stores	2,227
Household furniture stores (with appliances and furnishings)	1,978
Florist shops	1,877
Paint, glass, and wallpaper stores	1,799

Source: Statistics Canada, *Retail Chain and Department Stores,* Cat. 63-210, December 1995, p. 12.

($136,000/$1,000 = 136). Table 11–1 gives an idea of the average sales per square metre for various types of stores.

Build-up (model stock) method   Let us use a ladies' blouse department to illustrate this space allocation method. The build-up method would proceed as follows:

1. Determine the ideal stock balance necessary to achieve expected sales volume. The merchant, based on past experience, may believe that sales of $30,000 per year are obtainable. Trade sources indicate that in the price line planned, three turns per year are realistic. Within the price-line structure, the average price of a blouse is $15. Given these assumptions, approximately 666 blouses will be needed as a normal offering during each turnover period ($30,000/3 = $10,000 in merchandise; $10,000/$15 = 666 blouses). Normally, 666 blouses must be in stock. However, the merchandise planner may vary from this number during high- and low-sales-volume months. Under this method, planning ties merchandise needs to actual seasonal variations rather than yearly averages. For example, Mother's Day might be the yearly peak sales period and should be considered in layout planning.

2. Decide how much merchandise should be kept on display, and how much should be kept in reserve stock. How many of the 666 blouses should actually be displayed? Ideally, 100 percent should be on display, because goods do not sell if they are not seen. Since this is not realistic and since the decision is arbitrary, assume that two-thirds of the stock—approximately 444 blouses—will be displayed and one-third will be in reserve.

3. Decide the best method of displaying the merchandise. This decision depends on the merchandise display equipment available and the afford-able opportunities for display. Let's decide that we will hang the less expensive blouses on circular steel racks that have a glass top for display purposes. The most expensive blouses will be displayed in glass cases where they can be accessorised with jewelry, scarves, and other small items. Reserve stock will be stored in drawers beneath the display cases. Only one of each style will be displayed.

4. Decide how many display racks and cases are necessary to display the items. The physical size and capacity of the fixtures must be determined to answer this question. Scale models of fixtures are often placed on floor plans to assist in the layout planning process.

5. Determine the best way to handle the reserve stock. We have already determined that the reserve stock for the expensive blouses will be main-tained under the display cases. Space can be allocated for the remaining items in special storage fixtures on the selling floor or in a stock area as close to the selling area as possible.

6. Decide what service requirements are necessary for the department. Fitting rooms and a point-of-sale terminal or register will be needed. Likewise, depending on the nature of the operation, space for packaging may be required. Finally, all departments need aisles.

7. The total space needs can be determined by summing the space require-ments found in steps 4, 5, and 6.

Evaluation of space use

Good use of space involves more than creating an aesthetically pleasing environment, although such a goal is important. Effective use of space can also translate into additional dollars of profit. Thus, retailers must evaluate whether store space is being used in the most effective way. Management can use a variety of measures to evaluate space utilization. The gross-margin-per-square-metre method is discussed below to illustrate one method retailers can employ.

To determine whether a department can "afford" the space it occupies, the gross margin per square metre of the department should be measured. Big-ticket items may ring up more sales than lower-priced goods, yet the ratio of gross margin to square metre may be smaller for high-priced merchandise.

As shown in Table 11–2, three calculations are involved in evaluating space utilization by the gross-margin-per-square-metre method. Sales per square metre less cost of merchandise sold per square metre yields the gross margin per square metre figure.

With this gross-margin-per-square-metre figure, departments of varying sizes selling different types of goods can be compared. Gross margin per square metre can show management which departments are doing well, which are not,

Table 11–2   Calculating Gross Margin per Square Metre

Three calculations are involved in figuring gross margin per square metre:

1. $\dfrac{\text{Total sales}}{\text{Total square metres}}$ = Sales per square metre

2. $\dfrac{\text{Cost of merchandise sold}}{\text{Total square metres}}$ = Cost of merchandise sold per square metre

3. Sales per square metre − Cost of merchandise per square metre = Gross margin per square metre sold

Example

	Department A	Department B
Sales	$50,000	$70,000
Cost of merchandise sold	$30,000	$35,000
Square metres of space	50 m²	70 m²
Sales per square metre	$ 1,000	$ 1,000
− Cost of merchandise sold per m²	$ 600	$ 500
= Gross margin per square metre	$ 400	$ 500

which might improve if expanded, and which can be reduced in space allotment.

For example, based on the calculations shown in Table 11–2, management might be tempted to decrease the selling space allocated to department A and increase the selling space devoted to department B. However, the decision to reallocate space is not a simple one. Advertising and selling costs may rise when selling space is increased. After the reallocation, the merchandise mix may change, which can result in either higher or lower gross margins. Management thus needs to simulate the likely changes in the three variables used in the calculations as a result of possible shifts in space allocation and determine whether reallocations are likely to increase the overall profitability of the firm.

An evaluation of space utilization may not only lead to a reallocation of space among selling departments. Some stores are converting unproductive retail space to other uses.

Locating departments and activities

Management must decide where to locate selling and sales-supporting activities within the store. Several guidelines are available to retailers to aid in making these decisions.

Locating selling departments

The convenience of customers and the effect on profitability are the primary concerns of management in locating selling departments within the store. With these factors in mind, the following suggestions are offered:

- *Rent-paying capacity.* The department with the highest sales per square metre is best able to pay a high rent. Thus, this department should be placed in the most valuable, highly travelled area of the store. If a number of departments are equally good, the decision should be made based on the gross margins of the merchandise.

- *Impulse versus demand shopping.* **Impulse merchandise** is bought on the basis of unplanned, spur-of-the-moment decisions. Departments containing impulse merchandise normally get the best locations in the store. **Demand merchandise** is purchased as a result of a customer coming into the store to buy that particular item. Departments containing demand merchandise can be located in less valuable space because customers will hunt for these items.

- *Replacement frequency.* Certain goods, such as health and beauty aids, are frequently purchased, low-cost items. Customers want to buy them as conveniently as possible, so the department should be placed in an easily accessible location.

- *Proximity of related departments.* Similar items of merchandise should be displayed close together. In a superstore, for example, all household items—such as paper products, detergents, kitchen gadgets—should be placed together, so customers will make combination purchases. Similarly, the men's furnishings department—such as shirts, ties, and underwear—should be placed near the suit department in a department store. A customer wanting a new suit often needs a matching shirt and tie as well. Combination selling is easier when related items are close together. Location of related goods is even more important in a self-service store because no salesperson is around to help the customer.

- *Seasonal variations.* Items in some departments are big sellers only a few months or weeks of the year. Toys and summer furniture are examples. Management might decide to place these departments next to each other. When toys expand at Christmas, extra space temporarily can be taken from summer furniture, and vice versa.

- *Size of departments.* Management also may want to place very small departments in some of the more valuable spaces to help them be seen. A very large department could use a less desirable location in the store because its size will contribute to its visibility.

- *Merchandise characteristics.* In a supermarket, bakery products (especially bread) should be near the checkout. Customers avoid crushing these items in the carts by selecting bakery products at the end of their shopping. Products such as lettuce are usually displayed along a wall to allow more space and to better handle wiring for cooling.

- *Shopping considerations.* Items such as suits and dresses are often tried on and fitted. They can be placed in less valuable locations away from heavy traffic. Also, they are demand, not impulse, items and can be placed in out-of-the-way areas since shoppers will make an effort to find them.

- *New, developing, or underdeveloped departments.* Assume management has added a new department, such as more "nonfoods" in a superstore. Management may want to give more valuable space to the new department to increase sales by exposing more customers to the items.

Locating sales-supporting activities

Sales-supporting activities, such as credit departments, can be thought of in several ways:

- Activities that must be located in a specific part of the store: Receiving and marketing areas should be located near the "dock" area, usually at the back of the store.

Retail Highlight 11–4

Effective and Imaginative Merchandise Displays Improve the Shopper's Experience

Retailers need to constantly rethink their displays in order to make the shopper experience a pleasant one, not a chore. Examples of innovative approaches are:

• Food retailers have known for years that proper food presentations are key to sales volume. They have used mirrors behind vegetables, and empty boxes under piles of fruits to give the impression of abundance. Also, loose fragile fruits, such as strawberries, are perceived to be more fresh, and the customer who bags his own selection ends up buying more strawberries, increasing sales, and reducing spoilage. But retailers like Provigo, the third largest grocery chain, are testing other methods such as using wooden stands on wheels (some refrigerated), and placing shelves at an angle for special effects.

• The same principle is true for department stores, like The Bay at Yonge and Bloor, which spent $10 million trying to make the customer feel happy, upbeat, and comfortable. For instance, in the men's department, the fixtures and the colours are there to direct attention to the merchandise in custom-millwork display shelving. In the women's department, an unusual ironwork tree is used to display handbags hanging from the branches; an atrium is full of mannequins, in a French Art Deco style, dressed in various designer clothes.

Sources: Jean Benoît Nadeau and Julie Barlow, "Shopping for Wow!" *Report on Business Magazine,* October 1995, pp. 58–67; Gerald Levitch, "Memories of Versailles," *Globe and Mail,* November 30, 1995, p. D4

• Activities that serve the store only: Such activities are office space and personal services for employees of the store. These departments can be located in the least valuable, out-of-the-way places.

• Activities that relate directly to selling: Cutting areas for fresh meat need to be close to the refrigerators. Both refrigeration and cutting need to be close to the display cases. Drapery workrooms in department stores need to be close to the drapery department.

• Activities with direct customer contact: In a supermarket, customers often want to check parcels, cash a personal cheque, or ask for information about an item. Credit departments and layaway services are needed in department stores. Such activities can be located in out-of-the-way places to help increase customer movement in the store.

Merchandise Presentation

Merchandise displays are part of the so-called silent language of communication. They can be used to excite, entertain, and educate consumers. If effectively used, they can have a profound influence on consumer behaviour, as illustrated in Retail Highlight 11–4.

Often entire courses are devoted to the technical aspects of merchandise display. Because of space limitations, however, we must limit our discussion and will provide a brief overview of the following topics: the principles of display, interior displays, and shelf-space allocation.

Displays and in-store signs attract customer attention by featuring well-known brands, a wide selection, and good prices.

Photo by Betty McDougall

Principles of display

Customers in a retail store stop at some merchandise displays, move quickly past some, and smile at others. Shoppers are professional display watchers and know what they like. However, customers usually do not consciously judge displays. So the job of the retail manager is to "prejudge" for the purchaser. Managers need to be clever and creative enough to affect behaviour by display. Displays should attract attention and excite and stimulate customers.

In spite of the basically artistic and creative flair needed for display, some principles do exist.[18] The following basic principles have been developed from years of experience:

1. Displays should be built around fast-moving, "hot" items.
2. Goods purchased largely on impulse should be given ample amounts of display space.
3. Displays should be kept simple. Management should not try to cram them with too many items.
4. Displays should be timely and feature seasonal goods.
5. Colour attracts attention, sets the right tone, and affects the very sense of the display.
6. Use motion. It attracts attention.
7. Most good displays have a theme or story to tell.
8. Show goods in use.
9. Proper lighting and props are essential to an effective display.[19]
10. Guide the shopper's eye where you want it to go.

Hoping to catch customers with a great display of fresh and exotic foods. Notice that clean legible signs complement the products.

Photo by Betty McDougall

Interior displays

Interior displays can take a variety of forms, depending on the type of merchandise and image to be projected by the firm. Although space does not permit an in-depth discussion of the principles of interior display, we do offer several guidelines for planning the effective arrangement of merchandise in departments.

Consider the following suggestions regarding interior merchandise display:[20]

- Place items so that choices can readily be made by customers. For example, group merchandise by sizes.

- Place items in such a way that "ensemble" (or related-item) selling is easy. For example, in a gourmet food department, all Chinese food components should be together. In a women's accessories department, handbags, gloves, and neckwear should be together to help the customer complete an outfit.

- Place items in a department so that trading up or getting the customer to want a better-quality, higher-priced item is possible. Place the good, better, and best brands of coffee, for example, next to each other so customers can compare them. Information labels on the package help customers compare items displayed next to each other.

- Place merchandise in such a way that it stresses the wide assortments (choice of sizes, brands, colours, and prices) available.

- Place larger sizes and heavy, bulky goods near the floor.

- If the firm carries competing brands in various sizes, give relatively little horizontal space to each item and make use of vertical space for the different sizes and colours. This arrangement exposes customers to a greater variety of products as they move through the store.

- Avoid locating impulse goods directly across the aisle from demand items that most customers are looking for. The impulse items may not be seen at all.

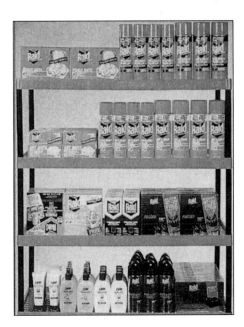

An example of a manufacturer-supplied display fixture where products are arranged for best effect, and promotional material can be presented to customers.

Courtesy S.J. Johnson & Son, Inc.

- Make use of vertical space through tiers and step-ups, but be careful to avoid displays much above eye level or at floor level. The area of vertical vision is limited.
- Place items in a department so that inventory counting (control) and general stockkeeping are easier.
- Finally, make the displays as attractive as possible.

Use of manufacturer-supplied display fixtures

Retailers are reacting more positively to the use of manufacturer-supplied display fixtures—one reason being that manufacturers are attempting to be more sensitive to the retailers' needs when designing such fixtures. In the past, retailers complained that many displays were ineffective for inventory control, used space poorly, and were unattractive.

Today, manufacturers are attempting to design display fixtures that overcome these problems. The in-store display fixture for Raid insecticide features various Raid products arranged under a colour code to help consumers pick the right spray for the right bug. A flip chart gives information on the habits of insects and suggests ways to "knock 'em dead." The unit can be arranged in various configurations to accommodate various store sizes.

In the self-service environment of mass marketing, manufacturer-provided displays can be used effectively as a selling tool.[21]

Shelf-space allocation

A very important merchandise presentation issue is determining the amount of space that should be allocated to individual brands or items in a product category. A number of rules have been devised for allocating facings to

Table 11–3   Computing Direct Product Profitability

Retail price	$9.50
Less cost of goods sold	7.30
Equals gross margin	$2.20
Plus discounts and allowances	
Merchandise allowance	.25
Payment discount	.10
Less direct handling costs	
Warehouse direct labour	.20
Retail direct labour	.75
Warehouse inventory expense	.05
Retail inventory expense	.06
Warehouse operating expense	.10
Retail operating expense	.50
Transportation to stores	.05
Equals direct product profitability	$ .84

competing brands. One rule frequently stressed by major consumer goods manufacturers is that shelf space should equal market share. Thus, a brand with 20 percent market share in a category takes 20 percent of shelf space.

For a retailer, however, this rule makes little sense. It takes no account of the profit margins or direct costs associated with each item. Some retailers thus allocate space according to gross margin. Other retailers apply the concept of **direct product profitability** (DPP). Direct product profitability equals a product's gross margin (selling price minus cost of goods sold) plus discounts and allowances, less direct handling costs (see Table 11–3). More space should be allocated to brands or items with greater DPP. The use of DPP was limited until the development of the personal computer and spreadsheet programs such as Lotus 1-2-3, which have made the calculations much easier. DPP is actually a better measure of a product's performance than the product's gross margin and is thus replacing gross margin in merchandising decisions. The greater accuracy of DPP is shown in Table 11–3, which indicates that gross margin overstated the product's financial performance by $1.36 ($2.20 – 0.84 = $1.36). As shown in Table 11–4, item A initially appeared to be more profitable than item B based on gross margin. However, in using DPP, discounts and allowances for item B were found to be higher and handling costs lower. The result is that DPP is higher for item B than item A.

Computer applications for shelf-space allocations are becoming more widespread. With the aid of software such as Superman III and AccuSpace, retailers can develop complete categories of products (*planograms* or shelf layouts) and experiment with efficient space use based on financial evaluation, product movement, profit yields, and other information. One area of great interest among chains is store-specific systems, whereby a retailer can identify the categories and products that best fit a specific store's customers. Retailers input information on package size, past sales history, projected sales, store deliveries, and other relevant data, and out comes an exact representation of the planogram schematic. The computer works to establish merchandising placement based on products that have the highest turnover or gross margins or other criteria that will allocate shelf space to best influence the consumer's behaviour. During the planogram

Table 11–4 Direct Product Profitability Comparison

	Item A	Item B
Retail price	$19.00	$18.00
Less cost of goods sold	7.25	8.20
Equals gross margin	$11.75	$ 9.80
Plus discounts and allowances	.60	1.80
Less direct handling costs	3.50	1.70
Equals direct product profitability	$ 8.85	$ 9.90

simulation, adjustments can be made to the database or planogram to best serve the retailer. For example, products tied to seasonal movement can be adjusted to reflect a temporary space allocation, or several planograms can be generated revealing layouts of different heights or widths.[22]

A particularly thorny problem is assigning space to new products. Some manufacturers, having conducted marketing tests, are able to recommend facing levels. The new item problem is simpler for a line extension. A new flavour of potato chips, for example, is invariably located with existing products in single-carton quantities until increased sales demand otherwise. In the case of a completely new category, facings can be provided only by creating new space or by destocking one or more lines from another category. Some firms tackle the new item problem by placing it in a special display until demand has stabilized at a predictable level of trial and repurchase. Because of the numbers of new products manufacturers attempt to introduce into the market each year and because of limited shelf space, some retailers (especially food retailers) are requiring manufacturers to pay slotting fees in order to gain shelf space for new products. These fees range from $250 to $3,000 per store.[23]

Chapter Highlights

- Store layout and design and merchandise presentation are important aspects of a firm's positioning strategy. The major goal of store design and layout and merchandise presentation is to get the shopper into the store to spend as much money as possible on a given shopping trip.
- Store design is a reflection of two elements: the interior design and the exterior design. Both should be in harmony with the store's merchandise and customers. Exterior design includes the building's architecture and entrances, display windows, and signs. Today, there is a renewed interest in window displays, especially among department stores and higher-priced retailers and in cities where walking and window shopping are in style. Window displays can be used to enhance store image, to expose shoppers to new products, or to introduce a new season.

- Some retailers view the interior of the store as a theatre and realize that theatrical elements can be used to influence customer behaviour. Interior design includes everything within the store walls that can be used to create an atmosphere, such as colours, lighting, scents, and sound.

- Store layout is a very important part of store planning. One aspect of store layout is the arrangement of the store. Typical arrangements are the grid, the free-flow or open plan, the boutique concept, and the racetrack layout.

- Another element of store layout is space allocation. Dividing total space between selling and sales-supporting areas is the first step in space allocation. Management can use three basic methods for allocating selling space: industry averages by type of merchandise, sales productivity of product lines, and the build-up (model stock) method.

- Effective use of space can translate into additional dollars of profit. Thus, retailers must evaluate whether store space is being used in the most effective way. The gross-margin-per-square-metre method is one method retailers may use.

- Management must decide where to locate selling and sales-supporting activities within the store. Several guidelines are available to aid in making these decisions.

- Merchandise displays can be used to excite, entertain, and educate consumers. If effectively used, they can have a profound influence on consumer behaviour. In spite of the basically artistic and creative flair needed for merchandise display, some guidelines and principles do exist.

- Interior displays can take a variety of forms, depending on the type of merchandise and image to be projected by thc firm. A number of guidelines to the use of interior merchandise displays are offered.

- An important aspect of merchandise display is determining the amount of space that should be allocated to individual brands or items in a product category. Some retailers allocate shelf space according to gross margin; others use the concept of direct product profit. Some retailers use computer software packages to determine optimum formulas for deciding how much shelf space each item should be allocated.

Key Terms

boutique layout 309	planogram 322
demand merchandise 317	racetrack layout 310
direct product profitability 322	store design 300
free-flow layout 308	store layout 300
grid layout 308	store planning 300
impulse merchandise 317	

Discussion Questions

1. Define store planning, store design, and store layout.
2. What are the decision areas that comprise layout planning?
3. Compare the following layout arrangements: the grid layout, the free-flow or open plan, and the boutique concept.

4. Describe the three methods retailers can use for allocating selling space in a store among the various departments.

5. Explain the gross-margin-per-square-metre method of evaluating space use.

6. What various factors do retailers need to consider in deciding where to locate selling departments and sales-supporting activities within the total store space?

7. Discuss the guidelines retailers can use relative to interior display of merchandise.

8. What information can retailers use in making the shelf-space allocation decision?

Application Exercises

1. Select three different types of stores (e.g., a traditional department store, a discount department store, a specialty apparel shop) and carefully observe their displays, fixturing, appearance—all the elements that make up the interior design of the stores. Write a report describing differences between the stores and how these differences relate to image projection and market segmentation.

2. Visit the following types of stores: a multilevel department store, a supermarket, a national chain, a national specialty chain outlet, and a discount department store. Describe the overall arrangement of the stores (e.g., grid, free-flow, boutique, racetrack). Evaluate the layout of each store and comment on the impact of each layout on the general image of the outlets. What changes, if any, would you suggest and why?

3. Visit several department stores and interview store management. Determine the method(s) used to allocate selling space to the various departments and how management evaluates space use. Based on what you learned in the chapter, evaluate the location of selling departments and sales-supporting activities within each store.

4. Use the following information and calculate the product's direct product profitability (DPP):

Selling price	$20.00
Cost of product	14.50
Payment discount	.40
Merchandise discount	.25
Warehouse direct labour	.10
Warehouse inventory expense	.05
Warehouse operating expense	.08
Transportation to stores	.60
Retail direct labour	.88
Retail inventory expense	.05
Retail operating expense	.20

Suggested Cases

22. The Best Display?

23. Noble Foodstuffs

24. Jim's Sporting Goods

Notes

1. A. Bokma, "Makeover Magic," *Retail Directions,* May/June 1989, pp. 34–37; K. Hannon, "The 1992 Store of the Year," *Money,* December 1991, pp. 156–60.

2. A. J. Stokan, "Design: The Silent Salesperson," *Retail Directions,* May/June 1989, pp. 45–55; K. Pocock, "Supermarket Makeover," *Canadian Grocer,* September 1994, pp. 37–40.

3. J. Margolis, "Windowonderlands," *Globe & Mail,* December 8, 1994, p. D11.

4. Stokan, "Design," p. 46.

5. W. R. Swinyard, "The Effects of Mood, Involvement, and Quality of Store Experience on Shopping Intentions," *Journal of Consumer Research* 20, no. 2 (September 1993), pp. 271–80.

6. J. Baker, M. Levy, and D. Grewal, "An Experimental Approach to Making Retail Store Environmental Decisions," *Journal of Retailing* 68, no. 4 (Winter 1992), pp. 445–60.

7. G. Levitch, "Memories of Versailles," *Globe & Mail,* November 30, 1995, p. D4.

8. E. Garel, "How to Select a Store Designer," *Retail Directions,* January/February 1989, pp. 25–28.

9. K. Pocock, "Supermarket Makeover," *Canadian Grocer,* September 1994, pp. 37–40; J. A. Bellizzi and R. E. Hite, "Environmental Colour, Consumer Feelings and Purchase Likelihood," *Psychology and Marketing* 9, September-October 1992, pp. 347–63.

10. "Office Depot Puts Spotlight on Its Goods," *Chain Store Age Executive,* September 1991, p. 94.

11. C. Miller, "The Right Sound in the Air Can Boost Retail Sales," *Marketing News,* February 4, 1991, p. 2; R.F. Yalch and E. Spangenberg, "Effects of Store Music on Shopping Behaviour," *Journal of Services Marketing* 4, no. 1, Winter 1990, pp. 31–39.

12. J. Baker, M. Levy, and D. Grewal, "An Experimental Approach to Making Retail Store Environmental Decisions."

13. C. Miller, "Scent as Marketing Tool," *Marketing News,* January 18, 1993, pp. 1–2; C. McCarthy, "Aromatic Merchandising: Leading Customers by the Nose," *Visual Merchandising and Store Design,* April 1992, pp. 85–87; C. Miller, "Research Reveals How Marketers Can Win by a Nose," *Marketing News,* February 4, 1991, pp. 1–2.

14. G. Robins, "The Logistics of Overseas Expansion," *Stores,* April 1990, p. 22.

15. M. Kuntz, K. Naughton, G. DeGeorge, and S.A. Forest, "Reinventing the Store," *Business Week,* November 27, 1995, p. 86; A. Salomon and S. Hume, "Hot Fast-Food Ideas Cool Off," *Advertising Age,* September 30, 1991, p. 42.

16. L.M. Grossman, "Hypermarkets: A Sure-Fire Hit Bombs," *The Wall Street Journal,* June 25, 1992, p. B1.

17. A. Willis, "Canadian Tire Goes Flat for Investors," *Financial Times,* June 1, 1992, p. 1.

18. C. Schefler, "Effective Presentation—the Art and Science of Merchandising," *Retail Merchandising,* October 1987, p. 5.

19. J. Pellet, "The Power of Lighting," *Chain Store Age Executive,* July 1992, p. 90.

20. Schefler, "Effective Presentation."

21. F. Brookman, "Fixtures Add Flexibility to Product Display," *Stores,* May 1992, pp. 84–85.

22. T. Steinhagen, "Space Management Shapes Up with Planograms," *Marketing News,* November 12, 1990, p. 7; B. Cohen, "How Micromerchandising Can Work for Big

Chains," *Chain Store Age Executive,* February 1992, p. 58; D. Raftery, "The Interest Behind Space Management," *Distribution Management,* November 1990, pp. 76–77.

23. C. Duff, "Nation's Retailers Ask Vendors to Help Share Expenses," *The Wall Street Journal,* August 4, 1993, p. B4; K. Deveny, "Displays Pay Off for Grocery Marketers," *The Wall Street Journal,* October 15, 1992, p. B1.

Merchandise Planning

1. **Understand the need to make merchandise decisions that support the overall competitive strategy of the firm.**

2. **Explain how merchandise strategies can be implemented to obtain a competitive advantage.**

3. **Describe the process of developing a merchandise budget to make inventory investment decisions.**

4. **Identify the issues to consider in making merchandise width and depth decisions.**

A new Future Shop soon to open; this superstore differentiates itself from the competition on the basis of price and selection.

Photo by Betty McDougall

A good example of a retailer with a competitive advantage is Future Shop, the Canadian electronics chain operating in Canada and the United States. The chain has grown from a single store in Vancouver in 1982 to over 70 stores and $1.5 billion in sales by the end of 1995. The stores feature wide and deep inventories of electronic products, from television sets to VCRs to compact discs to stereo systems, to achieve assortment dominance. This retailer wants consumers to come to its shops for all their electronic needs and encourages them with extensive advertising of their products and competitive prices.

Future Shop sells two things—selection and price. The retailer differentiates itself by offering a dominant assortment of merchandise at the best prices in the market. It promises to match any lower price within 30 days of a purchase at its stores. The strategy of Future Shop has led them to be leaders in the field, the ultimate goal in retailing.[1] ■

High-performance retailers such as Future Shop are credited with having a "compelling competitive advantage." Consider also Shopper's Drug Mart with its "Everything you want in a drugstore" strategy, which commits the retailer to carry an extensive product assortment to satisfy customer needs. Then there is "There's a lot more to Canadian Tire," which builds on Canadian Tire's dominance in automotive products for its other major product categories. Each of these examples illustrates the important role that merchandise management plays in the overall competitive strategy of the firm.

Development of the merchandise plan is the logical place to begin a discussion about competitive advantage in the marketplace, because without merchandise (or some offering), a retail establishment cannot exist.

Merchandise Management

Merchandise planning includes all the activities needed to balance inventory and sales. The major portion of this chapter is directed toward the merchandise plan at the department classification level. Although the function of merchandise planning is somewhat technical, the concept of merchandising is not. Traditionally, merchandising has been defined as offering the right merchandise at the right price at the right place in the right quantities at the right time. We support these "rights," but we see merchandising in the 1990s as much more. We see merchandising as a part of the strategic plan—the creative positioning tactics that support the long-run mission and objectives of a firm. Merchandising today must include short-term creative tactics based on management philosophies that can provide the firm with a different advantage.

Merchandise management is the management of the product component of the retailing mix; it comprises planning and control activities. Its purpose is to ensure that the inventory component of the mix supports the overall merchandising philosophy of the firm and meets the needs of target customers. The following sections provide examples of merchandising philosophies that can create a competitive advantage for their firms.

Merchandise management—the management of change

Canadian Tire manages change through its strategic planning process. Management must recognize change and identify it in a way that is compatible with the firm's merchandising strategies. Faced with new competitors like Wal-Mart and other environmental changes, Canadian Tire developed a new strategic direction to improve the company's growth and profits.

Components of the new strategy included a concentration on three product categories—auto parts, sports and leisure goods, and housewares; opening of a new format store—larger, brighter, more modern; improvements in customer service—including a no-hassle return policy; and improving the cost of operations—major productivity gains were achieved.

An important part of Canadian Tire's strategy is continually refining the value package they offer to their customers. Their goal is to offer the most value; to offer the best combination of quality, service, convenience, loyalty programs, *and* price.

Canadian Tire illustrates a focussed and deep assortment in sporting goods, one of the three main product areas in its new strategy.

Courtesy Canadian Tire

Canadian Tire's merchandising philosophy is based on its strategy and customer value. In focussing on the three product areas and introducing new format stores, Canadian Tire reviewed all of the chain's 50,000 "stock-keeping units," eliminated non-performing products, and added thousands of items. It significantly broadened product lines in home entertainment, pet food, personal security, and floral arrangements. Canadian Tire plans to offer its customers a highly focussed assortment (in the three product categories), a deeper and more competitive assortment (by adding product lines and more brands within each category) and the best value for the customers' dollar (through offering the best value combination).[2]

Progressive retailers like Canadian Tire recognize the importance of identifying merchandise trends and responding to them quickly. Retailers must be extremely alert to the particular phase of the merchandise trend so that inventories can be adjusted accordingly. In fact, merchandising planning is managing change, particularly meeting the changing needs (value changes) of customers, and interpreting the trends and adapting to the volatile elements of customer value.

Merchandising strategies: capitalizing on the momentum of change

The following examples illustrate retailing efforts to understand, anticipate, and capitalize on the momentum of change through implementation of their individual merchandising strategies. Our focus here is on brand strategy and licensing.

Private-label versus national-brand strategy

One of the more difficult problems facing merchants today is the optimal balance between private and national brands and, in some instances, generics. **Private brands (or private labels)** are owned by a retailer (e.g., Canadian Tire's Mastercraft tools). **National brands,** often called "manufacturer" brands, are owned by a manufacturer and can be sold to whomever the owner desires (e.g., Procter & Gamble's Tide laundry detergent). The issue is not limited to the general merchandise sector of retailing. The grocery and drug trades have struggled with such decisions for many years. In all merchandise categories and lines of trade, the position of the ideal mix is critical. Additionally, the drug and grocery trade face the *generic* program issues. Generics are unbranded merchandise offerings that carry only the designation of the product type on the package, such as "salt."

One retailer that has aggressively used a blend of generic, private, and national brands is Loblaws. To differentiate itself from its competitors, Loblaws has introduced over 1,500 "no name" and 400 "President's Choice" store-branded products. As well, it has introduced the "Club Pack" line, the environmentally friendly "Green" line, and the "Too Good to Be True" line. This merchandising strategy allows Loblaws to offer customers a product assortment that cannot be duplicated by competitors. Loblaws' executives believe that these products provide their customers with a powerful combination of excellent quality and low price. Loblaws' store brands now account for $1 billion in sales, of which about $200 million is in its Club Pack line,[3] or 20 percent of Loblaws' revenues. It is estimated that about one-quarter of all grocery sales in Canada are private brands.[4]

Retailers promote private-label programs to (1) defend themselves against off-price competition, (2) offer an alternative as the upscale catalogue companies feature virtually all competitive national labels, (3) guarantee some market exclusivity, (4) achieve a degree of control over merchandising programs, and (5) protect their profit margins.

In deciding on the best mix of national, private, and generic brands to carry, the retailer should consider a number of factors. National brands are well known and are usually supported by advertising. Additionally, many consumers regard national brands as superior to either private or generic brands in terms of reliability and quality. Private brands generate higher margins for retailers, offer economic benefits to consumers because they are usually cheaper than national brands, and may assist in developing store loyalty. Private brands do require the retailer to invest time and money and could damage the store's image if the brand is viewed by consumers as having poor quality. For the retailer, generics share some of the same risks as private brands but they appeal to price-conscious customers. Generics can help to create a strong competitive price image for a retailer.

Even though many retailers are introducing private brands and others are adding to their line of private brands, some retailers have reduced the ratio of

Courtesy Loblaw Company Ltd.

private to manufacturer brands in their stores. For example, Sears Canada's shift from private labels to a strong manufacturer brand statement has been attributed largely to its new philosophy of appealing to a broader range of consumers by offering more choices to more people. Sears Canada has added BOCA, Petites by Tan Jay, Nygard Collections, and Le Château national brands to its clothing line, and IMAN to its cosmetics line, to broaden its appeal and respond to changing consumer tastes.[5] Thus, the private versus national brand issue is a challenge for both retailers and manufacturers (Retail Highlight 12–1).

Licensing as a merchandising strategy

Licensing is a strategic marketing tool in which the *licenser* or owner of a "property" (the concept to be marketed) joins with a licensee (the manufacturer of the licensed product) to sell to retail buyers who offer the goods through retail organizations. Licensing is an important retail merchandising strategy.

Licensing is gaining widespread acceptance as a merchandising strategy among retailers because it provides the opportunity to capture a market whose customer is younger, richer, better educated, and willing to pay more than the average consumer for what he or she wants. The challenge for the merchant strategist is to choose the right licensees, weed out the weak ones, and cut back on those that are always popular but may, from time to time, lose momentum.

When considering licensing as a merchandising strategy, retailers must evaluate the opportunity in terms of the partnership that must evolve. The licensee who offers the property must be strong, have a good product, and provide sufficient advertising and marketing effort for the offering. The Esprit line of clothing is an example of licensing that has been profitable for both the licenser and licensee. In fact, it has been so successful that Esprit is also opening its own retail outlets in Canada and around the world.

Retail Highlight 12–1

Private Labels versus National Brands: The Issues

From the manufacturer's viewpoint, private label products pose a serious threat for a number of reasons:

- Private label products have improved in quality in the past 10 years.
- Retailers have developed premium private label brands that compete directly with national brands.
- New distribution channels are emerging (e.g., warehouse club/mass merchandisers) and they carry an increasing number of private label lines.
- Private labels are moving into new categories such as clothing and beer and creating more acceptance among consumers for private label purchases.

In response, national brand manufacturers have advantages:

- Brand names provide consumers with an assurance of quality and simplify consumers' decisions.
- Brand name firms have a solid foundation (quality, name recognition) on which to build their business.
- National brands have value for retailers—consumers expect them in stores, the brands have traffic-building power, and retailers can use them, with promotions, to create a store image.
- Retailers who carry large numbers of private brands dilute their strength because consumers have difficulty believing that a store can provide quality private brands across a wide range of categories.

From the retailer's viewpoint, private brands pose some threats:

- If the private brand varies in quality, particularly in categories where sophisticated manufacturing and automation are required, then consumers may be dissatisfied with both the brand and store.
- If the comparative quality of the private brand relative to national brands is low, then consumers may be reluctant to purchase any of the store's brands.

The retailer is likely to have success with private labels where:

- The product quality is consistent and relatively similar to national brands, thus offering consumers a high-value proposition.
- The product category is large and profitable, thus attracting less competitive response from national brands.
- There are few national brands and there are relatively low advertising expenditures by those brands.

Sources: John A. Quelch and David Harding, "Brands versus Private Labels: Fighting to Win," *Harvard Business Review,* January-February 1996, pp. 99–109; and Stephen J. Hoch and Shumeet Banerji, "When Do Private Labels Succeed?" *Sloan Management Review,* Summer 1993, pp. 57–67.

The Bay has established licensing partnerships with a number of cosmetics firms—including Estée Lauder, Clinique, Lancôme, MAC, and Christian Dior—and introduced new personalized cosmetics installations to many stores across Canada. The fashion emphasis provided by these installations complements The Bay's merchandise assortments of national and private brand clothing and accessories for their target customers.[6]

Summary

The objectives of this initial part of the chapter have been threefold: (1) to place merchandise management within the context of strategic planning, (2) to introduce merchandising as a concept integral to manage change, and (3) to provide real-world evidence of various ways that merchandise strategies, especially brand and licensing, are being implemented. The final objective of the chapter is to assist you in understanding merchandise management at the store level, with particular emphasis on the development of the merchandise budget.

Merchandise Planning

As defined earlier, merchandise planning includes those activities needed to ensure a balance between inventory and sales. The other element of the total management process is, of course, control. The control aspect is addressed in Chapter 18. Control efforts provide information on how effective the planning has been.

Basic terms

A **product** is simply a tangible object, service, or idea, such as a dress or a dress-cleaning service. A **merchandise line** refers to a group of products that are closely related because they are intended for the same end use (dishwashers), are used together (knives and forks), or are sold to the same customer group (children's footwear). Two important decisions the retailer makes are the breadth and depth of the merchandising lines carried by the store. **Breadth (or width)** is the number of different merchandising lines carried.[7] **Depth** is the number of items that are carried in a single merchandise line. Breadth and depth, illustrated in Figure 12–1, define the merchandise mix, which is the total of all the merchandise lines.

Assortment means the range of choices (selection) available for any given merchandise line. Assortment can also be defined as the number of **stockkeeping units (SKUs)** in a category. For example, a litre package of Nabob coffee is one SKU; a 500 ml bag of Maxwell House coffee is another SKU. Do not confuse, however, the number of items with a SKU. In other words, a food store might have 100 packages of the 1 litre Nabob coffee, but this represents only one SKU.

Merchandise (or inventory) **turnover** is the number of times the average inventory of an item (or SKU) is sold, usually in annual terms. Turnover can be computed on a dollar basis in either cost or retail terms, or in units.

The major focus of this section is merchandise assortment planning, the purpose of which is to maintain *stock balance*—a balance between inventories and sales. Figure 12–2 is a diagram of the merchandise planning process. Reference will be made to this diagram throughout most of this chapter.

Stock balance

Retailers may consider merchandise assortment in three different ways: width, depth, or dollar planning. Let's assume that we are planning for the men's sport shirt assortment in the furnishings department of a department store.[8]

Figure 12–1 The Merchandise Mix			
		Number of Merchandise Lines **Breadth**	
		Few	Many
Number of Merchandise Items **Depth**	Few	Narrow and shallow (Fast-food restaurant)	Broad and shallow (Convenience store)
	Many	Narrow and deep (Golf specialty store)	Broad and deep (Department store)

Laura Secord offers a narrow and deep merchandise mix to attract the chocolate and sweet lovers market.

Photo by Anne Laroche

Ways to look at stock balance

The three aspects of stock balance as shown in Figure 12–2 are: (1) width or breadth, point 5; (2) depth, point 6; and (3) total dollars, point 4.

Width. Width (breadth) of merchandise assortments refers to the assortment factors necessary to meet the demands of the market and to meet competition. Decisions must be made on the number of brands, sizes, colours, and the like. In our example for shirts, the following might be a planning process in terms of width:

Brands (Arrow, Forsyth, Manhattan)	3 SKUs
	×
Sizes (small, medium, large, and x-large)	4 = 12 SKUs
	×
Prices ($39.95; $49.95)	2 = 24 SKUs
	×
Colours (white, grey, blue)	3 = 72 SKUs
	×
Fabrics (knit, woven)	2 = 144 SKUs

Thus, we see that there are 144 SKUs necessary to meet customers' wants and the offerings of competition.

Depth

The next question is: How many units of merchandise do we need to support our expected sales of each assortment factor? This decision must be based on expectations of the sales importance for each assortment factor. For example, how many small Arrow shirts, at $49.95, in blue knit do I expect to sell? Such decisions involve the art of merchandising. Knowledge of the customer market,

Figure 12–2   The Merchandise-Planning Process

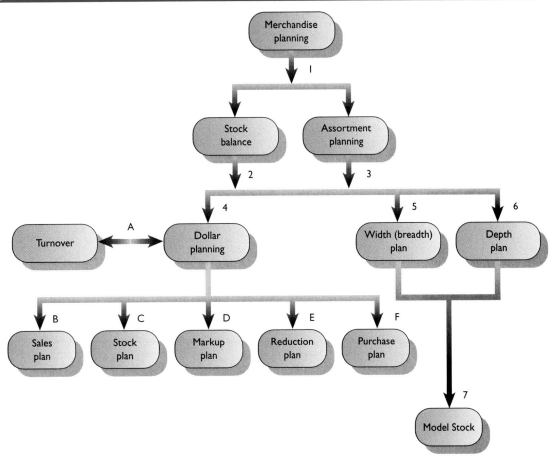

the segment appealed to, the image of the store and/or department, and other factors all enter into this subjective decision.

Only experience in planning the composition of stock will give retailers confidence in this activity.

Dollar planning of inventory

Assume that 1,000 shirts are needed for the ideal stock level. This number, however, does not tell the manager how many dollars need to be invested in stock at any one time. Thus, the total dollar investment in inventory is the final way to look at stock balance.[9] Here merchandise turnover comes into play.

Figure 12–3 shows how to calculate turnover. For turnover goals to be meaningful, they must be based on merchandise groupings, which are as much alike as possible. Planning on the basis of large, diverse merchandise groupings is unwise. Also, it is impossible to tell whether a particular turnover figure is good or bad unless it is compared to something. The retailer can compare turnover rates to average rates for various merchandise classifications or to the firm's own rates for past periods. The goal, however, is to have a turnover rate

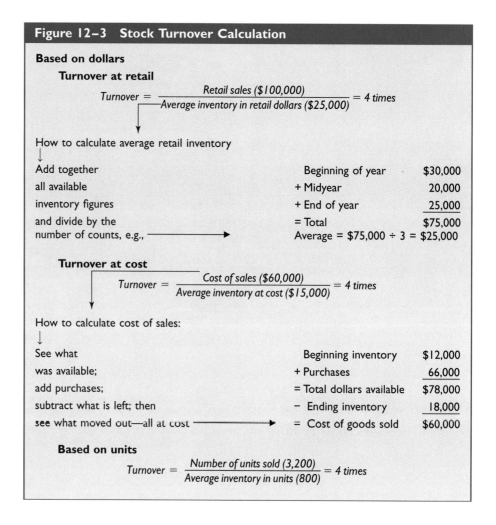

Figure 12–3   Stock Turnover Calculation

Based on dollars

Turnover at retail

$$\text{Turnover} = \frac{\text{Retail sales (\$100,000)}}{\text{Average inventory in retail dollars (\$25,000)}} = 4 \text{ times}$$

How to calculate average retail inventory

Add together	Beginning of year	$30,000
all available	+ Midyear	20,000
inventory figures	+ End of year	25,000
and divide by the	= Total	$75,000
number of counts, e.g.,	Average = $75,000 ÷ 3 = $25,000	

Turnover at cost

$$\text{Turnover} = \frac{\text{Cost of sales (\$60,000)}}{\text{Average inventory at cost (\$15,000)}} = 4 \text{ times}$$

How to calculate cost of sales:

See what	Beginning inventory	$12,000
was available;	+ Purchases	66,000
add purchases;	= Total dollars available	$78,000
subtract what is left; then	− Ending inventory	18,000
see what moved out—all at cost	= Cost of goods sold	$60,000

Based on units

$$\text{Turnover} = \frac{\text{Number of units sold (3,200)}}{\text{Average inventory in units (800)}} = 4 \text{ times}$$

that is fast enough to give the retailer a good return on money invested in inventory, but not so fast that the retailer is always out of stock.

Figure 12–4 recaps what has been discussed thus far in the chapter. Students should understand the material before proceeding to the next section, which discusses how to set up a merchandise budget.

The Merchandise Budget

This section of the chapter focusses on merchandise planning in total dollars. Later sections look at planning in terms of width and depth.

Approaches to preparing the merchandise budget

Traditionally, merchandise planning has been structured around either a bottom-up or a top-down approach. The bottom-up approach starts with estimates at the classification level. These estimates are then combined into a

Figure 12–4   How to Look at Stock Balance

Ways to Look at Stock Balance	Examples	Things to Consider in Assortment Planning
Width (or breadth)	Number of brands, sizes, colours.	What customers want. What competitors offer.
Depth	How many units are needed to support expected sales of each size, etc.	The sales importance of each size.
Total dollars	How many dollars are inventory?	Look at turnover. a. Fast enough to get good return. b. Not so fast that out-of-stocks occur.

departmental merchandise budget and finally into a total company plan. The **merchandise budget** is a plan of how much to buy in dollars per month based on profitability goals. The top-down approach starts with a gross dollar figure established by top management. This dollar figure is then allocated to the various merchandise classifications. A third method of merchandise planning is the interactive approach. Interactive means that management sets broad guidelines, and the buying staff then follows the bottom-up approach with reviews by management. The interactive approach probably results in the most accurate merchandise plan.

The merchandise budgeting process

The following items affect profit return and are included in the merchandise budget:

1. Sales: Figure 12–2, point 4B.
2. Stock (inventory): Figure 12–2, point 4C.
3. Reductions: Figure 12–2, point 4E.
4. Purchases: Figure 12–2, point 4F.

Figure 12–5 presents a diagram of these profit factors. References will be made to this diagram as each of these factors is discussed in more detail.

Sales planning

The starting point in developing a merchandise budget is the sales plan. Note from Figure 12–5 that sales are first planned by season and then by month. In discussing sales planning by season and month, let's assume we are planning a merchandise budget for sporting goods.

By season. A *season* is the typical planning period in retailing, especially for fashion merchandise. Assume that the merchandise budget is being planned for the 1997 spring season (February, March, April, May, June, and July). The retailer would start planning in November 1996. The factors the retailer needs to consider in developing this seasonal plan are given in Figure 12–6.

In planning seasonal sales, the retailer begins by looking at last year's sales for the same period. Assume sales were $15,000 for the spring of 1996. Too many retailers at this point merely use the past period's figure as their sales forecast for the planning period. However, recent sales trends should be considered. For

Figure 12–5 Schematic Diagram of Merchandise Budget

| | Components to Be Budgeted | | | | | |
| | Sales | | | Reductions | | |
	Season	Month	Stock	Season	Month	Purchases
Quantitative (factual) data						
Qualitative (subjective) data: trends and environmental factors						

example, if sales for the 1996 fall season have been running about 5 percent ahead of fall 1995 and this trend is expected to continue, the retailer would project spring 1997 sales to be $15,750 ($15,000 × 1.05 = $15,750).

But the retailer cannot stop here. Now one must look at *forces outside the firm* that would have an impact on the sales forecast. For example, the retailer's projections would be affected if a new sporting goods store opened next door, carrying similar assortments (especially if this new store was part of a national chain with excellent management), or a major manufacturer in the community was planning a large expansion. Next the retailer must look at *internal conditions* that might affect the sales forecast. Moving sporting goods to a more valuable location within the store is an example of an internal condition.

Exact numbers cannot be placed on all these external and internal factors. Retailers must, however, use judgment and incorporate all factors into the sales forecast. Assume that the retailer has decided sales should increase by 10 percent. The sales plan for the 1997 spring season is now $16,500 (15,000 × 1.10 = $16,500).

By month

The planned seasonal sales must now be divided into monthly sales. Figure 12–6 presents those factors that must be considered.

Again, the starting point is spring 1996. Assume the following sales distribution by month for this season: February - 10 percent; March - 20 percent; April - 15 percent; May - 15 percent; June - 30 percent; and July - 10 percent. Further assume that the retailer has considered all internal and external factors that would affect this distribution and has decided that no adjustments need to be made. Based on this breakdown, the season's sales plan by month for spring 1997 would look like that in Figure 12–7.

Stock planning

The next step in developing the merchandise budget is to plan stock (inventory) levels by month. In planning monthly stock needed to support monthly sales, several different techniques can be used. Because the **stock-to-sales ratio** method is often used to plan monthly stock levels for fashion merchandise and for highly seasonal merchandise, it will be used to illustrate the concept of stock planning. The formula is:

BOM inventory = Planned monthly sales × stock-to-sales ratio.

	Sales	
	Season	**By Month**
Information available for planning	1. Sales for spring 1996. 2. Recent trends in sales.	1. Sales percentages by month, 1996. 2. Check distribution against published trade data.
Judgment applied in certain issues	1. Factors outside the store such as new competition. 2. Internal conditions such as more space available.	1. Factors outside the store such as new competition. 2. Internal conditions such as more space available.

Figure 12–6 Diagram of the Sales Budget, 1997

The stock-to-sales ratio reflects the relationship between the dollar amount needed in inventory at the beginning of a month (BOM) to support planned sales for that month. For example, if $30,000 in inventory is needed at the BOM to support sales of $10,000, the stock-to-sales ratio would be 3 ($30,000/$10,000 = 3).[10]

To determine the BOM inventory, the retailer multiplies the month's planned sales figure by the month's stock-to-sales ratio figure. For example, as shown in Figure 12–7, planned sales for February are $1,650. If the retailer knows from past experience and industry trade data that 4.7 times more dollars in inventory than planned sales are needed, the BOM inventory for February would be $7,755 ($1,650 × 4.7 = $7,755). The 4.7 figure is the stock-to-sales ratio figure for the month of February.[11]

In determining monthly stock-to-sales ratios, retailers can use existing stock-to-sales ratios from past performance. However, retailers must judge whether the prior periods' stock-to-sales figures need to be adjusted. To help with this judgment, trade data may be used along with the retailer's own information. Stock-to-sales ratios can also be calculated directly from the turnover goal set for the line of merchandise. To do this, the retailer simply divides the desired annual turnover figures into 12 (the number of months in a year). For example, if the turnover goal is 2.5, the average monthly stock-to-sales ratio for the year would be 4.8 (12/2.5 = 4.8). If the desired turnover rate were 4, the average monthly stock-to-sales ratio for the year would be 3 (12/4 = 3). As one can see, the lower the turnover rate, the higher the average monthly stock-to-sales ratio.

Figure 12–8 provides information on needed monthly BOM stock for spring 1997, using planned monthly sales for spring 1997 from Figure 12–7 and the monthly stock-to-sales ratios for past years. In reality, the retailer would use judgment in deciding whether to use last year's monthly stock-to-sales figures or whether any conditions exist that would require them to be changed.

The end-of-the-month (EOM) inventory for a particular month would be the BOM inventory for the following month. For example, as shown in Figure 12–8, the BOM inventory for February is $7,755. The EOM inventory for February would be $13,860, which is also the BOM inventory for March.

Reductions planning

Reductions are anything other than sales that reduce inventory value.

Employee discounts are reductions. If an item sells for $100 and employees receive a 20 percent discount, the employee pays $80. The $80 is recorded as a

Figure 12–7 Spring Sales Plan, 1997				
Month	Percent of Total Season's Business in 1996	× Season's Sales Forecast	=	Planned Sales for Months of 1997 Season
February	10	$16,500		$ 1,650
March	20	16,500		3,300
April	15	16,500		2,475
May	15	16,500		2,475
June	30	16,500		4,950
July	10	16,500		1,650
Total	100			$16,500

sale. The $20 reduces the inventory dollar amount but is *not* a sale. It is an employee discount—a reduction.

Shortages (shrinkage) are reductions. A shoplifter takes a $500 watch from a jewelry department. Inventory is reduced by $500 just as if it were a sale. But no revenues come from shoplifting. If a salesperson steals another watch (internal pilferage), the results are the same. A $1,000 watch is received into stock and marked at $500 because of a clerical error. Fewer inventory dollars are in stock than the retailer thinks.

Markdowns are reductions. For example, assume a $50 tennis racket does not sell during the season and is marked down to $30. The $20 markdown is counted as a reduction of inventory and only $30 is counted as a sale.

Why plan reductions as a part of the merchandise budget? Note from Figure 12–8 that a planned BOM stock of $13,860 for March is needed to support March sales of $3,300 (with a 4.2 stock-to-sales ratio). However, suppose that the retailer's reductions during February amount to approximately $5,000. The EOM inventory in February (BOM for March) is $5,000 less than if no reductions had been taken. Reductions must be planned and accounted for so the retailer will have sufficient BOM inventory to make planned sales.

Assume that reductions for the spring season in the department are planned at 8 percent or $1,320 ($16,500 seasonal sales × .08). Figure 12–8 could be used to allocate the reductions by month (e.g., February would be $1,650 × .08 or $132, and March would be $3,300 × .08 or $264). Reductions normally vary by month.

Planned purchases

Up to this point, the retailer has determined planned (1) sales, (2) stock, and (3) reductions. The next step in developing the merchandise budget is to plan the dollar amount of purchases on a monthly basis. Planned purchases are figured as follows:

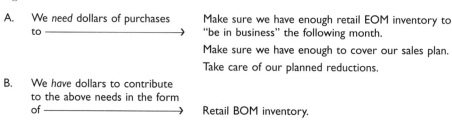

A.   We *need* dollars of purchases to ⟶   Make sure we have enough retail EOM inventory to "be in business" the following month.

Make sure we have enough to cover our sales plan.

Take care of our planned reductions.

B.   We *have* dollars to contribute to the above needs in the form of ⟶   Retail BOM inventory.

Figure 12–8 BOM Stock, Spring 1997			
Month	**Planned Sales** ×	**Stock-to-Sales** =	**Planned BOM Stock**
February	$ 1,650	4.7	$ 7,755
March	3,300	4.2	13,860
April	2,475	4.3	10,640
May	2,475	4.4	10,890
June	4,950	3.2	15,840
July	1,650	6.9	11,385
Total	$16,500		$70,370

Stated more concretely;

> Planned purchases = Planned EOM stock + Planned sales
> + Planned reductions – Planned BOM stock

To calculate planned purchases for March, look at Figure 12–8 to get the needed information.

Planned Purchases	=	$10,640	(EOM March or BOM April)	(Figure 12–8)
		+ 3,300	(Planned sales, March)	(Figure 12–8)
		+ 264	(Planned reductions, March)	(see above)
	=	$14,204	(Dollars *needs*, March)	
		−13,860	(BOM March-what you *have*)	(Figure 12–8)
	=	$ 344	(Planned purchases)	

One additional point. Purchases are planned in terms of *retail* dollars. However, when buying merchandise, the buyer must think in terms of the *cost* of merchandise. Thus, it is necessary to convert the planned purchase figure at retail to a cost figure. This conversion process will be explained in detail in Chapter 14. At this point simply remember: To convert retail dollars to cost dollars, multiply retail dollars by the complement of the initial retail markup. For example, assume that planned purchases for a given month are $1,000 at retail, and that the planned initial markup is 40 percent of retail. To convert retail dollars to cost dollars, multiply $1,000 by 60 percent, the complement of the planned initial markup. (100 percent – 40 percent = 60 percent.) Thus planned purchases at cost would be $600 ($1,000 × .60 = $600).

We have now worked through the dollar merchandise-planning process.[12] Figure 12–9 is a planning form for a typical six-month merchandise plan that includes all the factors just discussed. However, as Figure 12–2 shows, the retailer still needs to plan the width and depth factors of stock balance (points 5 and 6). The following sections of the chapter describe how to plan these parts of the merchandise budget.

Planning Width and Depth of Assortments

Now that the retailer knows how much to spend for stock, a decision still must be made on (1) what to spend the dollars for (width) and (2) in what amounts (depth). The goal here is to set up a **model stock plan** (Figure 12–2, point 7). A

Figure 12–9   Six-Month Merchandising Plan

Department name_____   Department no._____

Six-Month Merchandising Plan			Plan (this year)	Actual (last year)
		Stock turnover		
		Workroom costs		
		Etc.		

Spring 19--		Feb.	Mar.	Apr.	May	June	July	Season Total
Fall 19--		Aug.	Sep.	Oct.	Nov.	Dec.	Jan.	
Sales	Last year							
	Plan	1,650	3,300	2,475	2,475	4,950	1,650	16,500
	Percent of increase							
	Revised							
	Actual							
Retail Stock (BOM)	Last year							
	Plan	7,755	13,860	10,640	10,840	16,830	11,385	71,360
	Revised							
	Actual							
Markdowns	Last year							
	Plan (dollars)	132	264	198	198	396	132	1,320
	Plan (percent)							
	Revised							
	Actual							
Retail Purchases	Last year							
	Plan	344						
	Revised							
	Actual							
Percent of Initial Markup	Last year							
	Plan							
	Revised							
	Actual							

model stock plan is the retailer's best prediction of the assortment needed to satisfy customers.

The width plan

Figure 12–10 is a model stock plan for a sweaters classification in a sporting goods department. Assume that only two customer-attracting features are important—synthetic and natural fibres. Even though the illustration is simple, it shows that to offer customers only *one* sweater in each assortment *width* factor (in both synthetic and natural fibres), 270 sweaters (2 × 5 × 3 × 3 × 3) are needed (column 1 of Figure 12–10).

The depth plan

The depth plan involves deciding how many sweaters are needed in each of the five assortment factors (Figure 12–10). Assume that 800 are needed for one turnover period. (If turnover is to be 3, then 800 sweaters are needed for 4 months - 12 months divided by 3 is 4.) Also remember that the retailer is planning dollars at the same time as assortments. Thus, the amount of dollars will affect support.

If the retailer believes that 90 percent of sales will be in synthetic fibres, then 720 sweaters will be needed (800 × .90 = 720). Following Figure 12–10, one sees that the retailer will have 144 of size A, 58 in colour A, 29 at price point A, and 12 in design A.

The art of planning

The foregoing illustration of the formulation of the width and depth (model stock in units) appears to be a rather routine approach to planning. In fact, the decisions as to the percentage relationships among the various assortment factors are based on many complex factors relating to store objectives and to the merchandising art of retailing. In planning the assortment width factors, the entire merchandising philosophy and strategic posture of management assume critical importance. The factors would be significantly different for a classification in a unit of Eaton's than for the same classification in a Zellers outlet. The Eaton's merchandiser would consider the most unusual styles and fashion colours. Also, price points would greatly exceed those of Zellers.

In other words, the total image management wants the store to project and the strategy assumed to accomplish the store's objectives affect decisions on width factors and the relative importance of each. Certainly the target market of the store affects planning decisions, as do environmental conditions of the planning period. For example, as technological advances in textile fibres allowed more vibrant colourfast materials to enter the menswear industry, the width of offerings was expanded. The technology was a response to changing lifestyles, which dictated a more fashion-conscious male market for sportswear in general. In addition, changing styles of living and utilization of time for such activities as tennis and golf were reflected in sportswear offerings.

We have focussed on the "how to" rather than the "what" and "why" because of the artistic and creative nature of merchandising, the variability among differing types of merchandise classifications, and especially the virtual impossibility of teaching the *art* of merchandising. Our major concern is that you appreciate how the operating and the creative aspects of merchandise planning relate.

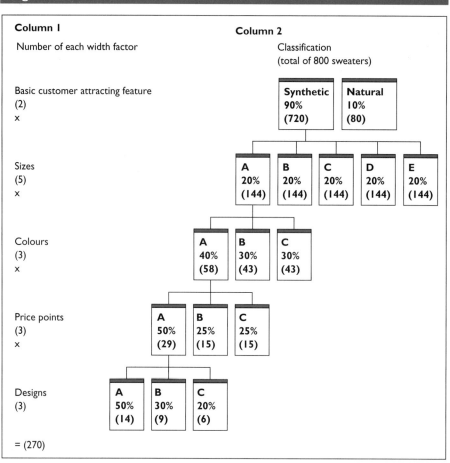

Figure 12–10   Model Stock of Sweaters

Note: The percentage in each factor is the expected importance of that assortment factor. Numbers in parentheses represent the share of the 800-sweater total: for example, 90% × 800 = 720; 20% × 720 = 144, and so on.

Chapter Highlights

- **Merchandising management is the management component of the marketing mix. The key to successful merchandising is to ensure that the customer is offered the right merchandise, at the right price, at the right place, at the right time, and in the right quantities (the five "rights" of merchandising). Merchandising is also part of the strategic plan—the creative positioning tactics that support the long-run mission and objectives of the firm.**

- Two of the merchandising strategies retailers use to gain a competitive advantage are branding (private-label versus national) strategies and licensing strategies.

- One of the more difficult problems facing merchants is the optimal balance between national, private, and generic brands. The question affects most types of retailing.

- Preparing a merchandise budget is a challenging and important task. It includes ways to look at stock balance (width, breadth, total dollars).

- Merchandise planning can be structured around either a bottom-up or a top-down approach, and perhaps best by the interactive approach.

- The following items affect profitability and are included in the merchandise budget: (1) sales, (2) inventory or stock, (3) reductions, and (4) purchases.

Key Terms

assortment 335
breadth (or width) 335
depth 335
licensing 333
merchandise budget 339
merchandise line 335
merchandise management 330
merchandise planning 330
model stock plan 343

national brand 332
private brand (or private label) 332
product 335
reductions 341
SKU (stockkeeping unit) 335
stock-to-sales ratio 340
turnover 335
width (or breadth) 335

Discussion Questions

1. By using examples, distinguish among the following: product, product line, variety, and assortment.

2. Describe the three points that go together in planning stock balance.

3. Explain "merchandise turnover;" indicate how it is useful in planning total dollars in inventory.

4. What factors must a retailer consider in deciding how many dollars to spend on inventory?

5. Discuss the following: sales planning, stock planning, reductions planning.

6. Explain the relationship between stock-to-sales ratios and turnover. How are stock-to-sales ratios used as a guide to stock planning in the merchandise budget?

7. How does a retailer plan purchases? Give an example of the process.

8. Explain the difference in the purposes of merchandise budgeting and expense budgeting.

Problems

1. If net sales for the season (6 months) are $48,000 and the average retail stock for the season is $21,000, what is the annual stock-turnover rate?

2. If cost of goods sold for the first four months of operation is $127,000 and average stock at cost for this same time period is $68,000, what is the annual stock-turnover rate?

3. Given the following figures, what is the stock-turnover rate for the season?

	Retail Stock on Hand	Monthly Net Sales
Opening inventory	$16,000	
End of: 1st month	16,450	$7,500
2nd month	16,000	6,900
3rd month	17,260	7,250
4th month	16,690	6,840
5th month	15,980	6,620
6th month	16,620	7,180

4. What is average stock if the stock-turnover rate is 4 and net sales are $36,000?

5. What is the cost of goods sold if the stock-turnover rate is 2.5 and the average stock at cost is $8,700?

6. A new department shows the following figures for the first three months of operation: net sales, $150,000; average retail stock, $160,000. If business continues at the same rate, what will the stock-turnover rate be for the year?

7. Last year a certain department had net sales of $21,000 and a stock-turnover rate of 2.5. A stock-turnover rate of 3 is desired for the year ahead. If sales volume remains the same, how much must the average inventory be reduced (a) in dollar amount and (b) in percentage?

8. A certain department had net sales for the year of $71,250. The stock at the beginning of the year is $22,500 at cost and $37,500 at retail. A stock count in July showed the inventory at cost as $23,750 and at retail as $36,250. End-of-year inventories are $25,000 at cost and $38,750 at retail. Purchases at cost during the year amounted to $48,750. What is the stock-turnover rate (a) at cost and (b) at retail?

9. Given the following information for the month of July, calculate planned purchases:

Planned sales for the month	$43,000
Planned BOM inventory	60,250
Planned reductions for the month	1,200
Planned EOM inventory	58,000

10. Given the following information for the month of October, calculate planned purchases:

Planned sales for the month	$198,000
Planned EOM inventory	240,000
Stock-to-sales ratio for the month of October	1.2
Planned reductions for the month	3,860

11.   Given the following figures, calculate planned purchases for January:

Stock on hand - January 1	$36,470
Planned stock on hand - February 1	38,220
Planned sales for January	21,760
Planned reductions for January	410

Application Exercises

1.   Contact a local buyer of a line that interests you. If possible, do a full six-month merchandise plan for a specific merchandise classification. Utilize the text format for your process of planning. You will need to get information from the buyer. If such information is not available from the store, you may have to make certain assumptions to come up with your planned purchases.

2.   Attention is given in the text to formal merchandise planning. Select some stores and find out how they handle this function. How much planning? Levels of sophistication? Does the degree differ by merchandise lines? See if you can develop some generalizations from your investigations.

3.   Visit two competing supermarkets and list the SKUs in one product category (e.g., laundry detergents). Analyze the lists and prepare a short paper on the two supermarkets' apparent merchandising strategies.

Suggested Cases

25.   Betty's Fashions

26.   Roger's Department Store

Notes

1.   John Schreiner, "Dirty Tricks Alleged in B.C. Retail Showdown," *Financial Post*, August 5, 1995, p. 4.

2.   Sources include Canadian Tire, *Annual Report*, various issues, and John Lorinc, "Road Warriors," *Canadian Business*, October 1995, pp. 26–43.

3.   Loblaw Companies Limited, *Annual Report*, 1994.

4.   Marina Straus, "Private Labels Serve Up 'Dynamic Growth," *Globe & Mail*, September 21, 1995, p. B6.

5.   Sears Canada, *Annual Report*, 1994.

6.   Hudson's Bay Company, *Annual Report*, 1994.

7.   The term *variety* can also be used to describe the number of different merchandise lines that a store carries.

8.   The men's furnishings department would include all shirts, ties, underwear, etc., the planning can be in terms of classifications, or subdepartmental units, or for a

small department; but for illustration we will look at the sport shirt classification only as we are illustrating a procedure.

9. Obviously, dollars invested in inventory relate to width and support. In fact, the dollars planned become the controlling decision. How many dollars the retailer has will determine investment in SKUs. But planning width, depth, and dollars does not guarantee the optimal stock. Many of the questions about how well the planning is being carried out will be answered in Chapter 18.

10. Stock-to-sales ratios designate the amount of inventory necessary to support sales for a particular period of time (e.g., a month). This discussion assumes a going concern with last year's figures available. In a budget process for a new store, estimates/projections based on trade figures and/or experience are particularly valuable.

11. Readers may wonder why 4.7 times more dollars of inventory than sales are needed. This relates to the support factor. An example can help illustrate this point. If customers were individually predictable—that is, if retailers needed only one jacket to satisfy each customer's demand—then they might get by with a one-to-one ratio. But people want to select from many colours, designs, fabrics, and so on. Thus, retailers need many more SKUs to support planned sales. The more fashion oriented (or the less stable) the merchandise, the more stock is needed to support sales.

12. Chapter 18 discusses setting up a control system (open to buy) to measure how well the plan is working. Readers may want to look at that part of the book now.

Buying, Handling, and Inventory Management

Chapter Objectives

After reading this chapter you should be able to:

1. Identify factors influencing the buying cycle.

2. Calculate desired inventory levels.

3. Describe alternatives in the selection of merchandise suppliers.

4. Explain how retailers negotiate price, discounts, datings, and transportation charges.

5. Evaluate issues related to the management of physical handling activities.

6. Discuss the key issues in inventory records management.

7. Discuss problems associated with shoplifting and employee theft and preventive measures available.

Technology, starting with scanning equipment, is having a major impact on consumers, manufacturers, and retailers.

Courtesy Arthur Andersen & Co.

*T*echnology is having a major impact on the way that Canadian retailers manage buying, handling, and inventory. With the advent of high-powered computer systems, customized software, and electronic data interchange, retailers are reducing distribution and handling costs, improving merchandise selection for customers, and increasing inventory turnover.

A key element is the electronic link between the retailer and its suppliers. For example, Sobeys operates over 120 supermarkets in the Maritimes, Quebec, and Ontario. It has introduced Efficient Consumer Response (ECR), aimed at coordinating the operations of manufacturers, distributors, and retailers to improve efficiencies. The purpose of ECR is to eliminate inefficient processes that add nothing to the value of Sobeys' products and services and to develop programs in which the supplier, the customer, and Sobeys will win. The installation of an advanced electronic data interchange with key suppliers has led to paperless transactions, an electronic inventory replenishment system, and lower operating costs.

Sears Canada has re-engineered its entire merchandise procurement process from the initial ordering of merchandise to the receipt of goods in the selling unit or delivery to the customer. The objectives of this program are to improve customer service and in-stock position, increase inventory turnover, decrease costs and overhead, and reduce merchandise procurement cycle times. Implementation included the adoption of a supplier compliance program that supported the implementation of electronic data interchange, quick response, and just-in-time ordering systems.

These two examples reflect the impact of technology and the new partnerships being formed between Canadian retailers and their suppliers. By working more closely together, the two parties can improve customer value and reduce their costs, benefiting everyone.[1,2] ■

The buying function is critical to the success of any retail firm. Buyers can be viewed as investment specialists and can be responsible for millions of dollars in merchandise. They must forecast demand for the merchandise, negotiate with vendors on a variety of issues such as price and transportation, and work as partners with the vendors in the sale of the merchandise. As shown above, buying relationships are changing, and as new technology makes more and better information available to retailers, it will allow them to work with manufacturers and wholesalers in new and creative ways.

Goals of Good Buying

For people not acquainted with retailing, the work of a buyer may seem to be a relatively simple one—finding and purchasing the needed merchandise at a good price. But there is more to buying than bargaining with vendors. Not only are there other functions to consider, but good buying involves buying the right merchandise for customers at the best price, in the right quantity, of the right quality, and from vendors who will be reliable and provide other valuable services. Many considerations are involved in doing this thoroughly and competently. These are all described in the buying cycle (Figure 13–1).

The process of buying involves four major steps. They are:

1. *Determining needs.* The buyer must determine for each line of merchandise what will be needed until the next time the line is reviewed. Determining

Figure 13–1   The Buying Cycle

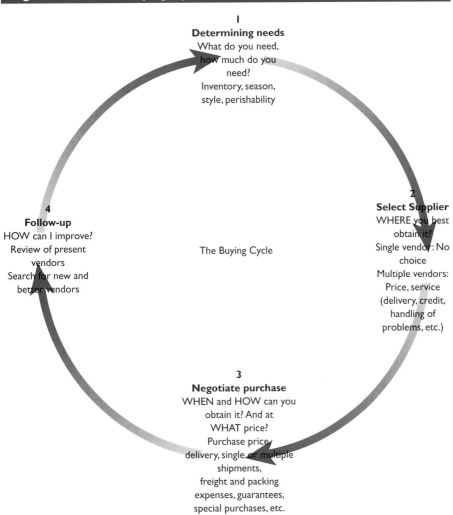

what is needed involves, for some items, merely looking at inventory and past sales. For other lines, it concerns risky decisions—*which* styles to select and *how much* of each to buy. One thing management does not want is a lot of merchandise in stock when a style is outmoded or the season is past.

2. *Selecting the supplier.* After determining the merchandise needs, the buyer must find a vendor(s) who can supply the merchandise. Some merchandise can be bought only from one vendor; in this case, the only decision to be made is whether to carry the line. For most merchandise lines, several suppliers are available. In these instances the buyer must evaluate price as well as service in terms of reasonable and reliable delivery, adjustment of problems, and help in emergencies and in other matters, such as credit terms, spaced deliveries, and inventory management assistance. For a

retailer like Canadian Tire, supplier selection is a major task as the company deals with more than 4,000 Canadian and international suppliers.

3. *Negotiating the purchase.* This crucial third step involves not only the purchase price but also quantities, delivery dates, single or multiple shipment deliveries, freight and packing expenses, guarantees on the quality of the merchandise, promotion and advertising allowances, special offers on slightly damaged materials or sellouts, and so forth.

4. *Following up.* Finally, to improve service, the buyer must review the relationship with each vendor from time to time to determine if changes should be made. If necessary, a search for alternate or new suppliers should take place.

Determining Needs

Different types of merchandise require different techniques to determine what is needed. It is therefore important to recognize, for the various merchandise lines in the store, whether they are primarily *staples, seasonal items,* or *style* and *perishable items.*

The goal in each case, whether the merchandise is primarily staple, seasonal, style oriented, or perishable, is to establish or maintain inventory at the lowest possible level and still have a sufficient variety of colours, sizes, or models available from which customers can choose. Such a practice will minimize losses due to obsolescence and spoilage, while freeing capital that may be put to other worthwhile uses.

Timeliness

Progressive retailers continue to refine the buying process, shorten lead times in ordering merchandise, maintain the minimum inventory level needed to meet customer needs, and have sufficient flexibility to quickly respond to changing customer tastes. These retailers have established faster buying than other retailers and are able to maintain less inventory than competitors, be more responsive to customer needs, and maintain higher gross margins than the norm.

Forecasting sales

Staples   **Staple** or semistaple **merchandise** is generally in demand year-round, with little change in model or style. Basic appliances, hardware, housewares, books, and basic clothing items like underwear and pyjamas fall into this category. Staples, even if the store is primarily focussed on seasonal fashion, generate extra profits and bring customers into the store who may then purchase some of the primary merchandise. Department stores, like Eaton's and The Bay, that focus much of their efforts on seasonal fashions would still have a large portion of their sales in staple or semistaple items.

The important characteristic of staples is steady usage. Deciding how much to buy, therefore, depends primarily on:

- *Sales trends.* Taken from records showing how much of each staple sold during the past two or three months, and also how much sold during the same period in the previous year. From this, the buyer can tell whether the

Table 13–1   Merchandise Item Record

Merchandise item:	Sales Record 1996	1997	1998	1999	2000
January	$ 0				
February	50				
March	700				
April	2,200				
May	1,000				
June	300				
July through December	0				
Total units bought	300				
Sold below cost	20				

item has increased in popularity or not and can then determine inventory levels based on this information.

- *Profitability.* Items that bring a better return on investment in space and capital are the more desirable items to buy.

- *Discounts.* These are usually available with quantity purchases.

The combination of these factors provides a general indicator of needs in staple merchandise.

Seasonal merchandise   **Seasonal merchandise,** as implied, is in demand only at certain times of the year. Obvious examples include sleds, snow tires, bathing suits, toys, sunglasses, lawn equipment, holiday greeting cards, and patio furniture. Although some seasonal items can be secured during peak demand to replenish inventory, many are unavailable or cannot be obtained quickly enough at this time. Therefore, such merchandise is bought well in advance of the season. Most clothing stores in Canada would have a seasonal component to their merchandise mix, reflecting the different clothes worn in the four seasons.

Forecasting needs for seasonal items relies heavily on *knowing* past customer demand for that item or merchandise line. One method is to maintain a month-by-month tally of units sold, either by dollar value or volume count. These records then can be examined on a yearly basis, enabling the buyer to identify selling trends and make buying decisions accordingly.

One method of maintaining records is to use a separate sheet or computer record for *each* merchandise *item, group of items,* or *entire line.* In the example shown in Table 13–1, note that in 1996 most of the sales on this item took place in April, and at the end of the season, the 20 remaining items in inventory had to be sold below cost.

No foolproof method exists for accurately predicting future sales, although a good prediction of future sales can be made by considering these factors:

- Past experience with the movement of the merchandise.

- Records of previous sales.

- Length of the season.

- Planned selling price.

- Planned advertising and promotion effort, including sales.

- The extent to which there is an increase or decrease in competition.
- Predictions of consumer buying from trade journals.

These factors together can give a fairly good idea of the quantity of each item likely to sell during the upcoming season.

Style and perishable items   Items of style include such merchandise as apparel and sportswear. Stylish items are usually more expensive than staples and seasonals. Because the demand for any particular style tends to increase rapidly, then drop off rapidly, overbuying can have a disastrous effect on profits. Once a style is "out," it is often difficult to sell at a profit.

Le Château, a specialty clothing chain with over 150 stores in Canada, has an interesting approach to forecasting and purchasing fashion merchandise. Using a reporting system that provides fast information on inventory and style performance, the company can identify and react quickly to trends in clothing style and colour. It then manufactures more of the items in its Montreal-based facility and uses the information in the design and buying of the next season's collections.[3]

Perishable merchandise has similar characteristics. If management buys more than can be sold, some of it will begin to spoil and bring only a fraction of the normal price.

Management can plot the progress of different styles to see how they usually behave. A few examples of such graphs are shown in Figure 13–2. They can help to predict how much to buy and when to buy.

When plotting graphs, it is important to note all special, significant events such as sales, including those of major competitors. These events also have to be planned or predicted and kept in mind when forecasting merchandise needs. These graphs may not predict sales very accurately, but they usually will narrow the amount of buying error.

Establishing buying guidelines

Determining the amount of stock that should be ordered is an important decision. In some cases, product shelf life may be the deciding factor. If the grocer stocked more than a two-days' supply of muffins, the muffins would lose their freshness and the grocer would lose customers. Delivery is immediate. The grocer gives the order directly to the bakery truck driver, and the driver fills the order in minutes.

More often, there are many other factors to consider. Take the case of the retailer who may require two weeks to receive delivery from suppliers on most items. On an emergency basis, the retailer may be able to replenish inventory more promptly, but only by forfeiting quantity discounts or incurring extra delivery charges. For most items, it is better to accept normal delivery, taking full advantage of all available discounts and minimizing freight charges. Lead time and needed levels of safety stock influence the amount or frequency of purchase.

Lead time   The length of time between order placement and receipt of goods is called **lead time.** If the lead time is two weeks, would it be sufficient to establish a minimum inventory level of a two-weeks' supply? Probably not. If no order were placed until the supply of a certain item reached two weeks, there would probably be just enough stock on hand to cover expected sales until the

Figure 13-2   Sales of Different Styles

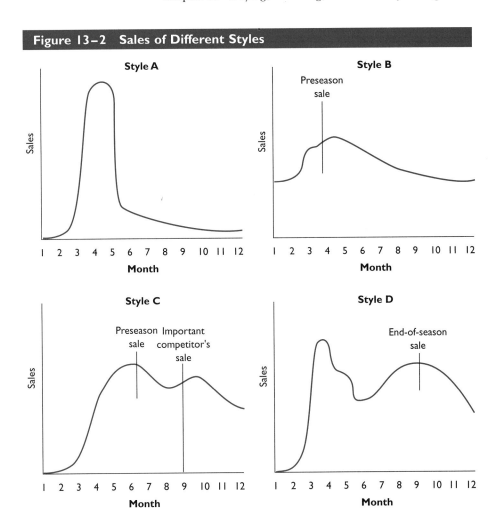

order arrived. However, if anything went wrong (and it usually does), there would be a stockout before the order was received. An unexpectedly large request from a customer might not be filled because of insufficient inventory. A strike, shipping delays, manufacturing problems, or unforeseen weather conditions could seriously delay the arrival of the merchandise so that the stockout could last for several weeks. Therefore, most businesses maintain a **safety stock** as protection against such occurrences. For many Canadian retailers who purchase merchandise from Europe and the Far East, lead times may be measured in months, not weeks. In these cases, the purchase of seasonal merchandise could be made up to six months before it is expected to go on sale.

Safety stock   The size of the safety stock will depend on the number and extent of the factors that could interrupt deliveries. Suitable guidelines have to be based on experience in the industry. Additionally, many items require a **basic stock,** an amount sufficient to accommodate regular sales, offering customers a reasonable assortment of merchandise from which their selection can be made.

For retailers selling perishable items, shelf life is important.

Photo by Betty McDougall

Assume that the lead time for a particular item is two weeks. The safety stock that the business wishes to maintain is a four-week supply. Additionally, a one-week basic stock is required. The desired inventory level would be established as the sum of these factors:

Lead time	2 weeks
+ Safety stock	4 weeks
+ Basic stock	1 week
= Inventory level	7 weeks

When to buy   The **order point** is the amount of inventory below which the quantity available should not fall or the item will be out of stock before the next shipment arrives. For example, if a camera shop wishes to maintain an eight-week supply of film as safety stock and lead time is two weeks, and average sales of a particular film type are 50 rolls per week, the order point is 500 (50×10 rolls). When inventory drops below 500 rolls, more film should be ordered.

How much to buy   The quantity of film to purchase depends on the usual time between orders, called the **order interval** (in the film example, assume the order interval is two weeks). In this way, sufficient supplies are maintained so that inventories between orders average out to the desired level.

A stock equal to expected sales during the camera shop's two-week order interval should be added to the order point to determine the **order ceiling.**

Order ceiling = Order point + Order interval sales

Order ceiling = 500 + (50×2)

Order ceiling = 600

An order quantity can then be determined as follows, assuming 450 rolls are on hand:

Order quantity = Order ceiling – Stock on hand

Order quantity = 600 – 450

Order quantity = 150 rolls

If an order for 50 rolls had already been placed, but had not yet been received, the present order should be *reduced* by the 50 rolls on order. The new order would then be 100 (150 – 50) rolls.

Review   Let us review the steps involved in establishing order quantities using a hardware store as an example. The store wants to maintain a basic tool stock equal to one week's sales and a safety stock of one week's sales for hammers. Average weekly sales are three hammers. Lead time for order placement and delivery is two weeks. Orders are placed every four weeks.

A desirable inventory level, or order point, is then calculated as follows:

Lead time	2 weeks
+ Basic stock	1 week
+ Safety stock	1 week
= Order point	4 weeks or 12 (4 × 3) hammers

Whenever the supply of any tool drops to a four-weeks' supply or below (i.e., 12 hammers), an order should be placed.

To determine the order quantity, management must first calculate the order ceiling:

Order point	4 weeks
+ Order interval	4 weeks
= Order ceiling	8 weeks or 24 (8 × 3) hammers

Assume that an order is being prepared for hammers. Average weekly sales are 3 hammers, and the stock on hand is 10 hammers. This is below the order point of 12 (4 × 3) hammers.

The order quantity would then be calculated as follows:

Order ceiling	24
– Stock on hand	10
= Order quantity	14

The hardware store should order 14 hammers. If any are already on order, the outstanding order quantity should be subtracted.

Information partnerships

Electronic data interchange (EDI), quick response (QR), and just-in-time (JIT) delivery are changing the way merchandise is ordered and shipped. New partnerships are emerging between retailers and vendors that are making the buying and replenishment process more timely and cost effective, as we discussed in the chapter introduction.

Ingredients   The ingredients of these emerging partnerships include the following:

- **Electronic data interchange.** EDI consists of software systems that allow for direct communication of standard business documents between retailers and vendors. Electronic sharing of information enables retailers and vendors to reduce reorder cycle times and speed delivery of replenishing inventory.

- **Just-in-time.** JIT systems are designed to allow delivery of only the quantity of a specific product needed at the precise time it is needed. For example, Eaton's might provide manufacturers with a six-month forecast of demand but a one-week lead time forecast of sizes, designs, and colours.

- **Quick response.** This is an information-sharing partnership between retailers and vendors (often manufacturers) that provides retailers with timely replenishment of inventory sufficient to meet customer demand without the necessity of carrying high levels of inventory in anticipation of customer demand. These partnerships will not work without a strong alliance between the vendor and the retailer. The level of trust and information sharing required in such relationships is very high.

QR consists of several interrelated technologies and partner initiatives. Six factors are considered essential:[4]

- Sharing inventory data among trading partners.
- Sharing sales and marketing data among trading partners.
- Using bar coding on packaging to track sales and inventory.
- Enabling customers to order through EDI.
- Managing stock replenishment for key customers.
- Using automated stock replenishment systems.

Although retailers such as Wal-Mart and Zellers have used it for several years, the system is becoming affordable and cost effective for small and medium-sized retailers and manufacturers.

Quick delivery and rapid merchandise turns provide several benefits. They can ensure both a high level of profitability and a low level of stockout, the most desirable dimensions of an inventory strategy. Short lead times can also ensure that the merchandise is more likely to be fashionable and, for perishables, fresh. Shorter lead times can help the retailer influence the size, colour, and style mix closer to the fashion season.

Large companies such as Canadian Tire link their databases directly to the manufacturers of the merchandise. Small manufacturers and independent regional retailers typically link through third-party providers, such as Transcare Supply Chain Management of Toronto. Either way, the results are improved efficiency, stronger relationships, and higher profits for suppliers and retailers alike.

For suppliers, EDI provides added service to retailers—a step beyond the usual merchandising, order-taking, shipping, and billing process. It strengthens the bonds between the companies as the suppliers become more important players in the retailers' merchandising plans.

For sales reps, it eliminates the tedium of frequent order taking and paper shuffling, which in turn enables them to focus on presenting new and special products and promotions, learn more about their customers by developing stronger interpersonal relationships, meet each customer's special needs, and call on more customers.

For retailers, it provides added efficiency and effectiveness. It enables them to serve their customers better by ensuring adequate, reliable stock. It also improves profitability by increasing stock turns and minimizing stock of slow items. For small retailers, the system relieves the mathematical drudgery of estimating turnover, forecasting demand, and determining economic order quantities.

Finally, it frees everyone to concentrate on business activities other than inventory maintenance. It clearly shows how improved marketing improves other business functions.

Selecting Suppliers

The first step in supplier selection is to obtain a list of those to consider. Awareness of available suppliers and their services will place the buyer in a position to choose the best one.

Sources of information concerning suppliers are plentiful. They include:

1. *Salespeople.* Salespeople of existing suppliers often provide excellent information concerning possible sources of supply. Many are well informed of alternative sources of noncompeting lines, and they can often suggest new services and new products. Salespeople are also a good source of information concerning merchandise selection practices of similar stores in different parts of their territories.

2. *Trade magazines.* General and specialized trade journals often contain advertisements placed by suppliers and articles that provide clues to desirable new sources. For example, the *Canadian Grocer* carries ads for new supermarket products.

3. *Business contacts.* Customers or other business contacts may be able to provide useful information concerning potential suppliers.

4. *Trade exhibits.* These provide an excellent opportunity to see a variety of new products and compare similar products of different manufacturers. A host of trade shows are held in Canada ranging from grocery products to children's fashion wear to hardware, housewares, and home improvements.

5. *Yellow Pages.* The Yellow Pages in the telephone directory contain listings of local suppliers.

How to make vendor contacts

Vendor contact may begin through catalogues and price lists. These documents are available to all potential retailers. Another source of vendor contact is the sales representative who calls on the retailer. In such lines as groceries and drugs, where item turnover is very fast, salespeople may call on the retailer almost weekly. For fashion lines, the representative will call on a seasonal basis.

Another source of vendor contact is a central market, a place where a large number of suppliers concentrate. Because of the close proximity of the United States, many Canadian retailers will visit central markets such as New York for women's fashion goods and High Point, North Carolina, for furniture. Some merchandise, as noted previously, may be purchased directly from the manufacturer. Most of the large Canadian chains will purchase a substantial portion of their merchandise on a direct basis.

Supplier evaluation criteria

Factors to be considered in determining the best supplier are: price and discounts, quality, reliability, services, and accessibility.

1. *Price and discounts.* Price is the most important consideration in the selection of a supplier, provided that quality and service are equivalent to that of other vendors. Price has many dimensions since it includes quantity discounts, special allowances, the chance to buy special lots, seconds, or sellouts, and dating of invoices.

2. *Quality,* and assurance of consistent quality, is almost as important as price and closely linked to it. Obviously, in selecting a supplier buyers want to be certain that they will rarely, if ever, receive a poor-quality shipment.

3. *Reliability* of delivery from a supplier is important as unreliable delivery can create problems of stockout, which result in lost sales. In addition, slow or unreliable delivery also requires the buyer to maintain larger average inventories, which results in increased carrying costs. A good supplier will be reliable when the store has a sudden emergency and needs some quick supplies and will protect the store when there are shortages of material due to a strike or disaster.

4. *Services* suppliers might provide are many and include spacing of deliveries that allows the buyer to purchase a larger quantity than the store may immediately handle, thus giving the advantage of quantity discounts; recycling of packaging to reduce overall freight and packing expenses and to help protect the environment; providing advertising and promotional materials and displays to help promote merchandise; and giveaways, such as literature and bags for the customers.

5. *Accessibility* is another factor on which suppliers should be judged. It is often important to contact the supplier concerning special problems that may arise. A supplier who is difficult to contact is clearly not as desirable as one easy to reach.

Methods of buying

Group buying

Group, or cooperative, buying is the joint purchase of goods by a number of noncompeting, nonaligned stores such as independent hardware stores in different areas of a province. By combining their orders into one large order, the stores hope to get lower prices. These group arrangements can be beneficial in other ways, too, because the noncompeting buyers can share knowledge about markets, fashion trends, and so forth.

There are disadvantages to group buying. Members of the group give up some of their individuality, which they may not want to do. Fashion merchants, particularly, find cooperative buying difficult because they feel their customers are unique.[5]

In Canada, buying groups have been formed by independent sporting goods stores (Sports Distributors of Canada), grocery and convenience stores (Distribution Canada), and drugstores (Drug Trading Company). For many of these independents, the buying groups provide the opportunity for volume discounts and are an important source of merchandise and marketing information.

Retail Highlight 13–1

What Makes Canadian Prices High?

A six-month, $400,000 study on cross-border shopping concluded that Canada has an inefficient distribution system that results in higher prices for consumer goods in Canada, relative to the United States. The study focussed on products that show marked price differences and are most often shopped across the border—clothing, appliances, bedding and linen, electronics, hardware, footwear and groceries, lumber and building products, sporting goods, and toys.

The study tracked 49 products as they moved from the manufacturer to store shelves on both sides of the border. It found prices in 40 of the 49 products were an average of 21 percent higher in Canada. The retail markup, for example, on a medium-priced men's dress shirt imported from Korea is $34.80, whereas a U.S. retailer takes a US$23.30 markup.

Three of the areas that lead to higher retail prices in Canada are:

- Canadian wholesalers are considerably smaller than their U.S. counterparts, which reduces their bargaining power with manufacturers. The problem is made worse by the high number of multinational subsidiaries that are forced to buy from their foreign parent at unfavourable terms.
- U.S.-made goods often pass through an additional level of distribution once they arrive in Canada, whereas U.S. manufacturers typically sell directly to major U.S. retailers.
- Manufacturers often charge more for identical goods that enter the Canadian distribution system because, for example, they face higher costs of doing business here or consider the domestic market less strategically important.

Among the recommendations contained in the report is the development of closer partnerships between suppliers and retailers to eliminate layers of bureaucracy and, as a result, lower costs. As well, the system should be examined to see if there are more efficient ways to operate using fewer middlemen.

Sources: John Heinzl, "What Makes Canadian Prices High?" *Globe & Mail*, May 15, 1992, p. B6, and Mark Evans, "Shopping Study Faults Mark-ups," *Financial Post*, May 15, 1992, p. 9.

Central buying

Central buying is most often practiced by chains such as Canadian Tire. As branch-store organizations grow in size, central buying is also logical for them. Central buying means that one person or department handles the buying of goods for all stores in the firm.

In firms where central buying occurs, most of the authority for buying lies outside any one retail outlet. In some firms, store managers are given limited authority to purchase locally produced items. For example, in a food store, locally grown produce might be bought by the local store instead of by the central buyer.

One of the major recommendations of a study on cross-border shopping was that Canadian retailers should band together in buying groups to increase their clout with manufacturers. The study found that grocery retailers have buying groups, which have resulted in a very efficient distribution system.[6] Retail Highlight 13–1 provides a summary of the study.

Because they order in such large quantities, central buyers hope to get favourable prices. Zellers, with its 300-store chain, uses centralized buying to obtain excellent prices, which are necessary to support its price image.[7] Technology is important in central buying, as the buyer must have adequate and rapid information from individual stores. Canadian Tire is in the forefront of Canadian retailers who use technology to improve their buying practices (see Retail Highlight 13–2).

Retail Highlight 13–2

Technology Improves the Buying Process

Progressive retailers, like Canadian Tire, Eaton's, and Sears Canada, are linking both stores and vendors into a computer system that allows for buying and ordering without sending "paper" through the mail or fax machines. Called electronic data interchange (EDI), companies can trade and "talk" electronically and they can exchange business documents, like cheques, invoices, and purchase orders, for different transactions via computer on standard forms.

Canadian Tire has installed or converted more than 600 vendors to its EDI system. By the end of 1997, virtually all of Canadian Tire's 2,000 suppliers will be electronically linked to the retailer. The benefits of EDI include: (1) more efficient order processing, (2) saving time preparing and delivering purchase orders, and (3) reducing invoice errors.

Canadian Tire has more than 420 associate stores that can select and stock more than 44,000 items through EDI. With EDI, Canadian Tire has (1) reduced its inventory safety stock (saving five days lead time), (2) almost completely eliminated paper handling in its buying transactions, and (3) allowed buyers to take action immediately if there is a problem.

The EDI project leader for Canadian Tire has stated that EDI is a prerequisite for retailers and that success in the 1990s will depend on how you do it, not whether. EDI facilitates their Quick Response Strategy (a program to ensure faster delivery, reduce administrative expenses, and turn inventory faster), and that for an initial investment of 1.9 percent of sales, and an annual cost of

0.28 percent of sales, they are realizing a savings of 5.1 percent of sales.

Eaton's has used EDI to cut inventory and improve customer service. For example, Eaton's just carries samples of mattresses on the floor and holds no inventories. Eaton's mattress suppliers, such as Bedford Furniture, Simmons, and Serta, are linked to Eaton's through EDI. When an Eaton's salesperson sells a mattress, the order is electronically sent to the supplier and moved right into manufacturing. Orders arriving by 7 A.M. are ready by the end of the day.

Everything—from the individual item to the carton it's packed in—gets bar-coded. Input at Eaton's warehouse records receipt of the goods, and indicates which store or truck they're destined for. They also trigger an inventory update, and alert accounts payable. When it's time for payment there's no cheque issued. The money is simply put in the client's account on the correct date. There are no invoices, no bills of lading, no shipment notices, no receipt notices. When the supplier gets the order, nothing has to be re-keyed.

While the benefits to the retailer, like Canadian Tire and Eaton's, are clear, suppliers like Bedford Furniture also benefit. With EDI, Bedford devotes fewer resources to order processing and other administrative functions, makes fewer errors, does a greater volume of business using the same number of employees, and has happier customers.

Sources: Serge Fortier, "EDI Efficiency," *Retail Directions,* January/February, 1989, pp. 21-22; "EDI or Die," *Issues for Canada's Future,* June 1992; John Heinzl, "Canadian Tire Wants to Go On-Line," *Globe & Mail,* September 21, 1995, p. B10; and Sandy Fife, "E-Commerce," *Challenges,* Summer 1995, pp. 8–11.

Committee buying

Committee buying is a version of central buying. It is a way to achieve the savings of central buying while having more than one person share the buying responsibility. This type of buying is common in firms selling staples, such as hardware stores.

Consignment

In consignment, suppliers guarantee the sale of items and will take merchandise back if it does not sell. University and college bookstores often purchase textbooks on this basis. The retailer assumes no risk in such an arrangement. Merchandise from an unknown supplier or a high-risk item might require such an arrangement. If a buyer has overspent the assigned budget, consignment can be attractive. But the buyer must be aware that most vendors would not offer consignment if the goods could be sold any other way.

Leased departments

If retailers do not have the skills to operate a specialized area, they may choose to lease departments. Shoe, camera, jewelry, and optical departments, as well as beauty salons and restaurants, are often operated under lease arrangements. By leasing to an expert, the retailer can provide customers with specialized items without fear of failure caused by inexperience.

Negotiating the Purchase

A good relationship between buyer and vendor may be one of the most important assets of the retail business.[8] If a strong, friendly, yet professional, relationship exists with suppliers, negotiations can go smoothly. Of course, bargaining with vendors does not begin until the buyer is sure that the items are truly what are needed for the store.

The buyer should be prepared to sacrifice something during a negotiation. Then the buyer can ask the supplier, "What are you willing to give up?" Remember, the buyer is trying to get the best deal, while the vendor is trying to hold the price up to protect profits.

Buyers normally attempt to negotiate on the following elements; cost (list) price of the items, discounts, datings, and transportation charges.

Cost price (list price)

Suppliers typically provide retailers with a price list of the merchandise available for sale. These list prices form the starting point for negotiations. Whereas some suppliers are flexible in the negotiating process, other suppliers will not negotiate price.

Discounts

Even though identical list prices may be offered by various vendors, they may offer different discounts and different provisions as to who will be responsible for paying transportation charges. An understanding of these purchase terms is necessary to negotiate the best price.

Trade

A **trade discount** is a reduction off the seller's list price and is granted to a retailer who performs functions normally the responsibility of the seller.

A trade discount may be offered as a single percentage or as a series of percentages off list price. If the list price on a sport shirt is $14.95, with a trade discount of 40 percent, the retailer will pay $8.97 ($14.95 − $5.98). The $5.98 ($14.95 × .40) is the trade discount. The same buyer might be offered a similar sport shirt from another manufacturer at a list price of $14.95 less 30 percent, 10 percent, and 5 percent. The three discounts (30 percent, 10 percent, and 5 percent) offered by the manufacturer could be for advertising support, transportation charges, and other promotional activities. The net price in this case would be computed as follows:

$$
\begin{array}{rcl}
\text{List price} & = & \$14.95 \\
& - & 4.48 \quad (\$14.95 \times 0.30) \\
& = & 10.47 \\
& - & 1.05 \quad (\$10.47 \times 0.10) \\
& = & 9.42 \\
& - & 0.47 \quad (\$9.42 \times 0.05) \\
\text{Net price} & = & \$8.95
\end{array}
$$

An alternative way of calculating the net price in the example above is to use the *complement* of the discount percentages. In this case, the net price would be calculated as: $\$14.95 \times .70 \times .90 \times .95 = \$8.95$.

Quantity

A **quantity discount** is a reduction in unit cost based on the size of the order. Such discounts may be noncumulative, meaning the reduction is based on each order, or cumulative, meaning the reduction is computed over the sum of purchases for a specified period of time.

When deciding whether a quantity discount is worthwhile, the buyer must compare the money saved with the extra inventory carrying cost.

To determine the *value* of a quantity discount, use the following steps:

1. Determine the savings from the quantity discount.
2. Determine how much extra merchandise the store would have to carry in inventory, and for how long.
3. Multiply the average extra stock by the carrying charge (which is usually 20 to 25 percent) to obtain the additional cost of carrying the extra stock for a year.
4. Determine the additional carrying costs for the period of time it will take to work off the extra stock.
5. Compare the savings from the quantity discount with the cost of carrying the extra inventory and decide whether it is worthwhile to buy the larger quantity.

For example, if the buyer can save $500 by taking an extra $6,000 of merchandise into stock, and if it will take six months to work off the extra stock, the calculations are as shown below:

$$\text{Cost savings (discount)} = \$500$$

Extra inventory would be $6,000 in the beginning and zero six months later; therefore:

Average extra inventory	=	$3,000
Carrying costs of average extra inventory	=	$3,000 × 25% × ½ year
	=	$750 × ½ = $375
Actual savings	=	Cost savings – Carrying costs
	=	$500 – $375 = $125

Since the real savings from taking the discount would be only $125, this deal is worthwhile only if the store can work the extra inventory off in six months without getting stuck with any hard-to-sell merchandise.

Seasonal

A **seasonal discount** is a special discount given to retailers who place orders for seasonal merchandise in advance of the normal buying period.

Promotional allowance

Vendors offer a **promotional allowance** to retailers as compensation for money spent in advertising particular items. This discount may also be given for preferred window- and interior-display space for the vendor's products. One form of a promotional allowance is co-op advertising. A manufacturer will pay for up to 50 percent of a retailer's advertising costs for ads that promote the manufacturer's products. For example, appliance manufacturers will allow a retailer an allowance of up to 50 percent if the retailer devotes at least 50 percent of the space or time in the ads to the manufacturer's products.

Cash

A premium is often granted by the vendor for cash payment prior to the time that the entire bill must be paid. The three components of the cash-discount terms are: (1) a percentage discount, (2) a period in which the discount may be taken, and (3) the net credit period, which indicates when the full amount of the invoice is due. A **cash discount** stated as 2/10, n/30, means that the retailer must pay the invoice within 10 days to take advantage of the discount of 2 percent. The full amount is due in 30 days.

A cash discount may be taken in addition to a trade or another type of discount. Returning to the earlier example, assume an $895 net bill for 100 sport shirts and that the invoice is dated May 22. The retailer has 10 days to take the discount. Payment is due June 1 (9 days in May and 1 in June). If the invoice is paid within this time, the retailer will remit $877 instead of $895 ($895 × .02 = $18; $895 − $18 = $877). If the retailer does not discount the invoice, the bill must be paid in full by June 21.

The 2 percent in the example represents an annual interest rate of 36 percent. Why? The full invoice payment is due in 30 days. Since the 2 percent cash discount can be taken if the invoice is paid within 10 days, the discount is allowed for paying the bill 20 days earlier than necessary. Since there are 18 20-day periods in the year (using 360 days as a year), this comes to 36 percent annually (18 × 2 percent).

Datings

The agreement between vendor and the retailer as to the time the discount date will begin is known as dating.

Cash datings

Technically, if the terms call for immediate payment, the process is known as **cash dating** and includes COD (cash on delivery) or CWO (cash with order). Cash datings do not involve discounts.

Two reasons may cause a negotiation to include cash terms. First, the seller may have a cash flow problem and many insist on cash on delivery (or with the order) to meet the bills incurred in the processing or distribution of the goods. Second, the retail buyer's credit rating may be such that the seller will deal with the firm only on a cash basis.

Future datings

There are four main types of **future datings:** end-of-month, date-of-invoice, receipt-of-goods, and extra dating.

- *End of month (EOM).* If an invoice carries EOM dating, the cash and net discount periods begin on the first day of the following month rather than on the invoice date.

- *Date of invoice (DOI).* DOI, or ordinary dating, is self-explanatory. Prepayments begin with the invoice date, and both the cash discount and the net amount are due within the specified number of days from the invoice date.

- *Receipt of goods (ROG).* With ROG datings, the time allowed for discounts and for payment of the net amount of the invoice begins with the date the goods are received at the buyer's place of business.

- *Extra.* Extra datings allow the retailer extra time to take the cash discount.

Transportation charges

The final aspect of negotiation relates to who will bear the responsibility for shipping costs. The most favourable terms for the retailer are *FOB (free-on-board) destination.* In this arrangement, the seller pays the freight to the destination and is responsible for damage or loss in transit. A more common shipping term is *FOB origin,* which means the vendor delivers the merchandise to the carrier, and the retailer pays for the freight.

Small retailers typically do not have the power to bargain with a vendor on discounts or the transportation charges. On the other hand, large retailers may be able to obtain price concessions from the supplier by bargaining on discounts even though the list price of the merchandise does not change.

Follow-up

The last step in the buying cycle is follow-up. Follow-up consists of continuous checking to find more desirable suppliers, merchandise, and buying and merchandise control practices.

Finding better suppliers can be accomplished only by getting to know existing suppliers and being alert to information sources on new ones who may come into the market. Improving merchandise selection is a matter of merchandise management, as discussed in Chapter 12. Better buying practices evolve from experimentation with improved methods whenever a problem appears.

Lastly, maintaining good merchandise control practices, as described below, will ensure success while operating within the buying cycle.

Two tasks remain to ensure success while operating within the buying system. The first is to develop an effective merchandise handling system and the second is to design a good inventory management system. Each is discussed in turn.

An effective merchandise distribution system in a multiunit retail organization can be an important element of competitive strategy and can have a positive impact on profitability. The first part of the next section focusses on **merchandise distribution**—getting merchandise from consolidation warehouses/distribution centres to the individual stores. The second part focusses on the physical handling aspect of merchandise management, including the receiving, checking, and marking of goods.

Merchandise Handling

Merchandise distribution in multiunit organizations

Some multiunit retailers operate under a system of direct store delivery (DSD), whereby merchandise is shipped from vendors directly to the individual stores in the chain. The possibilities of direct store deliveries have received increasing attention among multiunit retailers as a result of the efficiencies of vendor marking and electronic data interchange (EDI) between vendors and retailers. With EDI and vendor marking in place, stores do not have to do any checking or ticketing of goods. Shipments arrive in floor-ready condition, so goods can flow directly from the receiving dock to the selling floor. Disadvantages to DSD for some retailers may be additional payroll costs, increased transportation costs, and lack of receiving facilities at the stores.

Many chain operations, however, employ a merchandise distribution system involving the use of consolidation warehouses or distribution centres. Merchandise is shipped from vendors to the retail chain's distribution centres and from there is redirected to the individual store units. Many of these centres are computerized and highly automated, using the most recent innovations in merchandise handling and moving equipment including automatic guided vehicles and computerized sorting systems.

Multiunit retailers, like Canadian Tire and Wal-Mart, are also using a new distribution approach called cross-docking. For example, with cross-docking, designated products on incoming trailers to Canadian Tire's main distribution centre are immediately loaded onto scheduled outbound trucks taking shipments to the individual stores. Cross-docking effectively reduces handling costs by eliminating the typical storage and retrieval of goods.[9]

Advantages of using highly automated, computerized, distribution centres include more effective inventory control and merchandise reordering, more rapid movement of merchandise to increase turnover and margins at the stores, and cost efficiencies. The specific advantages resulting from retailers' implementation of distribution technology include the following benefits.

Operating efficiencies and cost reduction   Developing effective distribution systems can be an important factor in helping a retail firm lower its cost structure, which, in turn, leads to lower prices and higher levels of profitability.

Faster movement of merchandise   Retailers are finding that the speed with which they respond to change in the market—the **cycle time**—is a critical element in being more competitive. Highly automated, computerized distribution centres enable faster movement of merchandise to the individual stores, which results in higher sales and margins.

Loblaws' has developed its own efficient distribution system.

Courtesy Loblaw Company Ltd.

Greater accuracy   Common errors in multiunit organizations include individual stores' receiving the wrong merchandise from the distribution centre, or receiving the right goods but in the wrong quantities. Chains using a computerized system allow individual stores to know exactly what is on the way from the distribution centre before it arrives at the stores. These systems not only provide greater accuracy in the movement of goods to individual stores but also lead to reduced paperwork and labour savings at the store level.

Physical Handling Activities

As noted, **physical handling** involves receiving, checking, and marking merchandise. Although these activities are often performed in distribution centres, the following sections focus on these activities being performed in the retail store.

The receiving activity

Receiving is that phase of physical handling in which the retailer takes possession of the goods and then moves them to the next phase of the process. When the goods reach the store, packing cartons are inspected for damage. After the cartons are opened, individual packages in the cartons must also be inspected for damage. A receiving record must also be prepared. This record normally includes date and hour of arrival, weight, form of transportation, number of cartons, receiving number, invoice number, condition of packages, delivery charges, name of deliverer, amount of invoice, and department ordering the goods.

To ensure the effectiveness of the receiving department, the retailer must determine the most efficient methods for performing specific operations and then standardize these methods. In determining layout, management should plan for the straight-line movement of materials with as little backtracking as possible and the shortest distance possible. An attempt should be made to maximize machine operations and minimize hand operations. Sufficient equipment and standby equipment must therefore be purchased. Personnel working in the receiving area should be carefully selected, trained, and provided with adequate supervision. Finally, enough records must be maintained for control purposes.

The checking activity

Checking involves matching the store buyer's purchase order with the supplier's invoice (bill), opening the packages, removing the items, sorting them, and comparing the quality and quantity of the shipment with what was ordered. Let us focus on the activities of quality and quantity checking.

Quality checking

The decision to "check or not to check" for quality resides with the buyer. When quality checking is considered to be important, the responsibility is assumed by the buying staff. Remember—buyers are merchandise specialists; checkers are not.

Quantity checking

The two basic methods of quantity checking are:

1. The **direct check.** The shipment is checked against the vendor's invoice. The goods under this system cannot be checked until the invoice arrives. This method can result in items accumulating in the checking area if invoices have not arrived.
2. The **blind check.** This system is designed to avoid carelessness and merchandise accumulation problems associated with the direct check. The checker lists the items and quantities received without the invoice in hand. The system is slower than the direct check, because the list prepared by the checker must then be compared to the invoice.

The marking activity

Marking is putting information on the goods or on merchandise containers to assist customers and to aid the store in the control functions.

Various methods are used for establishing the price information to be marked on the goods. One common method is **preretailing.** Under this system, the buyer places the retail price on the store's copy of the purchase order at the time it is written. The buyer may also **retail the invoice.** In this practice, the buyer places a retail price on the copy of the invoice in the receiving room.

Goods can be marked either within the store or by a vendor. In **source marking,** the vendor rather than the retailer marks the merchandise. Source marking involves the use of codes such as the Universal Product Code (UPC). This technology was discussed in detail in Chapter 2. The remainder of the chapter discusses various aspects of the inventory management system.

Inventory Management

To manage inventory successfully, management should maintain accurate and up-to-date records of sales and stock on hand for every item. Inventory records tell you what you have. Sales records tell you what you need. Inventory records are used for making the following decisions: (1) purchases for inventory replenishment, (2) scrapping or clearing of obsolete items that are no longer in demand, and (3) addition of new items to inventory.

Electronic data processing

Although some retailers may use a manual inventory control system, with the advent of inexpensive microcomputers and software packages, the vast majority of retailers use some form of electronic data processing system. The system records all transactions and keeps a continuous record of changes in inventory. The system also prepares a sales summary. This information is needed for determining the adequacy of inventories and for order preparation. The sales summary can be compared periodically with stock on hand so that items that are not showing sufficient sales activity can be cleared through price reductions, scrapped, or otherwise disposed of. In this way, space and dollars invested in inventory are available for more active and potentially more profitable items.

Physical inventory

A physical inventory should be taken periodically to be sure that the actual quantities on hand equal those shown on the inventory records. The inventory records must then be adjusted to reflect any difference between "physical inventory" and "book inventory," the quantities shown on the inventory records. The actual quantity of each item on hand must be counted and compared with that shown on the inventory records. Necessary adjustments should be made immediately.

Differences between book and physical inventory arise for many reasons. The most easily understood, of course, are shoplifting and employee theft. Any business naturally wants to maintain an inventory control system to detect this situation as early as possible. This is the topic of the final section of the chapter.

Other reasons for inventory shortages are somewhat more subtle but equally damaging, if not worse. For example, if receiving procedures are faulty, a receiving clerk may not be counting actual quantities received and comparing them with those on the vendor's packing list or invoice. If the quantity actually received is less than that invoiced to the store, management is paying for the difference.

Merchandise may be sold to customers without being billed to them, through oversight or carelessness. In these cases, management will take a loss equal to their cost of the product and also lose the profit they should have earned on the sale.

Clerks may be accepting customer returns of merchandise that are no longer saleable because of damage, stains, or packing defects. Management may be ignoring opportunities to return merchandise to vendors when it arrives in an unfit condition for resale.

Any of these factors can result in inventory shortages. Although most businesses take careful steps to guard against theft, relatively few adopt serious procedures for protection from inventory shortages caused by such factors as poor receiving procedures, poor billing procedures, and merchandise damage.

Controlling Shoplifting and Employee Theft

An important aspect of inventory management is controlling for merchandise shortages. As shown by many surveys, the main causes of shortages are shoplifting and employee theft. In one survey, retailers attributed approximately 80 percent of inventory shrinkage to employee theft and customer shoplifting, and 20 percent to poor paperwork control. It was estimated that in 1994 Canadian retailers lost $3 billion (over $8 million a day) to shoplifters ($1 billion), paperwork errors ($600 million), and employee theft ($900 million). In the previous two years, total merchandise shortages in Canada were estimated at $2.75 billion.[10] The following sections will focus on shoplifting and employee theft, how they occur, and what actions can be taken to control and prevent them.

Shoplifting

In Canada, shoplifting accounts for 1.84 percent of sales. It affects retailers' profits, so plans should be made to control shoplifting.

Controlling shoplifting

Time and money are better spent in preventing shoplifting than in prosecuting the offenders. There are several areas where retailers can take action to control shoplifting.

Educate employees   Retailers know that salespeople are the most effective tool against shoplifting. Management can do a number of things to use salespeople effectively as a way of reducing shoplifting. Here are five key points:[11]

1. *Create awareness and concern.* Managers must communicate their concern about shoplifting and keep employees constantly aware of the problem. For example, shoplifting and its effects should be discussed periodically at staff meetings.

2. *Provide employee training.* Salespeople will respond to shoplifting only when they feel comfortable in doing so. Thus, they need to be taught to recognize shoplifters and how to respond to the situation. Retail Highlight 13–3 provides some practical advice on how to recognize shoplifters.

3. *Motivate salespeople to get involved.* Store managers should remind salespeople that shoplifters cost them personally. Salespeople must be aware that shoplifting affects their paycheque and benefits. Shoplifting makes the salesperson's job more difficult and diverts time from customers who are buying merchandise.

4. *Support the salesperson.* Salespeople need to know they are not alone in controlling shoplifting. Management needs to support salespeople's efforts by giving them the tools and devices they need to detect shoplifters and by providing backup assistance when needed.

Retail Highlight 13–3

How to Recognize Shoplifters

Be on the lookout for customers carrying concealment devices such as bulky packages, large pocketbooks, baby carriages, or an oversized arm sling.

Be on the lookout for shoppers walking with unnatural steps—they may be concealing items between their legs.

Employees should be alert to groups of shoppers who enter the store together, then break up and go in different directions. A customer who attempts to monopolize a salesperson's time may be covering for an associate stealing elsewhere in the store. A gang member may start an argument with store personnel or other gang members or may feign a fainting spell to draw attention, giving a cohort the opportunity to steal merchandise from another part of the store.

Shoplifters do not like crowds. They keep a sharp eye out for other customers or store personnel. Quick, nervous glances may be a give-away.

Sales help should remember that ordinary customers want attention; shoplifters do not. When busy with one customer, the salesperson should acknowledge waiting customers with polite remarks such as, "I'll be with you in a minute." This pleases legitimate customers—and makes a shoplifter feel uneasy.

Salespeople should watch for a customer who handles a lot of merchandise, but takes an unusually long time to make a decision. They should watch for customers lingering in one area, loitering near stockrooms , or other restricted areas, or wandering aimlessly through the store. They should try to be alert to customers who consistently shop during hours when staff is low.

---

5. *Show appreciation.* Salespeople need positive feedback; they need to know that their efforts are meaningful and recognized by management. Salespeople should be provided with periodic information on progress being made toward controlling shoplifting. Individual performance should be recognized by certificates of merit, monetary awards, notations on personal evaluations, and similar means.

Plan store layout with deterrence in mind   Retailers should maintain adequate lighting in all areas of the store and keep protruding "wings" and end displays low. In addition, display cases should be set in broken sequences and, if possible, run for short lengths with spaces in between. Small items of high value (e.g., film, cigarettes, small appliances) should be kept behind a counter or in a locked case with a sales clerk on duty. Display counters should be kept neat; it is easier to determine if an item is missing if the display area is orderly. If fire regulations permit, all exits not to be used by customers should be locked. Noisy alarms should be attached to unlocked exits. Unused checkout aisles should be closed and blocked off.

Use protective personnel and equipment   Protective devices may be expensive, but shoplifting is more expensive. Table 13–2 presents information related to retail use of shrinkage control devices. The table shows frequency of use of selected devices as well as the effectiveness of the devices according to retailers.

Electronic tags are judged by retailers to be the most effective protective device. Retailers using such devices, however, should be sure that salespeople and cashiers are diligent in their use. If an employee forgets to remove the tag and the customer is falsely accused, the retailer could be held liable.

Table 13–2 Shrinkage Control Devices		
Devices by Frequency of Use	**Devices Judged to Be Most Effective**	**Devices Judged to Be Least Effective**
Mirrors	Electronic tags	Mirrors
Limited-access areas	Guards	Visible TV cameras
Lock-and-chain devices	Point-of-sale systems	Guards
Guards	Observation booths	Observation booths
Point-of-sale systems	Visible TV cameras	Concealed TV cameras
Observation booths	Fitting-room attendants	Lock-and-chain devices
Electronic tags	Limited-access areas	Fitting-room attendants
Visible TV cameras	Lock-and-chain devices	Limited-access areas
Concealed TV cameras	Concealed TV cameras	Point-of-sale systems
Fitting-room attendants	Mirrors	Electronic tags

Source: *6th Annual Study of Security and Loss Prevention Procedures in Retailing 1984* (New York: National Mass Retailing Institute and Arthur Young, 1984), p. 18.

Guards are also considered by retailers to be powerful visual deterrents to shoplifters. Although mirrors are the most frequently used device, they are judged by retailers to be the least effective. The nearest runner-up in lack of effectiveness is visible TV cameras.

Apprehending, arresting, and prosecuting shoplifters

To make legal charges stick, retailers must be able to: (1) see the person take or conceal the merchandise; (2) identify the merchandise as belonging to the store; (3) testify that it was taken with the intent to steal; and (4) prove the merchandise was not paid for.

If retailers are unable to meet all four criteria, they leave themselves open to countercharges of false arrest. False arrest need not mean police arrest; simply preventing a person from conducting normal activities can be deemed false arrest. Furthermore, any physical contact, even a light touch on the arm, may be considered unnecessary and used against the retailer in court.

It is wisest to apprehend shoplifters outside the store. The retailer has a better case if it can be demonstrated that the shoplifter left the store with stolen merchandise. Outside apprehension also eliminates unpleasant scenes that might disrupt normal store operation. However, retailers may prefer to apprehend a shoplifter inside the store if the merchandise involved is of considerable value or if the thief is likely to elude store personnel outside the store premises. In either case, one recommended procedure is for store employees to identify themselves, then say, "I believe you have some merchandise you have forgotten to pay for. Would you mind coming with me to straighten things out?" Many Canadian retailers are taking a more aggressive stance and are prosecuting all shoplifters to reduce this cost.

Employee theft

Employee theft is a major problem facing retailers. One study revealed that the large majority of dishonest employees steal only occasionally. The study also found that 10.6 percent of dishonest employees steal at a weekly frequency or more and that these individuals are responsible for nearly 79 percent of total theft incidents.[12] In Canada, on average, employees steal around $200 worth of merchandise in each incident.[13]

How do employees steal?

Discount abuse is the leading form of retail theft by employees. Most frequently, employees will purchase merchandise for friends and relatives who are not eligible for a discount. The amounts of merchandise purchased often exceed limits set by company policy. Employees may purchase merchandise at a discount and then have it returned by a friend for full value. Some employee theft may be carried out in collusion with customers (who are acquaintances), or with a vendor. Theft of merchandise and cash can also occur.

Because of the magnitude of the problem, retailers must establish prevention and detection procedures for controlling employee theft.

Controlling employee theft

Some of the ideas discussed earlier for controlling shoplifting, such as use of guards and detection devices like mirrors and TV cameras, also serve to detect and prevent employee theft. This section thus looks at some of the things retailers are doing specifically to control employee theft.

Obviously the greatest deterrent to internal theft is to hire honest people. Traditionally, retailers have used the polygraph in employee screening. Now, however, they are turning to written honesty tests and better background checks because of some controversy surrounding the use of polygraph tests. Some retailers are using the Reed report, which consists of 90 psychologically oriented questions whose yes/no answers classify a person as prone or not prone to theft.

Another way to reduce employee theft is to run awareness programs. Such programs show how employees can hurt themselves by stealing. Through awareness programs, management points out the store's policy on dealing with employee theft and how important honesty is to job security and to a good reference when an employee changes jobs. Letting employees know that management cares about them is an effective way to prevent theft.

Peer pressure and use of a reward system can be effective. For such a system to work, however, management must assure employees that confidentiality will be respected and anonymity ensured—that their efforts in helping catch employee thieves will not place them in danger of termination, retaliation, lawsuits, or reputation as a "snitch."

Other deterrents to internal thievery include use of (1) employee identification badges; (2) restriction on employee movement within the store before, during, and after selling hours; (3) regular internal audits; (4) surprise internal audits; and (5) tight controls over petty cash, accounts receivable, payroll, and inventory.[14]

Chapter Highlights

- **The buying cycle consists of determining needs, selecting suppliers, negotiating purchases, and following up after the purchase. Buyers face different problems depending on whether the merchandise bought is primarily staples, seasonal items, or style or perishable items. The goal in each** instance is to establish or maintain inventory at the lowest level and still have a sufficient assortment from which customers can choose.

- The primary factors influencing the level of staples to be purchased include sales trends, profitability on various items, and discounts available. One way to establish buying levels for style and perishable items is to plot the sales of different styles in the past to see how they typically behave and use the resulting information as a guide in future purchasing decisions.

- A variety of factors determine desired inventory levels and when stock should be ordered. Product shelf life may be the determining factor for some items. The length of time between order placement and receipt of goods is also important. Most businesses maintain a safety or cushion stock as a protection against variation in demand and delivery.

- Merchandise suppliers can be identified by using salespeople, trade magazines, business contacts, trade exhibits, and the Yellow Pages. Factors to be considered in determining the best supplier include prices and discounts, quality, reliability, services, and accessibility.

- Technology is having a major impact on the buyer-seller relationship, including closer relationships and more effective ordering and distribution of merchandise. Electronic data interchange (EDI) and quick response (QR) mechanisms are at the heart of the emerging retailer-vendor relationships today. The application of such techniques has led to shorter lead times in merchandise delivery, and less on-hand inventory because of rapid replenishment schedules, especially for staples.

- The physical handling process involves receiving, checking, and marking merchandise. Receiving is that phase of the physical handling process that involves taking possession of the goods and then moving them to the next phase of the process. Checking means matching the store buyer's purchase order with the supplier's invoice, opening the packages and removing the items, sorting them, and comparing the quality and quantity of the shipment with what was ordered. Marking is putting information on the goods or on merchandise containers.

- Successful inventory management requires retailers to maintain an accurate and up-to-date record of sales and stock on hand for every item they sell. A physical inventory should be taken periodically to be sure that the actual quantities on hand equal those shown on the inventory records.

- Shoplifting is a very large monetary crime in Canada. Retailers, however, can take a number of actions to detect and prevent shoplifting.

- Employee theft is also a major problem retailers face. Because of the magnitude of the problem, retailers must establish prevention and detection procedures for controlling internal theft.

Key Terms

basic stock 359
blind check 373
cash datings 370
cash discount 370
checking 373

cycle time 371
direct check 373
future datings 370
lead time 358
marking 373

Discussion Questions

1. **Discuss the roles and responsibilities of a buyer.**

2. **Discuss each element of the buying cycle.**

3. **Describe the different methods of buying.**

4. **Explain the types of discounts available to retailers.**

5. **Explain the types of datings available to retailers.**

6. **What are the most favourable transportation terms for the retailer? Explain your answer.**

7. **Explain the two methods of quantity checking.**

8. **What are the various types of shoplifters? What can retail managers do to control shoplifting? What can retail managers do to control employee theft?**

Problems

1. A manufacturer of tables offers terms of 2/20, n/60. A furniture store places an order for a dozen tables at $27 each and receives an invoice dated July 2. The invoice is paid August 10. Failure to obtain the discount is equivalent to paying what annual rate of interest? (Use 360 days as a year.)

2. An invoice dated June 5 in the amount of $1,800, with terms of 3/10, n/30, EOM, and a trade discount of 20 percent, arrives with the merchandise on June 8. The invoice is paid July 2. What amount is due the vendor?

3. An invoice dated January 3 in the amount of $12,200, with terms of 2/10, n/30 ROG, and a trade discount of 10, 5, and 2 percent, arrives with the merchandise on January 10. The invoice is paid January 30. What amount is due the vendor?

4. A manufacturer of women's blouses quotes terms of 2/20, n/30, and grants retailers trade discounts of 10 and 5 percent. The list price of a blouse is $140 per dozen. A retailer receives an invoice dated July 7 for eight dozen of these blouses. The invoice is paid July 10. What is (*a*) the net cost per blouse and (*b*) the net amount of the cash discount taken?

5. A manufacturer of women's skirts quotes terms of 2/10, n/30 EOM, and grants retailers trade discounts of 10, 5, and 2 percent. The list price of the skirts is $360 per dozen. A retailer receives an invoice dated September 16 for 10 dozen of these skirts. The invoice is paid October 2. What is the net cost per skirt to the retailer?

Application Exercises

1. To clarify the relationships between the buyer and the supplier, the text approaches the subject from the retail point of view. It may be valuable to approach the subject from the other point of view. Make contacts with local suppliers (wholesalers, agents, or local manufacturers who sell to retailers), and see what they attempt to do to strengthen relationships with their customers. What problems do they incur in these relationships? What efforts do they make to "improve" the relationships?

2. Select a product line in which you are particularly interested. Identify merchants in your area who handle this line. Set up interviews after you have devised a questionnaire to determine how important the merchants believe relationships with suppliers are. Administer the questionnaire to the managers of the stores. Attempt to find out how these managers implement their philosophy of relationships with vendors. If you can get measurements of the various stores' success, see whether you can attribute some of that success to the "programs" for vendor relationships you discover. This will be a difficult project, but attempting to carry it out will be a beneficial experience, regardless of the outcome.

3. In interviews with retailers with whom you establish good rapport, attempt to find out (*a*) what special problems have been encountered with vendors; (*b*) what kinds of special "concessions" are offered to the retailers; (*c*) whether any particular plans have been effective in improving relations; and (*d*) why vendors are dropped.

Suggested Cases

27. The Lyon's Den

28. Ashley's

Notes

1. Empire, *Annual Report*, 1995; and Sears Canada, *Annual Report*, 1994.

2. For more on channel partnerships, see Robert D. Buzzell and Gwen Ortmeyer, "Channel Partnerships Streamline Distribution," *Sloan Management Review*, Spring 1995, pp. 85–96; and Mark Stevenson, "The New Computer Revolution: Canada's Smartest Corporations are Bonding with Their Customers," *Canadian Business*, September 1993, pp. 20–26.

3. Château Stores of Canada, *Annual Report*, 1994.

4. For more on quick response systems, see J.H. Hammond, "Quick Response in Retail/Manufacturing Channels," in S.P. Bradley, J.A. Hausman, and R.L. Nolan, *Globalization, Technology, and Competition* (Boston: Harvard Business School Press, 1993), pp. 185–214.

5. For more on the pros and cons of group buying, see Kenneth G. Hardy and Allan J. Magrath, "Buying Groups: Clout for Small Businesses," *Harvard Business Review*, September-October 1987, pp. 16–24.

6. John Heinzl, "What Makes Canadian Prices High?" *Globe & Mail*, May 15, 1992, p. B6.

7. Jay L. Johnson, "Zellers Fights Back," *Discount Merchandiser,* January 1996, pp. 24–30.

8. For more on negotiation, see Shankar Ganesan, "Negotiating Strategies and the Nature of Channel Relationships," *Journal of Marketing Research* 30, May 1993, pp. 183–203.

9. For more on Wal-Mart's use of cross-docking, see C.K. Prahalad and Gary Hamel, "The Core Competencies of the Corporation," *Harvard Business Review,* May-June 1990, pp. 79–97, and George Stalk, Philip Evans, and Lawrence E. Shulman, "Competing on Capabilities: The New Roles of Corporate Strategy," *Harvard Business Review,* March-April 1992, pp. 57–69.

10. John Heinzl, "Retailers Lose $2.4 Billion to Shoplifters, Employees," *Globe & Mail,* April 11, 1995, p. B13.

11. "Five Key Steps to Reducing Shoplifting," *Shrinkage Control,* September 1985, pp. 1–2; see also *Shrinkage Survey* (1985), Retail Council of Canada.

12. "Facts Continue to Show that Shoplifting Exceeds Employee Theft," *Shrinkage Control,* September 1987, p. 1.

13. John Heinzl, "Retailers Lose $2.4 Billion to Shoplifters, Employees," p. B15.

14. For more information on shrinkage protection, see Philip P. Purpura, *Retail Security and Shrinkage Protection,* Butterworth-Heinemann, Boston, 1993.

Retail Pricing Strategy

Chapter Objectives

After reading this chapter you should be able to:

1. Understand the role of price in the retailer's competitive strategy.

2. Discuss the store policies, consumer issues, and external factors that affect pricing decisions.

3. Understand a simple way to handle the arithmetic of pricing.

4. Discuss the kinds of price changes that may be made after the original pricing decision.

The battle for market share is reflected in the pricing strategies of Zellers, Canadian Tire and Wal-Mart.

Photo by Jim Hertel

In early 1994 when Wal-Mart, the world's largest discount retailer, entered the Canadian retail market, it brought a number of retail innovations to Canada including its use of technology, its distribution strategy, and its human resources policy. One key innovation was its pricing strategy, often considered the foundation of this retailer's success.

Since it began, Wal-Mart has followed an everyday-low-pricing (EDLP) policy. Unlike many other retailers who offer regular sales, Wal-Mart only marks down merchandise to clear it out at the end of the season. EDLP at Wal-Mart is to offer very competitive prices on most of the 80,000 items it carries, which may be slightly above or slightly lower than its discount store competitors.

However, Wal-Mart is always lower on the 500 to 600 items that are price sensitive—laundry detergent, paper towels, motor oil—products that consumers frequently purchase and know a bargain when they see one. On these items Wal-Mart will not be beaten and store managers are free to drop prices when they see a competitor underselling them.

Many consumers feel that everything is cheaper because the most frequently purchased products are discounted. When shoppers at discount stores are asked which discounter has the lowest prices, over 75 percent say Wal-Mart. As one retailing expert states, "The battle is won on perception. Most people perceive that Wal-Mart is a lot lower. It's a subtle thing." In Wal-Mart stores, prices are posted in black and yellow, the colour combination retail studies have shown to be the most eye-catching. Customers never have to pick up a product and search for a price tag.

Although its pricing strategy is just one element of Wal-Mart's overall strategy, it is a critical appeal aspect of this discounter's success. Pricing is also critical for its major competitors. Wal-Mart's entry into Canada led to retailers like Zellers and Canadian Tire lowering prices on thousands of products to maintain a competitive price image. Whether the competitors can master the Wal-Mart approach to pricing remains to be seen, but it will be a major weapon in the continuing battle for market share.[1,2] ■

The Wal-Mart example illustrates that its managers understand the important role price can play in a firm's competitive strategy and the need to make price decisions that support that strategy. Price decisions must be compatible with the overall marketing strategy for the firm.

Pricing Strategy

A retail pricing plan should start from explicitly defined objectives. For example, management must decide whether financial goals will be achieved by higher margins on merchandise and thus perhaps lower turnover, or lower margins and higher turnover. Various trade-offs are in order in such decisions. For instance, if management's objectives are short-run profit maximization, pricing should maximize cash flow. A policy of strengthening market position, on the other hand, probably would call for prices that are not above those of the market leader.

The absence of a distinct pricing policy often reflects a lack of strategic focus. For example, traditional department stores are being squeezed from both above and below their traditional market segments. They are being squeezed at the lower end by discount chains such as Zellers and Wal-Mart and at the higher end by specialty chains such as Holt Renfrew. In response, in the early 1990s Eaton's emphasized its everyday prices to be as good as or better than its competitors'— even their sale prices. Eaton's used the slogan "Why Wait for Sales" to focus on its competitive prices. This strategy was abandoned in the mid-1990s because consumers expected department stores to have sales and Eaton's returned to its previous strategy of using sales to attract customers.[3]

One way of relating price to competitive strategy is to differentiate among retailers that price above the market level, at the market level, and below the market level.

Pricing above the market level

Some firms price above the competition. Reasons that stores are able to follow this strategy include the following: they carry unique or exclusive merchandise; they cater to customers who are not price conscious and who want the

Holt Renfrew, a successful above-the-market retailer, focusses on consumers who value exclusive, quality merchandise.

Courtesy Holt Renfrew

highest-quality and style goods; they provide unusual services; they have a prestigious image customers are willing to pay for; they develop professional salespeople who are customer oriented and knowledgeable and who wish to develop long-term customer relationships; and they offer conveniences such as location and time.

Ziggys St. Clair Market in Toronto is an example of a merchant with above-the-market pricing. The firm caters to shoppers who want quality merchandise and personal attention. The store stocks an extensive selection of gourmet and specialty foods, employs more people than the average supermarket, and uses colour, lighting, and other design components to create an atmosphere unusual for a food store. Other examples of above-the-market retailers include Tilley Endurables and Holt Renfrew, both of whom offer exclusive, quality merchandise to customers who are not price conscious.

Pricing at the market level

At-the-market pricers offer prices roughly the same as their competitors. When following such a strategy, the retailer tries to make the store different in ways other than price and thus competes on a non-price basis. Department stores such as Eaton's and The Bay are examples of middle-of-the-road pricers. Typically, these types of retailers are willing to give up the top and bottom price points. The top price points require a level of expertise and acceptance of risks in high fashion that these retailers do not wish to pursue. The lower price points reflect merchandise quality levels below their standards and would require them to compete directly with discount stores. Other examples of at-the-market pricers are drugstores such as Shoppers Drug Mart and Pharma Plus.

IKEA uses effective cost-reducing strategies to keep prices low.

Courtesy IKEA

Pricing below the market level

Below-the-market pricers offer acceptable quality merchandise at low prices. Examples include off-price retailers, warehouse clubs, factory outlet stores, and discount houses. Competition in these operations is primarily on a price basis. Specific retail firms that are successfully emphasizing consistently low prices are Wal-Mart, Zellers, Home Depot, Toys "Я" Us, Business Depot in office products, and IKEA in contemporary furniture.

Below-the-market pricing is a difficult pricing strategy to carry out and maintain. To successfully implement such a strategy, the firm must focus on lowering its cost position. Many retailers have failed using this strategy because they have been unable to constantly monitor and adjust their cost components. To reduce costs, firms attempt to obtain the best prices possible for their merchandise; locate the business in an inexpensive location or facility; closely control inventory and limit the lines to fast-moving items; offer no or limited services; and, in general, monitor all cost components on a continuous basis to determine where cost savings can be realized. IKEA has even been highly successful in shifting a variety of cost burdens onto consumers. Shoppers select merchandise, pay for it at a central location, and then pick up the merchandise from a separate distribution area or select it from warehouse shelves. Often consumers assemble the product, like a bedroom set, themselves when they get it home.

While Zellers competes primarily on a price basis ("Where the Lowest Price is the Law"), it also provides a nonprice element to its core strategy. Zellers has Club Z, a customer loyalty program, in which members collect points based on purchases that can be redeemed for merchandise. This differentiates Zellers from the other discounters and offers consumers an additional benefit to continue shopping at Zellers.

Store Policies Affecting Retail Pricing

One-price versus variable-price policy

The majority of retail firms in Canada offer goods at one take-it-or-leave-it price. Bargaining with customers is unusual. In other countries, such as Mexico and Italy, varying prices with "haggling" are expected. In Canada, some stores selling big-ticket items such as automobiles, appliances, and furniture follow a variable-price policy and bargaining occurs over the price paid for the product. If this practice is usual and expected, consumers may form a negative view of retailers who do not engage in this bargaining process. However, many consumers appear to favour one price when it comes to buying automobiles and a number of automobile dealers have adopted a one-price policy.

Certain advantages exist in a store with a one-price policy. Customers do not expect to bargain, so salespeople and customers save time. Salespeople are not under pressure to reduce prices. Of course, self-service would not work where there is bargaining.

Retailers can follow a variable price policy even when they do not negotiate with consumers on the price itself. Negotiating over whether to charge for delivery and installation and varying the price of warranties can all result in a variable price policy.

Price-lining policy

Retailers practising **price lining** feature products at a limited number of prices, reflecting varying merchandise quality. A price-lining strategy can be implemented either in the context of rigid **price points** or more flexible **price zones.** Using suits as an example, the merchant might establish a limited number of price points to indicate quality difference between merchandise. The "good" suits might be priced at $175, the "better" suits at $225, and the "best" suits at $300. Alternatively, the retailer may decide to use "price zones" instead of rigid price points. For example, prices for good suits might fall between $175 and $200.

Price lining offers certain advantages. For example, some customers become confused and cannot make up their minds when they see too many prices. Price lining makes shopping easier for consumers, since there are fewer prices to consider. The merchant can offer a greater assortment of depth and width with fewer price points. In addition, inventories can be controlled more easily.

With price lining the salesperson can more easily become familiar with the merchandise. And it is much easier to explain differences between the merchandise when it is carefully planned and priced to show differences. In addition, the retail buyer may reduce the number of suppliers needed to provide merchandise in specific retail price ranges.

Certain disadvantages do exist in price lining. The retailer may feel "hemmed in" by the price line and lose some flexibility. Also, selection may be limited. If wholesale prices rise and fall rapidly, it may be difficult to maintain rigid price points. This is a reason for the use of price zones.

Leader pricing policy

In **leader pricing** the retailer takes a less-than-normal markup or margin on an item to increase store traffic. Some call this loss-leader pricing, implying a loss of the normal amount of markup or margin. In using leader pricing, the retailer is trying to attract customers to the store who will also purchase items carrying normal profit margins. Canadian supermarket chains, like Loblaws, Sobeys, and Safeway, use leader pricing to attract customers with the objective of having customers purchase all their grocery needs at the store. If customers only buy the "leaders," the retailer is in trouble. Thus, in selecting the leader item, retailers should choose products that will stimulate purchases of other, perhaps complementary, goods. For example, a food retailer may lower the price of ribs, which, in turn, might stimulate the sale of barbecue sauce, charcoal, starter fluid, and food products typically eaten with barbecued ribs. In a department store, using dresses as leaders might stimulate the sale of shoes, jewelry, and other accessories. Other characteristics of good price leader products are as follows:

- They are well-known and widely used items.
- They are items that are not usually bought in large quantities and stored.
- Such items have a high price elasticity of demand.
- They are priced low enough to attract many buyers.

Price discount policy

Retailers may offer a variety of discounts, such as cash discounts and frequent shopper discounts to attract and retain customers.

Cash discounts   Cash discounts can be profitable if retailers have (1) a high proportion of credit sales, (2) a high proportion of credit customers who are willing to pay by cash or cheque as a result of a discount, and (3) large ticket items or large volume purchases.

A variation of cash discounts is offered by Canadian Tire. If a customer pays cash or uses a Canadian Tire credit card for payment, the customer receives Canadian Tire "money" in proportion to the purchase. The "money" can be used to purchase merchandise at Canadian Tire stores. This tactic encourages customers to pay cash instead of using a Visa or MasterCard credit card, draws traffic to the stores, and provides an incentive for customers to return to the store and spend their Canadian Tire "money."

Frequent-shopper discounts

Some retailers are experimenting with frequent-shopper discounts, much like the frequent-flyer programs offered by the airlines, to generate greater sales volume and customer loyalty. Shoppers' cumulative purchases are tracked throughout the year and bonuses are offered after shoppers reach a specified dollar volume of purchase. Additional bonuses are sometimes given to stimulate shopping on slow days or to clear out slow-moving merchandise. Zellers, the discount department store chain, launched Club Z, a frequent-buyer program in 1986. It now has over six million members and Club Z is one of the most successful customer loyalty programs in North America. Sears Canada also has a large customer loyalty program with over four million members in its Sears

Club. In an interesting twist on customer loyalty programs, the Loyalty Management Group started the Air Miles co-op program. Consumers join the program and accumulate points when they purchase goods and services from retailers who participate in the program. The points can be used for air travel on several airlines, including Canadian Airlines. Sears Canada, along with other retailers including a supermarket chain and a bank, are participating in the program.[4]

Product and service issues

Retailers' pricing decisions are affected by type of products carried, brands carried, and services offered.

Type of products

One product issue affecting pricing decisions relates to whether the products offered by the retailer are primarily convenience, shopping, or specialty goods. The nature of the product carried affects a retailer's flexibility in establishing prices that are different from those of other retailers carrying the same goods. If products are viewed by consumers as convenience goods, prices do not vary greatly from store to store. Consumers do not believe it is worth their time to shop around for a better price (or quality) for convenience items because the savings are not likely to be worth the extra effort of comparison shopping. The retailer has only a little latitude in the pricing of convenience goods. A retailer has more leeway in setting prices for shopping goods. These are items for which consumers carefully compare price and quality differences before making a purchase decision. Finally, the retailer has the greatest latitude in pricing specialty goods. Specialty items are products consumers know they want and are willing to make an effort to acquire because they will not accept a substitute. To them, price is not particularly important.

Type of brands   Another product-related issue concerns the extent to which a retailer carries private brands and generics in addition to manufacturers' brands. Many retailers, such as Sears, Eaton's, Canadian Tire, The Bay, and Loblaws, have their own private brands (also referred to as dealer brands). Private brands are owned by the retail firm, rather than by a manufacturer. A private brand may be carried only by the owner or the owner's designee. A manufacturer's brand (often referred to as a national brand) may be carried by anyone who buys from the manufacturer of the brand. President's Choice is a private brand of coffee owned by Loblaws, Maxwell House is a manufacturer's brand owned by General Foods.

If private brands are featured, the retailer may offer them at prices lower than national brands and still make a good profit. This is possible because the retailer can pay less for the private brand merchandise than for comparable manufacturer brands. Consequently, the merchant has more freedom in pricing private-brand items.

Department stores, grocery chains, and some specialty retailers are increasingly turning to private brand merchandise as a source of competitive advantage, especially in the face of the challenges posed by off-price retailers. Private brands, such as Mastercraft at Canadian Tire, and President's Choice at Loblaws, are not subject to the price cutting that may occur with national brands.

Loblaws' private brand strategy includes a large selection of President's Choice products.

Courtesy Loblaw Company Ltd.

The question of generic merchandise and pricing is also important. **Generics** are "no-brand-name" goods. For example, if a supermarket offers generic paper products, the identification might read *paper napkins.* Customers may be willing to accept lower quality in some types of goods in return for lower prices. They rely on the reputation of the store and figure, If my supermarket has generics for sale, they must be OK for the price. More profits may be made on generics than on private brands, because even though generics are priced lower, they cost less to manufacture. Typically generics are produced at a lower cost than private brands or national brands because of economies of scale in manufacturing, lower-quality ingredients that reduce manufacturing costs, and reduced packaging costs. Generics are strongest in low-involvement merchandise such as paper products and other staples.

Loblaws pioneered no-name generic brands in Canada in 1978 and, at one time, during the early 1980s offered 1,500 private-label products. As the Canadian economy improved in the mid-1980s, consumers began switching back to brand names. Then Loblaws began introducing its own private label, President's Choice, in many product categories. As the economy declined in 1990, Loblaws began to reemphasize its generic "no-name" products and introduced Club Pack, products at reduced prices for large sizes. During 1991, at the height of the recession, sales of generics surged and represented almost 50 percent of Loblaws' private brand sales. This private-brand strategy offered four potential benefits for Loblaws: (1) to meet price-cutting with "no-name" and Club Pack, (2) to avoid the price-cutting that often occurs with national brands by maintaining President's Choice prices, (3) to position Loblaws as a store that offers consumers more variety ("no-name," Club Pack, President's Choice, G.R.E.E.N.), and (4) to gain greater control over distribution by selling more retailer brands (both private and generic). Loblaws continues to use private-brand strategy to compete against the warehouse clubs and discount chains.

Retail Highlight 14–1

Sam Walton on Price Elasticity

Sam Walton, called America's most successful merchant, built the Wal-Mart chain into a retail dynasty, based on a number of simple but powerful concepts like price elasticity. In his own words talking about his early days in retailing: "Here's the simple lesson we learned—which others were learning at the same time and which eventually changed the way retailers sell and customers buy

all across America. Say I bought an item for 80 cents. I found that by pricing it at a dollar I could sell three times more of it than by pricing it at $1.20. I might have made only half the profit per item, but because I was selling three times as many, the overall profit was much greater."

Source: "Sam Walton In His Own Words," *Fortune*, June 29, 1992, p. 100.

Consumer Issues Affecting Retail Pricing

A variety of consumer issues affect price decision making in retail operations. The following sections will focus on the issues of consumer demand and price sensitivity, price perceptions, psychological pricing, and consumer pressures.

Consumer demand and price sensitivity

Retailers must consider consumer reactions to different prices. In general, consumers will purchase more of a product at a lower price than at a higher price. Thus, the retailer needs to understand the effects of different price levels on consumer demand. Known as **price elasticity,** or the elasticity of demand, it is the ratio of the percentage change in the quantity demanded to a percentage change in price:

$$\text{Price elasticity} = \frac{\text{Percent change in quantity demanded}}{\text{Percent change in price}}$$

Elastic demand is a situation where the change in price strongly influences the quantity demanded (consumers are sensitive to price changes). For example, demand for many convenience products like soap and toothpaste is elastic; consumers will stock up on these items at a lower price. Inelastic demand is a situation where the change in price has little influence on the quantity demanded (consumers are relatively insensitive to price changes). For example, demand for gasoline tends to be inelastic because consumers typically do not increase or decrease their driving if the price of gasoline decreases or increases. Retailers should understand which products are sensitive, or not, to price changes (Retail Highlight 14–1).

Price perceptions

Consumer perceptions are important factors in establishing prices. For example, consumers have ranges of acceptable prices for products: prices outside the acceptable range—whether too low or too high—are objectionable. Demand provides not only an upper constraint on pricing decisions—pricing what the market will bear—but also a lower constraint. Cost-plus pricing may thus lead to a pricing error even if the price satisfies the cost and competition requirements. Optional price ranges are a function of market demand. Below certain price points, which vary widely from category to category, there is no elasticity of demand; lowering prices further does not have the classic effect of adding sales.

When buyers are given a range of prices they may choose the middle-priced item because it is perceived, relative to the other items, as a reasonably priced item. Retailers thus can influence the choice of products that are perceived as middle prices. In particular, retailers who use price lists or price catalogues can influence the price perceptions of consumers this way.

In judging prices, customers who find it difficult to compare the prices of individual items generalize from the overall price image of a store. Price images tend to be relatively stable, even in the face of special promotions. Management should thus consider not only the pricing of individual items but also the need for a favourable overall price image. A store may not need to place low prices on every item to have a "low-price" image; only certain key items need to be priced lower than expected. This was illustrated by Wal-Mart's strategy in the introduction to the chapter.

Consumer price perceptions tend to be imprecise about exact amounts, though reliable within well-defined ranges. Price-conscious shoppers perceive prices more accurately than less-price-conscious shoppers.[5] The number of stores shopped and frequency of shopping trips also affect price perception accuracy.

Retailers need to understand consumer sensitivity to price discounts: A price discount of less than 10 percent appears to have only a limited effect on consumer response. The reason, in part, is that consumers consider price differences in percentage terms (e.g., 10 percent) rather than absolute terms (e.g., $100). Small percentage differences may not be noticed by consumers.[6] One study of Canadian consumers' reactions to retail "price-offs" found that consumers thought the "best deal in town" was more likely when substantial savings were announced (for example, 50 percent off), and depended on the particular store doing the advertising (for example, a discount store).[7]

Psychological pricing

A retailer can price merchandise too low. A blouse might not sell at $20; but marked up to $27, it might. The reason for this phenomenon is that, for some goods, customers believe that price reflects quality (or value).[8] This situation may occur when the consumer has difficulty judging the quality of the product (e.g., fashion merchandise).

Odd price endings are believed by many to have psychological value. Odd ending prices are set just below the dollar figure, such as $1.99 instead of $2.00. Although the phenomenon is not verified, retailers practicing odd pricing believe that consumers perceive odd-ending prices to be substantially lower than prices with even endings, despite the fact that the prices are only slightly lower in actual dollar terms. Odd pricing may suggest that the price has been established at the lowest level possible.

Courtesy Black's

Black's uses odd pricing to encourage customers to purchase additional services.

Consumer pressures

Consumer pressures for unit pricing, individual item pricing, and similar consumer shopping aids also affect retail pricing practices. **Unit pricing** is the practice of stating price both in terms of the total price of an item and the price per unit of measure (e.g., $.83/l). For example, some provinces now require retailers to price mark each item instead of shelf marking only. Such a requirement adds to their cost structure. This situation has occurred because of scanning technology, which allows retailers to "read" the price from universal product codes instead of manually entering the price into the cash register. Similarly, activist consumer groups often publish market basket prices, especially for food, of competing stores in efforts to force down prices.

External Factors Affecting Retail Prices

A variety of external (environmental) factors affect retail price setting. The following sections focus on the issues of supplier policies, economic conditions, government regulations, and the level of competition in which the retailer operates.

Supplier policies

Suppliers will often suggest prices to retailers. If the retailer depends heavily on a particular supplier, then the supplier may have some influence over price decisions. However, as noted in Chapter 2, the Competition Act prohibits suppliers from requiring retailers to offer products at stipulated prices.

Often manufacturers will offer retailers distributor allowances, which are discounts or extended payment terms or a combination designed to encourage the retailers to purchase additional merchandise. Such discounts enable retailers, in turn, to lower their prices to stimulate sales. These allowances are often used by manufacturers of home entertainment products such as stereos, television sets, and VCRs.

Economic conditions

Retailers must be conscious of economic conditions and their impact on pricing decisions. During periods of inflation, increases in prices are expected (though not welcomed) by consumers. In times of recession, as Canada experienced in the early 1990s, prices often go down. For example, during 1992, the Consumer Price Index increased by only 1 percent, one of the lowest increases in 30 years. Prices of many grocery products actually decreased during that period. Part of the decrease was due to the extensive price-cutting that many retailers were using just to remain in business or to meet competitive prices.

In addition, the retailer must be aware of any voluntary or required governmental price controls that can limit price decisions. Clearly, changing and uncertain economic conditions make pricing complex.

Government regulations

Retailers are restricted from certain kinds of pricing actions, most of which are covered by the federal Competition Act. Chapter 2, presents a full discussion of the legal impacts on pricing.

One government regulation that had a major impact on retailers was the federal government's introduction of the goods-and-services tax (GST) in January 1991. The GST, at 7 percent, coupled with the recession, dealt a heavy blow to Canadian retailers. Total retail sales declined dramatically in the first three months after the introduction of the GST. A number of retailers also felt that the GST led to the significant increase in cross-border shopping at that time.

Level of competition

The degree of competition in the market will greatly affect pricing decisions. If little competition exists, pricing decisions are easier than if there is a great deal of competition. For example, a retailer with an "exclusive" on a brand in a market can probably price with greater freedom.

In addition, competitors' actions in the pricing area must be monitored. A good retailer is aware of prices being charged by competitive outlets. A word of caution is in order, however. To focus too much on the competition means you're relying on them to do their marketing job right.

When competition is severe, retailers must run efficient operations as their prices need to reflect the competitive nature of the market. The entry of the giant United States warehouse clubs, Price Club and Costco, to the Canadian market created tremendous competition in the grocery trade and the home improvement business. With the entry of Wal-Mart and Home Depot, the competition intensified even further. Price Club/Costco are generating sales of over $4 billion annually with their no-frills warehouse stores, and Home Depot racked up over $600 million in sales in 1995. Canadian supermarket chains have responded by opening up their own warehouse type outlets (Loblaws), match-

Retail Price Wars: The Battle for the Low Price Image

In 1994, when Wal-Mart came to Canada with their "Everyday Low Prices ... Always" campaign, it was the beginning of a retail price war that hammered a number of retailers, led to substantial changes in strategy for some retail chains, and pleased consumers who benefited from lower prices.

Zellers, with its "Where the Lowest Price Is the Law," responded with aggressive price cutting on thousands of items in its 300-store chain. Paul Walters, Zellers' president, felt that Zellers could not give up its position as the lowest price retailer to Wal-Mart and survive. In the second half of 1995, Zellers took its price-matching strategy a step further and significantly undercut Wal-Mart prices on key items, sparking a price war that escalated through the Christmas season. Wal-Mart continued to match Zellers' prices with the following dramatic results:

- K mart, with 127 stores in Canada, tried to sell its Canadian operation but was unsuccessful. K mart replaced its president in early 1996 and, in March, it hired a liquidator to unload more than $100 million worth of inventory and it dropped a number of merchandise lines from its stores.
- Sears Canada's profits dropped 73 percent in 1995 to $12.2 million from $44.7 million in 1994. It attributed the drop to the poor economic climate, the high debt levels of Canadian consumers, and relentless price competition.
- Zellers' president, Paul Walters, resigned in March 1996, in part because of a consolidation of some Zellers' operations with The Bay (both are owned by

the Hudson's Bay Company) and in part, because of a change in strategic direction for Zellers (an easing of its price cutting strategy). For the year ending January 31, 1996, Zellers' operating profit fell to $106.7 million from $215.6 million for the previous fiscal year.

- Wal-Mart Canada replaced its president in early 1996, and although operating results were not known, it was rumoured that sales and profits were considerably below expectations. In the spring of 1996, Wal-Mart changed its slogan from "Everyday low prices ... always" to "Where every day costs less."
- In March 1996, Canadian Tire, who had been aggressively cutting prices for the past year, changed its slogan from "There's a lot more to Canadian Tire for a lot less" to "Canadian Tire. Everyday low prices made better." Its new ad campaign also emphasized Canadian Tire money, the availability of brand-name products, and the convenience of shopping at Canadian Tire.

Some industry experts believe the aggressive pricing strategies of these chains will "cool off" but others feel that it will continue because consumers are expecting low prices and won't settle for less.

Sources: John Heinzl, "Canadian Tire Ad Campaign Takes Aim at Wal-Mart," *Globe & Mail,* March 14, 1996, p. B2; John Heinzl, "American to Run Wal-Mart Canada," *Globe & Mail,* January 31, 1996, p. B17; John Heinzl, "Sears Canada Profit Plunges 73%," *Globe & Mail,* January 30, 1996, p. B5; Paul Brent, "Bay Shakes up Zellers," *Financial Post,* March 15, 1996, pp. 1–2; Paul Brent, "K mart Scrambles with $100m Inventory Selloff," *Financial Post,* March 2, 1996, pp. 1–2; and John Heinzl, "Did Zellers Discount the Wal-Mart Threat?" *Globe & Mail,* March 28, 1996, p. B9.

ing Price Club/Costco's prices (Loeb, IGA), and modifying the merchandise selection in existing outlets (Oshawa Group).[9] Canadian Tire, Sears Canada, and Zellers have reduced prices on thousands of items to remain competitive. During 1995, the discount chains engaged in a price war that led to dramatic decreases in profits for a number of retailers (Retail Highlight 14–2).

The Arithmetic of Retail Pricing

This section presents information to help you understand the arithmetic of pricing. Every retailer is faced with the issues explained in this section.

Table 14–1 Price Concepts	
Original retail price	$1,000
Less reductions	−200
Sales retail price	$ 800

Concepts of price and markup

To begin, several terms need to be defined. First, as shown in Table 14–1, the **original retail price** ($1,000) is the first price at which an item (or a group of items) is offered for sale. The **sales retail price** ($800) is the final selling price, the amount the customer paid. Before the item was sold, a reduction or markdown ($200) occurred. (In a classification of merchandise, reductions also include employee discounts and shortages or shrinkage. See the section "Reductions Planning" in Chapter 12 for a review of these concepts.)

Table 14–2 shows that markup can be viewed in two ways. **Initial markup** is the difference between the cost of the merchandise and the original retail price ($1,020 – $800 = $220). Initial markup as a percentage of the original retail price is 21.6 percent ($220/$1,020). The concept of initial markup is used when planning a total classification or department (as discussed in Chapter 12).

Maintained markup, shown in Table 14–2, is the difference between invoice cost and sales retail price ($1,000 – $800 = $200). In percentage terms, maintained markup is related to sales retail price ($200/$1,000 = 20 percent).

Maintained markup covers operating expenses and provides the retailer with a profit. Maintained markup and initial markup differ by the $20 reduction. For purposes of the present discussion, maintained markup can be considered the same as gross margin.

Planning markup goals

Retailers must determine the initial markup to be placed on merchandise as it goes on the sales floor. Some retailers do not use a planning process to establish initial markup percentages. They simply add a fixed percentage to their invoice costs. If the goods do not sell at that price, the retailer marks them down. This approach is not likely to maximize sales or profits.

Other retailers use a planning process to establish initial and maintained markup goals. As part of this planning procedure, the retailer develops projected figures for sales, operating expenses, reductions, and profits for the operating period. These figures can then be used in the following formula to calculate the initial markup percentage that should be placed on merchandise as it comes into the store:

$$\text{Initial markup percentage} = \frac{\text{Expenses} + \text{Profit} + \text{Reductions}}{\text{Sales retail} + \text{Reductions}}$$

Assume that management has forecast sales of a merchandise line at $100,000, expenses of $15,000, and a profit return of 5 percent of sales or $5,000, and reductions as 2 percent of sales ($2,000). As shown in Table 14–3, a planned initial markup of $22,000, or 21.6 percent ($22,000/$102,000), is necessary to maintain a markup of $20,000, or 20 percent ($20,000/$100,000).

Table 14–2 Markup Concepts	
The Concept of Initial Markup	
Original retail price	$1,020
Less invoice cost	−800
Initial markup	$ 220
The Concept of Maintained Markup	
Original retail price	$1,020
Less planned reductions	20
Sales retail	1,000
Less invoice cost	800
Maintained markup	$ 200

Of course, a retailer cannot expect to have a uniform initial markup policy. This kind of policy would suggest that every item brought into a department would carry the same initial markup. Too many external factors and store policies exist for a uniform markup to make sense. As one example, retailers should consider consumers' sensitivity to prices (price elasticity of demand) when setting markups. When consumers are very sensitive to price, retailers should consider lower markups. When consumers are less sensitive to price, retailers should consider higher markups.

Planned initial markup figures become a good check. Actual performance in markup during an operating period can be checked against what has been planned.

Pricing computations

Every merchandiser needs practice in computing some routine relationships among cost, initial markup, and the original retail price. There is no need to memorize formulas, though formulas will follow examples for those who like them. Simply remember that *Cost + Initial markup = Original retail price*. Before working specific problems, let's first look at the ways markup percentages can be expressed.

Expressing markup percentages   The initial markup percentage can be expressed as a percentage of the cost of the item or as a percentage of the retail selling price. To illustrate, assume that a colour television set costs the retailer $500. The original retail selling price is set at $800. The dollar amount of the markup is $300. The initial markup percentage based on cost is 60 percent ($300/$500). Based on retail, the markup is 37.5 percent ($300/$800). Remember that the markup percentage on cost = $ markup/$ cost, and the markup percentage on retail = $ markup/$ retail.

In working with pricing, the buyer is often faced with the need to convert a markup on retail to a markup on cost or vice versa.

Conversion of markup on retail to markup on cost   Assume that a supplier quotes an initial markup of 42 percent on retail. What is the equivalent markup on cost? The formula is shown below:

$$\text{Markup percentage on cost} = \frac{\text{Markup percentage on retail}}{100 \text{ percent} - \text{Markup percentage on retail}}$$

Table 14–3   Planning Markup Goals

$$\text{Initial markup percentage} = \frac{\text{Expenses}+\text{Profit}+\text{Reductions}}{\text{Sales retail}+\text{Reductions}}$$

$$= \frac{\$15,000+\$5,000+\$2,000}{\$100,000+\$2,000}$$

$$= 21.6\%$$

$$\text{Maintained markup percentage} = \frac{\text{Expenses}+\text{Profit}}{\text{Sales retail}}$$

$$= \frac{\$15,000+\$5,000}{\$100,000}$$

$$= 20\%$$

If the retail markup is 42 percent, then retail is 100 percent and cost must be 58 percent. So, markup as a percentage of cost is .42/.58 = .724 or 72.4 percent. In other words, 42 percent markup on retail is the same as 72.4 percent on cost. Clearly, markup on cost will always be larger than markup on retail, because the cost base is smaller than the retail base.

Conversion of markup on cost to markup on retail   Suppose a vendor quotes an initial markup of 60 percent on cost. What is the equivalent markup on retail? Use the following formula:

$$\text{Markup percentage on retail} = \frac{\text{Markup percentage on cost}}{100 \text{ percent}+\text{Markup percentage on cost}}$$

If the cost markup is 60 percent, then cost must be 100 percent, and retail has to be 160 percent. So, markup on retail base is .60/1.60 = 37.5 percent. Or, 60 percent markup on cost is the same as 37.5 percent on retail.

Pricing problems   The following problems illustrate the various types of pricing decisions made by retailers.

1. A chair costs a retailer $420. If a markup of 40 percent of retail is desired, what should the retail price be? If 60 percent = $420, then 100 percent = 420/0.60, or $700, the retail price needed to achieve the desired markup of 40 percent on retail.
    Formula: Whenever the retail price is to be calculated and the dollar cost and markup percentage on retail are known, the problem can be solved with the following equation:

$$\$ \text{Retail} = \frac{\$ \text{Cost}}{100 \text{ percent}-\text{Markup percentage on retail}}$$

2. A dryer retails for $300. The markup is 28 percent of cost. What was the cost of the dryer? If 128 percent = $300, then 100 percent = $300/1.28, or $234.37, the cost that is needed to achieve the desired markup of 28 percent on cost.
    Formula: Whenever the cost price is to be calculated and the dollar retail and markup percentage on cost are known, the problem can be solved as follows:

$$\$ \text{Cost} = \frac{\$ \text{Retail}}{100 \text{ percent}+ \text{markup percentage on cost}}$$

3. A retailer prices a jacket so that the markup amounts to $36. This is 45 percent of retail. What is the cost of the item and its retail price? If 45 percent = $36, then 100 percent = $36/0.45, or $80. If retail is $80 and markup is $36, then cost is $80 – $36 = $44.

Formula: Whenever the dollar markup and the retail markup percentage are known, the retail price can be determined as follows:

$$\$ \text{Retail} = \frac{\$ \text{Retail markup}}{\text{Markup percentage on retail}}$$

Pricing Adjustments

In practice, retailers may raise or lower prices after the original pricing decisions have been made. These pricing adjustments may be (1) additional markups (markons) or (2) markdowns.

Additional markups

In inflationary periods, additional markups may be needed. Such adjustments are made when the retailer's costs are increasing.

Markdowns

A **markdown** is a reduction in the original selling price of an item. Most retailers take some markdowns, since this is the most widely used way of moving items that do not sell at the original price. Other things a retailer might do instead of taking a markdown are: (1) give additional promotion, better display, or a more visible store position to an item; (2) store the item until the next selling season; (3) mark the item up (discussed in "Psychological Pricing"); or (4) give the goods to charity.

One of the most famous retail department store organizations in the United States is Filene's Basement in Boston. This firm made its name through its widely known "automatic markdown policy." The policy operates as follows: When an item has been in the store for 12 days, it is marked down to 75 percent of list; after 6 more days, it is reduced to 50 percent; when 6 more days pass, it is reduced to 25 percent; and after 30 days, it is given to charity. Very little merchandise is given to charity.

Markdowns are also used for promotional reasons. The goods may not be slow moving, but markdowns create more activity. Smart merchants *plan* certain amounts of markdowns in order to protect profit.

Markdowns should be handled with care. If an item is marked down too often, the customer may come to view the markdown as the "normal" price and will not buy the item at the "regular" price. Consumers normally do not expect large markdowns on luxury items. Customers may question product quality if prices are slashed too much. Seasonal, perishable, and obsolete stock are exceptions. Further, excessive markdowns should be avoided. If markdowns are too high, the retailer should find out the reason. The causes can come from buying, selling, or pricing errors. A plan should be worked out to correct the errors once they have been determined.[10]

Chapter Highlights

- Price must be set to support the retailer's competitive strategy. As such, retailers may price above the market level, at the market level, or below the market level. In pricing above the competition, retailers must offer the consumer some benefit (for example, services, knowledgeable salespeople, or unique merchandise) to justify above-the-market prices. At-the-market pricers offer prices roughly the same as their competitors and attempt to make the store different in ways other than price. Below-the-market pricers offer acceptable quality merchandise at low prices. To effectively execute such a strategy, the firm must focus on lowering its cost structure.

- All stores have pricing policies that are often based on industry practices. Examples include a one-price versus a flexible-price policy, a price-line policy, a leader pricing policy, and a price discount policy.

- A variety of consumer issues affect price decisions in retail operations. Such issues include consumer demand and price sensitivity, price perceptions, psychological pricing, and consumer pressures.

- A variety of external (environmental) factors affect retail price setting. Examples include supplier policies, economic conditions, and the level of competition in which the retailer operates.

- Retailers must understand the arithmetic of pricing. In addition to planning markup goals, they must be able to perform a variety of mathematical calculations involved in making pricing decisions.

- In practice, retailers may raise or lower their prices after they have made the original pricing decisions. These pricing adjustments may be in the form of additional markups or markdowns.

Key Terms

generics 392	price elasticity 393
initial markup 398	price lining 389
leader pricing 390	price points 389
maintained markup 398	price zones 389
markdown 401	sales retail price 398
original retail price 398	unit pricing 395

Discussion Questions

1. Discuss the possible price level strategies available to the retailer. Give an example of a type of retail organization that follows each of the strategy options.

2. What are the advantages of instituting a one-price policy? What are the various ways a variable-price policy can be achieved?

3. Illustrate price lining and evaluate the concept.

4. Discuss the concept of leader pricing. What are the characteristics of products that are good price leaders?

5. How does a retailer's flexibility in setting prices depend on the extent to which he or she is selling primarily convenience, shopping, or specialty goods? How can a retailer offer private brands and generics at prices below manufacturer brands and still make a good profit?

6. What is meant by the concept of price elasticity of demand? Explain how a retailer can determine whether demand is elastic or inelastic by studying the directional changes in price and total revenue. How does the nature of demand elasticity affect retailers' pricing decisions?

7. Summarize the information presented in the text concerning external factors affecting retail price setting.

8. Define the following terms: original retail price, sales retail price, initial markup, and maintained markup.

Problems

1. If markup on cost is 36 percent, what is the equivalent markup on retail?

2. If markup on cost is 44 percent, what is the equivalent markup on retail?

3. If markup on retail is 18 percent, what is the equivalent markup on cost?

4. If markup on retail is 41 percent, what is the equivalent markup on cost?

5. A suit costs a retailer $36.80. If a markup of 43 percent on cost is required, what must the retail price be?

6. A lamp is marked up $168. This is a 61 percent markup on retail. What is (a) the cost and (b) the retail price?

7. The retail price of a ring is $7,800. If the markup on retail is 78 percent, what is the cost of the ring to the retailer?

8. The retail price of a picture is $48.50. If the markup on cost is 38 percent, what is the cost of the picture to the retailer?

9. Men's wallets may be purchased from a manufacturer for $300 per dozen. If the wallets are marked up 28 percent on cost, what retail price will be set per wallet?

10. Women's scarves may be purchased from a manufacturer at $81.60 per dozen. If the scarves are marked up 16 percent on retail, what is the retail price of each scarf?

11. Determine the (a) initial markup percent and (b) the maintained markup percent in a department that has the following planned figures: expenses, $7,200; profit, $4,500; sales, $28,000; employee discounts, $450; markdowns, $1,200; and shortages, $225.

12. Sales of $85,000 were planned in a department in which expenses were established at $26,000; shortages, $2,200; and employee discounts, $600. If a profit of 6 percent of sales were desired, what initial markup percent should be planned?

13. Department Z has taken $600 in markdowns to date. Net sales to date are $22,000. What is the markdown percentage to date?

Application Exercises

1. Devise a questionnaire to get consumer reaction to raising the price of goods already on display. Also get consumers' reaction to the fact that UPC codes allow supermarkets to change prices immediately even if old stock is still on the shelves. Do consumers feel these practices are fair or unfair? Why? Allow room for individual consumer comment on your questionnaire.

2. Assume that you are a management trainee for a major supermarket chain. Select a market basket of products that are available in all stores and easily comparable (for example, no private brands), and compare prices (including specials) in a conventional supermarket, a "warehouse-type" outlet, and a convenience store (a Mac's Milk). Keep your record over a period of time, present your data in an organized format, and draw conclusions about the pricing philosophy of the different types of food operations.

3. Health and beauty aids are carried in many different kinds of retail establishments, for example, conventional drugstores, supermarkets, discount drugstores, and department stores. Often, each type of establishment promises lower prices, better assortments, and so on, to establish a differential advantage. List selected items available in each store and group stores by type. Compare and contrast the items among the various types of stores. See what you find to be the "real" strategy of the competing stores in the market. Why is the lowest-priced store able to price as indicated? What are the specials? Are they similar for all stores?

Suggested Cases

29. Courtney's
30. Duncan Department Store

Notes

1. Sources include Mark Stevenson, "The Store to End All Stores," *Canadian Business,* May 1994, pp. 20–29; *Wal-Mart,* Laurier Institute Case Study, 1994; and Douglas J. Tigert, Stephen J. Arnold, and Terry W. Cotler, "K mart, Target and Wal-Mart: The Battle Is Joined in the Big Cities," *Babson College Retailing Research,* Report No. 76, 1993.

2. For more information on everyday low pricing see Stephen J. Hoch, Xavier Drèze, and Mary E. Purk, "EDLP, Hi-Lo and Margin Arithmetic," *Journal of Marketing,* October 1994, pp. 16–27.

3. Ian McGugan, "Eaton's on the Brink," *Canadian Business,* March 1996, pp. 38–73.

4. Stan Sutler, "Sears' New 'Club' Spots Outline Air Miles Tie-In," *Marketing,* May 4, 1992, p. 16.

5. For more information on how consumers perceive prices, see Gerald E. Smith and Thomas A. Nagle, "Frames of Reference and Buyers' Perception of Price and Value," *California Management Review,* Fall 1995, pp. 98–116; Donald R. Lichtenstein, Nancy M. Ridgeway, and Richard G. Netemeyer, "Price Perceptions and Consumer Shopping Behavior: A Field Study," *Journal of Marketing Research,* May

1993, pp. 234–45; and Valarie Folkes and Rita D. Wheat, "Consumers' Perceptions of Promoted Products," *Journal of Retailing*, Fall 1995, pp. 317–28.

6. Referred to as the Weber-Fechner Law, the law proposes that buyers perceive price differences in proportional terms rather than in absolute terms. The implication of the law is that there are thresholds (often referred to as just noticeable differences) above and below a product's price at which price changes are noticed or ignored. For more information, see Smith and Nagle, "Frames of Reference and Buyers' Perception of Price and Value," *California Management Review*, Fall 1995, pp. 98–116; and Kent B. Monroe and Susan M. Petroshius, "Buyers' Perceptions of Price: An Update of the Evidence," in H. Kassarjian and T.S. Robertson, eds., *Perspectives in Consumer Behavior*, 3rd ed., (Glenview, IL: Scott-Foresman, 1981), pp. 43–55.

7. Joseph N. Fry and Gordon H.G. McDougall, "Consumer Appraisal of Retail Price Advertisements," *Journal of Marketing*, July 1974, pp. 64–67. For more on retail price promotions, see John Liefeld and Louise A. Heslop, "Reference Prices and Deception in Newspaper Advertising," *Journal of Consumer Research*, March 1985, pp. 868–76; Abhijit Biswas and Edward A. Blair, "Contextual Effects of Reference Prices in Retail Advertisements," *Journal of Marketing*, July 1991, pp. 1–12; Abhijit Biswas, Elizabeth J. Wilson, and Jane W. Licata, "Reference Price Studies in Marketing: A Synthesis of Research Results," *Journal of Business Research*, July 1993, pp. 239–56; and Kiran W. Karanda and V. Kumar, "The Effects of Brand Characteristics and Retail Policies on Responses to Retail Price Promotions: Implications for Retailers," *Journal of Retailing*, Fall 1995, pp. 249–78.

8. For more information on the price-quality issue, see Valarie A. Zeithaml, "Consumer Perceptions of Price, Quality, and Value: A Means-End Model and Synthesis of Evidence," *Journal of Marketing*, July 1988, pp. 2–22; Kent B. Monroe and William B. Dodds, "A Research Program for Establishing the Validity of the Price-Quality Relationship," *Journal of the Academy of Marketing Science*, Spring 1988, pp. 151–68; Eitan Gerstner, "Do Higher Prices Signal Higher Quality?" *Journal of Marketing Research*, May 1985, pp. 209–15; Loren V. Geistfeld, "The Price-Quality Relationship-Revisited," *Journal of Consumer Affairs*, Winter 1982, pp. 334–46; and Benny Rigaux-Bricmont, "Influences of Brand Name and Packaging on Perceived Quality," in *Advances in Consumers Research*, vol. 9, Andrew A. Mitchell, (ed.), Ann Arbor, MI: Association for Consumer Research, 1982, pp. 472–77.

9. Daniel Girard, "The New Retail Giants," *Toronto Star*, February 9, 1992, pp. H1, H4.

10. For more information on price changes, see Peter R. Dickson and Joel E. Urbany, "Retailer Reactions to Price Changes," *Journal of Retailing*, Spring 1994, pp. 1–21.

Keys to Successful Retail Selling

Chapter Objectives

After reading this chapter you should be able to:

1. Describe the types of selling needed in retailing.

2. Understand the steps in the selling process.

3. Describe ways to increase sales force productivity.

4. Understand the need for sales training programs.

5. Understand how to help people in buying.

6. Understand the opportunities for motivating retail salespeople.

Salespeople are a critical factor in retailing, particularly when the customer seeks advice and assistance.

"As I paid for my Egg McMuffin, the teenager behind the counter smiled and said, "Thank you for coming." When I got back to the office around noon, I returned a call to my dentist. His answering machine responded: "We are out to lunch. Call back after one-thirty."

What a contrast in service! Getting my teeth cleaned costs a lot more than that Egg McMuffin, but the dentist's machine can't be bothered to thank me for calling. After all, I'm only a customer. Then, there is the salesman who has just sold me a $15,000 car but can't seem to locate the title. When I inquire about it, he tells *me* to call *him* tomorrow. Why can't he say something like, "I'm sorry about the mix-up. I'll look into it and call you in the morning?"

Many retailers seem to have forgotten about serving the customer. The good news, of course, is that there are some fine salespeople out there who make buying a pleasure. They know how to make you feel comfortable when you spend your money—a sure sign of being a pro. Pros know that investing money and time in a customer is far cheaper than finding a new

one. For instance, the other day I stopped by the local Sears to buy a lawnmower, only to discover that I no longer had a Sears credit card. I'd let the card lapse: there was no way I could take the new mower home with me. Fortunately, the manager did the next best thing, overlooking a couple of rules in the process. He had me reapply for credit and agreed to deliver the mower to my home gratis once the application was approved.[1] ■

A high-quality sales force can generate "plus" sales for a retail outlet. Consumers are increasingly frustrated over the poor quality of service they receive in retail outlets. One way to create strong customer loyalty is by offering a superior quality sales force as a complement to good merchandise and strong price/ value relationships. Creative selling differs dramatically from the image of the huckster or "sales clerk," which too many people have in their mind when they think of retail sales.

To the customer, the salesperson often is the business. The salesperson is the only person with whom the customer has contact. The salesperson encourages the customer to buy or, through a hostile or indifferent attitude, drives the customer away—forever. Salespeople can act as "sales prevention managers" by their rudeness or indifference.[2]

Building Sales and Profit

Salespeople can help build a business for greater sales and profit. They can:

- Sell skillfully to realize maximum sales and profit from each customer attracted to the firm.
- Provide customers with useful selling suggestions that will build sales and improve customer satisfaction.
- Assure that customers' needs are met so that returns are held to a minimum.
- Develop a loyal following of customers who will return to the store and will send their friends.
- Follow store policies and procedures so that losses through billing oversights, failure to secure credit approvals, and acceptance of bad cheques are held to a minimum.

Personal selling in retailing is essentially matching customers' needs with the retailer's merchandise and services. In general, the more skillfully this match is made, the better the personal selling. If salespeople make a good match, not only is a sale made, but a satisfied customer is developed (or maintained), as Retail Highlight 15–1 illustrates. Thus, a long-term, profitable relationship can be established. Figure 15–1 outlines this process.

In retailing, the top producers far outsell the average producers. The more top producers in a store, the more profitable it will be. Retailers cannot expect salespeople to become top producers by accident. There is no magic wand to wave or button to push to make this happen. However, there are a number of positive actions retailers can make to attract people with potential and, once hired, develop that potential so that maximum performance is achieved.

Retail Highlight 15–1

Finding the Right Merchandise Is Not Always Easy

It was an impossible request. One of Jan Dawe's regulars was begging her to find a certain pin-striped jacket made by American designer Donna Karan, an item last seen on Barbra Streisand in the March issue of *Us* magazine. Dawe, who manages the designer sportswear department at Holt Renfrew's flagship store in Toronto, did some research. Alas, the jacket for Streisand was one of a kind. Undaunted, Dawe found an equally attractive Karan blazer. The customer approved.

This is just one example of what makes Jan Dawe an excellent salesperson. Lynn Joliffe, Holt Renfrew's general manager, says: "Jan exemplifies what good service should be. She is sincere, hospitable, and truly wants to assist customers." To Holt Renfrew's emphasis on superior service, Jan Dawes adds her own rule: "Never high-pressure sell. Never put something on a customer that does not look right on her. Give the customer your undivided attention—you can't just stare off into a corner."

Source: Jared Mitchell, "I Can Sell You Anything," *Report on Business Magazine*, June 1992, pp. 48–49.

Basic Issues

When are salespersons needed?

The nature of the merchandise sold in the store is a factor affecting the extent to which salespeople are needed. For example, stores selling primarily convenience goods emphasize self-service. However, if the merchandise is expensive (such as furs) or technically complex (such as personal computers) and customers have little knowledge about the product, salespeople are needed. In such cases, consumers generally desire detailed information before making a purchase decision and expect to find knowledgeable salespeople to provide that information. Salespeople are also needed when negotiation over price is likely, as in car buying.

The overall strategy of the store affects the role assigned to salespeople. For example, in discount operations customers do not expect a fully staffed store. Of course, even discounters will assign salespeople to certain departments, such as those carrying more expensive, technically complex products (such as stereos and cameras) and merchandise that must be displayed in locked cabinets (such as gold jewelry). On the other hand, customers shopping in upscale, above-the-market retail stores expect high levels of customer service and expect personal selling to be emphasized.

What are the types of retail selling?

Several types of selling occur in retailing. A different type of person and different skill levels are needed for each type.[3]

Transaction processing

The easiest selling task is **transaction processing.** Employees simply serve as checkout clerks or cashiers and do little selling. Typical examples are personnel in discount department stores or supermarkets. Even though such employees do

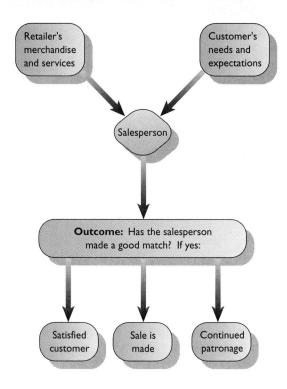

Figure 15–1   Matching Customer Needs with Retailer Merchandise and Services

not sell in the sense of presenting merchandise and relating how merchandise can fill needs, transaction processors can affect consumers' perceptions of a store and their eagerness to shop in that store. As a result, transaction processors should be trained to smile and pleasantly greet customers as they go through the checkout line, to ask whether they found everything they were looking for, and to thank them for shopping in the store. Such simple actions as these can do much to create a positive attitude among customers.

Routine selling

Routine selling involves more product knowledge and a better approach to the sales task. Often, people in routine selling are involved in the sale of non-technical items such as clothing. These salespeople assist the shopper in buying by giving them confidence in their judgment and answering simple questions.

Personnel involved in routine sales should also be trained in the techniques of suggestion selling. For example, a salesperson might suggest a shirt and tie to go with the suit a customer is trying. They should then be monitored closely to make sure they practice the concepts they have learned. Such techniques may increase sales by 10 percent or more, and additional sales are almost pure profit since they add little, if anything, to the cost structure of the firm. Retailers such as McDonald's

With warehouse retailers, like Price Club/Costco, most of the sales clerks are involved in transaction processing and do little selling.

Courtesy Price Club

consistently practice suggestion selling when the salesperson asks: "Would you like french fries or a Coke with your order?"

Creative selling

Creative selling is a type of higher-level selling in which the salespeople need complete information about product lines, product uses, and the technical features of products. They are often called sales consultants and may, for example, work as interior designers in a furniture store. Creative selling occurs when the product is highly personalized, and the primary selling activities revolve around determining customers' needs or problems and creatively helping them meet those needs.

Regardless of the type of selling involved, salespeople have a key role in the communications plan for a firm. Many extra sales can be made by creative sales efforts. The cost of retail selling is high, in spite of the low wages paid to sales personnel, and these costs must be offset by high productivity. A well-trained sales force can be a major advantage for a firm. Competing firms may duplicate price cuts and promotion, but may have difficulty in developing a quality sales force. The main differences in the three types of selling are summarized in Table 15–1.

An Overview of Personal Selling

A basic concept in retail sales is that a sale must first occur in the mind of the buyer. The job of the salesperson is to lead the customer into a buying situation. A successful salesperson should think of selling as a process consisting of the steps shown in Table 15–2.

Suggestion selling requires product knowledge and good selling skills.

Courtesy Sears Canada

Prospecting

Prospecting involves identifying and qualifying possible customers. Promotional, telephone, and direct mail programs often attract potential customers to the firm. Likewise, word of mouth can be effective when satisfied customers refer friends to the store.

Salespeople should try to know as much about their customers as possible before approaching them. This may seem difficult at first, but the concept of market segmentation discussed earlier may aid in identifying customers. The type of promotion program featured by the store is also a key. For example, most customers shopping at Zellers expect good price/value relationships and normally buy on the basis of price. These customers are often presold on products through national-brand advertising and do not expect many services. On the other hand, the customers of an exclusive store, such as Birks, expect personalized attention, a high level of product knowledge by the salesperson, and a wide variety of services.

Salespeople can also play an important role in getting customers into the store. Some firms keep lists of their good customers' likes and dislikes, measurements, and past purchases, as illustrated in Retail Highlight 15–2. Salespeople, as in the Harry Rosen example, often call these customers when a new shipment of merchandise arrives. Some salespeople, however, dislike using

Table 15–1   Types of Personal Selling in Retailing

Criteria for Comparison	Transaction Processing	Routine Selling	Sales Consultant
Purpose	Assist at check-out counter	Suggestion selling	Creative selling
Training required	Clerical training	Sales training	In-depth product knowledge
Source of sales	Impulse purchases	Maintain sales volume plus "add on" accessories	Creation of new sales volume
Type of products	Simple convenience items	Standardized with new options	Complex and customized
Primary activity	Order processing	Suggestion selling	Creative problem solving

the telephone to call customers and worry that they will be bothering their customers or that the customers will think they are being too pushy. Management should teach salespeople the proper techniques of telephoning customers and encourage and reward them for doing so.

Approaching the customer

A recent survey revealed that more than three-fourths of the 800 salespeople surveyed said that what they disliked most about their job was approaching strangers.[4] Even though many salespeople may feel negatively about this aspect of the selling process, the initial approach is a crucial variable affecting a sale. Research has shown that salespeople who exhibit poor approach skills also perform poorly on subsequent selling tasks. Similarly, those exhibiting excellent approach skills also perform well on the selling tasks that follow.[5]

The approach is designed to gain the customer's attention, create interest, and make a smooth transition into a presentation. Various approaches to customers are possible, but the most commonly used approaches are the service approach and the merchandise approach.

The service approach

With a **service approach,** the salesperson simply asks whether he or she can be of assistance to a potential customer with a question such as "Can I help you?" The greeting is especially useful if the customer has apparently made a selection and simply needs someone to ring up the sale. However, such an approach is weak because the customer is given the opportunity to quickly say no. It is better to approach by saying "Hi, if you need my help, let me know."[6] Even though it is weak, as shown in Table 15–3, the "Can I help you?" approach was found to be the most frequently used approach based on observations of salespeople in both specialty and department stores.

Thus, this greeting is useful when (1) the customer has apparently made a selection, (2) the customer clearly needs a salesperson to explain something about the merchandise, or (3) the customer needs someone to ring up a sale. Above all, sales personnel should always make the customer feel welcome. The customer needs to know that the salesperson is willing to serve him or her, and that the salesperson is knowledgeable about the merchandise.

Table 15–2   The Selling Process

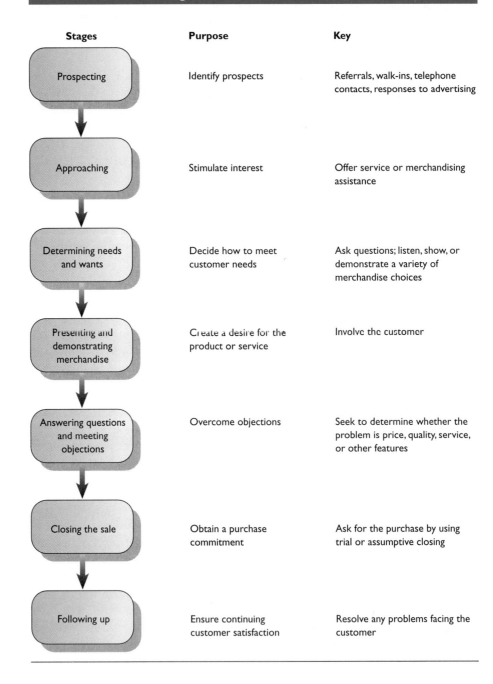

Stages	Purpose	Key
Prospecting	Identify prospects	Referrals, walk-ins, telephone contacts, responses to advertising
Approaching	Stimulate interest	Offer service or merchandising assistance
Determining needs and wants	Decide how to meet customer needs	Ask questions; listen, show, or demonstrate a variety of merchandise choices
Presenting and demonstrating merchandise	Create a desire for the product or service	Involve the customer
Answering questions and meeting objections	Overcome objections	Seek to determine whether the problem is price, quality, service, or other features
Closing the sale	Obtain a purchase commitment	Ask for the purchase by using trial or assumptive closing
Following up	Ensure continuing customer satisfaction	Resolve any problems facing the customer

Retail Highlight 15–2

Generating Sales through Good Customer Service

According to Harry Rosen, CEO of the menswear chain of the same name, good service does not mean having someone friendly standing by your elbow, ready to do your bidding; it's also knowing about the product and individual customer needs. And, adds Rosen, "it's imparting knowledge to the customer so that he can make an informed decision on his purchases."

In order to provide this level of service, all 24 Harry Rosen stores across Canada have been linked with a computer database. "Whenever a customer returns to one of our stores," says company president Bob Humphrey, "a sales associate can call up his name on a computer terminal and receive a detailed accounting of all his past purchases. In this way, we can ensure that our customer's wardrobe is kept well-rounded, that no duplications are made, and that he can always get the proper size and fit."

Source: Leslie C. Smith, "Dressing up Customer Service," *Globe and Mail*, June 11, 1992, p. D1.

The merchandise approach

The **merchandise approach** begins with a statement about the merchandise or an open-ended statement related to the merchandise. Questions such as: "The style you are looking at is very popular this year," or "For this style blouse, what size do you need?" The salesperson begins talking to the customer about the merchandise without asking whether he or she would like to be waited on. Such an approach is especially effective in making a smooth transition to the next stage of the selling process—determining customers' needs and wants.

Table 15–4 outlines 11 basic types of customers that salespeople are likely to meet in their day-to-day activities. The information in the table describes their characteristics and how to respond to their behaviour and actions.

Determining customers' needs and wants

A salesperson should quickly discover the customer's needs and wants after the greeting. Good questioning and listening skills are the key. Once the salesperson has the customer's attention and understands his or her needs, the salesperson can quickly move the customer into the interest and desire stage and on to the buying stage. Motives for buying generally are either emotional or rational.

Getting a customer to talk is important because it is the only way to find out his or her special problems, interests, and needs. Then, when making the sales presentation, the salesperson is in a position to stress the things that are important to the customer and to talk specifically about the situation. One way to develop information on customer needs and desires is to ask the customer about his or her planned use for the merchandise. This knowledge will help the salesperson better understand the buying problem and how the merchandise can help solve the problem. Such information can also provide insight into the price, styles, and colours that a customer may prefer.

Table 15–3   Frequency of Introductory Approaches Used by Salespeople

Approach	Specialty Store	Department Store
Verbal approaches		
"Can I help you?"	52	83
"How are you doing?"	22	14
"Are you looking for something special?"	18	9
"What size do you need?"	5	0
"If you need help, let me know."	3	8
Product presentation	2	0
"We are having a sale."	1	0
"Are you finding everything you need?"		10
"Hello!"		3
"Do you like that?"		2
"Can I get a price for you?"		1
Personal introduction		1
"Yes?"		1
Behavioral approaches		
Initial offer of a product demonstration	5	9
Smile	2	0
Interviewer had to seek out salesperson	12	21
Rep hovered	0	0
Total	122	164

Source: Lawrence B. Chonko, Marjorie J. Caballero, and James R. Lumpkin, "Do Retail Salespeople Use Selling Skills?" *Review of Business and Economic Research* 25 (Spring 1990), p. 41.

Knowing the *importance* of listening and actually doing it are two different things. Many salespeople keep planning what to say next instead of listening. A salesperson who is wrapped up in the sales pitch cannot hear the prospect. A good listener concentrates on what is being said. A good salesperson learns the attitudes and problems the customers have. Learning what is important to the individual may be important in selling to the individual.

By visualizing the person's problems, the salesperson understands. Eye contact is important. The salesperson should make a special effort to be attentive, not letting the mind wander to other subjects. To keep the prospects talking, salespeople should acknowledge that they are listening by prompting with nods, or commenting with "I see" or "I understand." Asking a question now and then helps. Salespeople should not worry about what to say next. If they listen carefully, their next move will usually be obvious. It is not easy to be a good listener, but it is important. Top salespeople listen to a prospect, show that they understand, and remember what is said.[7]

Presenting and demonstrating merchandise

Effective questioning and listening helps determine which merchandise to show the customer and which features of the merchandise will help solve the buying problems the customer faces. For example, if a salesperson discovers that a customer is buying apparel for a trip abroad, the salesperson might

Table 15-4   Recognizing Customers of All Types

	Customer			Salesperson
Basic Types	**Basic Characteristics**	**Secondary Characteristics**	**Other Characteristics**	**What to Say or Do**
Arguer	Takes issue with each statement of salesperson	Disbelieves claims; tries to catch salesperson in error	Cautious; slow to decide	Demonstrate; show product knowledge; use "yes, but ..."
Chip on shoulder	Definitely in a bad mood	Indignation; angry at slight provocation	Acts as if being deliberately baited	Avoid argument; stick to basic facts; show good assortment
Decisive	Knows what is wanted	Customer confident his or her choice is right	Not interested in another opinion—respects salesperson's brevity	Win sales—not argument; sell self; tactfully inject opinion
Doubting Thomas	Doesn't trust sales talk	Hates to be managed	Arrives at decision cautiously	Back up merchandise statements by manufacturers' tags, labels; demonstrate merchandise; let customer handle merchandise
Fact finder	Interested in factual information— detailed	Alert to salespersons' errors in description	Looks for actual tags and labels	Emphasize label and manufacturers' facts; volunteer care information
Hesitant	Ill at ease—sensitive	Shopping at unaccustomed price range	Unsure of own judgment	Make customer comfortable; use friendliness and respect
Impulsive	Quick to decide or select	Impatience	Liable to break off sale abruptly	Close rapidly; avoid oversell, overtalk; note key points
Look around	Little ability to make own decisions	Anxious—fearful of making a mistake	Wants salesperson's aid in decision—wants adviser—wants to do right thing	Emphasize merits of product and service, zeroing in on customer-expressed need and doubts
Procrastinator	"I'll wait 'til tomorrow"	Lacks confidence in own judgment	Insecure	Reinforce customer's judgment
Silent	Not talking—but thinking!	Appears indifferent but truly listening	Appears nonchalant	Ask direct questions— straightforward approach; watch for buying signals
Think it over	Refers to desire, but needs to consult someone else	Looking for another adviser	Not sure of own uncertainty	Get agreement on small points; draw out opinions; use points agreed on for close

Source: From C. Winston Borgen, *Learning Experiences in Retailing* (Santa Monica, Calif.: Goodyear Publishing, 1976), p. 293. © Goodyear Publishing Company, Reprinted by permission.

Good listening skills are key to discovering customers' needs and wants.

Courtesy Hudson's Bay Company Ltd.

point out items that are lightweight, that do not wrinkle easily, and that are most appropriate for the area of the world where the customer will be travelling.

Good salespeople have a mental outline they follow when presenting the merchandise. This mental outline differs from a canned sales presentation in which the salesperson repeats exactly the same statements to each customer. The salesperson is free to deviate from a fixed statement but still keeps key points from the outline in mind as a checklist. A mental guide should include the following points:

- *Begin with the strongest features of the product.* These features might be price, durability, performance, and so forth.

- *Obtain agreement on small points.* This helps the salespeople establish rapport with the customer.

- *Point out the benefits of ownership to the customer.* Salespeople should try to identify with the customer in making these points.

- *Demonstrate the product.* A demonstration helps the customer make a decision based on seeing the product in action.

- *Let the customer try the product.* Good salespeople get the customer involved as much as possible. The involvement pushes the customer toward the sale.

Other useful techniques include testimonials of customers who have used the product, discussion of research results, and discussion of product guarantees and case histories.

Answering questions and meeting objections

A customer may object to a point during the sales process. When that occurs, the salesperson should try to find the real reason for the objection, which may be based

Table 15–5   Overcoming Objections

Knowing *when* to answer an objection is almost as important as being able to answer it.

Timing is crucial! In general, it's wise to answer as many objections as you can *before* the prospect brings them up.

Putting the answers to objections into the sales talk saves time. But more important, when a salesperson, rather than the prospect, mentions an objection, the issue seems less important. It also makes the customer feel you're not trying to hide anything.

Sometimes a customer may hesitate to bring up a particular objection because he doesn't want to embarrass you. You can save the day by getting it out in the open, showing the customer you understand his or her concerns.

Another reason for discussing as many obvious objections as possible is that you avoid an argument. If the prospect brings up an objection, you may have to prove he's wrong in order to make the sale. That's a situation to avoid if you possibly can.

On the other hand, what if the customer *does* bring up an objection before you get to it? If you can give a satisfactory reply without taking attention away from your sales point— answer it immediately.

Sometimes you should delay your answer to a customer's objection. For example, you may not even need to answer if there's a good chance the objection will diminish in importance as you continue your presentation.

It's also best to delay answering if you would seem to be flatly contradicting the prospect. Rather than do this, wait and let the answer become clear as you proceed with your presentation. This gives the prospect a chance to save face.

There are some objections that it's best not to answer at all. If the prospect's statement is simply an excuse, or a malicious remark, don't bother trying to answer. This will only put you on the defensive.

Having good answers to objections and presenting them to the customer's satisfaction is important. But so is timing.

Choosing the right time and the right way to handle objections keeps you in control of the selling process.

Source: *On the Upbeat,* June 1982, pp. 11–13.

on price, quality of the product, service available, or various other reasons. The salesperson should try to get the customer to see the situation in a different way. The salesperson should acknowledge that he or she can understand why the customer holds a particular view. But the salesperson also should try to provide information that can overcome the objection. For example, an objection to a high price might be overcome by pointing out that the purchase is really an investment. Also, the salesperson might point out that the price of the product has not gone up any more than other items the consumer has recently purchased.

Above all, the salesperson should consider a customer's question as an opportunity to provide more information about the product or service. Salespeople should welcome objections as providing a way for overcoming obstacles to a sale. The key to handling objections is *timing*, as explained in Table 15–5.

Closing the sale

Salespeople often have a problem with the close. Based on observation of 122 salespeople in specialty stores and 164 in department stores, a researcher discovered that only 24 percent of the specialty store salespeople and only 32 percent of the department store salespeople attempted to close the sale.[8] These findings support the commonly held perception that few retail salespeople attempt to close the sale. They would rather wait passively for the customer to volunteer to purchase.

Customers, however, often give signals to alert salespeople that a buying decision is at hand. Such signals may include questions about the use of the item, delivery, or payment. Facial expressions may also indicate that the customer is close to the buying stage. More frequently, it's up to the salesperson to bring up the closing question. An easy way to approach the close is through use of a trial close.

Trial closes[9]

A **trial close** is a question that is asked to determine the prospect's readiness to buy. The following is an example of such a question: "Are you satisfied that our product will help you reduce your maintenance costs?" If the answer is negative, the salesperson can reemphasize how the product reduces maintenance costs or can ask the prospect to be more specific about the cause of his or her doubt.

Seeking agreement   If the prospect agrees with the salesperson on a series of points, it becomes difficult to say no when the salesperson asks for the order. However, the prospect who disagrees on a number of points will probably defend this position by also saying no when the salesperson asks for the order. The salesperson should **seek agreement** on a number of points such as:

- "Don't you think the self-defrosting feature of this refrigerator is a real convenience, Mr. Baker?"
- "You probably need a larger refrigerator than your present one, don't you?"

The salesperson probably knows the points to which the prospect will agree. The idea is to summarize them and ask them consecutively to establish a pattern of agreement, one that will make it difficult for the prospect to say no when the salesperson asks for the order.

Above all, salespeople should:

- Not make exaggerated claims.
- Use honest facts and figures to back up the claims they do make.
- Demonstrate and prove their points whenever possible.
- Use solid, legitimate testimonials that the prospect can check.
- Not promise what they cannot deliver.
- Back promises in writing and in performance.
- Show sincere interest in every customer's problems.
- Consistently and conscientiously put the customer's interest ahead of their own.[10]

Salespersons should not be pressed to act too quickly or make exaggerated claims because of potential legal consequences. Five categories of careless statements with potential legal consequences are: (1) creation of unintended warranties, (2) dilution of the effectiveness of existing warranties, (3) disparagement of competitive offerings, (4) misrepresentation of the firm's own offerings, and (5) unwarranted interference with business relationships.[11]

Table 15–6 summarizes the critical skills needed and common errors to avoid in the personal selling process.

Benefit summary   Another effective trial close is the **benefit summary,** which is a statement that summarizes **product benefits,** such as the following:

> "Ms. Perkins, I think you'll find that the Brand X washer has everything you're looking for. A partial load cycle saves you water, energy, and money. Temperature controls protect your fabrics. And Brand X's reputation for quality assures you that this machine will operate dependably for a long time with little or no maintenance."

Table 15–6   Critical Skills and Common Errors in Personal Selling
Critical Skills
Good listening to establish needs and to develop basic information Demonstrating how a product or service can meet an identified need Establishing good rapport with customers Skillfully handling objections or negative attitudes Summarizing benefits and actions required in closing the sale
Common Errors
Talking instead of listening Not seeking critical information from a customer by failing to ask crucial questions Failing to match customers' needs with product benefits Failing to handle objections Not knowing how or when to close the sale

Closing techniques

Now let us look at the most vital factor in the selling process—actually closing the sale. All previous steps have been taken with one purpose in mind—to close the sale and to get the prospect to buy. A variety of techniques can be used to close the sale, as shown in Table 15–7. The best approach often depends upon the salesperson's individual selling style, the prospect, the product or service that is offered, and the salesperson's earlier success in convincing the prospect of the advantages of the product and the benefits that it offers.

Direct close   The **direct close** assumes that the prospect is ready to buy. In closing, the salesperson asks a direct question such as the following:

- "We can deliver your sofa next week. What is the address that we should ship to?"
- "You want this in green, don't you?"
- "Will this be cash or charge?"
- "Would you like to put this on a budget plan?"

Assumptive close   The **assumptive close** is a modification of the direct close. The salesperson assumes that the prospect is ready to buy, but asks less direct questions, such as:

- "Which colour do you prefer, red or green?"
- "Which model do you prefer, the standard or the deluxe?"
- "Have you decided where you would like the machine installed?"
- "Shall I call an electrician to arrange the installation?"

Open-ended close   In the **open-ended close,** the salesperson asks open-ended questions that imply readiness to buy, such as:

- "How soon will you need the sofa?"
- "When should I arrange for installation?"

The prospect's answer to these questions leads to an easy close. If the prospect needs the sofa in three weeks, the salesperson can respond, "Then I'll need an order right away, to assure you of delivery on time."

Table 15–7   Salesperson Perceptions of Closing-Tactic Effectiveness

Closing Tactic	Mean Scale Value*
Summary: Restate major points or benefits and ask for the order.	4.2
Comparison: Compare product features with those of a well-known rival, then ask for the order.	4.0
Multiple choice: Reduce alternative offerings to two or three choices, then ask which one the prospect prefers.	3.4
Assumptive: Conduct oneself as if the prospect has decided to buy.	3.4
Ask for the order: In a straightforward manner, ask for the order.	3.2
Report: Describe situation where another prospect had a similar problem and benefited from the offerings, then ask for the order.	3.1
Close on an objection: Answer an important objection, then ask for the order.	3.1
Counselling: Advise the prospect to order an item, based on the sales representative's role as a counsellor or expert.	2.8
Contingency: Ask the prospect if he or she will order if a contingency is provided for by the sales representative.	2.7
Major point/minor point: Ask closing questions, then immediately ask questions on minor points. Agreement on minor points is taken as suggestive of making an order.	2.6
Contract: Fill out a contract and hand to prospect for signature.	2.5
Continuous affirmation: Seek agreement on minor points, then ask for the order.	2.5
Emotional: Show an emotional value of purchasing the product, then ask for the order.	2.4
Single obstacle: Get prospect to agree that only one obstacle prevents a purchase; remove obstacle and ask for the order.	2.3
Balance sheet: Make T-account and write reasons for purchasing in the left row and reasons for not purchasing in the right. Ask for the order.	2.1
Buy now: Raise anxiety by pointing out that delay by the prospect in placing an order may result in increased prices, out of stock conditions, or some other problem. Ask for the order.	2.0
Complimentary: Compliment prospect on the wisdom of making an order.	2.0
Concession: Give in to the prospect on one or more points in order to close the sale. Ask for the order.	1.6

*Scored on a 5-point scale ranging from very effective (5) to very ineffective (1).
Source: Robin Peterson, "Sales Representative Perceptions on Various Widely Used Closing Tactics," in *Educators Proceedings,* eds. Gary Frazier et al. (Chicago: American Marketing Association, 1988), p. 221.

Action close   The salesperson takes some positive step toward clinching the order (**action close**), such as:

- "I'll write up the order right now and as soon as you sign it, we can deliver."

- "I'll call the warehouse and see if they can ship immediately."

Urgency close   The salesperson advises the prospect of some compelling reason for ordering immediately (**urgency close**), such as:

- "That's a pretty tight schedule. I'll have to get an answer from you very quickly if we are going to be able to meet it."

- "That item has been very popular, and right now our inventory is running pretty low."
- "Our special price on this product ends the 15th of the month."

Dealing with delay   Not all closing attempts are immediately successful. The prospect may delay, unable to make a decision. If so, the salesperson should ask the reason for the delay. The reason will often help the salesperson plan the next course of action in reestablishing the presentation of the product or service.

For example, the prospect might say: "I think I'll stick with my present machine a while longer." If the salesperson has properly qualified the prospect earlier he or she might respond: "But didn't you say that repair costs were running awfully high? Isn't it worth a few dollars to know that you will save on maintenance costs and not have to worry about a breakdown at a critical time?"

The choice of the closing technique will depend on the salesperson, the salesperson's style, the customer, and the facts. Regardless of the technique chosen, the most important thing to remember is to pursue some closing technique and not avoid this critical step.

Following up

A note or telephone call to a customer after the sale is an important part of the selling process. Through such communications, the salesperson can again thank the customers for their patronage. They can provide additional information on the product purchased and assure the customers they have made wise product choices. For certain kinds of merchandise, such as major appliances and furniture, salespeople should make sure that the merchandise is delivered on time, that it arrived in good condition, and that installation, if needed, was satisfactory. Such communications can also be used to suggest other merchandise in which the customer might be interested and to invite him or her to visit the store again soon.

Above all, the salesperson should think back over the sale to determine what he or she learned that will help in future sales efforts. Also, the salesperson should think about why some sales were not made and what might have been done to overcome the lack of a sale. Salespeople should always be seeking to identify ways of achieving future sales by satisfying their customers, as Retail Highlight 15–3 demonstrates.

Increasing Sales Force Productivity

Productivity of the sales force can be generally defined as total sales divided by employee costs. More precise measures can be tailored to each type of salesperson. As noted earlier, the cost of retail selling is high, in spite of the low wages sometimes paid to sales personnel. However, these costs can be offset by developing a quality sales force and increasing its productivity. For example, management should know how many salespeople are needed at a given time and avoid overscheduling. They should avoid having too few personnel available at periods such as lunch time and think about split schedules to cover these busy periods. Management should consider having less overtime and hiring more part-time personnel. Keep in mind that salespeople should be used for selling;

Retail Highlight 15–3

Following up Is Showing Customers That You Care

Stan Rich gave up his coal-mining job to become a car salesman at Halifax's Colonial Honda. During his first 18 months, he moved 150 automobiles, a phenomenal achievement during a recession. According to Rich, the key to his success is showing customers that you care about their needs. Before hitting the sales floor each day, Rich consults index cards to see which of his previous customers he is scheduled to telephone. "How is the car?" he'll ask them in his Cape Breton drawl one week after they have driven away a new Prelude, Accord, or Civic. He'll do the same thing in a month's time, then in three months' time, and every six months after that, trouble-shooting where necessary, but always reminding customers that Stan Rich cares.

Source: Jared Mitchell, "I Can Sell You Anything," *Report on Business Magazine,* June 1992, p. 50.

such tasks as gift wrapping and shelf stocking should be done by non-selling personnel. The following sections discuss how better employee selection, effective training programs, appropriate compensation, and effective performance evaluation lead to increased sales force productivity.

Employee selection

Finding good salespeople is a problem for large and small retailers alike. What retailers fail to realize is that much of the problem is of their own making. They may not define clearly what they mean by "good" salespeople or specify what qualities they are seeking.[12] Therefore, to do a better job in finding and hiring salespeople, firms are doing several things.

First, many retailers are realizing that customers have more confidence in salespeople who are like themselves. As a result, some firms are attempting to hire salespeople that parallel as much as possible the firm's target customer. Firms that are doing so find that the result often leads to a rather diverse sales force.

Retailers should also develop *job descriptions* as discussed in Chapter 9. A job description is a written statement, often no longer than one or two paragraphs, spelling out the requirements for a particular job. For example, the job description for a retail sales position in a sporting goods store might appear as Table 15–8.

The job description forces the retailer to be more explicit about what a job requires and provides a guide for appraising the capabilities of prospective employees. For example, since the job discussed above emphasizes big-ticket items, the retailer should look for people who have this kind of experience. There are many instances of salespeople who can do an excellent job on low-unit-value merchandise but have trouble closing sales on the big-ticket items. Job specifications help to avoid such problems.

Job orientation

A job description and job specification can simplify the process of providing an orientation, or introducing a new employee into the business. An orientation will make the new employee feel at ease and better able to begin work. It is

Table 15–8   An Example of a Job Description

Type of job: Retail sales of sporting goods.
Requirements of the job: This job involves mainly in-store sales of a full line of sporting goods ranging from items of low-unit value (such as golf balls) up to higher-priced merchandise (such as complete sets of golf clubs and skiing equipment). The emphasis is on big-ticket items. Telephone follow-up selling is expected and there is occasional stock work.

important to note, however, that a job orientation only explains the job to the employee and does not train her or him to do it. A typical job orientation checklist is shown in Table 15–9.

After the period of formal job training and orientation is completed, management still faces the task of helping the salesperson perform successfully. One way to do this is a program of **management by objectives** that helps the person work to achieve tangible goals.

Sales training programs

Many people wonder why training salespeople is necessary, since their turnover is often so high. But effective training can increase employee sales levels, lead to better morale, and produce higher job satisfaction and lower job turnover. Training or retraining gives employees more knowledge about the items they sell and may make them feel more a part of the firm. Much training occurs on the job for the purpose of skills enhancement.

Retailers should budget dollars for training just as they budget dollars for hiring staff members, since training is a way to increase sales. Most people really want to succeed but no one can succeed without adequate training. Customers will show their appreciation by increased levels of buying. And add-on sales as a result of employee training are almost pure profit since they add little or nothing to expenses.[13]

Unfortunately, when the word **training** is mentioned, the retailer typically associates it with formalized programs conducted by large department stores and national chains. A good example is the Eaton's Professional Selling Skills (EPSS) seminars. However, sales training by smaller retailers does not have to be a formal and structured program. Actually, any conscious effort the retailer makes to improve the basic skills needed for effective retail selling is a form of sales training.

Sales training methods

Some of the frequently used retail sales training methods are: (1) role playing, (2) sales meetings, and (3) seminars.

Role playing   **Role playing** is an excellent method for developing a salesperson's skills at learning customer needs. In role playing, one person plays the part of the customer, while the other plays the part of the salesperson. Next time around, they reverse the roles. Role playing enables salespeople to see various sales situations from the customer's point of view. The skill necessary to quickly "size up" customers (learn about their needs) is rapidly sharpened through role playing.

Table 15–9   Job Orientation Checklist
• Explain background:
Company purpose
Company image
Kind of clients catered to
• Introduce to other employees and positions
• Explain relationship between new employee's position and other positions
• Tour the building:
Working areas
Management office
Rest facilities
Records
Employee locker room or closet
Other relevant areas
• Explain facilities and equipment
• Review the duties and responsibilities of the job from the job description
• Introduce to emergency equipment and safety procedures
• Questions and answers

Sales meetings   Knowledge of the merchandise and service can be improved with regularly scheduled **sales meetings.** Sales meetings offer an excellent opportunity to discuss the features of new products, changes in store policies, new merchandising strategies, or other matters relating to the store's merchandise and services. Sales meetings do not have to be formal and precisely scheduled events. Instead, they can be conducted right on the sales floor during slack periods or shortly before the store opens for business.

What is important is that management holds the meetings regularly and frequently and each has a specific theme or focus. For example, at one meeting management might discuss the features of a new line of products the store is now carrying and how to introduce them to the customer. The next meeting might focus on changes in the store's merchandise return policy. At another meeting, management might talk about the sales strategies for the upcoming inventory clearance sale. If meetings are held regularly, management may be pleasantly surprised at how much better informed salespeople will be about the store's merchandise and service offerings.

Seminars   Training aimed at improving the ability to convince customers that a store's merchandise and service offerings are superior is perhaps the most difficult. Some people believe that an individual either has this skill naturally or does not, and hence training makes little difference. Although there may be some truth in this position (people do differ in their natural communication abilities), training can still make a difference. Training can range from encouraging salespeople to take a formal course in salesmanship, to informal *sales seminars* organized by the store. These seminars may be no more elaborate than sitting down with salespeople for half an hour over a cup of coffee and discussing ways that merchandise and service offerings can be better communicated to customers.

If conducted informally (but regularly), these sessions may foster a constructive interchange of ideas about selling. For example, a salesperson may have developed a good argument that can be used successfully to close a sale when it looks as if the customer is ready to walk out.

What should training include?

Information about the company and its products   Who started the company? How long has it been in business? What lines of merchandise are sold? What are their main characteristics, uses, etc.

Expectations of the salesperson   A training program should outline such things as dress code, job skills expected, goals to be met, and how performance will be measured.

Basic training in selling techniques   Will the personnel need special technical skills? Management should also help employees to understand their non-selling duties.

The company's promotion and fringe-benefit policies   Management should explain promotion opportunities. Does the company pay for education for the employees? What are the sick leave and annual leave policies? What benefits such as health and life insurance does the company provide?

Training in telephone selling   Salespeople may call a list of regular and preferred customers when new merchandise arrives.

Equipment use   Nothing is more frustrating for a customer than to stand at the cash register for what seems an eternity, waiting for the salesperson to figure out how to use the cash register. Before being placed on the sales floor, sales associates should be trained thoroughly in how to operate such equipment as cash registers, credit card machines, and sensor tag removal machines.

Teaching selling skills[14]

Teaching selling skills consists of the three following steps:

- *Customer communications*. Developing a courteous approach to greeting customers and discussing their buying needs. This permits the salesperson to assist customers in their product selection and describe products in terms that show how they fulfill the customers' buying needs.

- *Feature-benefit relationship*. Understanding the reasons why customers buy, relating products or services to those reasons, and describing the products or services to the customers accordingly.

- *Suggestion selling*. Using customers' original purchase requests to develop suggestions for related or additional sales in which the customers might be interested.

Customer relations

Customer relations is the foundation of a successful selling effort, not simply because a courteous approach to selling is "nice," but because it can build sales and profit. In small businesses, it is particularly important because the customers of small retailers generally expect more personal service than they find in a major department or discount stores. The personal service could be advice on the colour, quality, or use of certain products. Or it might be just a friendly greeting and the confidence that comes with knowing that they are buying from people who are interested in them and their business, as Retail Highlight 15–4 demonstrates.

Retail Highlight 15–4

Showing Customers That They Are Important

Of all the 24 Walters Jewelers stores, the one in Barrie, Ontario, is the best, thanks to Karen MacPherson's selling skills. Once, when a necklace that a customer had brought in for repair failed to return from the factory a few days before an important wedding, MacPherson took the customer to the jewelry case and asked her to pick out a piece she could borrow for the big day. The woman chose a gold piece valued at $2,000. A few days after the wedding she came back to say that she'd received so many compliments about it that she'd decided to buy it.

Another time, MacPherson took 15 minutes to explain diamonds to a customer who admitted he knew nothing about gems. When he went to another jewelry store and started using the information to ask detailed questions, the saleswoman said she did not have a clue to what he was talking about. When he told her he had just received a crash course in diamonds at Walters, the clerk sniffed, "We don't do things like that here." This superior attitude was more than enough to persuade the man to hightail it back to MacPherson and buy a ring.

Source: Jared Mitchell, "I Can Sell You Anything," *Report on Business Magazine*, June 1992, p. 48.

The salesperson should try to know as much about the customer's buying interest as possible. This is done by asking questions such as:

- "Are you looking for a fall or a winter coat?"
- "How long has your daughter been playing tennis?"
- "How often do you need a power saw?"

The answers to these questions will help the salesperson direct the customer to the right product—perhaps the winter coat, the expert model tennis racket, or the most durable saw. The salesperson will be performing a service for the customer by matching the customer's needs to the right product and will be increasing the chances of closing the sale.

As in the hiring interview, the most effective questions are those that cannot be answered yes or no. Instead, the salesperson should try to use open-ended questions that require a more complete answer. These are usually questions that begin with why, what, or how, or offer a choice for the customer to make.

Even an apparently negative response can be useful. The customer who likes the style of a skirt but dislikes the colour can be shown another skirt in a colour she may prefer. The customer who objects to the price of an appliance can be shown a lower-priced model, or can be shown how the particular appliance justifies the apparently high price. Unless the salesperson is aware of the customer's objections, nothing can be done to overcome them.

Salespeople are responsible for *selling* products and services. Customers have no responsibility to buy them. It is up to the salesperson to find out what the customer wants and match a product or service to those wants.

Feature-benefit relationship　　Whenever a salesperson describes the product or service to a customer, it should be described in terms of the **feature-benefit relationship.** Features and benefits are defined as follows:

- A *feature* is any tangible or intangible characteristic of a product or service.
- A *product benefit* is the customer's basic buying motive that is fulfilled by the feature.

Table 15–10 Types of Buying Motives	
Rational	**Emotional**
Price	Life-style image
Convenience	Adventure and excitement
Warranties	Pleasure
After-the-sale service	"Keeping up with the Joneses"
Economy	Good provider for family
Length of service	Pride
Health and safety	Fantasy fulfillment
Quality	Status

For example, a salesperson says, "These all-leather hiking boots have waterproof seams. They are our highest priced line, but the leather will last a long time, look good, and keep you dry even on wet trails." The salesperson mentioned two features, "all leather" and "waterproof seams." The benefits that the owner can expect to derive from these features were also mentioned, as follows:

- "Last a long time."—Although they are higher priced, they represent value because they won't have to be replaced frequently.

- "Look good."—People want things that they wear to look good.

- "Keep you dry."—People are naturally interested in comfort and in preserving their health.

People's buying motives vary widely, as noted earlier. In fact, two people buying the same product might be looking for altogether different benefits. One man buys an expensive suit because of the status it confers upon him. Another man buys the same suit because its superior tailoring will make it more durable and long-lasting. A third buys it because he likes the styling.

The following are some typical benefits, as noted in Table 15–10, that people seek from the things they buy:

- *Safety.* The desire to protect their lives and property.

- *Economy.* Not just in the initial purchase price but in long-run savings through less frequent replacement or, in the case of certain products, lower maintenance and operating costs.

- *Status.* People buy things to be recognized. The woman buying an evening dress may consider the designer's name all-important. A 12-year-old boy might consider the brand of blue jeans or the autograph on a baseball bat to be equally important.

- *Health.* People buy exercise equipment, athletic equipment, and outerwear because they wish to preserve their health.

- *Pleasure.* People attend theatres, go to athletic events, eat at restaurants, and buy books and objects of art because they expect to derive personal pleasure from these pursuits.

- *Convenience.* People buy many things to make the routine chores of life easier. For example, the cook buys a cake mix because it is far more convenient than mixing the individual basic ingredients.

The list could go on indefinitely. The important question to consider is the customer benefits that are provided by the goods or services to be sold. Knowing these benefits, salespeople can describe products to customers in terms of the benefits that the customers can derive from them. Relatively few customers are interested in the technical or design details of a product. Customers are primarily interested in what the product will do for them. The principal reason for a salesperson to describe features of a product or service is to prove the benefits that the person can expect from it. For example, a salesperson might describe insulating material to a customer as follows: "This insulating material creates a thermal barrier." Impressive words, perhaps, but the statement tells the customer little or nothing about the reasons for buying.

Suggestion selling   In **suggestion selling,** the salesperson tries to build upon the customer's initial request in order to sell additional or related merchandise. For example, the salesperson might suggest that a woman buy two blouses to take advantage of a weekend special. If a man buys a dress shirt, the salesperson should suggest a complementary tie. With a tablecloth, a salesperson might suggest napkins that go well with it. With a stereo receiver, a skilled salesperson could suggest a pair of speakers matched to the output of the receiver.

The opportunities for suggestion selling are endless. Frequently, the benefit that a customer might derive from one product could be used to develop suggestions for others. Young parents buying one safety product for a baby would be interested in seeing others. Or the man who buys a designer necktie for status reasons could be persuaded to buy a belt, shirt, or eyeglass frames from the same designer.

Even a "no sale" or a return can become a sales opportunity through suggestion selling. The customer who is looking for a shirt to buy as a gift may not find the right shirt but could be persuaded to buy something else, perhaps a necktie or a sweater. The man who returns a raincoat because it doesn't fit properly still needs a raincoat and could be sold one if the salesperson takes advantage of the opportunity for a suggestion sale.

Involvement and feedback[15]   When training people in sales skills, it is relatively easy to get their involvement and the feedback needed to evaluate their progress to better shape the training needed. Instead of telling salespeople how you would sell a certain product, ask them how they would do it, and what they would say to a customer.

After management hears their presentation, they can explain any other features that should have been mentioned and any other benefits that are important. Then let the person try again, perhaps reviewing the basic technique of features and benefits if necessary.

Similarly, management can list a number of products that the store offers and have the salesperson write down a related product that he or she would suggest to every customer. In so doing, management will be gaining the trainee's active involvement and secure necessary feedback so they can see where review or correction is necessary. Management will also learn of the employee's strengths and weaknesses so they can perform their supervisory job more effectively.

Criteria for successful training

Regardless of the training method used, there are two key elements for success. These are as follows:

Trainee participation   The training process should directly involve the trainee. Listening to a person talk has little value. Few can absorb it. The passive role of reader or listener is seldom helpful in understanding and remembering. Reading a book or hearing a speech is fine for entertainment or intellectual stimulation, but these activities are seldom effective in a training environment. People learn by doing things. When new personnel are taught how to prepare an invoice or credit memo, it is not enough to tell them how or show them how. It is far more important to have them do it.

Feedback   Feedback is what a person learns by testing the employee's understanding of the facts that are being taught. It permits the trainer to measure the employee's progress at each step. Through feedback, management can recognize problems when they arise. Through early recognition of misunderstandings, they can correct them as soon as possible so that training can progress.

Feedback helps direct training efforts since management then knows those things that give the employee particular difficulty, such as arithmetic or trade terminology. In the remainder of the training effort, management can then be particularly careful and painstaking in teaching anything that involves trade terminology or arithmetic skills.

Compensation systems

The appropriate method of payment for a salesperson (for example, straight salary, straight commission, salary plus commission, or other options) depends on a number of factors. Because we discussed these factors in Chapter 9, we will not repeat the information here. However, an issue that is quite relevant today is the extent to which increasing numbers of retailers are attempting to link pay to performance.

Retailers must remember that incentive pay plans that work provide benefits for the company, the sales force, and customers. A proper balance must be struck between motivating employees and good customer service.

Performance evaluation systems

A well-designed performance evaluation system can result in improved customer relations and sales force productivity. In developing such a system, management must generate a set of standards against which sales associates' performance is to be measured. Actual performance should be compared to standards to determine areas where a salesperson is performing well versus those areas where improvement is needed. Management should personally meet with salespeople to give feedback. These sessions should be viewed as a mechanism for helping salespeople perform more effectively for their own benefit as well as that of the company. Thus, a well-designed performance evaluation system not only provides an objective way of evaluating and improving performance but also is often useful in helping management discover content areas where training programs need to be conducted.[16]

Chapter Highlights

- The trend today is toward more self-service. Improved signing, displays, packaging, and store layouts all make self-service possible. But retailers still need salespeople to answer customers' questions about the technical dimensions of products, to reassure customers about items of fashion apparel, and to help customers fit items such as shoes.

- The key to a good sales force is the right interaction between the merchandise, the customer, and the salesperson. A salesperson is needed when customers have little knowledge about the merchandise they plan to buy, when price negotiation is likely, and when the product is complex.

- The easiest type of selling is transaction processing. This means that employees simply serve as checkout clerks or cashiers and do little selling. Routine selling involves more product knowledge and a better approach to the sales task. Creative selling requires the use of creative sales skills by salespeople who need complete information about product lines, product uses, and technical features.

- The job of the salespeople is to lead the customer to a buying situation. Successful salespeople normally think of selling as a process consisting of the following steps: prospecting (preapproaching), approaching, determining needs and wants, presenting and demonstrating merchandise, answering questions and meeting objections, closing, and following up.

- The most vital step in the selling process is closing the sale. Techniques include the direct, the assumptive, the open-ended, the action, and the urgency closes.

- Developing a strong sales force is not a matter of luck. Training is needed; adequate incentives must exist to motivate personnel to high levels of performance; and supervision is necessary. Above all, management of the sales force means planning for increased sales. Sales per person can be increased by better employee selection, training, and supervision; improved departmental layout; more self-selection by customers; streamlining sales processing; improved merchandising and promotion; making sure salespeople are fully knowledgeable about the products they're selling; and following up where necessary after the sale (for example, with the service department).

- Retail sales managers should set up performance standards and let salespeople know what they are. Non-selling activities should be included if they are also expected to be performed by the employee. Finally, management should decide how to reward employees who exceed the established standards.

Key Terms

action close 422

assumptive close 421

benefit summary 420

creative selling 411

direct close 421

feature-benefit relationship 428

management by objectives 425
merchandise approach 415
open-ended close 421
product benefit 420
productivity of sales force 423
prospecting 412
role playing 425
routine selling 410

sales meetings 426
seeking agreement 420
service approach 413
suggestion selling 430
training 425
transaction processing 409
trial close 420
urgency close 422

Discussion Questions

1. What are the various types of retail selling? How do the skills required vary by type of selling? What is the difference between the service approach and the merchandise approach?

2. Under what conditions is the presence of sales personnel most essential in a retail store?

3. What are the various ways a salesperson can determine customer needs and wants?

4. Comment on the following statement: The best way for a salesperson to deal with a customer objection is simply to ignore it and continue with the sales presentation.

5. In closing a sale, how does an assumptive close differ from that which might be used during a special-sale event?

6. Why is sales-force productivity so important? How can it be increased? Why are self-selection and self-service becoming more common in retailing?

7. Assume that you have been asked by a retail store manager to describe what an effective sales training program should include and what sales training methods can be used. How would you respond?

8. Why should performance standards be established for sales personnel? List examples of performance standards for salespeople.

Application Exercises

1. Visit the personnel manager of the leading department store in your community and discuss briefly their training programs for salespeople. Find out their major problems with sales personnel. Do the same thing with the manager of a fast-food franchise. Be prepared to discuss the differences you find.

2. Interview 10 to 15 of your student friends and find out their overall impression of salespeople in your community. Are they satisfied? If yes, why? If not, why not? Get their thoughts on what can be done to improve the quality of service in retail outlets. Now, talk to several of your friends who have worked for or are working as part-time salespeople. Prepare a report based on their experiences. Get them to talk about their reactions to most customers in the stores where they work, their likes and dislikes about their jobs, and what could be done to make their jobs easier.

3. Visit three of the new car dealers in your community and act as a serious buyer. Develop a list of questions ahead of time about such things as miles per gallon of the auto, service requirements, and warranty and safety features. Compare and contrast the results you get in talking to the different salespeople about each of these points. Find out if they have what you consider the needed knowledge for selling the product. Do they conduct themselves in the way you would expect from persons who are selling items valued at $10,000 to $20,000? If not, make suggestions for improving their quality of service to customers.

Suggested Cases

5. Buying an Oriental Rug
6. A Buying Experience
7. York Furniture Company
31. How Good Are Tire Warranties?

Notes

1. M.C. Ramundo, "How the Pros Hang in There," *Sales & Marketing Management,* August 1987, p. 10.

2. M. Morris, A. Gold, and A. Camara, "Creating a Company," *Retailing Issues Letter* 4, March 1992, pp. 1, 3–4.

3. This material, including Figure 15–1, is adapted from B. Rosenbloom, *Improving Personal Selling* (Washington, DC: Small Business Administration), pp. 1–3.

4. T. Kabachnick, "Is Salesmanship the Dinosaur of the 90s?" *Retailing Issues Letter* 3, May 1991, p. 2.

5. L. Dawson, B. Soper, and C. Pettijohn, "The Effects of Empathy on Salesperson Effectiveness," *Psychology & Marketing* 9, July-August 1992, pp. 297–310; J.J. McClung, S.J. Grove, and M.A. Hughes, "An Investigation of the Impact and Situational Determinants of Customer Approach Skills in Retailing," in *Enhancing Knowledge Development in Markets,* Paul Bloom et al., eds., Chicago: American Marketing Association, 1989, p. 92.

6. M. Cartash, "Catch a Falling Store," *Profit,* December 1990, p. 22.

7. Dawson, Soper, and Pettijohn, "The Effects of Empathy on Salesperson Effectiveness"; S. Castleberry and C.D. Sheppard, "Effective Interpersonal Listening and Personal Selling," *Journal of Personal Selling and Sales Management* 1, Winter 1993, pp. 35–50.

8. L.B. Chonko, M.J. Caballero, and J.R. Lumpkin, "Do Retail Salespeople Use Selling Skills?" *Review of Business and Economic Research* 25 (Spring 1990), p. 41.

9. The material on closing the sale is adapted from *Marketing Strategy,* self-instructional booklet 1989 (Washington, DC: Small Business Administration).

10. Dawson, Soper, and Pettijohn, "The Effects of Empathy on Salesperson Effectiveness."

11. K.A. Boedecker and F.W. Morgan, "Managing the Salesperson—Prospect/Customer Interaction: Potential Legal Consequences of Salespersons' Statements," in *Enhanc-*

ing Knowledge Development in Marketing, eds. Paul Bloom et al. (Chicago: American Marketing Association, 1989), p. 307.

12. R. Henkoff, "Finding, Training and Keeping the Best Service Workers," *Fortune,* October 3, 1994, pp. 110–122; R. Henkoff, "Service is Everybody's Business," *Fortune,* June 27, 1994, pp. 48–60.

13. R. Williamson, "Motivation on the Menu," *Globe & Mail,* November 24, 1995, p. B7; D.E. Bowen and E.E. Lawler, III, "The Empowerment of Service Workers: What, Why, How and When," *Sloan Management Review* 33, 3, Spring 1992, pp. 31–39.

14. This material is adapted from *Managing Retail Salespeople,* self-instructional booklet No. 1019 (Washington, DC: Small Business Administration).

15. The material on involvement and feedback and criteria for successful training and job orientation is adapted from *Job Analysis, Job Specifications, and Job Descriptions,* self-instructional booklet no. 120 (Washington, DC: Small Business Administration).

16. B. Dalglish, "Snoops in the Shops," *Maclean's,* December 19, 1994, pp. 28–29.

Retail Advertising, Sales Promotion, and Publicity

Chapter Objectives

After reading this chapter, you should be able to:

1. Describe the communication process in the context of retail promotions.

2. Explain the role of advertising in attracting, informing, and motivating consumers.

3. Explain how to establish and allocate a budget.

4. Evaluate and select appropriate media alternatives for retail messages.

5. Understand how to determine the effectiveness of media.

6. Outline the stages involved in developing creative retail messages.

7. Explain how to measure the results of advertising.

8. Determine when to use an advertising agency.

9. Describe the role of sales promotion and publicity in the retail firm.

"Whooper, Hopper, Whopper, Wiper, etc., write it as you like, it is always good!"

Courtesy of Burger King/Marketel

*A*dvertising and sales promotion are an integral part of the market-ing strategy of many successful retailers. Consider the following example:

After 10 years of doing business in Quebec, Burger King's sales had gone from being flat to a 10 percent decline in 1991. While being second in the rest of Canada, it ranked a distant third to McDonald's and Harvey's. Quebecers either did not know the chain, or resented the fact that the "American" company failed to reach their heart. The major competitor, "McDo" (as it is affectionately called by Quebecers) had done very well thanks to its family-oriented campaigns targeted to the Quebec consumer.

In 1992, Burger King decided to improve its position on the Quebec market. Its advertising agency, Marketel, developed a "made-in-Quebec" campaign focussing on the most popular item, the Whopper, and it targeted the 18- to 34-years-olds, heavy consumers of fast foods.

The creative approach selected by the agency was to make fun of the name whopper (difficult to pronounce in French), using the humorist Marc-André Coallier. The selected media were television and radio, supported by print and POP advertising.

Within two weeks of the start of this very successful campaign, sales increased by 15 to 40 percent depending on the different markets in the province. After one year, top-of-mind awareness of Burger King went up 6 percent, unaided advertising awareness went from 8 percent to 40 percent,

and the number of new users went up 5 percent. Sales increased 11 percent in 1993 and 6.3 percent in 1994. Today, Burger King is a comfortable second in Quebec![1] ■

This example illustrates the role of advertising and other forms of promotion in conveying to a target market the retailer's strategy. Retailers use promotion as a major source of communication with consumers. **Promotion** includes the creative use of advertising, sales promotion, and publicity in providing information to customers. The purposes of communication may be to inform consumers of short-term price promotions, to help establish and maintain the desired image, and a variety of other tasks. The processes of developing promotion plans, establishing budgets, and evaluating the effectiveness of promotions are critical issues in the success of any retail firm. Retailers, such as Burger King, are constantly seeking new and creative ways of communicating with the consumer.

Promotion is an integral part of a firm's total merchandise process. If promotion efforts are not in harmony with decisions on pricing and other elements of the retail mix, the outlet will project a confusing and distorted image. Developing and maintaining store identity thus become the cornerstones of most retailers' promotion plans. Think about the successful positioning strategies these retailers promoted through their campaigns:

- Where the lowest price is the law—Zellers.
- Your money's worth . . . and more—Sears.
- From tune ups to tires, Goodyear takes you home.
- We do chicken right—Kentucky Fried Chicken.
- You deserve a break today—McDonald's.
- Where's the beef?—Wendy's.
- For the seafood lover in you—Red Lobster.

A sound promotion plan can be developed only in the context of the firm's marketing strategies. All promotion efforts should seek to tap the buying motivations of the target market groups selected by management. Sophisticated retailers develop promotion plans similar to those of leading non-retail firms. Each element of the retail plan should be supportive of the targeting and positioning of the firm. For example, media choice is affected by target market selection. Radio station audiences can be segmented on the basis of whether they appeal to teenagers, ethnic groups, or car drivers. Similarly, magazines can be chosen to reach boaters, hunters, tennis players, or the prospective bride. University or college newspapers are appropriate to reach students.

Promotion objectives may be either strategic or tactical. *Strategic objectives* are long term, broad based, and designed to support the overall competitive strategy of the retailer by developing and maintaining a favourable identity or image. *Tactical objectives* are short run and designed to achieve specific measurable goals that support the strategic objectives, for example, to liquidate last year's inventory or to launch a new line.

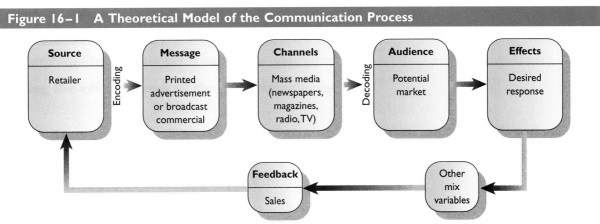

Figure 16–1   A Theoretical Model of the Communication Process

Source: Adapted from René Y. Darmon and Michel Laroche, *Advertising in Canada,* Toronto: McGraw-Hill Ryerson, 1991, p. 15.

The Communication Process

One role of retail communication is to *inform,* by providing information on store hours, brands carried, services available, and so forth. Retailers may also seek to *persuade* individuals to do a variety of things such as to make a purchase during a sale. A third role of advertising is to *remind* customers of the retailers' products and services.

A theoretical model of communication

A theoretical model of communication is shown in Figure 16–1. Communication takes place only when the individuals to whom the retailer is sending a message attach a meaning to the message similar to that intended by the retailer.

The **source** in the communication process is the originator of the message, normally the retailer. The retailer selects words, pictures, and symbols to present the message to the targeted audience. Composing the message is known as *encoding* and refers to putting together the thoughts, information, or ideas in a symbolic form that is familiar to and understood by the target audience.

The **message** is the idea to be transmitted. It may be either oral or written, verbal or non-verbal, or a symbolic form or sign as in the case of McDonald's golden arches. Often, the impression or image created by the advertisement is more important than the actual words.

The next decision after message content selection is the **channel** to be used to communicate the message to the receiver. The nature of communication may be either personal or non-personal. Personal channels such as salespeople include face-to-face contact with target individuals or customers. *Word-of-mouth communication* such as conversations with friends or associates is also a powerful source of information for consumers.[2] *Non-personal channels* of communication include mass media such as radio, television, newspaper, direct mail, or other means of message transmission.

The intended *receiver* is the target audience. Market segmentation plays a particularly important role in this process because segmentation ensures that the message is targeted to a relatively homogeneous audience. *Decoding* occurs when the receiver transforms and interprets the sender's message as part of the thought process. The process of decoding is influenced by the individual's experience, attitudes, and values. Active communication is most likely to occur when a common ground exists between the sender and the receiver.

Unplanned distortion in the communications process is known as *noise*. Noise may occur because of a lack of a common field of experience between the sender and receiver or a failure to properly encode messages, such as the use of signs, symbols, or words that are unfamiliar to the receiver or that have a different meaning than the one intended.

The *desired response* after seeing, hearing, or reading the message depends on the purpose of the promotion program and may include immediate sales, requests for further information, or success in establishing or reinforcing a desired image. Feedback can occur in a variety of ways. The potential customer may ask the salesperson specific questions or in some way reflect non-verbal responses by gestures or facial expressions. Customer inquiries, coupon redemptions, and reply cards are also examples of information feedback.

Market segmentation plays a particularly important role in the communication process because segmentation assures that the message is properly designed and is targeted at a relatively homogeneous audience. Retailers cannot be all things to all people. They must segment their messages, markets, and merchandise. Understanding the customer is the key in all such decisions. For example, The Bay has successfully used Quebec singing superstar Céline Dion in its advertising, all across Canada, singing: "I'm gonna make you love me." These commercials are not only liked by consumers all across the country, but they motivate them to purchase the advertised goods.[3]

Developing the promotion plan

Developing the **promotion plan** requires starting with the goals of the firm. Retailers must decide (1) whom they want to reach, (2) the message they want to get across to these customers, and with what effect, and (3) when and how often their message should reach this audience. Answers to the following questions can help in making such decisions:[4]

- What quality of merchandise do I sell?
- What kind of usage do I want to project?
- How do I compare with the competition?
- What customer services do I offer?
- Who are my customers?
- What are their tastes?
- What are their income levels?
- Why do they buy from me?

We will begin our discussion of promotion by starting with advertising, followed by sales promotion and public relations.

Advertising: Objectives and Budgets

The American Marketing Association defines advertising as "any paid form of nonpersonal presentation and promotion of goods, ideas, and services by an identified sponsor."

Goals of advertising

The basic goals of advertising can include:

- Communicating the total character or image of the store.
- Getting consumer acceptance for individual groups of merchandise.
- Generating a strong flow of traffic.
- Selling goods directly.

These goals can be combined with merchandising and store image objectives into the following framework:[5]

How much to spend	$\longrightarrow$	advertising budget
What to advertise	$\longrightarrow$	merchandise
When to advertise	$\longrightarrow$	timing
Where to say it	$\longrightarrow$	media
How to say it to achieve a campaign objective	$\longrightarrow$	copy
Whom to reach	$\longrightarrow$	audience
How to provide balance	$\longrightarrow$	planning

Communicating the total character of the store is known as **institutional advertising,** and the corresponding advertising campaign is called **image campaign.** Neither specific merchandise nor prices are featured. Rather, institutional advertising is designed to enhance the image of the outlet (such as "People's Choice Groceries") and to communicate targeting and positioning strategies to consumers. *Direct response advertising,* in contrast, persuades consumers to take a specific action, such as to purchase particular merchandise, increase the volume of store traffic, or participate in some type of contest or giveaway. The corresponding advertising campaign is called an **event campaign.** The A & P advertisement is part of an image campaign, while the Black's one is part of an event campaign.

Campaign objectives

In determining the particular objective of an advertising campaign, the retailer must understand that consumers respond to advertising according to various stages. Such a framework is called a **hierarchy of effect model.** The simplest such model is the **AIDA model**: this is, attract **A**ttention, develop **I**nterest, arouse **D**esire, and get **A**ction.

Institutional advertising in action: A & P advertises itself as the People's Choice. Notice there is no focus on individual items carried by the stores.

Courtesy Great Atlantic & Pacific of Canada

A more useful model is described in Figure 16–2. According to this model, the retailer must decide if the campaign objective is one of the following, and then decide the type of campaign that must be developed:

- To increase **awareness** of its name, and develop an attention-getting campaign.
- To increase *knowledge* about the store's assortment, location, services, etc., and develop a campaign that provides information.
- To increase *liking* of the store, and develop arguments to that effect.
- To increase *preference* for the store, with an aggressive campaign to attract new customers and convert them into loyal customers.
- To increase *conviction* by keeping current customers loyal to the store, with reminder advertising.
- To increase *purchase* through event advertising.

Developing the advertising budget

A budget helps retailers plan their promotions. This step alone can go a long way toward better campaigns. Why? There are at least three reasons: (1) a budget forces retailers to set goals so they can measure the success of the promotions; (2) retailers are required to choose from a variety of options; and (3) budgets are more likely to result in well-planned ads.

What should be in the budget?[6]

Promotion is a completely controllable expense, and the function of the budget is to control expenditures. By comparing the budget with actual financial

Figure 16–2 The Hierarchy of Effects Model			
Behavioural Dimension	**Campaign Objective**	**Target Audience**	**Type of Advertising Campaign**
Cognitive—the realm of thoughts; ads provide information and facts	AWARENESS ↓	All potential customers	*Attention-getting* (teasers, slogan, jingle, humour)
	KNOWLEDGE ↓	Potential customers aware of store	*Learning campaign* (description, demonstration, repetition)
Affective—the realm of emotions; ads change attitudes and feelings	LIKING ↓	Knowledgeable potential customers	*Competitive campaign* (reason why, endorsements, soft argumentation)
	PREFERENCE ↓	Customers of competitors	*Aggressive campaign* (comparative, testimonials, status, strong arguments)
Conative—the realm of motives; ads stimulate and direct desires	CONVICTION ↓	Present customers	*Reminder campaign* (image, reinforcements, new ideas)
	PURCHASE	Customers and potential customers	*Value-oriented campaign* (specials, price deals, rebates, direct-mail)

Source: Adapted from René Y. Darmon and Michel Laroche, *Advertising in Canada,* Toronto: McGraw-Hill Ryerson, 1991, p. 280; and Robert J. Lavidge and Gary A. Steiner, "A Model for Predictive Measurement of Advertising Effectiveness," *Journal of Marketing* (October 1961), p. 61.

reports coming from business activities of the firm, it is possible to compare planned activities with actual events.

What retailers would like to invest in advertising and what they can afford are seldom the same. Spending too much is obviously an extravagance, but spending too little can be just as bad in terms of lost sales and reduced visibility. Costs must be tied to results. It is necessary to be prepared to evaluate goals and assess capabilities, and a budget will help do this. The budget can help retailers choose and assess the amount of advertising and its timing. The budget also will serve as a benchmark for next year's plan.

Methods of establishing a budget[7]

There are three basic methods of establishing an advertising budget: (1) percentage of sales or profits, (2) unit of sales, and (3) objective and task. Management needs to use judgment and caution in deciding on any method or methods. The first two methods are "naive" in the sense that sales, in effect, help determine the advertising budget, while logically it should be the other way around. The third one is more in keeping with the logic that advertising affects sales, but is more difficult to apply.

Percentage of sales or profits   A widely used method of establishing an advertising budget is to base it on a percentage of actual sales. Advertising is as much a business expense as the cost of labour and should be related to the quantity of goods sold for a certain period.

The **percentage-of-sales method** avoids some of the problems that result from using profits as a base. For instance, if profits in a period are low, it might not be the fault of sales or advertising. But if retailers base the advertising budget on profits, they will automatically reduce the advertising allotment when

An example of event advertising: the focus of the ad is
on the Pentax camera, plus
related items (film, frame,
photofinishing).

Courtesy Blacks

profits are down. There is no way around it: 2 percent of $10,000 is less than 2
percent of $15,000.

If profits are down for other reasons, a cut in the advertising budget may
very well lead to further losses in sales and profits. This in turn will lead to
further reductions in advertising investment, and so on.

In the short run, it may be possible to make small additions to profit by
cutting advertising expenses. But such a policy could lead to a long-term
deterioration of profits. By using the percentage-of-sales method, it is possible to
keep advertising in a consistent relationship with sales volume. Sales volume is
what advertising should be primarily affecting. Of course, gross margin, especially over the long run, should also show an increase if advertising outlays are
being properly applied.

What percentage? The choice of a percentage-of-sales figure can be based on
what other similar retailers are spending. This can be done since these
percentages are fairly consistent within a given category of business. The
information may be found in trade magazines such as *Marketing,* association
publications, and reports published by financial institutions such as Dun and
Bradstreet. It can also be purchased from companies such as A. C. Nielsen
Canada.

Table 16–1 presents some of the retailers that are among the top 100
companies in advertising spending. Knowing the ratio for a particular industry
helps retailers put their spending into a competitive perspective. Then, depending on the situation, retailers can decide to advertise more than or less than
their competition. For example, compare Sears, Canadian Tire, and Woolworth,
both in terms of advertising expenditures and advertising-to-sales ratios. It may
be necessary to out-advertise competitors and forgo short-term profits. Growth
requires investment.

Retailers should not let any method bind them. The percentage-of-sales
method is quick and easy, and ensures that the advertising budget is not out of
proportion for the business. It may be a sound method for stable markets. But

Table 16–1 Some Canadian Retailers That Advertise Heavily

Rank in 1993*	Retailer	Spending ($000)	Revenues ($000)	A/S† (%)
6	Eaton's of Canada	47,136	N/A	N/A
7	Sears Canada	46,582	4,009,100	1.2
14	McDonald's Restaurants of Canada	35,476	1,520,363	2.3
22	Cineplex Odeon	28,884	549,270	5.3
23	Canadian Tire	28,558	3,232,836	0.9
32	Leon's Furniture	21,388	277,975	7.7
33	Brick Warehouse	21,209	N/A	N/A
39	Royal Bank of Canada	16,504	11,676,000	0.1
45	Canada Safeway	14,556	4,456,600	0.3
62	F.W. Woolworth	11,880	2,143,355	0.6
66	Le Mouvement Desjardins	11,115	411,000	2.7
74	Bank of Montreal	9,321	8,706,000	0.1
77	Majestic Electronic Stores	8,776	39,634	22.1
80	Multitech Warehouse Direct	8,735	N/A	N/A
74	Dylex	8,483	1,940,627	0.4
84	K mart Canada	8,238	1,235,072	0.7
91	Toronto Dominion Bank	7,309	6,366,000	0.1
94	20th Century Theatres	7,178	N/A	N/A
96	Rodale Books	7,136	N/A	N/A

*Based on the top 100 advertisers (the other ranks are non-retailers).
†In interpreting these figures one must remember that some companies have large wholesale or commercial sales.
Source: Adapted from "Canada's Top 100 Advertisers of 1993," *Marketing*, May 2, 1994, pp. 21–22; *Globe and Mail: Report on Business*, July 1994.

if retailers want to expand market share, they may need to use a larger percentage of sales than the industry average.

Which sales? The budget can be determined as a percentage of past sales, of estimated future sales, or as a combination of the two:

1. *Past sales.* The base can be last year's sales or an average of a number of years in the immediate past. Consider, though, that changes in economic conditions can make the figure too high or too low.

2. *Estimated future sales.* The advertising budget can be calculated as a percentage of anticipated sales for next year. The most common pitfall of this method is an optimistic assumption that the business will grow. General business trends must always be kept in mind, especially if there is the chance of a slump. The directions in the industry and in the firm must be realistically assessed.

3. *Past sales and estimated future sales.* Future sales may be estimated conservatively based on last year's sales. A more optimistic assessment of next year's sales is to combine both last year's sales with next year's estimated sales. It is a more realistic method during periods of changing economic conditions. This method allows management to analyze trends and results thoughtfully and predict more accurately.

Unit of sales In the **unit-of-sales method,** retailers set aside a fixed sum for each unit of product to be sold. This figure is based on their experience and trade knowledge of how much advertising it takes to sell each unit. For example, if it takes two cents' worth of advertising to sell a case of canned vegetables, and the object is to move 100,000 cases, management will plan to spend $2,000 on advertising. If it costs X dollars to sell a refrigerator, management will need to budget 1,000 times X to sell a thousand refrigerators. Managers are simply basing the budget on unit of sale rather than dollar amounts of sales.

Some people consider this just a variation of percentage-of-sales. The unit-of-sales method, however, does permit a closer estimate of what should be planned to spend for maximum effect. This method is based on a retailer's experience of what it takes to sell an actual unit, rather than an overall percentage of the gross sales estimate.

The unit-of-sales method is particularly useful where product availability is limited by outside factors, such as bad weather's effect on crops. The owners estimate the number of units or cases available to them. Based on a manager's experience, they advertise only as much as it takes to sell the products. The unit-of-sales method works reasonably well with specialty goods, where demand is more stable. But it is not very useful in sporadic or irregular markets or for style merchandise.

Objective and task   The most difficult method for determining an advertising budget is the **objective-and-task method.** Yet this method is the most accurate and best fulfills what all budgets should accomplish. It relates the appropriation to the marketing task to be achieved.[8] This method relates the advertising spending to the volume of expected sales. To establish a budget by the objective-and-task method, it is necessary to have a coordinated marketing program. This program should be set up with specific objectives based on a thorough survey of markets and their potential.

The percentage-of-sales or profits method first determines the amount retailers will spend with little consideration of a goal. The task method establishes what must be done in order to meet company objectives. Only then is the cost calculated.

It is best to set specific objectives, not just "increase sales." For example, a retailer wishes to "sell 25 percent more of product X or service Y by attracting the business of teenagers." First, the manager determines which media best reaches the target market. Then the retailer estimates the cost to run the number and types of advertisements it will take to get the sales increase. This process is repeated for each objective. When these costs are totalled, the projected budget is available. As this description indicates, applying this method requires an excellent knowledge of media planning principles, often not the case among retailers. The media representatives of each medium, an advertising agency, or a media buying service may often be of assistance to a retailer.

Of course, retailers may find that they cannot afford to advertise as they would like to. It is a good idea, therefore, to rank objectives. As with the other methods, managers should be prepared to change plans to reflect reality and the resources available.

Allocating the budget

Once the advertising budget has been determined, management must decide how to allocate the advertising dollars. A decision to use institutional (image) advertising or promotional (sales) advertising must be made. After setting aside money for the different types of advertising, retailers can allocate the promotional advertising funds. Among the most common breakdowns are: (1) departmental budgets, (2) calendar periods, (3) media, and (4) trading area.

Departmental budgets   The most common method of allocating advertising to departments is on the basis of their sales contribution. Those departments or product categories with the largest sales volume receive the biggest share of the budget. In a small business, or when the merchandise range is limited, the same percentage can be used throughout. Otherwise, a good rule is to use the average industry figure for each product. By breaking down the budget by departments or products, those goods that require more promotion to stimulate sales can get the required advertising dollars. The budget can be further divided into individual merchandise lines.

Calendar periods   Most executives usually plan their advertising on a monthly, or even a weekly, basis. Even a budget for a longer planning period, however, should be calculated for these shorter periods as well. This permits better control. The percentage-of-sales methods are useful to determine allocations by time periods. The standard practice is to match sales with advertising dollars. If February accounts for 5 percent of sales, it might get 5 percent of the budget. Sometimes, retailers adjust advertising allocations downward in heavier sales months in order to boost the budget of poorer periods. This is done only when a change in advertising timing could improve slow sales, as when competition's sales trends differ markedly from those of the firm.

Monthly percentages of annual sales differ by store type and region. Also, economic conditions can affect budget plans. Other ways for allocating funds focus on the traffic-drawing power of some items or on the growth potential of key lines. Sales variations by month normally have the largest effect on advertising. Almost three-fourths of the advertising budget by boating retailers, for example, is spent from March through July. In contrast, over 20 percent of the advertising budget for jewelry is spent in the month of December. Garden supplies retailers spend over 50 percent of their advertising budget from March through June. December is the largest advertising month for appliance dealers, bookstores, department stores, retail furniture dealers, hardware dealers, music stores, and shoe stores.

Media   The amount of advertising that is placed in each advertising medium—such as direct mail, newspapers, or radio—should be determined by past experience, industry practice, and ideas from media specialists. Normally, retailers use the same sort of media that competitors use, because it is most likely where potential customers will look or listen.

Trading area   Retailers can spend their advertising dollars in established trading areas or use them to try to stimulate new sales outside the primary trading area. It is wise to do the bulk of advertising in familiar areas. Usually, it is more costly to develop new markets than to maintain established ones.

Maintaining budget flexibility

Any combination of these methods may be employed in the formation and allocation of the advertising budget. All of them—or simply one—may be needed to meet the retailer's advertising objectives. However management decides to plan the budget, it must make it *flexible,* capable of being adjusted to changes in the marketplace.

The duration of the planning and budgeting period depends upon the nature of the business. If management can use short budgeting periods, they will find that advertising can be more flexible and that they can change tactics to meet immediate trends. To ensure advertising flexibility, management should have a contingency fund to deal with specials available in local media, or unexpected competitive situations.

Management should be aware of competitors' activities at all times. They should not blindly copy competitors, but analyze how their actions may affect business—and be prepared to act.

Cooperative advertising

Cooperative advertising is a situation in which a manufacturer pays part of the retailer's advertising costs under specific conditions. Many manufacturers and wholesalers state that a significant part of the reserves they set up for cooperative advertising are not used by their retailers. It has been estimated that $600 million of the $1.5 billion in co-op funds available to Canadian retailers goes unclaimed, and the reason is that many retailers do not know about these programs or are unsure of how they operate.[9] This is surprising. Cooperative advertising substantially lowers the cost for the retailer, since manufacturers or wholesalers pay part of the advertising cost.

For their own legal protection and to ensure the greatest return from their investment, manufacturers set up specific requirements to be observed in cooperative advertising. The retailer should consult each vendor about the requirements that must be met to qualify. The retailer must also be aware of the procedures to follow to apply for and receive payment. Some vendors relate cooperative dollars to the amount of the retailer's business. Others figure on a percentage basis. The amount and rules for payment of cooperative dollars are at the discretion of the vendor. For more details and examples, see Retail Highlight 16–1.

Cooperative advertising as a percentage of total advertising is approximately 50 percent for department stores, shoe stores, and clothing stores, and approximately 75 percent for food stores and electrical appliance stores.[10]

Advertising: Evaluating Media Options

Each medium has its strengths and weaknesses. Retailers normally use a media mix to give them the strengths of each. Media choices include radio, newspapers, TV, magazines, direct mail, and billboards. The characteristics of each medium are shown in Table 16–2. Other specialized forms of promotion not shown in the table are also available, and discussed later in the chapter.

Three general questions can help an advertiser evaluate media:

- Is the audience of the medium appropriate for the advertising campaign?

- Among the available media, which provides the largest audience at the lowest cost?

- Can the medium effectively communicate the sales message?

Retail Highlight 16–1

Understanding Co-op Advertising Programs

When Gary Kugler decided to get more aggressive about promoting his camera store in Ottawa (Focus Centre), he increased the advertising budget by 100 percent. Through co-operative advertising, Kugler's suppliers shared the costs of his newspaper and radio ads. In return, their products got greater exposure in the local market—and everyone benefited. As his co-op relationships developed, Kugler saw his annual sales increase by 20 percent. Adding a photo-finishing centre, he marked the expansion with a two-page insert in the *Ottawa Citizen,* for which most of his 20 suppliers contributed co-op funds. The ad cost $13,000, and Kugler's share amounted to $2,000.

In many co-op programs, as in the previous example, retailers earn co-op dollars based on a percentage of purchases made from a distributor or manufacturer: between 2 and 5 percent, although they can go as high as 10 percent. For example, if Kugler buys $10,000 worth of Canon cameras, his supplier will give him 5 percent

of that, or $500, to be spent in advertising Canon. The supplier then pays for a portion of advertising Canon cameras, up to the amount of co-op dollars his dealer accumulates. Most suppliers pay 50 to 75 percent of the cost for any one campaign (in some cases, they pay the full amount).

The suppliers' sales representatives are very important sources of information for these programs. Every manufacturer has different rules, from logo size to placement of the ad in the media. They can also provide ready-made ads or help retailers create their own.

Local media can also help. About 68 percent of co-op dollars are spent on newspaper advertising. In order to generate more co-op business, many newspapers handle much of the co-op paperwork, such as billing agreements. Finally, co-op dollars can also be used for a wide variety of promotions, such as direct mail or sales promotions.

Source: Jennifer Pepall, "Co-op Advertising Builds Strength from Numbers," *Profit,* November 1990, pp. 53–54.

Advertising can be tricky. However, by establishing specific goals, analyzing various media, and using proven techniques, a retailer can successfully promote merchandise.

Media information sources

For most media, information about rates charged to national advertisers and ad agencies (called **national rates**), as well as various conditions offered by the media, is published monthly in *Canadian Advertising Rates & Data (CARD).*[11] However, the rates charged directly to retailers (called **retail or local rates**) are not published in *CARD,* but in an individual Retail Rate Card that the retailer obtains directly from the local medium. For example, a quick phone call to the sales office of the local newspaper will get you the retail rate card for that newspaper such as *The Montreal Gazette.*

Two reasons for charging different rates are: (1) the medium does not pay the 15 percent commission to advertising agencies on retail rates, since most retailers do not use an advertising agency (because of a small budget and tight schedules); and (2) retailers do not normally need the total audience of a medium, as their trading area is more restricted.

Most retail advertising in Canada is spent on daily newspapers, followed by radio (Table 16–3) because it effectively reaches geographic targets. Table 16–4 provides two examples of media budget allocations for a retailer.

Table 16–2   Advantages and Disadvantages of Various Advertising Media

Medium	Advantages	Disadvantages
Newspapers	Good flexibility Timeliness Good local coverage Broad acceptance High believability	Short life Poor reproduction quality Small pass-along audience
Magazines	Good geographic and demographic selectivity Good credibility and prestige High-quality reproduction Long life Good pass-along readership	Long production lead time Some waste circulation Poor position guarantee
Radio	Mass audience Good geographic and demographic selectivity Low cost	Audio presentation only Lower audience attention than TV Non-standardized rate structure Fleeting Exposure
Television	Appeals to many senses Commands high attention levels High reach	High absolute cost High clutter Fleeting exposure Less audience selectivity Long production lead time
Direct mail	Best audience selectivity Good flexibility No clutter Good personalization	Relatively high cost Sometimes poor image
Outdoor	Good flexibility High repeat exposure Low cost Low competition	Poor audience selectivity Limited creativity

Media terminology

Before discussing the various media available to a retailer, a few definitions would be useful:

- **Reach** is the number of different persons exposed at least once to a message during an ad campaign. Reach is often expressed as a percentage of the total audience.

- **Frequency** is the average number of times a person will be exposed to a message during the advertising period.

- **Cost per thousand (CPM)** is the cost of reaching 1,000 members of a desired audience with one or several ads.

- **Selectivity** is the ability of a medium to reach only specific audiences, minimizing waste (e.g., only teenagers or men aged 24 to 45).

- **Spot advertising** refers to commercials shown on local (radio or television) stations, whereby the negotiation and purchase of time is made directly with the individual station. Network television advertising done by national advertisers during the prime time period is called **prime time advertising.**

Radio

Radio follows the listener everywhere: in the home, at the beach, and on the highway. Almost every Canadian owns at least one radio. There are currently 361

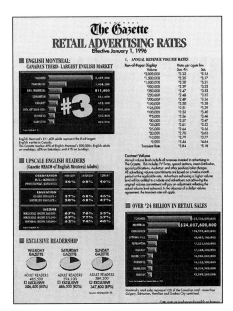

Courtesy Montreal Gazette

AM stations and 432 FM stations in Canada.[12] Radio advertising is characterized by comparatively low rates, little or no production costs, and immediacy in scheduling. Retailers spend about 25 percent of their advertising dollars for radio (Table 16–3), and radio stations depend on retail advertisers for 77 percent of their revenues.

Rates depend on the number of commercials contracted for, the time periods specified, and whether the station broadcasts on AM and/or FM frequencies. Usually, FM broadcasting is more localized and offers wider tonal range.

Strengths of Radio. Radio allows retailers to (1) direct ads to large target audiences; (2) reach people almost anywhere; (3) advertise at relatively low cost; and (4) work with short lead time.

Disadvantages of Radio. These are: (1) no pictures; (2) short messages; (3) the need to use several stations in large cities to reach a large target audience; (4) production problems, since most programming is local; and (5) large, wasted audiences for small local retailers.

Radio advertising is used to convey and reinforce distinctive images that draw shoppers to retail outlets. Such advertising typically is institutional, stressing features retailers believe customers are looking for. Humour, ad-lib dialogues, catchy music, and jingles increasingly are used to create bright images in radio advertising. Retailers prefer institutional advertising over price advertising because they believe that price/item advertising gets "lost" on air.

Buying radio time

Radio advertising time is typically sold in blocks of 30- or 60-second slots, with a few stations offering 15-second slots. The 60-second slots tend to be most popular. The price of advertising time varies by time of day, size of listening audience, and length of the spots.

Radio rate schedules vary by stations, as does the system of discounts. The most expensive time is known as "drive time," between 6 and 10 A.M. and 4 and

Table 16–3   Retail Advertising for Each Medium, and Share of Retail Advertising per Medium

Medium	Retail Expenditures (Millions)	Distribution (% Total Retail)	Retail Share (% Total Medium)
Television	$ 386	17.0	21.8
Radio	572	25.2	77.2
Daily newspapers*	785	34.6	70.0
Weekly papers	512	22.6	90.1
Weekend supplements	13	0.6	100.0
Magazines	0	0.0	0.0
Total retail	**$2,268**	**100.0**	**50.7**

*Excludes classified advertising.

Source: *The Canadian Media Directors' Council Media Digest, 1995/96,* p. 7.

7 P.M. on weekdays. Advertising is very inexpensive between midnight and 5 A.M., since few people are listening to the station. Weekend rates often differ from weekly rates, depending on the composition of the audience.

Other factors affecting cost include the frequency of advertising during a given week, the number of weeks the ad is aired, and the time of year the spot is on the air. The station may select the air time—this is called run-of-station (ROS)—or the retailer may choose a more costly fixed time slot. If the slots are part of a package, they probably consist of different time slots and frequencies for an extended period of time.

Television

TV has the visual impact of print and the sound impact of radio, plus colour, motion, and emotion. Canadians now spend as much time viewing TV as radio, newspapers, and magazines combined, for example, about 24 hours per week for adults, and 19 hours for children. Problems include the high cost of time and high production costs. Most people view TV at night after the stores are closed. Infrequent summer viewing is also a disadvantage as is the increasingly fragmented audience because of cable services, either part of the basic subscription such as The Learning Channel or the Youth Channel, or as pay-TV such as The Movie Network, The Family Channel, and others. Another major problem for advertisers is the high incidence of zapping and zipping, which lower the chance of the commercial being seen.

Local TV stations carry the programs of major networks. There are 2 English (CBC and CTV) and 1 French (Radio Canada) national commercial networks in Canada, 13 regional or provincial networks, and 18 specialty networks. Canadian network programs are viewed by 46 percent of the TV audience, against 21 percent for the U.S. stations (including U.S. pay-TV), 15 percent for the Canadian independents, 10 percent for the Canadian pay and specialty channels, and 8 percent for the others (including VCR).[13]

The network programs include commercials bought by national retailers such as Eaton's or Sears. The stations sell local commercial time during station breaks. Management probably should plan on using daytime, news program times, and early evening hours before TV prime time.

Table 16–4   Examples of Media Budget Allocations for Two Large Retailers

Medium	Sears Canada (in $000s)	%	Eaton's of Canada (in $000s)	%
Television	13,144	28.2	9,199	19.5
Daily newspapers	26,185	56.2	31,634	67.1
Magazines	4,735	10.2	2,070	4.4
Out-of-home	3	0.0	213	0.5
Radio	2,515	5.4	4,020	8.5
Total	46,582	100.0	47,136	100.0

Source: "Canada's Top 100 Advertisers of 1993," *Marketing*, May 2, 1994, p. 21.

TV ads are costly

The cost for a 30-second spot ad in a small local market such as Red Deer (Alberta) may be between $100 and $200, and in a major market such as Toronto a similar ad may cost between $700 and $2,000. The cost varies according to the time of the day, and the most expensive time is prime time (8 P.M.–11 P.M.).

Cost per viewer is the lowest for a national audience

However, few retail firms other than Eaton's, The Bay, Sears, and Wal-Mart have enough outlets to justify national TV ads. Use of local TV by large retailers is increasing, but about 14 percent of retail ad expenditures go to television. TV stations rely on local advertising for only 22 percent of their revenues (Table 16–3).

Few retailers feel that TV is the best overall medium by which to reach their audience. However, they are more prone to use television to reach a specific target audience like youth, which has been weaned on TV. Cable penetration in Canada is very high and reached 76 percent in 1994. Pay TV, with a low penetration of 5 percent, does not yet have a sufficiently large audience, particularly in major markets, to attract many national advertisers.[14]

Buying television time

Television time is normally sold in 15-, 30-, and 60-second time slots, with the 30-second slot being the most popular (76 percent). The cost of television advertising depends on the size of the audience, which can be described in terms of ratings and shares.

A **gross rating point (GRP)** is 1 percent of all homes with television sets in a market area. A program with a GRP of 10 is reaching 10 percent of the television homes. In contrast, a **share** is the percentage of television sets in use that are tuned to a given program. Thus, a program may have a GRP of only one, for example, at 4 A.M. on Sunday morning. But it may also have a share of 56.

Newspapers

About 35 percent of all retail ad dollars go to daily newspapers and another 23 percent go to weeklies and weekend supplements (Table 16–3). Daily newspapers rely on retail advertising for about 70 percent of their revenues. The other

Examples of radio scripts, using a spoof on popular Christmas songs to attract shoppers to First Canadian Place Shops in Toronto.

WE WISH YOU A MERRY HAIRCUT
SFX: *(Christmas music in background)*
TONY: *Hi, this is Tony of Tony's Barber Shop. All the other stores here at First Canadian Place Shops, like Fairweather, Benetton and Your Jewelry, are full of shoppers looking for novel gift ideas. So, I'd just like to say, consider the gift of a haircut. 'Cause you never have to worry about a loved one getting two haircuts for Christmas...ever.*
ANNOUNCER: *First Canadian Place Shops at King and Bay. One hundred and sixty stores full of gift ideas.*

WHEN DRY CLEANERS DREAM
SFX: *(Christmas music in background)*
RAJ: *Hi, this is Raj from Preeners Dry Cleaners. Other stores here at First Canadian Place Shops, like Bally Shoes, Cactus and Lipton's, are full of shoppers looking for unusual gift ideas. So, don't forget about us—Preeners Dry Cleaners—and give someone you love the gift of dry cleaning. Imagine the surprise when they open a gift and find their dry cleaning. Just imagine.*
ANNOUNCER: *First Canadian Place Shops at King and Bay. One hundred and sixty stores full of gift ideas.*

COME ALL YE HEELS
SFX: *(Christmas music in background)*
FRANK: *Hi, this is Frank from Mastercraft Shoe Repair. Here at First Canadian Place Shops, other stores like Costello, Kristy Allan and Town Shoes are full of shoppers looking for unique gift ideas. So don't forget us—Mastercraft Shoe Repair. Have a heel replaced for that special someone, or if you really love somebody, consider deodorized insoles. Merry Christmas.*
ANNOUNCER: *First Canadian Place Shops at King and Bay. One hundred and sixty stores full of gift ideas.*

Courtesy of Pirate Radio

types of newspapers depend on retail advertising for more than 90 percent of their revenues.

Daily newspapers

Most markets have some type of daily newspaper, and newspaper ad supplements are a popular advertising medium. **Supplements** are preprinted pages of ads that are inserted into the papers. Sunday papers are usually full of supplements, and local department stores are heavy users. There are about 108 daily newspapers in Canada with an average total daily circulation of 5 million copies and a penetration of 63 percent of households. Almost 8 million adults read daily newspapers and they spend about one hour reading them.[15]

Newspaper ad rates are quoted for short-term advertisers as weekly insertion rates, as monthly rates, and as yearly rates. Newspapers quote local retailers a *retail rate* that is below the **general rate** (charged to agencies for national advertisers).

Newspaper personnel speak in terms of modular agate lines when quoting prices. A **modular agate line (MAL)** is one (standardized) column wide and 1.8 mm deep. In addition, a **Canadian newspaper unit (CNU)** is a unit one column wide and 30 MALs deep. Newspapers have special rates for supplements, and rates for colour are higher than black-and-white rates.

The strengths of newspapers include: (1) broad market coverage; (2) short lead time for ads; (3) the capability of advertising a large number of items together; (4) wide readership; (5) high graphic potential; and (6) assistance in ad preparation (important for a small retailer).

Newspapers have their weaknesses, too. They include: (1) problems in reaching the younger market and children; (2) the chance that many readers will miss an ad; (3) accelerating ad rates; (4) limited ability to segment readers; and (5) lower suburban coverage by big-city papers.

The newspaper office can be helpful in planning the copy and layout. Many small retailers have few skills in these areas and rely on the newspaper professionals to provide the needed services.

Community newspapers

Community newspapers are published in almost every community in Canada, with the majority being published once a week. In Table 16–3, they are included in the 'weeklies' category, and rely almost exclusively on retail advertising. Their circulation has been increasing because their editorial coverage deals principally with local issues of interest to many readers. There are about 940 community newspapers in Canada with an average weekly circulation of 9 million.[16] They tend to be well read within the community and represent an attractive audience for local retailers, and often a very efficient buy, since there is little wasted circulation. The main drawback is the low frequency of publication.

Shoppers

Shoppers go by many names, including "shopping news," "pennysavers," or "marketplace." These papers are quite different from the traditional newspaper. They normally carry less than 25 percent editorial content. Virtually all news is syndicated feature material as opposed to local news, and shoppers are distributed on a free basis.

They offer retailers the opportunity for almost total coverage of a market area. Since they are primarily an advertising medium, the people who read them are already in a buying mood and seeking specific information. Still, the fact that the papers primarily contain advertising may cause some customers not to read them, and wasted advertising can occur.

More and more merchandisers are demanding the services of shoppers, however, since they want better market coverage. Each "shopper" has its own advertising rate schedule, and costs are often quite low. However, the coverage of markets in Canada is very uneven, with the majority in Ontario, and a handful in Quebec, New Brunswick, Manitoba, and Saskatchewan. Suppliers of "shoppers" in the Toronto metropolitan area provide about 10 different "shoppers." Each will cover only a selected portion of the metropolitan area, such as a specific suburban community.[17]

Special-purpose papers

There are newspapers for special-interest groups such as universities or community colleges (over 200), the farmers (about 100 publications), and ethnic groups (about 140). General information about these media is also available in *CARD,* and the retail rates from the publisher. These media are especially desirable advertising outlets for retailers who are seeking to reach highly specific audiences.

Magazines

As shown in Table 16–3, a negligible percentage of retail ad budgets are spent on magazines. Until recently, the only retailers using magazines were national firms such as Eaton's (4.4 percent) or Sears (10.2 percent), as illustrated in Table 16–4. However, local retailers can now place ads in regional editions of such magazines as *Reader's Digest, Maclean's,* and *Chatelaine.* There are over 500 consumer magazines in Canada, and about 30 of them offer geographic editions.

Magazine strengths include (1) carefully defined audiences, (2) good colour reproduction, (3) long ad life because they are not thrown away as quickly as newspapers, (4) low cost per thousand readers, and (5) good pass-along readership (as some magazines are read by people other than the subscribing household, such as friends and neighbours).

The primary problems are (1) high cost, (2) long closing dates (ads must be submitted several weeks before publication for monthly magazines), and (3) slower response.

Buying magazine advertising space

Advertising space is typically sold in pages or fractions of pages, such as one-half or one-sixth. The rates charged depend upon the circulation of the magazine, quality of the publication, and type of primary audience. Rates are higher for magazines with higher circulation. Magazines typically offer discounts for advertising depending upon the bulk and frequency of advertising. Higher prices are normally charged for special positions in the magazine and for special formats.

Direct promotion

Direct promotion will be covered in detail in Chapter 20. However, since direct mail is an important part of the retailer's media options, this particular form will be treated here for completeness.

Direct Mail is the most selective form of retail advertising. But the cost per person reached is high. According to retailers, direct mail is among the top three forms of retail advertising today. Most retailers use some form of direct mail such as catalogues. The strengths include (1) the high response rate by consumers, (2) the ability to send material to a specific person, (3) not being bound by media format (it is possible to use as much space as needed to tell the story of the product and use colours or other creative effects as the budget allows), and (4) the message does not have to compete with other editorial matter.

The weakness of direct mail is its high cost compared to other media. The cost per thousand is many times higher than for other media.

There are good reasons for the popularity of direct mail. Direct mail includes bill stuffers (which are about 70 percent of direct mail), catalogues, flyers for store openings, sales letters, and everything we normally call "junk mail." To cut costs, some retailers have resorted to hand-delivered flyers to selected targets. In addition to lower costs of printing and distribution (compared to a newspaper insert), the retailer can more effectively reach his or her customers.[18]

The procedure for direct mailing

Mailing lists can be rented from mailing houses. The list can be selected according to consumer tastes on a variety of bases including, for example, model of automobile, family income, tendency to buy through mail-order companies, and FSA code (Forward Sortation Area codes are the first three digits of the postal code) or census tract. A typical mailing list will cost between $30 and $50 a thousand. An occupant list (no personalized name) of all households in a designated area may cost as little as $5 per thousand. Understandably, the more precise and well-defined the list, the higher the cost.

The frequency of mailing depends on the purpose of the campaign. However, to generate new sales leads, one consulting firm recommends one mailing every other month for continuity and long-term effectiveness, or four

Photo by Jim Hertel

Catalogues, a form of direct promotion, are an effective advertising medium for many retailers.

mailings six weeks apart for maximum short-term impact. But one annual mailing may be sufficient for a seasonal operation or for a firm that occasionally needs a limited amount of new business.

Catalogues   Many merchants now operate catalogue sales departments. Sales through mail catalogues are growing. It is estimated that in 1994 there were about 620 catalogue firms in Canada, generating $1.8 billion in annual sales.[19] In addition, there is very strong competition from U.S. catalogue firms such as L.L. Bean, Spiegel, and Land's End, generating more than $200 million in Canadian sales.[20]

Catalogues are a special form of direct mail promotion and are often used as an advertising medium by department and specialty stores, for example, the Sears Catalogue or the Regal Gifts Catalogue. Most large department stores now have Christmas catalogues. Consumers like catalogues because of the convenience afforded by shopping at home, calling a toll-free number, and getting door-to-door delivery. There is even a *Catalogue of Canadian Catalogues* (Alpel Publishing). It has been estimated that about 60 percent of Canadians make a catalogue or mail-order purchase during a one-year period.[21]

The following are trends in catalogue marketing:

- New and better design/format. Upscale retailers like Holt Renfrew and Harry Rosen have developed new catalogue formats—Holt Renfrew a "magalogue" for men, and Harry Rosen a catalogue on CD-ROM. Launched in March 1995, the new Harry Rosen catalogue under the theme of "Get an attitude" allows customers to "try" various outfits in combination, in addition to providing the standard pricing and product information.[22]

- Emphasis on "lifestyle" merchandising, although the term itself is defined in almost as many different ways as there are catalogues.

- A stepped-up search for cost-cutting techniques, including charging a "subscription" to a series of catalogues, or offering the catalogue, via magazine advertising, at a charge to non-customers.
- Growth of separate catalogue operations, with full responsibility for inventory and controlling direct mail business.

The typical department store catalogue has a life of about six weeks. Two or three catalogues per year is not uncommon for some stores, and many are talking about 20 or more "specialogues." For example, Sears produces about 15 catalogues per year, almost like a magazine publication, and distributes 40 million copies.[23] A few have over 300 pages. The emphasis in all the stores is on "target mailing"—the use of catalogues to sell separate categories of merchandise. Stores are increasingly using computers to target prime customers instead of blanket mailings.

Directories

Every retail business normally advertises in one or more **directories.** The most common is the *Yellow Pages* in the telephone directory. Directories, however, are published by various trade associations and groups, and they reach more prospective customers than virtually any other medium. Consumers have normally already made a decision to purchase before turning to a directory for help in deciding where to buy. Also, directories have a longer life than most advertising media.

Most directories are published for a minimum of 12 months, which can serve as a drawback. Retailers do not have the option of changing the advertisement in any way until the appearance of a new directory. Thus, the advertisements can become obsolete rather quickly.

But costs are reasonable for ads such as the **Yellow Pages advertising** in a telephone directory. A half-column display ad can vary from $20 a month in an area with 20,000 residents to $200 a month or more in an area of 1,000,000.

Out-of-home advertising

Retailers are in a unique position to place advertisements near their stores, or along the roads leading to their stores. There are a large variety of **out-of-home media,** with the most important being transit advertising (e.g., buses) and outdoor advertising (e.g., billboards), but there are many other minor ones available at a relatively low cost (e.g., bench advertising).

Transit advertising

Transit advertising includes signs placed on buses, subway cars, and commuter trains, as well as advertising placed in the terminals, platforms, and stations for such vehicles. Total painted buses, where the whole bus is painted with the message, have become popular in the last few years, although they tend to be expensive.

Transit advertising has a captive audience in the people using the vehicles. Outdoor transit advertising (also on the outside of the vehicle) is especially effective for certain types of retailers. The vehicles carrying the advertising normally travel through the business area of a community and have a high level of exposure to prospective consumers. Transit advertising is typically a media option only for retailers in large metropolitan areas. Small areas normally do not have public transportation.

Outdoor advertising

Outdoor advertising signs are among the oldest form of advertising. Outdoor signs can be found along the roads, at the airports, in malls, and in the downtown areas of major cities.

Most retailers have signs outside their business even if they don't use billboards. Outdoor advertising signs have a large number of advantages, one of which is a high exposure rate. People tend to see the same outdoor billboard many times a month because they tend to follow the same traffic patterns each day. The signs are inexpensive but are heavily read by travellers and other customers seeking specific information.

The disadvantages are the relatively small amount of information that can be placed on a billboard, the large amount of display space needed, and the competition with other billboards in a community.

Buying outdoor advertising   Outdoor billboard advertising usually is bought from companies that specialize in leasing sign space to merchants. Outdoor signs come in a variety of sizes, shapes, and locations. The typical billboard size is 3.7 metres by 7.5 metres. Outdoor advertising signs are bought in terms of a set level of GRPs. A hundred GRPs weekly in a market means that advertising space was purchased on enough posters to deliver an *exposure* level equal to 100 percent of the population in an area on the average during a week.

Non-standard signs are normally those erected by the retailer. No standard size exists for such billboards. And the retailers arrange with each individual landowner for the space they want to lease. They have to be careful not to violate local regulations on the placement and construction of the signs, however. Billboards are becoming increasingly controversial in many communities because of concerns over quality of life and aesthetics.

Other out-of-home media

Other options for retailers include aerial advertising (e.g., balloons and sky writing), bench advertising, elevator advertising, sports advertising (e.g., in hockey arenas), taxicab and truck advertising, and theatre and videoscreen advertising.

Video tech

We discussed video technology in Chapter 2 and are highlighting it again as a reminder of its growing impact on promotion plans. Video involves promoting directly to the consumer by the use of cable TV, teletext, or video discs. Technological advances in two-way interactive cable are making shop-at-home services more feasible. The primary drawback still is the high cost per purchase. Nevertheless, merchants are looking at the new technologies as ways of expanding their profit centres.

There are a number of "Shopping Channels" in Canada, either in existence or in the planning stages. These continuous cable-television programs, like the revolutionary UBI system (*U*niversality, *B*i-directionality, and *I*nteractivity) being tested with 33,000 families in Chicoutimi (Quebec), are some of the most

An example of aerial advertising for a retailer. It costs $100,000, is 26 metres long, and gets about 100 flying days a year. Rides are occasionally donated to charitable groups.

Source: "Balloons Help Printer's Message Fly," *Marketing*, June 29, 1992, p. 15.

ambitious experiments in video shopping, and this innovation will have a profound effect in the retailing sector.[24]

Use of in-store audio and video promotion devices is one of the more rapidly expanding areas of opportunity for retailers. Such examples include the following:

- *Video screens.* In-store TV screens mounted at eye level, which are sometimes linked together to form a video wall for presenting brief brand and price identification messages lasting 7 to 10 seconds.
- *Audio systems.* Messages can be placed anywhere and typically are activated by motion or body heat. The devices contain a 10- to 20-second recorded selling message calling attention to a product and are typically placed within an aisle.
- *Shopping carts.* Some shopping carts today contain a video message that can be activated by the consumer.
- *In-store kiosks.* Such devices typically are placed next to a product and can operate either on constant play or be activated by a consumer who wants to see and hear a message about the product.[25]

Promotional products advertising

Promotional products (formerly called specialty) **advertising** uses gift-giving to customers as the advertising medium. Examples include clothing (caps, T-shirts), fountain pens, calendars, and key chains. The gifts typically contain the name of the firm, company address, and perhaps its logo or slogan. The business endeavors to build goodwill among customers by providing useful items that will remind customers of the firm each time they use them. The promotional products chosen should match the type of merchandise sold by the firm. For example, wallpaper and paint stores often will provide a tape measure. But promotional products advertising is more useful in retaining present customers than in attracting new ones.

Visual merchandising

Visual merchandising is often viewed as a form of non-media advertising. Visual merchandising was introduced in Chapter 11, but we want to remind you again of its critical role in communicating store image to consumers. Good displays inform the consumer about the merchandise offered and help to entertain and delight the consumer in such a way as to differentiate the outlet from competitors. As such, visual merchandising is part of a total store focus for communicating a unified image.

Evaluating the effectiveness of media

Media effectiveness is usually measured in terms of (1) cost per thousand and (2) reach and frequency, in order to establish a price/value relationship between media options.

Cost per thousand (CPM)

The most common method of evaluating the cost effectiveness of several media is the **cost per thousand (CPM).** The CPM is measured by dividing the cost of an advertisement (of given sizes, e.g., a full page, and options, e.g., four colours) by the number of households or persons reached within the target market. The general formula is:

$$CPM = \frac{\text{Ad cost}}{\text{Audience or circulation (in thousands)}}$$

The CPM allows comparing several different vehicles (e.g., different newspapers, magazines, radio, or TV stations) with different audiences, by standardizing the rates to the same 1,000 readers, viewers, or listeners. However, this calculation does not take into account other considerations such as quality of editorial matter or clutter (both could impact on ad readership).

This formula is useful only for intramedia comparisons, that is, for comparing one newspaper to another, and using it for media planning purposes.[26] Intermedia comparisons of radio and newspaper are less useful.

Example. For example, a 60-second spot on radio station A provides 100,000 impressions (the audience reached by each spot in the schedule) weekly and costs $500. The same size spot in radio station B provides 200,000 impressions weekly and costs $800.

The cost per 1,000 impressions is $5.00 for A and $4.00 for B.

$$CPM\ (A) = \frac{\$500}{100} = \$5.00 \qquad CPM\ (B) = \frac{\$800}{200} = \$4.00$$

Thus, B is a better buy, in addition to providing a bigger audience.

Reach and frequency

When comparing advertising programs it is important to select the most effective *balance* of reach and frequency. Although separate concepts, reach and frequency are closely related, and their product is the GRP (gross rating point) concept introduced earlier:

$$\text{Reach} \times \text{frequency} = \text{Gross rating points}$$

Consider a hypothetical situation as an example: an advertiser who uses magazines for an advertising campaign has two options:

- Buy one insertion in five different magazines.
- Buy five insertions in one magazine.

Assuming that each magazine has a reach of 10, and that both options have the same cost (i.e., magazine budget), both deliver the same level of GRP, i.e., 50 GRPs (5 times 10 in both cases). However, the first option tries to reach more people by using different magazines, while the second one will reach the same people several times. The first option emphasizes reach, and the second one frequency.

A major cause of failure in advertising programs is insufficient frequency. It is far more effective to reduce the reach of an advertising campaign and add frequency than to reduce frequency and add reach. Unless a product or service is well known and has no competition, increasing the frequency of the advertising message will increase overall effectiveness.

Advertising: Developing the Copy

Developing an effective message is as essential as using the right media, since the message is the one that has to produce results. Good messages get noticed: in surveys of advertising awareness, many ads from retailers score very highly, among them McDonald's, Sears, Eaton's, Mr. Submarine, Canadian Tire, and Provigo. In terms of product categories, among the top 10 one finds grocery stores, drug stores, department, furniture, and chain stores.[27]

Creative strategy and execution

The creative strategy is developed around the chosen level in the hierarchy of effects model introduced in Figure 16–4, and according to the corresponding type of campaign. Copy can be either rational (awareness or knowledge) or emotional (liking, preference, or conviction). The rational approach focusses essentially on the name of the store, merchandise, and various facts about it. The emotional appeal addresses the psychological benefits that one can obtain by visiting the store or using the product bought there.

Sometimes a combination of the two possibilities is effective. For example, product benefits could be both rational (economy) and emotional (appearance). *Headlines* in the ad can focus on benefits, promises, or even news to attract attention and/or transmit a message. Retail Highlight 16–2 describes some sample retail campaigns that have won awards in the past, and they illustrate the role of copy in the overall advertising strategy.

The body copy of the advertisement can do many things, including: (1) stating reasons for doing something (buying the product, patronizing the store), (2) making promises or giving testimonials, (3) publicizing the results of performance tests, (4) telling a story, (5) reporting a real or imaginary dialogue, (6) solving a predicament, or (7) amusing the audience.[28] For example, humour can help attract attention, increase awareness of the retailer, and develop some liking. If the need for the product is present, desire can be aroused, and the reader may be convinced to go and visit the store.

Retail Highlight 16–2

Award-Winning Retail Campaigns

Every year, professional organizations such as the Retail Council of Canada or the Association of Canadian Advertisers award retailers for their program excellence. The campaigns of some of the past winners are as follows:

- **McDonald's Restaurants of Canada** won an award for a highly humorous program promoting its low-calorie/light menu. The campaign used ads in newspapers, in-store translight signs, tray liners, buttons for the staff, and crew room posters. Another award went for a campaign to introduce a line of pizzas to McDonald's menus relied on billboards and store signs with the clever rendition of the word pizza with the chain's logo, a very simple message that communicates extremely well.

- **Metro Toronto Zoo,** won a Cassie award for a campaign entitled Cat-O-Rama featuring a "tiger talking to humans." It was used outdoors almost exclusively from May to September and created a lot of attention. Attendance in 1994 increased by more than 66,000 over 1993, bringing additional revenues of $400,000. About 54 percent of the public were aware of the campaign, and 27 percent were returned patrons.

- **The New Summerhill Hardware,** Toronto, won several awards for their newspaper ads announcing their reopening. The ads used humorous headlines such as: "What a Bunch of Knobs," and "The Only Good Bolt is a Deadbolt," and simple illustrations of the product to attract attention.

- **IKEA,** a home furnishing store, also uses humour to attract attention to their ads, such as "Just avoid bridges," a newspaper ad to announce "the-only-time-we-ever-have-a-sale," or The "Muchos glassias" ad.

Source: "The 1995 Cassie Awards," *Marketing*, June 12, 1995, p. 17; Gail Chiasson, "Cossette Collects Golds," *Marketing*, April 27, 1992, p. 2; "The Marketing Annual Advertising Awards," *Marketing*, Section II, March 9, 1992, pp. 18–19.

Illustrations are also important to convey a message to the audience, such as enhancing the prestige of the store, showing fashionable merchandise, or suggesting uses of the featured product.

Major creative principles

The following are some major creative principles that can be used when developing effective print advertisements or broadcast commercials.

- *Make each word count and avoid unnecessary words.* Keep sentences short, use action words, use terms the reader will understand, and do not use introductions. It is important to get right to the point of the message.

- *Make your ad easy to recognize.* Give the copy and layout a consistent personality and style. Avoid the cluttered look.

- *Use a simple layout.* The layout should lead the reader's eye easily through the message from the art and headline to the copy and price to the signature (i.e., name and logo of the store).

- *Use dominant illustrations.* Show the featured merchandise in dominant illustrations. Whenever possible, show the product in use.

- *Show the benefit to the reader.* Prospective customers want to know "what's in it for me." But do not try to pack the ad with reasons to buy—give customers one primary reason, then back it up with one or two secondary reasons.

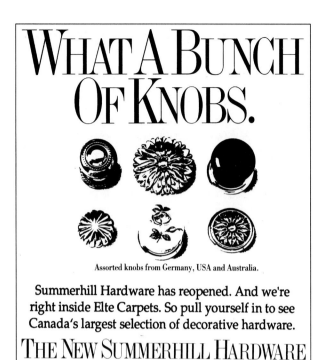

Great retail ads often use humour to attract attention and create a positive mood.

- *Feature the "right" item.* Select an item that is wanted, timely, stocked in depth, and typical of your store. Specify branded merchandise, and take advantage of advertising allowances and cooperative advertising whenever possible.

- *State a price or range of prices.* Don't be afraid to quote high prices. If the price is low, support it with statements that create belief, such as "clearance" or "special purchase."

- *Include store name and address.* Double-check every ad to make sure it contains store name, address, telephone number, and store hours.

The role of the ad agency

The function of an agency is to plan, produce, and measure the effectiveness of advertising. Larger retailers with outlets in several communities are more likely to use an ad agency's service. An agency helps them avoid the complication of having to deal with a variety of media in each community.

Advertising agencies typically earn their incomes from commissions. As an agent for the retailer, the agency will buy space in a medium. The agency then will bill the retailer for 100 percent of the cost and pay the medium, such as a newspaper, 85 percent. The 15 percent is the normal agency commission. Agencies may also take on the accounts of small retailers on a fee basis if the normal commission of 15 percent is too small to make the project worthwhile. Also in situations such as preparing direct mail advertising, the agency may charge a percentage of the cost involved.

However, it is important to note that retailers are normally entitled to *retail or local rates,* which are often much lower than *national or general rates,* provided that they are the ones purchasing the space or time from the media (no commission will be paid on retail rates). This often makes it uneconomical for a retailer to use an agency. In addition, retailers have to react very quickly to events in the marketplace, and agencies tend not to provide this service. For these reasons, retailers tend not to use an advertising agency for event advertising; when they use one, it is more likely to be for developing an image campaign.

Sales Promotion

Sales promotion has been defined as "marketing activities other than personal selling, advertising, and publicity that stimulate consumer purchasing and dealer effectiveness, such as displays, sales and exhibits, and demonstrations."[29] Examples are shown in Table 16–5. Perhaps the best way to introduce the varied nature of sales promotion possibilities is to highlight trends in sales promotion activities by retailers.

What are the trends in sales promotion?[30]

Couponing

Although coupon fraud and misredemption are serious problems,[31] couponing continues to be a very popular promotion device to introduce new products, stimulate trial, and increase purchase frequency.

Table 16-5 Examples of Retail Sales Promotion Programs

Gifts with purchase: Receipt of a gift with the purchase of an item—especially popular in the promotion of cosmetics.

Purchase with purchase: The offer of a second item at a reduced price after a minimum purchase—plush animals have been especially popular.

Price discount: Short-term reduction in the price of a product, normally marked on the product.

Coupons: Distributed via newspapers, product packages, door to door, magazines, or direct mail, they give the consumer an opportunity to purchase an item at a reduced price based on specified terms.

Contests: Skill-based competitions for designated prizes.

Sweepstakes: Games of chance for designated prizes.

Rebates: Refund of a fixed amount from the purchase price.

Premiums: The offer of something free or at a minimal price to induce sales—free glasses with the purchase of 25 litres of gasoline.

Self-liquidators: Incentives in which consumers pay part of the cost in cash plus submit product labels as proof of purchase to obtain an item such as a T-shirt.

In 1994, 15 billion **coupons** were distributed, 12 billion as retailer-initiated coupons or in retailer booklets. Of all the coupons distributed, 260 million were redeemed, and the average face value was 68 cents. This represents a large increase, since in 1986 less than 7 billion coupons were distributed, only 4 billion of which were by retailers (187 million redeemed). The redemption rate of coupons is about 4 percent for regular coupons, and 1 percent for retailer-initiated coupons (which have short expiration dates and are only valid at one retailer). There is still a great amount of potential since, on a per capita basis, Canadian consumers received only 15 percent as many coupons as U.S. consumers, and they redeem only 25 percent as many.[32]

Coupon distribution methods

The most important methods of coupon distribution are:[33]

- Free-standing newspaper inserts, usually in four-colours.
- Co-operative direct mail, distributed directly to households in non-addressed mail, according to selected postal codes.
- Selective direct mail, sent to specific customers.
- In/On pack, produced by manufacturers.
- Newspaper run-of-press, where the coupons are part of the newspaper advertisement.
- In-store coupons, distributed in-store through hand-outs, product demonstrations, at cash registers during checkout (e.g., Catalina coupons), in special retail booklets and calendars, on bulletin boards at the entrance (including electronic boards or kiosks).[34]
- Magazine coupons, usually in four colours, with the editorial support of the magazine, recipes, and so forth.

Trends in couponing

The following trends can be identified, and one can expect more creative uses to be made in the future:

- In general, more in- and on-pack coupon usage is likely, as is continued use of retailer-initiated coupons (retailer coupons paid by manufacturers), and more combination promotions with other devices—premiums, sweepstakes, and refunds.

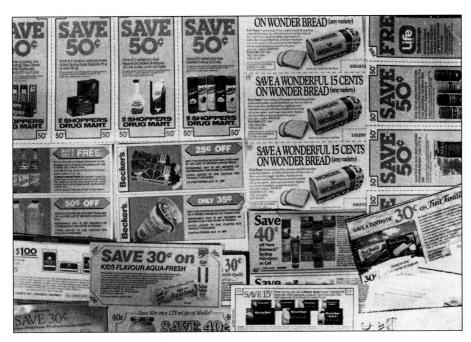

More than 15 billion coupons are distributed each year in Canada.

Photo by James Hertel

- Double coupons: to generate additional sales, and combat cross-border shopping, some retailers such as A&P and Miracle Food Mart have experimented with success with *double coupons:* these retailers double the face value of manufacturers' coupons for brand-name products.[35]

- An increased penetration and development of interactive electronic couponing. Safeway and K mart are experimenting with electronic kiosks. Canadian-developed technology by Qponyx International of Winnipeg allows the store to dispense coupons in 15 to 20 grocery categories, valid only the same day, at this store only. In addition, a seven-second message is played while the coupon selected by the customer is being printed. Other systems are also available in Canada.[36]

More sampling

Use of **sampling** is increasing, especially to new or non-users. Quite a few services now provide selective sampling. Retailers prefer saleable samples because they make a profit on them. Retailers don't profit from free samples. Saleable samples are good for manufacturers, too, because they save distribution costs.

Fewer cents-off bonus packs

Retailers generally resist these promotion devices because they necessitate additional stock-keeping units. They can also be quite costly to marketers because of the required special labelling and/or packaging. The advantages are that the benefit is passed on to the consumer, and the consumer readily sees the value in them.

More premiums

Some retailers are lukewarm to **premium** offers. This is especially true when they are used alone, rather than in combination with other promotion devices, such as coupons. In- and on-packs, special containers, and other forms of package-related or in-store premiums are sometimes resisted because of pilferage and handling problems. Nevertheless, consumers like these types of promotions. Retailers prefer premium offers that do not require their involvement but add excitement and impact to a promotion, create consumer interest, and generate increased product movement.

The general trends are toward more expensive self-liquidators, free premiums with multiple proofs-of-purchase, and brand logo premiums that are product or advertising related. One example of a timely premium program is the McDonald's/ Donruss MVP Series which offers customers four-baseball-card packs for 39 cents following the purchase of any pizza, sandwich, or breakfast. The 33-card set from the 26 major league baseball teams, also contains six special Blue Jays cards, a checklist card, and redemption vouchers for 1,000 Gold Series cards.[37]

More selective point-of-purchase material

Typical **point-of-purchase materials** include end-of-aisle and other in-store merchandising and display materials. Retailers like and want p-o-p materials, but generally feel that the material provided by manufacturers does not meet their needs. Retailers are highly selective in their use of p-o-p materials and prefer displays that merchandise an exciting and interesting promotion theme, support other promotion devices, adapt to storewide promotions on a chain-wide and individual store basis, harmonize with the store environment, sell related products, provide a quality appearance, install easily, are permanent or semipermanent, and guarantee sales success.

Some retailers develop and produce displays in accordance with the manufacturer's budget and guidelines. Some retailers are renting floor space to manufacturers.

More refunds/rebates

These devices, similar in intent and nature, continue to grow in popularity and use. Refunds and **consumer rebates** are usually handled as mail-ins with proofs-of-purchase. They are very effective promotion tools and will be used in more creative ways. Increasingly popular are rebates as charitable donations that show social concern, and higher price refunds for multiple products.

Fewer contests and more sweepstakes[38]

Sweepstakes are generally more popular than regular contests. However, the instant win contests are growing in use and importance. Retailers like both sweepstakes and instant wins, especially when they bring traffic into the store to look at product packages and obtain entry blanks.

More mailers and circulars

These promotion devices have been the biggest gainers in sales promotion over the past five years. Indeed, their share of sales promotion dollars has increased from one-third to almost one-half of the total dollars during this period, with the growth coming at the expense of newspapers.

More loyalty programs

A loyalty program is one that encourages the customer to keep coming back to the store to accumulate stamps or points. As mentioned earlier, one of the most

Table 16–6   Emerging Conclusions from Sales Promotion Research

1. Free-standing insert coupons are very effective in gaining incremental product sales, even among customers who do not redeem coupons.
2. Successful promotions depend heavily on trade support from the sales force.
3. The success factors are different between consumer promotions and trade promotions.
4. Promotions that are successful are the more expensive to launch, but they tend to pay out more than the unsuccessful ones.
5. The level of incentive by itself does not relate to support from the trade, i.e., a high level will not guarantee strong trade support, and conversely, a low level does not always prevent strong trade support.
6. For many companies, moving sales volume is more important than the profitability of the sales promotions.
7. About 50 percent of sales promotions are unprofitable.
8. Incentives to consumers tend to be less important to the success of a promotion than sales force support.
9. More of the promotional budget should be allocated to the sales force, and less to incentives for consumers.

Source: Adapted from Srini S. Srinivasan, Robert P. Leone, and Francis Mulhern, "The Advertising Exposure Effects of Free Standing Inserts," *Journal of Advertising* 24, 1, Spring 1995, pp. 29–40; Kenneth G. Hardy, "Key Success Factors for Manufacturers' Sales Promotion in Package Goods," *Journal of Marketing* 50, 3, July 1986, pp. 13–23.

successful loyalty programs is Zellers' Club Z. Another example for a smaller retailer is Odyssey Books and its discount stores Empire Books. Customers earn "Empire dollars," which they can use for their future purchases, and at Odyssey, they earn discount stamps on special customer cards; when the cards are complete, they can enter a monthly draw for a $25 gift certificate.[39]

When to use sales promotions

Table 16–6 highlights the conclusions about the effectiveness of sales promotion research based on 216 Canadian sales promotions.[40] Higher emphasis of manufacturers on the trade and the sales force would imply a different role for retailers.

Staple products exhibit the highest degree of price elasticity and are thus the most responsive to point-of-purchase displays. Sugar, vinegar, ketchup, coffee, and canned/powdered milk are all in the top 10 price elastic product categories for human consumption.[41]

Suppliers often advertise directly to retailers and inform them of upcoming national campaigns so the retailer can stock sufficient merchandise to meet consumer needs and coordinate local advertising with the national advertising program.

Cooperative promotions

Manufacturers also offer co-op funds for promotions in the same way they often offer advertising co-op dollars. Suppliers often advertise directly to retailers informing them about promotion allowances available for a product line. Suppliers then seek a commitment from the retailers for an increased volume of purchases because of the accelerated promotional program for the product line.

Measuring the Results of Advertising and Sales Promotions

Sales response to ads can be checked daily during the ad period. The effects of image ads are harder to measure. It is not always possible to tie a purchase to image advertising. However, the message may stay in the minds of people who have heard it. Sooner or later, it may help trigger a purchase. Research is needed to measure the success of image.

Tests for immediate-response ads[42]

In weighing the results of the immediate response to advertisements, a number of measurements have been used in the past.

Coupons redeemed

Usually, coupons represent sales of a product. Where coupons represent requests for additional information or contact with a salesperson, management may ask if enough leads were obtained to pay for the ad. If the coupon is dated, it is possible to determine the number of returns for the first, second, and third weeks. It is possible to design a low-cost couponing experiment to determine the profitability of retailer couponing.[43]

Phone or letter inquiries

A "hidden offer" can cause people to call or write. For example, included in the middle of an ad is a statement that on request the product or additional information will be supplied. Results should be checked over periods of one week through 6 months or 12 months, because this type of ad may have a considerable carry-over effect.

Testing advertising executions

Retailers can prepare two ad executions (different in some way that they would like to test) and run them during the same period. Management can identify the ads by the message or with a coded coupon so they can tell them apart. They can ask customers to bring in the coupon or to use a special phrase. Broadcast ads can be run at different times or on different stations on the same day with varying "discount phrases." Some consumer magazines can provide a "**split run**"—that is, to print "ad A" in part of its press run and "ad B" in the rest of the run. The responses to each can then be counted.

Sales made of a targeted item

If the ad is on a bargain or limited-time offer, retailers can consider that sales at the end of 1 week, 2 weeks, 3 weeks, and 4 weeks came from the ad. They may need to make a judgment as to how many sales came from in-store display and personal selling.

Store traffic

An important function of advertising is to build store traffic. Store traffic also results in purchases of items that are not advertised. Pilot studies show, for example, that many customers who were brought to the store by an ad for a blouse also bought a handbag. Some bought the bag in addition to the blouse, while others bought it instead of the blouse.

Testing the effectiveness of the advertising campaign

When advertising is spread over a selling season or several seasons, part of the measurement job of campaign effectiveness is keeping records. Retailers' records of ads and sales for an extended time should be compared.

An easy way to set up a file is by marking the date of the run on tear sheets of newspaper ads (many radio stations now provide "radio tear sheets," too), keeping log reports of radio and television ads, and keeping copies of direct mail ads. The file may be broken down into monthly, quarterly, or semiannual blocks. By recording the sales of the advertised items on each ad or log, management can make comparisons.

In institutional (image-building) advertising, individual ads are building blocks of the campaign, so to speak. Together they make up the advertising campaign over a selling season. A problem is trying to measure the effects of the ads, since they are designed to keep the name of the store before the buying public and to position the outlet in a way that harmonizes with the overall marketing strategy. In contrast to institutional advertising, product advertising is designed to cover a short period of time and increase sales.

One approach to testing is making the comparisons on a weekly basis. If a retailer runs an ad each week, management can compare the first week's sales with sales for the same week a year ago. At the end of the second week, managers can compare sales with those of the end of the first week, as well as year-ago figures, and so forth. Of course, the retailer should try to take into account other factors that may have influenced the sales, such as price reductions, advertising by competitors, or other environmental changes (e.g., a heat wave may boost the sales of fans).

Publicity and Public Relations

Publicity has been defined as "any nonpersonal stimulation of demand for a product, service, or business unit by planting commercially significant news about it in a published medium or obtaining favourable presentation of it upon radio, television, or stage that is not paid for by the sponsor."[44] Publicity and public relations are known by various names. Regardless, such activities normally fit into three categories: (1) merchandising events, (2) entertainment, and (3) education or community service.

Merchandising events

Special events create publicity. Often they may be featured in the editorial section of a newspaper, may result in an interview on a talk show, or generate other free promotion. Merchandising events require careful coordination between merchandising, advertising, and publicity. Such events can include fashion shows, bridal fairs, cooking demonstrations, celebrity authors, cartoon characters, or sports heroes. They can include exhibits of art, costumes, antiques, or rarities. Merchandising events may also be staged in conjunction with designers such as Lise Watier or sports figures such as Wayne Gretzky.

For example, in 1991 (during the recession) Ogilvy, a Montreal department store, sponsored 74 special events, including book-signings with authors, concerts broadcast live over CBC radio, and celebrity appearances, such as U.S. super-model Cindy Crawford, which attracted 2,200 people in one afternoon. During a 110-day period, these special events attracted 19,000 people into the store.[45]

Entertainment

Retailers seek to build goodwill, store image, and name awareness through entertainment programs. For example, several retailers participate in such events as the Quebec City Winter Carnival, the Calgary Stampede, or Canada Day festivities across the country. The results from such activities are hard to measure. Free publicity from such events can be worth hundreds of thousands of dollars.

Education or community service

Retailers sometimes sponsor education or community service activities. For example, Sears Canada is extensively involved in many community activities, including support for United Way/Centraide and childhood literacy campaigns. Such activities are provided free of charge during lunch hours. Other retailers offer fashion advice, career counselling, and even cooking courses, all on the store premises. For example, Elte Carpets of Toronto runs the "University of Fuzzy Side Up," a series of Saturday-morning courses on broadloom and rugs held at its showroom. About 20 people attend each week, learning about different kinds of carpets and how they are installed.[46]

Advertising Regulation and Ethics

The retailer must be more and more concerned with the effects of consumer protection regulations, both at the federal and provincial levels.

At the federal level, advertising is regulated by a number of agencies, including the CRTC, Health and Welfare Canada, and Consumer and Corporate Affairs. Among the regulations of the greatest importance to retailers are those concerning the use of false or misleading advertising resulting in "bait and switch" practices, forbidden by the Competition Act. There are also a number of codes, such as the Canadian Code of Advertising Standards. The media can also exercise judgment in refusing to carry an advertisement that they deem misleading, sexist, or in bad taste.

At the provincial level, retailers must contend with bureaus of consumer affairs, the Better Business Bureaus, and the small claims court.

Sears Canada is extensively involved in community activities, including supporting children's literacy.

Courtesy Sears Canada

Chapter Highlights

- Promotion should be viewed as a sales-building investment and not simply as an element of business expense. When promotion is executed correctly, it can be an important factor in the future growth of a business.

- Promotion is communication from the retailer to the consumer in an effort to achieve a profitable sales level. Promotion includes mass media advertising, coupons, trading stamps, premium offers, point-of-purchase displays, and publicity.

- Promotion is a key element of the marketing mix. All promotion should be in harmony with pricing, product lines, and store-location decisions (place). Otherwise a poor image for the firm can result.

- Developing promotion plans begins with the goals of the firm. Retailers must decide on whom to reach, the message to get across, the number of messages to reach the audience, and the means for reaching the audience.

- After defining the goals, retailers must carefully establish their advertising budget. Typical methods include the percentage-of-sales, the unit-of-sales, and the objective-and-task methods. The budget must also be carefully allocated, and cooperative advertising programs should be used to stretch the impact of the budget on sales.

- Numerous options exist for retail advertising, and each medium has its strengths and weaknesses, which must be studied carefully before a choice is made. Media choices include direct mail, magazines, billboards, transit ads, newspapers, radio, and television. The most commonly used media are newspapers, radio, direct mail and distribution, and out-of-home media. Large retail chains also use television and magazines. Nonmedia advertising includes point-of-purchase displays and promotional products advertising.

- Media effectiveness is normally measured in terms of cost per thousand and reach and frequency. Results tests for immediate response ads can be in terms of coupons redeemed, requests by phone or letter referring to the ad, sales made of a particular item, or an analysis of store traffic.

- Advertising copy can be either rational or emotional. The rational approach focusses on the merchandise, while an emotional appeal focusses on the psychological benefits obtained from using the product. Headlines in an ad can focus on benefits, promises, or news.

- Some retailers use an advertising agency. The function of an agency is to plan, produce, and measure the effectiveness of advertising. Agencies earn their commissions on advertisements placed for the retailers. However, retailers qualify for very advantageous retail rates (non-commissionable), if they buy directly from the media.

- Retail sales promotions include such activities as couponing, product sampling, cents-off bonus packs, premiums, point-of-purchase materials, refunds or rebates, contests and sweepstakes, and trade-in allowances.

- Publicity includes media exposure that is not paid for by the sponsor. Such activities normally fit into three categories: merchandising, entertainment, and education or community service.

Key Terms

AIDA model 441
awareness 442
Canadian Advertising Rates & Data (CARD) 449
Canadian Newspaper Unit (CNU) 454
catalogues 457
community newspapers 454
consumer rebate 468
cooperative advertising 448
cost per thousand (CPM) 450
coupons 466
direct promotion 456
direct mail advertising 456
directories 458
event advertising 441
frequency 450

general rate 454
gross rating point (GRP) 453
hierarchy of effects model 441
image campaign 441
institutional advertising 441
magazine advertising 455
message 439
modular agate line (MAL) 454
national rates 449
newspaper advertising 453
objective-and-task method 446
out-of-home advertising 458
outdoor advertising 459
percentage-of-sales method 443
point-of-purchase material 468
premiums 467
prime-time advertising 450

Discussion Questions

1. Is it possible to increase advertising expenses as a percentage of sales, yet increase the profitability of the firm?

2. Comment on the following statement: "The only goal of advertising is to increase sales and profitability."

3. Discuss the following approaches to establishing an advertising budget (be sure to include in your discussion the advantages and disadvantages of each): the percentage-of-sales method; the unit-of-sales method; and the objective-and-task method.

4. What are the reasons a retailer should consider using a multimedia mix?

5. Evaluate the following media in terms of their strengths and weaknesses: billboards, radio, television, newspapers, transit advertising, and magazines.

6. Why should a retailer consider the use of co-op advertising funds?

7. What are the various ways by which retailers can measure advertising results?

8. Comment on the use of the hierarchy of effects models for determining advertising objectives, the type of campaign to use, and the creative strategy to select. Give some examples with retail ads from your local newspaper.

Application Exercises

1. Imagine you work for the promotion division of a department store and have been told that you are to prepare a campaign for a new product. Select your own "new product." Plan the campaign, select the media, and prepare the message.

2. Make contacts with dealers in a specific product line (e.g., electronics) which have definite differences in product image, price, quality, and so on. Through interviews with the store managers, attempt to determine the allocation of the advertising (promotional) budget among the various media. Compare and contrast among the group. If actual dollars of promotional expenditures are not available, then utilize percentage allocations. Additionally collect national and local ads for the same dealers and evaluate the differences and similarities noted.

3. Select several automobile dealerships that seem to project differing public images. Interview management of each to determine their particular image perceptions of themselves and perhaps of their competition. Prepare a portfolio of ads of each dealership and also of the national ads of that same dealership's make of auto. Compare the images that seem to be projected by the local versus the national promotions. Attempt to reach certain strategy conclusions from your investigation.

Suggested Cases

14. West Coast Furniture
32. An Advertising Plan
33. The M & G Advertising Agency
34. Shoe Kingdom

Notes

1. "The 1995 Cassie Awards," *Marketing*, June 12, 1995, p. 16.
2. J. McElgunn, "Study Says Nothing Beats Word of Mouth," *Marketing*, May 1, 1995, p. 2.
3. M. Strauss, "Vive la différence," *Globe & Mail*, November 2, 1995, p. B13.
4. O. Riso, "Advertising Guidelines for Small Retail Firms," *Small Marketers Aid*, No. 160 (Washington, DC: U.S. Small Business Administration), p. 4.
5. M.J. Rothenburg, "Retail Research Strategies for the '70s," in *Combined Proceedings*, ed. Edward M. Mazze (Chicago: American Marketing Association, 1975), p. 409.
6. Riso, "Advertising Guidelines for Small Retail Firms."
7. The material on establishing and allocating the budget is based on S.H. Britt, "Plan Your Advertising Budget," *Small Marketers Aid*, No. 164 (Washington, DC: U.S. Small Business Administration).
8. G. Cestre, M. Laroche, and L. Desjardins, "Current Advertising Budgeting Practices of Canadian Advertisers and Agencies," *Canadian Journal of Administrative Sciences*, vol. 9, December 1992, pp. 279–293.
9. J. Pepall, "Co-op Advertising Builds Strength from Numbers," *Profit*, November 1990, pp. 53–54.
10. Pepall, "Co-op Advertising Builds Strength from Numbers."
11. *Canadian Advertising Rates & Data (henceforth referred to as CARD)* is a monthly publication of Maclean Hunter. For each medium the date for which the information was updated is indicated in the corresponding listing. For more complete information, you should request the Retail Rate Card from the medium itself.
12. *Canadian Media Directors' Council Media Digest, 1995/96 (henceforth referred to as CMDCMD)*, p. 21.
13. *CMDCMD, 1995/96*, p. 8.
14. *CMDCMD, 1995/96*, p. 16.
15. "NADbank '95, the Past, the Present and the Future," *Advertising Supplement to Marketing Magazine*, 1995, p. 4.

16. *CMDCMD*, p. 27.

17. *CARD*, October 1995, pp. 62–63.

18. R. Scotland, "Resurgence in Home Shopping Boosts Catalogue Sales," *Financial Post*, March 23, 1995, p. 19; M. Strauss, "Grocers Find New Ways to Reach the Masses," *Globe & Mail*, January 14, 1992, p. B4.

19. J. Pollock, "Lists of Opportunity," *Marketing*, May 22, 1995, pp. 14–15; "U.S. Apparel Catalogue Debuts in Canada," *Marketing*, November 6, 1995, p. 1.

20. G. Blackwell, "Just What the Armchair Shopper Ordered," *Globe & Mail*, July 18, 1992, p. B22.

21. Ibid.; J. Pepall, "Selling by the Book," *Profit*, December 1990, pp. 40–41.

22. L. Mills, "From Print to Bits and Bytes," *Marketing*, May 22, 1995, pp. 14–15; R. Scotland, "Menswear Ads Tailored to Tradition and High-Tech," *Financial Post*, April 4, 1995, p. 13.

23. R. Scotland, "Resurgence in Home Shopping Boosts Catalogue Sales."

24. J. Sinclair, "The New Media: Are High-Tech Innovations Likely to Bring Rapid Change?" *Marketing*, January 2/9, 1995, p. 14; "Windows on the Interactive Future," *Stores*, April 1995, pp. 57–58.

25. K. Riddell, "Reaching Consumers In-Store," *Marketing*, July 13/20, 1992, p. 10.

26. Y. Boivin, "Media Planning with the CPM Rule," *Marketing*, vol. 10 (ed. A. d'Astous), ASAC, 1989, pp. 39–47.

27. J. Lipman, "Consumers' Favoured Commercials Tend to Feature Lower Prices or Cuddly Kids," *The Wall Street Journal*, March 2, 1992, p. B1.

28. R.Y. Darmon and M. Laroche, *Advertising in Canada*, Toronto: McGraw-Hill Ryerson, 1991, pp. 308–317.

29. Committee on Definitions, *Marketing Definitions*, Chicago, IL: American Marketing Association, 1963.

30. W. Mouland, "Coupons and Loyalty Cards," *Marketing*, October 23, 1995, pp. 29–30; W. Mouland, "How Couponing Can Boost Brand Sales," *Marketing*, July 3/10, 1995, p. 21; C. Berneman and I. Fenwick, "Using the Multinomial Logit Model to Predict the Effectiveness of In-Store Promotion," *Marketing*, vol. 10, op. cit., pp. 21–30.

31. D. McClellan, "Desktop Counterfeiting," *Technology Review*, February/March 1995, pp. 32–40.

32. K. Riddell, "Couponers Show Record Year," *Marketing*, February 10, 1992, p. 2.

33. Darmon and Laroche, *Advertising in Canada*, pp. 196–99.

34. Riddell, "Reaching Consumers In-Store."

35. K. Riddell, "Double Coupons Perform Well for Miracle," *Marketing*, February 24, 1992, p. 7.

36. Riddell, "Reaching Consumers In-Store."

37. K. Riddell, "McDonald's Joins the Card Craze," *Marketing*, July 13/20, 1992, p. 3.

38. W. Mouland, "More Exciting Times Ahead for the Consumer Promotions Industry," *Marketing*, February 20, 1989, Section CP & I, pp. 6-7.

39. M. Cartash, "Catch a Falling Store," *Profit*, December 1990, p. 27.

40. K.G. Hardy, "Key Success Factors for Manufacturers' Sales Promotions in Package Goods," *Journal of Marketing* 50 3, July 1986, pp. 13–23.

41. "Not Everyone Loves a Supermarket Special," *Business Week*, February 17, 1992, pp. 64–65; "Price and Promotion Strategies for Impact at Retail," *Marketing Communication*, October 1985; C. Berneman and A. Carson, "Caution: Coupo-

Holics and Bargain-Hunters Ahead," in *Marketing,* vol. 11 (ed. J. Liefeld), ASAC, 1990, pp. 46–54.

42. This material is condensed, with modifications, from E. Sorbet, "Do You Know the Results of Your Advertising?" *Management Aid,* no. 4020 (Washington, DC: U.S. Small Business Administration).

43. R.G. Chapman, "Assessing the Profitability of Retailer Couponing with a Low-Cost Field Experiment," *Journal of Retailing* 62, no. 1, Spring 1987, pp. 19–40.

44. Committee on Definitions, op. cit.; M.A. Charlebois, "Putting a Value on Your Program," *Marketing,* October 23, 1995, p. 16; J. McElgunn, "Study Says Nothing Beats Word of Mouth," *Marketing,* May 1, 1995, p. 2.

45. J. Zeidenberg, "Is upscale dead?" *Profit,* October 1991, pp. 44–45.

46. Cartash, "Catch a Falling Store."

Developing a Customer-Focussed Culture

Chapter Objectives

After reading this chapter, you should be able to:

1. Understand the meaning of "customer service" versus "customer focussed."

2. Define the meaning of customer service and reasons for the gap that often exists between customer expectations and perceptions.

3. Understand the strategic role of customer support services in the retailer's overall marketing plan.

4. Describe the various types of retail credit.

4. List the various types of retail credit cards.

5. Understand the laws affecting customer support services.

6. Describe customer support activities, such as shopper services, educational programs, delivery, and extended hours.

Understanding the customer is critical to delivering excellent customer service.

Courtesy Hudson's Bay Company Ltd.

*R*emember the story in Chapter 9 about the customer who complained to Christine Renner, manager of Vancouver's Fortes Seafood House, that her favourite lunch selection, black bean fried rice, was not in the menu anymore? The way Christine responded to this loyal customer is illustrative of a real customer-focussed culture.

What this story also deals with is what Hubert Saint-Onge, the head of the CIBC leadership centre, calls "human capital," defined as the capabilities of a company's employees to provide solutions for customers, as in the case of Christine Renner. Human capital is different from "customer capital," the depth, breadth, and loyalty of the company's franchise, but high human capital helps increase customer capital. According to Hubert Saint-Onge, "If an employee's attitude is low—if he or she does not feel ownership of the job—the customer knows that right away, and if employees are well treated by the company, this is reflected in excellent customer service."[1] ■

As noted in the introduction, services offer retailers the opportunity to differentiate themselves from the competition. Services are expensive, however, and many retailers do not agree on what services should be offered.

Customer support services include such functions as credit, layaway, delivery, personal shopping programs, and a variety of other activities designed to attract new customers and to strengthen relationships with existing ones. Customer support services are a primary way in which retailers can differentiate from competitors. Many retail outlets offer essentially the same merchandise at the same price with similar merchandising programs. Services provide the opportunity to create a unique image in the minds of consumers.

Many customers now bag their own groceries, price mark goods at warehouse outlets, serve themselves in restaurants, handle their own delivery, and pump their own gas. Shifting these functions to customers is the result of efforts by retailers to lower their costs and increase profit margins.

Retailers probably cannot eliminate all basic services if they want to stay in business. Such services include credit, repair, warranty service, and others (depending on the merchandise sold). No service should be offered, however, unless it contributes directly or indirectly to profit.

A high-fashion store such as Holt Renfrew that appeals to the upper-income shopper will usually offer more services than a discount store. Also, two different stores may offer wide variations in the same service. For example, a discount store may accept a bank credit card as the only means of payment other than cash, but a department store may also accept the store's credit card or a travel and entertainment card such as American Express, or offer a customer a charge plan. Department stores may deliver large items such as furniture free of charge,

In addition to exclusive merchandising, Holt Renfrew offers a variety of services for the upscale shopper.

Courtesy Holt Renfrew

Figure 17–1   Customer Service Evaluation Model

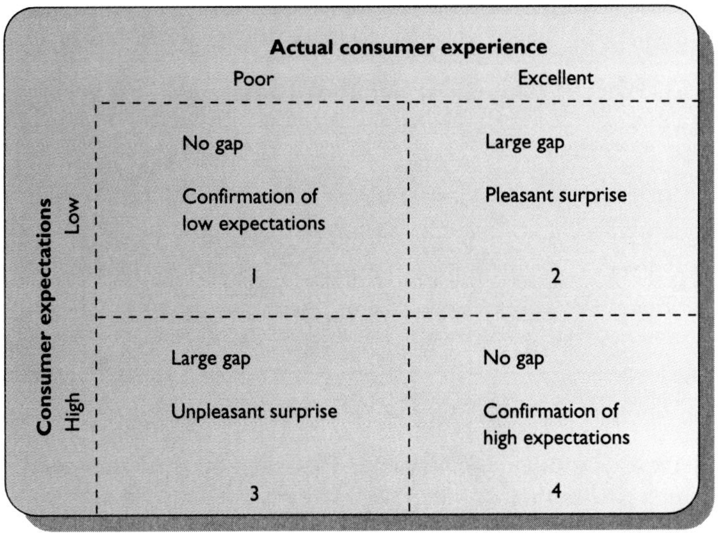

Actual consumer experience

	Poor	Excellent
Consumer expectations Low	No gap Confirmation of low expectations 1	Large gap Pleasant surprise 2
Consumer expectations High	Large gap Unpleasant surprise 3	No gap Confirmation of high expectations 4

Source: Reproduced with permission from Barry Berman, "Customer Service Strategy," *The Retailing Strategist,* no. 2, 1991, p. 10.

whereas a warehouse furniture store such as Leon's may charge extra for delivery.

A full-service specialty outlet such as Parachute stores offers a full array of customer services, often through special promotions. In contrast, a discount outlet such as Zellers Plus may offer identical merchandise, but without supporting services, at reduced prices. The use of services is thus part of the positioning strategy by merchants in targeting key market segments, as discussed in Chapter 6.

Understanding Customer Service Expectations

The difference between customer service expectations and experiences, if any, results in a customer expectations gap, as shown in Figure 17–1. The size of the gap depends on the difference between expectations and experiences.[2] Most of Harry Rosen's customers have high expectations and experience excellent service. Therefore, no service gap exists.

Customer assessments of retailer response depend on their perceptions—which may differ from reality. Customer service expectations are different during the busy Christmas season, for example, than during the slower times of the year. Expectations may also vary by customer.

Management can most effectively address the issue of customer support services by focussing on both customers and processes, which, in turn, translates into focussing on the outcome. Focussing on the customer means listening to his or her ideas about what constitutes satisfactory service. Focussing on the process means understanding the things necessary to meet customer expectations such as length of time waiting in line, personnel friendliness, and store cleanliness.

Retail Highlight 17–1

Providing Good Customer Service Pays Off

Since opening three stores in Toronto in September 1991, Talbots, a $500 million specialty retailer and cataloguer of women's apparel, has been very successful and plans to open 25 additional stores in Canada. Its formula includes offering classic merchandise to professional women, at reasonable prices, and with excellent customer service. For example, Talbots offers wardrobe consulting, alterations, free gift wrapping, full refund on returned merchandise, delivery anywhere in Canada, and a highly trained sales staff. Its clubby atmosphere appeals to professional women, by providing a conservative assortment of private-label merchandise, meeting their needs from head to toe: from hats to blazers, handbags to cologne, and jewelry to footwear.

Source: Anne Bokma, "Raking in the Dough," *Financial Post Magazine*, January 1992, p. 34.

Focussing on the outcome directs attention to the reliability of the service delivered such as accuracy in repair, delivery when promised, and so forth.

Nurturing the customer-focussed culture[3]

The only constant in retailing is change—in fashion, distribution channels, organization, buying patterns, customer wants and lifestyles, and in retail format.

Because of these constant changes, some retailers have lost sight of their primary mission—satisfying the customer. Two of the most misunderstood words today are *customer service*. Do they refer to an attitude, a function, or a result? With increased competition, many retailers are placing greater emphasis on customer service to differentiate themselves from the competitive pack. The traditional approach to customer service, however, is not broad enough to accomplish this objective or to satisfy the needs of today's customer. To find new areas of opportunity, retailers must go beyond customer service to a customer-focussed culture.

Traditional approach

Traditional customer service program objectives generally fall into four categories:

- *Integrity*—warranties, product quality, return, and exchange policies.
- *Convenience and shopping ease*—store layout, convenient parking, store hours, mail- and phone-order service, etc.
- *A pleasant shopping environment*—valet parking services, decor and lighting, fitting-room privacy, music, and credit account confidentiality.
- *Personal shopping services*—knowledgeable sales personnel, merchandise availability, and informative product signing.

The traditional customer service approaches include a variety of organizational structures and policies aimed at ensuring customer satisfaction, as illustrated in Retail Highlight 17–1.

Organizations range from a large central customer service staff, to a service/return desk at each store, to an authorized manager at each individual point-of-sale location in department and specialty stores. Policies range from very lenient to a policy of no returns without a sales receipt to no returns at all.

Customer service

When the term **customer service** is used, it usually refers to cashing cheques, handling bill adjustment transactions, or managing complaints. Some stores handle complaints at the store level when they arise and provide no feedback to management on complaint types, volumes, and frequency. Some companies have no clearly defined responsibility for pinpointing customer service, and resolve complaints slowly. Other stores have elaborate and well-defined systems for handling complaints, including procedure manuals, time standards for resolution, performance audits, and management reporting of complaints by type, store, work centre, and merchandise area. But the customer service program is always receptive, based on some function that is not meeting the customer's expectations.

Customer expectations

Retailers play a role in the development of customer expectations through advertising, store operations, and everyday marketing. When there are inconsistencies between what retailers say and do and what the customer expects, there is a gap, as indicated in Figure 17–1. At best, the result is customer confusion and, at worse, the loss of a customer. The situation is further complicated by the fact that customer expectations vary, not only by type of store, but also by major category of merchandise within a given store type. To make customer service proactive, retailers need to anticipate customer expectations and take action to meet or exceed them.

One simple way to identify these expectations is a customer expectation matrix by broad merchandise category. This approach identifies customer expectations of fashion, value, service, and the store facility for several types of retail store categories. It assigns a numerical value to each category as perceived by a customer. The higher the cumulative total, the higher the expectation.

By completing this format for various categories of products, one can assess how to fulfil the customers' expectations, thus reducing customer service problems.

Confusing the customer

One of the most common ways retailers confuse the customer is by doing one thing and saying another, thus creating large gaps. The following are examples of such practices:

- *Discontinuing services* such as delivery, cheque cashing, wrapping for mailing, alterations, and various repair services without offering the customer an alternative.
- Establishing *fees for support services* that are not in line with competition or that are disproportionately high for that particular service.
- Preaching customer service, but *posting restrictive negative signs* throughout the store (for example, "no cheque cashing," "please do not handle the merchandise," "we honour only manufacturers' warranties"). These signs are most negative when posted near a "service" desk.
- *Aisles that are narrow or cluttered with merchandise:* no natural grouping of merchandise categories, entering and exiting traffic collides, or high interior fixtures restrict visibility.

- Restrooms are difficult to find, dirty, out of supplies, or a combination of all three.

- *Department and merchandise signing is inadequate:* lack of up-to-date store directories, inadequate department signing, inadequate product information signing, using sales sign headers on non-sale merchandise, using a single-price sign on a fixture containing various-priced merchandise, not highlighting advertised merchandise, excessive variety of sign headers.

- *Inadequate merchandise or shelf-marking:* no price on merchandise or shelves, size information difficult to find, no standard location for merchandise tickets, merchandise tickets applied over product-to-size information.

- *Advertising lacks integrity:* fictitious or overstated comparative regular prices, advertising limited quantity merchandise without a disclaimer, unstated restrictions that apply to a special-price ad.

- Merchandise is out of stock and *the customer is not helped* by calling a different store to fill the order; providing similar merchandise at the same price (even if a markdown is involved).[4]

When measuring customer service it is the customer's perception of a company's actions that counts, not the actions themselves.

The customer-focussed culture

A **customer-focussed culture** is one that primarily focusses on customer concerns. Some retailers with already strong reputations for customer service are reluctant to reveal their secrets to success. Other retailers may try to remedy their customer service problems by copying their competitors, erroneously believing that they will then have joined a customer-focussed culture.

They miss the point. A combination of many positive programs produces positive results, not a limited mix of them. For example:

- Knowing the particular customer of the store.
- Planning an integrated approach to customer acquisition and service.
- Developing a clear statement on customer focus that is commonly shared and committed to.
- Hiring knowledgeable, consistent, motivated employees.
- Using customer information in an effective manner.
- Monitoring and measuring the results of all the combined efforts.

As mentioned, the examples provided in the introduction to this chapter clearly reflect a customer-focussed culture.

Customer definition and knowledge

The most critical starting point is a precise definition and in-depth knowledge of the customer base. One needs to know:

- Who are they?
- What are their values and attitudes?
- What are their lifestyles?
- What do they need?

- How can they be reached?
- Where do they buy?
- What do they expect?
- What are their perceptions of your customer service compared with that of the competition?

To answer these questions, a retailer must use both primary and secondary research on demographics, psychographics, media preferences, and purchasing. Primary research derives its information directly from potential customers; secondary research derives its information from third parties. For obtaining research material, retailers have a variety of sources to choose from (Chapter 5 has covered these in detail). However, a retailer's own customer information base can provide useful information if it is properly coded. The closer this information can be fine-tuned to the customer base of a given store, the better the results.[5]

A planned integrated approach

A well-planned approach to customer service includes the integration of the strategies used to attract, serve, and keep customers. Strategies to attract customers generally fall into the categories of *fashion* (newness, uniqueness, broad assortments), *value* (product/service quality, convenience, price), and *dominance* (assortment, effective presentation, strong in-stock position).

Strategies to serve customers, that is, high-quality customer services, include:

- Qualified sales personnel in quantity.
- In-stock position.
- Integrity—"We do what we say we will do."
- Consistent, timely handling of customer complaints.
- Support services including gift wrap, delivery, repairs, credit services, child care, package checking, and consolidation.
- Clean, easy access and exit, easy flow, pleasant facilities.
- Kiosk and free-standing product information and other placement terminals.

There are many programs that when properly timed and implemented help to keep the customers you already have. One example is to make it easier for customers to shop and, more importantly, to purchase. Management might extend store hours (when it is legally possible); add mail- and phone-order services; develop bridal, pregnancy, and baby registry programs; or add various financial services. All of these conveniences will make established customers happy to return to the store; they will be able to take care of many chores in the same place at the same time.

Another way to keep them coming back is to develop programs that build self-esteem in both customers and employees. Incentive programs can be successful as can programs designed to enhance personal appearance via cosmetics. Customers will feel good when they leave the store, and employees will feel good for having satisfied the customers.

Retail Highlight 17–2

Big Does Not Have to Mean Poor Customer Focus

For women who like wearing jeans, shopping for a pair is very frustrating, since the ready-made jeans rarely fit: they may be too long (short) in the rise, too big (small) in the waist, and too long (short) in the legs. A large company like Levi's cannot mass-produce and distribute the huge variety of sizes to satisfy all these varied combinations.

Advances in technology have helped Levi's answer this call for help. First, go to the Levi's Only Store, like the one in Mississauga, Ontario, and a fit consultant will take four key measurements: waist, hip, inseam, and rise. By entering these measurements into a computer, it suggests one of 478 prototype pairs available in the store (the system is programmed for 4,200 combinations of measurements). The customer can then try one of the

suggested prototypes, and the fit consultant may finalize the measurements, and offer additional options such as slim leg or boot cut, and stone-washed blue, stone-bleached blue, or white. The final act is to send all the measurements through phone lines to the Levi's plant in Stoney Creek. They are first cut and sewn according to the customer's measurements, then sent to Brantford for finishing and labelling, then to the store in Mississauga, for example, within 21 days of receiving the measurements. The custom-made, perfectly fitting jeans are now ready to be picked up, or they can be delivered (for a small extra charge).

Source: Miles Socha, "Jeans That Fit," *The Kitchener Record,* May 11, 1995, p. E1.

Basically, the way to retain customers is to be creative and anticipate as many of their needs as possible. Retail Highlight 17–2 indicates that a customer-focussed culture can also thrive in a warehouse-type operation.

Commitment and communication

Underlying all these strategies is the key factor that initiates and nurtures a customer-focussed culture—a statement of customer focus. That will produce the drive, incentive, and awareness and must include:

- Top management commitment.
- Clear organizational goals.
- Specifically assigned responsibilities to each area.
- A focal point for questions and problems.
- Ongoing communication and positive examples.

Once a clear "customer-focus" statement has been developed containing all these elements, all participants will have a game plan by which to achieve the goals. For example, Elte Carpets of Toronto has a clear customer focus of staff availability to customer questions on carpets: for that goal, it set up a 24-hour hotline service that responds to customers' questions within six hours; customers may request the salesperson's home number written on their receipt for future queries; it also set up a shop-at-home service, staffed by two sales representatives who answer customer queries by phone, then take carpet-sample books (and sometimes full rugs) to their homes. Customers can make a selection, or ask them to return with more samples, or come into the store to look at full rugs.[6]

Customized targeted marketing

Another important key to developing a customer-focussed culture is to effectively use marketing information. Business strategies are market driven—not product driven. Thus, one current approach toward successful marketing is to serve the needs of the customers by offering services that enhance their daily lives. The objective here is to design a shopping experience for each customer type, while offering a personal approach to the sale and handling of each individual customer. Individuality and personal preference are the hallmarks of today's consumer.

The growth of the "niche" catalogues and other non-store approaches tells us that customers welcome this type of marketing. Targeted direct mail is a growing medium capitalizing on some important lifestyle trends; for example, one-stop shopping is becoming more and more desirable because consumers have far less leisure time; home delivery during off hours has become an important consideration. Chapter 20 will provide more detail about this trend to non-store retailing.

Analysis for action

There is a lot of consumer information available from both inside and outside the company. It is easier and less costly to sell to current customers than it is to attract new ones. With this in mind, there are several things that need to be accomplished in order to improve the use of customer information:

- Focusing on customer needs, not on merchandise department's needs.
- Developing a list of merchandise classifications that customers are not buying.
- Cross-analyzing lists to use by merchandise type.
- Merging and updating lists with external lists.
- Determining where and how a given customer buys each product. (Department stores tend to approach all products the same way. One solution is to develop stores comprised of privately owned shops.)

Anticipation—the next level

With improvements in the content and administration of customer databases, the next opportunity to develop a competitive edge in customer service is to anticipate what the customer wants. To successfully accomplish this goal, one must have a pre-planned action based on information in the company's files. Here are some promotional ideas:

- If a customer books a vacation through the store's travel service, send a promotional package including information on camera and film, camcorder and videotape, photo finishing, luggage and accessories, and so on.
- When a customer buys a carpet, automatically send information on carpet cleaning, drapery services, decorating services, and so on.

Using files in this manner allows management to anticipate other related customer needs. This is where proper use of the computer can actually personalize the relationship with customers and offer additional sales opportunities.

Organizing for the customer

Management must have a focal point by which to gather, maintain, analyze, interpret, market, and measure the use of customer service information within the company. Functions include:

- Who buys what and where?
- Share of market surveys.
- Consumer shopping panels.
- Analysis of what current customers are buying elsewhere.
- Customer lists consolidation, development, administration, and potential communication.
- Employee feedback.
- Sales-results analyses including test mailings and promotions.

Summary

Traditional customer service (as it is currently practised or not practised) in the retail industry is no longer sufficient. A broader customer-focussed culture is called for today that incorporates customer lifestyles and buying patterns into the strategy. The results can provide a wide range of creative, competitive opportunities. But using this information to the greatest advantage requires planning, commitment, a focal point, a merger of inside and outside information, communication, and careful measurement.

Strategic Dimensions of Services

Given the preceding framework, services can now be analyzed on two critical dimensions—value to customers and cost. Four categories of services emerge from such an analysis, as shown in Figure 17–2: support services, disappointers, basics, and patronage builders.[7]

Support services

Support services directly support the sale of the retailer's merchandise. They have high value to consumers but also a high cost to the retailer. Such services include home delivery, child care, gift wrapping, and personalized shopper services. Retail Highlight 17–3 provides some examples of support services.

Disappointers

Disappointers include layaway and parcel pick-up. These services require high labour effort but return little value to the customer. They are candidates for elimination from the services offered by some retailers. An alternative possibility is to restructure them in such a way as to reduce their cost and increase their value to customers.

Figure 17–2   Retail Customer Services Profile

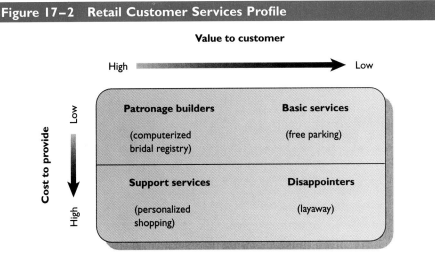

Source: Based on Albert D. Bates and Jamie G. Didion, "Special Services Can Personalize Retail Environment," *Marketing News*, April 12, 1985, p. 13.

Basic services

Customers take some **(basic) services** for granted. An example is free parking. Retailers often provide such services without giving much thought to their cost content, particularly if they are a competitive necessity.

Patronage builders

Patronage builders are the services that receive the most strategic attention from retailers. They include such services as birthday reminders and gift certificates. The services have high consumer value and can be provided at nominal cost. As such, they provide the opportunity to increase the store's customer base, especially if competitors are unable to provide comparable service at the same price. Computers have allowed retailers to shift some services from the high-value/high-cost category to one of high consumer value but low cost. Computerized bridal registries, for example, can be accessed from multiple store locations and purchases can be entered on virtually a real-time basis today.

Management may want to charge for support services, eliminate disappointers, and use patronage builders as a way to expand the customer base. Regardless, management needs to periodically re-evaluate services and make sure that patronage builders do not drift into the support services category.

Services audit

A services audit can help management evaluate the firm's services offerings relative to competition and on the basis of value to customers, as discussed above. The end result likely will be a more customer-driven services program. Identifying what services consumers really value is no simple task, partly because consumers may have difficulty articulating their preferences. Additionally, customers often form opinions about the quality and quantity of services by using competitors as a reference point.[8]

Retail Highlight 17–3

Examples of Excellent Support Services

Helping adults and children with special needs

- McDonald's reintroduced Braille and picture menus in 1992, emphasizing its commitment to serving the more than 3 million Canadians with vision, speech, or hearing impairments.
- Toys "Я" Us is distributing 175,000 copies of a 16-page brochure entitled *Toy Guide for Differently-Abled Kids!* featuring 50 toys assessed as helping disabled children. The guide is targeted to the parents of disabled children and is distributed at the 56 Canadian locations of Toys "Я" Us, and through agencies such as Easter Seals Canada, the Canadian Institute for the Blind, and the Canadian Down Syndrome Society.

Personalized services

- Harry Rosen's 24 stores across Canada are all linked by computer, with a database of their customers that allows salespeople to know what a particular customer has bought in the past, and to assist him in selecting the proper sizes, fit, and items (to avoid duplication). These data are also used to improve the merchandise mix, so that the right items are always in stock.
- Korry's Clothiers to Gentlemen will offer a potential client a free one-hour wardrobe analysis, and this information will be stored and used whenever the client has a need.
- When someone buys a new Mazda Miata, that person receives a one-year free subscription to a magazine specializing in after-market products for the Miata.

Sources: "Face to Face: A Look at McDonald's Customer Satisfaction," *First Quarter 1992 McDonald's Shareholders Newsletter;* James Pollock, "Toys "Я" Us Reaches out to Differently-Abled Kids," *Marketing,* October 16, 1995, p. 2; Leslie C. Smith, "Dressing up Customer Service," *Globe & Mail,* June 11, 1992, p. D1.

Customer services cannot be an afterthought. A quality services program can help to differentiate the firm from competition, generate new sales leads, discourage consumers from switching to alternative retail outlets that may offer the same merchandise, and reinforce customer loyalty. Asking questions such as these listed below help management integrate services as a strategic element of their customer support plan:

1. What are the company's customer service objectives on each service offered—to make a profit, break even, or, in order to remain competitive, to sustain the loss?

2. What services does the company provide (i.e., customer education, financing arrangements, pre-delivery preparation, complaints handling, repair service, etc.)?

3. How does the company compare with the competition on the customer services provided?

4. What services do customers want?

5. What are the customer service demand patterns?

6. What trade-offs in terms of cost versus service are customers prepared to make?

7. What level of service do customers want and at what price? For example, is an 800 or 888 telephone number adequate or is a salesperson necessary?[9]

Effective implementation of the services program is critical after the completion of the audit. Services response systems should be standardized

Table 17–1	Advantages and Disadvantages of Retail Credit	
Option	**Advantages**	**Disadvantages**
Maintaining in-house credit	Builds strong identification with customer. Retains customer loyalty. Facilitates customer purchase decision. When outside agency purchases credit contract, bad debt risk is transferred. Special consumers may be targeted with credit plan.	Bad debt may be incurred. Must staff and equip credit department. Clerical work involved with transaction. When credit contract is sold to outside agency, retail firm loses a percentage of credit contract.
Accepting bank cards	Attracts more diverse clientele. Outside agency may accept responsibility for collection of bad debts. Reduces pressure on sales personnel to grant credit. Loss due to bad debts accepted by outside agency. Credit offered to customers who otherwise would not qualify. Steady cash flow can be maintained. Broadens customer base. Supplements firm's credit options.	Fees paid to third party. Clerical work involved with transaction. With large purchases liability for non-payment may rest with retail outlet if proper authorization, signature, or both are not obtained. Depersonalizes relationship between firm and customer.
Accepting travel and entertainment cards	Attracts more diverse clientele. Cardholders are usually more affluent customers. Broadens customer base. Supplements existing credit options. Responsibility for processing applications, credit authorization, and collection rests with outside agency.	Fee charged to firm for using card. Clerical work involved with transaction. Proper authorization and/or signatures must be secured from cardholder (firm may be liable for debt if not). Depersonalizes customer/firm relationship. Types of purchases may be restricted.
Buying a private-label credit system	Bank handles details of processing, promotion of plan, credit authorization, and collections. Identity of third party is hidden because name of retail firm is on card. Customer loyalty is retained. Strong identity with retail firm is built. No fee assessed firm outside of cost for program.	Up-front fee assessed by firm sponsoring bank.

whenever possible and a pricing policy should be established in those situations where management decides to charge for various services.

Let's now look at the range of services offered by many retailers to see how they fit into a customer-focussed culture.

Retail Credit

Understandably, credit in one form or another is one of the most basic customer support services many retailers can offer. **Consumer credit** can be defined as sums that are borrowed, or financial obligations incurred, for a relatively short period of time. Historically, retailers have used a number of forms of retail credit to encourage patronage and purchases in their premises. The advantages and disadvantages of the various types of retail credit systems are shown in Table 17–1.

Credit is expensive, and write-offs are very costly, as illustrated in Table 17–2. However, well-managed, large-scale credit operations can be very profit-

Table 17–2   Every Dollar Written Off Requires a Fortune in New Business to Break Even

Your Profit Percent	Write-Offs of							
	$250	$500	$1,000	$2,000	$3,000	$5,000	$7,500	$10,000
	Equivalent to Sales of							
2%	$12,500	$25,000	$50,000	$100,000	$150,000	$250,000	$375,000	$500,000
3	8,333	16,667	33,333	66,667	100,000	166,667	249,975	333,333
4	6,250	12,500	25,000	50,000	75,000	125,000	187,500	250,000
5	5,000	10,000	20,000	40,000	60,000	100,000	150,000	200,000
6	4,165	8,333	16,667	33,333	50,000	83,333	124,950	166,667
7	3,572	7,143	14,286	28,571	42,857	71,429	107,145	142,857
8	3,125	6,250	12,500	25,000	37,500	62,500	93,750	125,000
9	2,778	5,556	11,111	22,222	33,333	55,556	83,340	111,111
10	2,500	5,000	10,000	20,000	30,000	50,000	75,000	100,000

Example: If you decide to write off $2,000 in bad debts and are averaging 6 percent profit, you must sell an additional $33,333 to recover that $2,000.

Source: I.C. Systems, Inc., St. Paul, Minnesota.

able. Most retailers believe that granting credit is necessary. Consumers apparently feel the same way since they often shop only in stores where credit cards are honoured.

Types of credit

A retailer has two choices in offering credit: (1) in-house credit or (2) third-party credit.

In-house credit

As shown in Figure 17–3, management has six choices in offering store credit: (1) installment payments, (2) open-charge credit, (3) revolving credit, (4) deferred billing payment, (5) layaway, and (6) store-issued credit card.

Installment credit (a monthly payment account) means that a customer pays for a product in equal monthly installments, including interest. Automobiles and major appliances are often paid for in this way.

Open charge credit means that the customer must pay the bill in full when it is due, usually in 30 days. Credit limits that the customer cannot exceed are set; also, partial payments on the account are not allowed.

Revolving credit means that a customer charges items during a month and is billed at the end of that month on the basis of the outstanding balance. Such a plan allows the customer to purchase several items without having a separate contract for each purchase.

A business can also offer **deferred billing credit.** Deferred billing occurs when a retailer allows customers to buy goods and defer payment for an extended time with no interest charge. Many stores advertise during the Christmas season, touting, "No down payment, and first payment not due for 90 days."

A layaway plan is another type of credit. This plan allows a customer to make a small deposit, perhaps two or three dollars, to hold an item. The retailer retains possession of the item until the customer completes paying for it. The

Figure 17–3   Types of In-House Credit

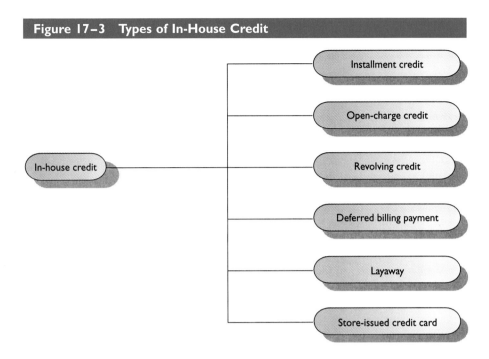

advantage to the customer is not having to worry about whether the item will be in stock when needed. And retailers do not have to worry about collection problems.

Most larger retailers historically have offered a **store-issued credit card.** The reason is clear. Store cardholders, compared to bank card customers, spend more per year in using their card, and also are more frequent card users.[10] The next section puts this method in context.

The credit card phenomenon in retailing   A **credit card** is basically a convenient way for customers to obtain credit without having to go through the approval process. It is in fact a modern form of revolving credit. Credit cards were first introduced in 1968 by the Royal Bank as the Chargex card (which became VISA). In 1995, an estimated 58.5 million credit cards were in circulation in Canada (i.e., 2.6 for each adult), of which about 28 million were MasterCard and Visa cards. In 1995, credit card balances exceeded $100 billion, of which $61 billion were accounted for by the 840 million transactions done with MasterCard and Visa cards.[11] In addition to bank cards, there were 26.6 million retail store cards and 3 million cards from gasoline retailers.[12]

Most retailers today honour some type of credit card. A retailer has two basic choices with credit cards. They can (1) have their own card or (2) participate in a third-party program.

Today, independent department stores and petroleum companies are practically the only stores that have internal credit operations (and even those are declining). These stores believe they get a strong marketing advantage from in-house credit. Many have added bank credit card plans to their programs, primarily to take advantage of out-of-town business. Others have sold their credit card business to financial institutions. Thus, in-house credit probably is on its way out for many merchants.

Managing internal credit   Most firms issuing credit use an application form. The application requests information that allows the firm to decide whether the person should be granted credit. The forms may ask for such information as the size of savings and chequing account balances, extent of debts, and various other personal information. Often information on the credit worthiness of the applicant is obtained from a credit bureau.

Credit scoring   Many firms use **credit scoring** in screening credit applicants. This method gives points about various types of personal information concerning the applicant. The points are determined through a study of information obtained from other good and bad accounts. Depending on the number of points received, a person may be given a credit limit or may be rejected. Experience can help decide on the minimum number of points necessary to approve an application. A credit application is considered by summing the points received based on the application characteristics evaluated. The score may be part of either a single cutoff method or a two-stage process.

In the single cutoff method, credit is granted if the points meet or exceed the cutoff. Otherwise, credit is denied. In a two-stage analysis, credit is automatically awarded if the credit score exceeds the cutoff point and is automatically denied if it is below the cutoff. Additional information is gathered on applicants who meet the cutoff exactly and is added to the initial score based on the application information. A decision on whether to accept or deny credit is then made.

Scoring gives the retailer the following advantages: (1) better control over credit, (2) ease in training new personnel, (3) lower cost of processing loan application, and (4) a more legally defensible way of granting or denying credit.

Key legislation   On this last point, retailers must comply essentially with the antidiscrimination sections of the Canadian Human Rights Act and some provincial Human Rights Codes, some provisions of the Bank Act and the Interest Act, as well as the appropriate provincial Consumer Protection Act and Cost of Credit Disclosure Act. To a lesser extent, the Competition Act (section 49) and the Small Loan Act may apply to credit.

Credit authorization   The retailer also needs to decide how credit will be verified when a credit purchase is made. Some firms still have *manual credit verification,* where a clerk calls the credit department when a sale is made and asks for approval. Most credit authorization is now done electronically. The clerk enters the account number and the amount of the sale at the cash register. The system then automatically cheques the accounts receivable information stored in the computer and indicates whether a credit charge should be approved. The stand-alone credit authorization terminal, however, is rapidly becoming a thing of the past. Instead, high credit volume retailers are integrating credit authorization into POS terminals.[13]

Added-value programs   Retailers often entice their core credit customers to remain loyal by creating purchase incentives for them. The key is adding value to the credit card.[14] Examples are:

- Eaton's sends its credit customers a mail-order catalogue invitations to special charge customers to shopping evenings before Christmas, special notices of private sales, and postcard mailings with special merchandise offers.

- Zellers' Club Z program allows charge customers to accumulate 100 points for every dollar in charge purchases. Customers begin receiving benefits and rewards based on their point totals earned.

- Canadian Tire has a new program, called "options," which can be used instead of receiving Canadian Tire "money" (3 percent of cash purchases). With the Canadian Tire card, customers receive 10 points per dollar in charge purchases, and they begin receiving benefits at the 3,000 point mark at the cash register, either in terms of percentage discount on merchandise or dollar rebates.

- Another successful loyalty program, called Air Miles, provides points for shopping at participating sponsors, and in 1995 there were more than 7 million Air Miles cards in circulation, in 3.7 million households, representing 37 percent of all Canadian households.[15]

Promoting credit   In spite of the possible losses from a credit operation, many retailers aggressively promote their credit plans because they can result in increased merchandise sales. College students are often a special target. They are perceived as upwardly mobile, soon-to-be-young-professionals with high income potential. As well, the population turnover in a community can easily equal 15 percent per year, and an ongoing program of credit promotion is necessary to maintain a strong customer base for a retail outlet.

Third-party credit

Third-party credit can consist of (1) a *bank card* such as Visa or MasterCard, (2) a **private-label credit card** for the store, which is issued by a third party such as a bank, (3) *travel and entertainment cards* such as American Express or Diner's Club. Bank credit cards, such as Visa, or travel and entertainment cards such as Diner's Club are not controlled by the merchant. Rather, the bank or the entertainment company receives applications and issues cards and is responsible for customer billing and collection. The firms then bill the merchants accepting the card a flat percentage of all credit sales.[16]

In a third-party program, banks handle (1) credit applications, credit processing, and authorization; (2) customer inquiries; (3) promotion; and (4) issuing each customer a card with the name of the participating store on it.

A *co-branded* card is a dual-purpose card combining the features of a private-label card and a bank card.[17] The issuer and the retailer each have their logo on the card. Recently, Visa has gone this route and will place a store name on the face of their card. Such programs allow consumers to reduce the number of cards they carry and to use the card at outlets that might not accept bank cards. Another advantage is consolidated billing. As with other third-party cards, the retailers focus on their skills—selling merchandise and services—while financial institutions handle the consumer credit issues.

In summary, more and more retailers are dropping in-house credit as a service. Many are (1) going to a private-label third-party system, (2) honouring bank cards such as Visa, (3) honouring travel and entertainment cards, or (4) structuring a program to encourage the use of cheques and cash. Some retailers, for example Canadian Tire, give rebates of 3 to 5 percent in the form of "store money" on cash purchases. This discount is the equivalent of what merchants pay the banks for the right to allow customers to make purchases with a bank credit card such as Visa.

Handling cheques

Historically, a customer with a chequebook at the head of a cheque-out line was sure to bring moans and grumbling from customers waiting in line. The process of paying by cheque can easily take 5 to 10 minutes and create great customer frustration. Stores have turned to on-line cheque acceptance services, which make payment by cheque as simple as using a credit card and just as quick.

Many retail customers still prefer to pay by either cash or cheque. Making it easy for them to pay by cheque generates customer goodwill and a substantial amount of "plus" business. Some supermarkets such as Provigo offer cheque-cashing privileges to their customers with the store card, that is, a customer cannot only pay for groceries with a cheque (no hassle for approval), but write a larger amount to obtain cash in return.

Shopping Services

Retailers are always trying to make it possible for customers to buy goods without having to spend an extended time in the store. Shopping services thus are being experimented on by large food retailers like Provigo. The most common shopper services are (1) telephone shopping, (2) in-home shopping, and (3) personal shopping.

Telephone shopping

Telephone shopping is encouraged by retailers because many people have less time for shopping. Often, the store will issue a catalogue to the consumer. After looking at the catalogue, the customer calls the store, orders the merchandise, and charges the goods to an account or credit card. The goods are then delivered to the shopper's home. Some retail outlets also offer toll-free 800 or 888 services as a way of increasing sales. Harrod's Department Store in London, England, was the first store in Europe to join AT&T's international 800 service. Shoppers were able to order goods during the store's post-Christmas sale by dialing direct—even before the store opened for business to Londoners.[18]

In-home shopping

In-home demonstrations remain popular for such services as home decoration. Employees bring samples of draperies, carpeting, and wallpaper to a customer's home and the customer can then see how the materials look under normal lighting conditions. One such example is Elte Carpets, discussed earlier.[19]

Personal shopping services

Personal shopping is one of the fastest-growing services. The customer goes to the store and provides a list of needed measurements, style and colour preferences, and lifestyle information. After that, the person can call the store and indicate the types of items wanted. The store personnel then assemble several choices and have them ready at the customer's convenience.[20]

Other Customer Support Services

The customer service possibilities are almost limitless. The type and level of services vary depending on the positioning strategy of the retailer. Some are quite unique, as in the case of the "people greeters" who meet shoppers at the front doors of Wal-Mart. The people greeters are one of the most popular customer support services offered by Wal-Mart.

Warranties

A strong customer satisfaction warranty forces the retailer to provide high-quality service and merchandise. Anything less than excellence will entice the customer to invoke the guarantee, which can be an expensive process. Thus, guarantees and warranties serve a two-fold purpose: to identify problems with the quality of service delivered, and to force the organization to meet consistently high standards of customer service.[21]

Some retailers also offer an *extended warranty* or a service contract.[22] The store agrees to extend a manufacturer's warranty for a period of time, commonly a year or so. The customer does not have to pay a repair bill during the agreed period of time regardless of how much the repair service may cost. Extended warranties are common on major household appliances and television sets.

Retailers should be aware of warranty legislation, however, when offering extended warranties, in particular the Competition Act, and the appropriate provincial Consumer Protection Act. *Satisfaction guaranteed* is a phrase often heard, but today such a statement is more of a contract than a courtesy. Some laws also determine where and how warranty information must be displayed. Many retail catalogues inform consumers that warranty information is available by mail before purchasing from the store.

Delivery

Delivery can be a large expense item for big-ticket items such as furniture and household appliances. Stores are often pressured not to charge extra for delivery. Retailers can help their image as full-service retailers by having their own trucks for delivery. The delivery schedule can then be more flexible, but the cost of having delivery trucks is high.

Another method of delivery is to use parcel post and service express. Retailers may want to use these services in addition to independent delivery services. Parcel post is a good way to deliver small packages to customers who may live a long distance from the store. Mail-order retailers often arrange delivery in this way.

Extended shopping hours

Where it is legal, more and more retailers are offering consumers longer shopping hours, either late-night or 24-hour shopping. Utility charges are about the same since the equipment runs most of the time anyway. Additional sales generated by longer hours can help spread the fixed costs over a larger sales base.

Merchants may do very well with such a service since in many communities only a few stores are open 24 hours a day. But it is important to study such a move carefully before making a decision. Retailers will have to pay overtime to employees or add part-time workers. The chance of being robbed is greater, and energy bills will go up somewhat.

Retailers should also remember that **blue laws** (laws against opening on Sunday) are enforced in some areas. Enforcement is spotty, but a retailer can be fined if a pressure group pushes the police to enforce the law. Blue laws are likely to be a thing of the past in the next few years since most consumers seem to want Sunday shopping.

Automatic bill payment

Retailers are increasingly offering bill-payment programs that allow bills to be paid by telephone, by pre-authorization, or by electronic terminals as an alternative to paying by cheque.

One such system is the **debit card** introduced in Canada in 1986 by several banks such as the National Bank, the Toronto-Dominion Bank, and the Canadian Imperial Bank of Commerce. At the retail level, the transaction is as follows:

1. The client presents the debit card to the cashier.
2. The cashier hands over a keyboard attached to the cash register.
3. The card is inserted into the terminal.
4. The client verifies the amount of purchase indicated, then chooses the bank account from which the withdrawal should take place, and then authorizes the transaction by keying in a personal identification number (PIN).
5. The money is transferred electronically from the client's to the retailer's bank account.
6. The client receives a statement of the full transaction.

The whole operation lasts only a few minutes. With the system, the debit card works within the network of merchants signed on by the issuing bank. An increasing number of banks and merchants have adopted this type of service, now integrated with the Interac banking system, allowing customers to use their card almost anywhere, including grocery stores and even corner stores. By 1994, the number of transactions reached 325 million.[23]

The advantages of such systems include (1) the elimination of bad cheques, (2) lower labour costs to the retailer, (3) lower cheque-processing fees because of a smaller cheque volume, and (4) reduced postage.

The disadvantages include (1) the loss of direct contact with the consumer, (2) the loss of the opportunity to send stuffers with monthly statements, (3) misunderstandings with consumers over the timing of the payments, which can lead to loss of goodwill, and (4) the loss of an audit trail that would help in catching dishonesty and fraud. Automated bill paying is very popular because consumers react positively to saving time by this means of payment. Also, banks are developing plans for a "smart" card that will be more efficient and will cut on fraud.[24]

Customers with special needs

Special opportunities exist to meet the needs of "special" consumers, including those who don't speak English, or French (in Quebec), the aged, and the infirm (including people who are deaf, blind, or confined to wheelchairs).[25]

The federal government mandated the push toward barrier-free environments in education, employment, and nonemployment situations. Now many provinces also have legislation requiring architectural compliance in developing barrier-free environments. Some progressive stores offer programs to assist and inform disabled and aged shoppers.

Large retailers in such metropolitan markets as Toronto, Vancouver, and Montreal, or in places popular with tourists such as Banff, Niagara Falls, or Charlottetown offer multilingual signing to attract and serve foreign tourists. They also maintain lists of employees with foreign language ability. In addition, store directories and information pamphlets are sometimes printed in foreign languages.

Registries

Computerization is giving department stores a convenience and flexibility in their registry system that was previously unavailable. The benefits these retailers have seen in a computerized bridal registry are broadbased. The most obvious advantage is in access and updating capabilities. Because a complete registry can be printed from the computer within a matter of minutes, stores on the system can provide customers with an instant "shopping list" for a betrothed couple—a list they can carry with them from department to department as they make their selections.

But perhaps of most interest to store executives is the merchandising aspect, providing buyers and merchandise managers with complete, up-to-the-minute sales information, right down to details on vendor, patterns, size, or colour of each gift purchased.

Nursery services

Some retailers are adding nursery services as part of their customer support programs. IKEA, the Swedish-owned home furnishings chain, has been widely noted in the trade press as having an excellent child-care program to encourage parents' shopping.[26] Sears has also added a play area in the Kids & More departments in its new power format stores.

Responding to Complaints

Invariably, in spite of a retailer's best efforts, complaints about the merchandise or store policies will arise. The tendency too often is to treat complaints as a nuisance. Such a viewpoint is shortsighted, however. Management should strive, within reasonable limits, to retain customers whenever possible. Customer loyalty and profitability go hand in hand because it costs less to serve repeat customers than to attract new customers.[27]

Customer service breakdowns are especially likely in the following situations: (1) when the service process involves complex scheduling; (2) when a new customer support service is being introduced; (3) when the customer support activity involves high employee turnover; (4) when front-line employees are inadequately trained; and (5) when the retailer is forced to rely on suppliers or other uncontrollable external factors such as the weather.[28]

Retailers need a policy for dealing with customer complaints. Customers are allowed to return items in most stores, and some retailers feel the customer should be satisfied at any price. Almost all retailers, while not guaranteeing satisfaction, do try to be fair to the customer. There may be many problems in addition to returns, including complaints about products, poor installation, problems with delivery, damaged goods, errors in billing, and so forth.

Complaints and returns can be handled on either a centralized or decentralized basis. Stores with a *centralized policy* handle all issues at a central level in the store; in this way they can be sure that a standardized policy is followed for all departments. In a *decentralized approach,* problems are handled on the sales floor by the person who sold the item, and the customer gets greater personal attention.

Stores normally prefer not to give a cash refund when handling a complaint or return. Most retailers try to get the customer exchanging an item to accept a slip (or "due-bill"), which allows him or her to purchase an item at the same price in the future. This policy is designed to keep the customer coming back to the store. Some retailers may feel, however, that the consumer should be given a refund. They believe this better satisfies customers and builds better customer relations.

Stores also have to make a decision in handling complaints and returned merchandise about whether to put the emphasis on the customer or the store. Again, a cost-benefit analysis is required. Providing an elaborate system for handling complaints and returns is costly, especially when the consumer wants money instead of merchandise upon returning an item. Still, stores may be better off viewing returns primarily from the viewpoint of the consumer and generating goodwill by going out of their way to have a liberal returned-goods policy, as illustrated in Retail Highlight 17–4.

Evaluating the Cost-Effectiveness of Services

All services offered cost the firm money. Employees may need to be added to offer certain services. The cost must be balanced against anticipated revenues or the loss of goodwill if the services are not offered.

It is not possible to precisely determine the revenue-generating effects of each service. Also, if certain services are offered by the competition, the firm may have to offer them to remain competitive.

Many factors must be considered in deciding to offer or discontinue a service. The same is true when the retailer is deciding whether to charge for a service such as merchandise returned through no fault of the retailer. Let's consider the issue of credit. Management must balance the additional revenue from additional customer sales against the cost of offering credit. For example, interest is lost because the funds are not available to management.

Other costs of credit include the discounting of receivables such as when a financial institution buys the credit accounts from a retailer at a discount. The

Retail Highlight 17–4

Proper Handling of Customer Complaints and Returns Requires a Conversion of Faith

- The following story illustrates a customer-focussed perspective on complaints and returns: Tom Sieciechowicz pondered service long and hard after he and his wife Anna opened their first Odyssey Books store in Kanata, Ontario, 11 years ago. After deciding that he was doing most things wrong by using his own preferences, he concluded that his store would have to capture loyal book buyers first, and adjust inventory to suit their tastes. He then began a policy of exchanging any book a reader found to be unsatisfactory—for whatever reason. But *carrying out* the policy required a conversion of faith. He recalls a pitch battle with a customer over a refund. In mid-argument, he suddenly realized that he had to stand behind his policy and give the refund. The experience changed his thinking: "What is service? It's what the customer thinks is service. The customer wanted to be able to return books without questions being asked. Whether he even bought it at a different store, he wanted to have a fair trade, to feel that everything was guaranteed. That was logical from the customer's point of view, so it became logical from mine."

Source: Marlene Cartash, "Catch a Falling Store," *Profit*, December 1990, pp. 26–27.

advantage to the retailer is that the cash is immediately available and no risks of collection are assumed. Still, the discount paid to get quick access to the funds can result in lower net profit. Other outside costs include the time sales clerks spend in charging a sale to a bank credit card or a travel and entertainment card.

Chapter Highlights

- **Customer service expectations vary by type of retailing. The differences between customer expectations and experiences, if any, result in a customer expectations gap. Management can most effectively address the issue of customer support services by focussing on both customers and processes which, in turn, translates into focussing on the outcome.**

- **Traditional customer service in the retail industry is no longer sufficient. A broader customer-focussed culture is called for today that incorporates customer lifestyles and buying patterns into the strategy. The results can provide a wide range of creative, and competitive opportunities. But using this information to the greatest advantage requires planning, commitment, a focal point, a merger of inside and outside information, communication, and careful measurement.**

- Services can be analyzed on two key dimensions: value to customers and cost to retailers. Four categories of services emerge from such an analysis: support services, disappointers, basics, and patronage builders.

- A services audit can help management develop a customer-focussed culture. Identifying what services customers really value is no simple task, partly because customers may have difficulty articulating their preferences.

- Retailers face a variety of decisions in deciding whether to offer credit. They can offer in-store credit or have credit handled by an outside agency such as a bank by honouring bank credit cards. They may also issue a store credit card of their own or have a card with their name on it, but have the bank handle the administrative details. Consumer pressure in favour of bank credit cards is increasing, and most stores now honour them.

- Most types of credit are offered by the retailer at a loss. However, credit normally is a necessary customer service.

- Retailers can offer a variety of other services as part of the customer support mix. These include warranties, extended hours and Sunday openings, delivery, automatic bill payment, nursery services, services to customers with special needs, and registries. However, it is important to try to balance likely revenue against the cost of the services.

- Retailers should closely monitor the legal issues relating to many of the services they offer.

Key Terms

basic services 491
blue laws 500
consumer credit 493
credit card 495
credit scoring 496
customer-focussed culture 486
customer service 485
debit card 500
deferred billing credit 494
disappointers 490
installment credit 494

layaway plan 494
open charge credit 494
patronage builders 491
personal shopping service 498
private-label credit card 497
revolving credit 494
store-issued credit card 495
support services 490
third-party credit 497

Discussion Questions

1. What might be the major reasons for a retailer to offer selected services? Why are many retailers cutting down on the number of services they offer?

2. Why should a retailer offer a store's own card for credit? What problems or disadvantages exist with a store having its own card?

3. What are some retailers doing to encourage customers to pay cash for purchases?

4. What are some of the methods retailers use to determine to which applicants credit should be extended?

5. **What are the advantages and disadvantages of offering customers liberal merchandise return privileges?**

6. **Explain the concept of a debit card. Describe its advantages and disadvantages for both the customer and the retailer.**

7. **What are some of the things retailers are doing to be more responsive to customers who have special needs?**

8. **What are the advantages and disadvantages of a centralized versus a decentralized procedure for handling consumer complaints?**

Application Exercises

1. Talk to the credit manager at a couple of the local department stores in your community and to the loan officer at a couple of banks to determine how they evaluate customer applications for credit. Try to get a copy of the forms they use, if possible. Find out if they use credit scoring. If not, what do they do in order to be objective in their evaluations? Find out if they are reasonably current on the regulations about granting credit to women.

2. Interview a group of students at random and select a department store, supermarket, discount store (e.g., Zellers), and national chain like Sears. Develop a list of services that the stores might offer (from the text listing). Then, have each student check the services that they perceive are offered by each type of store chosen. Write a report on the findings and suggest what they mean to you in terms of the material included in the chapter.

3. Discuss with several friends complaints that they may have had against a store or stores. Describe how each was handled by (1) the customer and (2) the store. Evaluate the process that you discover in this project.

Suggested Cases

Notes

1. R. Williamson, "Motivation on the Menu," *The Globe & Mail*, November 24, 1995, p. B7; G. Pitts, "The Vision of Saint Hubert," *Report on Business*, May 30, 1995, p. B10.

2. D.E. Headley and B. Choi, "Achieving Service Quality through Gap Analysis and a Basic Statistical Approach," *Journal of Services Marketing* 6, 1 (Winter 1992), pp. 5–14.

3. This section on customer service versus customer focus is reproduced with permission from R. Burns, "Customer Service vs. Customer-Focused," *Retail Control*, March 1989. © National Retail Merchants Association. All rights reserved.

4. "Their Wish Is Your Command," *Business Week/Quality*, 1991, pp. 126–27.

5. L.C. Smith, "Dressing up Customer Service," *Globe & Mail*, January 11, 1992, p. D1.

6. M. Cartash, "Catch a Falling Store," *Profit*, December 1990, p. 29.

7. A.D. Bates and J.G. Didion, "Special Services Can Personalize Retail Environment," *Marketing News*, April 12, 1985, p. 13.

8. G.H.G. McDougall and T. Levesque, "The Measurement of Service Quality: Some Methodological Issues," in *Marketing, Operations and Human Resources Insight into Services*, ed. P. Eiglier and E. Langeard, Aix, France: I.A.E., 1992, pp. 411–31; J.J. Cronin, Jr. and S.A. Taylor, "Measuring Service Quality: A Reexamination and Extension," *Journal of Marketing* 56, July 1992, pp. 55–68; G. LeBlanc, "The Determinants of Service Quality in Travel Agencies," in *Marketing*, vol. 11 (ed. J. Liefeld), ASAC, 1990, pp. 188–96.

9. A. Markowitz, "Technology Fills Multitude of Roles in Improving Customer Service," *Discount Store News*, May 3, 1993, pp. 48–49.

10. "Store Card Still Strong," *Stores*, January 1991, p. 169.

11. A. Mitchell, "Household Debt Reaching Historic High," *Globe & Mail*, November 18, 1995, p. A1; "Credit Card Interest Charges," *Information* (December 1995), Minister of Supply and Services Canada, pp. 2–6.

12. J. Partridge, "Canadians Set Visa Record of $43.5 Billion," *Globe & Mail*, February 14, 1995, p. B1; "Credit Card Interest Charges," p. 2.

13. G. Robins, "Wireless POS Systems," *Stores*, February 1994, pp. 47–48.

14. P. Gill, "Added Value. Relationship Marketing Is One Way for Retailers to Build Loyalty," *Stores*, October 1991, pp. 39–40; M. Strauss, "The Downside of Cultivating Loyalty," *Globe & Mail*, June 29, 1995, p. B4.

15. *Database Marketing* 3, 2, February 1995, p. 7.

16. D. Del Prete, "Credit Card Companies to Retailers: Use Us," *Marketing News*, March 4, 1991, pp. 1, 6.

17. "Co-Branding on the Rise," *Stores*, February 1992, p. S7; D. Alaimo, "Wegmans to Use Co-Branded Credit Cards," *Supermarket News*, February 25, 1991, p. 15.

18. "London's Harrods Department Store," *Sales and Marketing Management*, January 13, 1986, p. 83.

19. M. Cartash, "Catch a Falling Store," p. 29.

20. Smith, "Dressing up Customer Service."

21. C.W.L. Hart, J. Heskitt, and E. Sasser, *Service Breakthroughs* (New York: The Free Press, 1990), p. 89.

22. L. Freeman, "Service Contracts and Warranties Impact Bottom Line," *Stores*, January 1992, pp. 122, 124; D. Del Prete, "Looks Like a Hot Summer for Extended Car Warranties," *Marketing News*, August 8, 1991, p. 9.

23. G. Rowan, "Mixed Media," *The Globe & Mail*, August 15, 1995, p. B8.

24. R. Blackwell, "Visa Plans 'Smart' Cards," *Financial Post*, February 14, 1995, p. 8.

25. "Face to Face: A Look at McDonald's Customer Satisfaction," *First Quarter 1992 McDonald's Shareholders Newsletter;* J. Pollock, "Toys "Я" Us Reaches out to Differently-Abled Kids," *Marketing*, October 16, 1995, p. 2.

26. "Caring: IKEA Sets the Pace," *Stores*, November 1990, pp. 54–55.

27. Hart, Heskitt, and Sasser, *Service Breakthroughs*, p. 31.

28. Ibid.

PART

Evaluating the Retail Strategy

In Part 4, Evaluating the Retail Strategy, the tools and approaches to evaluation and control of the firm's strategy are discussed. The critical aspects of evaluating and controlling merchandise planning is covered in Chapter 18. Overall performance evaluation, including the strategic profit model and inventory turnover assessment, are discussed in Chapter 19.

18.   **Evaluation and Control of Merchandise Planning**

19.   **Performance Evaluation**

Evaluation and Control of Merchandise Planning

Chapter Objectives

After reading this chapter, you should be able to:

1. **Explain the relationship between planning and control.**

2. **Illustrate how to establish a dollar control and open-to-buy system to control dollar merchandise investment.**

3. **Explain unit control of inventory investment.**

Loblaws' inventory computer system is critical in evaluating and adjusting the merchandise mix to satisfy customer needs and maximize inventory turnover.

*T*he task of merchandise planning in a supermarket—a store that typically carries between 8,000 and 12,000 items—is easier today than a few years ago, thanks to computer systems. Loblaws is among the 1,100 supermarket outlets in Canada that have computerized check-out price scanners and in-store computers. Loblaws stocks more than 1,000 new national brand products each year, but it also drops an equal number. Computer systems allow Loblaws to identify both high- and low-volume items and make adjustments to shelf allocation—the low-volume items may be dropped and the high-growth products get more space. As well, computer systems can track inventories and allow the retailer to adjust quickly to changes in consumers' buying patterns.

Sears Canada has approximately 1,400 catalogue stores across Canada to handle the sales generated through its catalogues. The company has continued to fine-tune its catalogue systems, including the installation of a fully integrated, on-line, inventory control system. This allows Sears to closely monitor and improve inventory levels, ensure prompt delivery of goods to customers, and provide up-to-date information about merchandise availability.[1] ■

Figure 18–1   The Relationship between Planning and Control

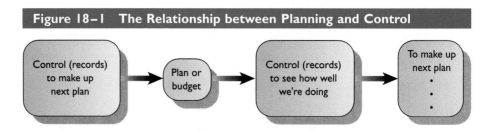

These examples illustrate the importance retailers place on merchandise management in the competitive struggle in today's marketplace. A good merchandise planning and control system allows the retailer to monitor what's going on so that better decisions can be made to attain a productive investment in inventory (i.e., not too much or too little). This chapter emphasizes the basics of the control of merchandise and expense management. Of primary interest is the evaluation of planning activities through control. Planning, discussed in detail in Chapter 12, was presented as an effort to obtain competitive advantages in the marketplace. The merchandise and expense budgets were noted as key plans utilized by management to reach specific objectives.

This chapter is a companion to the Chapter 12 material since it approaches the evaluation of these plans to achieve certain objectives. Planning is useless unless retailers monitor operating results to determine whether goals are being met. If plans are not being followed, corrective action must be taken to improve the situation. The monitoring process is the *control* aspect of retail management. Without control, planning is a wasted effort.

The Relationship between Planning and Control

The relationship between planning and control is essential, direct, and two-way. As shown in Figure 18–1, control records are needed to develop plans. Once a plan is developed, control records are needed to determine how well the retailer is doing.

In Chapter 12, the merchandise plan was discussed in terms of developing the following aspects of stock balance: (1) dollars, (2) width, and (3) depth. A merchandise budget in dollars and a model stock were developed for planning the width and depth factors. In this chapter, attention is given to the systems used to control the merchandise budget. Figure 18–2 illustrates the relationships between the merchandise planning and control systems.

Note from Figure 18–2 that two systems are used for controlling the merchandise plan. **Dollar control** is the way of controlling dollar investment in inventory. **Unit control** is used to control the width and depth aspects of stock balance. Figure 18–3 shows how these two types of control—dollar and unit—work together.

Dollar merchandise inventory control

To control dollar inventory investments, the retailer must know the following:

1. The beginning dollar inventory.
2. What has been added to stock.

Figure 18–2 From Planning to Control

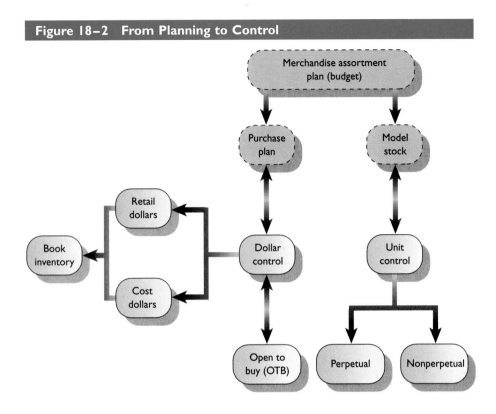

3. How much inventory has moved out of stock.

4. How much inventory is now on hand.

A more detailed statement appears in this section, but the following example shows the basic facts the retailer must know to control dollar inventory investments:

	1.	Inventory at beginning of period	$10,000
+	2.	Total additions to stock	2,000
=		Stock available for sale during period	$12,000
−	3.	Total deductions from stock	2,500
=	4.	Inventory at end of period	$ 9,500

To determine the value of inventory at the end of the period (number 4 in the example above), the retailer may (1) take a *physical inventory* (actually count all the inventory on hand) or (2) set up a book inventory or *perpetual inventory system.* A **book inventory** is the recording of all additions to and deductions from a beginning stock figure to continually have an ending inventory figure. It is impractical to take a physical inventory every time the manager wants to know how much inventory is on hand. Thus, retailers set up a book inventory system. This enables them to know the dollar value of inventory on hand without having to take a physical inventory.

A book inventory system is needed for efficient and effective dollar control. Information must be collected and recorded continually; it can be recorded in retail dollars or in cost dollars, manually or by computer.

Figure 18–3   Diagram of Merchandise Planning and Control

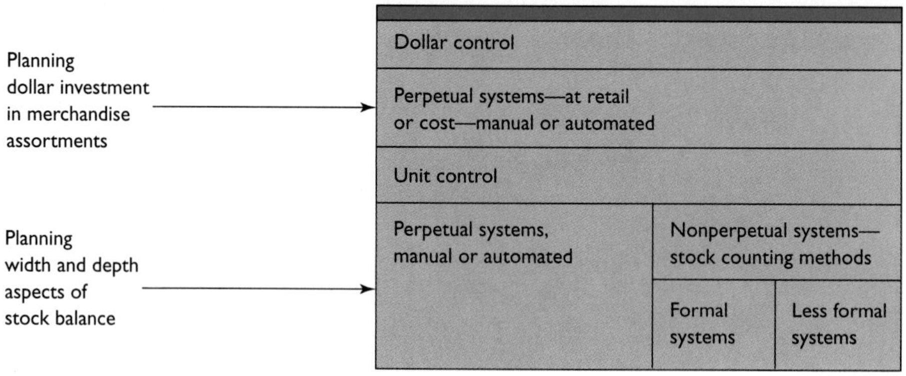

Retail dollar control

Table 18–1 includes the typical items included in a retail dollar control system. The system is a perpetual one and provides answers to the following questions:

- *What dollar inventory did the retailer start with?* The BOM (beginning of month) inventory dated 3/1 gives the answer to this question. This March BOM inventory figure is the EOM (end of month) February figure, or $10,000.

- *What has been added to stock?* The additions to stock are purchases, transfers, and additional markups that add dollars to the beginning inventory. Total additions are $2,300. The total available for sale is $12,300.

- *How much inventory has moved out of stock?* The deductions from stock are sales, markdowns, and employee discounts, which reduce the total dollars of inventory available for sale. Total deductions are $3,000.

- *How much inventory is on hand now?* The EOM inventory, dated 3/31, is the difference between what was available and what moved out of stock. This is the book inventory figure or $9,300.

The explanations in Table 18–1 should be studied carefully since it is important to fully understand the items that affect retail book inventory. This information, however, should not be confused with an accounting statement discussed in the next chapter. The information comes from accounting data, but it is for control purposes only.

Note in Table 18–1 the notation "including shortages" at the end of the illustration. Since these are "book" figures, a chance for error exists. The only way to determine the accuracy of the book figure is by taking a physical inventory.

The retail book figures indicate the value of on-hand inventory to be $9,300. Assume that when a physical inventory is taken, the retail value of on-hand stock is $9,000. This situation represents a shortage of $300. A **shortage** occurs when the physical inventory is smaller than the book inventory. Shoplifting, internal theft, short shipments from vendors, breakage, and clerical error are common causes of shortages. If, on the other hand, the physical inventory had indicated the value of stock on hand to be $10,000, then the retail

Table 18–1   Illustration of Retail Dollar Book (Perpetual) Inventory (Sweat Suits) for Month of March

Items Affecting Dollar Value of Inventory during Month				Necessary Explanations of Certain Items	Where to Get Information
BOM inventory, 3/1			$10,000		EOM February inventory
Additions to stock:					
Purchases	$2,000				Purchase records or invoices
Less: Vendor returns	(100)			Goods go back to source	Vendor return records
Net purchases		$1,900			
Transfers in	$ 200			In multistore firm, goods transfer from one store to another	Interstore transfer forms in multistore firm
Less: Transfers out	(100)				
Net transfers in		100			
Additional markups		300		Price increase after goods in stock	Price change forms
Total additions			2,300		
Total available for sale			$12,300		
Deductions from stock:					
Gross sales	$2,500				Daily sales report
Less: Customer returns	(100)				Return forms
Net sales		$2,400			
Gross markdowns	$ 500			Reduction from original price	Price change forms at start of a sale
Less: Markdown cancellations	(100)				Price change cancellation at end of sale to bring prices back to regular
Net markdowns		400			
Employee discounts		200		Employee pays less than merchandise price	Form completed at sale
Total deductions from stock			$ 3,000		
EOM inventory, 3/31 (including shortages)			$ 9,300	A book inventory figure so actual amount is somewhat different (physical inventory necessary for actual)	Derived figure from additions and deductions from BOM inventory

classification has incurred an overage of $700. An **overage** occurs when the physical inventory is larger than the book inventory. In retailing, an overage situation is usually caused by clerical errors or miscounts.

Open-to-buy

One of the most valuable outputs of a retail dollar control system is **open-to-buy** (OTB) (see Figure 18–2). OTB exists to "control" the merchant's utilization of the planned purchases figure (see Chapter 12, section on planned purchases). Dollar control provides the essential information to set up an OTB system. These essentials are the BOM and EOM inventories.

Table 18–2 Open-to-Buy Illustration

Planned purchases	=	$25,000	(EOM February or BOM March at retail)
	+	2,500	(Planned sales – February)
	+	600	(Planned reductions – February)
	=	$28,100	(Dollars needed)
	–	24,000	(BOM February at retail)(EOM January)
	=	$ 4,100	(Planned purchases)
Commitments against planned purchases during the month of February:			
On order to be delivered in February: $1,000			
Merchandise received as of February 15: $1,500	–	$ 2,500	(Commitments against planned purchases)
OTB as of February 15	=	$ 1,600	(Note: The $1,600 figure is in retail dollars and must be converted to cost to use as a buying guide in the market.)

Table 18–2 illustrates how OTB as of February 15 can be calculated. As shown in the figure, OTB is determined by deducting from planned purchases *commitments* that have been made. The two commitments are: (1) merchandise on order that has not been delivered and (2) merchandise that has been delivered. Remember, planned purchases relate to one particular month (in the example, to February). So, OTB relates to only one month. If, for example, merchandise was ordered in January to be delivered in March, that amount would not be a February commitment and would not affect OTB for February.

From the illustration, one can see that as of February 15, the buyer has $1,600 (in retail dollars) to spend for merchandise to be delivered in February. At the beginning of any month with no commitments, planned purchases and OTB are equal. Assume, however, that by February 20 all of the OTB has been used up and that, in fact, the buyer has overcommitted by $100. This situation is called *overbought* and is not a good position to be in. This leads to another point that must be made about OTB.

OTB must be used only as a guide and must not be allowed to actually dictate decisions. A retailer, however, always wants to have OTB to take advantage of unique market situations. The system must also allow for budget adjustments. If the buyer needs more OTB for certain purposes, management approval must be obtained. This can be done by: (1) convincing management of the importance of a contemplated purchase and obtaining a budget increase for planned sales; (2) increasing planned reductions or taking more markdowns than have been budgeted; or (3) increasing the planned EOM inventory in

Table 18–3   Example of an Open-to-Buy Report

Open-to-buy report

Department _____   Classification _____   Date prepared   February 15

Last Month (January)

Line				
1	**Sales**	–	actual last year	_____
2		–	adjusted plan this year	_____
3	**Stock**		actual this year	_____
4		–	adjusted plan EOM this year	_____
5		–	actual EOM this year	24,000
6		–	actual last year	_____
7	**Sales**	–	adjusted plan this year	2,500
8		–	month to date this year	_____

This Month (February)

9	**Stock**	–	balance of month this year	_____
10		–	actual EOM last year	_____
11		–	adjusted plan EOM this year	25,000
12		–	actual as of this report	_____
13	**Markdowns**	–	actual last year	_____
14		–	adjusted plan this year	600
15		–	actual as of this report	_____
16		–	balance of month this year	_____
17	On order to be received and received to date			2,500
18	**Open-to-buy**			1,600

anticipation of an upswing in the market. Each of these is a legitimate merchandising option and indicates that the OTB control system is flexible, as any budget control system must be.

Table 18–3 presents a sample open-to-buy report form. Of course, this form would vary by company based on what the retailer feels is needed for decision making. By using this form, OTB could be derived by: Line 11 + Line 7 + Line 14 – Line 5 = Planned purchases – Line 17 = OTB (Line 18). (Numbers from Table 18–2).

Cost dollar control

Retail dollar control is used more often than cost dollar control. The major problem in using cost versus retail control is *costing* each sale. Costing means converting retail dollars to cost dollars after a sale has been made.

Because of this costing problem, a cost dollar control system is used only when (1) merchandise is of an unusually high unit value and (2) there are relatively few transactions. With merchandise such as furniture or automobiles, cost-dollar control is practical. However, for merchandise classifications such as the sweat suits illustration in Table 18–1, retail dollar control is used. Table 18–4 shows the kind of information needed for a perpetual cost control system. When using a cost dollar control system, it is not possible to record additional

Table 18–4 Perpetual Cost Dollar Control					
Date	BOM Inventory	Cost of Items Received	Cost of Items Sold	–	Net Change
	$	$	$		$
March 1	15,000	1,500	1,000	+	500 (1,500 – 1,000)
March 2	15,500	—	2,000	–	2,000
March 3	13,500	400	1,200	–	800 (+400 – 1,200)
March 4	12,700				

markups and reductions such as markdowns and employee discounts because all the figures are in cost dollars.

Unit merchandise inventory control

Unit control is the system used to control the width and depth aspects of stock balance (see Figures 18–2 and 18–3). Unit control is simpler than dollar control since fewer factors affect units than affect dollars invested. The difference is that the price changes do not affect units carried. As Figures 18–2 and 18–3 indicate, the two types of unit control are perpetual and non-perpetual (or stock-counting) systems.

Perpetual unit control

Perpetual unit control, like perpetual dollar control, is a book inventory. Table 18–5 provides an illustration of perpetual unit control.

A perpetual book inventory for unit control is the most sophisticated of the unit systems. Because perpetual book systems require continuous recording of additions and deductions from stock, they are more expensive to operate. However, the use of point-of-sale systems reduces costs and saves time in collecting the information needed. If the system is manually maintained, sales information is recorded in the office, detaching a part of a sales ticket to be counted later, or deducting items sold from a tag on a floor sample.

Note in Table 18–5 the notation "including shortages," which appears at the end of the illustration. As with dollar control, this is a book figure—thus, there is chance for error. Again, the only way to determine the accuracy of the book figure is to take a physical inventory. The concepts of shortages and overages apply here just as they do in dollar control. The only difference is that shortages and overages are expressed in terms of number of units rather than in dollars.

Non-perpetual unit control

Non-perpetual unit control systems are also called stock-counting systems. These systems are not book inventory methods. Thus, the retailer will not be able to determine shortages or overages because there is no book inventory against which to compare a physical inventory.

Non-perpetual systems for unit control are actually a compromise. Perpetual control is better and the retailer gets more and better information. But

Table 18–5 Illustration of Perpetual Unit Control (Sweat Suits) for Month of March

BOM inventory			1,000
Additions to stock:			
Purchases	250		
Less—vendor returns	(40)		
Net purchases		210	
Transfers in	41		
Less—transfers out	(20)		
Transfers in		21	
Total additions			231
Total available for sale			1,231
Deductions from stock:			
Gross sales	225		
Less—customer returns	(8)		
Net sales		217	
Total deductions from stock			(217)
EOM inventory, 3/31 (including shortages)			1,014

sometimes the benefits simply do not justify the cost. Non-perpetual unit control systems include formal and less formal systems.

Formal systems

The requirements of formal, non-perpetual systems are as follows: (1) a planned model stock, (2) a periodic counting schedule, and (3) definite, assigned responsibility for counting. Let's use a tie classification as an example. Every tie in stock might be counted once a month. The retailer might select the first Tuesday of each month for the count schedule. Based on the stock on hand, the stock on order, and the stock sold, the buyer will place a reorder as the information is reviewed each count period.

For formal, non-perpetual systems to be used effectively, the rate of sale of the items being controlled must be predictable. Further, the items controlled by formal systems should not be of such a fast-moving, fashionable nature that the retailer needs to know the status of stock more often than the periodic count schedule will permit. The alert retailer will spot-check between count dates to catch any out-of-stocks that might occur. Formal systems do account for items on order (which less formal systems do not).

Less formal systems

Some kinds of merchandise can be controlled with a less formal system. If immediate delivery of goods is possible, there is no need to account for merchandise on order. However, the retailer still must have a planned model stock and a specific time for visually inspecting the stock.

Under a less formal system, there will be a minimum stock level (e.g., shelf level or number of cases in the stockroom) below which the stock must not go. When the stock reaches that level, a reorder is placed. In the canned goods department in a supermarket, this system might be used quite effectively.

A less formal system is suitable for this retailer because
of the limited product line
and the availability of fresh
product.

Photo by Betty McDougall

Chapter Highlights

- Planning is useless unless retailers monitor operating results to determine whether goals are being met. If plans are not being followed, corrective action must be taken to improve the situation. The monitoring process is the control aspect of merchandise and expense management.

- The relationship between planning and control is essential, direct, and two-way. Control records are needed to develop plans, and plans are evaluated by these control data.

- Two systems are used for controlling the merchandise plan: *dollar control* for controlling dollar investment and *unit control* for controlling the width and depth aspects of stock balance.

- To control dollar inventory investments, the retailer must know: (1) the beginning dollar inventory, (2) what has been added to stock, (3) how much inventory has moved out of stock, and (4) how much inventory is now on hand.

- One of the most valuable outputs of a retail dollar control system is open-to-buy (OTB), which exists to control the retailer's utilization of the planned purchase figure.

- Retail dollar control is used more often than cost dollar control because of the problems of "costing" each sale for the latter system.

- Unit control is the system used to control the width and depth aspects of assortments and is simpler than dollar control since fewer factors affect units than affect dollars invested. For example, price changes do not affect units.

- The two types of unit control are perpetual and non-perpetual (or stock-counting systems); the latter can be formal or less formal.

Key Terms

book inventory 513
dollar control 512
non-perpetual unit control 518
open-to-buy 515

overage 515
perpetual unit control 518
shortage 514
unit control 512

Discussion Questions

1. Explain the relationship between *planning* and *control*.

2. Explain open-to-buy (OTB). Why would a retailer attempt to have OTB always available? How can a retailer who has overbought make adjustments to get more open to buy?

3. What is the difference between a retail dollar control system and a cost dollar control system? Under what conditions might a cost dollar control system be used effectively?

4. What is the difference between a shortage and an overage? How are they determined? What are causes of each?

5. What is the purpose of unit control? What is the difference between perpetual and non-perpetual unit control systems? What is the difference between formal and less formal non-perpetual unit control systems?

Application Exercises

1. If you have a friend who is a retailer, make an appointment with that person and ask to see (a) the types of controls that are used in the store and (b) what they are used for. Report your findings to the class.

2. Visit a local grocery store. See if they have "scanning" equipment at the check out. If they do, ask to see the manager and tell that person you are a student and want to ask him/her a few questions. Design your questions so you can find out if information received from the new equipment is being used for control. If not, what is it being used for?

3. Interview several small retailers and perhaps a large one (e.g., several dress shops, men's stores, and a department store). Ask if you could speak with the person in charge of the accounting records. Find out if any of them is using the retail method of accounting. If not, find out how they operate the cost

method. How do they determine shortages? Try to strike up a conversation about the subject of this chapter; report back your findings.

Problems

1. Given the following data for a certain department as of June 10, calculate (a) planned purchases and (b) open-to-buy:

Planned sales for the month	$47,000
Planned reductions for the month	1,500
Planned EOM inventory	52,550
Planned BOM inventory	47,800
Merchandise received to date for June	14,980
Merchandise on order, June delivery	6,850

2. The following data are for a certain department as of January 20. Calculate (a) planned purchases and (b) open-to-buy:

Planned sales for the month	$142,000
Planned BOM inventory	177,000
Planned reductions for the month	4,200
Planned EOM inventory	165,000
Merchandise received to date for January	130,000
Merchandise on order, January delivery	4,200
Merchandise on order, February delivery	2,200

3. Given the following data for a certain department as of September 20, calculate (a) planned purchases and (b) open-to-buy:

Planned sales for the month	$9,200
Planned reductions for the month	100
Planned BOM inventory	14,600
Planned EOM inventory	15,500
Merchandise received to date for September	9,800
Merchandise on order, September delivery	500

4. Given the following information for the month of July, calculate (a) planned purchases and (b) open-to-buy:

Planned sales for the month	$27,000
Planned reductions for the month	650
Planned EOM inventory	36,000
Stock-to-sales ratio for July	1.5
Merchandise received to date for July	13,800
Merchandise on order, July delivery	5,250

5. Find open-to-buy for March, given the following figures:

Stock on hand, March 1	$72,500
Planned stock on hand, April 1	80,000
Merchandise on order for March delivery	49,875
Planned sales for March	63,500

6. Given the following information for November, calculate open-to-buy (a) at retail and (b) at cost:

Planned sales for the month	$24,600
Planned reductions for the month	300
Planned EOM retail stock	32,300
Planned BOM retail stock	30,800
Merchandise received for the month of November	16,300
Merchandise on order, November delivery	4,000
Merchandise on order, December delivery	2,575
Planned initial markup at retail	35%

7. Given the following information for August, calculate open-to-buy (a) at retail and (b) at cost:

Planned sales for the month	$57,000
Planned reductions for the month	1,200
Planned EOM retail stock	72,000
Stock-to-sales ratio for the month of August	1.2
Planned initial markup at retail	42%
Merchandise received for the month of August	35,000
Merchandise on order, August delivery	16,400

Suggested Case

35. JKA Department Store

Note

1. Sears Canada, *Annual Report,* 1994.

Performance Evaluation

Chapter Objectives

After reading this chapter, you should be able to:

1. **Review the key financial statements.**

2. **Utilize the strategic profit model (SPM) as a framework for monitoring performance results.**

3. **Explain how inventory turnover affects profitability (performance) by utilizing the concept of gross margin return on inventory investment.**

4. **Examine the problems that management faces in determining the cost and value of merchandise inventory.**

Performance evaluation led Mark's Work Wearhouse to
revise its strategy and introduce a new store format.

Courtesy Mark's Work Wearhouse

During the recession of 1990-1993, Mark's Work Wearhouse, the Canadian retail chain, had a difficult time and did not meet its financial objectives of (1) earning a 20 percent return on shareholders' equity and (2) earning a 20 percent contribution margin by region. In fact, Mark's Work Wearhouse suffered losses in all three years—$6.4 million (fiscal 1991), $8.7 million (fiscal 1992), and $2.7 million (fiscal 1993). During these years the retailer had a plan to return to profitability based, in part, on an extensive performance review and a revision of its retail strategy. In 1994, Mark's turned the corner and achieved a profit on operations of $1.2 million and made substantial gains in fiscal 1995 with profits of $6.3 million. Throughout these years, Mark's set objectives and evaluated performance against these objectives. For example, consider the following comparisons between 1994 and 1995 based on the company's performance review:

- Total chain sales—increased by 24 percent (from $200 million to $248 million) due, in part, to the improved economy and improving market share in the markets it serves.

- **Gross margin rate—remained constant (from 36.7 percent to 36.8 percent) due to changing its product mix and sourcing the same quality products at better prices, not by significant retail price increases.**

- **Sales per square metre—improved by 8 percent (from $2884 to $3110), which reflected an improved product mix and new store formats.**

- **Front line expenses (staff, advertising, occupancy, etc.) as a percentage of sales—improved by 1.2 points (from 27.7 percent to 26.5 percent) due to holding these expenses below the increase in sales.**

The continuing target for Mark's Work Wearhouse is to achieve an annual after-tax profit on sales of 5 percent and a return of 20 to 25 percent on average shareholders' equity. By constantly monitoring performance and making the appropriate strategy adjustments, the target is attainable.[1] ■

Firms such as Mark's Work Wearhouse strive for success by devising effective strategies to attract customers and to compete, and also by monitoring and evaluating performance to determine whether their strategies are being implemented effectively and whether changes in strategy and operations are needed.

This chapter focusses on monitoring and evaluating performance. The tools presented in the chapter help retailers assess their effectiveness in implementing strategy and provide a framework for determining shortcomings and identifying areas that need improvement.

Key Financial Statements and Ratios

The balance sheet, the income statement, and the various ratios derived from them give management the information needed to evaluate the effectiveness of strategy in financial terms.

The balance sheet

The **balance sheet** is a snapshot of a firm's financial health on a specific date. Table 19–1 lists the components of the balance sheet—**assets (current** and **fixed), liabilities,** and **net worth** (the owners' claim on the assets of the business—that is, the owners' investment or equity). The simplest expression of the balance sheet equation is: assets = liabilities + net worth.

The income statement

The **income statement** shows operating results over a period of time and indicates whether investments in assets and strategy have been successful and profitable (see Table 19–2). The income statement indicates net sales, **gross margin** (the difference between net sales and cost of goods sold), total expenses, and after-tax profit. Cost of goods sold is computed as follows:

```
  Beginning inventory
+ Purchases
= Goods available for sale
- Ending inventory
= Cost of goods sold
```

Table 19–1   Balance Sheet December 31, 19__

Assets

Current assets:		
Cash	$15,000	
Accounts receivable	24,000	
Merchandise inventory	84,000	
Prepaid expenses	10,000	
Total current assets		$133,000
Fixed assets:		
Building	$85,000	
Furniture and fixtures	23,000	
Total fixed assets		108,000
Total Assets		$241,000

Liabilities and Net Worth

Current liabilities:		
Accounts payable	$20,000	
Wages payable	18,000	
Notes payable	32,000	
Taxes payable	5,000	
Interest payable	3,000	
Total current liabilities		$ 78,000
Fixed liabilities:		
Mortgage payable	$75,000	
Total fixed liabilities		75,000
Total Liabilities		$153,000
Net Worth:		
Capital surplus	$80,000	
Retained earnings	8,000	
Total net worth		88,000
Total Liabilities and Net Worth		$241,000

Information from the income statement assists management in making any adjustments deemed necessary. For example, if expenses are higher than in the past and higher than in similar stores, the manager may decide that corrective action is needed. In general, the income statement is a valuable tool for measuring the results of operations.

Ratio analysis

Retailers establish ratio goals as part of their financial plan. They can then compare performance with objectives. Comparison over time is valuable, as is comparison of performance ratios with trade data for similar firms. Monitoring selected financial ratios can help determine whether problems are developing.

Table 19–3 presents a summary of key financial ratios, their methods of calculation, and the information they show. Many of these ratios were first discussed in Chapter 7 (see Tables 7–2 and 7–3) with respect to evaluating the purchase of an existing retail business. The ratios are presented again as many

Table 19–2 Income Statement Year Ending December 31, 19__			
Gross sales	$208,600		
Less returns and allowances	16,300		
Net sales		$192,300	100.00%
Cost of goods sold:			
Opening inventory	$ 21,650		
Net purchases	113,500		
Goods available for sale		$135,150	
Less closing inventory		28,495	
Cost of goods sold		106,655	55.46
Gross margin		$ 85,645	44.54
Expenses:			
Rent	$ 19,400		
Payroll	32,950		
Advertising	8,825		
Insurance	1,475		
Travel	2,160		
Utilities	5,265		
Miscellaneous	580		
Total expenses		70,655	36.74
Profit before taxes		$ 14,990	7.80
Income tax		4,950	2.57
Net profit after taxes		$ 10,040	5.22%

will be discussed in later sections of this chapter. Two of the ratios appearing in the figure—return on total assets (net profit after taxes divided by total assets) and the current ratio (current assets divided by current liabilities)—can often predict the success or failure of retail firms. Too high a current ratio and the inability to make a profit, as reflected by return on assets, can lead to the failure of a retail business.

We also call your attention to leverage ratios. **Leverage** is a situation in which a business unit acquires assets worth more than the amount of capital invested by the owners; the higher the ratio, the higher the amount of borrowed funds in the business. As shown in Table 19–3, leverage can be measured in various ways. Regardless of how it is measured, however, too high a leverage ratio can be dangerous, especially in periods of economic instability and high interest rates.

The Strategic Profit Model

An important purpose of this section is to utilize the **strategic profit model (SPM)** as a framework for monitoring performance results. The SPM is derived from information obtained in the balance sheet and the income statement. The SPM provides the essential ratios for performance evaluation needed here, as illustrated in Figure 19–1.

The objective of all retailers is to make a profit, but exactly what does "making a profit" mean? Perhaps the most common way to describe profit is net

Table 19–3   A Summary of Key Financial Ratios, How They Are Calculated, and What They Show

Ratio	How Calculated	What it Shows
Profitability Ratios:		
1. Gross profit margin	$$\frac{\text{Sales} - \text{Cost of goods sold}}{\text{Sales}}$$	An indication of the total margin available to cover operating expenses and yield a profit.
2. Operating profit margin (or return on sales)	$$\frac{\text{Profits before taxes and before interest}}{\text{Sales}}$$	An indication of the firm's profitability from current operations without regard to the interest charges accruing from the capital structure.
3. Net profit margin (or net return on sales)	$$\frac{\text{Profits after taxes}}{\text{Sales}}$$	Shows aftertax profits per dollar of sales. Subpar profit margins indicate that the firm's sales prices are relatively low or that its costs are relatively high, or both.
4. Return on total assets	$$\frac{\text{Profits after taxes}}{\text{Total assets}}$$ or $$\frac{\text{Profits after taxes} + \text{Interest}}{\text{Total assets}}$$	A measure of the return on total investment in the enterprise. It is sometimes desirable to add interest to after-tax profits to form the numerator of the ratio because total assets are financed by creditors as well as by stockholders; hence, it is accurate to measure the productivity of assets by the returns provided to both classes of investors.
5. Return on stockholders' equity (or return on net worth)	$$\frac{\text{Profits after taxes}}{\text{Total stockholders' equity}}$$	A measure of the rate of return on stockholders' investment in the enterprise.
6. Return on common equity	$$\frac{\text{Profits after taxes} - \text{Preferred stock dividends}}{\text{Total stockholders' equity} - \text{Par value of preferred stock}}$$	A measure of the rate of return on the investment the owners of the common stock have made in the enterprise.
7. Earnings per share	$$\frac{\text{Profits after taxes} - \text{Preferred stock dividends}}{\text{Number of shares of common stock outstanding}}$$	Shows the earnings available to the owners of each share of common stock.
Liquidity Ratios:		
1. Current ratio	$$\frac{\text{Current assets}}{\text{Current liabilities}}$$	Indicates the extent to which the claims of short-term creditors are covered by assets that are expected to be converted to cash in a period roughly corresponding to the maturity of the liabilities.
2. Quick ratio (or acid-test ratio)	$$\frac{\text{Current assets} - \text{Inventory}}{\text{Current liabilities}}$$	A measure of the firm's ability to pay off short-term obligations without relying on the sale of its inventories.
3. Inventory to net working capital	$$\frac{\text{Inventory}}{\text{Current assets} - \text{Current liabilities}}$$	A measure of the extent to which the firm's working capital is tied up in inventory.

(continued)

profit after taxes—the bottom line of the income statement. Profit performance is often evaluated in terms of sales volume—that is, profit as a percentage of sales. For strategic purposes, the most valuable way to view profit, however, is in terms of a return on investment (ROI).

The two ways of looking at ROI from a strategic point of view are: (1) return on assets (ROA) and (2) return on net worth (RONW). The ROA reflects all funds invested in a business, whether they come from owners or creditors. The

Table 19–3   (continued)

Ratio	How Calculated	What it Shows
Leverage Ratios:		
1. Debt-to-assets ratio	$\dfrac{\text{Total debt}}{\text{Total assets}}$	Measures the extent to which borrowed funds have been used to finance the firm's operations.
2. Debt-to-equity ratio	$\dfrac{\text{Total debt}}{\text{Total stockholders' equity}}$	Provides another measure of the funds provided by creditors versus the funds provided by owners.
3. Long-term debt-to-equity ratio	$\dfrac{\text{Long-term debt}}{\text{Total stockholders' equity}}$	A widely used measure of the balance between debt and equity in the firm's long-term capital structure.
4. Times-interest-earned (or coverage) ratio	$\dfrac{\text{Profits before interest and taxes}}{\text{Total interest charges}}$	Measures the extent to which earnings can decline without the firm becoming unable to meet its annual interest costs.
5. Fixed-charge coverage	$\dfrac{\text{Profits before taxes and interest} - \text{Lease obligations}}{\text{Total interest charges} + \text{Lease obligations}}$	A more inclusive indication of the firm's ability to meet all of its fixed-charge obligations.
Activity Ratios:		
1. Inventory turnover	$\dfrac{\text{Sales}}{\text{Avg. inventory (in retail dollars)}}$	When compared to industry averages, it provides an indication of whether a company has excessive or inadequate inventory.
2. Fixed assets turnover	$\dfrac{\text{Sales}}{\text{Fixed assets}}$	A measure of the sales productivity and utilization of plant and equipment.
3. Total assets turnover	$\dfrac{\text{Sales}}{\text{Total assets}}$	A measure of the utilization of all the firm's assets; a ratio below the industry average indicates the company is not generating a sufficient volume of business, given the size of its asset investment.
4. Accounts receivable turnover	$\dfrac{\text{Annual credit sales}}{\text{Accounts receivable}}$	A measure of the average length of time it takes the firm to collect the sales made on credit.
5. Average collection period	$\dfrac{\text{Accounts receivable}}{\text{Total sales/365}}$ or $\dfrac{\text{Accounts receivable}}{\text{Average daily sales}}$	Indicates the average length of time the firm must wait after making a sale before it receives payment.
Other Ratios:		
1. Dividend yield on common stock	$\dfrac{\text{Annual dividends per share}}{\text{Current market price per share}}$	A measure of the return to owners received in the form of dividends.
2. Price-to-earnings ratio	$\dfrac{\text{Current market price per share}}{\text{After-tax earnings per share.}}$	Faster growing or less risky firms tend to have higher price-to-earnings ratios than slower-growing or more risky firms.
3. Dividend payout ratio	$\dfrac{\text{Annual dividends per share}}{\text{After-tax earnings per share}}$	Indicates the percentage of profits paid out as dividends.
4. Cash flow per share	$\dfrac{\text{After-tax profits} + \text{Depreciation}}{\text{Number of common shares outstanding}}$	A measure of the discretionary funds exceeding expenses that are available to the firm.

Note: Industry average ratios against which a particular company's ratios may be judged are available in *Modern Industry* and *Dun's Reviews* published by Dun & Bradstreet (14 ratios for 125 lines of business activities), Robert Morris Associates, *Annual Statement Studies* (11 ratios for 156 lines of business), and the FTC-SEC's *Quarterly Financial Report* for manufacturing corporations.

Source: Arthur A. Thompson and A. J. Strickland III. *Strategic Management: Concepts and Cases,* 6th ed. (Burr Ridge, IL, Richard D. Irwin Co., 1992), pp. 282–83. Adapted with permission. Copyright Richard D. Irwin, Co.

Figure 19–1   The Strategic Profit Model Process

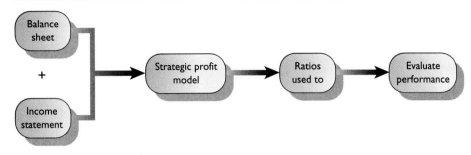

RONW is a measure of profitability for those who have provided the net worth funds—that is, the owners.

Purposes of the SPM

Figure 19–2 diagrams the SPM. Boxes 1 through 5 provide the basic ratios (derived from the key financial statements) that comprise the model. A simple algebraic representation of the model would look like this:

$$\underset{(1)}{\frac{\text{Net profit}}{\text{Net sales}}} \times \underset{(2)}{\frac{\text{Net sales}}{\text{Total assets}}} = \underset{(3)}{\frac{\text{Net profit}}{\text{Total assets}}} \times \underset{(4)}{\frac{\text{Total assets}}{\text{Net worth}}} = \underset{(5)}{\frac{\text{Net profit}}{\text{Net worth}}}$$

Figure 19–2 also indicates the various paths to profitability and indicates what each component of the model measures. Specifically, the purposes of the SPM are as follows:

1. To emphasize that a firm's principal financial objective is to earn an adequate or target rate of return on net worth (RONW).

2. To provide an excellent management tool for evaluating performance against the target RONW and high-performance trade leaders.

3. To dramatize the principal areas of decision making—margin management, asset management, and leverage management. A firm can improve its rate of RONW by increasing its profit margin, raising its rate of asset turnover, or leveraging its operations more highly.

Please note that in the SPM, leverage is calculated differently from the methods shown in Table 19–3 and is probably different from methods you learned in any accounting or finance courses you have taken. The ratio in the SPM is another way of calculating leverage; this ratio enables management to determine the extent to which debt is being used to support the asset base of the firm.

Gross margin return on inventory (GMROI) investment

Gross margin return on inventory (GMROI), another performance evaluation indicator, is stated as follows:

$$\text{GMROI} = \frac{\text{Gross margin dollars}}{\substack{\text{Average inventory investment} \\ \text{(expressed in retail dollars)}}}$$

Figure 19–2   The Strategic Profit Model

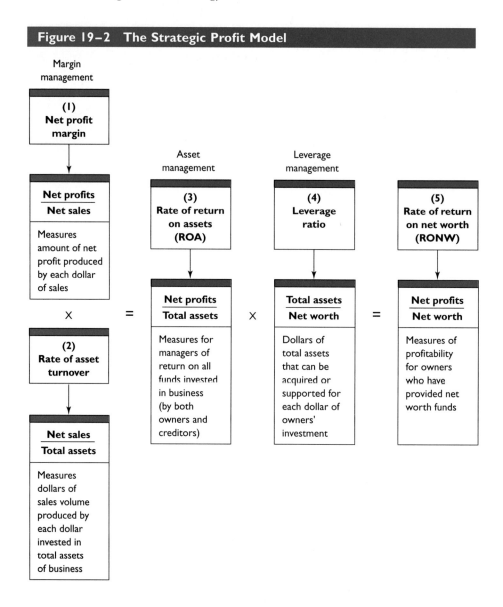

This single ratio does not indicate clearly the focus we want to emphasize—that of the important relationship between profit return (margin) and sales-to-retail stock (which is inventory turnover). Consequently, it is more useful to express GMROI as follows:

$$\text{GMROI} = \frac{\text{Gross margin dollars}}{\text{Total sales}} \times \frac{\text{Total sales}}{\substack{\text{Average inventory investment} \\ \text{(expressed in retail dollars)}}}$$

We must emphasize that gross margin return on retail inventory investment is not a real measure of return on investment because investment is in cost dollars. But many retail managers with a planning focus maintain retail book inventory figures. Thus, retail value GMROI can be calculated more frequently using the more common and more easily obtainable turnover component. Sales-to-cost

Table 19–4   Examples of Differing Retail Operations, Margins, and Turnovers Resulting in Identical GMROI

Type of Store	Gross Margin (percent)	×	Turnover Ratio	=	GMROI (percent) (retail)
Discount store sport shirt classification	25.0		4.0		100.0
Specialty store sport shirt classification	40.0		2.5		100.0
Department store sport shirt classification	33.3		3.0		100.0

inventory ratios are more accurately ROI ratios. In this particular discussion, however, the value of utilizing retail GMROI outweighs the somewhat different terminology. Our intent is to focus on the impact of turnover on profitability—thus, retail value is important.

The value of the turnover and margin components of the GMROI concept can be seen in Table 19–4. Three hypothetical retail classifications each produce the same GMROI, although they have differing gross margin percentages and turnover components. This table illustrates that measurement can focus on either turnover or gross margin in strategic planning to obtain identical GMROI results.

Determining Cost and Value of Inventory

The focus of this section is on the importance of merchandise inventory in performance evaluation and the problems that arise in determining its cost and value. The importance of merchandise inventory is reflected in several ways. Merchandise inventory is typically the largest current asset on the balance sheet. The value of ending inventory is also used to calculate cost of goods sold—a figure reported on the income statement. An error in determining the inventory figure will cause an equal misstatement of gross profit and net income in the income statement. Errors of this nature, due to faulty information and a bad accounting system can lead to disaster, as was the case in the bankruptcy of Bargain Harold's (Retail Highlight 19–1). The amount of assets noted on the balance sheet also will be incorrect by the same amount. The effects of understatements and overstatements of inventory at the end of a period are demonstrated in Table 19–5, which includes an abbreviated income statement and balance sheet.

Determining inventory cost

A major problem in determining inventory cost arises when identical units of a product are acquired over a period of time at various unit cost prices. Consider the purchase of sport shirts during the spring season. With the example shown in Table 19–6, the average cost per unit has increased by over 28 percent in just three months.

Bargain Harold's: Faulty Performance Evaluation Leads to Bankruptcy

In early 1992, Bargain Harold's, a 160-store discount chain, went bankrupt throwing over 4,000 people out of work and leaving suppliers with over $52 million in unpaid bills. Although a number of factors led to its demise, including poor management and a recession, a central cause of the failure was a faulty performance evaluation system.

In 1990, a group of investors led by Dean Muncaster purchased Bargain Harold's from K mart in a highly leveraged financial arrangement. Among the many changes introduced at Bargain Harold's by the new management team was a computerized information system that was installed in just 21 of the 160 stores. Management decisions were based on the information from this system, which proved to be wrong. As it turned out, information coming into the head office from the other stores often was inaccurate, inflating margins.

Stores using the old system could, for example, charge $3.79 for a box of detergent while head office was assuming that the price was $3.99. Miscalculations were made on everything from inventory to profits. The results were excess inventory, inadequate analysis of financial data, and unreliable profit projections. In a year-end audit at the end of 1991, management discovered the error but by then it was too late. The weight of decisions based on a faulty information system wrecked a company. As one retail expert noted: "It's a textbook case of a company that had a great concept and just blew it."

Sources: John Heinzl, "Good Strategy Gone Awry, Top Retailer's Tale of Woe," *Globe & Mail*, March 7, 1992, pp. B1, B4; Harvey Enchin, "Bargain Harold's in Receivership," *Globe & Mail*, February 29, 1992, p. B5; and Dunnery Best, "The Man Behind Bargain Harold's Mess," *Financial Times*, April 13, 1992, pp. 1, 4.

In some departments and/or classifications, it may be possible to identify units with specific expenditures. This can occur when assortments and varieties of merchandise carried and the sales volume and transactions are relatively small. More often, however, as in the sport shirt classification, specific identification procedures are too complex to justify their use.

Consequently, one of the two costing methods, FIFO or LIFO, may be adopted to simplify the problem of inventory costing.

FIFO

The assumption of the **first-in, first-out (FIFO)** method of costing inventory is that costs should be charged against revenue in the order in which they were incurred—that is, the first shirts purchased are the first ones sold. Thus, the inventory remaining at the end of an accounting period is assumed to be of the most recent purchases. Assume the following represents purchases of sport shirts for the year:

	Units	Unit Cost	Total Cost
February 1 (Beginning inventory)	50	$ 9	$ 450
April 15 (Purchases)	40	13	520
May 1 (Purchases)	30	14	420
October 1 (Purchases)	100	16	1,600
Available for sale during year	220		$2,990

Further, assume that 90 shirts were sold. Thus, the physical inventory at the end of the fiscal year (January 31) is 130 shirts. Based on FIFO and the

Table 19–5 Effects of Correct Statement, Understatement, and Overstatement of Ending Inventory on Net Profits

Income Statement — 19__			Balance Sheet — 19__	
Net sales		$200,000	Merchandise inventory	$ 20,000*
Beginning inventory	$ 30,000		Other assets	80,000
+ Purchases	110,000		Total	$100,000
= Available for sale	140,000		Liabilities	30,000
− Ending inventory	20,000*		Net worth	70,000
= Cost of goods sold		120,000	Total	$100,000
Gross profit		80,000		
− Expenses		55,000		
= Net profit		$ 25,000		
Net sales		$200,000	Merchandise inventory	$ 12,000†
Beginning inventory	$ 30,000		Other	80,000
+ Purchases	110,000		Total	92,000
= Available for sale	140,000		Liabilities	30,000
− Ending inventory	12,000†		Net worth	62,000
= Cost of goods sold		128,000	Total	$ 92,000
Gross profit		72,000		
− Expenses		55,000		
= Net profit		$ 17,000		
Net sales		$200,000	Merchandise inventory	$ 27,000‡
Beginning inventory	$ 30,000		Other assets	80,000
+ Purchases	110,000		Total	$107,000
= Available for sale	140,000		Liabilities	30,000
− Ending inventory	27,000‡		Net worth	77,000
= Cost of goods sold		113,000	Total	$107,000
Gross profit		87,000		
− Expenses		55,000		
= Net profit		$ 32,000		

*Ending inventory correctly stated.
†Ending inventory understated $8,000 (thus income, assets, capital also).
‡Ending inventory overstated $7,000 (thus income, assets, capital also).

assumption that the inventory is composed of the most recent purchases, the cost of the 130 shirts is as follows:

October (most recent purchases)	100 shirts	@	16	=	$1,600
May 1 (next most recent)	30 shirts	@	14	=	420
Inventory, January 31	130 shirts			=	$2,020

If we deduct the end-of-period inventory of $2,020 from the $2,990 available for sale during the period, we get $970 as the cost of merchandise sold. FIFO is generally in harmony with the actual physical movement of goods in a retail firm. Thus, FIFO best represents the results that are directly tied to merchandise costs.

Table 19–6 The Effect of Increasing Unit Costs				
Sport Shirts		**Units**	**Unit Cost**	**Total Cost**
February 1	Inventory	50	$ 9	$ 450
April 15	Purchases	40	13	520
May 1	Purchase	30	14	420
Total		120	$11.58	$1,390
Average cost per unit				

LIFO

The costing method known as **last-in, first-out (LIFO)** assumes that the most recent cost of merchandise should be charged against revenue. Thus, the ending inventory under LIFO is assumed to be made up of earliest costs. Refer to the previous example.

February 1	50 shirts	@	$ 9	=	$ 450
April 15	40 shirts	@	13	=	520
May 1	30 shirts	@	14	=	420
October 1	10 shirts	@	16	=	160
Inventory, January 31	130 shirts				$1,550

If we deduct the inventory of $1,550 from the $2,990 of merchandise available for sale during the accounting period, we get $1,440 as the cost of merchandise sold.

We can now compare FIFO and LIFO:

	FIFO	**LIFO**
Merchandise available for sale	$2,990	$2,990
Inventory, January 31	2,020	1,550
Cost of merchandise sold	$ 970	$1,440

FIFO yields the lower cost of merchandise sold and thus yields higher gross margin and net income as well as higher inventory figures on the balance sheet. On the other hand, LIFO yields a higher figure for cost of goods sold and lower figures for gross profit, net income, and inventory. For income determination purposes, Revenue Canada accepts FIFO but LIFO is not accepted.

Conservative valuation of inventory

Another problem in determining the cost of merchandise inventory is placing a conservative value on the inventory—that is, at cost or market, whichever is lower. This approach is an alternative to valuing inventory at cost. With either course, it is first necessary to determine the cost of inventory. *Market* means the cost required to replace the merchandise at the time of the inventory, whereas *cost* refers to the actual price of merchandise at the time of its purchase. Table 19–7 demonstrates the impact on profits of valuing the ending inventory at (1) actual cost, (2) depreciated value, and (3) appreciated value. In addition, it provides a rationale for the acceptance of the conservative practice of valuation—at cost or market, whichever is lower. At any given time, some merchandise in stock may not be valued at the amount originally paid for it. The merchandise may have declined in value because of obsolescence, deterioration,

Table 19–7 The Impact on Profits of Valuation of Ending Inventory at Actual Cost, or Depreciated or Appreciated Market Value

	(1) Actual Cost		(2) Depreciated		(3) Appreciated	
Net sales		$100,000		$100,000		$100,000
Merchandise available for sale	$70,000		$70,000		$70,000	
Ending inventory	10,000		4,000		12,000	
Cost of goods sold		60,000		66,000		58,000
Gross profit		$ 40,000		$ 34,000		$ 42,000
Expenses		35,000		35,000		35,000
Net profit		$ 5,000		$ (1,000)		$ 7,000

or decreases in wholesale market prices. It may have increased in value because of inflation, scarcity of materials, and the like. The first column in Table 19–7 indicates that the profit is $5,000 after the valuation of inventory at its actual cost (determined by one of the methods discussed earlier). The second column indicates that, if the retailer were to replace the same inventory at the time of valuation, it would be depreciated to $4,000 (a $6,000 decline in value from the actual cost); instead of a $5,000 profit, a $1,000 loss has been incurred. The information in the third column reflects a $12,000 valuation of the ending inventory resulting in a $7,000 profit, rather than a $5,000 profit based on actual cost.

The depreciated ending inventory value relative to the actual cost results in an increased cost of goods sold and thus reduces gross profit. The appreciated ending inventory relative to the actual costs results in a decreased cost of goods sold, an increased gross profit, and, with the same expense amount, an increased net profit. Comparing each method with the actual cost, the conservative rule would dictate that the inventory value should be taken at the depreciated value [column (2)] and at actual cost [column (1)] when compared with market increase. Let's investigate the logic of such a practice.

Rationale for the conservative rule

If management values the ending inventory at $4,000 rather than the cost of $10,000, the loss resulting will be taken in the period in which it occurs. This is logical, because the ending inventory of one period becomes the beginning inventory of the next. Thus, by placing a realistic depreciated market value on ending inventory, the lowered figure, which will be the next beginning inventory value, will give the merchant the opportunity to reflect a proper beginning inventory cost in the next period. This lets the merchant show realistic, and perhaps profitable, performance in the next period. This ending inventory figure also becomes an asset item on the balance sheet.

A realistic valuation reflecting declining value is wise because otherwise the assets, and consequently the net worth of the firm, will be overstated. Finally, if the market value were declining and the inventory were taken in at cost, the firm would show a profit, as illustrated in Table 19–7. Income taxes would be paid on "paper profits."

To emphasize the concept of "paper profits," consider what the results would be if the inventory were valued at an appreciated value [column (3)] of $12,000, rather than a cost of $10,000. The $7,000 profit, rather than the $5,000, represents anticipated profits on merchandise that has not been sold and thus should not be reported.

In summary, retail inventories should be valued at cost or market, whichever is lower. As with the method chosen for the determination of inventory cost (LIFO or FIFO), the method elected for inventory valuation (cost, or lower of cost or market) must be consistent from year to year.

Methods of Valuation of Inventory

The final objective of this chapter is to introduce the accounting practices that assist management in valuation decisions. Retailers invest large sums of money in merchandise and must know at all times the value of this inventory investment. The information is needed for tax reasons, to compute gross margins as measures of performance, and to make day-to-day decisions. How is a value placed on inventory in retailing? The two main ways are the cost method and the retail method.

The cost method

The cost method provides a book evaluation of inventory and the system uses only cost figures. All inventory records are maintained at cost. When a physical inventory is taken, all items are recorded at actual cost including freight. The cost of sales and cost of markdowns (depreciation) are deducted from the total merchandise available to provide the book inventory at the lower of cost or market value, which can be checked by means of a physical inventory. The limitations of the cost method are: difficulty in determining depreciation; difficulty for large retailers with many classifications and price lines; daily inventory is impractical; and costing out each sale, allocating transportation charges to the cost of the sales, and reducing markdowns to cost are extremely difficult. The cost method is appropriate in operations with big-ticket items, where there are few lines and few price changes, where the rate of sale is rapid, and/or where management has very sophisticated computer expertise.

The retail method

Because of the limitations with the cost method, the retail method of inventory costing is more widely used. The retail method is a logical extension of a retail book (perpetual) inventory utilized for dollar control (see Chapter 12). These steps, illustrated in Table 19–8, are described in the following section. The retail method is in actuality an income statement that follows certain programmed steps in the final determination of net profits. These steps, illustrated in Table 19–8, are described next.

Table 19–8   Statement of Retail Method of Inventory

Calculations	Step	Items	Cost	Retail	Cost	Retail	Percent
	1	Beginning inventory			$ 60,000	$105,000	
		Gross purchases	$216,000	$ 345,000			
		Less: Returns to vendor	(9,000)	(14,100)	207,000	330,900	
		Transfers in	3,000	4,800			
		Less: Transfers out	(4,500)	(7,200)	(1,500)	(2,400)	
		Transportation charges			4,500		
		Additional markups		2,100			
		Less: Cancellations		(600)		1,500	
		Total merchandise handled			270,000	435,000	
($270,000 ÷ $435,000)	2	Cost multiplier/cumulative markup					62.069/37.931
	3	Sales, gross		309,000			
		Less: Customer returns		(9,000)		300,000	
		Gross markdowns		12,000			
		Less: Cancellations		(1,500)		10,500	
		Employee discounts				1,500	
		Total retail deductions				312,000	
($435,000 − $312,000)	4	Closing book inventory @ retail				123,000	
		Closing physical inventory @ retail				120,750	
($123,000 − $120,750)		Shortages				2,250	0.75
($120,750 × 0.62069)		Closing physical inventory @ cost			74,949		
($270,000 − $74,949)	5	Gross cost of goods sold			195,051		
($300,000 − $195,051)	6	Maintained markup			104,949		35.0
		Less: Alteration costs			(3,000)		
		Plus: Cash discounts			6,000		
($104,949 + $3,000)		Gross margin			107,949		36.0
		Less: Operating expenses			(75,000)		25.0
		Net profit			32,949		11.0
	5	Gross cost of goods sold			195,051		
		Less: Cash discounts			(6,000)		
		Net cost of goods sold			189,051		
		Plus: Alteration costs			3,000		
		Total cost of goods sold			192,051		
($300,000 − $192,051)	6	Gross margin			107,949		36.0
		Less: Operating expenses			75,000		
		Net profit			32,949		11.0

Steps of the retail method

1. *Determine the total dollars of merchandise handled at cost and retail.* As indicated in Table 19–8, we start with a beginning inventory that we assume is an actual, physical inventory from the end of the previous period. To this figure we add purchases (minus vendor returns and/or allowances), any interstore or departmental transfers, and transportation charges (at cost only). The price change, which is a part of step 1, is additional markups. Suppose the retailer has a group of sport shirts in stock that were recently received. They are carried in stock at $14.95. Wholesale costs have increased since the delivery, and the wholesaler suggests that we take an additional markup of $3.00 per unit, bringing the retail price to $17.95. We take a physical count and find we have 700 shirts in stock; thus, we take an

additional markup of $2,100 to accommodate the price increase. Immediately after processing the price change, we find that the count was incorrect, or the amount of the additional markup was too high due to a misunderstanding. At any rate, the retailer wants to cancel $600 of the additional markup so that the mistake can be corrected (see Step 1 in the statement for the handling of this situation.) Cancellation of an additional markup is *not* a markdown, which reflects market depreciation. Cancellation is rather a procedure for adjusting an actual error in the original additional markup. Summing all the items that increase the dollar investment provides the total merchandise handled at cost and retail ($270,000 and $435,000, respectively).

2. *Calculate the cost multiplier and the cumulative markup.* As indicated in Table 19–8, the computation of the cost multiplier (sometimes called the cost percentage or the cost complement) is derived by dividing the total dollars handled at cost by the total at retail (that is, $270,000 ÷ $435,000 = 62 percent). This is a key figure in the retail method and in fact involves the major assumption of the system. This cost multiplier says that for every retail dollar in inventory, 62 percent or 62 cents, is in terms of cost. The assumption of the retail method is that if cost and retail have this relationship in goods handled during a period, then that same relationship exists for all the merchandise remaining in stock (that is, the ending inventory at retail).

    The *cumulative markup* is the complement of the cost multiplier (that is, 100.00 – 62.07 = 37.93) and is the control figure to compare against the planned initial markup. (See Chapter 14, where this planned figure is discussed). For example, let's assume that the planned initial markup is 38 percent. If our interim statement shows, as ours does, that our cumulative markup is 38 percent, then management will consider that operations are effective, at least as they relate to the planned markup percentage. The initial markup is planned so as to cover reductions (markdowns, employee discounts, and shortages) and provide a maintained markup (or gross profit or margin) at a level sufficient to cover operating expenses and to assure a target rate of profit return.

3. *Compute the retail deductions from stock.* Step 3 includes all the retail deductions from the total retail merchandise dollars handled during the period. Sales are recorded and adjusted by customer returns to determine net sales. Markdowns are recorded as they are taken.

    As an example, let's assume that during this period a group of 1,200 sport shirts retailing for $25.95 are put out for a special sale at $15.95. We would thus take a markdown, of $12,000 before the sale. After the sale, we want to bring the merchandise back to the regular price; an additional markup is not appropriate since we are merely cancelling an original markdown. Consequently, we put a markdown cancellation through the system for the remaining number of shirts—in this case, 150 that were not sold, making a cancellation of $1,500, which will reestablish the original retail price of $25.95. Employee discounts are included as deductions because employees receive, for example, a 20 percent discount on items purchased for personal use. If a shirt retails for $19.95, the employee would pay $15.96. If the discount were not entered as a separate item in the system, the difference between the retail price and the employee's price would cause a shortage. Recording employee discounts as a separate item also gives management a good picture of employee business obtained and affords a measure of control over use of the discount.

4. *Calculate the closing book (and/or physical) inventory at cost and retail.* The statement thus far has given us a figure for the dollars at retail that we had available for sale ($435,000) and what we have deducted from that amount ($312,000). Thus we are now able to compute what we have left ($435,000 – $312,000), or the ending book inventory at retail – $123,000. We are assuming, in this particular illustration, that this is a year-end statement and that we have an audited, physical inventory of $120,750. Consequently, we can now determine our shortages by deducting the amount of the physical inventory from the book inventory ($123,000 – $120,750 = $2,250) or 0.75 percent of sales.

   Let's assume that we were working with an interim statement rather than a fiscal-year statement. If this were the case, we would include in our retail deductions from stock (Step 3) an *estimated* shortage figure, which would give us as accurate a figure as possible for total deductions, and thus a figure for closing book inventory at retail. If we have an interim statement, then the cost multiplier is applied to the book inventory at retail to determine the cost value: if there is a physical retail inventory figure, as in Table 19–8, then we use that figure for cost conversion, since the physical inventory figure is accurate.

   The key to the retail method, as noted, is the reduction of the retail inventory to cost by multiplying the retail value by the cost multiplier ($120,750 × 0.6207). In our illustration, we get a value of $74,949. We can now go to the next step with this figure.

5. *Determination of gross cost of goods sold.* Since we know the amount of the merchandise handled at cost ($270,000) and know what we have *left* at cost ($74,949), we can determine the cost dollars that have moved out of stock ($195,051).

6. *Determine maintained markup, gross margin, and net profit.* Two procedures may be followed at this step. (We prefer the first method because of the emphasis given to the concept of maintained markup in Chapter 14). The gross margin and net profit figures in either case are identical; slightly different accounting philosophies are the determining factor, and the justification of either method is neither appropriate nor valuable here. We simply show the two ways to let you see the differences between them. Gross cost of goods sold is deducted from net sales to determine maintained markup ($300,000 – $195,051). Alteration costs (or workroom expenses) are traditionally considered in retailing as merchandising, non-operating expenses and in this first method are offset by cash discounts earned (non-operating income). The net difference between the two is added or subtracted from the maintained markup to derive the gross margin ($104,949 – $3,000 + $6,000 = $107,949), from which operating expenses are deducted to calculate net profits before taxes ($107,949 – $75,000 = $32,949). The various percentages appearing on the statement are all based on net sales (with the exception of the cost percentage and the cumulative markup).

   The second process for determining gross margin and net profit differs in that cash discounts earned are deducted from gross cost of goods sold ($195,051 – $6,000) to derive *net* cost of goods sold ($189,051). Alteration costs are added to that figure to obtain *total* cost of goods sold ($189,051 + $3,000 = $192,051). Total cost of goods sold is deducted from net sales ($300,000 − $192,051) to obtain the gross margin figure of $107,949.

Evaluation of the retail method

The retail method of inventory valuation offers the retailer many advantages:

1. The method is easily programmed for computer systems, and accounting statements can be drawn up at any time.

2. Shortages can be determined. The retail method is a book inventory, and this figure can be compared to the physical inventory. Only with a book inventory can shortages (or overages) be determined.

3. The retail method, through its book inventory, serves as an excellent basis for insurance claims. In case of loss, the book inventory is good evidence of what should have been in stock. This reason, as well as the two previously mentioned, are advantages that exist because the retail method is a perpetual, book inventory method. The following two advantages are uniquely related to the system of the retail method of inventory.

4. The physical taking of inventory is easier with the retail method. The items are recorded on the inventory sheets only at their selling prices, instead of their cost and retail prices.

5. The retail method gives an automatic, conservative valuation of ending inventory because of the way the system is programmed. This means that the retail method gives a valuation of ending inventory at cost or market, whichever is lower.

Even though there are many advantages to using the retail method of inventory it has been criticized. A major complaint is that it is a "method of averages." This refers to the determination of the cost multiplier as the "average relationship" between all the merchandise handled at cost and retail, and the application of this average percentage to the closing inventory at retail to determine the cost figure. Such a disadvantage, more real in the past than today, can be largely overcome by classification merchandising or dissection accounting—that is, breaking departments into small subgroups with similarity in terms of margins and turnover. The new technology in point-of-sales systems affords unlimited classifications and thus allows the similarity necessary for implementation of the retail method, giving management a good measure of the actual effectiveness of operations.

The retail method of inventory is not applicable to all departments within a store. For example, unless the purchases can be "retailed" at the time of receipt of the goods, the system will not work. The drapery workroom could not be on the retail method. Consequently, there are certain cost departments within many establishments. Such a condition does not lessen the value of the system where it is appropriate.

Departmental Performance Evaluation

Individual departments within a retail firm must be analyzed to evaluate performance and to determine whether changes need to be made in any aspect of the departments' operations. An important component of departmental

Table 19–9 Example of the Full Costing Approach						
		Department				
		A		**B**		**C**
Sales		$20,000		$10,000		$15,000
Cost of goods sold		5,000		5,000		3,000
Gross margin		$15,000		$ 5,000		$12,000
Expenses:						
Direct	$5,000		3,000		5,000	
Indirect	6,000		5,000		3,000	
Total expenses		11,000		8,000		8,000
Net profit (loss)		$ 4,000		($ 3,000)		$ 4,000

evaluation is the assignment of costs to the individual departments. But before discussing approaches that may be used to assign costs to departments, we direct your attention to the nature of costs in a retail operation.

Types of costs

Direct costs are costs directly associated with a department. Such costs would cease to exist if the department were eliminated. An example of a direct cost is advertising in support of products sold in a given department. **Indirect costs** are costs that cannot be tied directly to a department. An example is the store manager's salary.

In conducting a departmental performance evaluation, management must first redefine costs from natural accounts to functional accounts. **Natural accounts** are companywide accounts defined by the accounting department and include such categories as salaries, rent, promotion, and cost of supplies. **Functional accounts** reflect the retailing function involved. An example would be the allocation of salaries to administrative support, sales personnel, and so forth. Management must then determine which of two approaches (the contribution margin approach or the full costing approach) will be used to assign costs to individual departments.

Cost allocation approaches

In the **full costing approach,** both direct and indirect costs are assigned to departments (see Table 19–9). Each department's direct costs and its allocation of indirect costs are deducted from the department's gross margin to determine its net profit or loss. The store's indirect costs can be allocated to departments in several ways, including equal allocation to all departments or allocation based on the sales volume of each department. Advocates for the full costing approach argue that all the costs of operating a department should be included so that management has an accurate picture of how each department contributes to the overall profitability of the firm. However, the approach has been criticized because of the arbitrary bases sometimes used to assign indirect costs to departments and because it can lead managers to erroneous conclusions about whether a department should be abandoned or deleted. Let's look at the issue of deleting a department in more detail.

Table 19–10 Example of the Contribution Margin Approach ($ millions)	
Sales	
Department 1	16.2
Department 2	12.4
Department 3	11.6
Total	40.2
Merchandise costs	31.0
Gross margin	9.2
Expenses	
Promotion	2.6
Sales salaries	3.0
Overhead	1.2
Net profit before taxes	2.4

As shown in Table 19–9, the full costing approach shows that Department B is operating at a loss. Management's initial reaction might be to delete the department. However, several factors should be considered before making such a decision. First, Department B is covering all its direct costs and is contributing $2,000 toward the coverage of store indirect costs. If Department B were deleted, the initial costs currently being allocated to the department would have to be reallocated between Departments A and C, which would negatively affect their profit pictures. Thus, management might want to consider to what extent equitable bases are being used to allocate indirect costs to the departments. For example, Department B may be receiving a disproportionate share of indirect expenses. Several other factors should be considered in deciding to delete a department. For example, some departments are important because of their traffic-drawing ability. Their profit performance may be poor but they are important in drawing customers who then make purchases in other departments. Furthermore, sales in one department often affect sales in some other department. Thus, if management were to delete a department, the action could negatively affect sales in other departments. Before deleting a department, management should carefully consider not only the accounting data but also these other factors.

In the **contribution margin approach** only direct costs are assigned to departments. The department's direct costs are deducted from its gross margin to determine its contribution to the store's indirect costs. Advocates of this approach argue that even if a department is showing a loss under the full costing approach, it may still be making some contribution toward indirect costs and thus should not be abandoned or deleted. Advocates also argue that focussing only on direct costs in evaluating departmental performance is logical because indirect costs will continue even in the absence of the department.

Let's look more closely at the process of departmental evaluation, using the contribution margin approach. Assume that sales in Departments 1, 2, and 3 of a retail store are as shown in Table 19–10. Total store sales for the three departments are $40.2 million, and the cost of merchandise is $31.0 million. Storewide net profit before taxes is $2.4 million. The natural accounts of

Table 19–11   Transformation of Natural Accounts to Functional Accounts ($ millions)

Natural Accounts	Total	Functional Accounts	Dept. 1	Dept. 2	Dept. 3
Merchandise costs	31.0		10.0	11.3	9.7
Salaries	3.0				
		Sales personnel	0.8	1.0	0.6
		Administrative	0.2	0.3	0.1
Promotion	2.6				
		Department signing	0.1	0.2	0.1
		Newspapers	0.8	0.9	0.2
		Radio	—	0.2	0.1

merchandise costs, promotion costs, and sales salaries (all of which are direct costs) must be transformed into functional accounts in order to assign the costs on a departmental basis. All costs except overhead, which is an indirect cost and thus not assignable to the departments, are assigned to the three departments, as shown in Table 19–11.

A departmental performance evaluation can now be conducted for each department, as shown in Table 19–12. Department 1 contributes $4.3 million towards coverage of indirect costs and thus is responsible for the majority of the contribution margin. Even though Department 3 contributes $800,000, it is not a strong department in comparison to Department 1 and may need an evaluation to check where improvements could be made. Department 2 is showing a negative contribution margin and, thus, is in serious need of a detailed evaluation. Salespeople might need retraining, advertising and sales promotion efforts and expenditures may need to be reevaluated, and alternative vendor relationships may need to be established. Management may even consider deleting Department 2; however, before doing so, it should carefully consider the issues discussed earlier in this section.

Space Evaluation

The final performance evaluation issue we will discuss is that of space within the store. Effective use of space translates into additional dollars of profit. Retailers must therefore evaluate whether store space is being used in the most effective way. Management can use a variety of measures to evaluate space utilization, but we will discuss the gross margin per square metre method to illustrate one method retailers can employ.

Table 19–13 shows the calculations involved in evaluating space utilization by the gross margin per square metre method. Sales per square metre less cost of merchandise sold per square metre yield the gross margin per square metre figure.

With this figure, management can compare departments of various sizes selling different types of goods. Such an analysis can show management which

Table 19–12   Contribution Margin Analysis by Department ($ millions)

Department 1

Sales	16.2
Merchandise costs	10.0
Gross margin	6.2
Direct expenses	
Salaries	1.0
Promotion	0.9
Contribution to indirect costs	4.3

Department 2

Sales	12.4
Merchandise costs	11.3
Gross margin	1.1
Direct expenses	
Salaries	1.3
Promotion	1.3
Contribution to indirect costs	(1.5)

Department 3

Sales	11.6
Merchandise costs	9.7
Gross margin	1.9
Direct expenses	
Salaries	0.7
Promotion	0.4
Contribution to indirect costs	0.8

Summary

Contribution	
Department 1 contribution to indirect costs	4.3
Department 2 contribution to indirect costs	(1.5)
Department 3 contribution to indirect costs	0.8
Less overhead (shown in Table 19–10)	(1.2)
Net profits before taxes (as shown in Table 19–10)	2.4

departments are doing well, which are not, which might improve if expanded, and which can be reduced in space allotment.

For example, based on the calculations shown in Table 19–13, management might be tempted to decrease the selling space allocated to Department A in order to increase the selling space devoted to Department B. However, the decision to reallocate space is not a simple one. Advertising and selling costs for a department may rise when its selling space is increased. After the reallocation, the merchandise mix may change, which can result in either higher or lower gross margins. Management thus needs to stimulate the likely changes in the variables used in the calculations as a result of possible shifts in space allocation and determine whether reallocations are likely to increase the overall profitability of the firm.

Table 19–13 Calculating Gross Margin Per Square Metre

Three calculations are involved in figuring gross margin per square metre:

1. $\dfrac{\text{Total sales}}{\text{Total square metres}}$ = Sales per square metre

2. $\dfrac{\text{Cost of merchandise sold}}{\text{Total square metres}}$ = Cost of merchandise sold per square metre

3. Sales per square metre − Cost of merchandise sold per square metre = Gross margin per square metre

Example

	Department A	Department B
Sales	$50,000	$70,000
Cost of merchandise sold	$30,000	$35,000
Square metres of space	500 square metres	700 square metres
Sales per square metre	$ 100	$ 100
− Cost of merchandise sold per square metre	60	50
= Gross margin per square metre	$ 40	$ 50

Ziggys illustrates an effective use of space through its shelving, layout, and displays.

Courtesy Loblaw Company Ltd.

Chapter Highlights

- The balance sheet, the income statement, and various ratios derived from them give management information needed to evaluate the effectiveness of strategy in financial terms.

- The strategic profit model (SPM) emphasizes that a firm's principal financial objective is to earn an adequate or target rate of return on net worth (RONW) and dramatizes three areas of decision making (margin management, asset management, and leverage management) for improving RONW.

- Gross margin return on inventory investment (GMROI) is a performance evaluation indicator that focusses on turnover and gross margin percentage.

- Merchandise valuation is an important factor in performance evaluation. One of two methods—first-in, first-out (FIFO) and last in, first out (LIFO)—may be adopted to determine the cost value of inventory. According to the conservative rule, however, inventories should be valued at the lower of cost or market.

- In terms of accounting practices that assist management in inventory valuation decisions, retailers may use the cost method or the retail method. The cost method provides a book evaluation of inventory in which only cost figures are used. However, because of the limitations of the cost method, the retail method is more widely used.

- Individual departments within a retail firm must be analyzed to evaluate performance and to determine whether changes are needed in any aspect of the departments' operations. In evaluating departments, management may use either the contribution margin approach or the full costing approach.

- Effective use of space can translate into additional dollars of profit. Thus, retailers must evaluate whether store space is being used in the most effective way. The gross-margin-per-square-metre method is one method retailers may use.

Key Terms

assets, current 526
assets, fixed 526
balance sheet 526
contribution margin
    approach 543
direct costs 543
FIFO (first-in, first-out) 534
full costing approach 543
functional accounts 543
gross margin 526

GMROI (gross margin return on
    inventory) 531
income statement 526
indirect costs 543
leverage 528
liabilities 526
LIFO (last-in, first-out) 536
natural accounts 543
net worth 526
strategic profit model (SPM) 528

Discussion Questions

1. Distinguish between the balance sheet and the income statement. Illustrate an advocated format for each.

2. Explain the problems related to defining the terms *profit* and *investment*.

3. What are the significant purposes of the strategic profit model (SPM)?

4. Discuss the practical value of the strategic profit model.

5. Discuss your reaction to the following statement made by the manager of a large, full-line department store: "I am very pleased that my store had a 3.6 turnover rate for 1996."

6. Discuss the impact that turnover and margin planning have on the return of each dollar invested in inventory using a GMROI format.

7. Why is it difficult to determine cost of ending inventories? How do (a) FIFO and (b) LIFO relate to this problem? Explain the assumptions of and contrast the two methods.

8. Describe the cost method of inventory valuation. What are the limitations of the cost method? Under what conditions would this method be more appropriately used?

Application Exercises

1. With clearance from your instructor, interview at least three types of retailers, such as managers of department stores or catalogue showrooms. Discuss the issue of LIFO versus FIFO methods of inventory valuation. See if they understand the advantages and disadvantages of each. Summarize their perceptions and degree of sophistication. Try to draw some conclusions from this exercise.

2. Secure an annual report of a retail firm and construct (to the best of your ability) an SPM for that organization.

Problems

1. Use the retail method of accounting. Prepare a well-organized statement and determine for each of the three problems the following sets of figures:
    a. Cumulative markup percentage.
    b. Ending inventory at retail.
    c. Ending inventory at cost.
    d. Maintained markup in dollars and percent.
    e. Gross margin of profit in dollars and percent.
    f. Net profit in dollars and percent.

1. Item

	Cost	Retail
Beginning inventory	$20,000	$ 35,000
Gross purchases	72,000	115,000
Purchase returns and allowances	3,000	4,700
Transfers in	1,000	1,600
Transfers out	200	400
Transportation charges	1,216	
Additional markups		700
Additional markup cancellations		400
Gross sales		111,000
Customer returns and allowances		11,000
Gross markdowns		4,500
Markdown cancellations		1,000
Employee discounts		500
Estimated shortages, 0.4 percent of net sales		
Cash discounts on purchases	1,600	
Workroom costs	800	
Operating expenses	16,000	

2. Item

	Cost	Retail
Additional markup cancellations		$ 620
Estimated shortages, 0.05 percent of net sales		
Gross markdowns		8,000
Workroom costs	$ 500	
Sales returns and allowances		12,000
Transportation charges	2,094	
Beginning inventory	44,000	64,000
Purchase returns and allowances	2,200	5,200
Markdown cancellations		1,200
Gross purchases	65,600	105,240
Gross additional markups		2,480
Gross sales		102,000
Employee discounts		1,400
Cash discounts	1,500	
Operating expenses	11,000	

3. Item

	Cost	Retail
Gross sales		$ 27,200
Beginning inventory	$14,300	20,100
Sales returns and allowances		200
Gross markdowns		2,200
Gross additional markups		650
Transportation charges	418	
Purchase returns and allowances	830	1,720
Employee discounts		500
Gross purchases	17,200	27,520
Markdown cancellations		300
Operating expenses	3,800	
Cash discounts on purchases	200	
Additional markups cancelled		150
Alteration and workroom costs	300	
Ending physical inventory		16,500

2. Given below are the balance sheet and the income statement for a retail firm. Use this information to work Problems 4 and 5.

Balance Sheet

Assets		Liabilities and net worth	
Current assets	$342,000	Current liabilities	$252,000
Fixed assets	300,000	Long-term liabilities	170,000
Total assets	$642,000	Total liabilities	$422,000
		Net worth	$220,000
		Total	$642,000

Income Statement

Net sales	$752,000
Cost of goods sold	480,000
Gross margin	$272,000
Operating expenses	182,000
Profit before taxes	$ 90,000
Taxes	30,000
Profit after taxes	$ 60,000

4. Calculate the current ratio.

5. Using the strategic profit model (SPM) format, calculate the (a) net profit margin, (b) rate of asset turnover, (c) rate of return on assets (ROA), (d) leverage ratio, and (e) rate of return on net worth (RONW).

6. Given the following information, calculate each department's gross margin per square metre:

	Department A	Department B
Sales	$56,000	$43,800
Cost of goods sold	39,200	31,200
Selling space	54 square metres	30 square metres

7. Given the following information for a department in a retail store, calculate gross margin return on inventory investment (GMROI):

Net sales	$246,000
Cost of goods sold	98,400
Retail inventory (beginning of year)	120,000
Retail inventory (mid-year)	126,000
Retail inventory (end of year)	123,000

8. You are given the following information (for shirts) concerning beginning inventory and purchases during the year:

	Number of Shirts	Cost per Shirt	Total Cost
Beginning inventory	60	$ 6	$360
May purchases	70	8	560
September purchases	80	10	800

Assume that, during the year, 110 shirts were sold and that you want to determine the value of ending inventory. Calculate the cost dollar value of ending inventory using (*a*) the FIFO method and (*b*) the LIFO method.

Suggested Cases

10.   Clean Windows Inc.

11.   Donna Holtom

36.   Anne's Boutique

Note

1.   Mark's Work Wearhouse, *Annual Report,* 1995.

PART

New Dimensions in Retailing

In *Part 5, New Dimensions in Retailing*, Chapter 20 develops two important emerging issues in retailing: the retailing of services and the various types of nonstore retailing, including retailing through the World Wide Web.

Services and Non-store Retailing

Chapter Objectives

After reading this chapter you should be able to:

1. **Cite differences between service and tangible goods firms.**

2. **Describe unique aspects of consumer behaviour as related to the purchase of services.**

3. **Discuss various decisions involved in developing competitive plans and managing a retail service organization.**

4. **Highlight alternative forms of non-store retailing.**

Molly Maid, satisfying a variety of needs, including saving time for two-income families.

Photo by Michael Polselli

Demographic shifts, such as the sharp increase in two-income families and households headed by singles, are driving the growth of retail operations designed to meet the needs of consumers for whom time is scarce. A host of new businesses (from those that perform household chores, manicure the lawn, and fine-tune the car, to those that tend to kids and older family members) have sprung up to take care of life's many chores. These businesses have discovered that many people are willing to buy time at a fairly high price.

There seems to be no end to ideas for service businesses to meet the needs of the growing numbers of "time-pressed" consumers. Molly Maid Home Care Services will clean houses on demand and at a reasonable price. A company in Montreal will check the house every two days; pick up the mail, newspapers, and fliers; and water the plants while the owners are away on vacation, on business, or on sabbatical for a full year! There are hotels designed only for children, and even for pets. Catalogues allow families to order merchandise from the comfort of their homes. A whole array of new services is now available through the Internet in an interactive fashion.

This convenience retail industry is experiencing growth in other countries as well as in Canada. A most interesting service is that offered by Japan Efficiency Headquarters. People too busy to visit their aging parents can hire actors to take their place. The retailer charges $385 for a five-hour

visit by a "son" or "daughter," $769 for a couple, and $1,155 if a rental baby or child is included. The donors and recipients don't always live that far apart. A Tokyo computer salesperson, for example, sent a family unit of actors to visit his parents, who live only 10 minutes away. The parents enjoyed the visit so much that they decided to forego a vacation in order to treat themselves to a return visit.[1] ∎

The introduction to this chapter illustrates that not all retail organizations sell tangible products. Some market services. Because of the growing importance of service retail organizations to the Canadian economy, a separate chapter is devoted to this area. This chapter also presents information on non-store retailing—another segment of the Canadian economy that is experiencing growth. One factor causing this growth has been increasing time constraints among consumers, as described above.

Services Retailing

As mentioned previously, the selling of services is more important to the Canadian economy than ever before. Currently, services represent approximately three-quarters of the Canadian gross domestic product. By the year 2000, the service sector of the economy is forecasted to provide four out of five jobs.[2] Services are also taking on increasing importance in international marketing. In many countries, the names of such firms as American Express, McDonald's, and Hilton have become widely familiar.

The American Marketing Association defines a **service** as "activities, benefits, or satisfaction which are offered for sale, or are provided in connection with the sale of goods." Therefore, a service may have both tangible (high goods content) and intangible (low goods content) attributes. Based on the combination of tangible and **intangible** attributes provided, service firms may be placed along a continuum of no goods content to high goods content. At one end of the continuum would be services that are very low in goods content, such as the services provided by a psychiatrist. On the other hand, services provided by a janitorial service would be high in goods content (physical removal of dirt and trash).

In order to have a better understanding of service organizations, let's look at some of the differences between tangible goods firms and service firms.

Differences between tangible goods firms and service firms

Understanding the differences between tangible goods firms and service firms is important in developing successful competitive strategies for service organizations. The following sections highlight important differences between the two types of organizations.[3]

Perishability

Many services are essentially **perishable**. If a Four Seasons Hotel room is empty for an evening, or if a Canadian Airline plane leaves with empty seats, the revenue is lost forever. Dentists, physicians, attorneys, and accountants similarly cannot recover revenue lost because of an unfilled schedule. In contrast, tangible goods not sold on any given day can be held in inventory and sold at a later point to capture the revenue.

Lack of transportability

The inability to transport many services means that they often must be consumed at the point of production. Medical care essentially is available only at the doctor's office, hospital, or clinic, as are many other professional services.

Small firm size

Most service firms are small, single-unit operations. Small firm size limits the service firm's ability to achieve economies of scale. Changes are occurring, however. Sears, for example, offers a variety of services through its department stores. Tremendous growth is also occurring in the franchising of service organizations, such as real estate firms, travel firms, and dental, medical, and legal clinics. Some experts predict that one of the biggest growth areas in the future in franchising will be service organizations in the convenience industry such as child-, car-, and home-care franchises.

Difficulties in establishing large market share

Service industries typically are characterized by low barriers to entry. Competitors can quickly enter service markets, which keeps any one firm from establishing a dominant market share. The inability to experience economies of scale also negatively affects the service firm's ability to acquire a large market share. Some question whether economies of scale are possible because the cost of some services increases as the firm gets larger. Large, comprehensive-care hospitals, for example, have far greater per-unit overhead costs and labour costs than smaller, more flexible institutions such as emergency clinics and one-day surgery centres.

Labour intensity

Many service firms are labour intensive—another factor preventing economies of scale. The output of an attorney or a medical doctor, for example, cannot easily be increased. Many services must be personally produced and tailored to the needs of each individual client, which makes application of assembly line techniques and reduction of labour content difficult. Furthermore, the non-repetitive nature of many services minimizes learning curve effects. Thus, learning and experience do not drive down per-unit costs.

Difficulty in quality control

Because service firms are labour intensive and because many services are offered only at the point of sale, standardization in the level of service and quality is difficult to achieve.[4] Fast-food operations, offering a combination of tangible goods and services, are an exception. Such firms have been able to introduce essentially assembly-line techniques to the fast-food business.

Unpredictability of demand

The demand for services is often more difficult to predict than the demand for tangible goods. Demand for some services can fluctuate widely by the month, the day of the week, or even the hour of the day. Medical offices and ambulance services have problems predicting the number of patients needing their services. The same difficulty exists in forecasting the demand for using telephone services, visiting museum exhibits, and watching ballet performances.

As indicated earlier, competitive strategies of service firms are affected by the fact that they possess some unique characteristics that differentiate them from tangible goods firms. In addition, consumer behaviour differences in the purchase of services versus tangible goods affect competitive strategy development in retail service firms.[5]

Consumer behaviour in the purchase of services

Many studies on consumers' behaviour when buying goods versus services clearly establish that customers view the purchasing of services differently from the purchasing of goods. Some research has found, for example, that consumers seem to feel that purchasing services is frequently a less pleasant experience than buying goods and that consumers perceive higher levels of risk in buying services than tangible goods.[6]

Consumers often face an information gap when purchasing services. A lack of reliable data on vendors, be they garage mechanics or savings banks, exists. Especially lacking is information to help consumers choose professionals such as doctors and lawyers.

Furthermore, because services are often intangible, consumers find it difficult, if not impossible, to evaluate the service before purchase and also, in many instances, even after purchase and use. This particular issue has been examined in terms of three types of product properties: search qualities, experience qualities, and credence qualities.[7] Tangible goods possess **search qualities,** or attributes that a consumer can see, feel, or touch, and can thus determine before purchasing a product. Services, on the other hand, possess experience and credence qualities. **Experience qualities** are attributes such as taste that can be discerned only after purchasing or during consumption. Restaurants and theatres are examples of services with experience qualities. **Credence qualities** are attributes that consumers may find impossible to evaluate even after purchase and consumption, usually because they do not have the knowledge or skill to do so. Services provided by professionals such as doctors and lawyers are examples of services possessing credence qualities.

The fact that services primarily possess experience and credence qualities suggests that the service encounter extends beyond the service-production process. Service retailers should communicate with the consumer beyond the decision by the customer to buy the service and even beyond the completion of the service process. In this communication process, the retailer should establish the evaluative criteria and provide information to help the buyer know what to look for before, during, and after the service encounter. In addition, the use of reference groups to present favourable information about the use of a service is an important surrogate for evaluative criteria.

Many other implications exist in developing competitive strategy as a result of the unique characteristics of service retailers and the buying behaviour of consumers in purchasing services. These will be addressed in the following section, which focusses on the development of competitive strategy in retail service firms.

Developing competitive strategies

In developing a competitive strategy, the service retailer must have a clear definition and understanding of its market and must then develop a positioning strategy to attract this market and to distinguish itself from competitive firms.

Defining and analyzing target customers

Understanding the market is as critical for the service firm as for the tangible goods firm. Management must understand the demographics of the firm's market and the needs, perceptions, and expectations of its client base.

A growing trend is for service firms to segment the market and to target their markets carefully. For example, banks are increasingly trying to build customer loyalty by bundling their services into packages targeted to segments of the population, such as young people. An airline, on the other hand, may aim at businesspeople. For some time, banks have been aiming packages at the elderly, the demographic segment with the highest savings. Now, some banks are targeting subsegments within the elderly market because of various age, geographic, and lifestyle differences.

A study on customer behaviour found that there were two major segments of banking services: those who want convenience and those who want performance from their bank.[8] Recently, the CIBC has designed a prototype branch network that segments its customers into two basic categories: *(1)* convenience users who do mostly basic transactions, and *(2)* sophisticated users who have more complex needs. The convenience segment will be served by automatic teller machines and telephone, while the sophisticated user can visit "financial centres" for personal advice on how to manage their money.[9]

The service offering

The **core service** of a service firm is the primary benefit customers seek from the firm. **Peripheral services** are secondary benefits sought by customers. The core service for Federal Express, for example, consists of picking up the package, transporting it overnight, and delivering it the next morning. Peripheral services include providing advice and information, providing labels and certain types of packaging, documentation of shipments, and problem solving.

Most service organizations originate with a single core service offered to a single market segment. Initial growth opportunities normally occur through the addition of peripheral services and expansion into new geographic markets. Some service firms have been successful by following a strategy of offering new core services for existing market segments, and some have followed a strategy of **concentric diversification,** or moving into different, but closely related, services. Thus, services strategy includes deciding what new services to introduce to which target markets, what existing services to maintain, and what services to eliminate. Decisions on the service offerings then set the stage for decisions on other components of competitive strategy, such as price, promotion, and distribution (delivery) strategies.

In judging a company's service offering, research has shown that consumers are primarily concerned that the service providers give consistently high levels of quality service. However, customers are also concerned with tangibles, such as the appearance of physical facilities, equipment, personnel, and communica-

The Royal Bank targets young people for its Visa Gold card, while British Airways tells businesspeople that with the new Club World, they will be pampered.

Courtesy the Royal Bank and British Airways

tion materials. The following sections focus on these issues.[10] We also turn your attention to the extent to which service firms can engage in activities designed to achieve greater economies and efficiency without jeopardizing the level of personal attention and quality of service provided to customers.

Service provision   One characteristic of service firms, as discussed earlier, is the principal role people play in the delivery of the service.[11] How can service firms ensure that employees are providing consistently high levels of quality service to their customers? Some companies rely on careful selection and training of employees and the development of programs to build a sense of pride in the service and a sense of identification with the company. Organizations often use both monetary and non-monetary incentives to encourage employees to provide good service. One incentive is the employee-of-the-month award. The effectiveness of using such an award is enhanced when it is based on customer feedback.

Making the person who delivers the service more visible is another technique. For example, in Japanese-style steak houses, the chef cooks at a grill in front of the restaurant guests in an elaborate show of dexterity with knifes. The chef's visibility and proximity to customers promote a consistently high quality of service.

Often effective in achieving and maintaining quality is peer group control. This is especially relevant where professional standards have been established for a task. In an architectural firm, the existence of a policy requiring partners' review of every piece of work can keep partners and associates on their toes. Surgeons are sometimes assigned in teams to encourage peer group control.

Over the past few years a growing number of service organizations have found that a most effective way to affect customers' perceptions of reliable service is to offer an unconditional guarantee of satisfaction. Such a guarantee

Retail Highlight 20–1

Hampton Inn's Unconditional Guarantee of Satisfaction

In October 1989 Hampton announced its unconditional 100 percent satisfaction guarantee—a first in the hotel industry. The guarantee states that if guests have a problem or complaint at any time during their stay and are not satisfied when they leave, they will be given one night's stay for free.

Management believed that the secret to making the guarantee work was to give employees the authority to implement it. Thus, the program authorizes all employees—not just the manager or front-desk personnel—to take whatever action is necessary to keep the customer satisfied. For example, if a housekeeper notices that a guest is getting frustrated because the door key won't work, the housekeeper won't refer the problem to the front desk or the maintenance department. Instead, the housekeeper will take responsibility for getting a new key, changing the lock, or arranging for a different room. If the guest still isn't happy, the housekeeper may offer, without contacting management, to refund the cost of the room for the night. Before launching the program, training seminars were held for employees. Management also assured employees that they would stand behind their decisions completely.

When customers invoke the guarantee, their complaints are sent to company headquarters in Memphis. The operations staff is thus alerted to quality and service weaknesses and can initiate changes throughout the Hampton Inn chain. In this way, a single customer complaint in one location can contribute to improved service nationwide.

Since implementing the program, management has noticed a definite improvement in employee retention and employee morale. In addition, the program has positively affected the company's bottom line. Research indicates that approximately 2 percent of the system's total room nights are customers who said they stayed specifically because of the guarantee. Research also reveals that the guarantee strengthens customer loyalty—about half of all guests who complain about service problems after their stay indicate they will come back to Hampton Inn. Of the guests who invoke the guarantee before leaving the hotel (the guarantees are in the form of a reimbursement, not a voucher for later use), 86 percent say they will return to Hampton Inn and 45 percent of them already have.

Source: Adapted from "Satisfaction Guaranteed for Customers and Crew," *The Wall Street Journal*, January 28, 1991, pp. A3 and A10.

---

promises complete customer satisfaction and, at a minimum, a full refund or complete, no-cost problem resolution to dissatisfied customers. For many firms, such a guarantee has proven to be a powerful tool for building customer loyalty and market share and for improving overall service quality (to see how one firm, Hampton Inn, a low- to mid-priced hotel chain, has implemented such a concept, see Retail Highlight 20–1). Management should, however, carefully assess both the benefits and the risks of providing unconditional guarantees. For example, because of the complex nature and unpredictable results of professional services, payouts could be higher than with other services and each payout could be more painful, considering the higher fees and smaller number of clients typical of such firms. Of course, such risks can be managed, but doing so requires great care in the guarantee's design and implementation, as well as in achieving and maintaining exceptionally high service quality.[12]

Importance of the physical environment   Because consumers often find the offerings of service organizations difficult to comprehend and evaluate because they are largely intangible, consumers often look for tangible evidence of the intangible to help them determine just what the offering is. Service retailers can provide such tangible surrogate features. For example, a hotel puts drinking glasses in clean paper bags, provides wrapped tablets of soap, and attaches "cleaned" bands across the toilets as tangible evidence that the room has been specially cleaned and prepared for the new occupant. The decor of the salon, the appearance of the staff, and the quality of the appointment cards are all tangible, surrogate product features for the basically intangible product of hairdressing.

Standardization and specialization in service delivery   Increasingly, managers in service firms are engaging in activities to achieve greater economies and higher levels of efficiency. Such activities enable service firms to enjoy not only economies of scale but also more consistent, predictable quality in service delivery. As mentioned earlier, fast-food restaurants have introduced an assembly-line approach to what is a combination of tangible goods and services delivery in an effort to improve efficiency. Other examples of standardized consumer services range from quick auto service providers (such as oil change, muffler, and tune-up shops) to highly specialized medical services, such as centres that treat only one ailment such as hernias or cataracts. For example, Shouldice Hospital in Toronto only performs hernia operations, about 8,000 a year.[13]

Standardization of service does not necessarily mean the end of personal attention, which is often a key element the customer seeks from a service firm. For example, trade-offs are successfully being made between standardization and personal service in the chains of legal and dental clinics that offer routine, standardized services to customers in essentially an assembly-line fashion. Emergency medical care centres follow a similar approach. Overhead is low because of the absence of costly equipment, treatment is limited to routine cases, and paraprofessionals are used whenever possible. Other efforts at standardization are evident in banks that offer only routinized services at the branches and handle unusual or complex transactions only at a central office. Banks' use of technology such as automatic teller machines is another way to standardize service delivery and increase efficiency.

Service delivery

Although service retailers are less concerned with issues such as transportation, inventory, and warehousing than are tangible goods firms, service delivery is an important element of a service retailer's competitive strategy and involves such decisions as channel structure and location.

Channel structure   Most services are provided directly by the producer to the end user, without an intermediary. Most physicians deal directly with patients, as do attorneys with their clients. Still, some indirect channels are used in service delivery. Tickets to ball games, concerts, and similar events are often sold at locations in addition to the place of performance. Travel agencies serve as intermediaries between the airline and the consumer. Banks extend credit to retail customers who use the bank's credit card, so the bank becomes a third party to any credit transaction a customer has with a retail outlet.

The importance of location   Location is an important element of the competitive strategy in a service business. Frequent air travellers are more likely to use

Courtesy Four Seasons Hotels

Advertisement for the Four Seasons Hotels, with its "Defining the art of service" theme

auto rental agencies with the largest number of airport locations because such firms are most likely to have an outlet in a major airport. Fitness centres seek locations easily accessible to customers. Dental and legal clinics have found that location is important in attracting customers and are now increasingly moving to shopping mall locations.

Promoting the service offering

Effective use of promotion is extremely important for service retailers. Promotion is important in providing tangible "cues" for an intangible offering, in communicating the image of the firm and promoting its individual services, and in communicating with the customer after the service encounter. Let's look at these and other issues in more detail.

Promotion plays an important role in making a service more tangible to consumers. For example, some advertisements associate the service with some tangible object to establish a psychological association between a vaguely perceived intangible and a more easily perceived tangible object. Prudential Insurance's association with the rock of Gibraltar is an example. The rock signifies the solid, unwavering security and peace of mind a consumer desires from insurance. The Royal Bank uses a similar approach with the lion in its logo. In addition, advertisements may focus on the physical environment in which the service is to be performed in an effort to make services more tangible. For example, a hospital's ad might show pictures of its pleasant birthing rooms, or an ad for the Four Seasons Hotels shows the various amenities, the decor, the doorman, the valet, and the room service for busy and successful business-people.

Service marketers should also try to create a strong organizational image through their promotional efforts. Retailers have long recognized that the quality of a store's services is an important determinant of its image and that store image strongly affects shopping and patronage behaviour.

In addition, service retailers should make post-purchase communication a part of promotional strategy. This can be accomplished with postcards, surveys, telephone calls, brochures, or a variety of other devices to show customers that their input is sought and their patronage is appreciated.

Finally, marketing research suggests that consumers of retail services do not rely heavily on traditional, source-controlled information sources.[14] Instead, they prefer more personal sources for obtaining information. Hence, service retailers should try to stimulate positive word-of-mouth communication among present and potential customers.

Pricing

Price is a key element of a service retailer's competitive strategy. Price setting for a service firm, however, may prove to be a challenging task, and in some instances pricing issues have even become the source of controversy and criticism.

Research has shown that consumers may often perceive a stronger relationship between price and quality for services than for goods. This, together with the difficulties that customers encounter in evaluating services, suggests a greater emphasis and reliance on price as an indicator of quality. It thus becomes crucial that service retailers' prices are set appropriately.[15] However, sometimes there may be no sure way of knowing just what the provision of a service will entail until it is completed; there may be no way of telling the customer what the exact price of the service will be until the service has been provided. In addition, research shows that service retailers use cost-oriented pricing strategies more than competition- and demand-oriented pricing strategies. Costing a service, however, is a difficult and imprecise task because of service intangibility and flexibility. How does one place a value on such things as skill, expertise, and knowledge? Although service costs may be difficult to calculate, service companies are apparently making estimates of costs to be sure that they are covered.[16]

Because of intense competition, slow growth, and other conditions, many service firms are focussing heavily on price as a competitive weapon. Intensive price competition has been evident, for example, in deregulated service industries such as financial services, telecommunications (see Retail Highlight 20–2), and transportation. Air travellers today, for example, are faced with a bewildering array of different prices. In fact, the lowest fare may even differ from one ticketing agent to another. Such aggressive pricing is not limited to the service industries just cited.[17]

Non-store Retailing

Non-store retailing has experienced rapid growth with sales of more than $3 billion in 1992, or 2.5 percent of total retail sales. A number of environmental dynamics explain this growth. Demographic and lifestyle changes, for example, have affected the demand for non-store retailing. Single-person or single-parent household members lack the time to shop, as do those in two-career families.

Retail Highlight 20–2

Pricing Wars in Telecommunications

Following the deregulation of telephone services in the United States and in Great Britain, the Canadian Radio and Telecommunications Commission (CRTC) followed suit in 1987 and in 1992. In the long-distance market, several resellers (including Sprint, ACC, and Fonorola) and Unitel Communications are competing for a share of the market that, previously, belonged exclusively to the Stentor Group (primarily Bell Canada and affiliates). This market of $7.5 billion is expected to reach $10 billion in the year 2000.

At first, the new companies tried to take a large share of the market by cutting price, and hoping that the old monopolies would not react. But, unfortunately for them, Bell Canada reacted vigorously by cutting its prices by an average of 40 percent. Initially, the battle was for large customers, then shifted to small businesses, and finally the residential sector. By acting swiftly and decisively, Bell only lost 10 percent of its long-distance business.

This pricing war used advertising extensively in a battle of images. From 1992 to 1993, Bell Canada increased its advertising budget by 35 percent, and it used humour (with a well-known actor playing Mr. Bell) effectively to increase awareness to 22 percent. On the other hand, Unitel relied on comparative advertising to demonstrate that its prices were lower than Bell Canada's, while Sprint used its U.S. campaign with Candice Bergen (of Murphy Brown fame).

In spite of its successes, Bell Canada's share is expected to continue eroding, and analysts expect that by the year 2000, Stentor's share will be 70 percent, Unitel's 13 percent, and Sprint's 10 percent, with several resellers gone. To protect itself from this war, Fonorola is targeting very specific needs of users who want high-quality services and services related to computer applications.

Source: Adapted from Laurent Fontaine, "La téléphonie à l'heure du marketing," *Commerce* (April 1994), pp. 56–64.

The "grey market," or the senior segment, is growing and, although such consumers have more disposable income, they are less mobile. Furthermore, some people are afraid to go downtown or to malls and prefer shopping in the safety of their homes. Many consumers also like the idea of shopping 24 hours a day, seven days a week. In addition, advances in the technological environment have spurred the growth of some forms of non-store retailing. Let's look at the issue more closely by discussing the following forms of non-store retailing: direct-mail retailing, direct-response retailing, in-home retailing, telephone retailing, electronic retailing, and vending-machine retailing.

Direct-mail retailing

Direct-mail retailing is a significant part of non-store retailing. The catalogue industry in Canada is estimated at $2 billion annually and growing at about 5 percent per year. Catalogue merchandising in Canada is widespread with over 620 titles in 1994, selling anything from seeds to silks. Sears Canada alone distributes 40 million catalogues a year to Canadian households.[18] As well, many U.S. catalogue retailers have entered the Canadian market including Land's End, L.L. Bean, and recently Spiegel, which began delivering its 1.5 kilogram, 600-page doorstop catalogue to Canadian homes. Canadians can order Spiegel's upscale clothing and accessories through a 1-800 number.[19]

Retail Highlight 20–3

Three Examples of New Direct-Marketing Methods

Tilley Endurables: The 60-page catalogue of Tilley Endurables of Toronto can be seen around the world thanks to the Internet on the World Wide Web: it includes pictures, prices, and descriptions of its merchandise. Products can be ordered through e-mail, fax, or an 800 number. On April 29, 1995, the company received a request from a man in Perth, Australia!

Harry Rosen: Headquartered in Toronto, Harry Rosen has 22 stores in Canada and one in Buffalo, New York. On March 14, 1995, it launched its first **CD-ROM catalogue** provided free to customers. Two weeks later, it had already distributed 1,000 copies of the CD catalogue. The CD provides information and prices, but also allows customers to point and click various outfits and play with them singly or in combination to see how they would look! One customer came into the store and said: "I saw this page on the CD-ROM, could you show me this outfit?"

Grand & Toy: This Toronto office-supply company developed a software program (OrderPoint) for its numerous commercial clients, which not only helps them order supplies, but reduces the number of procedures for placing an order, and can be tailored to the needs of a client. The company catalogue is built into the software itself. Updates and upgrades will be sent later.

Source: Adapted from Lara Mills, "From Print to Bits and Bytes," *Marketing* (May 22, 1995), p. 14.

As the number of catalogues has changed, so has their content. Whereas the earlier catalogues contained a wide variety of merchandise, ranging from farm supplies to lingerie, the typical contemporary catalogue presents a tightly focussed assortment of goods designed to meet the needs of a specific market segment. For example, Spiegel is targeting Canadian women aged 25 to 44, in dual-income families with household incomes of more than $70,000.[20]

In addition to focussing the content of their catalogues, companies are using consumer data and technology to develop highly targeted mailing lists. With the use of **selective binding,** for example, a customer and her next-door neighbour might get two different catalogues. Another option is **ink jetting,** which enables the company to print personalized messages within a catalogue. Techniques such as these enable a company to treat each customer as an individual. Some industry analysts believe that in a few years, the industry will be at the point where almost every catalogue will be for a specific customer.

An exciting development in mail-order retailing is the *videolog,* a shop-at-home video catalogue. Not only do videologs provide a novel method for reaching the consumer, but the approach seems especially appropriate for selling expensive or complicated products.[21] Even though videologs have attractive benefits, they are not without their drawbacks. An individual tape costs anywhere from $7 to $10. Furthermore, they require more effort to use than a printed catalogue. Retail Highlight 20–3 provides some examples of the use of new technologies for direct selling.

Even though direct-mail retailing is experiencing growth, it is not without its critics. Environmentalists are concerned not only with disposal issues but also with the destruction of trees. Some direct-mail companies are attempting to respond to these concerns.[22]

Direct-response retailing

Instead of soliciting customers through the mail, some companies have used mass media (billboards, newspapers, magazines, radio, and television) to carry their selling proposition, and the customer can order merchandise through the mail, a fax machine, the telephone (with an 800- or 888-number), or cable (through an interactive system).

In-home retailing[23]

In-home retailing is a method of distribution of consumer goods and services through personal contact (salesperson to buyer) away from a fixed business location. Major modes of personal selling include one-on-one selling and the party plan, in the home or elsewhere. The significance of in-home retailing is underscored by the fact that it is has been outselling mail-order for many years, with total sales of $895 million or 29.5 percent of total non-store sales.[24]

Four major categories of products and services are sold by in-home selling firms:

1. Household products, including cookware, tableware, kitchen and decorative accessories, vacuum cleaners and other appliances, household cleaning products, and foods and beverages.[25]

2. Personal care and beauty items, including cosmetics, fragrances, skin care items, jewelry, and clothing. Well-known firms in the cosmetics and skin care line include, for example, Mary Kay and Avon.

3. Leisure and educational products, such as encyclopedias and other educational publications, toys, craft and hobby items, computers and software, and self-improvement or vocational training programs.

4. Services and product lines that vary widely in character such as cemetery property, foliage plants, and photographic supplies.

Of interest is the fact that many of the environmental dynamics discussed earlier that have led to an increase in demand for non-store buying have adversely affected in-home selling. As the public's fear of crime has increased, fewer people are willing to open the door to strangers. With more single-person and dual-income households, there are fewer people at home. Many personal sellers are therefore attempting to reach consumers during the evening hours and at locations other than consumers' homes, such as work sites. Some are using direct-mail pieces and are printing 800 or 888 numbers in their literature as well as on product packages to assist customers in reordering products or making contacts. Such companies are quick to point out, however, that customer orders generated by the toll-free numbers or direct-mail pieces are turned over to their salespeople to fill. In an attempt to increase sales, some companies are moving into international markets. Amway, for example, has more than 100,000 salespeople in Japan. Avon is sold in more than 100 countries today and earns a substantial portion of its profit from its international operations.

Telephone retailing

The use of telephones for selling products or services has become increasingly popular. **Telephone retailing**, or **telemarketing**, can be either *inbound* when the

Women taking classes at an Avon training centre in Guangzhou, China, to become Avon representatives

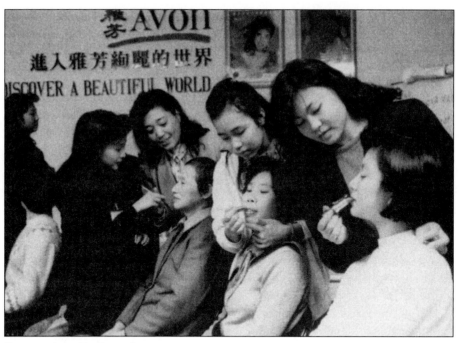

Courtesy Avon Products, Inc.

retailer receives orders or requests from customers thanks to the use of 800 or 888 numbers; or *outbound* when the retailer calls customers or potential customers to sell merchandise or services.[26]

Consumers are buying virtually every type of product and service via the telephone—from prescriptions to computers to prepared foods. Telemarketing not only gives companies a practical, cost-effective way of interacting personally with customers, but it also gives consumers a chance to ask questions and seek information about a company's offering.[27]

Although some consumers welcome telephone selling, others view it as an interruption and an invasion of privacy. Especially objectionable to many consumers are computerized machines that automatically call and relay messages. They are concerned, for example, that some consumers must pay for calls—people with car phones and pagers are charged for every minute they use a telephone line even if they don't initiate the call.

In an attempt to be more sensitive to the needs and concerns of consumers, more and more telemarketers are developing policies and guidelines in order to protect privacy and prevent exploitation. MCI, for example, has developed such guidelines. The company makes all contact through a live operator, they use only equipment that allows immediate disconnection, and they limit hours of calling from 9:00 A.M. to 9:00 P.M., Monday through Saturday, and noon to 5:00 P.M. on Sunday. The company never engages in random dialling, and the company's telemarketers are trained to politely reschedule or terminate a call if the consumer does not wish to take the call. MCI also maintains an up-to-date list of consumers who have asked not to be called and routinely receives the Canadian Direct Marketing Association's Telephone Preference Service, a national no-call list to which any consumer may subscribe. Because unsuspecting consumers can be exploited by telephone sales if they misunderstand the conditions of a sale, MCI has developed a verification process to ensure the accuracy of its telemarketing efforts. If a consumer agrees to become an MCI subscriber, an independent company contacts the customer to verify that MCI has accurate information identifying him or her and that he or she understands the terms of MCI's service. If any problems are detected by the independent company, the sale is terminated.[28]

Electronic retailing

Electronic retailing can assume a variety of forms, including phone shopping from computerized listings, such as Comp-U-Card International Inc.; cable television programs with product and service presentations and demonstrations, such as the Canadian Home Shopping Network which claims to reach 5 million households; and electronic ordering of merchandise from retailers or manufacturers through nationwide computer networks such as Prodigy or Netscape. The **Internet** *World Wide Web* has already attracted the attention of numerous retailers who have developed complex web sites, including all the major banks, and most universities. In an advertisement for the Bank of Montreal, the small businessperson is invited to visit its Web site for information on the new HQ program (for virtual headquarters). In another example, the TD Web site has attracted new customers for the Toronto Dominion Bank from countries such as Finland and Australia; over 25 percent of the traffic on the TD Web site is from outside North America.[29] The Internet is expected to revolutionize the retail business of the future, with the addition of better graphic designs, 3-D effects, and two-way picture and voice interactions.[30]

The most ambitious project is called UBI (for *U*niversality, *Bi*-directionality, and *I*nteractivity). It is currently being tested in Chicoutimi, Quebec, with 33,000 households who received free equipment (a set-top device, a receipt printer, a PIN pad, a smart card and a remote control) and access to interactive services (such as banking, paying bills, interactive games and sports, and buying lotteries).[31]

Regardless of the format, electronic shopping has taken on increased significance as a form of non-store retailing. Over 200 companies are experimenting with ways to use personal computers, videodisc players, and other technologies to improve customer service and provide convenient access to merchandise and product information. More than 5,000 electronic shopping systems now provide information and transaction services to consumers. More than 500,000 consumers shop electronically from their homes through personal computers.

Some market analysts believe that the impending fusion of fibre-optic technology with computer and video technology should make electronic shopping relatively commonplace by 2010. By the year 2000, 70 percent of Canadian households are projected to have computers. Some envision that several basic formats will be widely used then and that electronic shopping will account for 20 to 25 percent of retail sales.[32] Some believe that such estimates are overly optimistic, but no one can doubt the increasing significance of electronic shopping as a form of non-store retailing.

Vending-machine retailing

Historians believe that the first **vending machine,** created by Hero of Alexandria in 215 B.C., was a five-drachma machine that dispensed holy water. Since that time, vending machines have been used to sell a wide variety of merchandise,

An advertisement from the Bank of Montreal inviting small businesses to visit its Web site for information on the HQ program

Courtesy Bank of Montreal

ranging from soft drinks and snack food items to blue jeans to freshly baked pizza. Vending machines have even been used to vend names and telephone numbers of ladies of the evening.

The vending machine industry had revenues of about $400 million in 1992. Because of increasing competition, however, profit margins are usually around 2 to 3 percent. There are over 700 vending machine firms in Canada, ranging from mom-and-pop firms to larger companies competing for about 200,000 vending locations.[33]

The largest categories of products sold through vending machines are coffee, non-alcoholic beverages, cigarettes, and confectionaries. Most vending machines can be found in industrial plants, business offices, hospitals, universities, schools, etc.

Chapter Highlights

- **The service sector of the Canadian economy is becoming increasingly important. This is evidenced by the fact that four out of five jobs will be in the services area by 2000. There are strategic differences between tangible goods firms and service retailers. The competitive strategies of service firms must conform to their unique characteristics. In addition, consumer behav-**

iour differences in the purchase of services versus tangible goods affect competitive strategy development in retail service firms.

- Service firms must develop competitive strategies just as firms selling tangible goods do. The service retailer must have a clear definition of its target market and an understanding of that market.

- An element of positioning strategy is the decision regarding the service offering. Here, the retailer must determine not only the core service to be offered but also the peripheral services. Because of the intangible nature of many service offerings, the people involved in service delivery and the physical environment are key ingredients of a service firm's competitive strategy.

- In terms of service delivery, service retailers are involved in channel structure decisions. Although most services are provided directly by the producer to the end user without an intermediary, some indirect channels are used in service delivery. Location is also an important element of service delivery.

- Effective use of promotion is important for service retailers. Promotion is important in providing tangible "cues" for an intangible offering, in communicating the image of the firm and promoting its individual services, and in communicating with the customer after the service encounter.

- Pricing is also a critical element of a service firm's competitive strategy. Because the offering of a service firm may largely be intangible, price is often used by consumers as a surrogate for quality. Price must therefore be set appropriately. However, some unique aspects of service retailing make price setting a challenging task.

- Non-store retailing has experienced rapid growth. Forms of non-store retailing include direct-mail retailing, direct response retailing, in-home retailing, telephone retailing, electronic retailing, and vending-machine retailing.

Key Terms

CD-ROM catalogue 568
concentric diversification 561
core service 561
credence qualities 560
direct-mail retailing 567
direct-response retailing 569
electronic retailing 571
experience qualities 560
in-home retailing 569
inbound telemarketing 569
ink jetting 568
intangibility 558
internet 571

non-store retailing 567
outbound telemarketing 570
peripheral service 561
perishability 558
physical environment 563
search qualities 560
selective binding 568
service 558
telemarketing 569
telephone retailing 569
vending-machine retailing 571
World Wide Web 571

Discussion Questions

1. Summarize the differences between tangible goods firms and service retailers.

2. Discuss the unique aspects of consumer behaviour in the purchase of services that affect competitive strategy development in service firms. Be sure to include in your discussion the differences between search, experience, and credence qualities of products.

3. What is the difference between core services and peripheral services?

4. What are some service organizations doing to increase service standardization? Are there any disadvantages in following such a strategy? If so, what are they?

5. Comment on the validity of the following statement: "Channel structures in service industries are always direct from producer to user."

6. Why is promotion such an important part of a service retailer's competitive strategy?

7. Discuss why pricing is an important element of competitive strategy for service retailers. What difficulties do service firms encounter in price setting?

8. How do present-day catalogues and their use differ from earlier catalogues? What controversial issues surround the use of direct mail as a form of non-store retailing?

9. What is in-home retailing as a form of non-store retailing? What environmental dynamics are affecting in-home retailing firms and how are these firms responding?

10. What are the advantages of telephone retailing from the perspectives of companies and consumers? What controversial issues are related to the use of telemarketing?

Application Exercises

1. Review the recent business press regarding the competition among hotel chains.
   a. What has motivated hotels to engage in price competition?
   b. Are there any negative repercussions from competing on the basis of price? If so, what are they?
   c. Is there any way a full-service hotel could maintain prices and promote its services when competitors are reducing prices and advertising price specials? Or is its only effective response to likewise lower prices?

2. Find a local direct seller in your community or by reading about that company in the library. Interview the manager of that company with respect to the following issues:
   a. What are the environmental dynamics that have negatively affected the company?
   b. What motivated the company to stay with its distribution system of direct selling rather than selling its products through stores?
   c. What are the future prospects about direct selling in this sector?

Suggested Cases

8. Diego's
10. Clean Windows Inc.
11. Donna Holtom
13. Wing and a Prayer

Notes

1. Randall Scotland, "Resurgence in Home Shopping Boosts Catalogue Sales," *The Financial Post,* March 23, 1995, p. 19; Ricardo Sookdeo, "Too Busy with Your Career," *Fortune,* June 29, 1991, p. 13.

2. M. Wagner, "Good News for the Service Economy," *Fortune,* May 3, 1993, pp. 46–52.

3. C.H. Lovelock, *Managing Services: Marketing, Operations and Human Resources,* Prentice-Hall, Englewood Cliffs, 1992.

4. L.L. Berry, *On Great Service,* Free Press, New York, 1995.

5. D.J. Showell, Jr. and J.J. Cronin, Jr., "Service Marketing Strategies for Coping with Supply/Demand Imbalances," *Journal of Services Marketing* 8, 4, 1994, pp. 14–24.

6. T.J. Levesque and G.H.G. McDougall, "Profiles of Complainers and Switchers in Retail Banking," in *Marketing* 15, ed. Brock Smith, ASAC (1994), pp. 97–106; G. LeBlanc, "The Determinants of Service Quality in Travel Agencies: An Analysis of Customer Perceptions," in *Marketing* 11, ed. John Liefeld, ASAC (1990), pp. 188–196.

7. V.A. Zeithaml, "How Consumer Evaluation Processes Differ Between Goods and Services," in *Marketing of Services,* J.H. Donnelly and W.R. George, eds., Chicago, Illinois: American Marketing Association, 1981, pp. 186–90.

8. G.H.G. McDougall and T.J. Levesque, "Benefit Segmentation Using Service Quality Dimensions: An Investigation into Retail Banking," *International Journal of Bank Marketing* 12, 2, 1994, pp. 15–23.

9. J. Partridge, "CIBC Testing Two-tier System of Branch Banking," *Globe & Mail,* January 19, 1996, pp. B1, B5.

10. L.L. Berry, V.A. Zeithaml, and A. Parasuraman, "Five Imperatives for Improving Service Quality," *Sloan Management Review,* Summer 1990, pp. 29–38.

11. For more, see B. Schneider and D.E. Bowen, *Winning the Service Game,* Harvard Business School Press, Boston, 1995.

12. C.W.L. Hart, L.A. Schlesinger, and D. Maker, "Guarantees Come to Professional Service Firms," *Sloan Management Review,* Spring 1992, pp. 19–29.

13. J. L. Heskett, W. E. Sasser, Jr., and C. W. L. Hart, *Service Breakthroughs: Changing the Rules of the Game* (Toronto: The Free Press, 1990), pp. 43, 51.

14. J. McElgunn, "Study Says Nothing Beats Word of Mouth," *Marketing,* May 1, 1995, p. 2.

15. R. E. Hite, C. Fraser, and J. A. Bellizzi, "Professional Service Advertising: The Effects of Price Inclusion, Justification, and Level of Risk," *Journal of Advertising Research,* August–September 1990, pp. 23–31.

16. K. H. Bacon, "Banks' Services Grow Costlier for Consumers," *The Wall Street Journal,* November 18, 1993, pp. B1, B12.

17. See W. J. Glyns and J. G. Barnes, eds., *Understanding Service Management,* (New York: John Wiley & Sons, 1995).

18. J. Pollock, "List of Opportunity: The Catalogue Business Looks to Its Entrepreneurs for Growth," *Marketing*, July 3/10, 1995, pp. 14–15; R. Scotland, "Resurgence in Home Shopping Boosts Catalogue Sales," *Financial Post*, March 23, 1995, p. 19; M. Lavin, "Have Contemporary Consumers Integrated Mail/Phone Order into Their Categorization of Goods and Retailers?" *Journal of Direct Marketing* 6 (Summer 1992), p. 23.

19. P. Brent, "Spiegel Lands at Canadian Doors," *Financial Post*, January 19, 1996, p. 8.

20. Brent, "Spiegel Lands at Canadian Doors"; K. Helliker, "Fashion Catalogues Focus on Consumers' Special Physical Needs," *The Wall Street Journal*, November 29, 1990, p. B1.

21. L. Mills, "From Print to Bits and Bytes," *Marketing*, May 22, 1995, p. 14.

22. M. W. Miller, " 'Greens' Add to Junk Mail Mountain," *The Wall Street Journal*, May 13, 1991, p. B1.

23. See T. R. Wotruba, "Direct Selling in the Year 2000," in *The Future of U.S. Retailing*, ed. Robert Peterson, (New York: Quorum Books, 1992), p. 188.

24. Statistics Canada, *Direct Selling in Canada, 1992*, cat. 63–218, p. 7.

25. G. Stricharchuk, "Making Money the Old-Fashioned Way: Door to Door," *The Wall Street Journal*, February 19, 1991, p. B2.

26. M.W. Miller, "When the 'Junker' Calls, This Man Is Ready for Revenge," *The Wall Street Journal*, June 24, 1991, p. A1.

27. *Telemarketing and Privacy: Are Consumers Being Exploited?* (Washington, D.C.: Direct Selling Education Foundation, August 1992), p. 5.

28. *Telemarketing and Privacy*, pp. 5 and 7.

29. D. Hopkins, "Building an Internet Presence," *Marketing*, May 29, 1995, p. 18; D. Menzies, "TD Bank opens a branch in cyberspace," *Marketing*, June 19, 1995, p. 11; J. Long, "On Line and Onside," *Marketing*, May 15, 1995, p. 16.

30. A. Kainz, "The Future of Shopping: Cyberspace meets Rodeo Drive on the Internet," *The Montreal Gazette*, January 28, 1995, p. B6; M.H. Martin, "Why the Web is Still a No-shop Zone," *Fortune*, February 5, 1996, pp. 127–128.

31. "Window on the Interactive Future," *Stores*, April 1995, pp. 57–58.

32. Kainz, "The Future of Shopping."

33. Statistics Canada, *Direct Selling in Canada, 1992*, cat. 63–218, p. 7.

Appendix A
Careers in Retailing

Retailing has been, and will continue to be, an important sector in the Canadian economic scene. Retailing offers many career opportunities for those interested in a dynamic, ever-changing field. As well, there are opportunities available for retail entrepreneurs. Budding entrepreneurs should consider the field of retailing as a likely, long-term choice for one's own business. We hasten, however, to encourage all students not to go into retailing immediately following an educational experience. We are strong believers in "making mistakes for someone else" before investing one's own capital in any business, especially retailing.

This appendix addresses the concerns of the average student who will probably go into the job market to seek a job with someone else. Consequently, the purposes of this appendix are to:

1. Focus your attention on career orientation.
2. Review the characteristics of retailing careers.
3. Stress the job skills needed to succeed in retailing.
4. Offer tangible tips on job search.
5. Offer suggestions for career planning and progress.

Students considering retailing as a career possibility may not realize where the jobs really are. Department stores, although highly visible, are just one source of entry-level opportunities. Retailing takes place in many kinds of operations—specialty stores (Future Shop), off-price (BiWay), and discount firms (Nabours); the national chains (Sears and Eaton's); national, regional, and local food organizations (Safeway, Loblaws, and Sobeys); the specialty chains (Toys "Я" Us); and many other types of firms. Students interested in retailing careers may also consider direct sellers (Mary Kay and Tupperware); shopping centre developers and managers (Cambridge); mail-order firms (Eddie Bauer); and services retailing (Century 21 and the Toronto Blue Jays). This is quite a list, though still incomplete, to add to Wal-Mart and Zellers.

The skills gained in retailing can be transferable to other fields. Retailing can be a good experience for anyone who enjoys buying and selling merchandise. If you are excited about "making your day"—seeing how well you did compared to the same day in the previous year—retailing can be a challenge.

Not everyone who studies retail management wants a career in the field. For those of you who are curious about retailing opportunities, however, this appendix can help you discover what to expect after graduation.

Career Development

Students are at various stages of career development. The continuum below suggests the degrees of career development or orientation that you may be experiencing. You probably have friends who are at each phase. A student who is "career disoriented" may not have given any thought to the future; the student may be less disoriented than unconcerned. This apparent casual attitude may seem immature, and indeed this may be the case. Career development is, after all, part of total human development:

x ——————————————————— x ——————————————————— x
Disoriented   Initial orientation   Definitive orientation

We encourage you to seek career counselling at all phases of your career development, especially when a concern about careers surfaces. Also, don't confuse "getting a job" with "career development." We suspect that a great deal of early attrition in first jobs results from both a desire to get a job simply to earn money and uncertainty about a career. A job without a career direction is likely to prove unsuccessful in the long run.

The following sections offer information on careers in retailing and in general to assist you in finding the right direction for your career.

Characteristics of Retailing Careers

Employment in retailing exceeds 1.4 million people in Canada. The diversity of opportunities is staggering and can fulfill almost every kind of ability, ambition, and desire. Retail establishments are located in the smallest rural village and the most sophisticated metropolitan area.

Security

Security in a job is important to many people. Traditionally, even during periods of economic stagnation, retailing usually suffers fewer employment declines than manufacturing or wholesaling. Consumers must continue to buy goods and services regardless of the state of the economy. However, in the wake of the recession of the early 1990s, the low growth of the Canadian economy and the number of retail bankruptcies, job security is less certain than in the past.

Decentralized job opportunities

No matter where they live, people must purchase goods and services on a regular basis to maintain their standards of living. This means you can have a successful career in retailing even if you do not want to move far from home. On the other hand, people who want to move frequently can find the opportunity for employment in retailing wherever they go.

Opportunities for advancement

Many executive positions exist because of the large number of retail establishments in Canada. Even in a low-growth economy, successful retailers continue to expand, and positions in management are created in these firms.

Reward for performance and entrepreneurship

Retailing offers a daily performance measure because sales and profits can be evaluated daily. For high performers, such tangible measures are a delight; for the non-performers, each day is painful. Obviously, not everyone is right for retailing (and the same can be said for all career options). A graduate who performs may become a buyer for a high-dollar-volume department in a large department-store organization within two or three years. As a buyer responsible for producing a profit in the department, such an achiever will really be acting as an entrepreneur in the security of an established firm.

Salaries in retailing

Starting salaries for graduates entering retail training programs vary widely—from $17,000 to $30,000 annually. The contrast in starting salaries reflects the variation in training programs, location, cost of living, and the competitive market for trainees.

Non-monetary rewards

A person's ability and effort—or their absence—are quickly recognized in retailing. The position of store manager appeals to people with the ability to organize and direct the activities of others. As store manager, you set your own sales and profit goals as well as control expenses, compensate employees, and perform other vital management functions. In effect, you have the opportunity to manage your own business with someone else's money. A management career in retailing also offers the opportunity to work with ideas. Managers create ways of increasing sales and profit through imaginative use of the retail mix.

Job Skills in Demand

Mention retailing and many people think of selling or working as a cashier. Yet these positions make up only a small portion of total job opportunities. Consider the need for fashion experts, accountants, advertising and personnel specialists, market researchers, and lawyers. Go even further and think in terms of public relations, engineering, data processing, real estate analysis, and physical distribution. Think beyond the people you typically see when making purchases. Visualize the complex organization behind most retail outlets. Consider the increasing role of technology, which has opened up career opportunities that simply didn't exist a few years ago. Retailing is indeed high tech.

Tangible Career Tips

For this discussion to be meaningful, we must assume that you have moved along the career orientation continuum to at least the initial orientation phase. We also want to note here that this section is rather "generic." We think the tips herein are valuable even if retailing is not your career objective.

Job search plan

We urge you to develop a job-search plan; Exhibit A–1 provides a seven-step plan.

Exhibit A–1   Job Search Plan

Here are seven steps that will help in your job search.

1. **Who Am I Really?**
   If you do not know where you are going, any road will take you there. In a job search, it is crucial to determine what you want from a position, as well as what you have to offer an employer, before you take any other steps. To do this, remove all labels (e.g., Teacher, Psych Grad, Music Major) and, instead, examine the skills you have acquired from past experiences, the interests and values you possess, how your personality might fit in with the position and organization, and your preferred working environment. Only after you have developed a list of your abilities and needs should you start looking for employment.

2. **The Paper Chase**
   With your self-assessment completed, you should have a range of prospective areas to investigate; the idea here is to find the environments that would offer conditions similar to those you have identified as "ideal." It is most important, at this stage, to start with a sense of what you want to *do*, rather than what you want to *be*. You will have more scope and depth to your search, and more options from which to choose.

   Now, begin your research—use libraries and your school's career placement office to learn about the occupations and companies that are of interest to you. When you have zeroed in on some possible career choices, information on the companies you might like to work for can be found in business magazines, annual reports, newspaper articles, and directories.

3. **Getting First-Hand Knowledge**
   Although some very good, basic information can be gleaned from libraries (written, video, and audio materials), the most valuable information comes from talking to people. Meeting with people who are in the field or occupation that interests you can provide information on the advantages and drawbacks to the field, the type of entry-level positions and who offers them, and inside "tips" on how to get started in the field.

4. **Preparing to Job Search**
   If you really dislike the thought of looking for work, you are not alone. Job search is hard work; it's a full-time job. In many ways, it's a gamble. Therefore, we need to learn how to improve our odds and take control of the parts we can control. There will be rejection, so build it into your plan—expect it, so it doesn't catch you off guard. Perseverance is critical to move you, step by step, closer to that YES. Be positive and realistic. Two books that can help with this phase are:

   - *What Color Is Your Parachute,* by R. N. Bolles.
   - *Guerilla Tactics in the New Job Market,* by Tom Jackson.

Questions to ask in an interview

If you really want the job, you ask probing, intelligent questions. The following questions are suggested:

How was this position created?

Will I be able to work with the person I am replacing?

What kind of training will be provided?

How much responsibility will I be given in this position?

What is the first task I would be undertaking?

Does the company promote from within?

Can you tell me about the organization's training policies/incentives?

In your opinion, what is the most difficult part of this job?

How would you describe the work atmosphere in this organization?

What do you like about working here?

Does the company have any plans for expansion?

Exhibit A–1   (Concluded)

Finally, a very important tool in conducting a successful job search is a well-prepared resume and cover letter. A good resume and cover letter probably will not get you a job, but they could lead you to the most important phase—the job interview (see Exhibit A–2 for an example of a resume).

5. Looking for Work
The three main techniques in looking for work are reactive, online, and proactive. Reactive job search strategies target positions that are advertised in some form. The job opening exists, and job seekers respond to the request for applications. Online computer search strategies use the Internet to identify employment opportunities and job postings. Finally, a proactive job search strategy involves contacting firms that you think best suit your skills and experience and where hiring opportunities may exist. The outcome of step 5 is an interview (see Exhibit A–3).

6. Follow-Up
An organized follow-up program is essential to a successful job search. Always keep a detailed log, recording all information in one place so you can easily monitor the process of your search. Make note of each time you contact an employer and flag each organization for future contact. Follow-up is critical in a number of situations:

- After an informational interview, always send a thank-you note.
- After submitting a resume or broadcast letter, follow up with a telephone call 7–10 days later.
- After a job interview, it is wise to write a brief follow-up letter expressing your pleasure at having had the opportunity to meet with the interviewer(s). Refer to some topic of interest discussed during the interview, and reiterate your interest in the position/organization.
- After receiving a rejection letter, contact the employer to indicate your desire to be considered for future positions. Also ask for feedback on your interview presentation and your qualifications, as well as advice on your job search.

7. The Job Offer
Your creativity, perseverance, determination, and efforts have finally paid off—you receive one or more job offers. Take some time to analyze whether or not accepting this job is the best move for you. Does this position meet most of the needs you addressed in your original self-assessment? If not, have your priorities changed, or should you reject this offer? Can you realistically expect to find something that better meets your needs in an acceptable time frame? This is a major decision for you, so take some time to reflect before saying yes or no.

Source: *Job Search,* Wilfrid Laurier University, Career Services, booklet.

Have a good, up-to-date résumé

Check with the placement office for ideas, but above all, make sure that the resume is neat, has no spelling errors, and points out your skills and work-related background. Focus on the jobs you have held and on your skills, talents, and interests. Exhibit A–2 shows you the organization of a typical resume for a person in college seeking retailing employment. Exhibit A–3 provides some ideas on the job interview, and other useful tips are found in Exhibit A–4—the interview "dos and don'ts," presented along with typical interview questions to contemplate in the job interviewing process.

Training Programs and Career Paths

Thus far, the appendix has focussed on career orientation, the characteristics of retailing careers, the job skills needed to succeed in retailing, and some generic, tangible career tips. This concluding section is concerned with training programmes and career paths.

Exhibit A–2   Example of a Résumé

Julie K. Ashman
215 Old Post Road
Prairie City, Saskatchewan
S4S 0K7
(306) 588-1234

HIGHLIGHTS OF QUALIFICATIONS

- Served two years on Board of Directors for U. of P. Students' Union
- Attentive to detail, with strong analytical skills
- Able to work effectively with a wide variety of people

EDUCATION

Bachelor of Business Administration, The University of the Prairies, Prairie City, Saskatchewan (199_–199_)
Relevant Courses: Retailing, Industrial Marketing, Marketing Strategy

RELATED EXPERIENCE

Small Business Consultant, Small Business Consulting Services, The University of the Prairies, Prairie City, Saskatchewan (Summer 199_, Part-time 199_–199_)

- Designed, administered, and analyzed market research survey for two retail stores
- Developed an advertising plan for a small manufacturer
- Performed a feasibility study for a restaurant
- Interviewed prospective clients and prepared written reports
- Presented a seminar to a group of local citizens

Sales Clerk, Stereo Warehouse, Regina, Saskatchewan (Summer 199_, Part-time 199_–199_)

- Received two awards for outstanding monthly sales
- Provided customers with comparative technical information about television and stereo components
- Corresponded with suppliers and other dealers in the chain

OTHER EXPERIENCE

Cashier, J and L Supermarket, Regina, Saskatchewan (Summers and part-time, 199_–199)

- Operated computerized cash register

UNIVERSITY ACHIEVEMENTS

Student Senator (199_–199_)

- Participated in decisions related to academic policies

Member, Varsity Ski Team (199_–199_)

- Attended regular practices and entered annual slalom races

SKILLS

Software: WordPerfect, Lotus 1-2-3, Quattro Pro, CorelDraw
Languages Spoken: English, French

REFERENCES

Available upon request.

Exhibit A–3   The Job Interview

The job interview is critical as it is the final stage in the job search process. It is a time during which both you and the employer are exchanging information relating to employment, and it requires both interpersonal and information presentation skills.

The interview should meet *your* objectives to:

1. Market your transferable skills, experience, interests, and personality to meet the requirements of the employer.
2. Assess the appropriateness of the position and the employer in relation to your career goals.

It should also meet the *interviewer's* objectives to:

1. Assess the knowledge, abilities, self-confidence, motivation, initiative, teamwork, and communications skills you possess to fulfill the employment needs of the organization.
2. Promote his/her organization to you, the applicant.

To prepare for the interview, first, you need to research yourself (know your abilities, interests, goals, skills, experience, and personality and your strengths and weaknesses in each of these areas). Second, you need to be informed about the occupation you are interested in; and third, you need to research the organization you are interviewing (products and services offered, history, future plans, etc.).

In the interview, you should present information in a coherent, sequenced, and dynamic manner. In preparation, decide what information you want your interviewer(s) to have about you at the close of the interview. Plan your comments and examples accordingly. As questions are asked, you can respond using this material.

Source: *The Interview,* Wilfrid Laurier University, Career Services, booklet.

Training programmes

Training programmes involve rotation among the various departments/ functions within a firm until the trainee is familiar with the operations. Programmes vary in detail and reflect the philosophy of the particular retail organization.

Career paths

A career path can be thought of as the route taken within a particular company. The progression through a retailing organization depends at least in part on the organizational structure. For example, in a highly centralized structure, more executive-level opportunities exist in the corporate or division headquarters. In a more decentralized operation, where most of the necessary functions are at the local level, additional opportunities may exist in the individual stores.

A career path can also be viewed as a life-time pattern of advancement. This longer time frame will undoubtedly involve multiple organizations, different industries, and apparent total changes in direction.

Exhibit A–4   Interview Dos and Don'ts

Ninety-nine out of 100 bright-as-a-penny candidates who are wearing their best dressed-for-success outfits and have all the credentials necessary to impress St. Peter at the gate of heaven won't make the effort necessary to answer the following typical interview questions:

- How did you happen to select X as a career choice?
- What are the qualities necessary for success in X?
- What do you consider your chief strengths in this profession?
- What are some of the weaknesses that might hinder your success?
- Why should we hire you rather than one of your equally competent classmates?
- What are your long-term career objectives at this point?
- Why do you think you would like to work for our company?

There is no way you can answer these questions without also revealing whether or not you have done your homework about yourself, your career decisions, and the company.

Do:

- Anticipate probing questions about any obviously difficult career episode on your résumé, such as a job briefly held or a summer job that did not result in a permanent offer.
- Control your desire to run the interview. Instead, concentrate on adopting a pleasant and cordial tone throughout.
- Be succinct.

Don't:

- Oversell and make promises you will live to regret once you are actually on the job.
- Project a self-centered perspective, such as "What's in this for me?"
- Be negative about any employer or company. Don't blame others in the course of explaining situations.

Allan Sarn, an executive search consultant who sees the mistakes that experienced candidates make while interviewing for executive jobs, emphasizes that candidates must know the following about the company before an interview:

- The dollar volume of the company's annual business.
- The number of employees who work for the company.
- The products manufactured or services provided by the company.
- The names of the top executives in the company.
- The scope of the business—whether domestic or international.
- The general content of the company's most recent annual report as well as information contained in major articles written about the company.

Source: Reprinted from the Spring/Summer 1984 issue of *Business Week's Guide to Careers* by special permission. © 1984 by McGraw-Hill, Inc. All rights reserved.

Conclusions

We do not believe it is our role to sell you on a retailing career. We have presented information for you to think about. Retailing career paths are rather definite and understandable, and can result in high-level performance for the right person. Retailing offers many excellent training programs. Evaluate them in terms of your own career aspirations. Consider retailing as a career possibility—we ask no more.

Cases

1. Videofile

Ms. Alice Chaffe, the owner of Videofile, an independent video rental store located in a neighbourhood shopping plaza, was deeply concerned. She had just received a call from Murray Blain, the owner of another neighbourhood video store about 3 kilometres away. Mr. Blain told her he was closing his store. "I can't make a go of it," he told Ms. Chaffe. "My customers are all going to the superstores like Jumbo and Blockbuster. I'm renting less than 20 movies a day." He finished the conversation by wishing her luck. "I'll need it," Alice thought to herself. "I'm doing better than Murray, but not by much." Alice had opened the store in early 1985 to cash in on the rapidly growing video rental market. However, in the past year or two, the market had changed significantly and competition had increased. Sales at Videofile had been declining and Alice wondered if there was still room in this dynamic market for a neighbourhood video store.

Video Industry in Canada

The market for video rentals developed as an offshoot of the videocassette recorder (VCR) market. Since 1980, the number of households owning VCRs—and, so, in a position to rent videos—has escalated from approximately 45,000 in 1980 to about 7.8 million in 1996. This represents about 84 percent of all the households in Canada. Until recently, growth in video rentals had paralleled VCR sales. Typically, nearly 60 percent of a VCR's user-time was spent playing rented videos. Surveys had indicated that VCR households rented an average of about two videos per week. However, in the past two years, total revenues from video rentals had actually declined in North America, due in part to the increase in the pay-per-view market offered by cable companies, and an increase in sales of videos.

The Video Business

Ms. Chaffe reflected on the changes that had occurred in the business since she began operations in 1985. The most common type of video store at that time was like hers—neighbourhood video stores that were located in strip malls. Her store was located in such a mall, which included a supermarket, hairdresser, bank, pizza take-out, convenience store, and laundromat. Her customer base was the immediate neighbourhood. Typically, people would rent a movie on their way home from work and return it the following day.

While many competitors entered the market—including major department stores like Eaton's and, on the other extreme, gas stations—her major competition was the convenience store in the mall that introduced video rentals in 1986 and other neighbourhood stores (the closest being her competitor who had just closed).

Source: This case was prepared by Arlene Bennett and Gordon McDougall, Wilfrid Laurier University.

However, in 1987 the market changed significantly. The first superstore in the area, Rogers Video, opened five kilometres away. Rogers Video was one of the first operations to begin franchising on a regional—then a national—basis. Rogers carried a wide range of titles and benefited from economies of scale (mass media advertising, quantity discounts on movie purchases), expertise in store/ strategy development, and convenience to customers (drop-off of videos at any location). Efficiencies were also gained through computerized inventory systems.

If that wasn't enough, in early 1988, Jumbo Video, another developing national chain, opened a store just six blocks from her location in another strip mall. Then in late 1994, Blockbuster Video opened a store 10 blocks away (in the opposite direction from the Jumbo Video store). Now she faced two video superstores, both in close proximity to her store.

Both Blockbuster and Jumbo were large (approximately 740 square metres) and stocked over 5,000 titles. Jumbo was open 24 hours a day; Blockbuster was open 14 hours a day.

These superstores used free membership cards to keep track of customers and their rentals. They also used economies of scale and efficiency through computerization to keep their costs down.

A further threat was new technologies: CD-ROMs, special compact discs, and other new formats that were supposed to be the wave of the future. As one example, fibre-optic technology allowed consumers to order pay-per-view movies at the time they wanted to see them. While some experts saw this trend as happening in the next few years, other experts saw it as not happening for 5 to 10 years.

Recent Trends

When Alice returned home that night, she mentioned the closing of Mr. Blain's store to her husband, Jack, a plant manager for a metal fabrication factory. Jack had encouraged her to go into the business and had a continuing interest in the progress of the store. He responded, "Maybe you should think about the future of the store. Last weekend I made some notes on the articles I found on the video business. Let me read some of them." With that, Jack began reading his notes, which included the following comments about the video industry.

- The neighbourhood stores are being squeezed on the one hand by the big chains and on the other hand by convenience stores and gas stations that rent videos as a sideline. It is estimated that Canada has between 4,500 and 5,000 video outlets, most of them small "mom-and-pop" stores like Videofile. However, if all stores that rent videos are included, somewhere between 18,000 and 30,000 stores of one kind or another rent videos. The top 10 chains in Canada, including Blockbuster, Jumbo, and Rogers, have about 25 percent of the total market share.

- The video rental industry is in transition. Up until about 1991 it was dominated by unsophisticated operators. Since then there has been a consolidation of the market. Many "mom-and-pop" stores are going out of business, the video chains are increasing their market share, and the largest chains are now advertising. The industry is changing to larger stores, larger selections, and more convenient hours.

- Another major change that is occurring is the increase in sales of videos as opposed to rentals. Estimated at $320 million, or 20 percent of the total Canadian video market, video sales were made primarily by department stores like Zellers and the large video chains.

- Video store rentals have flattened due to the increase in pay-per-view films being offered by cable companies and because the price of buying the popular videocassettes (e.g., the "blockbuster" movies) has dropped sharply, from a regular price of $89.95 a few years ago to less than $20 today. The majority of movies were priced at around $30.

- The strategies of the large chains are changing to reflect the new environment. For example, Blockbuster Video is devoting less space to video movie rentals and more space to video game rentals, video sales, and other entertainment products, including audio books, compact disks, film merchandise, relaxation tapes, and computer software. Other chains are rearranging their space to make their stores more entertaining.

Jack paused for a moment, then said, "That's the bad news. But some people see some hope for the independent." With that, he read the following notes:

- Some customers who switched from the neighbourhood to the superstores are returning and willing to pay higher prices for better service. These customers are overwhelmed by the size of the superstores and they can't find anything. As well, they may be willing to drive four or five miles to get a video, but they are not keen about returning them. Also, the superstores may advertise a large selection, but most of their titles are "B" movies or "C minus" movies that are low quality, "straight-to-video" movies, and customers quickly become disappointed.

- The key for the independent operator to keep a strong customer base is a knowledgeable sales staff and personalized service—service with a smile.

Alice reflected on the comments and then responded, "I'm going to take a close look at what I offer versus Jumbo and Blockbuster. Let's talk about this again tomorrow night."

The current situation

The next day, Alice prepared a sheet listing the major characteristics of Videofile, Jumbo, and Blockbuster (Exhibit 1). She then did some rough calculations on her costs and revenues.

Videofile had 1,800 members, although many were inactive—they had not rented a movie in the past six months. Videofile was open 75 hours a week, and Alice worked 40 of those hours and had part-time help whom she paid $8 an hour to cover the remaining hours. While the cost per movie varied, she calculated she bought three new movies a week at an average price of $25. Occasionally, a discount of 15 percent was offered if a video store purchased six copies of a new movie. Alice had never purchased more than two copies of any movie. She estimated that total monthly fixed costs including rent, insurance, and so on were $500.

Alice then looked at her sales for the last two months. She found that she had rented an average of 40 movies a day at $2.50. As well, the rental of VCRs

Exhibit 1 Profile on Videofile, Jumbo Video, and Blockbuster Video

	Videofile	Jumbo Video	Blockbuster Video
Hours	Mon.–Sat., 10:00 A.M. – 9:00 P.M. Sunday, noon – 9:00 P.M.	Open 24 hours	Daily, 10:00 A.M. – midnight
Rental rates	$2.99/day Classics $1.49/day Children's $1.99/day	$2.99/day Children's and "specials" $.99/day $3.99 for three-day rental	Hot new arrivals $3.99/day New arrivals $3.79/day Special Interest $1.99/day Kids $.99/day
VCR rentals	$4.99/day	$4.99/day	$9.99/day
Video game rentals	$2.99/day	$.99 to $2.99/day	$3.99/day
Video game cartridge rentals	$3.99/day	$2.99/day	$6.99/day
Membership	Free	Free	Free
Number of movies available	2,000	Thousands	Thousands
Physical size	5.5m × 9.1m	21.3m × 21.3m	21.3m × 27.4m
Other Features/ Services	Reservations Small selection of snack foods	Free popcorn Camcorders for rent ($19.99/day) Snack foods and drinks Movies for sale Blank tapes, posters for sale	Selection of snack foods, drinks Movies for sale CDs for sale Blank tapes, posters for sale

(she had six in stock) added another $500 a month to her revenues. "If I pay myself $8 an hour, this store is barely breaking even," she thought.

The Future

That night, she showed Jack her analysis. "Maybe I should get out before things get worse," she said. "Before you do that," said Jack, "let's look at all the options, then decide." With that, they did some brainstorming and listed a number of ideas that included the following:

- Video rental stores compete on the basis of convenience, service, selection, and price. Convenience includes store hours, location, parking, and store layout. Service includes the attitude of the staff, their knowledge of the movies (and customers), a reservation policy, and when movies are returned. Selection includes the number and quality of titles and the availability of a movie on a particular night. Pricing includes the price of the movie on a weekday or weekend and whether it is a new release, older movie, or a children's movie.

- With price, a number of further options exist, including selling coupons for movies, a monthly price that would allow a customer 30 movies for the month, and reduced prices for older movies. As well, prices could be varied during the week (weekends are more popular for renting movies than Monday through Thursday).

- With promotion, options include mailings to customers, signs within the store, neighbourhood pamphlets, and temporary signs.

- With product, options include selling the older movies at reduced prices, considering new product lines (compact discs, VCRs, other accessories, and snacks, and selling new movies).

After they generated the list, Alice and Jack agreed to think about it for a day and make the decision the next night. As Alice turned out the lights, she thought, "I really want to make a go of this, but I'm not sure. There must be something I can do to turn this around and make it a viable operation."

Questions

1. **What further changes, if any, will take place in the video rental market?**
2. **Recommend a strategy for Ms. Chaffe, assuming she plans to stay in the business.**
3. **Should Ms. Chaffe stay in the business?**

2. Retailing Newswatch

Choose an article from a business magazine that addresses a topic/event/issue of importance to retail management. The topics can be wide-ranging, but *must* be related in some way to the *practice* of retail management.

The article must have been published over the last two years. Likely sources for the articles include the following:

Business Week	*Globe & Mail*
Business Quarterly	*Harvard Business Review*
Canadian Business	*Marketing*
Financial Post	*Marketing and Media Decisions*
Forbes	*Marketing News*
Fortune	*Report on Business Magazine*

There are *many* possibilities for topics: profiles of retailing entrepreneurs, shopping malls, warehouse retailers, box-stores, Canadian retailers in the United States, U.S. retailers in Canada, strategic and operational analysis of a retailing operation (e.g., Wal-Mart, Zellers, The Bay, Canadian Tire, McDonald's, etc.), Sunday shopping, cross-border shopping, auxiliary services, universal product code, display/merchandising techniques (e.g., planograms), home shopping, shrinkage, retailing and the Internet, and so on. You may also know of some issues in finance, accounting, industrial relations, or MIS that have a bearing on retail management. The more wide-ranging the topics, the greater the contribution to the class!

Your Task

1. Sign up for a presentation date.
2. Choose one article, as described above.

Source: This application was prepared by Rosemary Polegato, Saint Francis Xavier University.

3. Prepare a 10-minute presentation on the content of the article *and* on the implications for retail management.

4. *Five days before your presentation,* please deliver to the instructor a legible copy of the article.

5. Have fun choosing your topic and figuring out what it's all about!

3. Canadian Lifestyles

Compusearch, a Canadian market research firm, has evaluated over 200 different demographic and socio-economic variables and, by clustering neighbourhoods, has isolated 10 major urban groups and three major rural groups. The percentage of Canadian households by province in each of these lifestyles and the lifestyle definitions are contained in Tables 1 and 2.

Table 1 Canadian Lifestyles—1995											
Percentage of Households, by Province											
	Canada	**Nfld.**	**P.E.I.**	**N.S.**	**N.B.**	**Que.**	**Ont.**	**Man.**	**Sask.**	**Alta.**	**B.C.**
Affluent	2.01	.34	.05	.73	.36	1.34	2.84	1.33	.98	4.05	1.00
Upscale	8.78	4.36	2.86	4.17	2.19	5.26	13.07	7.22	5.11	10.39	7.20
Middle class	18.80	11.79	7.61	11.48	13.74	20.10	20.35	15.08	12.48	19.10	18.81
Working class	14.77	17.50	18.78	22.94	17.87	20.71	11.10	8.05	8.86	14.42	14.31
Lower income	5.89	1.47	3.44	3.18	3.82	7.74	6.22	6.49	4.27	4.06	4.58
Older and retired	4.28	1.41	3.53	1.56	1.78	3.78	4.80	4.60	2.51	1.60	7.73
Empty nesters	9.68	5.36	8.55	9.00	6.98	6.11	11.18	14.40	9.36	8.36	13.80
Young singles	4.46	.07	.64	2.73	1.34	4.01	3.37	4.84	5.58	8.11	7.39
Young couples	4.23	.58	.00	2.24	.80	6.86	3.80	3.93	1.26	3.42	3.46
Ethnics	2.45	.00	.00	.21	.00	1.14	4.94	.62	.21	.42	2.06
Rural upscale and middle class	9.86	6.91	10.79	11.41	8.27	5.68	10.25	10.50	14.66	14.66	11.50
Rural working class	11.91	48.57	38.32	29.20	42.30	15.99	5.78	14.77	19.22	4.99	6.98
Farming	1.96	.65	4.17	.52	.20	.64	1.31	7.11	14.51	4.92	.25
Other	.93	.99	1.27	.64	.36	.67	.99	1.01	1.01	1.49	.92
Total	100.00	100.00	100.00	100.00	100.00	100.00	100.00	100.00	100.00	100.00	100.00
Total number of households ('000)	10,625	182	46	338	266	2,768	3,927	416	364	969	1,349

Source: "Canadian Markets 1995," *Financial Post,* 1995.

Questions

Provide examples, by analyzing the data, as to how this lifestyle information can be useful for retailers in the following situations:

- **A regional chain of clothing stores, carrying mid-range prices, wishing to go national.**

- A successful sporting goods store in Toronto targeting upper-income households wants to expand to another province.

- A franchise concept that plans to market lower-priced home furnishings wants to rank the provinces in terms of attractiveness.

- A Nova Scotia home improvement centre targeting households with incomes under $30,000 wants to expand into other provinces.

Table 2   Definitions of Canadian Lifestyles

Affluent—Extremely wealthy, highly educated households living in exclusive neighbourhoods; parents mostly over 35 years of age with teenaged children; average household income, $128,000.

Upscale—Wealthy, well educated, middle-age families with school-aged children living in expensive, single detached houses. Average household income, $71,600 to $84,800.

Middle (and upper-middle) class—Families with children living in suburban single detached houses, moderate education level, and average household income of $50,200 to $61,400.

Working class—Families with children, often living in rented multiple dwellings, generally working in blue-collar jobs; average household income of $37,100 to $45,100.

Lower income—Low education level and average household income of $18,600 to $39,900 (a high percentage of income comes from government transfer payments), young households with blue-collar or low-level white-collar positions in rental units, higher than average unemployment rate.

Older and retired—Older couples and widow(er)s living in condominiums and high-rise apartments; low education levels and a wide range of incomes from $15,400 to $41,800.

Empty nesters—Husband-and-wife families over 55 years of age whose children have left home; wide range of incomes and types of dwellings. Average income, $50,500.

Young singles—Highly mobile young one- or two-person households in rented dwellings. Highly educated with a wide range of incomes averaging $27,100; many working women.

Young couples—Young two-person households in rental high-rise accommodation; usually both members employed and average household income of $35,700.

Ethnics—Large ethnic families whose primary language is neither English nor French; low education, wide range of incomes averaging $47,000, and many blue-collar workers.

Rural upscale and middle class—Large families with young children, above average incomes for small urban and rural areas, primarily white-collar positions. Equivalent of Affluent, Upscale, and Middle class living in a more rural setting. Average household income, $47,200.

Rural working class—Large households with children, below average income, living in older inexpensive single detached houses. Low mobility households with much-below-average education levels. Average household income, $34,000.

Farming—Households whose primary source of income is agriculture. Large families with children, middle-aged and older parents, living in older single detached farm houses. Farmers with a wide range of household incomes from $30,700 to $66,600.

Source: "Canadian Markets 1995," *Financial Post,* 1995.

4. Canadian Population, Household, and Retail Sales Trends

An important aspect of retailing is to determine the future implications of population and household trends. The four tables that follow provide past and future data on the Canadian population by age group, by geographic area, and by household and retail sales by region.

Table 1	Population, Actual and Projected by Age Group 1951–2011 (Thousands)						
Year	Population	9 and Under	10–19	20–34	35–49	50–64	65 & Over
Actual							
1951	14,010	3,120	2,190	3,260	2,610	1,740	1,090
1956	16,080	3,790	2,600	3,540	3,020	1,890	1,240
1961	18,240	4,340	3,290	3,670	3,400	2,150	1,390
1966	20,020	4,500	3,930	3,950	3,630	2,470	1,540
1971	21,570	4,070	4,420	4,790	3,760	2,780	1,750
1976	22,990	3,620	4,620	5,760	3,850	3,140	2,000
1981	24,340	3,560	4,240	6,560	4,220	3,400	2,360
1986	25,600	3,630	3,730	6,940	4,980	3,590	2,730
1991	26,610	3,570	3,610	6,750	5,820	3,690	3,170
1996E	29,880	3,980	4,030	6,840	7,170	4,200	3,660
Projections							
2001	31,360	3,770	4,210	6,570	7,770	5,070	3,970
2006	32,510	3,480	4,240	6,620	7,800	6,050	4,320
2011	33,420	3,400	3,990	6,780	7,430	7,000	4,820

Source: Statistics Canada, *Marketing Research Handbook,* Catalogue 63-224, various years. Projections based on moderate fertility rates, average net international migration, and a migration flow within Canada that partially reflects the late 1960s pattern.

Table 2	Population, Actual and Projected by Geographic Area 1951–2011 (Thousands)					
Year	Total Population	Maritime Provinces	Quebec	Ontario	Prairie Provinces	B.C. & Yukon/N.W.T.
Actual						
1951	14,010	1,620	4,050	4,600	2,550	1,190
1956	16,080	1,760	4,630	5,410	2,850	1,430
1961	18,240	1,900	5,260	6,230	3,180	1,670
1966	20,020	1,980	5,780	6,960	3,380	1,920
1971	21,570	2,060	6,030	7,700	3,540	2,240
1976	22,990	2,180	6,240	8,260	3,780	2,530
1981	24,340	2,230	6,440	8,630	4,230	2,810
1986	25,600	2,320	6,630	9,110	4,510	3,030
1991	26,610	2,360	6,750	9,410	4,800	3,290
1996E	29,880	2,410	7,400	11,270	4,910	3,890
Projections						
2001	31,360	2,410	7,620	12,030	5,070	4,230
2006	32,510	2,410	7,760	12,660	5,200	4,480
2011	33,420	2,360	7,840	13,210	5,310	4,700

Source: Statistics Canada, *Marketing Research Handbook,* Catalogue 63–224, various years. Projections based on moderate fertility rates, average net international migration, and a migration flow within Canada that partially reflects the late 1960s pattern.

Table 3 Households, Actual and Projected by Geographic Area 1966–2011 (Thousands)

Year	Total Households	Maritime Provinces	Quebec	Ontario	Prairie Provinces	B.C. & Yukon/N.W.T.
Actual						
1966	5,180	450	1,390	1,880	910	550
1971	6,030	500	1,600	2,230	1,020	680
1976	7,170	600	1,900	2,640	1,190	840
1981	8,280	670	2,170	2,970	1,450	1,020
1986	9,220	750	2,340	3,430	1,590	1,110
1991	10,110	820	2,510	3,780	1,760	1,240
1996E	10,500	840	2,690	3,890	1,750	1,330
Projections						
2001	11,100	880	2,830	4,170	1,820	1,400
2006	11,650	910	2,960	4,420	1,890	1,470
2011	12,130	940	3,050	4,660	1,960	1,520

Note: Households include: single-detached, single-attached, apartments and flats, and mobile homes.

Source: Statistics Canada, *Marketing Research Handbook,* Catalogue 63–224, various years. Projections based on moderate fertility rates, average net international migration, and a migration flow within Canada that partially reflects the late 1960s pattern.

Table 4 Retail Sales, by Geographic Area 1951–2000 ($ millions)

Year	Total Retail Sales	Maritime Provinces	Quebec	Ontario	Prairie Provinces	B.C. & Yukon/N.W.T.
Actual						
1951	10,693	898	2,443	4,130	2,122	1,100
1956	14,774	1,209	3,463	5,734	2,728	1,640
1961	16,073	1,380	4,108	6,207	2,774	1,604
1966	22,678	1,861	5,881	8,621	3,810	2,505
1971	30,660	2,533	7,682	11,883	4,929	3,633
1976	58,468	4,795	14,529	21,629	10,522	6,993
1981	92,821	7,098	22,578	32,428	18,248	12,469
1986	138,131	11,084	34,246	53,054	23,967	15,780
1991	213,975	16,324	53,971	83,110	34,101	26,469
1996E	224,078	15,652	53,984	81,173	36,840	36,429
Projections						
2000	270,306	18,653	64,307	101,290	43,946	42,110

Note: Data for the 1951 and 1956 years are not strictly comparable with data for later years.

Source: Statistics Canada, *Canadian Statistical Review,* Catalogue 11–003, various years and "Survey of Markets," *Financial Post,* various years.

Questions

1. **Analyze the tables and prepare a discussion on the retailing implications for the decade from 1996 to 2006. Contrast these changes with those that occurred in the decade from 1986 to 1996.**

2. **Between now and 2001 which retail sectors should experience the greatest growth? The least growth? Why?**

5. Buying an Oriental Rug

Janet Gordon was admiring her three new rugs and feeling a little bit guilty at spending so much money. Trying to understand these mixed emotions and her own behaviour, she looked back at the events of the past few weeks.

Janet, a recent university graduate, is employed as a computer programmer in Calgary. Soon after she started working, she married John Gordon, a young production supervisor. They bought a small older house in a well-maintained neighbourhood about two kilometres from the city centre. Shortly after moving in they felt the need to do some decorating. They bought some traditional style furniture, but Janet thought the rooms felt empty without rugs. She remembered that her parents had wall-to-wall solid colour carpets, and how she came to dislike them. Janet also remembered the neighbours' house, and how the furniture was enhanced by the use of patterned rugs. Looking for ideas in home magazines, she kept noticing the use of patterned rugs in the decorating ideas presented in the articles and advertisements.

During her lunch hour, she visited the rug department in a leading department store. She was quickly overwhelmed by the quantity and variety of rugs displayed on the floor. She had some trouble lifting them up, and no salesperson was available to offer assistance. Confused about what to do, she left the department store. On her way back to the office, she passed by Ali Baba, a small store specializing in patterned rugs. A sign on the window advertising "One-Third Off" attracted her attention. She decided to take a look inside and was met by the store owner, who asked what she was looking for. In the ensuing discussion, she learned that there were a variety of rugs of different quality and prices. Some were machine made and tended to be cheaper, while others were hand-made in various countries such as Iran (Persian rugs), Pakistan, India, Turkey, China, and Morocco. Some were made of pure wool, others (more expensive) of silk, and others were blends. As the time was passing quickly and the owner kept pressuring her to buy, Janet said that she needed to talk to her husband, and went back to the office.

In the afternoon she had trouble remembering and trying to sort out all the information the store owner had provided. That evening she related her experiences to her husband. They agreed that a patterned rug would be nice in the dining and living rooms, but that they had to be careful about their finances since they were carrying a large mortgage, and still paying for the furniture. They also found it difficult to decide on a particular design. They decided to postpone the decision.

Janet realized that she was talking more and more to her friends and colleagues about decorating with rugs and noticing ads about them in the newspaper and magazines. The following Saturday, they were invited to dinner at the home of John's boss. As they arrived, they immediately noticed that all the rugs in the house were beautiful Bokharas. They found out later that the rugs were from Pakistan. The following week Janet talked to two friends who seemed knowledgeable about decorating, read articles in magazines about oriental rugs, and compared prices in newspaper ads. She noticed that the department store she had previously visited was having a one-third sale beginning the following Saturday. Janet and John decided to see what was on sale.

Source: This case was prepared by Anne H. Laroche.

On Saturday morning, they went to the store and noticed that the rug department was very busy. This time a young clerk offered some help and was able to answer most of their questions. Both he and John were able to lift the rugs, so that all of a rug could be seen for its effect. At one point, he left for a minute and came back with the department manager, Mr. Barton. The manager was much more at ease discussing the advantages and prices of different types of rugs. After asking a few questions about their furnishings and decor, Mr. Barton asked them where they lived and realized that they were neighbours. He suggested that the simplest thing would be for him to bring a few rugs over to their house so that they could see what style and size of rug would do best.

On the following Monday evening, Mr. Barton arrived at their house with several rugs. Both Janet and John were impressed with Mr. Barton's advice on decorating. After trying out these rugs in different rooms, they found three rugs they liked very much, two Bokharas and one Kirman. Mr. Barton suggested that they keep them for a few days to see how they liked "living" with them. He emphasized that they were under no obligation to buy any rug from him. If they decided not to buy any, they had only to call the store and a delivery truck would pick them up. He also indicated that they could pay in four instalments without interest.

After having the three rugs on the living room and dining room floors for two days, they decided that they liked them all and called Mr. Barton to announce that they were keeping all three. Looking at each other, they seemed surprised by their decision. They were also pleased that they had bought three rugs for the price of two.

Questions

1. **What needs were Janet and John attempting to satisfy in purchasing the rugs?**

2. **What and who influenced Janet and John in purchasing the rugs?**

3. **What were the major events that occurred in the buying process?**

4. **Evaluate the actions of the salespeople in the two retail stores. What were the advantages and disadvantages of their actions?**

6. A Buying Experience

"I really enjoyed that last movie," Doug said to his wife Jean. Doug Bell and his family had just finished watching four movies on a weekend in mid-January, something they had done once a month or so for the past five years. Typically, they rented a VCR and four or five movies from Steve's TV, a local store, and had a "weekend binge" where the four family members (Doug, Jean, and the two children, Kathy, age 15, and Jason, age 11) each picked out a movie and spent much of the weekend watching the shows.

Source: © David Gillen and Gordon McDougall, School of Business and Economics, Wilfrid Laurier University, 1992.

As they were returning the VCR and movies to Steve's TV, Doug mentioned to Jean that over the course of a year they probably did this eight or nine times, at a cost of $30 to $40. He thought that maybe they should buy a VCR instead of renting one. "We'd probably pay for it in a couple of years. I've been watching the prices on VCRs in the paper and they've come down a lot in the past two years but the prices don't seem to be getting lower." Jean agreed and after returning home they mentioned the idea of buying a VCR for the children, and both Kathy and Jason thought it was a great idea.

The Bells owned a colour TV set and had the basic cable service that provided 10 channels. They had not purchased any of the seven pay TV channels available, nor did they have the converter system that added eight more channels to the basic service. They had never discussed purchasing these extra services.

Doug, an associate professor in the Economics Department at the University of Waterloo, knew very little about VCRs. Many of his friends had VCRs and he knew they had paid as much as $900 for them two years earlier. Often when he was reading the daily newspaper he looked at ads for VCRs and observed that the prices had come down to around $500 for a basic unit but had not declined further. He thought that VCR prices probably wouldn't go much lower and, in fact, had noticed that new model VCRs had more features, such as stereo. He felt that prices might start going up a bit because of these features.

Doug wanted to get some information on VCRs and the type of machine he'd probably buy before he visited any stores. On January 20, Doug went to the university library and spent about an hour looking up all the articles he could find on VCRs. He photocopied two he thought were useful, went back to his office, and spent about an hour reading them. He noted the wide range of options available and the strengths and weaknesses of the various types of machines.

The next day Doug picked up a recent copy of *Consumer Reports* that had an extensive article on VCRs and listed the characteristics and strengths and weaknesses of over 40 machines. While reading the article, Doug was amazed at the number of features available in VCRs. He also noted that the article emphasized that an important factor to consider in buying a VCR was that the instructions and programming were easy to follow and do. It struck Doug that as more features were added—the bells and whistles—it became increasingly complex to use the recording features. He knew that he wanted to use a VCR for recording and he didn't want to get a machine where he'd have to spend hours learning how to program it.

After reading the article, Doug felt comfortable with what he had learned. The article had pointed out the key questions a buyer should ask himself, explained the technical jargon, and described the features to get for a good basic VCR, including on-screen programming and one-touch recording. Doug examined the extensive list of models received and decided that Magnavox and Panasonic looked like good brands. These two brands were rated highly for both the high-priced, full-feature models and the low-priced basic units. As well, both brands had excellent repair records. Doug thought he'd like to buy a VCR that had multiple channels, more than two tracks to increase the clarity, and easy programming. He did not want any other features such as "stop action" because he wasn't going to be taping sports like football where that feature might be useful.

In early February, Doug felt he was ready to buy a VCR, and one night he told his family what he had learned. They talked about what they'd use the VCR for and Doug suggested the kind of features he thought were important, what was available, and what they shouldn't get. He pointed out that it would be nice to get stereo but it was difficult to get stereo on a VCR without having all the bells and whistles. Since stereo was a new feature, it was also the most expensive and they probably wouldn't get their money out of it. The family finally concluded that what they really needed was a VCR that was capable of getting multiple channels, provided clarity, was easy to record, and had a good repair record.

At work the next day, Doug was talking with one of his students who knew a lot about stereos and VCRs. Doug mentioned what he was looking for and asked him where he could pick up a good quality VCR with those features. The student said that he often dealt with Natural Sound and it was a good store. On his way home from work Doug went into Natural Sound, where he found only a few VCRs on display. He talked to the owner of the store who said that Natural Sound was getting out of the VCR business: "We can't compete with places like Steve's TV and Krazy Kelly." Doug decided that if Natural Sound wasn't going to service it, he wasn't going to buy it there and he left.

Doug had planned to go to Steve's TV but it was getting late and he went home for dinner. At dinner he mentioned he was going over to Steve's TV to buy the VCR, and the family decided they'd all go. They drove over to Steve's and went to the aisle where the VCRs were located. The newer stereo VCRs were set up on the right side of the aisle and the basic VCRs were on the left side of the aisle. The movie *Back to the Future,* was playing on the top-of-the-line stereo VCR. The four stereo models on display were all made by Panasonic and ranged in price from $750 to $1,100. Doug and his family were immediately attracted to the movie, which had a very catchy soundtrack, and stood watching it.

A salesman approached and asked if he could help them. Doug told him they were interested in buying a VCR. The salesman then went to the lowest priced stereo VCR ($750) and asked if they were familiar with all the features. Doug replied that he had talked to a number of people who had owned VCRs and had read a lot about them in *Consumer Reports.* Jean said that she knew very little. Doug said; "I'm interested in three features: easy programming, multiple channels, and a good repair record." The salesman replied: "This low-price VCR has linear stereo and is not true hi-fidelity. Do you know the difference?" "No," replied Doug and Jean. "With linear stereo you can record and play back in stereo but the sound range is narrower than the true hi-fi." The salesman then moved to the next model, priced at $850. "This model has on-screen programming, an MTS decoder, and four heads for better picture clarity. It has on-screen programming, which makes it easy to program." He then moved to the next model which was priced at $1,000. "Now, this model has true hi-fi." Doug interjected that they were not interested because it was too much money. They then moved back to the two lower-priced stereo models. The salesman compared the two models and explained that the higher-priced one has a number of features that made it very compatible with the new stereo television sets that were coming on to the market. Jean said, "We don't watch much TV, and we probably won't buy a stereo TV."

Doug and Jean then said they did like some of the features on this mid-range model priced at $850.

At that point, Jean and the children began talking and thought that the difference between a basic $500 VCR and an $850 stereo VCR was probably going to be worth it because of the added features they would get in addition to stereo. Jean said; "You know, we're renovating the basement and we plan to move two stereo speakers down there and attach them to the television. Once we get the stereo speakers hooked up it wouldn't cost much more to get the stereo VCR."

Doug was a little unhappy with this turn of events. He had planned to spend $500; he didn't watch much television and felt that $850 was more than they should spend. He thought to himself that if they watched a lot of television and rented movies every week, then he might feel different. Maybe, he thought, with a stereo unit we'll use it more. Doug then asked the salesman; "How easy is it to get these VCRs repaired?" The salesman replied, "We can do all the repairs here in the store."

After some discussion the Panasonic model they chose was the "one-up" from the lowest-priced stereo VCR. They were impressed with the stereo sound and agreed it had the features they wanted. Doug then gave the salesman a credit card. The total price, including tax, came to $909. The salesman brought out a boxed VCR, Doug put it in the trunk, and five minutes later the VCR was home and downstairs. Doug and his son began to hook it up. They set up the VCR and immediately discovered that in order to hook up the stereo speakers you needed an amplifier. Unfortunately, their amplifier was located upstairs. This was something that Doug was not aware of and they stopped setting up the VCR. Doug decided to think about it a little bit more and find out what it would cost to buy an amplifier. The whole family went to bed that night somewhat disappointed.

At work the next day he spent an hour phoning several stores asking about prices of amplifiers and found out he would have to spend at least $100 to $150 to even get a used amplifier. He then decided buying the stereo VCR was a mistake. He was going to go home, take the VCR back, and get what he wanted to get in the first place, which was a basic VCR.

He went home and packed up the VCR, making sure he had all the materials in the box and that it was packed properly and protected. He took it upstairs and was about to leave when Jean and the children came up and asked him what he was doing. He told them that he felt they had made the wrong decision. "We're spending way too much money, we don't really need this, it's got too many features, and the whole cost is adding up much too quickly." They agreed and Doug said, "I'm going to take it back and get the VCR we went to buy in the first place."

On the way over to Steve's TV, Doug was a little hesitant. He had unpacked everything and wondered if he'd have any problems returning it. He was upset with himself in that he hadn't known how these stereo systems worked. "I should have known that," he thought.

He took the VCR into Steve's TV and found the salesman from whom he'd purchased it. The salesman asked what the problem was, Doug explained what had happened, and the salesman immediately said, "No, we don't have a policy about taking these machines back." Doug's heart sank at that point because he didn't want to end up spending another $150 for an amplifier. The salesman brought out the manager. Doug explained his problem to him and he immediately tried to sell him an amplifier. Doug knew at this point that he was not going to have his mind changed—he wanted to return the VCR.

The sales manager told Doug he was making the wrong decision and that Doug was getting a lot of new features and extra technology in this VCR. He pointed out that if he wanted to upgrade the system in a couple of years, the additional cost would be much higher than what Doug would pay now. Doug told him his family didn't watch that much television and didn't rent movies that often. Doug also said he didn't want all of this extra technology because he felt the cost was simply too high. "What I want is a basic VCR, I'm more than happy to purchase it here, and I'm sorry to have caused this kind of problem." The manager said, "Fine, that's what we will do." The salesman took Doug over to the basic VCR models. There was a large selection of brands and models available. Doug remembered the reason why he had agreed to buy the stereo Panasonic was that Panasonic was rated very well in *Consumer Reports*. He knew Panasonic was a good name and said that he was interested in the Panasonic basic VCR. The salesman showed him two different Panasonic models, and Doug took the lower-priced one without any bells and whistles on it, but with the features he wanted, including easy programming.

Doug gave the salesman his credit card, the purchase was rung through, and Doug got a credit receipt for $350, the difference between his original purchase ($909) and the basic VCR ($559). Doug felt good because now he was getting the product he wanted in the first place. He was also pleased with the way in which the store had handled the matter. He didn't feel that there had been any upmanship on his part. He was going home with what he wanted, but it simply took him a long time to get there. On the way home, Doug thought the salesman had been very kind. After the transaction had been completed, he gave Doug two free VCR movie tickets. When he got home, Doug and his son immediately took the VCR downstairs and hooked it up. Jean and Kathy decided that it would be a nice night to have popcorn and watch their first movie on the new VCR. They took one of the tickets, went over to Steve's, got a movie, brought it home, and had a very enjoyable night. They commented on the terrific sound, how easy it was to program, and how much they enjoyed it.

About a month later Doug and Jean were talking about the VCR. Doug said, "I'm happy with it. The best thing is, we can rent movies when we want—and we're not paying for the VCR." Jean replied, "I agree, but I wonder how we would feel if we had the first VCR we bought?" Doug laughed and said, "That's a good question—I'm glad I don't have to think about that."

Questions

1. **What needs was Doug attempting to satisfy in purchasing a VCR?**

2. **Evaluate the salesperson's performance at Steve's TV.**

3. **Evaluate the sales manager's performance at Steve's TV.**

4. **What implications does Doug and his family's behaviour have for retailers of VCRs?**

7. York Furniture Company

Mrs. Carol King has been operating the York Furniture Company for 10 years and has slowly built the sales to $900,000 a year. Her store is located in the downtown shopping area of a city with a population of 150,000. It is basically a factory town, and she has deliberately selected blue-collar workers as her target market. She carries some higher-priced furniture lines but places great emphasis on budget combinations and easy credit terms.

Mrs. King is concerned because she feels the store may have reached the limit of sales growth—sales have not been increasing during the last two years. Her newspaper advertising seems to attract her target customers, but many of these people come in, shop around, and then leave. Some of them come back, but most do not. She feels her product selections are very suitable for her target market and she is concerned that her salespeople do not close more sales with potential customers. She has discussed this matter several times with her salespeople. They say they feel they ought to treat all customers alike—the way they personally want to be treated. They feel their role is just to answer questions when asked—not to make suggestions or help customers arrive at their selections. They feel this would be too much of a "hard sell."

Mrs. King argues that this behaviour is interpreted as indifference by the customers who are attracted to the store by her advertising. She feels that customers must be treated on an individual basis—and that some customers need more encouragement and suggestions than others. Moreover, she feels that some customers will actually appreciate more help and suggestions than the salespeople themselves might. To support her views, she showed her salespeople the data from a study about furniture store customers (Tables 1 and 2). She tried to explain to them about the differences in demographic groups

Table 1						
In Shopping for Furniture I Found (Find) that	**Demographic Groups**				**Marital Status**	
	Group A	Group B	Group C	Group D	Newlyweds	Married 3–10 yrs.
I looked at furniture in many stores before I made a purchase	78%	57%	52%	50%	66%	71%
I went (am going) to only one store and bought (buy) what I found (find) there	2	9	10	11	9	12
To make my purchase I went (am going) back to one of the stores I shopped in previously	48	45	39	34	51	49
I looked (am looking) at furniture in no more than three stores and made (will make) my purchase in one of these	20	25	24	45	37	30
No answer	10	18	27	27	6	4

Source: This case was prepared by E. Jerome McCarthy, Michigan State University.

Table 2   The Sample Design

Demographic Status

Upper class (group A): 13% of sample

This group consisted of managers, proprietors, and executives of large businesses. It also includes professionals, including doctors, lawyers, engineers, college professors and school administrators, and research personnel. Sales personnel, including managers, executives, and upper-income salespeople above level of clerks.
Family income over $50,000.

Middle class (group B): 37% of sample

Group B consists of white-collar workers including clerical, secretarial, sales clerks, bookkeepers, etc. It also includes school teachers, social workers, semiprofessionals, proprietors or managers of small businesses, industrial foremen, and other supervisory personnel.
Family income between $25,000 and $50,000.

Lower middle class (group C): 36% of sample

Skilled workers and semiskilled technicians were in this category along with custodians, elevator operators, telephone linemen, factory operatives, construction workers, and some domestic and personal service employees.
Family income between $15,000 and $40,000.
No one in this group had above a high school education.

Lower class (group D): 14% of sample

Non-skilled employees, day laborers. It also includes some factory operatives and domestic and service people.
Family income under $18,000.
None had completed high school; some had only grade school education.

and pointed out that her store was definitely trying to aim at specific groups. She argued that they (the salespeople) should cater to the needs and attitudes of their customers—and think less about how they would like to be treated themselves. Further, she suggested that she may have to consider changing the sales compensation plan if they don't "do a better job." Now they are paid a salary of $13,000 to $20,000 per year (depending on years of service) plus a one percent commission on sales.

Question

1. **What recommendations would you make to Mrs. King? Why?**

8. Diego's

Dr. Albert Collins, a Montreal physician, faced a difficult decision as to whether or not to invest in a new fast food franchise concept specializing in Mexican food. Dr. Collins had made several good business investments and while he thought this was a great opportunity he recognized that there was a chance it wouldn't succeed. He decided to discuss the concept with his friend Jack Timlin, a marketing consultant, who had advised him on a number of earlier ventures. Dr. Collins arranged a meeting and presented the following information to Mr. Timlin.

The Concept

About six months ago, Dr. Collins had read an article in a major U.S. magazine about a relatively new but already successful fast-food franchiser based in Phoenix, Arizona. In operation for less than five years this franchiser had opened 55 locations (some franchised, some corporately owned) in Arizona and several other Southwestern states and had sold (to one firm) the franchise rights for 80 locations in Florida and sold many other, soon to be built, franchises in the Midwestern states.

Although Mexican food is very popular in the southern United States, this firm in all of its advertising and store signs, always uses the phrase "We serve marinated charbroiled chicken and Mexican food" to indicate that it offers a choice of items so that people who don't like Mexican food can also patronize the chain.

On the door of each location is a sticker stating that this restaurant is approved by the American Heart Association as a healthy place to eat away from home. Dr. Collins believed that this endorsement was obtained because of the manner in which the chicken is prepared. First it is marinated in a secret recipe of natural fruit juices and herbs and then it is charbroiled so that the fat drips out of the meat. Chicken prepared this way is lower in cholesterol than fried chicken and is juicier than barbeque (B.B.Q.) chicken. To further enhance its healthy image the chain does not serve french fries but does offer baked potatoes and an assortment of salads.

A quote from the article provided a very strong endorsement from at least one customer: "I do not have a great deal of experience in eating Mexican food, but the dishes were different than what I expected. The chicken was tender and juicy and had a subtle flavour—for my taste it was better than B.B.Q. chicken. The other dishes were very tasty and definitely not spicy. If this is what Mexican food is like, I am a convert."

Dr. Collins investigated further and found out that the recipes could not be protected by patent or copyright. In fact, he learned that the Arizona chain found out how a California chain of chicken restaurants marinated their chicken and then they used the recipe themselves. Dr. Collins then purchased some of the American marinated chicken, had it analyzed by a laboratory and then had a food technologist develop and test the formula and the correct procedures to cook the chicken.

He gathered a group of investors (primarily friends and acquaintances) who liked the concept and were willing to put up most of the money required to open up one or two locations to show that the concept would be successful in Canada. The plan was to sell franchises across the country.

For each location, franchisees would be charged an initial fee plus an ongoing five percent royalty on the gross sales of the franchises. In return for these fees the franchisee would have the right to use the trade name, which the investors decided would be Diego's. The franchisee's staff would be trained to prepare the food as per set procedures and the franchisee would purchase the chicken marinade from the franchisor. The franchisee would be assisted in site selection, construction of the restaurant, and the purchasing of the required equipment and would receive ongoing managerial assistance. In addition, the franchisee would benefit from a co-op advertising programme to be funded by a charge of four percent of gross sales levied on each location—franchised or corporately owned.

Preliminary Research

Dr. Collins met with the investment group several times and although nothing was formalized, a considerable amount of preliminary research had been conducted. A location was found for the first Diego's restaurant in a relatively new suburban residential area where most of the homes have been built in the last 10 years. New homes were still being built in the area and there was enough vacant land to more than double the population of the area. Most of the homes sold for $140,000 to $225,000 (compared to the current Montreal average price of $89,500 per home). Census data suggested that the typical home owner in this area was raising a young family and had a managerial job or was a professional with a practice that had not yet developed fully.

Studies have shown that most people will travel about 2.5 to 3.5 km (5 minutes) to go to a fast-food restaurant. Since Diego's would be very distinctive, the first few locations probably would draw customers from a slightly larger trading area. Information was obtained from recent census data for the census tracts that would likely constitute the trading area (Table 1).

Table 1 Trading Area Demographic Data	
Total population	108,725
Private households	37,445
Total families:	30,061
With 1 child at home	7,395
With 2 children at home	9,505
With 3 children at home	3,846
No children at home	9,315
Ages of children:	
0 to 4 years	7,430
5 to 9 years	7,810
10 to 14 years	8,355
15 to 19 years	7,710

Source: Statistics Canada, *Census of Canada, 1991*, Cat. 95-329, February 1993, Table 1.

Investor Group Meeting

After the information was collected, the investors held a meeting where a lively debate took place about the proposed image of Diego's, the target market, and other matters.

The investment group couldn't agree what image Diego's should have and what types of customers they should concentrate on satisfying. Some of the members wanted to concentrate the efforts on attracting and satisfying families with young children (e.g., offering free magic shows on selected evenings and on weekends, offering children free balloons, and perhaps offering a special children's menu of items that would appeal to children).

One member argued that this market segment appeared to be important. A recent newspaper article reported the results of an American study that, in 85 percent of the cases when parents go out to eat with their young children, the children make the final decision on which restaurant the family will go to.

Some of the group argued that children are known as very finicky eaters and maybe they won't like Diego's food. They suggested that Diego's should go after the teenage market or possibly Diego's should concentrate on the adult fast-food market.

One member of the investment group had conducted an analysis of the competition in the trading area (Table 2). He noted that at least two competitors in the trading area, McDonald's and Chi Chi's, had special strategies for attracting children. Another group member provided some data prepared by Statistics Canada that dealt with food purchased from restaurants (Table 3).

One of the members of the investor group was a practising accountant. He estimated that if the average bill at a restaurant was $4.99 (excluding tax) and the actual cost of the food and the packaging was 30 percent of the selling price, the restaurant would need to serve 225,000 meals a year to break even.

Information on traffic flows was also collected. One Thursday, Dr. Collins went to the proposed site and between 12:00 noon and 1:00 P.M. counted 2,000 cars moving in the four directions at the intersection. Between 5:00 P.M. and 6:30 P.M., the street heading north in front of the site became a "parking lot" as people headed home. He felt that this was a positive sign in that people could stop on the same side of the street as they were already travelling (and not have to cut across traffic), pick up food for supper, and then continue home.

Related to the decision as to which target market(s) to appeal to, some members wondered if people would be confused if the restaurant was simultaneously promoted as a chicken restaurant and as a Mexican food restaurant. That is, would potential customers perceive the chicken as a Mexican dish or would they consider the chicken to be a suitable alternative to B.B.Q. chicken or fried chicken?

Various members then raised the following questions and issues:

- Will consumers recognize the fact that Diego's is really two different restaurants in one and even if a person does not like Mexican food (or is afraid to try it) he or she can order a very tasty chicken or will some stay away because they view Diego's as a Mexican restaurant? Perhaps Diego's is too strong a Mexican name for what we would like to achieve?

Table 2   The Competition

The competition environment in the Dollard/Pointe Claire area (Montreal suburbs located about 30 minutes by car from downtown Montreal).

On the 2 km stretch of St. John's Road North from the TransCanada Highway to the proposed location of Diego's, there are 10 restaurants including:

McDonald's —	it is estimated that an average McDonald's has sales of between $2,000,000 and $2,500,000 per year. McDonald's places special emphasis on children, and some locations have playgrounds.
Chenoy's —	a deli that has been at this location for at least 15 years.
Chi Chi's —	a restaurant that features Americanized Mexican food. Runs special promotions to attract children, e.g., Shirley Temples (a non-alcoholic cocktail) and a special children's menu. It is estimated that Chi Chi's total sales volume is good, but it is thought that more than 50 percent of its revenue comes from its bar.
Le Vieux Duluth —	a Greek restaurant featuring popular-priced meals in the $8 to $12 range. Most Saturday evenings there is a line-up to get into this restaurant.
Nan Wah Restaurant —	located in the small shopping centre across the street from the proposed Diego's location. It has been there for several years. Monday to Friday they offer a nice lunch buffet for $4.95 plus tax. Based on eating there a few times, the lunch trade arrives just after 12:00 noon and a second small group arrives just after 1:00 P.M. On the days that we were there, it appears that their lunch volume was between 30 and 50 patrons per day. (Many businesses located on the TransCanada Highway are outside the 5-minute trading area.)

Along the 2 km further north from the proposed Diego's location to the end of St. John's Road, there are six additional restaurants including a St. Hubert B.B.Q. St. Hubert offers sit-down-at-the-table service and take out. A quarter chicken (dark meat), french fries, sauce, and bun costs $5.95 plus tax and tip. It is estimated that an average St. Hubert B.B.Q. has sales in the $1,000,000 per year range.

Sources Boulevard, about 1.5 km away from St. John's, is the next major artery that runs parallel to St. John's. On Sources there are many other restaurants including a Swiss Chalet B.B.Q. that has been at its location for at least 20 years and is considered to be a very successful operation. This restaurant is part of a chain that frequently uses coupons to offer very good value meals—e.g., a quarter chicken (dark meat), french fries, a bun, sauce, and a soft drink for $3.75 plus tax and tip. Swiss Chalet features sit-down-at-the-table service and take out.

Next to the Swiss Chalet on Sources Blvd. is one of the few Wendy's locations in Quebec that is currently profitable.

Note: Please remember that all this information is based on general discussions with various people and extrapolations of available facts. There is no assurance that any of the estimated sales figures are accurate.

- Both images should be positive. Diego's proposed first location is not far from Chi Chi's which exposed the consumer to and expanded the market for Mexican food. According to comparisons made by some of the group our Mexican dishes taste better and will cost less than the same items at Chi Chi's.

- On the other hand, for many years chicken has been more popular in Quebec than other parts of the country. It may be due to cultural differences or may be the result of the success of the St. Hubert B.B.Q. chain that started in Quebec (Table 4).

Table 3 Weekly Food Purchases from Restaurants per Family—Canada 1992

	Food Purchases	Income before Taxes
Average	$33.30	42,825
1st quintile	12.88	11,171
2nd quintile	22.51	23,807
3rd quintile	31.29	37,561
4th quintile	39.03	54,504
5th quintile	60.48	92,082

Note: The average weekly food purchases from restaurants in the Montreal Metropolitan Area were $34.87.
Source: Statistics Canada, *Family Food Expenditures in Canada, 1992,* March 1994, Tables 2 and 8.

Table 4 Per Capita Regional Differences in Food Consumption

	Chicken	Italian	Chinese	Greek
National	100%	100%	100%	100%
Quebec	125	120	145	130
Ontario	90	75	85	80
Prairies	90	165	35	25
B.C.	90	120	100	85
Atlantic Provinces	175	80	55	45

- In addition, over the last three or four years the consumption of chicken across Canada has increased significantly as people switched away from red meats, which are higher in cholesterol than chicken. This ties in very nicely with the emphasis that the American chain firmly places on the health aspect of its chicken meals.

Some members debated whether legally they could use an approach similar to the one Americans use and were not convinced that the "healthy" image will be a unique selling proposition that will cause people to pick this restaurant over the competition. They argued that the Canadian laws concerning food advertising were different and more restrictive than the U.S. laws. In Canada, the advertising of the cholesterol content of food (with the exception of vegetable oils such as Mazola) is prohibited. In addition, it appears that, even if it wanted to, the Canadian Heart Association would be unable, given the present legal environment, to endorse the restaurant. As well, they argued that many Quebecers are not especially health conscious when it comes to food.

One member had obtained a copy of a research study conducted in Montreal about bakery products. This study concluded that French-speaking respondents were less concerned with food additives than the English-speaking segment of the population. It was also found that older people were less concerned with this issue than the younger generation. Quebecers consumed large amounts of especially greasy french fries and poutine (French fries, sauce, and melted cheese). In other parts of Canada, the preference was for crispier, less oily french fries.

Some research conducted in the Montreal area by one of the members indicated that more than half of the respondents want french fries with their

B.B.Q. chicken. Consumers like and expect the combination and that is what the chicken restaurants offer with their meals.

In spite of this information, other members would like to follow the lead of the American firm and not serve french fries, but instead offer a choice of baked potatoes or Mexican rice.

One member pointed out that Quebecers love fine food and are receptive to ethnic foods. However, for some reason Mexican food has not caught on in Quebec. Taco Bell, a large U.S. Mexican fast-food chain that has opened in Ontario, does not, at this time, have any Quebec locations. In Montreal proper, several small Mexican restaurants have opened. None of them appears to be especially successful.

In addition, one member visited about a dozen supermarkets (some in the area of the proposed location, others in various parts of Montreal and other suburbs). Each store has a small section of packaged Mexican foods. The managers of these stores described the sales of Mexican foods as "slow but steady."

Because there is a lot of money at stake, the investors paid for some basic research. They conducted focus groups in a restaurant setting similar to what is being considered and the respondents had the chance to taste the food. (Table 5 provides a summary of the comments.) The results of the research were interesting in that in two cases the findings go against what the investors thought the consumer might want or accept.

First, it was planned to prepare the food out in the front of the restaurant where it could be seen by people inside and outside. This was intended to show that Diego's had nothing to hide and that the food was prepared under hygienic conditions. In addition, it was hoped that seeing the golden brown chicken on the grill and the aroma of cooking chicken would encourage people to order. According to the focus groups, some people viewed this as a strong negative.

Table 5   Focus Group Comments

Positive Comments:

- The food is delicious.
- Great food.
- I never tasted Mexican food before; it is really good and not at all spicy.
- I am happy that you don't serve french fries. My seven-year-old son just ate nutritious food, not the junk food that he prefers.
- I enjoyed the food. The chicken was moist but not greasy.
- I liked it. I would come back again.
- I hope it opens soon. I am bored and fed up with the traditional fast foods.

Negative Comments:

- The chicken looks yellow. What's wrong with it? Is it cheaper quality chicken?
- I don't think French Canadians are ready to eat B.B.Q. chicken on paper plates using plastic cutlery.
- I don't want to see the chicken being cooked. I don't want to know that it was once a living thing.
- The chickens were brought to the grill in a pail. Do they use the same pail to wash the floors?
- For me, B.B.Q. chicken and french fries go together. Something is missing and the meal is not enjoyable without french fries.

Secondly, while travelling through New England, Dr. Collins came across a very successful chain of seafood restaurants that, in order to keep prices low, serves on paper plates and provides plastic cutlery. This makes sense because Harvey's and other fast-food chains also use disposables. Again, based on the results of the focus groups, there seems to be resistance in Montreal to eating chicken in this way.

Another research finding was of special interest and requires more study. When respondents were offered a choice between traditional B.B.Q. sauce and salsa, a Mexican sauce, the vast majority opted for the B.B.Q. sauce. Was it because salsa was something unknown? Was it the fear of something spicy? Or perhaps it was just a habit.

The Decision

Dr. Collins concluded the presentation to Mr. Timlin with the following comments: "As you can see, there is a lot of information to consider. In fact, I am confused as to what I should do. I know that the concept is successful in Arizona, but I have also obtained a great deal of information, some of which is not positive, about duplicating this concept in Canada and particularly in Quebec.

"I don't know if I should invest in this project or not. If it succeeds, it will be the chance of a lifetime to make a lot of money. Should I go into it, or not? What, if anything, can be done to improve the concept so that the risk of failure will be reduced?"

Question

1. **What would you recommend that Dr. Collins do? Why?**

9. The Undercover Agency

In July of 1993, Bill Jones and Ruth McDonald had one of their many meetings to discuss a business venture. Over the past two years, Bill and Ruth had identified, studied, and finally rejected a variety of potential enterprises. At last they believed they had come across an idea that would be successful: a woman's intimate apparel store.

"Listen, Bill, we have conducted the market research and calculated the financial analysis. I believe this idea is sound and will make money. After all, your financial projections show we will meet our objective of showing a profit by the second year. I say we should go for it."

But Bill raised several objections. "I realize the financial projections and industry analysis do look good. But what if this trend toward intimate apparel is just a fad? Also, the rent for the store location is very high. Perhaps it would be better to find a different location. I think we should review our analysis and see if it is really as good an opportunity as we think."

Ruth agreed to further review the information; however, she reminded Bill that this was Friday night and that a decision would have to be made by Monday since the mall manager would not hold the lease option open any longer for them.

Source: This case was prepared by Scott Edgett, Brock University, with the assistance of Louise Gauthier.

Background

Bill and Ruth felt that together they formed a good business partnership, since they both held business degrees and their areas of interest complemented each other. For the past five years, Bill had been employed as a chartered accountant with a firm in St. Catharines, Ontario. He was able to contribute a strong financial background to the partnership. Ruth had a good knowledge of the retailing industry. After rapid advancement over the last five years, she had recently been promoted to assistant buyer with a major department-store chain.

Because of their business knowledge, both partners had actively participated in conducting the feasibility study for the lingerie store. Each was also willing to contribute $25,000 to the venture. Any further financing requirements would have to be met by borrowing from a bank. Neither Bill nor Ruth had actually owned or operated a business. However, given the nature of the product and Ruth's merchandising experience, both partners felt she would be able to manage the store, and that Bill would provide part-time assistance, primarily on the accounting side of the venture.

The Idea

Bill and Ruth first became interested in opening an intimate apparel specialty store they would call The Undercover Agency after Ruth read an article in *Marketing* about *Linrich,* a new fashion magazine catering specifically to women's intimate apparel. The article stressed consumer interest in intimate apparel was growing in Canada. They began to formalize plans for The Undercover Agency after conducting some initial investigations, as well as seriously discussing the proposal.

The product assortment they were considering would consist of bras, panties, camisoles, teddies, slips, nightwear, and matching sets. These items would be highly fashionable and would be offered in a variety of colours and sizes. Bill was uncertain whether he wanted the store to carry core products, which included mainly packaged bras; however, Ruth felt these items were a necessity. Suppliers would be mainly Canadian: Canadelle (Wonderbra), Warner's, and Vogue for intimate apparel products, as well as Kayser, Papillon Blanc, and French Maid nightwear. These suppliers offered high quality, high fashion products, ranging in price from medium to high. Bill estimated these prices would allow for gross margins in the range of 30 to 50 percent.

An ideal location for the store had become available in the Pen Centre, a regional shopping mall located in St. Catharines, Ontario. At the time Bill and Ruth were considering their business venture, the Pen Centre was the only large shopping centre in Ontario's Niagara Region. The traffic flow through the mall averaged 140,000 people per week.

The potential store location measured 100 square metres. Bill and Ruth estimated that 15 square metres would be sufficient for the storage room, as most of the products would be displayed on the sales floor. Ruth had designed a layout to provide maximum exposure to the fashion items located at the front of the store, while maintaining some visibility to the core products at the rear of the store. The fashion items at the front of the store obstructed the sight line to the rear. This would enable browsers to feel more comfortable while shopping. Ruth had suggested that the store be richly decorated in warm pastel colours, with wood coloured trim. The fixtures, racks, and change rooms would be custom made of wood and brass, and the lighting would be very soft. The store would be perfumed with mild fragrances, and relaxing music would be played.

Ruth felt a promotional plan would be needed to develop a strong position in the market as well as to gain a competitive edge. One idea she had been toying with was to start a registry system, which would include a customer's personal preferences, previous purchases, as well as her home address to enable the store to mail announcements of new product arrivals and upcoming sales. The customer would also be invited to disclose information regarding her husband/boyfriend, to facilitate the mailing of reminder notices to her male counterpart for events such as birthdays and anniversaries. Gift wrapping and delivery services would also be provided for male customers. Bill had suggested a grand opening be held to create a high level of initial awareness among consumers.

The Industry

The lingerie market in Canada was estimated to be worth more than $2 billion in 1991, with the intimate apparel segment estimated at $570 million in retail sales. This segment of the industry is currently at the maturity stage of its life cycle and experiencing limited growth. However, the specialty store segment of this industry is experiencing a growth in retail sales due to the increasing interest among women in stylish lingerie.

As Bill and Ruth collected information from discussions with various manufacturers and retailers, they were able to put together a profile of the intimate apparel market. Department stores accounted for about 30 percent of the market, discount stores another 15 percent, specialty stores 50 percent, and other types of outlets the remaining five percent. By combining St. Catharines/Niagara region population figures with the area's combined retail sales, Bill had determined that the total intimate apparel sales for the area were approximately $7 million. Although pantyhose accounted for another $300 million in industry sales, Bill and Ruth decided after a lengthy debate not to carry the product due to the diverse range of the line and the display space this type of product would require. With her experience and knowledge as a buyer, Ruth was able to provide a breakdown of industry sales by product line (Exhibit 1).

Exhibit 1	Total Women's Intimate Apparel Market
Product	**Percent of Market**
Bras	37%
Panties	18
Camisoles	5
Teddies	1
Full slips	4
Half slips	4
Hostess gowns, loungewear	2
Negligees	2
Nightshirts	4
Nightgowns	17
Pyjamas	6
Total	100%

The Competition

Recognizing that competition would be strong in a mature industry, the partners conducted a competitive analysis for the local trading area. After surveying local stores, Ruth categorized the competitors as direct and indirect competition. Direct competitors included all intimate apparel specialty stores, whereas indirect competitors consisted of a local department store called The Wright House, as well as all stores selling apparel in the Pen Centre. These were comprised mostly of department stores and discounters (Exhibits 2 and 3).

Exhibit 2   Direct Competition

Table of Attributes

Scale: 4 = Excellent selection   3 = Good selection
       2 = Fair selection   1 = Poor selection

Product	Annabelles	Charlott's	Intimate Memories	Phoebes
Bras	2	2	3	.5
Panties	1	1	3	.5
Camisoles	1	1	2	—
Teddies	1	1	3	1
Full slips	1	2	2	—
Half slips	2	3	1	—
Negligees	1	1	1	—
Nightshirts	1	1	5	2
Nightgowns	—	2	1	2
Pyjamas	—	2	—	—
Hostess/ loungewear	—	1	2	—
Pantyhose	1	1	—	—
Service	Good offered assistance	Good offered assistance	Good offered assistance	Good offered assistance
Location	Downtown	Lakeshore Plaza	Ridley Square	Downtown
Visibility	High	Low	Moderate	Low
Accessibility	Restricted	Good	Good	Restricted
Parking	Restricted Pay	Ample	Ample	Restricted Pay
Square metres	90	70	120	30
Hours	Mon.–Fri. 9:30–9:00 Saturday 9:30–5:30	Mon.–Fri. 9:30–9:00 Saturday 9:30–6:00	Mon.–Fri. 10:00–9:00 Saturday 10:00–6:00	Mon.–Wed. 10:00–5:30 Thur.–Fri. Sat. 10:00–5:00
Prices	Medium	Medium	Medium	High
Target	25–44 yrs.	35–45 yrs.	25–45 yrs.	30–45 yrs.

Exhibit 3   Indirect Competition

Table of Attributes

Scale:	4 = Excellent selection		3 = Good selection	
	2 = Fair selection		1 = Poor selection	

Product	Wright House	Eaton's	Robinson	Sears
Bras	4	4	4	3
Panties	4	4	3	4
Camisoles	1	1	1	1
Teddies	1	—	1	—
Full slips	4	3	2	3
Half slips	4	3	2	3
Negligees	2	1	1	—
Nightshirts	3	2	2	2
Nightgowns	3	3	2	3
Pyjamas	2	2	2	—
Hostess/ loungewear	1	1	3	2
Pantyhose	4	3	3	2
Service	Moderate assistance available	Moderate, only one salesperson for dept.	Moderate assistance offered	Poor, no salesperson available
Location	Fairview Mall	Pen Centre Plaza	Pen Centre Square	Pen Centre
Visibility	Moderate	High	High	High
Accessibility	Good	Excellent	Excellent	Excellent
Parking	Ample	Ample	Ample	Restricted
Square metres	210	270	280	270
Hours	Mon.–Fri. 9:30–9:00 Saturday 9:30–6:00	Mon.–Fri. 9:30–9:00 Saturday 9:30–5:30	Mon.–Fri. 9:30–9:00 Saturday 9:30–5:30	Mon.–Fri. 9:30–9:00 Saturday 9:30–5:30
Prices	Medium to low	Medium to low	Medium to low	Medium to low
Target	18–45 yrs.	13 and over	13 and over	13 and over

The St. Catharines Market

St. Catharines is located in Southern Ontario and is the main shopping area for the Niagara Region. This region accounts for 1.15 percent of all retail expenditures in Canada. The Pen Centre is no more than a 30-minute drive for Niagara Region residents. Population and income information from the 1991 Canadian Census is provided in Exhibits 4 and 5.

Ruth felt that further segmentation could be conducted but was unsure about how to do this. She wondered how important the ages of potential consumers would be. Although males purchase gifts for their wives/girlfriends, she was also unsure of the extent to which males should be considered potential customers.

Exhibit 4   St. Catharines/Niagara Population

Age Groups	Male	Female
14 and under	36,485	34,080
15–19 years	12,785	12,100
20–24 years	12,550	12,575
25–34 years	28,310	29,445
35–44 years	26,325	27,480
45–54 years	19,970	20,325
55–64 years	18,075	19,160
65–74 years	22,990	31,590
Total	177,490	186,755

Exhibit 5   Income Levels by Gender

Income Levels	Males, 15+	Females, 15+
Average income	$30,382	$15,864
Average employment income (full-time)	39,245	24,582
Average census family income	44,998	
Average household income	44,929	

Financial Analysis

Bill had estimated that the approximate start-up costs and operating expenses would be as follows:

Insurance	$ 1,000
Fixtures	60,000
Computer system	8,000
Office supplies	500
Professional fees	1,000
Rent	3,500/month plus ½ of 1% of gross sales
Salaries per year	26,000
Advertising	
opening	1,000
during year	4,500
Freight and shipping	1,400
Utilities	1,800
Interest (on loan principal)	11,500

Bill estimated that sales for the first year would be $240,000, and for the second year they would be $280,000. The cost of goods sold was calculated to average 58 percent of sales. It is an industry custom by manufacturers to allow 60-day terms for opening inventory requirements.

Summary

Bill and Ruth settled in for a long night. By Monday morning, a decision would have to be reached on whether to go ahead with the venture or not. If a "go" decision were to be made, the partnership would need a more tailored target market and a marketing plan before presenting a proposal to a bank for financing consideration.

Questions

1. **Conduct a situational analysis for the Undercover Agency business venture.**

2. **Conduct a segmentation analysis of the market. Who should the target market be?**

3. **Would you recommend a "go" or a "no go" decision for this business venture?**

4. **If the recommendation is "go," develop a marketing strategy; if "no go," write a report that will show the partners why the idea is not viable.**

10. Clean Windows, Inc.

It was January 1995, and Terry Gill and John Kelly, partners of Clean Windows, Inc. (CW), were contemplating a marketing strategy for expanding their operations in the window-cleaning market. Both were full-time students in the second year of their programs at the University of New Brunswick. They were committed to their studies and realized that their chosen strategy must allow them to complete their programs within the next two years.

They were optimistic that CW had the opportunity to grow very rapidly. Their optimism appeared justified, given the growth they had experienced in both residential and commercial contracts since they commenced operations in July 1994 (Table 1). Mr. Kelly attributed this growth to the current lack of serious competition in the greater Fredericton area.

When questioned about balancing school-work and the responsibilities of his business, Mr. Gill commented:

> We know we have a really great concept here, but our study schedule could result in a lack of attention to customer demands and administrative details. I think that we can pull it off, but we need to make the right choices and develop an appropriate marketing strategy. John and I even considered franchising as our means of growth because we have to grow to maximize profitability.

Table 1   Monthly Cleaning Gross Revenue

Month	Residential	Commercial	Total
July	$1,377	$ 37	$1,414
August	2,175	45	2,220
September	1,990	1,423	3,413
October	1,402	2,509	3,911
November	315	1,021	1,336
December	0	896	896

Source: Company records.

Source: This case was prepared and revised by Professor E. S. Grant, University of New Brunswick, assisted by G. T. Clarke and K. Dunphy. Copyright 1995.

Initial Strategy

Operations commenced June 20, 1994, with enough equipment for two cleaners. Initially, all labour activity was completed by Mr. Gill and Mr. Kelly. Business was relatively slow for the first two months (Table 1), as most of the owners' time was spent cleaning windows, not marketing and management activity. Advertising in these months was limited to the purchase of business cards and a direct mail campaign. The business cards were an important asset for business contacts, but the mailout resulted in limited success. It was thought that this was due to poor timing.

One thousand five hundred photocopied flyers were distributed just prior to a long weekend in July. Both partners and employees delivered the flyers to private residences in the downtown area and to a few upscale neighbourhoods.

By the end of July a display ad was run in the business directory section of the local newspaper and free air time was received on a local radio station interested in promoting student businesses. Unfortunately, neither of these two media proved successful. Lawn signs and T-shirts displaying the company logo and phone number were purchased. These media, combined with word of mouth, accounted for close to 85 percent of all new cleaning contracts.

The promotions were responsible for business growth in August and September. With this additional business, the need for extra staff became apparent. By August, six cleaners were employed. An increase in demand through September and October was experienced, but it became difficult for both partners to cope with the increased volume as university commenced in September. By then, CW had only two full-time employees, who were responsible for reducing the partners' workload.

In early November, Mr. Gill and Mr. Kelly realized that the two employees were not working out as anticipated and the decision was made to lay them off. This left only the partners to resume the labour-intensive duties of window cleaning. This was very difficult, since both maintained a rigorous cleaning schedule in addition to a full course load at the university.

With the summer quickly approaching, both partners agreed that this strategy would have to be reconsidered.

Competition

When questioned about the competition, Mr. Kelly commented:

> There is only one firm that cleans residential windows, but we don't see them as a serious competitor. We know that they do have some business, but they cannot have much. We have phoned them several times, but our calls were never returned. There are two firms that service only commercial accounts. One of these firms cleans high-rise buildings only, but they operate out of Moncton, which is more than a two-hour drive. The other is a local firm; they are not equipped to clean high-rises but they have a very significant share of the local commercial market. We are certain that we can compete with them; almost all of our commercial clients have experienced their service and have expressed relief that there is now an alternative available.

Mr. Kelly had obtained information on all three of these competitors (Table 2). Fredericton also had a number of maid and janitorial service companies, most of which cleaned windows. However, none cleaned external window surfaces, and they cleaned interior window surfaces on an irregular basis.

Table 2   Competition in Fredericton Window Cleaning Market

Company	Customer Type*	Bonded	Liability Insurance	Estimated Price
City Window Cleaners	Residential	?	?	?
Mr. Windows	Commercial	Yes	Yes	$15/hr
Gormay Cleaners	Commercial: high-rise buildings only	No	Yes	$40/hr
Other (janitorial and maid services)	Commercial† and residential†	N/A	N/A	N/A

* Residential customers are defined as single dwellings only; all other accounts are defined as commercial.
† Clean only interior window surfaces.
? = unavailable.
Source: Telephone directory and telephone enquiries.

Although Fredericton offers only a relatively small potential market size, both partners were certain that there was an attractive opportunity in both the residential and the commercial market.

Many customers have indicated they would use CW's service again. One customer stated that she had seen the lawn sign and then decided to request CW's service. Unable to find the phone number (a business number was obtained in September), she claimed to have driven more than 50 miles before finding the lawn sign that she needed to find the number.

Mr. Gill believed that the most profitable opportunity would be to service what he calls high-rise buildings (all those that require staging). He estimated that there are more than 350 such buildings in the Fredericton area.

Cost Data

Cost data are provided in Tables 3 and 4. All costs for 1994 (Table 3) were actual, based on the costs incurred to date. Costs for 1995 (Table 4) were estimated by the partners. Transportation costs have been excluded. A small van belonging to Mr. Kelly's father had been used and John was confident that this vehicle would be available for at least another year. Although CW incurs no rental fee for the use of this van, fuel would have to be purchased.

All estimated costs were believed to be reasonably accurate. However, the pricing of window contracts had been much more arbitrary. Mr. Kelly saw the pricing decision of key importance to CW's long-term profitability. To date, prices had been based on an estimated completion time for each potential contract.

The time estimate was multiplied by a charge-out rate of $15/hour per cleaner. Mr. Kelly confessed that the decision to use $15 per hour was arbitrary; however, he was confident that it was competitive and fair. This was thought to be the same charge-out rate used by Mr. Windows (Table 2). Mr. Kelly had difficulty deciding what to charge in the future. Although he believed their price was competitive, he had a hunch that many customers expected a lower charge-out rate given their status as students. He believed it was a serious issue and realized that many customers selected CW because of the altruistic satisfaction they received from supporting a student venture.

Table 3 Actual Costs—1994		
Variable Costs	**Per Hour**	
Wages		
One two-person crew	(2 × $5.50 each)	$11.00/hour
Supplies		
Fuel	$ .75	
Cleaning fluids	.50	
Cleaning materials	.90	2.15
Total variable costs		$13.15
Fixed Costs	**Per Month**	
Insurance (liability)	$ 15.00	
Telephone	55.00	
Advertising	110.00	
Bank charges	25.00	
Equipment depreciation	10.00	
Total fixed costs	$215.00	

Source: Company records.

Table 4 Estimated Costs—1995		
Variable Costs	**Per Hour**	
Wages		
One two-person crew	(2 × $5.70 each)	$11.40/hour
Supplies		
Fuel	$ .80	
Cleaning fluids	.50	
Cleaning materials	.90	2.20
Total variables costs		$13.60
Fixed Costs	**Per Month**	
Insurance (liability)	$ 20.00	
Telephone	60.00	
Advertising	200.00	
Bank charges	30.00	
Equipment depreciation	20.00	
Total fixed costs	$330.00	

Source: Company estimates.

Enough equipment (ladders, staging, buckets, etc.) to operationalize three two-person crews had been acquired. It was estimated that additional equipment would cost $300 per crew, but it was uncertain whether or not it would be necessary to hire additional crews.

Additional investment would be necessary in order to clean high-rise buildings. Staging that would allow one person to safely manoeuvre up and down the side of a high-rise would cost approximately $4,500.

Table 5   Selected Characteristics—Fredericton, NB

Dwelling characteristics	
Single detached house	10,230
Apartment, five or more storeys	275
Movable dwelling	50
All other types	5,890
Total number of occupied private dwellings	16,445
Population characteristics	
By industry division	
All industries	24,095
Primary industries (SIC divisions A,B,C, and D)	440
Manufacturing industries (division E)	1,290
Construction industries (division F)	1,160
Transportation, storage, communication and other utility industries (divisions G and H)	1,895
Trade industries (divisions I and J)	950
Finance, insurance, and real estate industries (divisions K and L)	950
Government service industries (division N)	4,565
Other service industries (divisions M, O, P, Q, and R)	9,365
Not applicable	480
Total labour force 15 years and over	24,570

Source: Statistics Canada, Cat. 94-107 and 108, 1986.

The Market

Mr. Gill had evaluated the Fredericton market and concluded that it was sizable enough to allow CW to realize satisfactory profits. He had collected select statistics at the university's library (Table 5). Although Mr. Gill was uncertain how many households and commercial customers were likely to use his services, he was certain that his competitors were not satisfying the current demand.

In the past, CW's window contracts were largely concentrated within a small geographic area. Both partners were uncertain why this phenomenon existed. Mr. Kelly wondered: "Is this because our lawn signs were displayed more often in this area? Are these people different, or is it related to other, undetermined causes?"

The Future

The partners faced a number of important decisions. They had to decide whether or not their current strategy was appropriate for the situation. If it was not, they would have to agree on appropriate changes. These changes would have to be made in light of both partners' commitment to expansion. They believed they could create a student-owned franchise operation similar to College Pro Painters and University Painters. However, they were uncertain how they should proceed.

They would need to make some decisions very soon. Exams finished in April, and they anticipated that April and May would be extremely busy months, given that many people plan to clean their homes and businesses in the spring. They realized there would be little time available for analysis and strategic planning after late March. Time would be spent hiring employees, selling, cleaning, and perhaps even studying for final exams.

1. How can the market (commercial and residential) for window cleaning be segmented?

2. What types of promotional activities would you suggest CW, Inc., use? How can the firm encourage repeat usage of its service?

3. How feasible is the venture?

4. Would you recommend that the partners attempt to sell franchise agreements? Explain.

11. Donna Holtom

Introduction

"Hello, Santé Restaurant." Donna Holtom, owner and manager, flipped open the reservation book. "Can I make a reservation for 4 at 7:30 tonight?" This used to be a simple question. But after three-and-a-half years in business, Donna found herself planning and replanning the reservation book before replying, "I could serve you at 8:30." It was Friday night, and once again she was losing potential revenues, even after setting four extra tables in the gym.

Santé is part of a group of businesses Donna operates at the corner of Sussex Drive and Rideau Street, in the heart of downtown Ottawa. The major business components are:

- The Sussex Club, a women's club centred around a fitness program but also offering its members access to a wide range of personal services (the spa, hair salon, and "dining-room").

- Santé Restaurant, a fine-dining facility offering an eclectic blend of Caribbean, Californian, and East Asian dishes.

- Holtz Health & Beauty Centre, a health spa offering aesthetic services (facials, manicures, pedicures, electronic muscle toning, etc.), massage, and hair styling.

Background

After three years' managing a women's credit union, and a dozen before that working as executive assistant to Alderman and later Mayor Marion Dewar, Donna's first step in establishing her own business had been a big one, starting the three businesses together, from scratch. She had expected the three businesses to develop a synergistic relationship—and they had.

The Sussex Club had developed a strong reputation as Ottawa's premier women's facility because it could offer its members a quality dining facility and a wide range of personal services that the membership of a private club just could not support. At the same time, the club members provided a solid core of regular clientele for the restaurant and spa, reducing their marketing requirements.

Santé had also been very successful in establishing a reputation based on its innovative cuisine, fine service, and central location. Donna takes full advantage

Source: This case was written by Brian Bourns under the supervision of Professor David S. Litvack, University of Ottawa.

by promoting the spa and club facilities to restaurant diners. Her most effective technique is the "fishbowl." Diners have the opportunity to win a complimentary massage (or some similar service) by dropping a business card into the bowl. Even the losers are called with the offer of a discount on the service being promoted at the moment.

Each of these entities attracts differing, but overlapping clientele. The Sussex Club services predominantly professional and business women 30 to 60 years old. The restaurant attracts diners of both sexes, but offers fine dining and an elegant decor attractive to the upper third in income terms. Ninety-five percent of spa clients are women (a few men utilize the massage services), but they cover wider age and income ranges than club members.

What Donna hadn't counted on was that the three businesses would be so diverse in their management and operating requirements. When the hired managers proved to be unsuccessful, she found herself learning three new business areas "on the job."

The start-up period was difficult, and the nature and range of services offered have gradually been refined with experience, adding some elements, and deleting others. Overall the group is now profitable (see Table 1), and the challenge is how to continue growing and avoid turning business away.

Table 1 Operating Income[1]		
Santé Restaurant		
Period Ending	**May 1991**	**May 1992**
Revenue		
Food	$ 484,200	$ 615,651
Liquor	143,114	201,976
Other	(8,523)	(10,827)
Total revenue	**$618,791**	**$806,800**
Cost of sales		
Cost of food	$ 177,835	$ 257,012
Cost of liquor	69,654	91,476
Credit card discounts	8,867	13,716
Miscellaneous	3,138	1,656
Total cost of sales	**$259,494**	**$363,860**
Contribution margin	**$359,297**	**$442,940**
Expenses		
Salary waiting	$ 75,397	$ 109,896
Salary kitchen	95,607	101,944
Other labour costs	3,486	3,885
Total wage and salary	**$174,490**	**$215,725**
Rent and occupancy	$ 79,011	$ 81,784
General administration	24,008	23,060
Advertising	27,197	14,617
Printing	0	8,736
Laundry	4,246	5,937
Equipment/smalls	8,822	33,132
Other	3,970	11,410
Total other expenses	**$147,254**	**$178,676**
Total expenses	**$321,744**	**$394,401**
Operating profit (loss)	**$ 37,553**	**$ 48,539**

Table 1 (concluded)

Holtz Health & Beauty (including The Sussex Club)

Period Ending	May 1991	May 1992
Health spa		
Revenue		
Retail sales	$ 82,058	$ 237,850
Aesthetic services	147,700	243,047
Massage services	54,802	91,939
Hair services	50,113	41,828
Prepaid items	91,342	245,285
Less certificates used	(62,118)	(129,321)
	$363,897	$730,628
Cost of sales		
Cost of products sold/used	54,362	140,188
Payroll aesthetics	61,532	120,292
Payroll massage	24,601	44,625
Hair commissions	29,687	21,826
Advertising	1,455	19,421
Supplies and expenses	11,605	9,812
Total cost of sales	**$183,242**	**$356,164**
Gross profit	**$180,655**	**$374,464**
Fitness program		
Revenue		
Membership sales	$ 110,563	$ 123,968
Other sales	19,103	10,553
	$129,666	$134,521
Cost of sales		
Payroll	65,937	66,035
Advertising	2,955	9,117
Services purchased from spa	7,835	12,012
Expenses	6,619	7,539
Total cost of sales	**$ 83,346**	**$ 94,703**
Gross profit	**$ 46,320**	**$ 39,818**
Other/unallocated	($ 350)	($ 11,104)
Total gross profit	**$226,625**	**$403,178**
Corporate expenses		
Salaries and benefits	$ 42,996	$ 69,126
Rent	116,475	118,605
Administrative	39,114	55,505
Advertising	14,798	14,238
Maintenance/cleaning	3,810	3,937
Credit card discounts	6,714	14,306
Bank charges	4,277	3,278
Other	15,463	3,429
	$243,647	**$282,424**
Operating profit (loss)	**($ 17,022)**	**$120,754**

[1]The data have been disguised.

The Facility

The businesses are located in a small eight-story office building at a major intersection, two blocks from the Parliament Buildings, with the By-Ward Market restaurant district a block behind, and a major downtown shopping centre across the street. The two best known downtown hotels (the Chateau Laurier and the Westin) and the convention centre are all within a block. As a result, there is considerable pedestrian, vehicle, and bus traffic at the corner and in the immediate area. Most downtown employment, however, is across the Canal, several blocks away.

There is no parking associated with the building, and although there is considerable parking in the immediate area, most of it is in parking structures and virtually no free parking is available.

The first floor of the building is occupied by a major bank branch. The businesses occupy all of the second floor, and part of the third. Customer access is by a stairwell and elevators common to the office floors further up.

The layout of the second floor is shown in Figure 1. There are two entrances to the complex, one for the restaurant, and one for the spa, hair salon, and fitness facility. This allows the restaurant to establish a somewhat separate identity, a useful approach, particularly in attracting male diners to a complex that is otherwise primarily female.

The restaurant offers a very pleasant, relatively formal atmosphere. There are very few "poor tables," with most of the seating along the floor to ceiling windows along both Sussex and Rideau, offering interesting views of some fine older buildings and the activity along the street below. There are 62 seats at 22 tables, and another six tables with 20 seats are set up in part of the gym most

Figure I Facility Layout, Main Floor

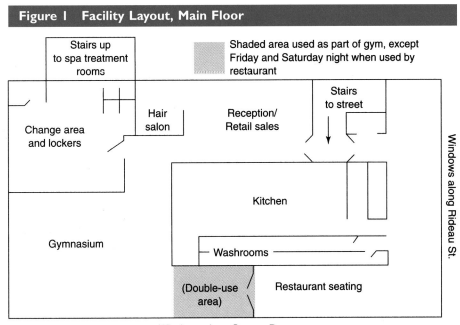

Windows along Sussex Dr.

Table 2	Space Allocation (in square metres)			
	Sussex Club	Santé Restaurant	Holtz Health & Beauty Spa	Rent/m²*
Second floor	163	279	70	$207.21
Third floor			186	$182.99

*Quoted as "net, net." Landlord charges an additional $86.11/sq. metre for taxes, maintenance, etc. Lease has three years to run, and a five-year option to renew, subject to arbitration on rent level.

Friday and Saturday evenings (on long weekends, and in January and February they generally weren't required).

This extra seating has helped deal with the rising demand in the evenings, but it can't be used when the gym program is running, and it could be filled by most Friday lunches. An average of 10 extra seats would be useful for Thursday lunches. It takes two waiters an hour and a half to "convert" the gym space to restaurant seating so it is not a useful response to an unexpected group of "walk-in" patrons. There are five evenings a month (on average) when the 20 seats could be used for walk-ins or large parties that cannot be accommodated now. In fact there are probably an equal number of Friday or Saturday evenings when another 20 seats could be useful.

The nicely decorated gym facility is relatively small, accommodating aerobic classes of 10 to 15 persons, and a small selection of Nautilus and Lifecycle equipment.

The spa originally had six treatment rooms and a small lounge area on the third floor. This space can be reached by a private stairway from the change area, which is used by aesthetic clients. As a result of the increasing demand for services, however, the spa recently took over some vacant space across the public hallway from the third floor treatment rooms, adding four treatment areas. However, the need to cross the public hallway to reach this area is a distinct disadvantage for clients dressed in housecoats between treatments. The space allocation for the three businesses is provided in Table 2.

The Spa

Holtz Health & Beauty is the largest aesthetic salon in Ottawa, and is unique in the regional focus of its market. Aesthetic salons are generally based on a clientele that works or lives in the area of the business, and uses it out of convenience. They tend to be small operations, usually an aesthetician/manager and two or three staff with gross revenues in the $80,000–$120,000 range. Although there were two other large salons with a more substantial staff and clientele, the central location of Holtz, the wide range of services it provides, and the promotional approaches it pioneered give it a different focus.

One-third of Holtz's revenues come from the sale of "gift certificates" and "prepaid" items, and about half of those sales come in the pre-Christmas period. If the revenues from repeat visits by clients introduced by gift certificates and the retail products purchased by those clients were included, the significance of this marketing approach would be even more obvious.

The gift certificates are specially promoted for Christmas, Valentines' Day, and Mothers' Day, but are also advertised throughout the year as "A Perfect Gift for the

Woman Who Deserves Everything" for birthdays, graduations, weddings, corporate recognition, and so on. Most of these sales are for the "Supreme Day of Beauty," a $165 package. The gift certificate sales are promoted through radio and newspaper advertising (the results from the newspaper are obvious, those from radio are not), by donations as door prizes for community events, through flyers and direct mail campaigns, and at the annual "Bridal Fair."

Effective promotion is part of the program's success, but so is Holtz's reputation as the "best and biggest" salon in the city, with the widest range of services. Donna plans to maintain this reputation by continuing to improve the facilities and expand the range of services offered. Holtz is still weak in the area of water treatments, for example, and a whirlpool used for treatments should generate at least two clients a day for a $35 treatment. The cost of a treatment is $6.

Although not all gift certificates are in fact redeemed for services, the success of the gift certificate program is having a dramatic impact on the level of activity in the spa. Holtz was the first salon to introduce this concept in Ottawa, and in the three years they have offered it, sales have increased dramatically. Although the facilities have been expanded once, they still cannot keep up with the demand, and the location of the manicure area (where clients tend to be fairly chatty) adjacent to the massage rooms (where clients tend to be fairly drowsy) is less than ideal.

The Sussex Club

The situation with the gym facility is quite different. Fitness facilities in the region fall into two categories:

- volume oriented, high-pressure sales, well-advertised "meet markets," focussed on weights and aerobic programs, and
- higher priced, generally suburban sports clubs that offer a wide range of facilities for racquet sports, swimming, running, weights, and so forth.

The Sussex Club is a very small facility, relative to the others, and has a totally female clientele that tends to be older, less fit, and higher income. It serves business and professional women who pay a little more to receive more individual attention, and to have their bodies shielded from the masses, at least until they are improved a little. But this part of the business has never been very profitable and after paying its share of the rent has never broken even. It certainly raises the question that perhaps this space could be used more profitably. On the other hand, Donna feels that with a more aggressive and effective sales effort, membership could be increased. The average price of a Sussex Club annual membership is $495. In the past, membership sales appeared to be related to the level of skills and motivation of the sales staff. Both newspaper advertising and door-to-door distribution of flyers had been used and did show some effect. The club also offers incentives to members to bring referrals (three extra months of your membership, etc.).

Santé Restaurant

The restaurant requires an entirely different promotional approach. The best promotions have been the least "in control"—nothing did more for business than a restaurant review in the daily newspaper. Another period of increased sales could clearly be related to the major exhibition that ran following the opening of the nearby National Gallery. A good week always results from a major production at the neighbouring National Arts Centre. Conversely, the newspaper advertising that works well for the other businesses produced no measurable results for the restaurant.

But one promotional activity had worked well. The "Entertainment Card" is a coupon booklet put out across North America, featuring a section in which restaurants could offer a free entrée with any dinner for two. Santé has been featured in each annual booklet. It had also placed the same offer in a widely distributed coupon booklet put out for "Wheelchair Sports."

The results are very noticeable. Particularly in the periods shortly after the books come out, and shortly before they expire, as many as half the tables in the restaurant any given night could be using a coupon as partial payment for their meals. This results in a higher cost of sales and lower profit margin than some restaurants show, and brings the average dinner bill down from $28/seat "sold" to $25/seat actually collected. For a while this resulted in poor service as overstretched waiters and kitchen staff tried to push tables through. More recently, it was resulting in reservations refused and walk-ins turned away. The coupons are less noticeable at lunch, and receipts are only marginally below the $12/head "sold" at menu prices.

Alternative Directions

"I think we are ready to expand," Donna said, "but I am not sure which direction we should take."

"Sometimes it seems we should eliminate the Sussex Club. The fitness program is not a big revenue generator; in fact if you take into account the rent on the space it occupies, it loses money."

Figure 2 shows one option for the re-allocation of this space. It would add 40 seats (including the 20 already used some evenings) and a corresponding expansion to the kitchen (56 square metres) of the restaurant.

The remaining 107 square metres would be allocated to the spa, relocating the hair salon and manicure areas to take advantage of the windows along Sussex Drive, and allowing the development of water treatment rooms and an expansion of the massage facilities. Donna estimates the hair salon revenues would double with the improved environment, while the water treatment facility should average $35/treatment, with two to three treatments per day.

This sounded like an excellent idea until the cost of making these changes was estimated as follows:

a.	Converting gym space to restaurant seating	$20,000
b.	Extending kitchen	15,000
c.	New hair salon/manicure area	15,000
d.	New water treatment area	10,000
e.	Changes to change area	10,000
f.	New massage treatment rooms	8,000
	Total cost	$78,000

Figure 2   Optional Facility Layout, Main Floor

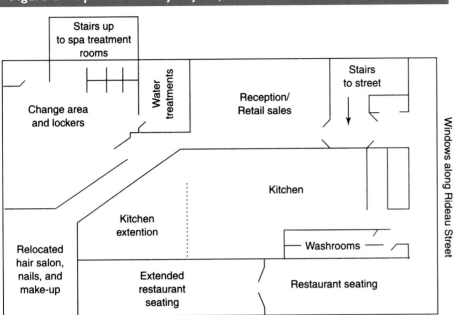

Windows along Sussex Drive

At current rates, a bank loan to finance these changes would cost 10 percent per annum. It would be nice to know the expenditure was worthwhile before taking on that kind of commitment. Since the lease has three years to run and a five-year option to renew, these improvements will be amortized over an eight-year period.

Although she feels that the above-mentioned estimates are realistic, she also wants to determine the effect that the proposed changes will have on profits under a more pessimistic scenario. She wonders what would happen if: hair salon revenues would increase by only 50 percent and if 25 percent of the members of Sussex Club would not return to take advantage of the spa and restaurant. Sussex Club members, on average, have been spending $200 per year at the spa and the same amount at the restaurant.

Donna is also considering an alternative strategy, one that would involve increasing promotion to get new members for the Sussex Club while leaving all other conditions unchanged. She would spend $25,000 for another salesperson and an additional $10,000 for newspaper advertising. The variable costs for each member are $80 per year and the average price for an annual membership is $495. Each new member can be expected to spend $200 per year at the spa and the same amount at the restaurant.

Before making any decision, Donna wants to know the effect of each of the scenarios on the operations' total profits.

Questions

1. **How will the proposed changes affect profitability (a) under the current scenario and (b) under the most pessimistic scenario?**

2. **How many new members would be needed to cover the cost of the proposed promotional campaign?**

3. **What recommendations will you offer Donna?**

12. Omer DeSerres: Artists' Supplies and Computers

From Hardware to Artists' Supplies

Omer DeSerres was 26 years old when he opened his first wholesale and retail hardware store on St. Laurent Street in Montreal in 1908. The store specialized in plumbing and heating supplies for both individual consumers and businesses. In the mid 40s, Omer DeSerres' son, Roger, took over the operations. Under his leadership, the company expanded as he added new stores and several new and diverse product lines. Customers at these stores purchased a variety of products including household appliances, gifts, renovation materials, artists' materials, and sporting goods.

The company experienced sustained growth until the early 1970s. At its peak, the company owned seven outlets, five hardware stores, a sporting goods store, and a heating and plumbing supplies store. The company had about 325 employees during the peak.

During the 1970s, the company suffered several setbacks forcing Roger DeSerres to downsize its operations. First, a very aggressive wholesaler of plumbing supplies entered the market resulting in a substantial reduction in sales of these products. In 1972, Roger DeSerres closed its wholesale plumbing division and withdrew all the plumbing materials from the stores, despite the fact that 50 percent of the company's sales were generated from plumbing supplies. Second, the competition in the hardware sector intensified with the arrival of new "large store" hardware chains (i.e., Pascal, Canadian Tire, and Beaver/Le Castor Bricoleur). These stores had an average selling area of 2000 square metres compared to an average of 1000 square metres for the Omer DeSerres stores. The Omer DeSerres stores lost customers to the new chains and sales fell substantially.

Finally, in 1974 the store located on St. Catherine Street received an expropriation notice for the construction of the Université du Québec à Montréal (UQAM) campus. As a result, the company was forced to relocate its main store, a company's landmark since 1913. The store was relocated to St. Hubert Street at the corner of Bélanger Street, where the family already operated a hardware store. This outlet was poorly located to satisfy the needs of the primary and the secondary markets. The 1000-square-metre store exceeded the size required to satisfy the needs of the neighbouring area, but, on the other hand, the size was not large enough to carry the selection of merchandise required to compete directly with the large chains.

Two years later, Roger DeSerres closed the hardware store on St. Hubert Street, thus ending the hardware activities he had developed during his career. Marc DeSerres, who had started working in the retail sector of the hardware store on St. Hubert Street, took over the family business. At that time, the company had only a small store of 150 square metres situated on St. Catherine Street, which sold artists' and graphic arts supplies. The boutique had four employees.

Source: Case written by Professor JoAnne Labrecque, École des H.E.C. (affiliated with the University of Montreal).

The Development of the Artists' Supplies Division

Marc DeSerres and the store faced an uncertain future. The store occupied a site belonging to UQAM and risked being expropriated at any time. He nevertheless went ahead and expanded its operations. In 1979, he moved the store to a larger site, still under the ownership of UQAM. He believed the site had good potential due to its proximity to UQAM, which represented an attractive target market. In 1985, the uncertainty facing the store was eliminated when the company acquired the building where the main store and head office of Omer DeSerres are currently situated, at 334 St. Catherine St. East. This choice location for the artists' and graphic arts supplies store, close to UQAM and in the heart of downtown Montreal, allowed the company to rapidly increase sales in a very short time. In the mid 1980s, most of the advertising agencies and graphic artists purchased their supplies, including brushes, technical rulers, and drawing tables, from Omer DeSerres. The store, which had 1000 square metre of selling space and carried 30,000 articles, could satisfy the needs of a very wide clientele including students, amateur artists, and graphic arts professionals.

Growth by Acquisition

In the mid 1980s, Marc DeSerres began expanding operations primarily through acquiring other stores. The major product line—artists' supplies—had changed little in many years and the overall market was in the maturity stage of its life cycle. Thus, growth came through acquisitions.

In 1986, Omer DeSerres acquired the Lizotte store in Old Quebec, a successful store dealing with artists' supplies. Shortly after the purchase, Marc DeSerres changed the name of the store to Omer DeSerres and made major changes to the store and to the product mix to conform to the Omer DeSerres image of quality and product specialization. Two years later, Omer DeSerres acquired its main competitor in Quebec City, the Trottier store. Since telephone orders represented the largest proportion of sales, Marc DeSerres closed the Trottier store and concentrated all his activities in the Old Quebec area.

In the 1987–88 period, Omer DeSerres opened two branches, one in Laval and another one in Pointe-Claire (both suburbs of Montreal). The stores were smaller than the main store on St. Catherine Street and carried a more limited product line (approximately 15,000 items).

In 1992, Omer DeSerres acquired its Montreal competitor, Loomis & Toles, located on Stanley Street. The store layout was changed as well as the product line to conform to the distinct character of Omer DeSerres. The store had an area of 400 square metres, employed seven people, and carried an inventory of 15,000 items. By the end of 1992, Omer DeSerres operated five stores in the province of Quebec (Exhibit 1).

The technological advances of the 80s revolutionized the graphic arts market. Each year, several products disappeared from the shelves as they were replaced by computer graphics packages. As these graphics packages were adopted by advertising agencies and the boutiques of graphic artists, Marc DeSerres knew that his business would suffer. As a strategic move, he expanded

Exhibit 1   Omer DeSerres Stores—1992

Location	m²	Number of Products	Number of Employees	Delivery	Competitors
Montreal, St. Catherine Street	1000	30,000	50	Yes	
Montreal, Stanley Street	400	15,000	7	No	
Laval	250	15,000	6	No	None
Pointe-Claire	250	15,000	6	No	None
Quebec	450	20,000	20	Yes	3 (Small)

into the computer market and in early 1990 opened two computer stores in Montreal. By becoming an Apple dealer, Omer DeSerres was adapting to the new needs of its clients. "Since our clients were using more and more computers," said Marc DeSerres, "we had to offer that service."

Contrary to the market of artists' supplies, which had reached maturity, the world of computer graphics was continually changing. In fact, it was a difficult task to forecast the growth of the computer division of Omer DeSerres six months ahead. Omer DeSerres—Computer Graphics was positioned in the market as a specialized store selling computer equipment and offering consulting services in imagery, computerized systems, computer-aided design and manufacture, data acquisition, and colour separation. Companies were its main target. According to Marc DeSerres, the future growth of the company lay in the computer division, which represented close to 50 percent of sales.

In 1993 Omer DeSerres acquired six stores specializing in artists' supplies owned by the S.P.R. RAPID-Graphic division of the CORRA group, a Dutch holding company that was well established in the French food industry. The CORRA group had set as an objective during the 1980s to penetrate new markets and had acquired 10 small stores of artists' supplies in Quebec. The S.P.R. acquisition represented a turning point for Omer DeSerres. The transaction involved several stores, located in six different cities (Montreal, Quebec, Chicoutimi, Ottawa, Burlington, and Sherbrooke). The management of S.P.R. was centralized in the Montreal store, but most of the stores were poorly organized. The stores did not offer the same product mix and had different names, some of which had been changed several times (see Exhibits 2, 3, and 4). The stores employed a large number of people, 85 in total. The CORRA group had given management the freedom to manage the stores in any way they felt was appropriate. The management team, composed of four people, had considerable latitude to decide on the choice of articles, the selection of suppliers, price policies, and promotions.

Although this move would strengthen Omer DeSerres' position of leadership in the market of artists' and graphic arts supplies, Marc DeSerres knew that the purchase of the six new stores would be a challenge for a company of 130 employees and seven commercial outlets, namely five stores selling artists' and graphic arts supplies and two stores selling computers. In order to integrate these newly acquired stores into the company, Marc DeSerres started by merging the management of the two companies to avoid overlapping of administrative tasks, with the assistance of three of the four members of the S.P.R. RAPID-Graphic management. Under the new organizational structure, all the strategic

Exhibit 2   Stores Acquired from S.P.R. RAPID-Graphic Division of CORRA Group

City	Store Names (including former names)
Montreal	• Le Pavillon des arts (corner of St. Denis/Ontario streets) • La spatule • RAPID-Graphic
Chicoutimi	• Le Pavillon des arts
Ottawa	• Eezee-Art et RAPID-Graphic • RAPID-Blue
Burlington (Ontario)	• RAPID-Graphic • Studio Gosselin • Rouillard
Sherbrooke	• RAPID-Graphic • Le Pavillon des arts
Quebec City	• Le Pavillon des arts

Exhibit 3   Product Mix of the S.P.R. RAPID-Graphic Division

	Graphic Arts Material	Artists' Material	Crafts Material	Framing	Lettraset	Reprographics	Delivery
Montreal	X	X	X	—	—	—	—
Chicoutimi	—	X	X	X	X	—	X
Ottawa	X	X	—	X	X	—	X
Burlington	X	X	—	—	X	X	X
Sherbrooke	—	X	X	X	—	—	—
Quebec City	X	X	—	—	—	—	—

Exhibit 4   Some Characteristics of the S.P.R. RAPID Stores

Location	m²	Number of Articles	Number of Employees	Delivery	Competitors
Montreal (St. Denis St.)	1000	20,000	35	No	Omer DeSerres
Chicoutimi	1500	15,000	10	Yes	None
Ottawa	700	15,000	12	Yes	1 (major)
Burlington	400	10,000	10	Yes	None
Sherbrooke	150	7,000	4	No	None
Quebec City	250	15,000	6	No	Omer DeSerres

decisions—promotional budget, store layout, choice of suppliers, price policies—would be made by the management. The store managers would be responsible for managing their personnel, restocking and selecting products as per the product mix authorized by the company's purchasing agents.

Shortly after the acquisition, Marc DeSerres made major changes to the stores located in the markets he knew well, namely Montreal and Quebec. In Montreal, he changed the layout of Le Pavillon des arts, but kept the same personnel. In Quebec City, he relocated Le Pavillon des arts to be near Laval University, an important target market. Few changes were made to the other stores. On the other hand, he wonders what retail strategy he should follow for the stores located in the other cities and what commercial name they should have.

In total, the Omer DeSerres network today has 13 outlets—two computer stores and 11 artists' supplies stores—and employs more than 200 people. According to Marc DeSerres, sales are expected to exceed $20 million in 1995.

Following the acquisition of the S.P.R. RAPID-Graphic, Marc DeSerres wonders what retail strategy he should follow for the new stores. In particular, he would like to know what your recommendations are to the following questions.

Questions

1. **Which commercial name (Omer DeSerres, Pavillon, Rapid, . . .) should he use for the new stores in Quebec, Montreal, Chicoutimi, Ottawa, Burlington, and Sherbrooke?**

2. **Should he modify the product lines carried by the stores?**

3. **Should he use the same positioning for all the stores?**

4. **Would you recommend the same promotional program for all the stores?**

13. Wing and a Prayer

Stefan Bakarich finally had found just the right name for his mobile bungee jumping operation—Wing and a Prayer. It was March 1994, and he had eight weeks to the May Victoria Day Weekend—the first long weekend of the summer—to get his operation "off the ground." If he had it figured correctly, Stefan would rent a construction crane, assemble a group of friends, and tour southwestern Ontario offering bungee jumps at tourist attractions. He and his friends could earn enough money to return to university in the fall while being paid to have fun and work on their tans over the summer.

Background

Bungee jumping started as a ritual practised by "land divers" on Pentecost Island in the New Hebrides, located in the South Pacific. To cleanse themselves of wrongdoing or as acts of courage, men constructed 30 metre towers from thin trees. Climbing to the top, they dove off with vines tied around their ankles. Their heads would just touch the ground as the vine became taut. In the 1960s, a group of Oxford University students (who called themselves the Oxford Dangerous Sports Club) brought bungee jumping to the modern world. As a commercial curiosity, the sport was born in New Zealand in 1988, where ancient vines were replaced with modern man-made fibre cords tested to withstand more than 3,000 pounds, and where bamboo pole towers were replaced with bridges spanning deep river gorges.

Source: This case was written by Marvin Ryder, McMaster University.

The sport became popular on the West Coast of the United States in the late 1980s and swept across the country in the early 1990s showing phenomenal growth. In 1991, only 20 companies in the United States offered bungee jumps. In 1992, that number had grown to 200 and by 1993, more than 400 companies were in the bungee jump business. Participation in the sport had also grown. In 1992, 1.5 million Americans experienced a bungee jump, spending more than $100 million for the thrill. In 1993, 2.5 million Americans participated, spending more than $125 million.

In Canada, the first commercial bungee operation (Bungy Zone) opened south of Nanaimo on Vancouver Island on August 4, 1990. By 1993, 30,000 people had jumped at this site. Some Bungy Zone statistics: oldest jumper 73; youngest 14; and heaviest 330 pounds. The most paid bungee jumps by one person was 30. The typical jumper was a thrill-seeking male aged 18 to 25. Ninety-nine percent of the people who paid the fee completed the jump. Ten percent of jumpers took a second jump on the same day. Participation statistics were not available for Canada but, in 1993, there were about 35 companies that arranged bungee jumps off bridges, towers, cranes, and hot air balloons. The West Edmonton Mall had introduced indoor bungee jumping and Nanaimo had even hosted bungee jumping in the nude.

Stefan had taken his first bungee jump in May 1993. He tried to describe his experience to a friend.

> I dove straight out, in my best imitation of Superman. At first, the free-fall was exhilarating. But it was also disorienting, and after a moment I panicked. I wished there were something to grab hold of. The sound of the wind was almost deafening. The ground below rushed toward me, until everything became a blur. It was hard to believe that I was feeling 3 G's—just like air force pilots.
>
> Suddenly, the world seemed upside-down. The ground was receding, and now I was completely confused. I was up in the air again when I realized that the cord had held.
>
> I started to descend once more. This time, there was no fear, just enjoyment. I rebounded up and down four more times, with each rise becoming smaller. Finally, the bungee cord had no more bounce, and I was lowered onto the pad where my feet were untied. Friends told me I had the Look—a certain glow common to those who had just found God or had escaped the electric chair.

During the summer of 1993, Stefan took a bungee jump training course, worked for two and a half months at an amusement park in the United States, and jumped 150 more times.

Operations

Stefan's experience with a crane-based company inspired him. He had taken careful notes about its operation so that he could replicate its success in Canada. For a typical jump, a patron would be taken, in a specially designed metal cage, 130 feet to the top of a crane—a ride of 60 seconds. These jump platforms were available for $500 to $1,000, though Stefan thought he could design and build one over the next eight weeks. At the top, the patron would be placed in one of two harnesses and given special instructions about jumping. One harness went around a person's ankles so that he or she would fall head first. The feet were tightly bound together with a towel and tethered to the bungee cord by a nylon strap and carabiner, a common piece of mountaineering equipment. The other harness could be strapped around a person's waist so that he or she would fall feet first. Each harness was commercially available at a cost of $150 to $300. While the patron took some time to build courage, the length of the bungee cord was adjusted to that person's weight. These "top of crane" activities could take between two and four minutes. Jumping out from the cage and away from the crane, the patron would take three seconds to fall until the bungee cord became taut and caused him or her to bounce. Waiting for the bounding to stop, lowering the basket, retrieving the jumper, and removing the harness from her or him would take another two minutes.

Stefan had researched potential suppliers so he had a firm estimate of costs. He would have to pay $100 per operating hour for construction crane rental, which included $1 million of liability insurance, fuel to run the generator, and a driver. Given the lack of office building construction, many companies had cranes parked in their compounds. These construction companies had been quite interested in Stefan's lease proposal. A crane operator would cost an additional $40 per operating hour. He felt the cost was justified as a skilled employee operating the crane would minimize the chances of something going wrong.

He and a jump assistant would be on the jump platform helping with instructions, adjusting the bungee cord, strapping on the harness, and communicating via walkie-talkie to the crane operator. On the ground, one person would use a microphone and sound system to speak to any crowd that had gathered and encourage them to participate. Two other people would assist on the ground by getting potential patrons to sign a liability waiver form, weighing jumpers to determine the proper bungee cord, collecting the jump fee, and talking personally with patrons in the crowd. While people under 18 could jump, a parent or guardian's signature would be required on the waiver form. Excepting the crane operator and himself, all staff would each be paid $8.00 per operating hour.

Of course, a bare crane was not very attractive so Stefan would have to invest in some cloth banners that, when hung on the crane, would also be used for promotion. Some portable tables, folding chairs, walkie-talkies, and a sound system would have to be purchased for $1,700. This cost also included portable "snow" fencing that would be used to limit public access to the crane, jump platform, and retrieval area. During less busy times, the sound system would play "hip hop," "dance," "house," and "rap" music to help attract and build a crowd. His major cost was an inflatable target pad that would be used to catch a jumper only if the bungee cord broke. Though pads came in many sizes, he felt it was a wise precaution to choose the largest size available at a cost of $12,000. As he thought the business would have a three- to five-year life, the pad and other equipment could be used year after year.

He had modelled his fee schedule on the American amusement park: $65 for the first jump and $55 for a second jump on the same day.

Realistically, the company would operate for the 110-day period from the Victoria Day Weekend in late May to the Labour Day Weekend in early September. As he did not want to be bothered with portable lighting, he would start operations no earlier than a half hour after sunrise and cease operations no later than a half hour before sunset. The company would never operate during a thunderstorm or in high winds and Stefan thought that the start of a weekend with overcast/rainy days would see less demand for the service.

Safety

Bungee jumping was not without its risks. In August 1992, a man was killed in Peterborough, Ontario, when he jumped from a crane. That same year, two people died in the United States and one in New Zealand from accidents. The Canadian Standards Association, a non-profit agency, had not determined any rules for bungee jumping so regulations varied by province. Some provinces had no regulations, but Ontario, working with the Canadian Bungee Association, had amended the Amusement Devices Act to regulate bungee jump operations starting in the spring of 1994.

In the legislature, Ontario Consumer and Commercial Affairs Minister, Marilyn Churley, said, "Operators can't just take a construction crane and set it up and have people jump off. We don't think that's safe. The government is committed to establishing and enforcing safety standards to minimize the risk to Ontarians who take part in this activity. Maintaining high standards of safety may also limit bungee operators' exposure to lawsuits and reduce the high cost of liability insurance."

Bungee jump operators were required to obtain a licence and permit ($310 fee) from the ministry prior to any jumps taking place. Before a licence could be issued, the equipment design first had to be approved by ministry engineers ($400 fee) after which a thorough on-site physical inspection of the bungee operation would be completed ($200 fee). The technical dossier of designs was to include: the jump height; a description of bungee cords including manufacturer, type of cord, and weight range of jumpers; an indication if the jump is static or portable; a description of the hoisting device including name of manufacturer, year, serial number, and safe working load; depth of water or air bag; type of harnesses to be used and types of jumps offered; wind speed restrictions; and number and functions of jump personnel.

A 40-page code for bungee jumping operations was also in place. The code had been recommended by the Task Force on Bungee Jumping, a working partnership between government and the Canadian Bungee Association. The code required a number of safety features that must be in place on bungee equipment and technical specifications for the structure, platform, bungee cords, harness, and all other equipment used in the activity. It also outlined the qualifications for bungee jump employees including certificates in First Aid and Cardio-Pulmonary Resuscitation (CPR) and training specific to bungee jumping. Another requirement was a good first aid kit with a spinal board and speed splints, which would cost an operator an additional $500.

These changes were introduced to regulate careless operators and were aimed primarily at mobile bungee operations as they had less-experienced staff and more failure-prone equipment because it was repeatedly set up and dismantled. Prior to the legislation, some operators had voluntarily introduced dual carabiners for ankle harnesses so there was a back-up if one failed.

Stefan planned his own set of rules. No pregnant women. No people with heart conditions. No people with high blood pressure. No people who suffered from epilepsy. No people with neurological disorders. Especially no people under the influence of alcohol and drugs. He would allow no reverse jumping (anchoring and loading the bungee cord from the ground to propel the jumper upward), no sand bagging (loading excess weight with the jumper to be released at the bottom to gain more momentum), and no tandem jumping (two or more jumpers harnessed together).

A bungee cord was made from several bound strands of latex rubber doubled back on itself thousands of times sheathed in cotton and nylon. The cost of these cords varied from $300 to $1,000. The cord could stretch to five times its original length. For safety, most operators retired a bungee cord after 150 jumps. Prior to the popularity of jumping, these cords were used by the U.S. Air Force on aircraft carriers so they were constructed to military specifications.

Some Decisions

To start his business, Stefan needed capital to acquire bungee cords, harnesses, the landing pad, and his operating equipment. He was aware of two Ministry of Economic Development and Trade loan programmes. As a returning Canadian university student, he could apply for a $3,000 interest-free loan. To qualify for this loan, he had to be over 15, returning to school, and operating a business in Ontario between April 1, 1994, and September 30, 1994. Whatever loan amount he received would be payable on October 1, 1994.

He had also heard of the Youth Adventure Capital Program. It provided loans of up to $7,500 to help unemployed Canadian youth aged 18 to 29 start a business in Ontario. The interest rate on the loan would be prime plus one percent and he would be expected to make principal and interest payments each month. He would also be expected to contribute a minimum of one-quarter of the loan amount to the operating capital of the firm. This pro-gramme was not intended to fund a summer job experience.

Neither programme would provide him with all the capital he required. He approached his parents. While not completely sold on the venture, his parents thought it would be a good learning experience so they agreed to loan him $3,000 interest-free, though they expected to be repaid at the end of the summer.

Needing more money, Stefan shared his plan with Zach Thompson, a friend on the university water-polo team and a recent bungee jumping enthusiast. Zach had also worked part-time with a bungee jump operator, but he had only jumped 40 times in the last year. He would act as a jump assistant. Zach proposed a partnership and a joint application for any government loan. Profits would be split 50/50. Like Stefan, he would replace a "paid" worker on the jump crew but would not draw any hourly wages. Of all people Stefan contacted, Zach asked the most questions.

Where would they operate the business? Stefan thought they could create a base of operations in Grand Bend, a popular beach location within an hour's drive of London, Ontario. When special events occurred, like the Western Fair in London, Ontario, or the Zurich Bean Festival, they could pull up stakes and move to that location for a few days.

Would they only offer bungee jumps? Zach thought they could sell some complementary products. A colourful logo could be designed for "Wing and a Prayer" and applied to T-shirts and baseball caps. Selling for $20 and $10 respectively, these items would have a 100 percent mark-up on cost and could add extra revenue. Zach had also thought about selling a personalized video. That would mean purchasing a camcorder ($1,800), developing some stock footage for opening and closing credits, and somehow editing/processing on site the video footage shot so the patron could quickly get her/his tape. Zach thought they could sell the videos for $25. Building on these ideas, Stefan thought about offering a colourful poster that might be especially popular among children. To produce 1,000 posters would cost $800, but they would be sold for $4 to $6, generating a very healthy profit margin.

Would they make any money? That required some financial analysis including a break-even analysis. Zach felt they needed to assess a second scenario: the likelihood that they would make enough money to return to university in the fall. These analyses would be needed along with their marketing plan when any loans were sought.

If this was going to be their summer occupation, they needed to get started right away.

Questions

1. **Based on financial analysis, how likely are the entrepreneurs to meet their profit targets?**
2. **Is their operational plan sound? Do you have any improvements to suggest?**
3. **Should they open a bungee-jumping business?**

14. West Coast Furniture

West Coast Furniture is a high-line furniture dealer active in the Vancouver area. The company specializes in expensive luxury furnishings that are purchased by upper-middle to high-income consumers who want fine craftmanship and quality—and who are prepared to pay for it. West Coast deals in products such as oak burl inlaid coffee tables ($4,000), dining room suites ($10,000–$15,000), bedroom suites ($6,000–$10,000), sofas and couches ($6,000), and executive desks ($8,000).

A slowdown in total company sales began in the late 1980s. With the onset of the 1990 recession, sales started to deteriorate seriously. This trend became apparent to the owners, Stan and Susie, when they reviewed the historical sales of their two main market segments (see Exhibit 1). West Coast had originally relied on its wholesaling operations to other retail furniture dealers, but the company also sold direct to consumers through its own discount retail show-room. Aside from the difficulties related to declining sales, West Coast was also under pressure from its retail dealers to stop selling direct to consumers. Retail dealers argued that West Coast was supposed to act as their wholesaler and that operating a discount retail showroom made it a direct competitor.

A review of West Coast's performance was definitely in order, so the owners together with a consultant examined the firm's two market segments. Their marketing mix analysis included the following insights.

Wholesale Distribution to Retail Dealers

Product

West Coast's retail distributors concentrated on the low and mid-range product lines in terms of quality and brand image. Retailers used a very limited selection of West Coast's luxury name brand product lines to provide an option to those

Source: This case was written by Dr. Lindsay Meredith, Simon Fraser University.

consumers who found the quality and craftmanship of their regular product lines to be unacceptable. While the retailers carried a good selection of the low and mid-range product lines in their showrooms (and in immediately available inventory), the brand names distributed by West Coast were available only through catalogue ordering. Retailers followed this policy to minimize their inventory carrying costs for the expensive West Coast product lines.

Price

The retailers' price structures were heavily concentrated in the low and medium ranges. For comparative purposes, a consumer could expect to pay approximately 40 percent more for the cheapest product lines distributed by West Coast than for the most expensive mid-priced products offered by the retailers. This price spread reflected the manufacturing costs and quality of materials used in the furniture. Low- and medium-priced furniture, for example, is made of a thin layer of oak veneer glued to particle board. The brands distributed by West Coast are made from solid oak.

Place

All of the retail dealers were located in the suburban areas of Greater Vancouver. The retailers preferred mall locations in regions where low-to-medium-priced townhouses and medium-priced single detached housing starts were increasing most rapidly. The general consensus in the industry was that these areas of new family formation represented the largest demand for potential furniture sales. Three of West Coast's retailers had declared bankruptcy in 1995, which left Stan and Susie with $18,000 in bad debts.

Promotion

The retailers supplied by West Coast had over recent years begun to rely heavily on advertising their price competitiveness as a means of attracting the young marrieds who comprised the family formation groups. Retail dealers rarely advertised the expensive furniture lines supplied by West Coast because they didn't wish to scare off potential customers who wanted to avoid high-priced home furnishings.

Direct Discount Retail Sales to Consumers

Product

West Coast's product lines were very high quality with a good assortment of name brand furnishings. Depth of the company's product mix was substantial. Approximately 12 percent of inventory in dining room suites averaged one to two turns per year. The total 1995 inventory in dining room suites was approximately $300,000.

Price

West Coast's retail discounting strategy gave customers an approximate 20 percent price advantage over their four major luxury furniture competitors.

Exhibit 1	West Coast Furniture Sales (000s $)						
	1989	**1990**	**1991**	**1992**	**1993**	**1994**	**1995**
Wholesale	$1,351	$1,329	$1,304	$1,271	$1,216	$1,137	$1,002
Direct consumer retail	821	831	843	867	905	983	951
Total company sales	$2,172	$2,160	$2,147	$2,138	$2,121	$2,120	$1,953

Prices weren't actually shown on the majority of stock on the showroom floor because Stan and Susie wanted the customers personally to approach the sales staff for help. The sales representatives could then provide price data as well as information about West Coast's fine product quality and competitive value.

Place

West Coast was strategically located in close proximity to three major upscale suburbs in the Greater Vancouver area. Other high-income areas in Vancouver were closer to competitors' locations, but Stan and Susie believed that people who were prepared to spend an average of $8,000 on a home furnishing item were also inclined to spend more search time looking for high quality at good prices.

West Coast's 2,500-square-metre showroom floor was a bit large, but necessary to carry its substantial product mix.

Promotion

West Coast relied solely on word of mouth for its advertising. The sales force was, by necessity, made up of Stan and Susie plus one receptionist/clerk because low cash flows coupled with poor retail sales didn't justify any more help.

The segmental analysis raised a number of questions and concerns regarding West Coast's total operations:

1. While the wholesale operation of the company still accounted for over slightly half of its revenues, what was causing the decrease in West Coast's sales to its retail dealers since 1990? (See Exhibit 1.)

2. Should the company get out of direct selling to consumers since a number of West Coast's retailers didn't like it acting as a competitor? If West Coast chose to remain a wholesaler as well as selling direct to consumers, what could it do about the negative reaction of those retailers who feared direct competition from West Coast?

3. Direct consumer retail sales (see Exhibit 1) indicated a moderate but consistent level of growth over the 1989 to 1994 period. But 1995 sales gave cause for concern. Stan and Susie couldn't understand why they weren't getting a better response from upper-income consumers of luxury home furnishings. After all, the other luxury furniture stores in Vancouver certainly appeared to be getting business. The owners wondered if all of the elements in their retailing mix were operating effectively.

4. Finally, Stan and Susie wondered if they should try advertising, but this involved answering a number of questions: What media should they use: direct mail, newspapers, radio, TV, or magazines? Even if they chose some of these media, where in the newspaper should they advertise, for example? What radio station should they use? If all of the magazines were similar, should they look for the cheapest one? Where would they get the money to pay for the advertising since poor sales meant that their cash flow was limited?

Questions

1. **Would you recommend that West Coast drop its own direct sales program?**
2. **If not, what changes would you make in that program?**
3. **What about advertising?**

15. The Maaco Franchise

Martin Klyne sat back and reflected on the analysis he had just completed. Now he had to make the decision—whether or not to obtain a Maaco auto painting and body work franchise. He was impressed with the franchise and his first-year financial projections for the Regina market looked great. However, he thought, I'll just review everything again before I decide.

The Idea

Mr. Klyne became interested in obtaining a Maaco franchise while working with the Canadian Imperial Bank of Commerce during a cooperative work semester. He was a finance major in the Bachelor of Administration program at the University of Regina. During his work semester he had been involved in approving loans, some of which were for individuals purchasing various franchises. In his spare time he studied the franchise field and identified Maaco as an up-and-coming franchise in Canada. He expressed his interest to a friend, Dale Schick, an experienced autobody repairman. Dale had 13 years' experience in all phases of the business from wreck dismantler, autobody man, painter, and estimator to shop supervisor. Together they agreed to investigate obtaining a Maaco franchise. Martin had a small inheritance and Dale had some money set aside, and they determined that each partner could invest $40,000 in the business.

The potential partners then gathered some information on the Maaco franchise concept, the Regina market, the competition, and the investment required for the franchise.

The Maaco Franchise Concept

The typical Maaco Centre focussed on quality, with job specialization and a production-line approach enhancing the centre's performance. In addition to

Source: This case was prepared by Jim Mason, University of Regina.

auto painting, a shop handled autobody repairs, from the minor fender bender to the most extensive collision repairs.

The highest profit resulted from completing as many total paint jobs as possible, with only minor or cosmetic body repairs. Retail paint jobs were the most lucrative, but to ensure the shop operated at full capacity year round, Maaco also sought trade or wholesale paint jobs (marginally less profitable). Collision repair, also profitable, kept the shop busy during the winter months. The high efficiency of the shop was complemented by aggressive advertising and promotion, quality service, reasonable prices, and particularly effective ways of closing sales.

Franchisor Support

The first Maaco franchise opened in 1972 and by 1995 there were more than 450 centres, including 36 in Canada. Based on accumulated knowledge and experience, Maaco had developed a uniform system for the financing, location, construction, and operation of its centres. The relationship between Maaco and the franchisee was thoroughly laid out in a 14-page franchise agreement. Maaco provided the following support:

1. Finance: Maaco assisted with obtaining and negotiating financing.

2. Site selection: Maaco assisted in locating and negotiating the lease for an existing location or a build-to-suit facility.

3. Education: Every new owner/manager attended a five-week training programme. There the owner/manager learned painting and auto-repair techniques, as well as how to make service estimates, close sales, evaluate technical performance, supervise personnel, and manage a shop environment. Maaco covered the training, travel, and lodging expenses as part of the franchise agreement.

4. Advertising: Maaco created and coordinated placement of all advertising for television, radio, local newspapers, and Yellow Pages. Franchisees contributed $400 per week to the advertising fund in the United States. Because Maaco advertising was in its infancy in Canada, Canadian franchisees coordinated their own advertising and promotions using American materials. With more Maaco centres, franchisees would be expected to pay $400 per week to a Canadian advertising pool.

5. Equipment: A Maaco service technician organized and supervised the installation of all equipment and utilities inside the centre. The franchise package covered this service along with equipment and installation costs.

6. Signs: Maaco furnished both freestanding and affixed outdoor signs. The package included the signs and all freight charges. The owner/operator paid for the pole, mounting attachments, electrical hookup, and installation.

7. Operations: Maaco furnished full operating support for a centre's first three weeks. Thereafter, their operations person constantly monitored the centre's operation and management. Within 20 days of month end, franchisees submitted monthly profit-and-loss statements. Maaco had an automated accounting system capable of complex statistical analysis.

Maaco's professional staff provided guidance, training, field, and telephone supervision and help was readily available from other centres. Maaco held regular operations meetings where franchisees exchanged ideas, resolved problems, and received additional training. Further, a weekly newsletter listed the performance of all shops and highlighted new ideas.

Business for a Maaco franchise came from three areas: the retail market (people repainting their cars), the trade and wholesale market (used car dealers, auto rental, etc. who wanted cars repaired or painted), and the collision repair market (cars that were in an accident and usually covered by insurance).

The Regina Market

Retail market

Martin and Dale contacted another Maaco franchisee, in operation for eight years, who advised them that a Regina Maaco Centre should easily secure a retail market (no-collision/claims repair) of $150,000 per year. The average retail complete job was $550 ($350 for paint plus $200 in cosmetic body work). Therefore, securing a market of $150,000 would mean painting 273 retail cars.

Martin did some quick calculation on the retail market. The population of Regina was 180,000 and the number of households was 58,695. Assuming that 90 percent of the households had cars and that 25 percent of these households had two cars, the total cars in Regina was 66,030.

How many of these cars would require completes? Perhaps 1 in 10, or 6,603. How many of these car owners could afford to or would care to paint these cars? How many could be enticed if the price were reasonable and the end product was a quality finish? Perhaps one in four, or 1,650 (2.5 percent of the total car population). How many of these 1,650 could be enticed by Maaco's aggressive advertising and marketing to inquire further? Maybe one in four, or 412. Maaco's retention rate, that is, how many inquiries they closed on, was 50 percent. In summation, then, Maaco Regina should attain 206 cars (0.31 percent of the total car population) at $550 each, for a total retail of $113,300.

This did not take into account cars repaired under an insurance claim. A good majority of these car owners would have their entire car painted while it was in for collision repair, if the price was right. As the car was already being handled for body work, paint preparation, and painting, Maaco could afford to reduce its rates.

Could a Maaco Centre handle 206 cars? The season for retail completes was April to August inclusive—22 weeks. This added up to 110 working days, of which perhaps 5 were statutory holidays, leaving 105 days available. This meant approximately two cars per day on average—well within a Maaco Centre's capacity.

Trade and wholesale market

Numerous trade sources (used car dealers, auto brokers, fleet and lease disposal specialists, and auto rental centres) were contacted by telephone to determine the amount of trade business available. This market excluded collision/claim repairs. Fleet owners (i.e., City of Regina, SaskTel, Genstar, federal and provincial supply and services, etc.) were not contacted. It was judged that they purchased new vehicles (paint finish, factory ordered) and would, therefore, fall into the collision/claim repair market. The resale (and refurbishing) of these fleets would be included in collision/repair business.

Individuals contacted were briefed on the concept: quality work, reasonable prices, and relatively quick turnaround time. Of those who responded favourably, only one (Regina Mazda Sales) would be reluctant to provide 100 percent of their available work. They considered it important to spread this around among those shops that purchase Mazda parts. Based on their survey, Martin and Dale estimated that the following work was available:

473	completes @ $380	$179,740
64	completes @ $425	27,200
325	touch-ups/half cars @ $175	56,875
862		$263,815

For those customers who would provide more than 25 complete paint jobs per annum, a discount was included. Average trade complete job was $425, which the 10 percent discount lowered to $380.

To be realistic, Martin reduced the total by 40 percent to approximately $150,000 per year. Thus, the forecast for trade work was 517 cars handled in one year over 249 working days. On average, the centre would have to handle approximately two cars per day—again, well within the capacity of a Maaco Centre.

Collision market

Regina's total collision market was $25,000,000. They estimated a Maaco franchise should get 1–2 percent of that market with an aggressive advertising and promotions budget. This would mean revenues of $250,000 to $500,000 from collision repairs. They felt they should be able to get at least $405,000 from this market. A typical Maaco Centre easily had the capacity for $675,000 of business in collision repair alone.

Competition

Leading competition in the autobody industry was A & B, Arcola, Queen City, Regina, and Western. In the best sense of the Maaco concept, competition was very limited. Maaco would ultimately be the industry leader. Most shops were averse to complete paint jobs versus collision repair due to perceived lower margins. Maaco's efficient operations welcomed both paint and collision markets. With an aggressive advertising budget and quality service at a reasonable price, Maaco would become a key player in short order.

The Investment

The summary of investment in Exhibit 1 was based on a Maaco "Analysis of Investment" and discussions with the franchisor's representatives, other Maaco franchisees, and local body shop owners and suppliers.

Exhibit 1 Summary of Investment	
Description	**Investment**
Licence and service fee	$ 15,000
Initial advertising	6,800
Working capital fee	6,000
Equipment, including installation, freight, rigging & provincial sales taxes, custom duties where applicable	106,890
Inventory: paint, supplies, and stationery	11,550
Sign package: not including installation	5,760
Total franchise package	$152,000
First month's rent and security deposit (est'd)	8,000
Miscellaneous start-up costs (est'd)	20,000
Total investment	$180,000

The total investment was $180,000—$80,000 cash investment and $100,000 in seven-year term debt that could be arranged under the Small Business Loans Act. This investment secured a turnkey operation.

With respect to the advertising, Maaco collected an initial $2,500 for classified advertising in *The Leader Post* to hire a start-up crew, and for preopening and grand opening retail advertising. With the support of the regional operations representative, Martin planned to ask Maaco to return the $2,500. He would then coordinate his own preopening and grand opening advertising.

With a budget of $6,800 he judged that he would be able to undertake the following:

- An educational brochure circulated to *Leader Post* subscribers in selected areas. The brochure would outline who and where they were, and what services they provided.
- An on-location radio set-up for the grand opening.
- A full-page ad in *The Leader Post* (grand opening) in conjunction with their suppliers and contractors.

Martin then worked out a couple of scenarios for the business. A "most likely" scenario projected gross sales at $665,000, resulting in a 60 percent return on the cash investment (Exhibit 2). Sales at $575,000 ("pessimistic" scenario—15 percent reduction, very conservative) resulted in a net loss of $2,405. However, this was after meeting all loan payments, having no accounts payable, and setting aside a $17,800 cash balance to start the second year of operations. Break-even revenue was approximately $584,000.

In these scenarios, Martin felt that expenses were projected very realistically and were overstated in some areas. The second year under both scenarios improved substantially, since one-time start-up expenses were not incurred. Under the "most likely" scenario, the returns were 15 percent and 33 percent; under the worst, the returns were 4 percent and 9 percent.

Exhibit 2 Financial Projections (First Year)	
Total sales	$665,000
Cost of sales	364,234
Gross profit	300,766
Operating expenses	238,913
Net income before tax	61,852
Tax	15,463
Net income	46,389
Add depreciation	10,400
Less principal	16,000
Cash flow	$ 40,789

The Decision

Martin knew that people brought their cars to an autobody shop for many reasons:

- To provide normal maintenance, like tune-ups, brakes, and tires
- To spruce up the family's second car
- To refurbish their present car until they decide on a new model
- To protect and restore the original beauty of a special car
- To repair damage from an accident

They would bring their car specifically to Maaco because it offered:

- Quality paint services for every budget
- Written warranties honoured at more than 400 locations
- State-of-the-art paint finishes
- Timely service
- Expert body repairs
- Full collision repair services, from the minor fender bender to the most extensive collision repairs
- Extensive experience from servicing more than three million customers.

The needs of the Regina market had never before been met economically. Auto dealers, body shops, and "cheap paint" shops had attempted to satisfy the market with various alternatives—limited colour selection, air-dry coating (an inferior process), spot or partial painting, and the high-priced paint job.

Martin was convinced of the merits of the Maaco franchise but wondered if his analysis was sound. Did he and Dale have the administrative and managerial skills and technical expertise to successfully operate the franchise? Should he obtain the franchise?

Questions

1. **Should the partners conduct any further analysis before making the decision?**

2. **What are the advantages and disadvantages of the Maaco franchise?**

3. **Should the partners invest in the franchise?**

16. Dans un Jardin Canada Inc. Beauty Shops

The retail franchise concept of Dans un Jardin was created in 1960 in France by the Countess Lucile de Baudry d'Asson. Specializing in exclusive perfumes, beauty products, and personal service, the franchise chain grew rapidly. Through a series of events, the ownership of this international chain was obtained by Jean-Claude Gagnon of Boucherville, Quebec. He owned the concept and the trademark, and handled the manufacturing and distribution of the entire product line.

Mr. Gagnon was actively involved in the Canadian franchise, Dans un Jardin Canada Inc., whose head office was also located in Boucherville. The chain had 25 beauty shops throughout Quebec offering exclusive perfume and beauty products.

In late 1992, at a monthly meeting of the Dans un Jardin Canada franchisees and Mr. Gagnon and his staff, concern was raised about the following issues:

- How to improve sales throughout the year. Peak sales occurred prior to major gift-giving holidays such as Christmas, Easter, Mother's Day, and Father's Day.

- As a related issue, how to improve sales to customers who will buy the product for themselves (i.e., their own personal use).

- Concern was also raised about the current product mix. Some items were not selling very well and there was a general feeling that the product line could more closely match the needs of the customer.

The Dans un Jardin Concept

"Luxury, calmness, and pleasure. . ." This verse from the poet Charles Baudelaire is clearly reflected in Dans un Jardin Canada. The corporate brochure expresses the exclusive concept of the company with an analogy: "the beauty shops where everything is fragrance and freshness, tenderness and pleasure. . ."

The concept has been well executed and has led to the success of the business to date. The elegance of the decor, the fine packaging, the top-of-the-line quality products, the personalized service, and the store location are all focussed to appeal to the discriminating customer. As an example, the company

Source: Case written by Michèle Bernard, under the supervision of Gunnar K. Sletmo. © 1992, École des Hautes Études Commerciales (H.E.C.), Montreal.

was a finalist in the retail section for the prestigious Mercure 1990 Award of the Quebec Chamber of Commerce.

Dans un Jardin International Inc. has an excellent staff of professionals—chemists, marketing specialists, buyers and merchandisers, and supervisors—who contribute to maintain the concept of quality and image for the franchise and its brands.

The Dans un Jardin Franchise

Dans un Jardin Canada offers franchisees the necessary financial and managerial assistance and supplies to allow them to operate the business without having previous business experience. Dans un Jardin Canada operates a distribution franchise where the relationship between the franchisor and the franchisee includes the strategic and managerial approach that is specified by the franchisor. The distribution franchise offers the most opportunities to individuals having an entrepreneurial flair.

The Dans un Jardin Canada franchisee benefits from a well-known name, brand awareness, an existing market, and the expertise of the franchisor, without necessarily requiring a large amount of start-up capital. On the other hand, the franchisor has certain requirements that a qualifying franchisee must meet. Dans un Jardin Canada Inc. requires franchisees to: operate the store (i.e., no absentee owners), be committed, have a favourable attitude toward the product concept, be ambitious and dynamic, be a team player and follow procedures, be financially and morally sound, and respect the contractual agreement.

In return, the franchisor will assist the franchisee in arranging a long-term loan, provide the initial inventory to start up the business, assist in the design of the store, and provide basic training in managerial and selling techniques and knowledge of the specialized products. The franchisor supplies the computer equipment to enable the franchisee to manage sales, purchases, inventory control, and the overall operation. The franchisor provides help in promoting the business. Franchisees benefit from cooperative advertising and also participate in the decision-making process through monthly management meetings. In 1992, the Dans un Jardin Canada Inc. shops were owned almost exclusively by women.

The Target Market

Dans un Jardin uses a lifestyle approach to segmentation. The target market appreciates the feeling of well-being and pleasure, loves to be pampered, and likes to associate with people of his/her same image. Research has identified the typical customer as 25 to 55 years old (95 percent are female), has a relatively high income, and makes a purchase either to please himself/herself, for his/her own personal use, or to please his/her relatives and friends by giving them a personalized gift. It is estimated that 50 percent of the purchases are for personal use and 50 percent are purchased as gifts.

The clientele appears to be brand loyal, but the purchases vary depending on the season: lighter flower and fruit fragrance products in the summer, and more spiced products during the remainder of the year. Customers are dynamic, demanding, and active, and have little free time. Often made up of couples where both spouses work outside the home, these customers face time pressures yet wish to increase the quality of their lives. For these people, the notion of pleasure is becoming increasingly important and little individual treats take on a whole meaning in their lives. To look after themselves and their body is important; to spend 20 minutes relaxing in a bath scented with quality products is a precious, important, and cherished moment.

The Product Line

Dans un Jardin offers eight different product lines: bath products, hair care, beauty care, cosmetics, various items for men and children, lingerie, accessories, and perfumes. More than 600 different products are produced at the Boucherville plant or imported from France (brand names such as Decléor, Yves Delorme, Mustela, Plisson, etc.) and are distributed exclusively in Dans un Jardin shops.

For its perfumes, Dans un Jardin gets its essential oils, indispensable for the production of its products, from Grasse, France, the real "mecca" of perfume manufacturers. This is how the legendary names like mimosa, coriander, bergamot and passion fruit, opopanax, musk, or grey amber are enough to make a customer dream.

Centralized purchasing by the franchisor provides significant economies of scale to the franchisees. Decisions to launch or drop a line of products or a fragrance are decided by a majority vote of the franchisees at the monthly management meeting. This approach meets one of the criteria for a successful franchise: to carry a product mix large enough to allow the franchisee the flexibility to adapt purchases to cater to the tastes of his/her own clientele.

Store Location

The location of a new franchise is determined by Dans un Jardin Canada Inc. based on market studies. Exclusive territories are established between the franchisor and the franchisee depending on whether the store is located in a shopping centre or is a "stand-alone" location.

The choice of district, and consequently the type of neighbourhood clients or "walk-by" shoppers, is an important selection criterion. Particular care was taken in locating the first store of the Quebec franchise. It was opened on Laurier Street in Outremont, a "chic" district in Montreal. This first boutique set the tone for many franchises that were opened after that time.

The interior design of the store is based on corporate specifications to always ensure an image of quality. Regulations and procedures from Dans un Jardin International Inc. specify the choice of furniture, and the layout and display of products in the windows and in the store.

The competition for Dans un Jardin consists of stores specializing in beauty care (i.e., Lise Watier), brands sold in large department stores and pharmacies, and direct competitors operating with the beauty shop concept. These direct competitors are the English chains of Crabtree & Evelyn and Le Body Shop. Although closer to the concept of Dans un Jardin, they do not target exactly the same clientele and thus do not have a significant impact on market share.

The Franchisor and Franchisee Relationship

Dans un Jardin Canada Inc. provides assistance and training for its franchisees in all aspects of their operations. The assistance includes, among other things: training through videos covering products and accessories, packaging, window displays, and store layout; extensive product training covering perfumes and care products; and a two-week training program in the franchisee's new boutique covering management of the store.

The corporate advertising program is operated jointly between the franchisor and the franchisees and makes use of various media: dailies, monthly publications, radio and television, billboards, direct mail, and so on. Franchisees pay a fee of 2 percent of sales to cover the marketing aspects of the franchise, which is the norm in the industry. Franchisees are responsible for the costs of launching and promoting the opening of the store. The franchisee may also cover his/her promotional costs for special events in his/her area in terms of samples or gift certificates.

The price structure established by the franchisor provides the franchisee a gross profit margin of 48 percent, a figure within the Canadian national average for retail outlets classified as "gifts."

Recent Trends

The concept of Dans un Jardin is based on the notion of pleasure. It owes its success to this concept, which will continue to be important in industrialized countries, hence in Canada and Quebec. The wish to take care of oneself, associated with the wish to alleviate the frantic pace of modern life, will continue to provide a large client base for the Dans un Jardin shops.

It is sometimes argued that a recession has a limited negative impact on luxury products. The little daily life treats have a better chance to survive in a sagging economy than a vacation to a sunny destination or a luxurious durable or semi-durable good.

While the chain had experienced reasonable success, franchisees were concerned about a number of issues regarding profitability. As one example of an attempt to increase sales and profits, some shops in the chain have started to offer the service of aesthetic cubicles for facial and body care. To date, it was not clear whether this service would be profitable.

After a number of monthly meetings where both the franchisees and Mr. Gagnon had discussed their profitability concerns, it was decided at the September 1992 meeting to form a task force of five people: Mr. Gagnon, his marketing manager, and three franchise owners. They would provide recommendations at the next meeting regarding the best strategy to accomplish three goals: (1) to balance sales over 12 months; (2) to increase sales per retail outlet; and (3) to improve the performance of the product mix.

Questions

The three issues raised at the meeting between Jean-Claude Gagnon, his staff and franchisees are:

1. **How to increase sales?**
2. **How to balance sales over the year?**
3. **How to improve the performance of the product mix?**

17. Who's the Best Candidate?

Howard Goldman, the president of David and Charles, a department store in Halifax, Nova Scotia, had a buying vacancy in his misses coat department, and three candidates to choose from to fill it.

The misses coat department was not in good shape. The previous buyer, who had just been let go, had left a lot of distress stock behind, following a season in which sales had dropped nearly 8 percent. Mr. Goldman recognized that the department needed new blood, which was why he was eager to make the best possible choice.

Paul Coward

The first candidate was the current assistant in the department, Paul Coward. Coward was 28 years old and had come to the store directly from school five years earlier. He had joined the training group, served as a branch manager, and worked in various coat departments since then. He was familiar with the coat market and the department's vendors, and of course knew all store people and systems thoroughly. He had consistently received excellent reviews, but had lost a chance to become misses dress buyer to a candidate with comparable qualifications six months earlier. He had a pleasant personality and was well liked throughout the store.

Marie Whipple

The second choice was Marie Whipple. Two years younger than Coward, she had been with the store three years, all of which had been in the children's area. Currently, she was associate buyer of children's wear, with full responsibility for buying girls' coats. She had bought these coats for one full season, and her figures showed a respectable 20 percent growth. She had only completed two years of college (as opposed to Coward's four), but was known as a hard-driving, no-nonsense kind of buyer. The children's executives thought extremely well of her and recommended her strongly to Mr. Goldman.

Frank Coyle

Finally, Goldman had received a résumé of an older candidate, Frank Coyle, from an employment agency. Coyle had just been released by one of the May Company divisions, which had recently undergone a belt-tightening. He had an impressive résumé—20 years of buying coats, and his sales figures and gross margin had always been superior, even in years when coat business had been difficult. He knew everyone in the coat manufacturing business and had many friends and supporters there. Goldman wondered, though, whether he might

Source: This case was prepared by David Ehrlich, Marymount University.

not favour too many of his old friends as he came to a new store. Coyle would also cost the store more to hire. His salary would be at least $10,000 higher than what Goldman would pay the other two, and there would be relocation and agency expenses.

Question

1. As Howard Goldman, which candidate would you pick and why?

18. Diamond Clothiers

Ruth Diamond, president of Diamond Clothiers, was concerned that sales in her store appeared to have flattened out, and was considering establishing a different method of compensating her salespeople.

Diamond was located in an affluent suburb of Toronto, Ontario. Ruth's father had founded the company 40 years earlier, and she had grown up working in the business. After his retirement in 1980, she moved the store into an upscale shopping mall not far from its previous location, and sales had boomed almost immediately, rising to just over $1 million in five years. However, once it had reached that level, sales volume remained there for the next three years, making Ruth wonder whether her salespeople had sufficient incentive to sell more aggressively.

Diamond's staff were all women, ranging in age from 27 to 58. There were four full-timers and four part-timers (20 hours a week), all of whom had at least three years of experience in the store. All of them were paid at the same hourly rate, which was $10.00; there was also a liberal health benefit plan. Employee morale was excellent, and the entire staff displayed strong personal loyalty to Mrs. Diamond.

The store was open 78 hours a week, which meant that there was nearly always a minimum staff of three on the floor, rising to six at peak periods. Diamond's merchandise consisted exclusively of designer coats and jackets, ranging in price from $750 to more than $5,000 each. The average unit sale was about $2,000. Full-timers' annual sales averaged about $160,000, and the part-timers were a little over half of that.

Mrs. Diamond's concern about sales transcended her appreciation for her people's loyalty. She had asked them, for example, to maintain customer files and call their customers when new styles came in. While some of them had been more diligent about this than others, none of them appeared to want to be especially aggressive about promoting sales.

So she began to investigate commission systems, and discussed them with some of her contacts in the trade. All suggested lowering the salepeople's base pay and installing either a fixed or a variable commission rate system.

One idea was to lower the base hourly rate from $10 to $7 and let them make up the difference through a 4 percent commission on all sales, to be paid monthly. Such an arrangement would allow them to earn the same as they currently did.

Source: This case was prepared by David Ehrlich, Marymount University.

However, she realized that such a system would provide no incentive to sell the higher-priced coats, which she recognized might be a way to improve overall sales. So she considered offering to pay 3 percent on items priced below $2,000 and 5 percent on all those above.

Either of these systems would require considerable bookkeeping. Returns would have to be deducted from commissions, and she was also concerned that disputes might arise among her people from time to time over who had actually made the sale. So she conceived a third alternative, which was to leave the hourly rates the same, but to pay a flat bonus of 4 percent of all sales over $1 million, and divide it among the people on the basis of the proportion of hours each had actually worked. This "commission" would be paid annually, in the form of a Christmas bonus.

Questions

1. **What is your opinion about the various alternatives Mrs. Diamond is considering?**

2. **Do you have any other suggestions for improving the store's sales?**

19. The Gourmet Palace

Beverly Long had just finished reviewing with her daughter Alison the results of a survey that she had conducted the previous week. She kept shaking her head, not really understanding the situation. She had thought all along that research will give her the answers she was looking for, but now she wasn't sure.

Mrs. Long is the owner of The Gourmet Palace, a food store specializing in gourmet foods and exotic items from around the world. It is located in an upscale shopping mall situated in the downtown area of an East Coast city with a total population of 103,000. The store was opened a year ago, and business has been very uneven and rather disappointing, with large variations during the week and during the year. She confided her problems to a friend and he suggested that she needed to do some customer research. Her friend worked for a company that often purchased marketing research. He did not have any expertise himself, but he strongly encouraged Mrs. Long to conduct a study of her customers. He added that it shouldn't be too hard for Beverly to design, distribute, and analyze a simple questionnaire on why people shop at her store.

After thinking about this idea for a few days, she sat down and developed the questionnaire shown in Exhibit 1, which seemed to deal with the questions that were bothering her. She had the questionnaires copied by the print shop located in the mall. The following Saturday, she put up a sign inside the store indicating that, in exchange for filling out the questionnaire, she would give the customer a free can of tuna. She collected 50 questionnaires that way, which she spent Sunday tabulating.

The results were very disappointing. Many questions were left unanswered, such as addresses, age, and income. In the questions about the store, respondents wrote down one or two words, often quite general and not very useful. About half the respondents shop there once a week, and the other half occasionally. In the second question, several answered milk, bread, and cheeses. In the third question, most said quality and freshness. What they liked least were

Exhibit 1   Questionnaire Used by Beverly

The Gourmet Palace

Hi! I am conducting a survey today in order to find out your impressions about the Gourmet Palace, and how I can better serve you. Upon completing this questionnaire, you will receive a free can of tuna.

Information about you: Please indicate below

Your address _____

Your age _____

Your sex _____

Your occupation _____

Your approximate family income _____

Size of your family _____

Information about the Gourmet Palace

1 How often do you shop here? _____

2 What kinds of food items are you looking for? _____

3 What do you like best about the Gourmet Palace? _____

4 What do you like least about the Gourmet Palace? _____

5 How did you find out about the Gourmet Palace? _____

6 How do you find the prices at the Gourmet Palace? _____

7 Are there other food products you would like to buy at the Gourmet Palace? _____

8 Have you recommended the Gourmet Palace to your friends? _____

9 Any other comments? _____

   Thank you very much.

the high prices. They found out about the store by walking through the mall. For question 7, very few provided a suggestion; among those who did, some said sushi, caviar, and quails. Most said yes to question 8, and question 9 was not answered by anyone.

Beverly then showed the questionnaire and the results to her daughter Alison who was visiting her from Fredericton. Alison had recently graduated from the University of New Brunswick with a Bachelor of Commerce. Alison immediately reacted with confidence and pride. She said to her mother that she would develop a set of hypotheses, a new questionnaire, a sampling plan, and a plan for analysis before she returned to Fredericton.

Questions

1. **Evaluate the research design and the questionnaire prepared by Mrs. Long.**

2. **Take the role of Alison and complete the assignment.**

20. F. B. Smith/McKay Florists Ltd.

In April 1990, Marie Robbins, owner of F. B. Smith/McKay Florists Ltd., of Hamilton, Ontario, was considering whether or not to relocate one of her retail stores. The lease was up for renewal at the end of August. Marie believed that any decision she made would have a profound impact on the future of that store, in particular, and her business, in general.

Source: This case was prepared by Marvin Ryder, McMaster University.

Company Background

In 1990, Smith/McKay Florists consisted of three separate outlets. Marie, a native of Hamilton, purchased F. B. Smith Florists in 1980 and McKay Florists in 1983. These two established florists were among the oldest flower stores in Hamilton having been opened in 1919 and 1907 respectively. Marie blended the two business names in 1985 before establishing a third outlet in 1988.

Prior to 1980, Marie had been a Family Studies teacher for grades 8 to 12 in the public school system. Although she had little experience in the florist business, Marie valued her independence and saw the store as an outlet for her entrepreneurial spirit and creative energies. Lacking both floral design and business experience, Marie worked over the summer of 1980 with the former owners before launching out on her own.

The location in question was the original site of F. B. Smith Florists. Located between the Pioneer Restaurant and the Canadian Imperial Bank of Commerce, the building was on the south side of King Street West, between James and MacNab Streets. Her other two locations were: 238 James Street North (the original site of McKay Florists); and 1685 Main Street West. All three locations had a reputation for quality, service, and rapid delivery.

In 1990, Marie had 12 employees at the King Street store who served customers and arranged flowers. The centre of her operations was the James Street store where she combined a retail outlet with storage, office space and a floral design production facility. Daily flower deliveries were handled by a local delivery service. Smith/McKay Florists belonged to the FTD (Florist Transworld Delivery), the AFS (American Florist Service), and the Teleflora networks. Phone-in sales accounted for 75 percent of the King Street store's current business.

The average customer spent $22 at Marie's stores—$28 at a holiday time. On average, Marie did $300 to $500 per day in business at the King Street store. Her product mix was relatively simple: cut flowers, silk flowers, potted plants, and arrangements. She had found that items priced under $5.00 tended to be purchased as impulse goods on a cash-and-carry basis. The King Street store was open from 8:00 A.M. to 5:30 P.M. daily and closed early at 4:00 P.M. on Saturday.

The Florist Business in Hamilton

Between 1985 and 1990, the florist business in Hamilton flourished. Approximately 33 shops were opened, bringing the total number to 95 stores. According to Marie, the rapid expansion of the market created a "neighbourhood phenomenon." Almost every neighbourhood in the city had at least one florist.

The flower business was seasonal by nature. The sales peaks were Valentine's Day, Easter, Mother's Day, and Christmas. The worst months for flower sales were June, July, August, October, November, January, February (except for February 14), and March. On the other hand, December flower sales accounted for 25 percent of her yearly revenue. For the remainder of the year, anniversary, funeral, wedding, birthday, and hospital arrangements accounted for the majority of the sales volume.

Smith/McKay Florists faced competition on three fronts. First, it competed directly for the phone-in business with any florist shops listed in the Yellow

Pages. Second, it competed for walk-in traffic with other nearby florist shops. Third, there was competition from the grocery stores, which carried both plants and cut flowers. Because of their buying power, they could offer flowers at a cheaper price. They did not offer arrangements or delivery. All the florist shops in Hamilton purchased their flowers from the same suppliers.

In some ways, Marie believed the grocery store sales might actually be beneficial. "Grocery stores may help encourage people to purchase flowers. Getting them into the habit of buying flowers will help my business. Further, when they visit my store, they should be able to see the extra quality that I offer."

Besides the Yellow Pages, Marie participated in many promotional activities. She placed a bi-monthly ad in the classified section of *The Hamilton Spectator* between the birth and death notices. She also used a limited amount of radio ads. She advertised during the "Garden Doctor" radio show on a local station for a couple of weeks prior to a special holiday. She also had occasion cards printed (with her company name and address) for customer use.

The Location Decision

Since Marie first bought the store, Smith/McKay Florists had been renewing its lease on an annual basis. The monthly rental, $800, had been unchanged since 1984. That figure included one-third of the property taxes on the store (the landlord paid the rest) and did not include heat ($2,500 per year) or hydro ($225 per month). However, as of August 1990, the monthly rent would increase 50 percent. In addition to the proposed rent hike, Marie was concerned about persistent rumours that the block in which the store was located would be torn down to make way for a large office building. She knew that the Canadian Imperial Bank of Commerce had been buying up the properties around the store for the last few years and had expressed an interest in this property too. Marie was anxious, therefore, to explore alternative locations for her shop.

Alternatives

Although in theory Smith/McKay Florists could relocate anywhere in the city, Marie had a preference for the downtown Hamilton area, where her target market—the upscale suburban consumer—lived and worked. She felt that she must stay downtown, so any potential location should be within four to five blocks of her current location. If she were too remote, loyal customers might not be able to find her. The alternative locations, therefore, were selected with this criterion in mind.

Park Place

Park Place, a recently opened shopping/office complex, was located on the northwest corner of King and Hughson Streets. The building had been home to a furniture store for nearly 75 years until it closed in 1987. Sand blasted and completely renovated inside, the mall was targeted to the luxury consumer.

Only a few stores and businesses had moved into the building so far. The complex managers had a prime 46-square-metre location that they felt was proper for a flower store. The King Street store had over 186 square metres of space.

The rent at Park Place was $355.00 per square metre per year and heating was included. Management indicated that there would be no trouble negotiating a five-year lease. Marie estimated hydro costs to be $70.00 per month. No parking was available at the mall but there were two large municipal lots within three blocks of the building. As the only florist in this mall, Smith/McKay would get all the florist business. Yet business would have to improve to cover her increased costs.

Starting with the concrete floors and unfinished walls and given the mall's luxury image, Marie estimated that her renovation costs would be about $40,000. As well, there would be a delay in the completion date of any renovations as the management was waiting for a special carpeting that all stores were supposed to use. This location was three blocks east of her current store and she estimated that moving costs would be about $3,000. All the one-way streets in the downtown core added to the total time a move would take.

Marie was uncertain about this location for two reasons. First, the mall was new. There was little traffic through the mall as there were very few stores. As far as business traffic was concerned, so few companies had taken office space that she was unable to predict any level of walk-in sales. She also questioned her ability to maintain a high profile in the larger Hamilton community. She felt that the downtown core was expanding to the west and a move to the east could really isolate her business.

Jackson Square

Jackson Square, a major development, first opened in 1972 and two expansions to the mall were completed in 1977 and 1989. The mall was situated opposite her current King Street location. The mall complex included the soon-to-be-opened Sheraton Hotel and Victor K. Copps Coliseum. The development was bounded by King, James, York, and Bay Streets. The density of housing was high with many apartments and condominiums nearby. Four office towers had been incorporated into the complex. As well, three underground parking lots were available for up to 1,000 cars.

The trading area for the mall was defined to be the downtown business community and apartment dwellers. Few people from outside the city or from the "Hamilton Mountain" area shopped at the mall on a regular basis. Over the past few years many suburban malls had opened (Eastgate Mall and Centre Mall in the east end and Lime Ridge Mall on the mountain), yet few customers had been lured away. There already was one florist, Brandi's House of Flowers, in Jackson Square that had just opened for business. Given the large number of shoppers who frequented the mall, Smith/McKay Florists, as the only other florist, would benefit substantially.

The length of the lease was negotiable, but Marie felt that five years would be the maximum that she could obtain. In spite of the obvious advantages offered by a dynamic mall, Marie was concerned about the monthly rent. Mall managers were asking $377.00 per square metre per year rent which included heating and air conditioning. She estimated that her hydro costs would be $75.00 per month. Marie wondered whether the potential increase in walk-in business would offset the incremental increase in rent.

Mall management were offering her a 39-square-metre space, which was about one-third the size of her current location. Even with that small size, she estimated that renovations to the location would cost $35,000 and could take up to two months to complete. Moving and purchases of new furnishings could cost another $1,500. Marie also wondered what impact extended mall hours (Monday, Tuesday, Wednesday, and Saturday—9:30 A.M. to 5:30 P.M.; Thursday and Friday—9:30 A.M. to 9:00 P.M.) would have on her staffing. She had found it difficult in the past to find and train good staff.

King Street

The King Street location was the bottom half of a car rental agency, situated at the very busy intersection of Caroline and King Streets, two blocks from the exclusive "Hess Village" shopping area of Hamilton. Marie would purchase the building for between $125,000 and $140,000 rather than lease. The top floor could be used for office and storage space and, perhaps, a one-bedroom apartment could be created and rented out. Marie estimated total renovation costs to be about $75,000. Other pertinent costs included a large illuminated sign ($1,500), property taxes ($7,750 per year), and heating and hydro (same as current location). Total useable floor space amounted to 150 square metres.

Marie believed that the volume of drive-by traffic would increase the store's visibility. King Street was one of the city's main traffic arteries. The traffic flow, at the end of the day when people might want to take flowers home to a loved one, was going the "correct" way. Ten parking spaces were available on the property and four major bus routes had stops nearby.

Although Marie felt that aesthetically the location had great potential, she had reservations. Though the property was zoned for commercial business, Marie felt that she would have to spend $4,000 in legal fees to purchase the building. As well, in light of her success downtown, Marie was concerned that the location was too isolated from other retail outlets and the office building workers that she relied upon for her business. A used car lot, a maternity clothing store, and a print shop occupied the other three corners of the intersection—residential housing, some of it newly renovated, apartments, and some small shops made up the rest of the immediate area.

Marie's friends and business associates urged her not to move away from the downtown core where Smith/McKay Florists was an established member of the retail community.

If she decided to move, Marie knew she would have to promote to tell people where the store was going. With the alternatives in mind, Marie wondered what she should do.

Question

1. **What location would you recommend? Why?**

21. Housewares Unlimited

Paul Crowne had a decision to make—which one of five possible locations to select within the Conestoga Mall for his new housewares store. After working for eight years as a buyer for Sears, Paul had returned to his hometown of Waterloo to open his own store.

With the experience gained at Sears, Paul had been able to identify many suppliers in both North America and Europe who manufactured top quality housewares at very competitive prices. In many cases these manufacturers were not well-known and, as a result, sold primarily on the basis of price, as opposed to brand name. Paul was convinced that a store that offered a wide and shallow range of housewares would succeed. His plan was to offer the best value product in each area with very limited choice. For example, he would offer only one line of coffee-makers—from a Swedish manufacturer—that were quality products at competitive prices. His total merchandise line would consist of all the items necessary in the preparation and serving of food (excluding major appliances). The line would include pots, pans, mixing bowls, utensils, kettles, small appliances, baskets, cannisters, place mats, napkins, table cloths, and other items in the houseware line.

Paul had grown up and gone to college in Waterloo, Ontario. During his years with Sears he had worked in Toronto and Montreal but always had the desire to return to Waterloo. While working he had saved sufficient funds to open his store, which he planned to call Housewares Unlimited, and in the summer of 1993 he resigned from Sears and returned to Waterloo.

Paul spent the next two months contacting the suppliers and establishing his merchandise line. As well, he looked for a site for his new store. Waterloo is one of the two twin cities (Kitchener being the other) located 100 kilometres west of Toronto. The population of Waterloo is 70,000 and of Kitchener is 130,000. Both cities are part of a census metropolitan area (CMA) that has a population exceeding 360,000. Both personal incomes and retail sales in the CMA are above the Canadian average.

After examining a number of possible sites, Paul decided that a shopping mall would be a desirable location because of the traffic volume generated by the mall. After studying each of the malls in the area, he decided that the Conestoga Mall, located in North Waterloo, would be ideal. Many new housing developments were springing up in the area and the majority of stores in the mall stocked medium-priced merchandise, which would be consistent with Paul's plan to sell quality items at competitive prices.

The Conestoga Mall was a regional enclosed mall that had 80 stores and parking for 1,868 cars. The primary market (within 5 kilometres of the mall) included 89,000 people and 44,000 households. The secondary market (within 7 kilometres of the mall) included 97,500 people and 22,000 households. The average household income in the prime market was $46,100 per year. The anchor tenants in the mall were Robinson's a department store chain, K mart, another department store chain, and Zehrs, a supermarket chain owned by Loblaws. Exhibit 1 provides a layout of the mall.

Paul's major competitor in the mall would be Robinson's, which offered medium-priced houseware goods. Although Robinson's would be a strong competitor, Paul felt that his merchandise line offered a unique alternative to customers. K mart was another competitor, but the houseware items offered

Exhibit 1 The Conestoga Mall

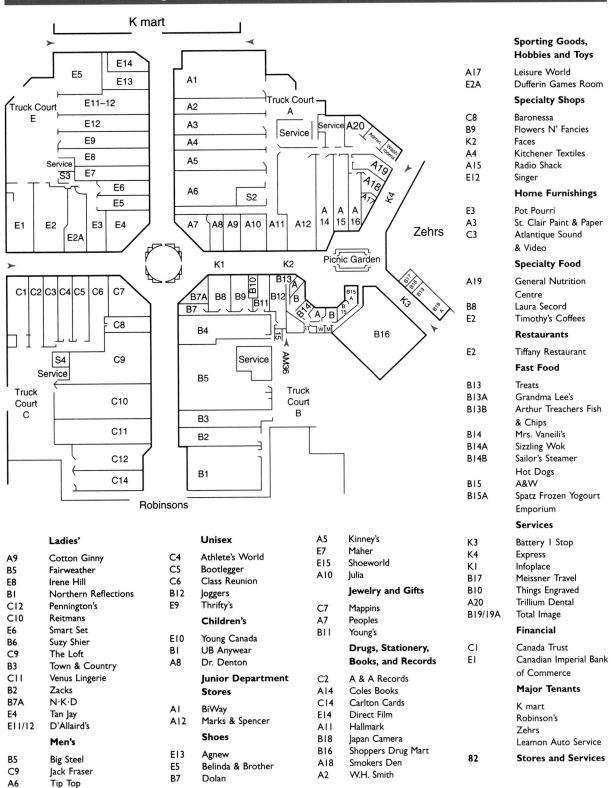

Sporting Goods, Hobbies and Toys

A17	Leisure World
E2A	Dufferin Games Room

Specialty Shops

C8	Baronessa
B9	Flowers N' Fancies
K2	Faces
A4	Kitchener Textiles
A15	Radio Shack
E12	Singer

Home Furnishings

E3	Pot Pourri
A3	St. Clair Paint & Paper
C3	Atlantique Sound & Video

Specialty Food

A19	General Nutrition Centre
B8	Laura Secord
E2	Timothy's Coffees

Restaurants

E2	Tiffany Restaurant

Fast Food

B13	Treats
B13A	Grandma Lee's
B13B	Arthur Treachers Fish & Chips
B14	Mrs. Vaneili's
B14A	Sizzling Wok
B14B	Sailor's Steamer Hot Dogs
B15	A&W
B15A	Spatz Frozen Yogourt Emporium

Services

K3	Battery 1 Stop
K4	Express
K1	Infoplace
B17	Meissner Travel
B10	Things Engraved
A20	Trillium Dental
B19/19A	Total Image

Financial

C1	Canada Trust
E1	Canadian Imperial Bank of Commerce

Major Tenants

	K mart
	Robinson's
	Zehrs
	Leamon Auto Service
82	**Stores and Services**

Ladies'

A9	Cotton Ginny
B5	Fairweather
E8	Irene Hill
B1	Northern Reflections
C12	Pennington's
C10	Reitmans
E6	Smart Set
B6	Suzy Shier
C9	The Loft
B3	Town & Country
C11	Venus Lingerie
B2	Zacks
B7A	N·K·D
E4	Tan Jay
E11/12	D'Allaird's

Men's

B5	Big Steel
C9	Jack Fraser
A6	Tip Top

Unisex

C4	Athlete's World
C5	Bootlegger
C6	Class Reunion
B12	Joggers
E9	Thrifty's

Children's

E10	Young Canada
B1	UB Anywear
A8	Dr. Denton

Junior Department Stores

A1	BiWay
A12	Marks & Spencer

Shoes

E13	Agnew
E5	Belinda & Brother
B7	Dolan
A5	Kinney's
E7	Maher
E15	Shoeworld
A10	Julia

Jewelry and Gifts

C7	Mappins
A7	Peoples
B11	Young's

Drugs, Stationery, Books, and Records

C2	A & A Records
A14	Coles Books
C14	Carlton Cards
E14	Direct Film
A11	Hallmark
B18	Japan Camera
B16	Shoppers Drug Mart
A18	Smokers Den
A2	W.H. Smith

Exhibit 2   Information on Store Sites

Store	Physical Size	Total Square Metres	Rent per Square Metre per Year
A16	7.3×15.8 m	116	$215.00
A3	7.3×20.4 m	149	$237.00
B7A	7.9×5.8 m	46	$269.00
C4	7.9×16.8 m	133	$247.00
B2	7.3×18.9 m	138	$237.00

were lower-priced and lower quality. Paul felt he was targeting a different group of customers from K mart. The only other competitor was Pot Pourri, which offered specialty houseware items at medium prices. However, Pot Pourri focussed mainly on kitchen items whereas Paul would offer a far wider range.

Much to Paul's delight upon inquiring about spaces for lease in Conestoga Mall, he discovered that due to a recent remodelling of the mall five locations would be available for lease. The locations that would be available were A3, B7A, C4, B2, and A16. The corresponding sizes and costs per square metre are given in Exhibit 2.

Rents are based, among other things, on the traffic flow in various parts of the mall. The shops in the centre square paid the highest rent per square metre as most people passed through the centre square at least once while in the mall. The largest parking lot is located outside sections E and C and therefore stores along that strip had the highest traffic flow. This is followed by the strips leading to K mart and Robinson's. The traffic flow was considered to be equal along these two strips and there were parking lots of equal size outside both K mart and Robinson's. The strip between section A and B was the least travelled section. People going to Zehrs generally parked in the lot outside Zehrs, did their shopping, and left.

Paul was somewhat concerned about the rental cost as his cash flow would be tight in the first few months of operation. However, he also felt that he needed a location with a reasonable amount of traffic flow to ensure people became aware that his store existed. Paul estimated that the ideal size for a store to hold his merchandise line would be around 120 square metres, but he also knew that a slightly smaller store would be more economical.

Question

1. **What store site would you recommend? Why?**

22. The Best Display?

A major department store, one of the three oldest in Canada, recognized that the first-floor selling fixtures in its main branch had become outmoded and had set aside funds to renovate. The main floor had not been changed appreciably

Source: This case was prepared by David Ehrlich, Marymount University.

since the store was built in the 1920s. There were a number of handsome mahogany-panelled counter islands, which had always given the store an aura of tasteful elegance.

Jim Lewis, director of store fixturing, was debating the merits of several possible display systems. The selling departments that would be affected by the renovation were cosmetics; fine and costume jewelry; women's handbags, scarves, and belts; men's shirts, ties, and furnishings; women's sweaters; and gifts.

As Lewis saw it, the two major issues surrounding his decision were incompatible. On the one hand, the store wanted to make merchandise as accessible to customers as possible; on the other hand, experience had indicated that open-selling fixtures inevitably lead to more shoplifting. As an experiment, the store had tried substituting self-service fixtures in its upstairs men's sweater department a year earlier. Sales jumped 30 percent, but inventory shrinkage in the department had gone from 2 to almost 5 percent.

A further consideration was that the size and quality of the staff on the selling floor had declined dramatically. In 1929, there were always two salespeople behind every counter, and customers could count on never having to wait for service. However, selling costs had since escalated, and the store's staff was less than half what it had been then. Furthermore, the store had instituted modern point-of-sale cash registers that enabled every salesperson to ring up a sale from any department in the store at any register. Most of the clerks were paid minimum wage and were only working there until something better turned up. Although some were able to provide useful selling information to the public, most could do little more than ring up sales.

The kind of open-selling fixtures Lewis was considering were contemporary and very attractive. They allowed the customer to pick up, unfold or unpackage merchandise, try it on if appropriate, and then return it to the fixture. Such fixtures would unquestionably lead to more sales, especially since the customer could merely look for any salesperson or perhaps go to a central cashier to pay. However, it was equally unquestionable that such easy access to merchandise, especially to small goods, would encourage shoplifting and increase the need for ongoing stockkeeping.

Another disadvantage to the new type of fixturing was that in addition to being contemporary, it was somewhat trendy, which would lead to the need to replace it in a few years, thereby adding to capital costs.

An alternative system would be to retain the old counter islands, or a portion of them, but to put more goods on the countertops to encourage a measure of self-service. The disadvantage here, of course, would be the blocking of sight lines. Salespeople could not see customers, customers could not see salespeople, and the store security personnel could not see either. There would also need to be more policing by the store's display and merchandising staff to be sure the countertops looked inviting at all times. Manufacturers often contribute countertop displays to stores as part of the merchandise buying, and many of them might not be in harmony with the store's overall appearance.

Lewis recognized that he would have to make some compromises. Every affected department has its own peculiarities, and his job was to minimize those differences, rather than allow them to get out of hand. Some merchandise, such as fine jewelry, would obviously have to remain behind glass, but other departments would probably do much better by opening up their stocks to the public.

Questions

1. **What display system would you recommend? Why?**
2. **Would you make the same recommendation for each of the affected departments? Why or why not?**

23. Noble Foodstuffs

James Noble was puzzled by the design layout he had just received for his new supermarket (Exhibit 1). He was very uncomfortable with it, but could not quite say why, and if it needed to be changed, what should be done?

James Noble is a young entrepreneur. He graduated two years ago from the University of Calgary with a bachelor of commerce. He immediately started working for a supermarket chain in Penticton, British Columbia. However, he soon realized that he did not like working for a large corporation, and that he really wanted to be his own boss. With money lent to him by his father and

Exhibit I   Proposed Layout for Noble Foodstuffs

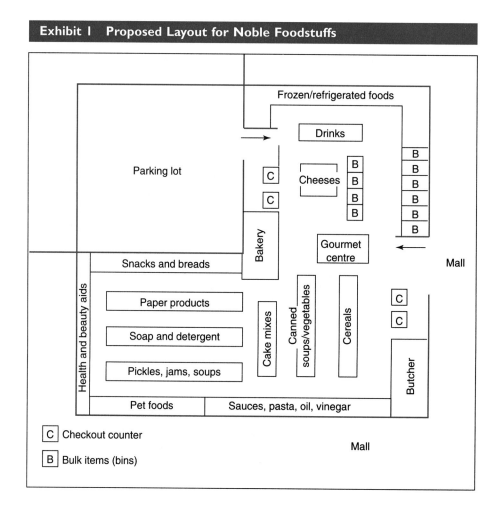

a bank loan, he had rented a corner location in a newly built shopping mall in a mixed working–middle-class neighbourhood of Calgary. The mall had rented all 18 stores. Noble Foodstuff was the only supermarket in the mall. There were also a small department store and several small boutiques. The mall had a 100-car parking lot.

James Noble decided to use a store design consultant to help in planning the layout for the new store. He had asked his designer to take into account a number of current trends that he found in various newspaper and magazine articles:

- The trend toward more bulk items, and items that are not damaging to the environment;
- The trend toward gourmet items, as well as freshly baked breads, muffins, and pastries;
- The trend toward fresh fish, seafood, and specialty cuts of meat;
- The trend toward adding non-food items in supermarkets.

The designer had just brought a first draft of her work, and James Noble needed to approve the layout before work could start. He was bothered by a number of decisions the designer had made, including the location of checkout counters, the placements and sizes of the different departments, and the flow of traffic in the store. He also has to decide on the interior design of the store, that is, what kind of atmosphere and image does he want to create inside his supermarket.

Questions

1. **Evaluate the design proposed by the consultant.**
2. **What changes, if any, would you recommend? Why?**

24. Jim's Sporting Goods

Jim's Sporting Goods, a large store, offers a complete range of sporting goods and accessories to both beginners and experts. The store consists of 16 departments (labelled A to P), each carrying a sports line (e.g., hockey, baseball) or types of clothing (e.g., beach wear, hiking). Recently an issue arose concerning space allocations for two departments.

The two adjacent departments have space, sales, and sales per square metre as follows:

	Square metres	Annual Sales	Sales per Sq. Metre
Dept. A	84	$ 63,000	$750
Dept. B	93	50,000	538
	177	$113,000	$638

Department A is in urgent need of 19 square metres of additional space to provide adequate display and storage space for a line that is enjoying an upward trend in popularity. There is considerable evidence that a good deal of potential business is being lost because of the inadequate space. The manager is

Source: This case was prepared by Aldo J. Cimpello, Algonquin College of Applied Arts and Technology.

convinced that he can generate $750 a square metre from the additional space requested.

The only practical way to do this is to take away 19 square metres from Department B where space does not seem to have been used to best advantage and where volume is barely holding its own. Better layout planning should increase the average sales per square metre in B to $592. But dollar sales, nevertheless, will be reduced considerably in B, to which the manager of that department objects.

Questions

1. **If management decides to make the proposed change, by how much may total sales of the two departments combined be increased?**
2. **What will be the increase in sales per square metre for the total area?**

25. Betty's Fashions

Anne Lemont, the buyer for Betty's Fashions, was preparing the merchandising plan for the store for the Spring season (February–July). Betty's Fashions is a women's fashion accessory store located in Charlottetown, Prince Edward Island. As a first step, Anne filled in the previous year's sales, stock, markdowns, and purchases as well as this year's targets (initial markup, gross margin, etc.) on the Six Month Merchandising Plan (Exhibit 1). She then reviewed the information she had, which included:

- The planned sales increase for the forthcoming season was 20 percent.
- The planned markdown rate was 15 percent.
- Last year Betty's Fashions underwent a major renovation and expansion that was completed on May 1st. This resulted in a 30 percent sales increase for that month, and an average 25 percent sales increase for the balance of the season.
- A new shopping centre located approximately 3 kilometres from the store is presently under construction and is scheduled to open on April 1st. Betty, the store owner, has estimated that it may attract up to 10 percent of the store's customers.
- Betty feels very strongly that for the type of merchandise (fashion accessories, i.e., jewelry/handbags/scarves/hats, etc.) the store offers, the major seasonal clearance should be held back until July—rather than June as it was done last year.
- Anne noted that she had just confirmed with one of the store's major suppliers that Betty's Fashions would be given an exclusive promotion of 50 percent off on a wide assortment of fashion jewelry for the month of March. Anne had bought $30,000 at retail for this promotion.
- A two-week strike at a major local plant last year in February resulted in a 5 percent decrease in sales for this period.

With this information in mind, Anne began preparing the merchandising plan.

Source: This case was prepared by B. Chevallier, Sheridan College of Applied Arts and Technology.

Exhibit 1   Merchandising Plan Form

						PLAN (This Year)	ACTUAL (Last Year)
	BETTY'S FASHIONS						
SIX MONTH MERCHANDISING PLAN	Initial markup (%)					48.0	47.5
	Gross margin (%)					42.0	41.7
	Cash discount (% cost purch.)					7.9	7.8
	Season stock turnover (rate)					3.0	2.8
	Shortage reserve (%)					1.6	1.7
	Advertising expense (%)					3.5	3.0
	Selling salaries (%)					8.4	8.6

SPRING 199_		FEB.	MAR.	APR.	MAY	JUNE	JULY	SEASON TOTAL
SALES	Last Year	105	140	160	225	175	155	960
	Plan							
	Percent of Increase							
	Revised							
	Actual							
RETAIL STOCK (BOM)	Last Year	330	360	360	410	340	290	320
	Plan							
	Revised							
	Actual							
MARKDOWNS	Last Year	20	24	28	20	25	20	137
	Plan (dollars)							
	Plan (percent)							
	Revised							
	Actual							
RETAIL PURCHASES	Last Year	155	164	238	175	150	205	1087
	Plan							
	Revised							
	Actual							

Note: All dollar figures in $000s.

Questions

1. Prepare the merchandise plan for the next six months.
2. Provide a rationale for each month's planned sales increase or decrease.

26. Roger's Department Store

A new general merchandise manager was recently appointed at Roger's large urban department store. He arrived with a reputation as an aggressive merchant and a believer in low inventories and high turnover, and in taking advantage of unusual buying opportunities whenever possible.

His credo was, "If we could fill our stores with new merchandise *every single day*, we would be the smartest buyers in the country. I want us to run *lean and mean*. I want us to be bringing in fresh goods every day. And I want everything we buy to be bought at the best possible prices."

The store had tended to be quite lax under the previous management, allowing inventories to pile up early in the season, and leaving little open-to-buy available to make advantageous late-season market breaks.

At his first meeting with his buyers, he issued the following instructions: "Please come back to me with a plan that will improve sales by at least 10 percent, and will reflect a stockturn of at least 3.25 times next fall season."

The handbag buyer took out her last year's sales figures and tried to put together a plan that she could achieve and that would also meet her new boss's guidelines.

Last year's results in sales dollars were as follows: ($000 omitted)

Month	Beg. Inv.	Purchases	Sales	End. Inv.
August	225	135	60	300
September	300	75	100	275
October	275	95	70	300
November	300	165	90	375
December	375	25	200	200
January	200	20	60	160
Total		515	580	268 (average)

Last year's stockturn, she calculated, was only 2.21 times, and she had to agree that she had been careless. However, she was concerned that she would only be able to meet the new guidelines if she were allowed several ads.

Questions

1. **As the buyer, work out a plan that will produce sales of $650,000, and that will meet the merchandise manager's goal of 3.25 turns.**

2. **After doing this, you feel the requirements are too tough without a lot of advertising. Work out an advertising program that you think will help you achieve the 10 percent sales increase. Be specific about what kinds of merchandise you will want to advertise and when.**

Source: This case was prepared by David Ehrlich, Marymount University.

27. The Lyon's Den

The Lyon's Den had been a winner ever since Jane and Jim Lyon opened their gift shop in an old renovated home in Victoria, British Columbia, and moved in over it. The business was started in 1950. Over the years it had become "the" place for gifts and, eventually, decorating services in a city of some 260,000. Their apartment was a showcase for the many lines of fine silver, china, crystal, and decorator furniture items that were carried in the shop.

Over the years, their lines expanded. To the traditional gift lines they added cosmetics and linens. Nothing in the shop was carried anywhere else in the trade area and were unique in the sense that they were all Canadian made. Jane and Jim felt that exclusivity was a major advantage for The Lyon's Den.

Several years ago, Jane, who does the bulk of the buying (whereas Jim is the decorator and takes care of the books), felt that she had secured a market exclusive for the area. She was able to acquire the finest and most prestigious lines of stainless Hensen. The name was not known in the market, but the quality was unsurpassed. Jane knew that, given an exclusive, she could develop a demand for the line that would make her a leading outlet for the merchandise. She had done this before; she knew good products and was a retailer with foresight—an entrepreneur who liked a challenge. The salesperson, whom she met at a regional trade show, assured her of market protection, and thus she set out to launch the new line.

She ran ads and invited special customers to attend a reception to meet the manufacturer. The market had probably never had such a dramatic introduction and perhaps never would again. After a year and a half, the line was one of the most profitable in the shop. Brides were convinced that, without Hensen from The Lyon's Den, marriage was out of the question. Jane had done what she set out to do—create a market demand for the line and bring in new customers because of it.

Just this morning, Jane got a phone call from the Toronto office of Hensen's. The national sales manager was on the phone with some distressing news for The Lyon's Den. Lucille's Table Top, a new market entrant carrying medium- to high-priced table accessories, had just been into the Toronto showroom and had bought the Hensen line. The sales manager felt that since Lucille's was in a shopping centre in Victoria some distance from The Lyon's Den, the competition would be negligible. In addition, the sales manager said that company policy was actually not to give exclusives in a market. The salesperson who originally opened the Lyon's account had not been aware of the policy.

Questions

1. **What options are available to Jane?**
2. **What are the advantages and disadvantages to a supplier of granting a retailer the exclusive right to sell a line of merchandise?**

28. Ashley's

Sally Jones, sweater buyer for the 10-unit department store Ashley's, was making her plans for a forthcoming buying trip to the Far East. Ashley's, an upper-crust store, had made its first direct buying venture to Hong Kong last year, had

Source: This case was prepared by David Ehrlich, Marymount University.

been quite successful with several knitwear purchases totalling some $1,000,000 at retail, and was anxious to expand its direct importing.

For this trip, Ashley's intended to examine the advisability of transferring its entire Shetland sweater business to this market, and Sally had been asked to evaluate the desirability of substituting Hong Kong Shetlands for a domestic program that had been successful for the last five years.

Last fall's Shetland sales were approximately 6,000 units (500 dozen), and the store hoped to increase sales to 7,200 pieces this year. The price was $32 each, and nearly all units were sold without a markdown.

Banner, Ashley's source last year, is a large domestic sweater producer, operating in an old Montreal mill. It buys its yarn abroad and turns out its production on somewhat antiquated machinery. It is known for an unusual colour sense and reliability for on-time delivery and ability to fill in sizes and colours on a one-week basis. Last fall, Ashley placed two orders for 2,400 units each on July 25 and September 25, as well as weekly fill-ins. This year's wholesale price has already been announced: $15.75 less 8 percent.

In a price list received from Yu Pei Mee, a Hong Kong supplier, Sally noticed Shetland sweaters that appeared of a quality comparable to Banner's being offered at $7.60 net. The colour range was just as broad as Banner's.

Making the Hong Kong buy would require accepting a single shipment of all 7,200 sweaters in July, and also that the store would have to tie its money up in a letter of credit from February until July.

Further investigation disclosed that Canadian customs duty on wool sweaters was 25 percent of the cost, and that airfreight and other expenses associated with buying abroad would come to about $10,000.

Her final consideration was that Shetland sweaters just might fall out of fashion favour next fall, causing huge markdowns, although she doubted that.

Her choice, therefore, was between the higher markup afforded by the Hong Kong sweaters and the reliable service provided by the domestic supplier.

Questions

1. **Figure the difference in gross margin between buying domestically and abroad, assuming all units are sold at full price.**

2. **As Sally, would you recommend buying: (1) in Hong Kong; (2) domestically; or (3) some kind of third option?**

29. Courtney's

For the last two years, Courtney's, an upscale gift store, has carried at Christmas-time a sweet-smelling potpourri in a plastic bag with an attractive ribbon. The mixture is heavily scented with cloves and gives a pleasant holiday aroma to any room, including the store at holiday time.

Two years ago, the mixture cost $4.50 a bag, and Courtney's, the only store in town that carried it, sold 300 pieces for $9.50. Courtney's supply ran out 10 days before Christmas, and it was too late to get any more.

Source: This case was prepared by Professor David Ehrlich, Marymount University.

Last year, the manufacturer raised the price to $5.00, and Courtney's raised its retail to $9.95. Even though the markup was lower than the previous year, the store owner, Linda Courtney, felt there was "magic" in the $10 price. As before, the store experienced a complete sellout, this time five days before Christmas. Sales that year were 600 units.

This year, the wholesale price has gone up to $5.50, and store personnel are trying to determine the correct retail price. Linda's feeling is once again to hold the price at $10 ($9.95), but the buyer, Jason Blue, disagrees:

> It's my job to push for the highest possible markup wherever I can. This item is a sure seller, as we're still the only store around with it, and we had some unsatisfied demand last year. I think we should market it at $12.50, which will improve the markup to 56 percent. Staying at $10 will penalize us unnecessarily, especially considering the markup would be even lower than last year. Even if we run into price resistance, we'll only have to sell 480 to maintain the same dollar volume.

Linda responded:

> This scent is part of our store's ambience. It acts as a draw to get people into the store, and its pleasant smell keeps them in a free-spending state of mind. I think we should keep the price at $9.95, despite the poorer markup. And if we can sell many more at this price, we'll realize the same dollar gross margin as last year. I think we should buy 1,000. Furthermore, if people see us raising the price of a familiar item by 25 percent, they might wonder whether our other prices are fair.

Questions

1. **What prices should Courtney's charge?**
2. **What do you think sales would be at each price level?**
3. **Which price would result in the most profits?**
4. **What other factors should Courtney's consider?**
5. **What price would you charge and how many units would you order?**

30. Duncan Department Store

Donald Claxton, the confectionary buyer for the Duncan Department Store, was concerned. He had purchased $35,000 (at retail) of candy for the Easter selling season. The initial markup was 30 percent, or $10,500. Here it was the Saturday morning following Good Friday and he was holding $16,000 worth of inventory he would have to sell in one day or "give it away" after Easter. Mr. Claxton quickly reviewed the events leading up to this situation. The purchase of $35,000 was an increase of $20,000 from the previous Easter season. He based this increase on two factors:

1. Last year he ran out of stock on the Thursday before Easter by 12 noon, thereby losing two full selling days.

Store Hours:	Thursday	9:00 A.M. to 9:00 P.M.
	Friday	Closed (Good Friday)
	Saturday	9:00 A.M. to 6:00 P.M.

Source: This case was prepared by Aldo J. Cimpello, Algonquin College of Applied Arts and Technology.

2. He recognized that the Thursday and Saturday before Easter represent approximately 65 percent of his total Easter candy sales.

The sales plan and actual results to date were:

	Plan	Actual
Weeks prior to Easter week	$ 4,500	$4,400
Monday	2,000	1,800
Tuesday	2,500	2,600
Wednesday	4,000	3,900
Thursday	10,000	6,300
Friday	—	—
Saturday	12,000	

Thursday at closing he pondered over the actual sales to date in comparison to his plan. Saturday morning on his way to work, he was still troubled by the amount of inventory remaining. He knew that after the store closed on Saturday, the remaining candy would be sold at 50 percent off the retail price during the following week.

Questions

1. **What options are available to Mr. Claxton?**

2. **What would you do in this situation?**

31. How Good Are Tire Warranties?

Jim Reed was really upset about the poor customer service and the inconsistent warranties from the Dunlop Tire Company and wondering if there is anything that can be done.

It all started when Jim Reed, a professor at the University of Ottawa, was returning from a sabbatical at San Diego State University. Jim and his wife Joan had taken her V.W. Jetta to San Diego, instead of Jim's Volvo, because the Jetta was still under warranty. The return trip, some 5,600 kilometres, was not a comfortable drive. The Jetta did not seem to be able to take the heavy load that was packed in the car, and Jim was convinced that the shocks would need to be replaced.

They arrived home in early June, and three days later Jim took the Jetta into Desjardins Inc., in Hull, to get it serviced. They changed the oil and the oil filter and added a litre of transmission fluid. The shocks were fine, but the manager claimed that the car needed four new tires. This bothered Jim since the tires had only 42,000 kilometres on them. He figured that he might have ruined them by overloading the car on the trip from California, or perhaps the manager was being overly cautious and saw a chance to make a large sale, especially during the recession when business was down. In any case, since he was planning to return to San Diego next January, Jim felt that he could replace them at a lower price and not have to pay the exorbitant 15.56 percent combined GST (goods and services tax) and PST (provincial sales tax). In the meantime, neither Jim nor Joan would do much driving in the Jetta.

Source: © 1991, Faculty of Administration, University of Ottawa. This case was written by Professor David Litvack.

At the end of July, their daughter Julie and son-in-law David found a job in Washington and asked to borrow the Jetta to carry their possessions to their new home. While driving to Washington, one of the tires exploded, and they replaced it. They were told that the other three tires were not very good.

When they returned with the car on August 12, Jim took it to Desjardins and bought three tires that would be compatible with the new tire. The invoice shows that three P185/60HR14 Dunlop D89 ETE tires were purchased at $84.92 each, and the total invoice, including taxes, was for $294.40. The odometre reading was 45,516 km. The same day, upon the advice of the technician at Desjardins, the car was given a four-wheel alignment, which with two small parts cost $83.27.

On December 11, Jim drove the Jetta to Swedish Garage to get it serviced. After 6,000 km, it was time to have the oil changed. On the way there, Jim felt a shimmy in the steering and he asked the mechanic to check it. He balanced the tires but the shimmy was still there. He looked at the tires and discovered that two of them were defective. The odometre reading was 48,640, or 3,124 km of driving on the tires.

After he left Swedish, Jim drove directly to Desjardins, where the defects were confirmed. Two new tires were ordered and an appointment was made for the following Tuesday to have them installed. That day, Jim arrived at 3 P.M., and within a half hour the car was ready to go. He was surprised to hear that he would have to pay for partial use of the defective tires. Since the tires had a 96,000 km warranty, Jim figured that he would owe Desjardins about $6. He became very upset when the cashier presented him with a bill for $44.50. He went to see the manager, who told him that he was being charged according to the policy of the Dunlop Tire Company, and that if he did not like it, he could replace the new tires with the old ones.

Jim argued that he was being treated unfairly, and that the policy did not make sense. He insisted that the manager get someone from Dunlop on the phone. The man at the other end of the line, who claimed to be in public relations at Dunlop, defended the policy, adding that he had been in the tire business for 38 years. After more discussions, he offered to cut the price in half, stating that he still did not agree with Jim that the policy was unfair. Since there seemed to be little choice, Jim decided to accept his offer, but deep inside, he was still angry.

When he got off the phone, two customers who had overheard the conversation approached him and told him that he was absolutely right. André Lefort, a service agent at Desjardins, joined the discussion and expressed some sympathy at Jim's predicament.

Feeling a little bit better, Jim returned home and put the invoices and receipts into his "car file." In flipping through the file, he discovered an invoice dated from early June (shortly after they returned from San Diego) for four new tires for his Volvo which had been sitting idle since the previous January. The invoice read: four 1 85/70R14 Dunlop Elite 4S BW at $85 each plus tax. Along with the tires came a warranty which states:

UP TO 50% WORN/NO CHARGE: If during the first five thirty-seconds of an inch (5/32″) of tread wear, the tire becomes unserviceable for a condition covered by this warranty, it will be replaced by a comparable new Dunlop tire. No charge will be made for mounting, balancing or taxes.

At this point, Jim was extremely angry but he did not know what to do next.

Questions

1. **Analyze the buying decision process of Jim Reed, using three decision cycles.**

2. **What lessons can a retailer learn from these events?**

3. **What other retailing concepts are illustrated in this case?**

32. An Advertising Plan

A major department store in the Toronto area is planning a major sale of rugs in its suburban Brampton warehouse over the three-day Labour Day weekend (Saturday through Monday). Nearly $4 million worth of rugs will be on sale, assembled both from the company's inventory and from various market purchases. The average sale price of each rug is approximately $500, and the company hopes to realize at least $1.8 million in sales during the three days.

This is the first time the store has sold rugs from its warehouse, but previous experience with coats and furniture has been successful. Two factors in particular were common to the previous events:

1. The first day's sales are 50 percent of the total; the second day's, 35 percent; and the last day's, 15 percent.

2. One of every two customers who come makes a purchase.

It is known further that large numbers of people always flock to such sales, some from as far away as 50 miles. They come from all economic levels, but are all confirmed bargain-hunters.

You are the assistant to the general merchandise manager, and he has asked you to plan the advertising campaign for this event. You have the following information at your disposal:

1. A full-page ad in the Toronto Star costs $14,000; a half-page ad is $8,000; and a quarter page is $4,000. Furthermore, in order to get the maximum value from a newspaper campaign, it is company policy to always run two ads (not necessarily the same size for such events).

2. Using the local Brampton paper, *The Brampton Guardian,* which is printed weekly and distributed free to some 60,000 households, costs $2,000 for a full page and $1,000 for a half page.

3. In order to get adequate television coverage, at least three channels must be used, with a minimum of eight 30-second spots on each at $500 per spot, spread over three or more days. The cost of producing a television spot is $5,000.

4. The store has contracts with three radio stations: one that appeals to a broad general audience aged 25–34; one that is popular with the 18–25 group; and a classical music station with a small but wealthy audience. The minimum costs for a saturation radio campaign (including production) on the three stations are $8,000, $5,000, and $3,000, respectively.

5. To produce and mail a full-color flyer to the store's 80,000 charge customers costs $10,000. When the company used such a mailing piece, its experience was that about 3 percent would respond.

Source: This case was prepared by Professor David Ehrlich, Marymount University.

Questions

Knowing that the company wants a mixed-media advertising campaign to support this event, prepare an advertising plan for the general merchandise manager that costs no more than $60,000.

1. **Work out the daily scheduling of all advertising.**
2. **Work out the dollars to be devoted to each medium.**
3. **Justify your plan.**

33. The M&G Advertising Agency

Sandra Malik has just been given a new assignment: to prepare and deliver a report to her vice president within a week on the various aspects of retail advertising.

Sandra is the account executive for the newly created account on retail operations within the M&G advertising agency. The agency has recently decided to expand its customer base into the retail field, and the assignment was given to Sandra. Her mandate was to develop a complete understanding of retail advertising, and to use this knowledge to develop new clients.

Sandra has been with the M&G agency for two years. She joined the firm after doing an internship during her Bachelor of Business Administration studies. Toward the end of the internship, one of the vice presidents came to appreciate her marketing savvy and her ability to work hard and produce effective results. After she obtained her degree, she was hired by the agency as a junior account executive and assigned small accounts, none in the retail field.

Sandra realized that retail advertising is very different from product advertising. Although products and services are sold by retailers, the main objective of a particular retailer is to make sure that product or service is bought at his or her store. In order to succeed, a retailer begins by carefully defining the target market, and learning as much as possible about these customers. Then, the retailer must know the role and goals of advertising within the overall mix decisions. There are a variety of goals that a retailer may want to pursue, including to:

- define or improve the image of the store, or some specific aspects of it;
- obtain customer acceptance for a particular merchandise line or group of lines;
- attract new customers to improve store traffic;
- create store loyalty;
- increase frequency of patronage by existing customers;
- promote special events;
- announce sales and clearances in order to smooth out sales during the year, increase inventory turnover, and liquidate old inventory.

Sandra also realizes that retailers use different kinds of media, partly because of smaller budgets, and partly because of their target audiences. Most print retail advertising can be found in daily newspapers and weekend supplements, community newspapers and shoppers, local magazines, out-of-home media (billboards, mall, transit), direct mail, catalogues, and directories. Retailers also use radio, and a few use television. However, due to the time constraint, it was agreed that for this initial assignment she will concentrate in her report on the print media only.

Sandra can see how she can structure her report as well as her oral presentation. However, she needs some examples to illustrate the various advertising goals that a retailer may have, and it would be more effective to have examples of "good" and "bad" retail advertisements. As she will be asked to justify her evaluation of each one, she must carefully examine each one of them in terms of intended target, goal, creative approach, and effect. Now she is reading to start working on her report.

Questions

1. **Assume the role of Sandra Malik and provide examples of "good" and "bad" retail print advertisements.**

2. **Include your justification along the lines indicated in the case.**

34. Shoe Kingdom

Sam McGuire was meeting this morning with Joan LeBlanc, the account executive of the small advertising agency that he hired to develop an advertising campaign for Shoe Kingdom. Both were relatively new to the game of advertising. Sam has just been hired as marketing manager, and Joan's agency had recently been established by a former vice president at McKim, Vancouver. Both parties were hoping to benefit from this relationship.

Shoe Kingdom was a national chain of 105 stores, situated in the 28 major metropolitan areas of Canada. It was founded in 1972 to provide good quality shoes at reasonable prices for every member of the family. It was a successful formula, and in 1992 the chain had total revenues of $30 million. In the past two years, sales had increased marginally, a reflection of the difficult economic times in Canada. However, during the same period a number of retail shoe chains had declared bankruptcy.

The retail chain had never advertised on a national basis, leaving it to the discretion of store managers to advertise special sales or events. However, when Sam took over as marketing manager, he realized that the chain did not have a very clear and consistent image across Canada. Also, individual store advertisements projected different images, which contributed to the lack of a strong identity. In the excitement of developing the business, no one had thought of even developing a slogan that would capture the chain's strategy. At this time, he approached Joan's agency for some help in developing a national advertising campaign for Shoe Kingdom. Sam had known the owner of the new agency for many years, since McKim had handled the advertising business for National Foods, where he had previously worked as a market analyst.

As Sam explained to Joan, his objective was to create a strong image for Shoe Kingdom, which in turn would generate consistent store traffic over the year, and make the cash register ring more often. Another objective was to attract some of the price-conscious consumers who were cross-border shopping in the United States.

Although the initial strategy had been successful, sales were uneven across the country and during the year (see Exhibit 1). Also, the initial target market

Exhibit 1   Sales Distribution by Province and Month

Province	Population	Sales	Number of Stores	Month	Sales
Newfoundland	2.1%	3.0%	1	January	2%
P.E.I.	0.5	0.0	0	February	4
Nova Scotia	3.3	3.6	2	March	5
New Brunswick	2.8	3.1	2	April	4
Quebec	25.8	29.1	36	May	10
Ontario	36.0	38.1	44	June	8
Manitoba	4.2	4.0	4	July	2
Saskatchewan	4.0	3.5	4	August	10
Alberta	9.3	8.1	5	September	19
British Columbia	11.4	7.5	7	October	15
Yukon	0.1	0.0	0	November	11
N.W.T.	0.2	0.0	0	December	10
Total, Canada	100.0	100.0	105		100

(i.e., every member of the family) did not fully materialize; most of the sales were for children's and younger women's shoes (see Exhibit 2).

What Sam wanted was a strong slogan that would project a positive image of Shoe Kingdom. He had made up one slogan: "Shoes fit for a king, at prices his servants would like." The messages should reflect a number of attributes such as:

- Comfort with quality
- Leadership and authority
- Fashionable yet practical shoes
- Reasonable prices and good values
- One-stop shopping for the whole family
- Very attentive superior service

In the past, store managers had mainly used newspaper advertisements, and some had distributed flyers, all announcing a special sale, for example, "Back to school sale." However, Sam felt there was some merit in using radio, television, billboards, mall posters, or even magazines. Exhibit 3 provides some rate benchmarks for a preliminary budget exercise. Of course, Joan would have access to more accurate information by looking at the last issue of *Canadian*

Exhibit 2   Distribution of Sales by Demographic Groups

Group	Age	Population	Sales
Women	13–19	4.7%	15%
	20–34	12.5	10
	35–54	13.5	8
	55+	11.2	7
Children	0–6	9.8	22
	7–12	8.4	27
Men	13+	40.0	11
Total	All	100.0	100

Exhibit 3	National Costs Guidelines
Television	$700 per GRP (30 sec. commercial)
Radio	$400 per GRP (60 sec. commercial)
Newspaper	$80 per modular agate line, black & white
Magazine	$20,000 per page, 4 colours (6 major magazines)
Outdoor/transit	$200 per GRP

Note: A GRP represents 1 per cent of the corresponding population that is reached by the medium (e.g., with TV sets, radio sets, access to outdoor/transit). A modular agate line (MAL) is a newspaper space 1.8 mm deep by one standard column. A full page is 1,800 MALs for a broadsheet and 900 MALs for a tabloid. For fractional sizes use the proportional rule. For more details, consult the appropriate sections in Chapter 16. For actual rates for vehicles, consult the latest *CARD* catalogue and discount them by 30 percent or ask each vehicle for its *Retail Rate Card.*

Advertising Rates and Data. Sam has figured that he could get final approval for a total budget of $300,000, with 15 percent of it devoted to preparing the ads, and the rest to media expenditures.

The meeting was coming to an end. Joan had agreed to come back in two weeks and present Sam with a preliminary advertising plan, complete with a slogan, some sample advertisements and/or commercials, and a rough media plan.

Questions

1. **Prepare a preliminary advertising campaign for Shoe Kingdom.**
2. **Be prepared to justify your recommendations.**

35. JKA Department Store

In his estimation, George Baker had the opportunity of a lifetime. George was an assistant buyer in the flagship store of a major full-line department store in Canada. His boss, Clarence Adams, senior buyer of home goods, was en route to the Orient for an extended buying trip. Adams had left George in charge—up to a point. George knew that if any really difficult problem arose, he should consult with Finus Cooke, the division's merchandise manager for the hard lines and all home store goods.

George was quite comfortable working with dollar control and open-to-buy (OTB) data, as he and Adams discussed their position weekly. Thus George knew, as of October 15, that the department was virtually overbought for the month. He also knew that it was important to keep some OTB available for fill-ins for the remainder of the month.

On October 18, a sales representative from one of the major suppliers of table linens called George to offer a remarkable lot of goods amounting to approximately $50,000 at retail. The merchandise could be sold, with a full markup, at half price. George was positive that it would be a terrific promotion. He had to let the sales representative know by the end of the day, as the offer would then be made to a competitor.

George went to his computer to recheck the store's OTB. No change—no dollars available to spend. The promotion had not been planned, but George knew linens would walk out of the store and a real profit would be made.

Questions

1. **Should George go to the divisional merchandise manager and try to get more open-to-buy? Why or why not?**

2. **Assuming that George does go to the divisional merchandise manager to try to get more open-to-buy, what arguments could he present?**

36. Anne's Boutique

Anne Lyton, a fashion designer for a large women's clothing manufacturer, had always had a desire to own and operate her own retail business. Her goal was accomplished when she purchased a small retail business that specialized in women's fashion clothing. She renamed the store, calling it Anne's Boutique, introduced a number of new fashion lines, and changed the interior of the store.

Anne's strengths were in design and product selection; she did not feel comfortable with the "numbers" side of the operation. At the end of the first full year of running her business, she hired an accountant to prepare a balance sheet and operating statement. When the accountant submitted the information, he also provided her with a table consisting of a number of ratios (Table 1). Anne looked at the table and wondered what it meant.

Question

1. **Interpret the data in the table. What are the strengths and weaknesses of Anne's Boutique and the areas that need particular attention?**

Table 1		
Ratio	Anne's Boutique	Industry Average
Net profit margin	4.8%	10.2%
Rate of asset turnover	1.7X	1.5X
Rate of return on assets	8.2%	15.3%
Leverage ratio	4.0%	2.8%
RONW	32.6%	35.1%

Glossary of Terms

achievers Successful career- and work-oriented people who like to, and generally do, feel in control of their lives.

action close A sale closing technique, where the salesperson takes a positive step toward clinching the order, such as immediate delivery.

action-oriented consumers Consumers guided by a desire for social or physical activity, variety, and risk-taking.

actualizers Successful, sophisticated, active, take-charge people with high self-esteem and abundant resources.

adaptive behaviour A theory about retail institution change based on the premise that institutions evolve when environmental conditions are favourable.

added-value programs Programs that provide purchase incentive for the retailer's core credit customers (e.g., loyalty programs such as Club Z).

advertising Any paid form of non-personal presentation and promotion of goods, ideas, and services by an identified sponsor.

AIDA model In advertising, consumers move from attention to interest to desire and to action.

ambience The quality of design that expresses the character of a store, resulting in an institutional personality immediately recognized by consumers.

anchor tenants The major tenants in a shopping centre that serve as the primary consumer attracting force.

arbitration The settlement of a dispute by a person or persons chosen to hear both sides of a dispute and come to a decision.

area-development franchise An individual purchases an extensive territory and then opens a large number of franchises within the territory.

area sampling A method of selecting respondents in a survey, where first the trading area is defined on a map; next, some blocks are randomly selected (for example, census tracts or enumeration areas); third, some streets are randomly selected; and finally, houses or apartments are either systematically or randomly selected.

assets, current Primarily cash, accounts receivable, and inventory. They are in varying states of being converted into cash within the next 12-month period.

assets, fixed Used in the operation of the business; they are not intended to be resold. They include real estate, leasehold improvements, machinery, equipment, and vehicles.

assortment The number of different choices available within a particular merchandise line.

assumptive close A sales closing technique that asks a question about preferred colours, method of payment, or type of delivery that can help the salesperson to quickly determine whether a customer is ready to make a purchase.

autonomous decision A decision within the family that is made over time independently by the husband and the wife.

awareness Knowledge of the brand name of the advertised product.

baby boomers Individuals born between 1946 and 1964, they comprise the largest population segment today.

backward integration A development that occurs when a retailer or wholesaler performs some manufacturing functions.

balance sheet The financial statement that expresses the equation: Assets = Liabilities + Net worth. (Net worth is the owners' equity or claim to the assets of the business.)

balanced tenancy A term that means that the types of stores in a planned shopping centre are chosen to meet all of the consumers' shopping needs in the trading area.

basic services Services that customers expect to have available at all retail outlets. An example is free parking.

basic stock The amount and assortment of merchandise sufficient to accommodate normal sales levels.

believers Conservative, conventional people with concrete beliefs and strong attachments to traditional institutions.

benefit summary A transition to the close technique, where the salesperson summarizes the product benefits to demonstrate that it is the right one for the customer.

benefits Holidays and paid vacations, insurance, health care, pensions, social security, disability payments, and various other forms of support for employees.

big-box store A huge store with a large variety and quantity of merchandise organized in one floor.

blind check A checking method in which the checker lists the items and quantities received without the invoice in hand and then compares the list to the invoice.

blue laws Provincial laws that prohibit retailers from opening on Sundays.

book inventory Recording of all additions to and deductions from a beginning stock figure to continually have an ending inventory figure. (Also called perpetual inventory.) The book inventory must be compared to the actual physical inventory to determine shortages or overages.

boomers *See* **baby boomers.**

boutique layout Merchandise classifications are grouped so that each classification has its own "shop" within the store.

breadth (or width) The number of different merchandise lines carried.

bridgers Consumers aged between 50 and 64.

business format franchising An ongoing relationship between a franchisor and franchisee that includes not only the product, service, and trademark, but the entire business format.

buy-for-one consumer A single-person household.

Canadian Advertising Rates & Data (CARD) A monthly publication providing updated general rates and other information for most medias in Canada.

Canadian Human Rights Commission An agency of the federal government with the responsibility to eliminate discrimination on the basis of race, national or ethnic origin, sex, colour, age, religion, or other variables in job hiring, retention, and promotion.

Canadian newspaper unit (CNU) A unit of measure of newspaper space that is one standardized column wide and 30 MALs deep.

cash datings Payment terms that call for immediate payment for merchandise. Cash datings include COD (cash on delivery) and CWO (cash with order). Cash datings do not involve cash discounts.

cash discount A premium granted by the supplier for cash payment prior to the time the entire bill must be paid.

catalogue Book containing items for sale by a retailer.

category killers Merchants offering great depth and breadth in one line of merchandise accompanied by low prices and good quality.

CD-ROM catalogue A catalogue presenting merchandise from a retailer using a compact disk, instead of being printed on paper.

census tract A permanent small census area established in large urban communities of 50,000 or more population; the population of a census tract must be between 2,500 and 8,000 people.

central business district The area of the central city that is characterized by high land values, high concentration of retail and service business, and high traffic flow.

chain A retail organization consisting of two or more centrally owned units that handle similar lines of merchandise.

channel of distribution A system through which products, commodities, or services are marketed.

checking A phase of the physical handling process that involves matching the store buyer's purchase order with the supplier's invoice (bill), opening the packages, removing the items, sorting them, and comparing the quality and quantity of the shipment with what was ordered.

classification dominance Displaying and arranging merchandise in such a way that psychologically the consumer is convinced the firm has a larger assortment of merchandise in the category than competitors.

cognitive dissonance A feeling whereby consumers, when making a major purchase, are afraid that they may have spent their money foolishly.

committee buying A form of central buying where more than one person shares the buying responsibility.

community newspapers Local newspapers that are usually published once a week.

community shopping centre A shopping centre in which the leading tenant is a variety store or junior department store. The typical leasable space is 10,000 square metres, and the typical site area is 40,000 square metres. The minimum trade population is 25,000 to 75,000.

compensation The amount of salary and fringe benefits to be paid for a particular job.

concentric diversification A strategy by which a service firm moves into different, but closely related services.

consumer cooperative A type of retail store owned by consumers and operated by a hired manager.

consumer-dominated information sources Information sources over which the retailer has no influence. Examples include friends, relatives, acquaintances, and others.

consumer rebates A situation in which a manufacturer pays the consumer a sum of money in the form of a price reduction when a purchase is made.

consumerism An organized expression of consumer dissatisfaction with selected business practices.

contest Skill-based competitions for designated prizes.

contribution margin approach An approach to departmental evaluation in which only direct costs are assigned to departments.

convenience goods Frequently purchased items for which consumers do not engage in comparison shopping before making a purchase decision.

convenience sample A non-probability sample in which researchers simply talk to the most readily available individuals.

cooperative advertising Promotional programs in which wholesalers or manufacturers pay a portion of the retailer's advertising cost under specified conditions.

core service The primary benefit customers seek from a service firm.

corporate culture The values of greatest importance to the organization.

corporate systems competition A type of competition that occurs when a single management ownership links resources, manufacturing capability, and distribution networks.

corporation A group of people who obtain a charter that grants them collectively the rights, privileges, liabilities, and legal powers of an individual, separate and apart from the individual making up the group. The corporation can sell, buy, and inherit property. The corporation owns assets and is liable for the debts it contracts.

cost per thousand (CPM) A measure of the relative cost of advertising that is determined by the number of households or persons reached.

coupon A sales promotion technique consisting of a certificate offering a given price reduction for a given item or service.

creative selling A type of higher-level selling in which the salesperson needs complete information about product lines, product uses, and the technical features of products.

credence qualities Attributes consumers may find impossible to evaluate even after purchase and consumption, perhaps because they do not have the knowledge or skill to do so.

credit scoring A method used by retailers to screen credit applicants based on various types of personal information about the applicant.

cross-border shopping A form of outshopping, where Canadians travel to the United States to make purchases on a regular basis.

culture A set of values, attitudes, traditions, symbols, and characteristic behaviour shared by all members of a recognized group.

customer-focused culture An integrated approach to dealing with customers that incorporates customer lifestyles and buying patterns into the overall strategy of the retail firm.

customer service Additional services provided to customers such as cashing cheques or managing complaints.

data sources Include internal data, secondary data, and primary data.

debit card A bank-issued card that allows, with the help of special terminals attached to the cash register, for a customer to pay for purchases by having an electronic transfer of funds from the client's to the retailer's bank account.

deferred billing credit A payment plan in which a retailer allows customers to buy goods and to defer payment for an extended period of time with no interest charge.

demand merchandise Merchandise purchased as a result of a customer coming into the store to buy that particular item.

departmentalization An organization principle that determines how jobs are grouped.

depth The number of items carried in a single merchandise line.

destination centres *See* **power strip centre.**

dialectic process A theory of change in retail institutional structure based on the premise that retailers mutually adapt in the face of competition from "opposites." When challenged by a competitor with a differential advantage, an established institution will adopt strategies and tactics in the direction of that advantage, thereby negating some of the innovator's attraction.

direct check A checking method whereby the shipment is checked against the vendor's invoice.

direct close A sale closing technique, where the salesperson takes the position that the customer is ready to buy.

direct costs Costs directly associated with a department; such costs would cease to exist if the department were eliminated.

direct mail retailing A form of promotion of the store and its merchandise directly to customers through the use of direct mail or catalogues (printed or electronic).

direct product profitability Reflects a product's gross margin (selling price minus cost of goods sold), plus discounts and allowances, less direct handling costs.

direct response advertising Advertising designed to induce consumers to take specific action such as make a purchase or participate in a contest or giveaway.

disappointers Services offered by a retailer that have a high labour content and that return little value to the consumer. An example is a layaway.

discount centre A shopping centre with a strong representation of discount merchants.

distributor allowances Discounts and/or extended payment terms to retailers designed to encourage them to purchase additional merchandise from a wholesaler or manufacturer.

distributorships Franchise systems whereby franchises maintain warehouse stocks to supply other franchises. The distributor takes title to the goods and provides services to other customers.

dollar control A system for controlling the dollar investment in inventory. To work, the system must record the beginning dollar inventory, what has been added to stock, how much inventory has moved out of stock, and how much inventory is now on hand. Involves perpetually recording additions and deductions at retail or cost.

electronic cash register A point-of-sale register that uses electronic light beams to enter information at a very high rate of speed.

electronic data interchange (EDI) Computer-to-computer exchange of data.

electronic retailing Retailing using electronic media (telephone, cable, and computer network).

employee compensation Wages or salary, commissions, incentives, overtime, and benefits.

energy costs Include carrying packages, fighting traffic, parking, and waiting in line.

enumeration area A small federal electoral area of about 100 to 200 households, the smallest geographic units for which census data are available.

environmental scanning Monitoring critical environments for decision-making purposes.

event advertising An advertising campaign to promote a very specific sale, during a specific period (e.g., after-Christmas sale).

exclusive dealing A situation in which a supplier prohibits a retailer from selling the product of a competitor.

experience qualities Attributes such as taste that can only be discerned after purchase or during consumption.

experiencers People who are young, vital, enthusiastic, impulsive, and rebellious.

experimental design A type of research design that allows management to make inferences about cause-and-effect relationships in variables of interest.

exploratory research A research process characterized by flexibility in design and the absence of a formal research structure.

extended warranty Warranties purchased by the consumer separate from the product and covering parts, labour, or both for a period of time beyond the duration of an express warranty.

extensive problem solving A thought process that consumers experience when faced with a first-time purchase in an unfamiliar product category.

external environment The political, technological, economic, and social forces that affect the organization.

external factors In a situation analysis, variables over which store management has no control.

factory outlet centre Shopping centres occupied by manufacturers selling directly to the public.

family life cycle It reflects the various stages individuals go through as they get married, have children, and so on until retirement.

fashion-oriented centres Shopping centres composed primarily of apparel shops, boutiques, and handicraft shops carrying selected fashion merchandise of high price and quality.

feature–benefit relationship Understanding the reasons why customers buy, relating products to those reasons, and describing the products or services to the customers.

festival/entertainment centres Centres with a strong representation of restaurants, specialty retailers, and entertainment facilities.

field work The steps involved in actually collecting information from respondents in a survey.

FIFO (first-in, first-out) An inventory costing method that assumes that costs should be charged against revenue in the order in which they were incurred; in other words, the first items purchased are the first ones sold. The method is generally in harmony with actual movement of goods.

financial risk The monetary loss from a wrong decision.

fixed-payment lease A rental agreement in which rent is based on a fixed payment per month.

flextime A system by which workers arrive at work on a variable schedule.

focus group A type of exploratory research, where a group of 8 to 12 suppliers, customers, or non-customers gather around a table to talk informally around the issue, with the assistance of a trained interviewer.

forward integration A situation in which a manufacturer establishes its own wholesale and retail networks.

franchisee An individual who pays a fee for the right to use a franchisor's product, service, or way of doing business.

franchisor An organization that has developed a unique product, service, or a way of doing business and allows another firm to use the product, service, or business concept in return for payment of a fee.

free-flow layout Merchandise and fixtures are grouped into patterns that allow an unstructured flow of customer traffic.

Free Trade Agreement (FTA) An agreement whereby, on January 1, 1989, Canada and the United States started a 10-year process of lowering tariff barriers and liberalizing trade practices.

frequency The average number of times a person will be exposed to a message during an advertising period.

fulfilleds Mature, satisfied, comfortable, reflective people who value order, knowledge, and responsibility.

full-costing approach Both direct and indirect costs are assigned to departments.

functional accounts Reflect the retail function involved; for example, the allocation of salaries to administrative support and sales personnel.

future datings A type of dating other than cash dating; includes DOI (date of invoice), ROG (receipt of goods), EOM (end of month), and extra datings.

general rate The advertising rate charged to agencies for national advertising.

general salary increases Increases granted to employees to maintain real earnings as required by economic factors and in order to keep pay competitive.

generation X The group of individuals born between 1965 and 1976.

generation Y The group of individuals born between 1977 and 1986, i.e., the children of the baby boomers.

generics Unbranded merchandise offerings carrying only the designation of the product type on the package.

get-my-money's-worth consumer A consumer activist looking for good values.

GMROI (gross margin return on inventory) Expression of the relationship between margin and sales-to-retail stock (turnover), stated to effectively indicate the impact on profitability as:

$$\frac{\$GM}{\$Sales} \times \frac{\$Sales}{\$Average\ inventory\ investment}$$

gravity models Methods for trading area analysis that are based on population size and driving time or distance as the key variables in the models.

green marketing Marketing products that do not harm the environment.

grid layout Merchandise is displayed in straight, parallel lines, with secondary aisles at right angles to these.

gross margin The difference between net sales and the cost of goods sold.

gross rating point One percent of all homes with television sets in a market area, or more generally, 1 percent of the target population in a market area.

group buying The joint purchasing of goods by a number of non-competing, non-aligned stores.

hedonic consumption Facets relating to the multisensory and emotional aspects of shopping and consuming

hierarchy of effects model A type of model often used in advertising where consumers respond to advertising according to various sequential stages. The simplest one is called AIDA (for attention—interest—desire—action).

high involvement Consumer's shopping characterized by a high level of search in an effort to obtain information about products or stores.

home improvement centres Centres featuring a concentration of home improvement or hardware specialty retailers.

husband-dominant decision A decision within the family that is made most of the time by the husband.

image The way consumers "feel" about a store or merchandise.

image campaign An advertising campaign by a retailer for the sole purpose to improve its image.

impulse merchandise Merchandise bought on the basis of unplanned, spur-of-the-moment decisions.

inbound telemarketing Telephone selling where the retailer receives orders or requests from customers through the use of 1-800 or 1-888 telephone numbers.

income statement Operating results of a period indicating if investments in assets and strategy have been successful and if a profit has resulted.

indirect costs Costs that cannot be tied directly to a department, such as a store manager's salary.

in-home retailing A method of distribution of consumer goods and service through personal contact away from a fixed business location.

initial markup The difference between the cost of merchandise and the original retail price.

ink jetting A technique that allows the inclusion of personalized messages in a retailer's catalogue.

instalment credit A payment plan in which a customer pays for a product in equal monthly instalments, including interest.

institutional advertising An advertising campaign to communicate the total character or image of the store, and no merchandise or prices are featured.

intangibility The characteristic of a service that indicates that a service cannot be seen, touched, smelled, or handled.

internal data Data that help management systematically determine what's going on in the firm.

internal environment Forces within the organization that affect the activities of the firm.

Internet A computer network that allows computers to communicate with each other.

intertype competition Competition between different types of retail outlets selling the same merchandise.

intratype competition Competition among retailers of the same type.

involvement The way in which individuals identify with a product, service, or outlet and the personal relevance of the purchase to them.

job analysis A method for obtaining important facts about a job.

job classification Comparing jobs with the aid of a scale that evaluates job complexity and the length of time the respective responsibility and qualifications are utilized during an average workday.

job description The part of a job analysis that describes the content and responsibilities of a job and how the job ties in with other jobs in the firm.

job evaluation A method of ranking jobs to aid in determining proper compensation.

job ranking Ranking jobs on the basis of how valuable they are to the organization and the complexity of the job.

job sharing A situation whereby two workers voluntarily hold joint responsibility for what was formally one position.

job specification The part of a job analysis that describes the personal qualifications required of an employee to do a job.

labelling violation A situation encountered by consumers where some important information, such as fibre content, is missing from the product label.

layaway plan A situation in which a customer can make a small deposit that assures that the retailer will hold the item until the customer is able to pay for it.

lead time The length of time between order placement and receipt of goods.

leader pricing A pricing policy in which merchandise is sold at less than the normal markup in an effort to increase store traffic.

leased departments Departments of a retail business that are operated and managed by an outside person or organization rather than by the store of which it is a physical part.

leverage When assets worth more than the amount of capital invested by the owners are acquired. Leveraging is the ratio of total assets to net worth. The higher the ratio, the higher the amount of borrowed funds in the business.

liabilities What is owed by the business.

licensing A tool of marketing in which the licenser or owner of a "property" (the concept to be marketed) joins with a licensee (the manufacturer of the licensed product) and attempts to sell to retail buyers.

life cycle The stages through which retail institutions evolve, including innovation, growth, maturity, and decline or stagnation.

lifestyle A person's pattern of living as reflected in the way merchandise is purchased and used.

lifestyle cluster Shopping in urban areas that cater to a specific lifestyle with a combination of food stalls, specialty shops, and restaurants.

lifestyle segmentation Dividing consumers into homogeneous groups based on similar activities, interests, and opinions.

LIFO (last-in, first-out) An inventory costing method that assumes that the most recent cost of merchandise should be charged against revenue. LIFO yields a higher figure for cost of goods sold than FIFO and thus lower figures for gross profit, net income, and inventory. LIFO is popular during inflationary periods.

Likert scale A type of scale that allows respondents to express their level of agreement or disagreement with a statement.

limited problem solving Shopping situations in which the consumer is already familiar with the class of product or service and makes a choice between brands or outlets.

low involvement Consumer's shopping characterized by a very low/no effort to compare products or stores; the product that will satisfy the consumer's needs will be purchased at the most convenient outlet.

macro environmental audit Monitoring the impersonal forces beyond the control of the firm, such as technology or social trends.

magazine advertising Selecting magazines for the retailer's advertising plan.

maintained markup The difference between invoice cost and sales retail.

makers Practical people who have constructive skills and value self-sufficiency.

management by objectives Goals established with salespeople that give direction to their efforts and permit them to evaluate their progress.

management information system The structure of people, equipment, and procedures necessary to gather, analyze, and distribute information needed by management.

manufacturer's brand A brand, often referred to as a national brand, owned by a manufacturer who may sell to anyone who wants to buy the brand.

margin The percentage markup at which inventory is sold.

markdown A reduction in the original selling price of an item.

market development A strategy option that focuses either on attracting new market segments or completely changing the customer base.

market penetration A strategy option whereby retailers seek a differential advantage over competition by a strong market presence that borders on saturation.

market positioning Developing a unique position in a market segment relative to other retailers by the use of merchandise, price, hours of operation, services offered, and a clear understanding of consumer demographics.

market saturation A situation that occurs when such a large number of stores are located in a market that low sales per square metre, compared to the industry average, are the result.

market segments The groupings of consumers based on homogeneous responses to merchandise offerings.

marketer-dominated information sources Sources of information under the control of the retailer. Examples are advertising, personal selling, displays, sales promotion, and publicity.

marketing The process by which individuals and groups obtain what they need and want through creating and exchanging products and value with others.

marketing concept A management philosophy stating that all activities of the firm should be organized and executed from the viewpoint of the customer in satisfying the needs identified.

marking A phase of the physical handling process that involves putting information on the goods or on merchandise containers to assist customers and to aid the store in the control functions.

master franchise An individual buys the right to an extensive geographic area and sells the rights within the territory to individual franchisees.

merchandise approach A retail sales approach that begins with a statement about the merchandise.

merchandise budget A plan of how much to buy in dollars per month by classification based on profitability goals.

merchandise distribution An aspect of merchandise management in multiunit organizations related to getting merchandise from consolidation points/ distribution centres to the individual stores.

merchandise information systems Computer-based systems that provide retail managers with better and faster information on their merchandising activities. The product of a merchandise information system is a series of computerized reports that can give almost instant answers to queries.

merchandise line A group of products that are closely related because they are intended for the same end use, are used together, or are sold to the same customer group.

merchandise management The management of the product component of the marketing mix.

merchandise planning Includes all the activities needed to plan a balance between inventories and sales.

merit increases Pay increases granted to recognize superior performance and contributions.

message The development of an idea in transmittable form.

mission statement A statement that describes what a firm plans to accomplish in the market in which it will compete for customers it wants to serve.

model building The practice of applying statistical principles and using computer analysis of data to help solve management problems.

model stock plan A fashion merchandiser's best judgment about what demand will be at specific times of the year.

modular agate line (MAL) A unit of measure of newspaper space that is one standardized column wide and 1.8 mm deep.

money costs Costs of goods purchased and costs of travel.

motivation Getting people to do what is best for the organization.

multiattribute model A model that explains how attitudes toward stores are formed based on a number of attributes and their stated importances and beliefs by consumers.

national brands The brands of a manufacturer such as Procter & Gamble that are sold through a wide variety of retail outlets.

national rates Advertising rates applicable to national (non-retail) firms.

national spot advertising Non-network advertising done by national retailers.

natural accounts Companywide accounts such as salaries, rent, promotion, and costs of supplies.

neighbourhood shopping centre A shopping centre in which the leading tenant is a supermarket or drugstore. The typical leasable space is 5,000 square metres and the typical site is 16,000 square metres. The minimum trade population is 7,500 to 25,000.

net worth The owner's investment or equity.

neutral sources of information Sources of information such as government rating agencies and state and local consumer affairs agencies that consumers perceive as trustworthy.

newspaper advertising Selecting newspapers for a retailer's advertising plan.

niche malls A type of mall targeted to a very specific group of customers, e.g., the Chinese or the working women.

non-perpetual unit control (Also called *stock-counting methods.*) This is *not* a book-inventory method. A non-perpetual unit system requires the retailer to have a planned model stock, a periodic counting schedule, and definite, assigned responsibility for counting. The beginning and ending inventories are counted and the differences are the sales (and shortages).

non-store retailing The sale of merchandise other than through retail stores. Examples include mail order, telephone shopping, door-to-door (direct selling), and vending machines.

non-store shopping The purchase of merchandise by use of catalogues, telephone, or ways other than physically entering an outlet.

nutritional labelling Information provided on the label that helps people with allergies or on some form of diet.

objective-and-task method A method of setting the advertising budget that relates the dollar appropriation to the advertising goals to be achieved.

objectives Statements of results to be achieved.

observation A type of primary data collection, where the behaviour of customers or competitors is monitored and analyzed.

off-price centre A centre with a high concentration of stores selling brand name goods at 20 to 70 percent off the manufacturer's suggested retail prices.

off-price retailers Outlets offering well-known brands of merchandise at substantial discounts compared to conventional stores handling the same products.

open charge account A charge account in which the customer must pay the bill in full when it is due, usually in 30 days.

open-code dating Information provided so that the consumer can tell the date after which a product should not be used.

open-ended close A sale closing technique, where the salesperson asks open-ended questions that imply readiness to buy.

open-ended question A type of question where the respondents are simply asked to give their opinions without a formal response structure.

open-to-buy A control system devised to "control" the retailer's utilization of the planned purchase figure. Dollar control provides the essential component of the system. OTB records the commitments made against the planned purchases amount.

open-to-spend report A report recording commitments against planned expenses for a period.

operating environmental audit Monitoring all organizations or groups that either directly or indirectly are affected by a firm's competitive strategy.

opinion leader A person whose product-specific competence is recognized by others.

order ceiling A level of stock sufficient to maintain a minimum order point level of stock and one sufficient to cover sales between ordering intervals.

order interval The amount of time between merchandise orders.

order point The level of stock below which merchandise is automatically reordered.

original retail price The first price at which an item is offered for sale.

outbound telemarketing A method of selling by contacting customers or potential customers by telephone.

out-of-home advertising All the advertising media that are physically outside the home, such as outdoor, transit, aerial, bench, taxicab, etc.

outshopping Travelling out of one's local area to make purchases.

overage The physical inventory (either in dollars or units) is larger than the book inventory.

panel A selected group of customers or suppliers who are asked to keep a record of their purchases over time or give their opinions about merchandising issues.

partnership A voluntary association of two or more persons to operate a retail outlet for profit as co-owners. The rights, responsibilities, and duties of the partners are stated in the articles of partnership.

patronage builders A classification of services that provide high customer value and can be provided by the retailer at nominal cost. An example is a computerized bridal registry.

people care programs Programs by some retailers to give employees paid time off to deal with personal matters such as taking a driving test, applying for a mortgage, or doing volunteer work in the community.

percentage of sales A method of establishing an advertising budget based upon a percentage of retail sales.

performance risk The chance that merchandise purchased may not work properly.

peripheral services Secondary benefits customers seek from a service firm.

perishability The characteristic of a service which indicates that a service is lost forever if not consumed within a specific period.

perpetual inventory control Is a book inventory.

personal motives Reasons for shopping that result from the internal needs of the consumer, distinct from other needs fulfilled in purchasing a good or service.

personal shopping service A situation in which a retailer will assemble wardrobes for men and women at their request and have the items ready for inspection when the customer comes to the store.

physical environment A tangible surrogate to a service to provide a concrete indication of the quality of the service.

physical handling Activities involved in receiving, checking, and marking merchandise.

physical risk The likelihood that a purchase decision will be injurious to one's health or will likely cause physical injury.

planned shopping centre A shopping centre developed with balanced tenancy, parking, and architecture.

planogram A visual plan for standardized in-store merchandise presentation showing the ideal physical location of products within a merchandise grouping.

point-of-purchase material A sales promotion technique that include end-of-aisle and other in-store merchandising and display material.

point-of-sale (POS) A cash register terminal that records a variety of information at the time a transaction occurs.

positioning The design and implementation of a retail mix to create an image of the retailer in the customer's mind relative to its competitors.

power retailers Retailers with sufficient financial strength, marketing skill, and reasonably priced, quality merchandise to establish dominance in any market, however saturated, and make a profit.

power strip centre An oversized strip centre typically anchored by destination-oriented retailers or superstores (e.g., Toys "Я" Us).

predatory pricing Setting prices to deliberately drive competition out of business.

premiums A sales promotion technique that offers something free or at a minimal price to induce sales.

preretailing The practice of determining merchandise selling prices and writing these prices on the store's copy of the purchase order at the time it is written.

price discrimination Varying the prices charged to different retailers for identical merchandise without an economic justification for doing so.

price elasticity The ratio of the percentage change in the quantity demanded to the percentage change in price.

price lining Featuring products at a limited number of prices that reflect varying levels of merchandise quality. Price lining may occur either in the context of rigid price points or price zones.

price points Offering merchandise at a small number of different prices. For example, a merchant might price all "good suits" at $175, all "better" suits at $225, and "best" suits at $350.

price zones Pricing strategy in which a merchant establishes a range of prices for merchandise of different quality. For example, prices for "good" suits might be between $175 and $200 while prices for "better" suits might be between $225 and $275.

primary data Needed information that is unavailable either internally or externally to the firm and that must be collected especially for the purpose at hand.

primary trading area The area around the store that includes the majority of the store's customers, who live within a certain range of the store.

prime time advertising Advertising that takes place during the prime time segments of television and radio programming.

principle-oriented consumers Consumers guided in their choices by beliefs or principles, rather than by feeling, events, or desire for approval.

private brands Brands of merchandise that retailers develop and promote under their own label.

private corporation A corporation owned by a few people. Persons outside the corporation cannot buy the stock on the open market.

private label credit card A credit card that is imprinted with the name of the issuing retail outlet but for which the administrative details of the credit transaction are handled by a third party such as a bank.

probability sample A sample in which each unit has a known chance of selection.

product A tangible object, service, or idea.

product and trade-name franchising An independent sales relationship exists between a supplier and a dealer, but the dealer acquires some of the identity of the supplier. Primary examples are automotive and truck dealers, gasoline service stations, and soft drink bottlers.

product benefit A customer's basic buying motive that is fulfilled by a product feature.

productivity improvement A strategy that focuses on improved earnings through cost reductions, increased turnover through an improved merchandise mix, and increased prices and margins.

productivity of salesforce Total sales divided by employee costs.

promotion Any form of paid communication from the retailer to the consumer.

promotion plan A written document detailing the complete promotional programme, including communication goals, targets, budgets, media, and messages.

promotional allowance A discount from list price given by suppliers to retailers to compensate them for money spent on promoting particular items.

promotional increases Salary increases given to employees assigned a different job and a higher pay level.

promotional products advertising Advertising that uses gifts to customers as an advertising medium (e.g., calendars, pens, or T-shirts).

prospecting The first step in the selling process that involves identifying and qualifying possible customers.

psychographics Ways of defining and measuring the lifestyles of consumers.

psychological risk The probability that the merchandise purchased or the store shopped will be compatible with the consumer's self-image.

public corporation A corporation in which the stock of a firm can be purchased on the open market.

publicity Any non-personal stimulation of demand for a product, service, or business unit by planting commercially significant news about it in a published medium or obtaining a favourable presentation about it on radio, television, or in other ways that are not paid for by the sponsor.

quantity discount A reduction in unit cost based on the size of an order.

quantity violation A situation encountered by consumers whereby the quantity of a product was significantly less than claimed by the retailer or the manufacturer.

questionnaire A sequence of questions that elicit from respondents the information to be collected to meet the objectives of the survey.

quick response (QR) A distribution method for responding rapidly to customer demands and for improving operations and profitability.

racetrack layout A store layout that encourages customers to visit several departments by providing a major aisle that loops through the store.

radio advertising Selecting radio stations for the retailer's commercials.

random sample A sample in which each unit has a known and equal chance of selection.

reach The number of persons exposed at least once to a message during an ad campaign.

rebates The refund of a fixed amount from the purchase price.

receiving A phase of the physical handling process that involves taking possession of the goods and then moving them to the next phase of the process.

reductions Anything other than sales that reduced inventory value, including employee discounts, shortages, and markdowns.

reference group Any group for which the consumer is a "psychological" participant, one with which she or he will identify and accept its norms or judgment.

regional centre A shopping centre in which the leading tenant is one or more full-line department stores. The typical leasable space is 20,000 square metres, and the typical site is 120,000 square metres. The minimum trade population is 75,000 or more.

regional dominance A location strategy whereby a retailer decides to compete within one geographic region, for example, the Maritimes.

resale price maintenance A situation in which manufacturers set minimum prices at which their products must be sold.

retail accordion A theory about institutional change based on the premise that retail institutions evolve from broad-based outlets with wide assortments to specialized narrow lines and then return to the wide-assortment pattern.

retail decision support system The structure of people, equipment, and procedures to gather, analyze, and distribute the data that management needs for decision making.

retail rate Rate given by the media to retailers and that are considerably lower than for a national advertiser or an ad agency.

retail saturation The extent to which a trading area is filled with competing stores.

retail structure The structure comprising all retail outlets through which goods and services move to the ultimate consumer.

retail the invoice The practice of determining merchandise selling prices and writing these prices on the copy of the invoice in the receiving room.

retailing Consists of all activities involved in the sale of goods and services to the ultimate consumer.

retailing mix Those variables—product, price, presentation, promotion, personal selling, and customer services—that can be used as part of a positioning strategy for competing in chosen markets.

reverse marketing A situation where the buyer works very closely with the seller to develop a mutually beneficial relationship.

revolving credit A customer is billed at the end of a month on the basis of an outstanding credit balance.

role playing A sales training situation in which one person plays the part of the customer, while another person plays the part of the salesperson.

routine selling A type of selling that involves the sale of non-technical items.

routinized response behaviour Situations in which consumers, because they are familiar with the product class, do not engage in external information search before making a purchase.

safety stock The level of stock sufficient to maintain adequate inventory for accommodating expected variations in demand and variations in supplier delivery schedules.

sales productivity Sales by square metre of selling space.

sales promotion Marketing activities other than direct selling, advertising, and publicity that stimulate consumer purchasing. Examples include displays, sales, exhibits, and demonstrations.

sales retail price The final selling price, or the amount the customer pays for the merchandise.

sales-to-expense ratio Sales divided by costs expended to obtain their sales.

sales variance analysis A technique that enables management to compare actual sales to sales goals.

sample A selected group of respondents in a survey.

sampling A sales promotion technique where the product is provided free or at nominal cost for trial.

scanner A device that emits a laser beam for scanning the bar codes on the merchandise and that can provide automatic price readouts, automatic updates of inventory, and similar features.

search qualities Attributes a consumer can see, feel, or touch and can thus determine prior to purchasing a product.

seasonal discount A special discount given to retailers who place orders for seasonal merchandise in advance of the normal buying period.

seasonal merchandise Merchandise in demand only at certain times of the year.

secondary data Existing data that have been previously collected for their own purposes.

secondary market expansion Development of retail outlets in communities with under 50,000 population.

secondary trading area The area around the store, beyond the primary trading area, which includes the majority of the store's customers who live within a certain range of the store (the rest is called the fringe trading area).

seeking agreement A transition to the close technique, where the customer is made to agree with the salesperson on a number of points, leading to making the order.

selective binding A method of producing individualized catalogues for different customers.

selectivity The ability of a medium to reach only specific audiences, minimizing waste (e.g., only teenagers or men aged 24 to 45).

self-liquidators Incentives in which consumers pay part of the cost of a promotion in cash in addition to submitting product labels as proof of purchase to obtain an item.

semantic differential scale A type of scale that allows respondents to select the point representing the direction and intensity of their feelings between two bipolar words.

service Activities, benefits, or satisfaction offered for sale, or provided in connection with the sale of goods.

service approach A weak approach in personal selling in which the salesperson simply asks if they can be of assistance to a potential customer.

service firm An organization that derives more than 50 percent of its sales from providing services that may involve a combination of both tangible and intangible offerings.

service-oriented centres Centres that depend heavily on service-oriented retailers such as optical, dental, repair, health, and legal services.

share The percentage of television sets in use that are tuned to a given programme.

shoppers Newspapers that carry primarily advertising and very little news. They are distributed free to the homes of consumers.

shopping goods Merchandise for which consumers will make comparisons between various brands in a product class before making a purchase.

shortage The physical inventory (either in dollars or units) is smaller than the book inventory.

single-price policy All merchandise in a store is sold at the same price.

single-theme centres Centres offering merchandise in a narrow range such as auto care, home decorating and design, or weddings.

situation analysis An assessment of internal strengths and weaknesses and external threats and opportunities.

social classes Divisions of society that are relatively homogeneous and permanent, and in which individuals or families share the same values, lifestyles, interests, and types of behaviour.

social motives Reasons for shopping that reflect the desire for group interaction of one sort or another.

social responsibility A belief of retailers that they have an obligation to society beyond making a profit and obeying the laws of the land.

social risk The likelihood that the merchandise or store will not meet with peer approval.

sole proprietorship A situation where the retail outlet is owned and operated by one person who has title to the assets and who is subject to the claims of all creditors.

solo location A location with no other retail stores nearby.

source The originator of the promotional message.

source marking The practice of the vendor rather than the retailer marking the goods.

span-of-control A principle of organization that addresses the question of how many persons should report to a supervisor.

specialization A principle of organization that states that the content of individual jobs should be narrowly defined.

specialized functional area Self-defining shopping urban areas such as entertainment districts, medical districts, or high-fashion districts.

specialty goods Products that consumers know they want and for which they are willing to make a special effort to acquire.

specialty store An outlet specializing in the sale of one item in a product line. An example is a store specializing in athletic shoes.

split runs A service offered by some print publications whereby the retailer can have two different ads in alternate copies of the same publication at the same time.

spot advertising Advertising shown on local stations whereby the negotiation and purchase of time is made directly with the individual station.

stability-seeking consumers Usually blue-collar middle-income households.

staple merchandise Items of merchandise generally in demand year round, with little change in model or style.

status-oriented consumers Consumers heavily influenced by the actions, approval, and opinions of others.

stockkeeping units (SKUs) One or more units of a distinctive item.

stock-to-sales ratio Used in planning monthly stocks in relation to expected sales for the month.

store design Refers to the style or atmosphere of a store that helps project an image to the market.

store layout Planning of the internal arrangement of selling and sales-supporting departments, and deciding on the amount of space for each department.

store planning Includes exterior and interior building design, the allocation of space to departments, and the arrangement and location of departments within the store.

strategic planning Defining the overall mission/purpose of the company, deciding on objectives that management wants to achieve, and developing a plan to achieve those objectives.

strategic profit model (SPM) A model from the basic ROI model that focuses on the firm's primary profit paths—margin, assets, and leverage.

strivers People who seek motivation, self-definition, and approval from the world around them.

strugglers Individuals who are chronically poor, ill-educated, low-skilled, and lacking strong social bonds.

suggestion selling Using a customer's original purchase decision as a basis for developing suggestions about related or additional items in which the customer might be interested.

supermarket retailing A type of retailing characterized by self-service and self-selection, large-scale, but low-cost physical facilities; strong price emphasis; simplification and centralization of customer services; and a wide variety and broad assortment of merchandise.

supplements Pre-printed pages of ads that are inserted into newspapers.

support The depth behind each assortment factor in a merchandise plan. Answers the "how many" question.

support services Services offered by a retailer that directly support the sale of the retailer's merchandise. Examples include home delivery and gift wrapping.

survey research Collection of data on the opinions or perceptions of people in a market segment by the use of a structured questionnaire.

sweepstakes Games of chance for designated prizes.

syncratic decision A decision within the family that is made jointly by both spouses.

syndicated services Services offered by firms that specialize in collecting and selling information to clients.

systematic sampling A type of probability sample in which researchers choose a random beginning and then choose every *n*th number thereafter.

target markets The markets that management decides to serve.

telemarketing Selling using the telephone (inbound or outbound).

telephone retailing *See* **telemarketing.**

television advertising Selecting television stations to carry the retailer's commercial.

tenure increases Pay increases given to employees for time worked with the company.

test market A selected testing area that allows the retailer to help decide on whether to make changes in the merchandise mix, decor, store layout, or similar variables.

theme or specialty centres Shopping centres characterized by common architectural themes that unite a wide range of retailers who repeat the theme in their spaces.

third-party credit A situation in which a customer uses a card such as Visa or MasterCard to charge merchandise purchased at a retail outlet.

time-buying consumers Households with two incomes and short of time for shopping.

time-loss risk The likelihood that the consumer will not be able to get merchandise adjusted, replaced, or repaired without loss of time and effort.

trade discount A reduction off the seller's list price that is granted to a retailer who performs functions normally the responsibility of the vendor.

trading area The area from which a store primarily attracts its customers.

traffic count A method used to determine the character and volume of traffic (both vehicular and pedestrian) passing a particular site.

transaction processing A situation in which employees serve as checkout clerks or cashiers and do little selling.

transit advertising Selecting bus routes or subway lines for the retailer's advertising.

trial close A transition to the close technique, where a question is asked to determine the customer's readiness to buy.

turnover The number of times the average inventory of an item (or SKU) is sold, usually in annual terms.

uniform communications standard A computer language used in retailing.

unit control System used to control the width and support aspects of stock balance. The system records (perpetual) beginning inventory and all additions and deductions to stock to obtain the ending inventory. (*See* **non-perpetual unit control** for the other system in use.)

unit of sales A method of establishing an advertising budget whereby retailers set aside a fixed dollar amount for each unit of the product to be sold.

unit pricing A situation in which price is stated in such terms as price per kilogram or litre.

unity-of-command A principle of organization that states that no person should be under the direct control of more than one supervisor in performing job tasks.

universal product code (UPC) A standardized form of product marking for electronic reading of price and other information that is used for food and health and beauty aids.

universal transverse mercator (UTM) A system that provides the coordinates of every location in Canada.

universal vendor marking (UVM) A standard vendor-created identification system for marking merchandise items at the vendor level.

unplanned shopping centre Typically a small group of stores and service establishments that have not been developed with a balanced tenancy in mind.

urban arterial development Shopping areas usually found in an older part of the city.

urgency close A sale closing technique.

VALS A trademark program, Values and Lifestyles, developed by Stanford Research International that places emphasis on the psychological underpinnings of consumer behaviour.

values Beliefs or expectations about behaviour shared by a number of individuals and learned from society.

variable-payment lease A situation in which the retailer makes a guaranteed monthly rental payment to the landlord in addition to a specified percentage of sales.

variety The width of a store's selection of merchandise.

vending machines Mechanical dispensers of goods or services placed in strategic locations.

vertical merchandising A form of displaying merchandise vertically instead of horizontally to increase space productivity.

video tech Reaching consumers with cable TV, teletext, and video discs.

wand An electronic device that can be passed over items for reading machine-coded information.

warehouse-style store *See* **big-box store.**

wheel of retailing A theory about institutional structure change based on the premise that institutional innovations in retailing penetrate the system on the basis of price appeal and gradually trade up over time in terms of store standing, quality, store services, and prices.

width *See* **breadth.**

wife-dominant decision A decision within the family that is made most of the time by the wife.

work sharing A situation that occurs during economic recessions where employees are required to cut back on their work hours rather than face layoffs and are paid accordingly.

World Wide Web The part of the Internet (information highway) where individual sites (electronic store fronts) can be found using software such as Netscape or Mosaic.

Yellow Pages advertising Using the Yellow Pages directory to advertise.

Name Index

Subject Index